Encyclopedic Dictionary
of
Accounting and Finance

Encyclopedic Dictionary
of
Accounting and Finance

Jae K. Shim, Ph.D.

and

Joel G. Siegel, Ph.D., CPA

PRENTICE HALL
Englewood Cliffs, New Jersey 07632

Prentice-Hall International (UK) Limited, *London*
Prentice-Hall of Australia Pty. Limited, *Sydney*
Prentice-Hall Canada, Inc., *Toronto*
Prentice-Hall Hispanoamericana, S.A., *Mexico*
Prentice-Hall of India Private Limited, *New Delhi*
Prentice-Hall of Japan, Inc., *Tokyo*
Simon & Schuster Asia Pte. Ltd., *Singapore*
Editora Prentice-Hall do Brasil, Ltda., *Rio de Janeiro*

This publication is designed to provide accurate and authoritative information in regard to the subject matter covered.
It is sold with the understanding that the publisher is not
engaged in rendering legal, accounting, or other professional service. If legal advice or other expert assistance is
required, the services of a competent professional person
should be sought.
. . . *From the Declaration of Principles jointly adopted
by a Committee of the American Bar Association and a
Committee of Publishers and Associations.*

10 9 8 7 6 5 4 3 2

Library of Congress Cataloging-in-Publication Data

Shim, Jae K.
  Encyclopedic dictionary of accounting and finance / Jae
K. Shim and Joel G. Siegel.
    p. cm.
  ISBN 0–13–275801–6
  1. Accounting—Dictionaries. 2. Finance—Dictionar-
ies.
I. Siegel, Joel G. II. Title.
HF1001.S525 1989
657′.03—dc19   89–3628
                                                        CIP

ISBN 0-13-275801-6 ISBN 0-13-275595-5 PBK

PRENTICE HALL
BUSINESS & PROFESSIONAL DIVISION
A division of Simon & Schuster
Englewood Cliffs, New Jersey 07632

Printed in the United States of America

To

Chung Shim,
dedicated wife

and

Roberta Siegel,
loving and wonderful wife

David F. Hawkins,
noted scholar, leading intellectual, and dear friend

Philip E. Levine,
dear and precious friend

ACKNOWLEDGMENTS

We wish to express our deep gratitude to Bette Schwartzberg for her outstanding editorial assistance during this project. Her input and efforts are recognized and greatly appreciated. Much thanks and appreciation goes to Christina Burghard for her highly professional and superb production editorial work.

We also thank Roberta M. Siegel for her help in preparing the data base of entries to be included in the book, as well as her reading of the computer topics and offering suggestions.

ABOUT THE AUTHORS

Jae K. Shim, Ph.D., is Professor of Accounting and Finance at California State University, Long Beach. He received his MBA and Ph.D. degrees from the University of California at Berkeley.

Dr. Shim, an accounting and financial consultant, has published numerous referred articles in such journals as *Financial Management, Econometrica, Decision Sciences, Management Science, Long Range Planning, OMEGA, Journal of Operational Research Society,* and *Advances in Accounting.* He has sixteen college and professional books to his credit, including *Handbook of Financial Analysis, Forecasting and Modeling; Accountants' Microcomputer Handbook; The Vest Pocket MBA;* and *The Vest Pocket CPA.*

Dr. Shim is the recipient of the 1982 Credit Research Foundation for his article on financial modeling.

Joel G. Siegel, Ph.D., CPA, is Professor of Accounting and Finance at Queens College of the City University of New York. He is an accounting and financial consultant.

Dr. Siegel was previously a member of the staff of Coopers and Lybrand, CPAs, and a faculty resident with Arthur Andersen, CPAs. He has acted as a consultant in accounting and financial issues to many organizations, including International Telephone & Telegraph, Citicorp, and Person-Wolinsky Associates.

Dr. Siegel is the author of 21 books and about 150 articles on accounting and financial topics. His books have been published by Prentice Hall, McGraw-Hill, John Wiley, Barron's, and the American Institute of CPAs.

He has been published in numerous accounting and financial journals, including *The CPA Journal, Computers in Accounting, National Public Accountant, Financial Executive,* and *The Financial Analysts Journal.*

In 1972, he was the recipient of the Outstanding Educator of America Award. He is listed in *Who's Where Among Writers* and *Who's Who in the World.*

WHAT THIS BOOK WILL DO FOR YOU

The *Encyclopedic Dictionary of Accounting and Finance* is written and compiled in such a way that working professionals engaged in the fields of accounting, finance, investment, and banking may use it in both their day-to-day practice and for technical research. The Encyclopedic Dictionary is a practical reference of proven techniques, strategies, and approaches that are successfully used by professionals to diagnose accounting and financial problems. The book covers virtually all important topics dealing with financial accounting, financial statement analysis, managerial/cost accounting, auditing, managerial finance, investments, financial planning, financial economics, and money and banking. It also covers such topics as computers, quantitative techniques and models, and economics as applied to accounting and finance. The Encyclopedic Dictionary will benefit practicing accountants, financial analysts and planners, financial managers, investment analysts, and professional bankers, among others.

The subjects are explained with

- Clear definitions and explanations, including step-by-step instructions
- Checklists
- Practical applications
- Tables and statistical data, as needed
- Charts, exhibits, and diagrams, where appropriate

The Encyclopedic Dictionary will enlighten the practitioner by presenting the most current information, offer important directives, and explain the technical procedures involved in the aforementioned dynamic business disciplines. This reference book will help you diagnose and evaluate accounting and financial situations you face daily. This library of accounting and finance will answer every question you may have. Real-life examples are provided, along with suggestions for handling everyday problems. The Encyclopedic Dictionary applies to large, medium, or small companies. It will help you to make smart decisions in all areas of accounting and finance. It should be used as an *advanced guide* for working professionals, rather than as a reference guide for laymen or a glossary of accounting and finance terms.

The Encyclopedic Dictionary is a handy reference for today's busy accountant and financial executive. It is a working guide to help you quickly pinpoint

- What to look for
- What to watch out for
- What to do
- How to do it
- How to apply it in the complex world of business

You'll find ratios, formulas, examples, applications, tables, charts, and rules of thumb to help you analyze and evaluate any business-related situation. New up-to-date methods and techniques are included. Throughout, you'll find this Encyclopedic Dictionary practical, comprehensive, quick, and useful. In short, this is a veritable cookbook of guidelines, illustrations, and how-to's for you, the modern decision maker. The uses of this handbook are as varied as the topics presented. Keep it handy for easy reference throughout your busy day.

There are approximately 500 major topics in accounting and finance covered in the Encyclopedic Dictionary, as well as about 100 related entries. Where appropriate, there is a cross-reference to another entry to explain the topic in greater detail. The entries are listed in alphabetical order for easy reference. The Encyclopedic Dictionary is so comprehensive that any subject area of interest to accountants and financial executives, as well as other interested parties, can be found.

CREDIT LINES

Permission to reprint Example 1 of Appendix C (pages 44–51) of *FASB Statement 95—Statement of Cash Flows* and the example on page 32 of *FASB Statement 96—Accounting for Income Taxes* were received from the Financial Accounting Standards Board, High Ridge Park, Stamford, Connecticut, 06905, U.S.A. Reprinted with permission. Copies of the complete document are available from the Financial Accounting Standards Board.

The CPA System and The Client System are trademarks of ICON Interactive Concepts. ATOM 1–3, Plus Plan, Statistical Techniques, and Estimation Sampling are trademarks of Deloitte, Haskins and Sells. Enterprise System is a trademark of BPI Corp. Crystal Payroll is a trademark of Crystal Software. Stock-Master is a trademark of Applied Micro Business Systems. Taxadvisor is a trademark of R. Michaelson. Auditor is a trademark of C. Dungan. TICOM is a trademark of A. Bailey, A. Whinston, and M. Gagle. Arborist Decision Tree, Natural Link, and Personal Consultant/Plus are trademarks of Texas Instruments. Audit Cube is a trademark of Blackman, Kallick & Co. Automated Workpapers is a trademark of Linton Shafer. Pre-Audit is a trademark of Coopers and Lybrand. dBase III+ and Framework are trademarks of Ashton-Tate. Sidekick is a trademark of Borland International. Expert Ease is a trademark of Human Edge Software. Planpower is a trademark of Applied Expert System. Expert Strategist is a trademark of Unitek Technologies. Interactive Easy Flow is a trademark of Haven Tree Software. PC Storyboard and Topview are trademarks of IBM. Harvard Presentation Graphics is a trademark of Software Publishing. Market Analyzer, Market Manager, Market Microscope, and Investment Evaluator are trademarks of Dow Jones. Value Pac is a trademark of Value Line. Winning on Wall Street is a trademark of Samna Software. Stockpac II is a trademark of Standard and Poor's. Option Strategy Calculation and Reporting is a trademark of ATS Software. Portfolio is a trademark of Software Option. Real Estate Analyzer is a trademark of Howard Software. Real Estate and Financial Software is a trademark of Taft Cameron. Property Management Plus is a trademark of Realty Software. Property Management is a trademark of Yardi Systems. Local Net is a trademark of Sytek. Managing Your Money is a trademark of Andrew Tobias. Scratch Pad is a trademark of SuperSoft. Note It is a trademark of Turner Hall Publishing. Spreadsheet Auditor is a trademark of Consumers Software. Spreadsheet Analyst is a trademark of Cambridge Software. SPSS/PC is a trademark of SPSS Inc. Strategic Management Game is a trademark of Strategic Management Group. Windows is a trademark of Microsoft. GEM Desktop is a trademark of Digital Research. Desqview is a trademark of Quarterback Office Systems. Amps Tax is a trademark of Amps Software. Volts Tax Software Pack is a trademark of Hanover Software. Micro-Tax is a trademark of Microcomputers Tax Systems. Tax-Plan is a trademark of Ernst and Whinney. A-plus Tax is a trademark of Arthur Andersen. The Tax Planning Template is a trademark of Permar Associates. Security Modem is a trademark of ITT. Think Tank is a trademark of Living Videotext. Time Management and Billing System is a trademark of Systematic Data Marketing Corp. Professional Time and Billing is a trademark of UniLink. Crosstalk is a trademark of Microstuf. Smartcom is a trademark of Hayes. SideTalk is a trademark of Lattice. Lotus 1-2-3 is a trademark of Lotus Development Corp.

A

ABC INVENTORY METHOD This is a method that categorizes items according to importance. Hence, greater attention is given to higher dollar merchandise (A's) than lower cost items (B's). The least essential items (C's) are lowest in priority order in terms of control and attention. Under this method, inventory evaluation is performed often. The steps involved follow:

1. A segregation is made of merchandise into components (e.g., varying models) based on dollar value.

2. Annual dollar usage is computed by inventory type (anticipated annual usage times unit cost).

3. A ranking is given to inventory in terms of dollar usage, ranging from high to low (e.g., A's in top 30%, B's in next 50%, and C's in last 20%.

4. Inventory is tagged with the appropriate classification so proper emphasis may be placed on them. A recording is made in the inventory records of the classifications.

See also Inventory Control and Management; Inventory Planning and Control.

ACCEPTANCE SAMPLING This involves an accept–reject decision, such as for inventory items and documents. It necessitates a precise advance decision regarding the error incidence mandating rejection. For example, if a company's internal control system is rejected after sampling, the entire system will be closely scrutinized.

In acceptance sampling, a group of data are examined to ascertain whether the number of sampled items possessing a specified attribute is greater than a stated percentage. One objective is not to reject acceptable batches. It is a useful approach for the internal auditor in gauging the quality of clerical work. Acceptance sampling tables are used to formulate a sampling plan to assure that errors will not exceed a stated percentage of the batch (tolerable error rate). However, a complete examination of rejected batches must be made. Also, documents may be examined for such things as mathematical computations. Acceptance sampling is primarily an internal audit technique rather than an external audit tool. For example, it is quite difficult to come up with a sampling plan that while rejecting, say, 95% of deficient batches does not also reject many good batches. Three considerations in a sampling plan are batch size, sample size, and maximum number of defects before rejection of the whole batch. *See also* Sampling.

ACCOUNTING CHANGES   The types of accounting changes provided for in APB 20 are principle, estimate, and reporting entity. Proper disclosure of accounting changes is necessary.

Change in Accounting Principle

Once adopted, it is presumed that an accounting principle should not be changed for events or transactions of a similar nature. A method used for a transaction that is being terminated or was a single nonrecurring event in the past should not be changed. Only where necessary should a change in principle be made.

A change in accounting principle is accounted for in the current year's income statement in an account called cumulative effect of a change in accounting principle. The amount equals the difference between retained earnings at the beginning of the year with the old method versus what retained earnings would have been at the beginning of the year if the new method had been used in prior years. The account is shown net of tax with EPS on it. The new principle is used in the current and future years. Consistency is needed to make proper user comparisons. The cumulative effect account is shown after extraordinary items and before net income in the income statement. Note that a change in depreciation method for a *new* fixed asset is *not* a change in principle. Footnote disclosure should be made of the nature and justification of a change in principle, including an explanation of why the new principle is preferred. Proper justification may take the form of a new FASB pronouncement, new tax law, new AICPA recommended practice, change in circumstances, and to conform more readily to industry practice. According to FASB 32, specialized accounting practices and principles included in the AICPA Statements of Position (SOPs) and Guides are "preferable accounting principles" for the application of APB 20.

In the case where summaries of financial data for several years are presented in financial reports, APB 20 applies to them.

Indirect effects are included in the cumulative effect only if they are to be recorded on the books as a result of a change in accounting principle. The cumulative effect does *not* include nondiscretionary adjustments based on earnings (e.g., employee bonuses), which would have been recognized if the new principle had been used in prior years.

If comparative financial statements are not shown, *pro forma* disclosures (recalculated figures) should be made between the body of the financial statements and the footnotes of what earnings would have been in prior years if the new principle had been used in those prior years, along with showing the actual amounts for those years. If income statements are presented for comparative purposes, they should reflect the change on a pro forma basis as if the change had been in effect in each of such years. Financial statements of prior years, presented for comparative purposes, are presented *as previously reported*. But income before extraordinary items, net income, and earnings per share for previous years presented are *recalculated* and disclosed on the face of the prior periods' income statements as if the new principle had been in use in those periods. If space does not allow, this information may be presented in separate schedules showing both the original and recalculated figures. If only the current period's income statement is presented, the actual and pro forma (recalculated) figures for the immediate preceding period should be disclosed.

In exceptional cases, pro forma amounts are not determinable for prior years even though the cumulative effect on the opening retained earnings balance can be computed. The cumulative effect of a change in principle is presented in the usual fashion, with reasons given for omitting pro forma figures. In a similar vein, when the cumulative effect of a change in principle is impossible to calculate, disclosure is given for the effect of the change on income data of the current period and explaining the reason for omitting the cumulative effect and pro forma amounts for prior periods. An example of a situation where the cumulative effect is not determinable is a switch from the FIFO to LIFO inventory pricing method.

If an accounting change in principle is deemed immaterial in the current year but it is anticipated to be material in later years, disclosure is necessary.

Certain types of changes in accounting principle instead of being shown in a cumulative effect account require the restatement of prior years as if the new principle had been used in those years. These changes are

• Change from LIFO to another inventory method.

• Change in accounting for long-term construction contracts (e.g., changing from the completed contract method to the percentage of completion method).

• Change to or from the full cost method used in the extractive industry. The full cost method is where both successful and unsuccessful exploration costs are deferred to the asset account and amortized. An alternative method is successful efforts where only successful costs are deferred while unsuccessful ones are immediately expensed.

Exempt from the requirements of APB Opinion 20 is a *closely held* business that for the *first time* registers securities, obtains equity capital, or effects a business combination. Such company *may* restate prior year financial statements.

Not considered a change in accounting principle are

• A principle adopted for the first time on new or previously immaterial events or transactions

• A principle adopted or changed due to events or transactions clearly different in substance

As per Interpretation 1, an *accounting principle* is not only an accounting principle or practice, but also includes the methods used to apply such principles and practices. *Changing the composition* of the cost elements (e.g., material, labor, and overhead) of inventory qualifies as an accounting change. Changing the composition must be reported and justified as preferable. The basis of preferability among the different accounting principles is established in terms of whether the new principle improves the financial reporting function. Preferability is not determinable considering income tax effect alone.

■ Example

X Company changed from double declining balance to straight-line depreciation in 19X7. It uses ACRS depreciation for tax purposes, which results in depreciation higher than the double declining balance method for each of the three years. The tax rate is 34%. Relevant data follow:

Year	Double Declining Balance Depreciation	Straight-Line Depreciation	Difference
19X5	$250,000	$150,000	$100,000
19X6	200,000	150,000	50,000
19X7	185,000	150,000	35,000

The entries to reflect the change in depreciation in 19X7 follow:

Depreciation	150,000		
Accumulated depreciation		150,000	

(For current year depreciation under the straight-line method.)

Accumulated depreciation (100,000 + 50,000)		150,000	
Deferred income tax credit (150,000 × 0.34)			51,000
Cumulative effect of a change in accounting principle			99,000

Change in Accounting Estimate

A change in accounting estimate is caused by new circumstances or events requiring a revision in the estimates, such as a change in salvage value or life of an asset. A change in accounting estimate is accounted for prospectively over current and future years. There is *no* restatement of prior years. A footnote should describe the nature of the change. Disclosure is required in the period of the change for the effect on income before extraordinary items, net income, and earnings per share. However, such disclosure is *not* required for estimate changes in the ordinary course of business when immaterial. Examples are revising estimates of uncollectible accounts or inventory obsolescence. If a change in estimate is coupled with a change in principle and the effects cannot be distinguished, it is accounted for as a change in estimate. For instance, a change may be made from deferring and amortizing a cost to expensing it as incurred because future benefits may be doubtful. This should be accounted for as a change in estimate.

■ Example

Equipment was bought on 1/1/19X2 for $40,000 having an original estimated life of 10 years with a salvage value of $4,000. On 1/1/19X6, the estimated life was revised to 8 more years remaining with a new salvage value of $3,200. The journal entry on 12/31/19X6 for depreciation expense is

Depreciation	2,800	
Accumulated depreciation		2,800

Computations follow:

Book value on 1/1/19X6:

Original cost		$40,000
Less: Accumulated depreciation		
$\dfrac{\$40,000 - \$4,000}{10} = \$3,600 \times 4$		14,400
Book value		$25,600

Depreciation for 19X6:

Book value	$25,600
Less: New salvage value	3,200
Depreciable cost	$22,400

$$\frac{\text{Depreciable cost}}{\text{New life}} \quad \frac{\$22,400}{8} = \$2,800$$

Change in Reporting Entity

A change in reporting entity (e.g., two previously separate companies combine) is accounted for by restating prior years' financial statements as if both companies were always combined. Restatement for a change in reporting entity is necessary to show proper trends in comparative financial statements and historical summaries. The effect of the change on income before extraordinary items, net income, and per share amounts is reported for all periods presented. The restatement process does not have to go back more than 5 years. Footnote disclosure should be made of the nature of and reason for the change in reporting entity only in the year of change. Examples of changes in reporting entity are

• Presenting consolidated statements instead of statements of individual companies

• Change in subsidiaries included in consolidated statements or those included in combined statements

• A business combination accounted for under the pooling-of-interests method

ACCOUNTING INFORMATION SYSTEM (AIS)

AIS is a subsystem of management information system (MIS) that processes financial transactions to provide scorekeeping, attention-directing, and decision-making information to management. The AIS is therefore the set of activities of the firm responsible for the preparation of financial information and the information obtained from transaction data for the purposes of (1) internal reporting to managers for use in planning, controlling, and decision making and (2) external reporting to outside parties such as stockholders, creditors, and government. *See also* Financial Information System; Management Information System (MIS).

ACCOUNTING POLICIES

Accounting policies of a business entity are the specific accounting principles and methods of applying them that are selected by management. Accounting policies used should be those that are most appropriate in the circumstances to fairly

present financial position and results of operations for the period. Accounting policies can relate to reporting and measurement methods as well as disclosures. They include
 • A selection from generally accepted accounting principles
  • Practices unique to the given industry
  • Unusual applications of generally accepted accounting principles

The first footnote or a section preceding the notes to the financial statements should be a description of the accounting policies followed by the company.

The application of GAAP requires the use of *judgment* where alternative acceptable principles exist and where varying methods of applying a principle to a given set of facts exist. Disclosure of these principles and methods is vital to the full presentation of financial position and operations so that rational economic decisions can be made.

Examples of accounting policy disclosures are the depreciation method used, consolidation bases, amortization period for goodwill, construction contract method, and inventory pricing method.

Some types of financial statements need not describe the accounting policies followed. Examples are quarterly unaudited statements when there has not been a policy change since the last year-end and statements solely for internal use.

ACCOUNTING PRINCIPLES These are guidelines, laws, or rules used in accounting practice to prepare financial statements. GAAP curtails the differences in accounting practice so that usefulness and comparability of financial statements are improved. GAAP is formulated by authoritative bodies, such as the Financial Accounting Standards Board. Applying accounting principles to a particular situation may require the accountant's judgment. Sources of GAAP include
 • FASB pronouncements
 • AICPA Interpretations, Audit Guides,

Accounting Guides, and Statements of Position
 • SEC regulations
 • IRS regulations
 • Accounting literature

ACCOUNTING SOFTWARE An accounting package must be selected given the client's circumstances and needs. Accounting modules include general ledger, accounts receivable, accounts payable, payroll, inventory, and fixed assets. The first four modules are the most common. There are many accounting packages on the market, with a wide range in cost, quality, features, applications, and sophistication. Select the one that best meets your needs as well as your client's requirements.

The client may acquire individual modules or an integrated package. A small business may find that a general ledger module is adequate. A large corporation would need several modules. *Note*: Integrated accounting software links a number of modules performing related tasks; data from one module are transferred to another module. With integrated accounting packages, you do not have to continually reenter information because the different modules communicate with each other, updating the data base. For example, updating accounts payable automatically updates the general ledger. Integrated accounting software centers around the general ledger and includes other modules for specific accounting purposes, plus spreadsheet and word processing. You can go from accounting programs and other software to answering questions even if you're in the middle of a batch of transactions. Compatibility, efficiency, expeditious learning, integration, and lower cost dictate purchasing an integrated package from one vendor. It would be a mistake to acquire individual packages from different vendors.

The better accounting software works in different business situations and on different types of computers. This kind of package is needed to meet changing circumstances. Lower priced general ledger software having such key features as accounts receivable, accounts payable, and report writing can be bought. However, inexpensive packages have fewer features and look only at the broadest accounting problems. Although the number of accounts might be restricted, there is still an automatic interface to the general ledger, along with adequate audit trails and controls.

ICON Interactive Concepts™ has compatible systems for CPAs and their clients. The CPA System™ includes audit, client write-up, tax preparation and planning, and practice management. The Client System™ includes general ledger, inventory control, accounts receivable/accounts payable, order entry/billing, sales analysis, and office automation. There is an instant rescue package to solve problems. Client data may be transferred to the CPA's computer automatically.

Deloitte, Haskins and Sells' ATOM 1-3™ has modules for trial balance, financial statements, and financial analysis. It maintains trial balance and financial statement information for many years. Items prepared include adjusting and reclassifying entries, working papers, ratio analysis, and financial statements. Information can be transferred to other programs such as Lotus 1-2-3.™

BPI's Enterprise Series™ generates an income statement for the company and income statements for departments. There are modules for accounts receivable, accounts payable, payroll, and inventory. It updates the control account and individual accounts automatically for a single transaction. Standard adjusting entries are made in the general ledger with a single command. Using information in the cash disbursements journal, checks may be written automatically. It has the ability to customize financial statements and produce ledgers with a full year's transactions.

Consolidation packages exist to prepare consolidations or foreign currency translations; an example is Deloitte, Haskins and Sell's Plus Plan.™

While there are specialized accounting programs for specific industries (e.g., Bristol Information Systems is a manufacturer of industry-specific software), general-purpose programs usually fit the bill.

The implementation of a new computerized system usually takes 6 to 12 months. Typically, one module is implemented at a time.

General Ledger Module

The general ledger module is central to the entire accounting system. It alone is sufficient for a small company. The general ledger module typically produces a chart of accounts, journals, trial balance, general ledger, and financial statements. The package should be flexible, allowing you to customize the system and report formats to the particular business requirements and preferences.

General ledger and financial statement programs should be used for client write-ups, whether for compilations, reviews, or audits, as well as to keep the practitioner's records. General ledger programs set up the chart of accounts and allow for entering beginning balances, budget amounts, and comparative prior period amounts. From a control point of view, these programs should also generate batch totals for input verification; display cumulative totals for both sides of a transaction, warning of any out-of-balance situation; and search for and reject any erroneous account numbers.

Accounts Receivable

An accounts receivable module is needed where there are significant amounts of sales transactions. The accounts receivable module assists cash flow and credit policy. Receivables from customers are tracked, reconciled, invoiced, and aged.

Desirable features in an accounts receivable package include

• Types of receivables accommodated
• Number of customers and general ledger accounts
• Highest transaction amount
• Number of invoices and payments
• Verification of customer information before transaction processing
• Proper adjustments to accounts receivable accounts
• Aging analysis
• Comparison of individual accounts to credit limits
• Sales analysis by salesperson, customer, and territory
• Sales tax reports

Accounts Payable

An accounts payable module is needed only when numerous checks are written. The frequency of the system may be weekly, semimonthly, or monthly, depending on the availability of cash discounts and the number of transactions. The accounts payable package makes out checks to vendors, assures the receipt of discounts, and prepares an aging of payables.

A quality accounts payable package should

• Accommodate many vendors, vouchers, checks, and invoices.
• Alphabetically list vendors
• Provide highest invoice amount allowed
• Calculate discounts and finance charges
• Pinpoint frequency and amount of payments and payables
• List recurring checks
• Show a due date register of payables along with their terms
• Analyze vendors
• Track lost discounts
• Compare receiving reports to supplier invoices

• List open purchase orders by vendor and item number

Payroll

A payroll package is feasible only if there are enough employees to justify the cost. Payroll software aids in determining the payroll deposit and offers needed payroll data at tax reporting time. Various packages exist. For example, Crystal Software's Crystal Payroll™ has user-defined pay types for hourly, salary, dollar, bonus, commission, tips, piece wage rates, expenses, and voluntary reductions, including 401Ks. There are multiple pay and deduction rates as well as allocation to multigeneral ledger accounts and departments. Quarterly and year-end reports are prepared.

Inventory

In evaluating an inventory package's quality, consideration should be given to

• Master files for inventory, customer, and vendor
• Number of inventory items handled
• Inventory records, including balances by item and category
• Inventory transactions for receipts, issuances, returns, and adjustments
• Interfacing with purchase orders and sales orders
• Comparing packing slips to purchase orders for quantity and part verification
• Processing adjustments to inventory quantities and price
• Reconciliation of promised date for delivery to actual delivery date
• Warehouse information
• Pricing determined by product, such as by using preestablished pricing methods
• Comparison of book to physical amounts
• Entry error-rejection capability
• Variance analysis for inventory discrepancies

• Calculation of economic order quantity and economic order point

• Calculation of lead time in receiving inventory

• Determination of safety stock

• Shortage reports

• Inventory turnover rates

• Actual inventory amounts compared with preestablished limits

• Back-order report

• ABC inventory classification

• Sales data by item for a given period

• Gross profit data by customer, item, and sales territory

An example of an inventory package is Applied Micro Business Systems' Stock-Master™, which provides stock status, trend analysis, purchase order tracking, quality control reporting, detail analysis, and Bill of Materials.

Fixed Assets

A good fixed asset package may provide the following features

• Description and categorization of assets

• Number and amount of assets accommodated

• Cost, life, and salvage value for fixed assets

• Allowance for different depreciation methods

• Pro rata depreciation calculations

• Fixed asset cost center

Best Programs' PC/Fixed Asset System™ manages fixed assets and provides necessary record keeping. Three sets of books are maintained for each fixed asset for the IRS, state, and internal use. Voluminous assets can be managed at once. It calculates depreciation, tracks asset location and "class," and indicates warranty expiration.

ACCOUNTS RECEIVABLE FINANCING (INCLUDING ASSIGNMENT AND FACTORING) Accounts receivable may be financed either through an assignment or factoring arrangement.

Assignment

When accounts receivable are assigned, the owner of the receivables borrows cash from a lender in the form of a note payable. The accounts receivable acts as collateral. New receivables substitute for receivables collected.

At a particular date, the transferor's equity in the assigned receivables equals the difference between the accounts receivable assigned and the balance of the line ($5,000). When payments on the receivables are received, they are remitted by the company to the lending institution to reduce the liability. Assignment is on a nonnotification basis to customers. It is made with recourse, where the company has to make good for uncollectable customer accounts.

■ Example

On 4/1/19X1, X Company assigns accounts receivable totaling $600,000 to A Bank as collateral for a $400,000 note. X Company will continue to receive customer remissions since the customers are not notified of the assignment. There is a 2% finance charge of the accounts receivable assigned. Interest on the note is 13%. Monthly settlement of the cash received from assigned receivables is made. During the month of April, there were collections of $360,000 of assigned receivables less cash discounts of $5,000. Sales returns were $10,000. On 5/1/19X1, April remissions were made plus accrued interest. In May the balance of the assigned accounts receivable was collected less $4,000 that were uncollectable. On 6/1/19X1, the balance due was remitted to the bank plus interest for May. The journal entries follow:

4/1/19X1

Cash	388,000	
Finance charge		
(2% × $600,000)	12,000	
Accounts receivable assigned	600,000	
Notes payable		400,000
Accounts receivable		600,000

During April:

Cash	355,000	
Sales discount	5,000	
Sales returns	10,000	
Accounts receivable as-signed		370,000

5/1/19X1

Interest expense	4,333*	
Notes payable	355,000	
Cash		359,333

During May:

Cash	226,000	
Allowance for bad debts	4,000	
Accounts receivable as-signed ($600,000 − $370,000)		230,000

6/1/19X1

Interest expense	488†	
Notes payable ($400,000 − $355,000)	45,000	
Cash		45,488

* $400,000 × 0.13 × 1/12 = $4,333
† $45,000 × 0.13 × 1/12 = $488

Factoring

In a factoring of accounts receivable, the receivables are in effect sold to a finance company. The factor buys the accounts receivable at a discount from face value, usually at a discount of 6%. Customers are typically notified. Factoring is usually done without recourse, where the risk of uncollectability of the customer's account rests with the financing institution. Billing and collection is typically done by the factor. On a factoring arrangement, the factor charges a commission of from 3/4% to 1½% of the net receivables acquired. The entry is

Cash (proceeds)
Loss on sale of receivables
Due from factor (proceeds kept by factor to cover possible adjustments such as sales discounts, sales returns, and allowances)
Accounts receivable (face amount of receivables)

Factoring is normally a continuous process. The seller of the goods receives orders and transmits the purchase orders to the factor for approval; on approval, the goods are shipped; the factor advances the money to the seller; the buyers pay the factor when payment is due; and the factor periodically remits any excess reserve to the seller of the goods. Once a routine is established, a continuous circular flow of goods and funds takes place among the seller, the buyers, and the factor. Once the agreement is in force, funds from this source are spontaneous.

■ Example

T Company factors $200,000 of accounts receivable. There is a 4% finance charge. The factor retains 6% of the accounts receivable. Appropriate journal entries are

Cash	180,000	
Loss on sale of receivables (4% × $200,000)	8,000	
Due from factor (6% × $200,000)	12,000	
Accounts receivable		200,000

Factors provide a needed and dependable source of income for small manufacturers and service businesses.

■ Example

You need an additional $100,000. You are considering a factoring arrangement. The factor is willing to buy the accounts receivable and advance the invoice amount less a 4% factoring commission on the receivables purchased. Sales are on 30-day terms. A 14% interest rate will be charged on the total invoice price and deducted in advance. With the factoring arrangement, the credit department will be eliminated, reducing monthly credit expenses by $1,500. Also, bad debt losses of 8% on the factored amount will be avoided.

To net you $100,000, the amount of accounts receivable to be factored is

$$\frac{\$100,000}{1 - (0.04 + 0.14)} = \frac{\$100,000}{0.82} = \$121,951$$

The effective interest rate on the factoring arrangement is

$$\frac{0.14}{0.82} = 17.07\%$$

The annual total dollar cost is

Interest (0.14 × $121,951)	$17,073
Factoring (0.04 × $121,951)	4,878
Total cost	$21,951

ACCOUNTS RECEIVABLE MANAGEMENT In managing accounts receivable, the financial manager should consider that there is an opportunity cost associated with holding receivables. Means to expedite collection should be explored. A key concern is the amount and credit terms given to customers. Receivable management bears on the bottom line.

Means of Managing Accounts Receivable
- "Cycle bill" to produce greater uniformity in the billing process.
- Mail customer statements within 24 hours of the close of the accounting period.
- Send an invoice to customers when the order is processed at the warehouse instead of when merchandise is shipped.
- Bill for services periodically when work is performed or charge a retainer. *Tip*: Bill large sales immediately.
- Use seasonal datings. *Recommendation*: When business is slow, sell to customers with delayed payment terms to stimulate demand for customers who are unable to pay until later in the season. *What to do*: Compare profitability on incremental sales plus the reduction in inventory carrying costs, which have to exceed the opportunity cost on the additional investment in average accounts receivable.
- Carefully analyze customer financial statements before giving credit. Also, obtain ratings from financial advisory sources such as Dun and Bradstreet.
- Avoid typically high-risk receivables (e.g., customers in a financially troubled industry).
- Modify credit limits based on changes in customer's financial health.
- Ask for collateral in support of questionable accounts. *Tip*: The collateral value should equal or exceed the account balance.
- Factor accounts receivable when net savings ensue.
- Use outside collection agencies where warranted.
- Consider marketing factors, since a stringent credit policy might result in a loss of business.
- Consumer receivables have greater risk of default than corporate receivables.
- Age accounts receivable to spot delinquent customers. Aged receivables can be compared to prior years, industry norms, and competitive norms. *Note*: Bad debt losses are typically higher for smaller companies than for larger ones.
- Accelerate collections from customers currently having financial problems.
- Have credit insurance to guard against unusual bad debt losses. *What to consider*: In deciding whether to get this insurance, take into account expected average bad debt losses, financial capability of the firm to withstand the losses, and the cost of insurance.

Attributes of a Good Credit System
- Clear, quick, and uniform in application.
- Does not intrude on customer's privacy.
- Inexpensive (e.g., centralization of credit decisions by experienced staff).
- Based upon past experience, considering characteristics of good, questionable, and bad accounts. *Tip*: Determine the correlation between customer characteristics and future uncollectability.

The financial executive often has to determine the dollar investment tied up in accounts receivable.

■ Example

A company sells on terms of net/30. The accounts are on average 20 days past due. Annual credit sales are $600,000. The investment in accounts receivable is

$$\frac{50}{360} \times \$600,000 = \$83,333.28$$

■ Example

The cost of a product is 30% of selling price and the cost of capital is 10% of selling price. On average, accounts are paid 4 months after sale. Average sales are $70,000 per month.

The investment in accounts receivable from this product is

Accounts receivable	
(4 months × $70,000)	$280,000
Investment in accounts receivable	
[$280,000 × (0.30 + 0.10)]	112,000

Should customers be offered a discount for the early payment of account balances? Compare the return on freed cash resulting from customers' paying sooner to the cost of the discount.

■ Example

The following data are provided

Current annual credit sales	$14,000,000
Collection period	3 months
Terms	net/30
Minimum rate of return	15%

The company is considering offering a 3/10, net/30 discount. We expect 25% of the customers to take advantage of it. The collection period will decline to two months.

The discount should be offered, as indicated in the calculations shown below.

Should the company give credit to marginal customers? Compare the earnings on sales obtained to the added cost of the receivables. *Note*: If the company has idle capacity, the additional earnings is the contribution margin on the incremental sales because fixed costs are constant. The additional cost on the additional receivables results from the greater number of bad debts and the opportunity cost of tying up funds in receivables for a longer time period.

■ Example

Sales price per unit	$120
Variable cost per unit	80
Fixed cost per unit	15
Annual credit sales	$600,000
Collection period	1 month
Minimum return	16%

If you liberalize the credit policy, you project that

- Sales will increase by 40%.
- The collection period on total accounts will be 2 months.
- Bad debts on the increased sales will be 5%.

Preliminary calculations:

Current units ($600,000/$120)	5,000
Additional units (5,000 × 0.4)	2,000

Advantage		
Increased profitability:		
Average accounts receivable balance before a change in policy		
$\dfrac{\text{Credit sales}}{\text{Accounts receivable turnover}}$ $\dfrac{\$14,000,000}{4}$		$3,500,000
Average accounts receivable balance after change in policy		
$\dfrac{\text{Credit sales}}{\text{Average receivable turnover}}$ $\dfrac{\$14,000,000}{6}$		$2,333,333
Reduction in average accounts receivable balance		$1,116,667
Rate of return		× 0.15
Return		$ 175,000
Disadvantage		
Cost of the discount 0.30 × 0.25 × $14,000,000		$ 105,000
Net advantage of discount		$ 70,000

The new average unit cost is now calculated:

	Units ×	Unit Cost =	Total Cost
Current units	5,000 ×	$95	$475,000
Additional units	2,000 ×	$80	160,000
Total	7,000		$635,000

New average unit cost =

$$\frac{\text{Total cost}}{\text{Units}} = \frac{\$635,000}{7,000} = \$90.71$$

Note that at idle capacity, fixed cost remains constant. Thus, the incremental cost is only the variable cost of $80 per unit. This will cause the new average unit cost to drop.

Advantage

Additional profitability:	
Incremental sales volume ×	2,000 units
Contribution margin per unit	
(Selling price − variable cost)	
$120 − $80	× $40
Incremental profitability	$ 80,000

Disadvantage

Incremental bad debts:	
Incremental units × Selling price	
2,000 × $120	$240,000
Bad debt percentage	× 0.05
Additional bad debts	$ 12,000

Opportunity cost of funds tied up in accounts receivable: Average investment in accounts receivable after change in policy:

$$\frac{\text{Credit sales}}{\text{Accounts receivable turnover}} \times \frac{\text{Unit cost}}{\text{Selling price}}$$

$\frac{\$840,000 @}{6} \times \frac{\$90.71}{\$120}$	$105,828

@7,000 units × $120 = $840,000

Current average investment in accounts receivable:

$\frac{\$600,000}{12} \times \frac{\$ 95}{\$120}$	39,583
Additional investment in accounts receivable	$66,245
Minimum return	× 0.16
Opportunity cost of funds tied up	$10,599

Net advantage of relaxation in credit standards:		
Additional earnings		$80,000
Less:		
Additional bad debt losses	$12,000	
Opportunity cost	10,599	22,599
Net savings		$57,401

The company may have to decide whether to extend full credit to presently limited credit customers or no-credit customers. Full credit should be given only if net profitability occurs.

■ Example

In deciding on a credit policy, the financial manager is appraising for different categories of customers what the percentage of uncollectability will be as well as the collection pool.

Category	Bad Debt Percentage	Collection Period	Credit Policy	Increase in Annual Sales if Credit Restrictions Are Relaxed
X	2%	30 days	Unlimited	$ 80,000
Y	5%	40 days	Restricted	600,000
Z	30%	80 days	No credit	850,000

Gross profit is 25% of sales. The minimum return on investment is 12%.

	Category Y	Category Z
Gross profit		
$600,000 × 0.25	$150,000	
$850,000 × 0.25		$212,500
Less bad debts		
$600,000 × 0.05	−30,000	
$850,000 × 0.30		−255,000
Incremental average investment in accounts receivable		
$\frac{40}{360}$ × (0.75 × $600,000)	$50,000	
$\frac{80}{360}$ × (0.75 × $850,000)		$141,667
Opportunity cost of incremental investment in accounts receivable	× 0.12 − 6,000	× 0.12 − 17,000
Net earnings	$114,000	$(59,500)

Credit should be extended to Category Y.

■ Example

The company is planning a sales campaign in which it will offer credit terms of 3/10, net/45. We expect the collection period to increase from 60 days to 80 days. Relevant data for the contemplated campaign follow.

	Percent of Sales Before Campaign	Percent of Sales During Campaign
Cash sales	40	30
Payment from		
1–10	25	55
11–100	35	15

The proposed sales strategy will probably increase sales from $8 million to $10 million. There is a gross margin rate of 30%. The rate of return is 14%. Sales discounts are given on cash sales.

	Without Sales Campaign	With Sales Campaign
Gross margin (0.3 × $8,000,000)	$2,400,000	0.3 × $10,000,000 $3,000,000
Sales subject to discount		
0.65 × $8,000,000	$5,200,000	
0.85 × $10,000,000		$8,500,000
Sales discount	× 0.03 − 156,000	× 0.03 − 255,000
Investment in average accounts receivable		
$\frac{60}{360}$ × $8,000,000 × 0.7	$933,333	
$\frac{80}{360}$ × $10,000,000 × 0.7		$1,555,555
Return rate	× 0.14 − 130,667	× 0.14 −217,778
Net profit	$2,113,333	$2,527,222

The company should undertake the sales campaign, because earnings will increase by $413,889 ($2,527,222 − $2,113,333).

ACCRUAL BASIS   This is an accounting method that recognizes revenue and expenses when earned or incurred rather than at the time of cash flow. The accrual basis is employed in the case of a manufacturer or dealer in inventory. *See also* Cash Basis.

ACCUMULATED BENEFIT OBLIGATION   The accumulated benefit obligation is the actuarial present value of future benefits to be paid to retired employees for services performed prior to a specified date and based on employee service and salary up to that date. The *existing* salary levels are used in the computation. *See also* Pension Plans.

ACTUARIAL COST METHOD   The actuarial cost method is a technique that actuaries use to compute annual employer contribution to the pension so that plan sufficient monies exist at employee retirement. An actuarial cost method is needed for pension expense and funding computation. Two general approaches are based on *cost* or *benefit*. The cost technique estimates total retirement benefit and then computes the adequate cost level (including expected interest) sufficient to provide retirement benefits. The benefit technique computes pension benefits applicable to service to date and then derives the present value of these benefits. *See also* Pension Plans.

ACTUARIAL GAINS AND LOSSES   These represent the difference between actual experience and estimates applicable to the pension plan. If, for instance, the actual return on pension assets is less than the estimated return rate, there is an actuarial loss. Actuarial gains and losses are deferred and amortized as an adjustment to pension expense. An actuarial gain decreases pension expense whereas an actuarial loss increases it. However, if an actuarial gain or loss arises from an occurrence not applicable to the pension plan (e.g., closing a plant), it is immediately recognized in the current year's income statement. *See also* Pension Plans.

ADDING OR DROPPING A PRODUCT LINE   The decision whether to drop an old product line or add a new one must take into account both qualitative and quantitative factors. Ultimately, however, any final decision should be based primarily on the impact the decision will have on contribution margin or net income.

■ Example

The ABC grocery store has three major product lines: produce, meats, and canned goods. The store is considering the decision to drop the meat line because the income statement shows it is being sold at a loss. Note the income statement for these product lines below:

	Produce	Meats	Canned Food	Total
Sales	$10,000	$15,000	$25,000	$50,000
Less: Variable costs	6,000	8,000	12,000	26,000
CM	$ 4,000	$ 7,000	$13,000	$24,000
Less: Fixed costs:				
Direct	$ 2,000	$ 6,500	$ 4,000	$12,500
Allocated	1,000	1,500	2,500	5,000
Total	$ 3,000	$ 8,000	$ 6,500	$17,500
Net income	$ 1,000	($ 1,000)	$ 6,500	$ 6,500

In this example, direct fixed costs are those costs that are identified directly with each of the product lines, whereas allocated fixed costs are the amount of common fixed costs allocated to the product lines using some base such as space occupied. The amount of common fixed costs typically continue regardless of the decision and thus cannot be saved by dropping the product line to which it is distributed.

The following calculations show the effects on the company as a whole with and without the meat line:

	Keep Meats	Drop Meats	Difference
Sales	$50,000	$35,000	($15,000)
Less:			
Variable cost	26,000	18,000	(8,000)
CM	$24,000	$17,000	($ 7,000)
Less:			
Fixed cost:			
Direct	$12,500	$ 6,000	($ 6,500)
Allocated	5,000	5,000	—
Total	$17,500	$11,000	($ 6,500)
Net income	$ 6,500	$ 6,000	($ 500)

We see that by dropping meats the store will lose an additional $500. Therefore, the meat product line should be kept. One of the great dangers in allocating common fixed costs is that such allocations can make a product line look less profitable than it really is. Because of such an allocation, the meat line showed a loss of $1,000, but it in effect contributes $500 ($7,000 − $6,500) to the recovery of the store's common fixed costs.

ADJUSTABLE RATE MORTGAGE (ARM) An
ARM is a mortgage where the interest rate is not fixed but changes over the life of the loan. ARMs are often called *variable* or *flexible rate mortgages*. Adjustable rate mortgages often feature attractive starting interest rates and monthly payments. But there is the risk that payments will rise. Pluses of ARMs include:
1. Lower initial interest (often 2 or 3 percentage points below that of a fixed rate) and lower initial payments, which can mean considerable savings. This means that ARMs are easier to qualify for.
2. Payments come down if interest rates fall.
3. Loans are more readily available and their processing time is quicker than fixed-rate mortgages.
4. Many adjustables are assumable by a borrower, which can help when it comes time to sell.
5. Many ARMs allow one to prepay the loan without penalty.

Some of the pitfalls of ARMs include:
1. Monthly payments can go up if interest rates rise.
2. Negative amortization can occur. Negative amortization occurs when the monthly payments do not cover all of the interest cost. The interest cost that is not covered is added to the unpaid principal balance. This means after making many payments one could owe more than at the beginning of the loan balance.
3. The initial interest rates last only until the first adjustment, typically 6 months or 1 year. And the promotional or tease rate is often not distinguished from the true contract rate, which is based on the index to which the loan is tied.

ARMs vs. Fixed Rate

A borrower should consider a fixed rate loan over an ARM if he or she
• Plans to be in the same home for a long time. It pays to get an ARM if buying a starter home or expecting to move or be transferred in 2 to 3 years.
• Does not expect income to rise.
• Plans to take sizable debts, like auto or educational loans.
• Prizes the security of constant payments.

Checklist for ARMs

When shopping for an ARM (or for any other adjustable rate loan), the following checklist of questions to ask lenders is helpful:
• What is the initial loan rate and the annual percentage rate (APR)? What costs besides interest does the APR reflect? What are the points?
• What is the monthly payment?
• What index is the loan tied to? How has the index moved in the past? Will the rate always move with the index?

• What is the lender's margin above the index? The margin is an important consideration when comparing ARM loans because it never changes during the life of the loan. Note that index rate + margin = ARM interest rate.

■ Example

You are comparing ARMs offered by two different lenders. Both ARMs are for 30 years and amount to $65,000. Both lenders use the 1-year Treasury index, which is 10%. But Lender A uses a 2% margin and Lender B uses a 3% margin. Here is how the difference in margin would affect the initial monthly payment:

	Lender A	Lender B
ARM interest rate	12% (10% + 2%)	13% (10% + 3%)
Monthly payment	$668.60 at 12%	$719.03 at 13%

• How long will the initial rate be in effect? Will there be an automatic increase at the first adjustment period even if the index has not changed? What effect will this have on monthly payments?

• How often can the rate change?

• Is there a limit on each rate change and how will the limit affect monthly payments?

• What is the ''cap,'' or ceiling on the rate change over the life of the loan?

• Does the loan require private mortgage insurance (PMI) and how much does it cost per month?

• Is negative amortization possible?

• Is the loan assumable?

• Is there a prepayment penalty?

AFTER-TAX RATE OF RETURN The after-tax rate of return is the return on an investment that has to be considered in after-tax dollars.

■ Example

An individual earns 12% interest and is in the 28% tax bracket. The after-tax return rate is

$$12\% \times 72\% = 8.64\%$$

Inflation can be incorporated into the analysis. Assuming an inflation rate of 4%, the real rate of return after taxes and inflation is

$$
\begin{array}{r}
8.64\% \\
- 4.0\ \% \\
\hline
4.64\%
\end{array}
$$

AGENCY THEORY This is a branch of law and economics applying to the contractual relationship between principals and their agents. An example of a principal is the owner, and his agent is the manager. The principal delegates authority for action to the agent.

AGING SCHEDULE An aging schedule shows the length of time an item has been outstanding or held. Examples are aging of accounts receivable, accounts payable, and inventory. For example, an aging of accounts receivable reveals how many days receivables have been outstanding. The longer receivables are uncollected, the greater is the likelihood for uncollectability. Thus, there are varying bad debt percentages applied to the various categories of receivables. The percentages used are based on prior experience.

■ Example

X Company
AGING SCHEDULE

Customer's Name	12/31/19X1 Balance	Under 60 Days	61–90 Days	91–120 Days	Over 120 Days
ABC Co.	$ 85,000	$ 60,000	$ 20,000	$ 5,000	
XYZ Co.	160,000	160,000			
TEL Co.	120,000	70,000	25,000	10,000	$15,000
Total	$365,000	$290,000	$ 45,000	$15,000	$15,000

AGING SCHEDULE—Continued

Age	Amount	Bad Debt Percentage	Needed Balance in Allowance Account
Under 60 days	$290,000	1%	$ 2,900
61–90 days	45,000	4%	1,800
91–120 days	15,000	8%	1,200
Over 120 days	15,000	10%	1,500
	$365,000		$ 7,400

ALLOCATION OF SERVICE DEPARTMENT COSTS TO PRODUCTION DEPARTMENTS

There are two basic types of departments in a manufacturing company: production departments and service departments. A production department (such as assembly and machining) is where the production or conversion occurs. A service department (such as engineering and maintenance) provides support to production departments. Before departmental overhead rates are developed for product costing, the costs of a service department should be allocated to the appropriate production department (as part of factory overhead). There are three basic methods of allocation:

1. Direct allocation method
2. Step down method
3. Reciprocal service method

Direct Allocation Method

Direct allocation method, also called *direct method*, is a method of allocating the costs of each service department directly to the production departments. Under this method, no consideration is given to services performed by one service department for another. This is perhaps the most widely used method because of its simplicity and ease of use.

▪ Example

Assume the following data:

	Production Departments		Service Departments	
	A Machining	B Assembly	General Plant (GP)	Engineering (E)
Overhead costs before allocation	$30,000	$40,000	$20,000	$10,000
Engineering hours by Engineering	50,000	30,000	5,000	4,000
Direct labor hours by General Plant	60,000	40,000	15,000	20,000

Using the direct method yields:

	Service Departments		Production Departments	
	GP	E	A	B
Overhead costs	$20,000	$10,000	$30,000	$40,000
Reallocation:				
GP(60%, 40%)[a]	($20,000)		12,000	8,000
E(5/8, 3/8)[b]		($10,000)	6,250	3,750
			$48,250	$51,750

[a] Base is (60,000 + 40,000 = 100,000); 60,000/100,000 = 0.6; 40,000/100,000 = 0.4.
[b] Base is (50,000 + 30,000 = 80,000); 50,000/80,000 = 5/8; 30,000/80,000 = 3/8.

Step Allocation Method

This is a method of allocating services rendered by service departments to other service departments using a sequence of allocation; also called the *step-down* method and the *sequential* method. The sequence normally begins with the department that renders service to the greatest number of other service departments; the sequence continues in step-by-step fashion and ends with the allocation of costs of service departments that provide the least amount of service. But no *reciprocal* service is considered. Using the same data, the step allocation method yields:

	Service Departments		Production Departments	
	GP	E	A	B
Overhead costs	$20,000	$10,000	$30,000	$40,000
Reallocation:				
GP(1/2, 1/3, 1/6)	($20,000)	3,333	10,000	6,667
E(5/8, 3/8)		($13,333)	8,333	5,000
			$48,333	$51,667

Reciprocal Allocation Method

Reciprocal allocation method, also known as the *reciprocal* method, the *matrix* method, the *double-distribution* method, the *cross-allocation* method and the *simultaneous equation* method, is a method of allocating service department costs to production departments, where *reciprocal* services are allowed between service departments. The method sets up simultaneous equations to determine the allocable cost of each service department.

Using the same data, we set up the following equations:

$$GP = \$20,000 + 50/85\ E$$
$$E = \$10,000 + 1/6\ GP$$

Substituting *M* from the second equation into the first:

$$GP = \$20,000 + 5/85\ (\$10,000 + 1/6\ GP)$$

Solving for *GP* gives *GP* = $20,791. Substituting *GP* = $20,791 into the second equation and solving for *E* gives *E* = $13,465.

	Service Departments		Production Departments	
	GP	E	A	B
Overhead costs	$20,000	$10,000	$30,000	$40,000
Reallocation:				
GP(1/2, 3/1, 1/6)	($20,791)	3,465	10,396	6,930
E(50/85, 30/85, 5/85)	791	($13,465)	7,921	4,753
	0	0	$48,317	$51,683

ALPHA VALUE Alpha value of a security is the excess return that would be expected on the security if the excess return on the market portfolio were zero. It is also called *average differential return*. In the context of a mutual fund, an alpha value is the value representing the difference between the return on a fund and a point on the market line that corresponds to a beta equal to the fund, where the market line describes the relationship between excess returns and the portfolio beta. It has been used to evaluate performance of mutual funds. Generally, a positive alpha (excess return) indicates superior performance, whereas a negative value leads to the opposite conclusion. ''Keep your alpha high and your beta low'' is a basic strategy for those who wish to generate good investment performance. *See also* Beta Coefficient; Mutual Fund; Portfolio Theory and Capital Asset Pricing Model (CAPM).

AMORTIZATION This is the periodic reduction of an amount over time. It can apply to the gradual write-down of an asset and the gradual extinguishment of a debt. Examples are periodically reducing an intangible asset or deferred charge and reducing loan principal by making monthly payments.

Assets having a limited life must be reduced gradually over the period benefited. In the case of intangibles, amortization is over a period not exceeding 40 years using the straight-line method. In the case of some intangibles, a legal life may exist, such as with patents that have to be amortized over a period not exceeding 17 years. *Note*: If an intangible asset is suddenly deemed worthless, it is immediately written off, reflecting a nonrecurring loss.

▪ Example

During 19X2 and 19X3 research costing $300,000 to discover a new product was incurred. On 1/1/19X4, a patent is registered for $20,000 on the product. The useful life of the patent is estimated at 10 years. On 1/3/19X6, legal costs incurred in the successful defense of the patent is $5,000. The amortization expense for 19X6 is computed below:

Initial cost of 1/1/19X4	$20,000	
Less: Accumulated amortization		
($20,000/10) × 2	4,000	
Book value on 1/1/19X6		$16,000
Add: Legal costs on 1/3/19X6		5,000
Book value on 1/3/19X6		$21,000
Amortization expense for 19X6		
($21,000/8)		$ 2,625

ANALYTICAL PROCEDURES AICPA Statement on Auditing Standards No. 56 deals with auditor involvement with analytical review. The auditor is required to employ analytical review procedures in the planning and final review stages of an audit. Analytical techniques at the planning stage typically employ data at a high level. The procedures employed will vary depending on the complexity associated with the client's operations and reporting system. Examples of procedures are appraising the trend in account balances over the years and careful evaluation of quarterly financial statements.

Analytical review procedures are a type of substantive testing relating to the study and comparison of the relationships among data. It is helpful in alerting the auditor to the possibility of certain kinds of material irregularities. When significant fluctuations exist that are unexpected or unusual, the auditor should determine the reasons therefore. For example, the auditor may compare total wages to the number of employees to identify unauthorized payments. If a relationship does not make sense, detailed evaluation is required.

Analytical review procedures may be based on dollars, quantities, percentages, and ratio analysis comparing current period financial information with prior period financial data, anticipated amounts, predictable pattern information, intra-industry information, and nonfinancial data. In looking at nonfinancial data, the auditor may consider sales volume (e.g., if volume declines, there may exist merchandise quality problems), area of selling space occupied in square footage, and number of employees.

Professional judgment is exercised in deciding on specific analytical review procedures to be employed in a particular client setting.

There is greater assurance and predictability to relationships in a stable environment relative to one in an unstable environment. There is more assurance associated with income statement account relationships relative to balance sheet items. The former involves transactions over a time period. On the other hand, balance sheet items are static as of the end of the accounting period. If management discretion exists, the relationship associated with the transaction is more uncertain. For instance, management may cut back on repairs instead of buying new fixed assets. *See also* Substantive Test.

ANNUAL PERCENTAGE RATE (APR) Different types of investments use different compounding periods. For example, most bonds pay interest semiannually. Some banks pay interest quarterly. If an investor wishes to compare investments with different compounding periods, he needs to put them on a common basis. The annual percentage rate (APR), or effective annual rate, is used for this purpose and is computed as follows:

$$APR = (1 + r/m)^m - 1.0$$

where r = the stated, nominal, or quoted rate,

   m = the number of compounding periods per year.

■ Example

Assume that a bank offers 6% interest, compounded quarterly, then the APR is

$$APR = (1 + 0.06/4)^4 - 1.0 = (1.015)^4 - 1.0$$
$$= 1.0614 - 1.0 = 0.0614 = 6.14\%$$

This means that if one bank offered 6% with quarterly compounding while another offered 6.14% with annual compounding, they would both be paying the same effective rate of interest.

Annual percentage rate (APR) also is a measure of the cost of credit, expressed as a yearly rate. It includes interest as well as other financial charges such as loan origination and certain closing fees. The lender is required to tell a borrower the APR. It provides him with a good basis for comparing the cost of loans, including mortgage plans.

ANNUAL REPORT A report prepared by a business entity at the end of its calendar or fiscal year. It presents a company's financial position and operating results for use by interested parties, including potential investors, creditors, stockholders, and employees. An audit report is prepared by an independent CPA to determine whether the financial statements fairly present the company's financial health. In addition, the president's letter appears outlining current status and future prospects. There is a section on ''Management's Discussion and Analysis of the Summary of Earnings,'' in which management explains the reasons for material changes in revenue and expenses.

ANNUITY An annuity is a series of equal receipts or payments. It is also called rent. Examples of an annuity are cash dividends from a preferred stock, semiannual interest receipts from a bond investment, and a retirement annuity from an insurance company. There are different types of an annuity, including
1. Ordinary annuity (or annuity in arrears),
where receipts or payments are made at the end of the period
2. Annuity due, where receipts or payments are made at the beginning of the period
3. Deferred annuity, where receipts or payments do not start until two or more periods have elapsed
4. Perpetuity, which is an annuity that continues for an indefinite period
See also Retirement and Pension Planning; Time Value of Money and Its Applications.

APPROPRIATION

1. Restricting retained earnings for a designated purpose, such as appropriation for retirement of bonds or appropriation for plant expansion.
2. Authorization of a municipality to expend money subject to legal restrictions. The appropriate account is credited when a budget is adopted and debited when the budget is closed. It is a nominal account.
See also Governmental Accounting.

ARBITRAGE This applies to earning a profit arising from the price difference of the identical stock, bond, commodity, or currency that is traded in more than one market. Arbitrage tends to equalize prices of the items in different markets, except for differences in the costs of transportation, risk, and so on.

■ Example

An arbitrageur buys one security in the New York market for $40,000 and sells that security in the Chicago market for $41,000, making a profit of $1,000 since the price of the security at that exact time is different in the two markets. Brokerage commissions will reduce the profit.

What some arbitrageurs do is purchase stock of a company that may be acquired by another and sell short the stock of the acquiring company. If the acquisition occurs, a profit will be made. If not, a loss may be incurred.

ARITHMETIC AVERAGE RETURN VERSUS GEOMETRIC AVERAGE RETURN

It is one thing to measure the return over a single holding period and quite another to describe a series of returns over time. When an investor holds an investment for more than one period, it is important to understand how to compute the average of the successive rates of return. There are two types of multiperiod average (mean) returns. They are *arithmetic average return* and the *geometric average return*. The arithmetic return is simply the arithmetic average of successive one-period rates of return. It is defined as

$$\text{Arithmetic return} = 1/n \sum_{t=1}^{n} r_t$$

where n = the number of time periods and r_t = the single holding period return in time t.

The arithmetic average return, however, can be quite misleading in multiperiod return calculations.

A more accurate measure of the actual return generated by an investment over multiple periods is the geometric average return. The geometric return over n periods is computed as follows:

$$\text{Geometric return} = \sqrt[n]{(1 + r)(1 + r)\ldots(1 + r)} - 1$$

Since it is cumbersome to calculate the nth root (although there is a formula for approximation), we will illustrate only the two-period return calculation ($n = 2$).

■ Example

Consider the following data where the price of a stock doubles in one period and depreciates back to the original price. Assume no dividend.

| | Time Periods | | |
	$t = 0$	$t = 1$	$t = 2$
Price (end of period)	$50	$100	$50
HPR	—	100%	−50%

The holding period return (HPR) for periods 1 and 2 are computed as follows:

Period 1 (t = 1)
$\text{HPR} = \dfrac{\$0 + (\$100 - \$50)}{\$50} = \dfrac{\$50}{\$50} = 100\%$

Period 2 (t = 2)
$\text{HPR} = \dfrac{\$0 + (\$50 - \$100)}{\$100} = \dfrac{-\$50}{\$100} = -50\%$

Therefore, the arithmetic average return is the average of 100% and −50%, which is 25%, as shown below:

$$\frac{100\% + (-50\%)}{2} = 25\%$$

Obviously, the stock purchased for $50 and sold for the same price two periods later did not earn 25%; it earned *zero* return. The geometric average return provides a correct return.

Note that $n = 2$, $r_1 = 100\% = 1$, and $r_2 = -50\% = -0.5$
Then:

$$\text{Geometric return} = \sqrt[2]{(1 + 1)(1 - 0.5)} - 1$$
$$= \sqrt[2]{(2)(0.5)} - 1$$
$$= \sqrt{1} - 1 = 1 - 1 = 0\%$$

See also Mean.

ARM'S-LENGTH TRANSACTION

In an arm's-length transaction, the seller and buyer attempt to maximize their best interest without any restrictions being placed. Some transactions do not satisfy this criteria, such as transactions between related parties and affiliated businesses. Arm's-length transactions are the basis for a fair market value determination in connection with recording the acquisition cost of an asset.

ARTIFICIAL INTELLIGENCE (AI)

Artificial intelligence software enhances the thinking process of accountants and financial executives so that optimum decisions can be made. In effect, microcomputers evaluate and solve problems requiring human imagination and intelligence that involve known and unknown information. Reasons for difficulties can be uncovered and expert advice furnished. *Note*: There is imitation of intelligent human behavior and learning from experience. Significant data are evaluated and relevant relationships, such as the determination of a warranty reserve, uncovered. The computer learns which kinds of answers are reasonable and which are not. AI performs complicated strategies that assist in determining the best or worst way to accomplish a task or avoid an undesirable result. Applications of AI include

• Tax preparation and planning, such as tax shelter options, given the client's financial status

• Financial ratio analysis, including what-if analysis for the effect of alternative assumptions on an outcome

• Planning and audit analysis, including testing, internal control, attestation of EDP systems, appraising evidence, formulating an audit opinion, scheduling and monitoring the audit engagement, and uncovering illogical relationships (e.g., promotion expense to sales)

• Management services, including providing pension plan advice

• Practice management involving making decisions about staff development and assignment

• Analyzing delinquent accounts receivable along with probabilities of collection

An expert system for estate planning called Taxadvisor™ was developed by R. Michaelson of the University of Illinois. A package called Auditor™ is for the examination of bad debts and was formulated by C. Dungan of the same school. For internal control evaluation, a package referred to as TICOM™ was developed by A. Bailey of the University of Minnesota and A. Whinston and M. Gagle of Purdue.

Artificial intelligence programming languages include LISP, PROLOG, OPS5, ESIE, and POPLOG. Artificial intelligence software basically searches a data base for certain characteristics and then extracts them. Inference and reasoning functions exist. LISP programs change nonnumeric symbols like words to present useful and meaningful associations and interrelationships. When the program lists are correctly integrated in terms of facts and associations, a rational solution to a problem can be generated. LISP packages can modify themselves and create new data lists. INTERLISP is a version of LISP containing many packaged routines.

Backward chaining is involved where the system begins with a hypothesis, finds a rule whose premise supports the hypothesis, and then attempts to verify the knowledge base for a relevant fact. The process verifies or disproves the hypothesis.

▪ Example

Lightyear™ is a decision software package that has the manager put into the microcomputer alternative solutions to a problem and evaluating criteria. Lightyear then ranks the alternatives from good to bad according to user weights. The manager can then go backward through the problem to reappraise the criteria. Comparison of decisions among different executives can also be made. The software permits the management and organization of decisions. Although the software does not make decisions, it has the financial executive organize and give the reasons supporting the decision already made. The user can also get a detailed evaluation for any of the alternatives.

▪ Example

TIMM-PC™ logically considers alternative ways to solve problems when essential data are missing or inadequate. A pattern-matching technique permits differentiation between statements that vary continuously and those that have an all-or-nothing quality. Solutions are provided to problems, with probabilities assigned. Various types of statistical forecasting formulas are provided in the model.

The user can specify the rules to be followed by the micro to solve the problem via interaction with it. Once the particular problem is solved, the micro is trained to solve similar problems with fewer indicators.

■ Example

Texas Instruments' Natural Link™ provides the financial executive with a selection of phrases at each point, representing possible alternatives. The executive chooses from the available options until a sentence has been constructed indicating what the program is supposed to do.

■ Example

Texas Instruments' Personal Consultant/Plus™ has a frames feature allowing a complex problem to be segregated into smaller, related subproblems. There is an external program interface so that other programs (e.g., spreadsheet, data base) can be used in the consultation process.

ASCII (AMERICAN STANDARD CODE FOR INFORMATION INTERCHANGE)   ASCII is a standard code for the conversion of a character to a binary number so that it is understandable by many microcomputers and on-line information systems. Because of this uniform code, varying models of microcomputers are capable of communication. Most computer terminals, microcomputers, and printers utilize ASCII. Included are control characters that are used by on-line data bases. Reference should be made to software and microcomputer books that contain a description of ASCII characters. ASCII aids in permitting information files produced by one kind of software (i.e., spreadsheet) to be used in a different kind of software (i.e., data base management, word processing).

■ Example

Information is downloaded from an on-line data base (i.e., AICPA NAARS) in ASCII and then loaded into word processing software. It is then modified, and data may also be transferred to a distant computer at another office via telecommunications. ASCII is also used for electronic mail so that letters may be sent among executives at different locations.

■ Example

A client may upload accounting files to his CPA in ASCII via MCI for audit-testing purposes.

ASSET MANAGEMENT OF BANKS   A commercial bank earns profits for stockholders by having a positive spread in lending and through leverage. A positive spread results when the average yield on earning assets exceeds the average cost of deposit liabilities. A high-risk asset portfolio can increase profits since the greater the risk position of the borrower, the larger the risk premium charged. On the other side of the coin, a high-risk portfolio can reduce profits because of the increased chance that it could become ''nonperforming'' assets. Favorable use of leverage (the bank's capital-asset ratio is falling) can increase the return on owners' equity. A mix of a high-risk portfolio and high leverage could result, however, in insolvency and bank failure. It is extremely important for banks to find an optimal mix. A bank is also threatened with insolvency if it has to liquidate its asset portfolio at a loss to meet large withdrawals. It can happen because, historically, a large proportion of banks' liabilities come from demand deposits—and therefore can easily be withdrawn. For this reason, commercial bank asset management theory focuses on the need for liquidity. There are three theories:

1. *The commercial loan theory*—contends that commercial banks should make only short-term self-liquidating loans (e.g., short-term seasonal inventory loans). In this way, loans could be repaid and cash could be readily available to meet deposit outflows. This theory lost much of its credibility as a certain source of liquidity since there is no guarantee

that even seasonal working capital loans can be repaid.

2. *The shiftability theory*—an extension of the commercial loan theory and states that by holding money market instruments, a bank could sell such assets without capital loss in the event of a deposit outflow.

3. *The anticipated-income theory*—holds that intermediate-term installment loans are liquid because they generate continuous cash inflows. The focus is not on short-term asset financing but on cash flow lending.

It is important to note that contemporary asset management hinges primarily on the shiftability theory, anticipated-income theory, and liability management. *See also* Liability Management of Banks.

ASSIGNMENT OF ACCOUNTS RECEIVABLE
See Accounts Receivable Financing.

ATTESTATION STANDARDS
The auditor may be engaged to prepare reports other than for historical cost financial statements, such as for supplementary financial data, compliance with regulatory requirements, statistical data on investment results, and evaluation of internal control. The guidelines for auditor involvement are contained in the AICPA's *Statement on Standards for Attestation Engagements*. The Statement defines an attest engagement as one when the CPA will express in writing an opinion on the reliability of specified information. The two types of attest assurance are

• *Positive assurance* contained in reports involving an *examination* engagement

• *Negative assurance* contained in reports based on a *review*

Attestation may be in accordance with agreed-upon procedures provided the report is limited to the individuals agreeing on such procedures.

The attestation standards are classified into general standards, standards of fieldwork, and standards of reporting.

1. General Standards
   a. The practitioner should have technical training and knowledge in order to perform the attest function.
   b. An engagement should be undertaken if the following conditions are present: (1) reasonable criteria exist to conduct an evaluation and (2) reasonable estimation or measurement can be made.
   c. The practitioner is independent.
   d. The practitioner shall conduct himself or herself with due professional care.
2. Standards of Fieldwork
   a. The engagement should be properly planned and staff adequately supervised.
   b. Sufficient evidence should exist as a basis to express an opinion.
3. Standards of Reporting
   a. The assertion being reported on should be stated along with the nature of the engagement.
   b. The practitioner should provide his or her conclusion as to whether the assertion is presented in accordance with established criteria.
   c. The practitioner's reservations should be given in the report.
   d. If the engagement is to apply agreed-upon criteria, there should be a statement in the report restricting its use to individuals who have agreed upon those criteria.

See also Audit.

ATTRIBUTE SAMPLING
An attribute is defined as a characteristic that a component of the population has or does not have. For instance, a customer's account is either past due or not. Authorization to pay a vendor has either been given or not.

In attribute sampling, an estimate is made of the proportion of the population that contains a particular characteristic. It can apply to a random sample of physical units or to a systemic sample that approximates a random sample. A sample item possesses or does not possess the specific characteristic. No consideration is given to the magnitude of the characteristic. Based on the sample result, it is found if the true occurrence rate in the population is not greater than a specified percentage expressed at a given reliability level. The auditor may test for several different attributes in a sample.

Attribute sampling is based on a binomial distribution. An estimation may be made of the probable occurrence rates of particular characteristics in a population, where each characteristic has two mutually exclusive outcomes. Software for attribute-sampling purposes is available from time-sharing vendors.

An application of attribute sampling is the auditor's substantiation of breakdown of control procedures. Examples are the measurement of the degree of breakdown of control procedures related to cash disbursements, cash receipts, sales, payroll, and the extent of incorrect entries and incorrect postings.

Attribute sampling of physical units cannot be employed to estimate the total of a variable characteristic (e.g., values).

In determining sample size, the auditor should select an acceptable risk level. In practical terms, auditors select either a 5% or a 10% risk because these levels will furnish the auditor with a 95% or a 90% confidence, respectively, that the sample is representative of the population. The lower the risk the auditor selects, the greater will be the sample size.

A tolerable error rate will have to be selected. It is the maximum rate of deviation the auditor is willing to tolerate and still be able to rely on the control. The tolerable rate depends on professional judgment and the extent of reliance placed on the control or procedure. The following guidelines exist:

Degree of Reliance	Tolerable Rate
Little	11–20%
Moderate	6–12%
Substantial	2–7%

An evaluation should be made of the anticipated deviation rate which may be based on deviations in prior years, taking into account corrective changes in the current year.

The actual deviation rate in the sample equals:

$$\frac{\text{Number of deviations}}{\text{Sample size}}$$

The auditor should ascertain whether the deviations are due to errors or irregularities (intentional). When the sample deviation is in excess of the tolerable rate, no reliance may be placed on the control.

In examining the population, the population should be complete so that representative testing is possible. For instance, in testing purchase transactions, unpaid as well as paid invoices should be included.

The auditor should define the period covered by the examination. If interim testing is involved, the period after testing to the end of the year should be reviewed. Consideration should be given to the nature and amount of transactions and balances, and the length of the remaining period. The working papers should contain definitions of attributes and occurrences.

Attribute sampling is helpful in tests of controls. An example is evaluating the appropriateness of accounting controls through transaction testing.

Tables are referred to in determining sample size given the risk of overreliance, tolerable occurrence rate, and anticipated occurrence rate.

■ Example

In ascertaining if the credit department is performing well, a CPA uses attribute sampling in examining sales orders through compliance testing. The CPA determines that (1) the deviation condition is the failure of the credit manager's initials on a sales order; (2) the population is comprised of the duplicate sales orders for the whole year; (3) the sampling unit is the sales order; (4) random number selection is used; (5) a 5% risk of overreliance on internal control is used; (6) the tolerable rate of deviation is 6%; and (7) the anticipated population deviation rate is 2%.

Using Table 1, 127 is the sample size. The CPA uses a random number table (Table 5) to select the sample. Because the population is comprised of sales orders numbered 1 to 500, the CPA decides to use the first three digits of items selected from the random number table. With a blind start at column 5, row 6, the auditor selects the following sales orders: 277, 188, 174, 496, 482, 312, and so on.

After carrying out the sampling plan, the auditor discovers that four sales orders are missing the credit manager's signature (apparently an error on the part of the credit manager). The sample deviation rate is thus 4/127, or 3.1%. The upper occurrence limit, determined by referring to Table 3, is 7.2. In evaluating the results, 127 is used for the sample size for conservative reasons. Because the upper occurrence limit exceeds the tolerable rate of 7%, the auditor rejects the control and attempts to identify a compensating control for further tests of compliance. *See also* Sampling.

AUDIT

1. Examination of accounting records by an independent CPA for the purpose of expressing an auditor opinion on the fairness of presentation of a company's financial statements in conformity with GAAP. It includes tests of transactions as well as analysis of records and supporting documents. Confirmation requests may be sent to outside parties (i.e., customers) for verification of account balances. Inspection and counting of assets is typically involved (i.e., inventory count). 2. Investigation and appraisal of an entity's operations and procedures by an internal auditor in order to ascertain conformity with prescribed criteria.

See also Audit Opinion; Audit Procedure; Auditing Standard.

AUDITING ACCOUNTING ESTIMATES

Statement on Auditing Standard No. 57 relates to the auditor's responsibilities with regard to accounting estimates. The auditor has to obtain and evaluate evidential matter dealing with significant accounting estimates. Although management makes the estimates, the auditor must assure himself of their reasonableness. The auditor must follow professional skepticism in examining the objective and subjective factors in the estimation process.

There is greater risk of an estimate being incorrect as the complexity and subjectivity of the situation increases. The estimation process is also more difficult when information is not readily available or is unreliable. If assumptions are significant, the estimate is more prone to the possibility of an error resulting in misleading financial statements. When estimation factors are difficult, a specialist in the area may be retained by management.

The auditor should examine and test the management process of making the estimate, consider events occurring after the estimate but before the audit report date, and determine whether he or she would come up with the same estimate that management did.

In appraising the management process, the auditor does the following:

• Analyzes the consistency of the assumptions

• Evaluates supporting information (e.g., documentation for estimates)

• Compares corporate data to industry information

• Compares previous estimates to current estimates

• Determines the effect of changes in the industry or business based on assumptions and estimates used

• Ascertains if alternative assumptions exist

Table 1

5 Percent Risk of Overreliance

Statistical Sample Sizes for Tests of Controls (for large populations)

Expected Population Deviation Rate	TOLERABLE OCCURRENCE RATE								
	2%	3%	4%	5%	6%	7%	8%	9%	10%
0.00%	149	99	74	59	49	42	36	32	29
.50	•	157	117	93	78	66	58	51	46
1.00	•	•	156	93	78	66	58	51	46
1.50	•	•	192	124	103	66	58	51	46
2.00	•	•	•	181	127	88	77	68	46
2.50	•	•	•	•	150	109	77	68	61
3.00	•	•	•	•	195	129	95	84	61
4.00	•	•	•	•	•	•	146	100	89
5.00	•	•	•	•	•	•	•	158	116
6.00	•	•	•	•	•	•	•	•	179

Table 2

10 Percent Risk of Overreliance

Expected Population Deviation Rate	TOLERABLE OCCURRENCE RATE								
	2%	3%	4%	5%	6%	7%	8%	9%	10%
0.00%	114	76	57	45	38	32	28	25	22
.50	194	129	96	77	64	55	48	42	38
1.00	•	176	96	77	64	55	48	42	38
1.50	•	•	132	105	64	55	48	42	38
2.00	•	•	198	132	88	75	48	42	38
2.50	•	•	•	158	110	75	65	58	38
3.00	•	•	•	•	132	94	65	58	52
4.00	•	•	•	•	•	149	98	73	65
5.00	•	•	•	•	•	•	160	115	78
6.00	•	•	•	•	•	•	•	182	116

•Sample size is too large to be cost effective.

Table 3

5 Percent Risk of Overreliance

Statistical Sample Results Evaluation Table for Tests of Controls

Upper Occurrence Limit
(for large populations)

Sample Size	ACTUAL NUMBER OF OCCURRENCES FOUND								
	0	1	2	3	4	5	6	7	8
25	11.3	17.6	•	•	•	•	•	•	•
30	9.5	14.9	19.5	•	•	•	•	•	•
35	8.2	12.9	16.9	•	•	•	•	•	•
40	7.2	11.3	14.9	18.3	•	•	•	•	•
45	6.4	10.1	13.3	16.3	19.2	•	•	•	•
50	5.8	9.1	12.1	14.8	17.4	19.9	•	•	•
55	5.3	8.3	11.0	13.5	15.9	18.1	•	•	•
60	4.9	7.7	10.1	12.4	14.6	16.7	18.8	•	•
65	4.5	7.1	9.4	11.5	13.5	15.5	17.4	19.3	•
70	4.2	6.6	8.7	10.7	12.6	14.4	16.2	18.0	19.7
75	3.9	6.2	8.2	10.0	11.8	13.5	15.2	16.9	18.4
80	3.7	5.8	7.7	9.4	11.1	12.7	14.3	15.8	17.3
90	3.3	5.2	6.8	8.4	9.9	11.3	12.7	14.1	15.5
100	3.0	4.7	6.2	7.6	8.9	10.2	11.5	12.7	14.0
125	2.4	3.7	4.9	6.1	7.2	8.2	9.3	10.3	11.3
150	2.0	3.1	4.1	5.1	6.0	6.9	7.7	8.6	9.4
200	1.5	2.3	3.1	3.8	4.5	5.2	5.8	6.5	7.1

Table 4

10 Percent Risk of Overreliance

Sample Size	ACTUAL NUMBER OF OCCURRENCES FOUND								
	0	1	2	3	4	5	6	7	8
20	10.9	18.1	•	•	•	•	•	•	•
25	8.8	14.7	19.9	•	•	•	•	•	•
30	7.4	12.4	16.8	•	•	•	•	•	•
35	6.4	10.7	14.5	18.1	•	•	•	•	•
40	5.6	9.4	12.8	15.9	19.0	•	•	•	•
45	5.0	8.4	11.4	14.2	17.0	19.6	•	•	•
50	4.5	7.6	10.3	12.9	15.4	17.8	•	•	•
55	4.1	6.9	9.4	11.7	14.0	16.2	18.4	•	•
60	3.8	6.3	8.6	10.8	12.9	14.9	16.9	18.8	•
70	3.2	5.4	7.4	9.3	11.1	12.8	14.6	16.2	17.9
80	2.8	4.8	6.5	8.3	9.7	11.3	12.8	14.3	15.7
90	2.5	4.3	5.8	7.3	8.7	10.1	11.4	12.7	14.0
100	2.3	3.8	5.2	6.6	7.8	9.1	10.3	11.5	12.7
120	1.9	3.2	4.4	5.5	6.6	7.6	8.6	9.6	10.6
160	1.4	2.4	3.3	4.1	4.9	5.7	6.5	7.2	8.0
200	1.1	1.9	2.6	3.3	4.0	4.6	5.2	5.8	6.4

•over 20%

Table 5

Random Number Table

Line	(1)	(2)	(3)	(4)	(5)	(6)	(7)	(8)	(9)	(10)	(11)	(12)	(13)	(14)
1	10480	15011	01536	02011	81647	91646	69179	14194	62590	36207	20969	99570	91291	90700
2	22368	46573	25595	85393	30995	89198	27982	53402	93965	34095	52666	19174	39615	99505
3	24130	48360	22527	97265	76393	64809	15179	24830	49340	32081	30680	19655	63348	58629
4	42167	93093	06243	61680	07856	16376	39440	53537	71341	57004	00849	74917	97758	16379
5	37570	39975	81837	16656	06121	91782	60468	81305	49684	60672	14110	06927	01263	54613
6	77921	06907	11008	42751	27756	53498	18602	70659	90655	15053	21916	81825	44394	42880
7	99562	72905	56420	69994	98872	31016	71194	18738	44013	48840	63213	21069	10634	12952
8	96301	91977	05463	07972	18876	20922	94595	56869	69014	60045	18425	84903	42508	32307
9	89579	14342	63661	10281	17453	18103	57740	84378	25331	12566	58678	44947	05585	56941
10	85475	36857	53342	53988	53060	59533	38867	62300	08158	17983	16439	11458	18593	64952
11	28918	69578	88231	33276	70997	79936	56865	05859	90106	31595	01547	85590	91610	78188
12	63553	40961	48235	03427	49626	69445	18663	72695	52180	20847	12234	90511	33703	90322
13	09429	93969	52636	92737	88974	33488	36320	17617	30015	08272	84115	27156	30613	74952
14	10365	61129	87529	85689	48237	52267	67689	93394	01511	26358	85104	20285	29975	89868
15	07119	97336	71048	08178	77233	13916	47564	81056	97735	85977	29372	74461	28551	90707
16	51085	12765	51821	51259	77452	16308	60756	92144	49442	53900	70960	63990	75601	40719
17	02368	21382	52404	60268	89368	19885	55322	44819	01188	63255	64835	44919	05944	55157
18	01011	54092	33362	94904	31273	04146	18594	29852	71585	85030	51132	01915	92747	64951
19	52162	53916	46369	58586	23216	14513	83149	98736	23495	64350	94738	17752	35156	35749
20	07056	97628	33787	09998	42698	06691	76988	13602	51851	46104	88916	19509	25625	58104
21	48663	91245	85828	14346	09172	30168	90229	04734	59193	22178	30421	61666	99904	32812
22	54164	58492	22421	74103	47070	25306	76468	26384	58151	06646	21524	15227	96909	44592
23	32639	32363	05597	24200	13363	38005	94342	28728	35806	06912	17012	64161	18296	22851
24	29334	27001	87637	87308	58731	00256	45834	15398	46557	41135	10367	07684	36188	18510
25	02488	33062	28834	07351	19731	92420	60952	61280	50001	67658	32586	86679	50720	94953
26	81525	72295	04839	96423	24878	82651	66566	14778	76797	14780	13300	87074	79666	95725
27	29676	20591	68086	26432	46901	20849	89768	81536	86645	12659	92259	57102	80428	25280
28	00742	57392	39064	66432	84673	40027	32832	61362	98947	96067	64760	64584	96096	98253
29	05366	04213	25669	26422	44407	44048	37937	63904	45766	66134	75470	66520	34693	90449
30	91921	26418	64117	94305	26766	25940	39972	22209	71500	64568	91402	42416	07844	69618
31	00582	04711	87917	77341	42206	35126	74087	99547	81817	42607	43808	76655	62028	76630
32	00725	69884	62797	56170	86324	88072	76222	36086	84637	93161	76038	65855	77919	88006
33	69011	65795	95876	55293	18988	27354	26575	08625	40801	59920	29841	80150	12777	48501
34	25976	57948	29888	80604	67917	48708	18912	82271	65424	69774	33611	54262	85963	03547
35	09763	83473	73577	12908	30883	18317	28290	35797	05998	41688	34952	37888	38917	80050
36	91567	42595	29758	30134	04024	86385	29880	99730	55536	84855	29080	09250	79656	73211
37	17955	56349	90999	49127	20044	59931	06115	20542	18059	02008	73708	83517	36103	42791
38	46503	18584	18845	49618	02304	51038	20655	58727	28168	15475	56942	53389	20562	87338
39	92157	89634	94824	78171	84610	82834	09922	25417	44137	48413	25555	21246	35509	20468
40	14577	62765	35605	81263	39667	47358	56873	56307	61607	49518	89656	20103	77490	18062
41	98427	07523	33362	64270	01638	92477	66969	98420	04880	45585	46565	04102	46880	45709
42	34914	63976	88720	82765	34476	17032	87589	40836	32427	70002	70663	88863	77775	69348
43	70060	28277	39475	46473	23219	53416	94970	25832	69975	94884	19661	72828	00102	66794
44	53976	54914	06990	67245	68350	82948	11398	42878	80287	88267	47363	46634	06541	97809
45	76072	29515	40980	07391	58745	25774	22987	80059	39911	96189	41151	14222	60697	59583
46	90725	52210	83974	29992	65831	38857	50490	83765	55657	14361	31720	57375	56228	41546
47	64364	67412	33339	31926	14883	24413	59744	92351	97473	89286	38931	04110	23726	51900
48	08962	00358	31662	25388	61642	34072	81249	35648	56891	69352	48373	45578	78547	81788
49	95012	68379	93526	70765	10592	04542	76463	54328	02349	17247	28865	14777	62730	92277
50	15664	10493	20492	38391	91132	21999	59516	81652	27195	48223	46751	22923	32261	85653

• Appraises the controls over the estimation process

• Ascertains the relevance and reliability of the estimates

• Tests management computations in translating assumptions to estimates

• Examines goals and plans of the entity to determine how they tie into the estimates used

AUDITING STANDARDS These provide guidance in assuring that audit performance is of high quality. CPAs have to conform to ten generally accepted auditing standards (GAAS), as promulgated by the AICPA. Interpretations of the standards are issued in the form of Statements on Auditing Standards (SAS). Audit Guides for specific industries are also issued by the AICPA.

GAAS consist of ten standards in the following three groupings: general standards, standards of fieldwork, and reporting standards. SASs are interpretations of these standards. The SASs are often called GAAS themselves. The ten standards are

General Standards

1. The examination must be conducted by individuals with sufficient audit training and expertise.
2. The auditor must be independent in performing his activities.
3. Due professional care must be exercised in conducting the audit and in preparing the audit report.

Standards of Fieldwork

1. The engagement must be properly planned and assistants adequately supervised.
2. There must be an adequate understanding of the internal control structure so that the audit may be properly planned and a determination made of the nature, timing, and degree of tests to be conducted.
3. Sufficient competent evidential matter must be obtained through observation, inspection, inquiries, and confirmations so that a proper basis exists for an audit opinion.

Standards of Reporting

1. The report should state if the financial statements are prepared in accordance with GAAP.
2. The report should identify those circumstances in which accounting principles have not been consistently observed in the current year relative to the preceding period.
3. Footnote disclosures should be deemed sufficient unless indicated otherwise in the audit report.
4. The report should contain an audit opinion or an assertion that no opinion can be expressed. If not, the reasons should be given. The nature of the audit examination and the degree of responsibility assumed should be contained in the audit report.

A brief summary of a few important SASs issued by the Auditing Standards Board of the AICPA follow:

SAS No. 42—Reporting on Condensed Financial Statements and Selected Financial Data This statement applies to reporting on a client-prepared document containing (1) condensed financial statements that are derived from audited financial statements and/or (2) selected financial data derived from audited financial statements.

The auditor's report on condensed financial statements should include

• A statement that the auditor has examined, in accordance with GAAS, the complete set of financial statements

• An indication that an opinion has been expressed on the complete set of financial statements

• The date of the auditor's report on the complete set of financial statements

• The type of opinion expressed on the complete set of financial statements

• An opinion as to whether the information

contained in the condensed financial statements is presented fairly in all material respects in relation to the complete set of financial statements

SAS No. 46—Consideration of Omitted Procedures After the Report Date In certain cases, such as peer review, the auditor may conclude after the issuance of an audit report that he or she omitted one or more auditing procedures. In these instances, the auditor has the responsibility to assess the importance of the omitted procedure(s) to his or her present ability to support the previously expressed opinion. In making this assessment, the auditor should consider any alternative auditing procedures performed. If the auditor still feels that the omitted procedure(s) impairs the present ability to support the audit report, he or she should undertake to apply the omitted procedure(s) or alternative procedures. If the auditor is unable to apply the necessary procedures, he or she should contact legal counsel in order to discuss the appropriate course of action to be taken.

SAS No. 50—Reports on the Application of Accounting Principles An accountant may be asked to prepare a written report on (1) the application of accounting principles to specified transactions; (2) the type of opinion that may be expressed on an entity's financial statements; or (3) the application of accounting principles not involving facts or circumstances of a particular principal (i.e., a hypothetical transaction).

The accountant's report should include
• The appropriate address (i.e., it should be addressed to the principal to the transaction or to the intermediary).
• A statement describing the engagement.
• An indication that the engagement was conducted in accordance with the relevant standards of the AICPA.
• A description of the transaction and its related facts, circumstances, and assumptions (including their source). Furthermore, an identification of the principals to the transaction should be made.

• A description of the relevant accounting principles.
• A statement fixing the responsibility for the proper accounting treatment with the preparers of the financial statements, who should consult with their continuing accountants.
• A warning that the report may change if differences of facts, circumstances, or assumptions are altered.

SAS No. 51—Reporting on Financial Statements Prepared for Use in Other Countries Generally accepted auditing standards as developed in the United States should be adhered to when examining financial statements of a U.S. entity prepared in conformity with accounting principles accepted in another country. Under certain circumstances the auditor may also have to adhere to the auditing standards of the foreign country.

If the financial statements are for use only in a foreign country, the auditor may issue (1) a U.S.-style report modified for reporting on the foreign country's accounting principles or (2) a report based on the foreign country's standards.

AUDIT OPINION AICPAs' Statement on Auditing Standards No. 58 deals with the audit report. The standard audit report takes the following form:

> We have audited the accompanying balance sheet of X Company as of December 31, 19XX, and the related statements of income, retained earnings, and cash flows for the year then ended. These financial statements are the responsibility of the Company's management. Our responsibility is to express an opinion on these financial statements based on our audit.
>
> We conducted our audit in accordance with generally accepted auditing standards. Those standards require that we plan and perform the audit to obtain reasonable assurance about whether the financial statements are free of material misstatement. An audit includes examining, on a test basis, evidence supporting the amounts and disclosures in the financial statements. An

audit also includes assessing the accounting principles used and significant estimates made by management, as well as evaluating the overall financial statement presentation. We believe that our audit provides a reasonable basis for our opinion.

In our opinion, the financial statements referred to above present fairly, in all material respects, the financial position of X Company as of [at] December 31, 19XX, and the results of its operations and its cash flows for the year then ended in conformity with generally accepted accounting principles.

In the introductory paragraph, there is mention of management's responsibility for the financial statements. In the scope paragraph (second paragraph), it is stated that an audit furnishes reasonable assurance within the context of materiality that the financial statements are free of material misstatement. An explanation of what an audit involves is also stated. The opinion paragraph provides the audit opinion. Note that the reference to consistency is no longer made. But if there is a lack of consistency, an additional explanatory paragraph should be given of that fact.

An unqualified opinion means that the financial statements present fairly the financial position and operating results of the company in conformity with GAAP.

A qualified opinion occurs in the following cases:

- A scope limitation exists where the auditor was not
  - Able to obtain sufficient evidential matter for an unqualified opinion.
  - Able to apply a necessary auditing procedure. (If the scope limitation is not severe, an "except for" qualified opinion may be issued instead of a disclaimer.)
- The financial statements have a departure from GAAP and the client refuses to make the needed modifications. In this case, an "except for" qualified opinion is rendered (assuming the effects are not so severe as

to require an adverse opinion). Departures from GAAP include an inappropriate accounting method that does not reflect the theoretical substance of a transaction and inadequate disclosure.

Statements on Auditing Standards Nos. 58 and 59 have eliminated "subject to" opinion qualifications. In disclaiming an opinion, the auditor is saying that he or she is unable to form an opinion on the fairness of the financial statements. One is allowed to disclaim an opinion on some of the financial statements while at the same time expressing an opinion on the other statements.

An adverse opinion occurs when the financial statements do *not* fairly present a company's financial position and operating results. The financial statements are therefore misleading.

AUDIT PROCEDURES These comprise detailed steps in performing an audit that change by audit engagement. The auditor obtains evidence to support recorded figures in the financial statements. The audit procedures followed depend on the complexity of the tasks to be performed, the type of client's accounting system, characteristics of the records, and nature of the company. Examples of procedures include confirming accounts receivable balances, physically inspecting assets, and testing the system of internal control. *See also* Audit Program; Workpapers.

AUDIT PROGRAM

1. Procedures carried out in the performance of an audit
2. Description and outline of work to be conducted in an audit

The audit program typically includes the estimated time for each task as well as the personnel to perform it. It gives an indication of the scope of the examination and provides guidance for staff. It serves for planning and control purposes as well as to document functions performed. Information is given on who performed the audit and when.

AUDIT RISK Statement on Auditing Standards No. 47, titled "Audit Risk and Materiality in Conducting an Audit," deals with the steps to take when to reduce audit risk when planning and conducting an examination. Audit risk refers to the possibility that the auditor may unintentionally fail to modify the audit opinion on materially misstated financial statements. Audit risk must be taken into account in ascertaining the nature, timing, and degree of audit techniques to be employed on the particular engagement. Also, an analysis of audit results must be carefully performed.

The auditor is required to

• Aggregate likely errors

• Compare estimates made by management to what the auditor believes is reasonable

• Take into account that undetected errors may exist even though proper audit procedures have been undertaken and, as a result, the financial statements may be materially misstated

• Preliminarily estimate materiality for the financial statements so that audit procedures may be properly planned

• Minimize audit risk through a thorough examination

• Conduct substantive tests based on evaluating control risks

In considering audit risk, the CPA must be aware of inherent risk, control risk, and detection risk.

Inherent risk is the "built-in" susceptibility of an account balance or class of transactions to errors, irrespective of the internal control system. For example, cash has greater risk due to its liquidity.

Control risk is the risk that an account balance or class of transactions may contain errors that may be undetected or prevented by the internal control system.

Detection risk is the risk that the auditor may fail to spot material errors. *Note*: There is no guarantee that a statistical sample will detect all errors that may exist.

There is an inverse relationship between detection risk and inherent and control risks. For example, the less the inherent and control risks, the more is the detection risk the auditor should accept.

The auditor can minimize detection risk through the application of necessary auditing procedures. On the other hand, it is management's responsibility to curtail control risk by formulating and maintaining a sound internal control system. *See also* Audit.

AUDIT SAMPLING Statement on Auditing Standard No. 39 provides recommendations as to planning, performing, and analyzing audit samples. Also, the AICPA has issued a related guide called "Audit Sampling." Audit sampling is the use of an audit procedure to part of the population being examined (e.g., similar transactions, account balances, documents, entries, lines in a voucher register) to derive a conclusion regarding characteristics of the population.

The two acceptable alternative approaches to audit sampling are nonstatistical (judgmental) and statistical. The prime distinction is that the former does not provide for a quantitative measure of sampling risk, whereas the latter does. The selection of the appropriate type depends on the particular circumstances, typically taking into account cost and effectiveness.

However, that choice (nonstatistical or statistical sampling) does not directly impact decisions regarding the audit approach to be used (systems-reliance or substantive) or particular audit procedures to be applied, the competence of evidential matter obtained with respect to sampled items, or the actions that might be taken when errors or irregularities are uncovered.

Some important sampling terms from the auditor's perspective are

• *Sampling risk*—The risk that sample results do not accurately reflect the population. A particular sample may contain proportionately more or less monetary errors or compliance deviations than in the balance or class as a whole. Sampling risk varies inversely with sample size. If sampling risk is unacceptable to undertake, the population should be tested in full.

• *Tolerable error*—an estimate of the maximum amount of error that may exist so that the financial statements are not materially misstated.

In determining sample size, the following factors should be considered:

• Purpose of the sample.
• Desired efficiency level.
• Tolerable error. A higher acceptable error rate will require a lower sample size.
• Frequency or size of expected errors. As more errors are anticipated, the sample size increases for a fixed tolerable error rate.
• Risk of improper acceptance.
• Population characteristics such as variation in items comprising the population. Wide variability requires a larger sample. Sample size can be reduced, however, through stratification (breaking down the population into subgroups).
• Extent of other audit procedures performed for the item under scrutiny. A lower sample size is needed if other audit techniques are being used in conjunction with the sample.

Computer software may be used to compute sample size and appraise sample results.

The auditor must be on guard against the possibility of reaching an incorrect conclusion regarding the population based on the sample result. For example, the sample may indicate that the population is correct when in fact it is not. The degree of risk of improper acceptance of a population varies depending on the appropriateness of the internal control structure or other substantive tests (e.g., analytical procedures) performed for the same particular audit objective.

In examining deviations, the auditor should consider the following:

• Frequency of errors.
• Nature and reason for errors, including whether they were intentional (irregularities).

• Effect of deviations on other aspects of the audit.

In reviewing audit sampling, consideration should be given to:

• Satisfaction of the audit objective.
• Appropriateness in defining the sampling unit.
• Whether the reported amounts in the financial statements were verified.
• Whether the sample selection is from the correct population.
• Whether internal control structure was supported by tests of controls. If not, substantive tests may have to be adjusted.

When engaging in audit sampling, items or groups are identified as having significance. For example, when evaluating accounts receivable, testing may be done of accounts with significant balances, unusual balances, or out-of-the-ordinary activity.

An acceptable method to project the results of a nonstatistical sample is

$$\frac{\text{Dollar amount of errors}}{\text{Total dollars tested}}$$

■ Example

The sample of a population being examined is $300,000. The sample results indicate $20,000 being in error. The incidence rate of error is therefore

$$\frac{\$20,000}{\$300,000} = 6.7\%$$

This should now be compared to the tolerable rate of error that was deemed acceptable.

With regard to tests of controls, the auditor should

• Take into account in the planning stage population the characteristics and deviation from prescribed controls.
• Formulate the objectives of the test and conditions of deviation.
• Determine a sampling method and appropriate sample size.
• Derive a representative sample so that

all items in the population have an equal chance for inclusion.

• Evaluate the sample results.

If sample results will not support the desired level of confidence in controls, substantive tests must be expanded to provide assurance.

In tests of controls, the following should be documented in the working papers:

• Prescribed control procedures being tested.

• Sampling method and means of selection.

• Application objectives.

• Relationship of tests of controls to planned substantive testing.

• Definition of the population, sampling unit, and deviation condition.

• Risk of overreliance.

• Tolerable deviation rate.

• Anticipated population deviation rate.

• Description of sampling procedure.

• Enumeration of compliance deviations found, including their nature.

• Appraisal of sample results, including sample errors found and whether the sample results indicate good controls in existence.

• Impact on planned substantive tests.

In substantive testing, the following items should be documented in the working papers:

• Objectives of the test.

• Description of audit procedures to meeting objectives.

• Sampling technique and method of sample selection.

• Description of the population sampling unit.

• Definition of the error.

• Rationale for the risk of (1) incorrect acceptance, (2) tolerable error, and (3) expected population error.

• Enumeration of errors found.

• Appraisal of sample results, including a projection of the errors uncovered in the sample and the population. Qualitative aspects of the errors should be considered.

• Sampling risk.

• Overall conclusion concerning the population.

See also Sampling.

AUDIT SOFTWARE   Audit software assists in examining and testing client accounting data. The packages combine general accounting, spreadsheet, and word processing to aid in the accounting, analysis, and reporting elements of the audit. Audit reports, footnote data, compilation and review reports, management letters, and other related auditing schedules and analyses are prepared.

Audit programs carry out mathematical and logical operations: sampling data from a population, comparing actual data to predetermined criteria and printing out exceptions (e.g., excessive inventory balances), appraising accounting data, reading and extracting information, comparing financial data on different files for consistency, integrating data from one file to another, sending out confirmations, and analytical review of the logic in reported figures.

Is the audit software performing correctly? Test the software periodically to assure reasonable results. Is the programming proper for the objectives to be accomplished? Current auditing pronouncements must be incorporated. *Warning*: Make sure the package is the one actually being used. Audit controls must exist over any modifications to the program or documentation.

Audit software should provide for preventing and correcting errors, including error messages. Does the error message suggest the cause and the appropriate corrective action? Audit software also exists to ask internal control questions to derive an audit program.

Audit software exists for flow chart preparation showing the movement of transactions in processing and control. As the need occurs, revised flow charts are prepared to assist in internal control evaluation.

Audit software should display control totals for checking purposes. Software should have processing checks. An example is the "next file version" on the file header. There should be sequential numbers in the control field such as 1/19 and then 1/20.

The CPA must check what each program does and how it impacts files. Files can be printed to assure correct processing. Updates and amendments to audit software must be tested to assure there has been no deterioration in internal control.

Packaged (canned) audit software exists for a particular application (e.g., general ledger). If the packed software cannot satisfy the application, a customized program should be written.

Canned packages can be employed to test transactions, appraise data processing, and examine records. Deloitte, Haskins and Sells has an appropriate package called Auditape.™ Packaged audit software may be used for different clients in terms of file data and characteristics. *Problem*: A canned package may not be able to access information from a data base management system. *Solution*: Put information on the data base to tape and then use the packaged program or utilize the querying ability of DBMS to conduct the audit function.

If a packaged audit program will not satisfy client needs, the auditor is forced to go the customization route. Some programming knowledge is thus essential to assure that the programmer is doing the right job in terms of logical flow. *Recommendation*: Consider customization in the following instances:

• Excessive limitations exist to the canned program.

• "Tailored" confirmations are required.

• There is a need to identify an unusual item.

• Client application is difficult.

• Integration with a data base management system is called for.

When compliance and substantive tests are being performed, utility programs can assist. For example, a useful utility function is changing and sequencing file data. The use of a utility program will reduce tests needed with audit software.

■ Example

Blackman, Kallick and Company's Audit Cube™ handles mechanical, computational, and sorting procedures on an audit. With the aid of a portable computer, the auditor can prepare a fully documented audit in the field. Statements and reports are printed automatically.

■ Example

Linton Shafer's Automated Workpapers™ has a main program and optional modules. It is structured for CPAs using the lead schedule approach for workpapers on audit engagements for clients who maintain their own general ledger.

■ Example

Coopers and Lybrand's Pre-Audit™ prepares financial statements, footnotes, and audit reports.

■ Example

Deloitte, Haskins and Sells' Statistical Techniques for Analysis Review™ program utilizes linear regression in conducting analytical review procedures. It identifies and quantifies the relationship between a dependent variable of audit interest and independent variables. The program computes the amount by which estimates differ from recorded values. Excessive differences require audit attention.

■ Example

Deloitte, Haskins and Sells' Estimation Sampling™ helps in designing, selecting, and appraising samples. Conclusions are drawn about the population based on sample results. Applications include valuing receivables, inventory, and estimated liabilities. Also, the auditor can evaluate the impact of employing alternative GAAP.

Workpaper information and analysis can be facilitated. Audit codes should be assigned to accounts to encourage later grouping for audit purposes. Computerized lead sheets should be used in the audit so that workpapers may be cross-referenced. The lead sheets can also serve as documentation of adjusted balances. Permanent workpaper information is carried forward, such as description of business activities and the accounting system. If data are altered, modifications may easily be made.

An audit program may be processed with the auditor's computer, on the client's premises, or with an outside service bureau. If it is on the client's premises, an appraisal must be made of the client's general controls to guard against unauthorized access to programs. Stringent audit control is needed. *Recommendation*: If the client's facilities are not adequate (e.g., bad geographic location, control problems), the service bureau may be the route to go.

Software can be used for analytical review by comparing corporate information with industry standards noting deviations, comparing the company's current year figures with prior years, and deriving financial ratios. *See also* Accounting Software.

AUDIT TRAIL   This is the total recording and documentation associated with a transaction (journal entry or posting) to source backup (i.e., document). A sound audit trail makes it easy and time efficient to trace a transaction to a source.

AUTOCORRELATION (OR SERIAL CORRELATION)   This is one of the assumptions required in a *regression* in order to make it reliable. It means that the error terms are independent of each other. The deviation of one point about the line (i.e., the error $= y - y'$) is unrelated to the deviation of any other point. When autocorrelation exists (i.e., the error terms are not independent), the standard errors of the regression coefficients are seriously underestimated. The problem of autocorrelation is usually detected by the Durbin-Watson statistic. *See also* Durbin-Watson Statistic; Regression Analysis.

B

"BAIT RECORD" A bait record is a fictitious record. If it is manually or electronically processed, it is indicative of a problem in internal control, which requires the attention of the external auditor. A determination should be made of when, how, and by whom this dummy record has been processed.

■ Example

There is a change in the account balance of a nonexistent supplier, such as that due to a recorded cash payment.

■ Example

A "dummy" inventory item has the balance changed by an employee. *See also* Internal Control Structure.

BALANCE OF PAYMENTS AND BALANCE OF TRADE The *balance of payments* is a statistical tabulation of all kinds of a nation's transactions with all other countries during a given period, such as a year. These transactions consist of exports and imports of goods and services, and movements of short-term and long-term investments, currency, gold, and gifts. The transactions may be classified into several categories, of which the two major ones are the current account and the capital account. The *balance of trade* (*trade balance*) is that portion of a country's balance of payments covering merchandise trade. A favorable balance of trade results when the value of exports exceeds the value of imports. An unfavorable balance of trade, more often called *trade deficit* results when the opposite is the case. A large number of trade deficits could drive interest rates higher and stocks and a country's currency lower as the country increases its reliance on foreign capital to finance the budget deficit.

BALANCE SHEET ANALYSIS In analyzing the balance sheet, the financial analyst is primarily concerned with the realizability of the assets, turnover, and earning potential. The evaluation of liabilities considers arbitrary adjustments and understatement.

Assets

If assets are overstated, net income will be overstated because the earnings do not include necessary charges to reduce earnings to their proper valuations. Asset quality depends on the amount of timing of the realization of assets. Assets should be categorized by risk category. Useful ratios are the percentage of high-risk assets to total assets and high-risk assets to sales. High asset realization risk points to poor quality of earnings due to possible future write-offs. For instance, the future realization of accounts receivable is better than that of goodwill. Multipurpose assets are of better quality than single-purpose assets resulting from readier salability. Assets lacking separable value cannot be sold easily and as such have low realizability. An example is work-in-process and intangibles.

In appraising realization risk in assets, the effect of changing government policies on the entity has to be taken into account. Risk may exist with chemicals and other products deemed hazardous to health. Huge inventory losses may have to be taken.

■ Example

Company A presents total assets of $6 million and sales of $10 million. Included in total assets are the following high-risk assets as perceived by the credit and investment analyst.

Deferred moving costs	$300,000
Deferred plant rearrangement costs	100,000
Receivables for claims under a government contract	200,000
Goodwill	150,000

Applicable ratios are:

$$\frac{\text{High-risk assets}}{\text{Total assets}} = \frac{\$750,000}{\$6,000,000} = 12.5\%$$

$$\frac{\text{High-risk assets}}{\text{Sales}} = \frac{\$750,000}{\$10,000,000} = 7.5\%$$

Cash

A high ratio of sales to cash may indicate inadequate cash leading to financial problems if additional financing is not available at reasonable interest rates. A low turnover ratio, on the other hand, indicates excessive cash being held.

A determination should be made as to whether part of the cash is restricted and unavailable for use. An example is a compensating balance that does not constitute "free" cash. Also, cash in a politically unstable foreign country may have remission restrictions.

Accounts Receivable

Realization risk in receivables can be appraised by studying the nature of the receivable balance. Examples of high-risk receivables include amounts from economically unstable foreign countries, receivables subject to offset provisions, and receivables due from a company experiencing severe financial problems. Further, companies dependent on a few customers have greater risk than those with a large number of important accounts. Receivables due from industry are typically safer than receivables arising from consumers. Fair trade laws are more protective of consumers.

A significant increase in accounts receivable compared to the prior year may indicate higher realization risk. The firm may be selling to more risky customers. The trends in accounts receivable to total assets and accounts receivable to sales should be evaluated.

The financial analyst should appraise the trends in the ratios of bad debts to accounts receivable and bad debts to sales. An unwarranted decrease in bad debts lowers the quality of earnings. This may happen when there is a decline in bad debts even though the company is selling to less credit-worthy customers and/or actual bad debt losses are increasing.

A company may purposely overstate bad debts to provide accounting cushions to report understated profits. Also, companies may have substantial bad debt provisions in the current period because improper provisions were made in prior years, distorting the earnings trend. A sudden write-off of accounts receivable may arise from prior understated bad debt provisions. Earnings may be managed by initially increasing and then lowering the bad debt provision.

Receivables are of low quality if they arose from loading customers up with unneeded merchandise by giving generous credit terms. "Red flags" as to this happening include

• A significant increase in sales in the final quarter of the year

• A substantial amount of sales returns in the first quarter of the next year

• A material decrease in sales for the first quarter of the next year

In a *seasonal* business, the accounts receivable turnover (credit sales/average accounts receivable) may be based on monthly or quarterly sales figures so that a proper averaging takes place.

The trend in sales returns and allowances is often a good reflection of the quality of merchandise sold to customers. A significant decrease in a firm's sales allowance account as a percentage of sales is not in conformity with reality when a greater liability for dealer returns exist. This will result in lower earnings quality.

■ Example

Company X's sales and sales returns for the period 19X3 to 19X5 are shown below.

The reduction in the ratio of sales returns to sales from 19X4 to 19X5 indicates that less of a provision for returns is being made by the company. This would appear unrealistic if there is a greater liability for dealer returns and credits on an expanded sales base.

Inventory

An inventory buildup may point to greater realization risk. The buildup may be at the plant, wholesaler, or retailer. A sign of buildup is when the increase in inventory is at a faster rate than the increase in sales.

A production slowdown may be indicated when there is a reduction in raw materials coupled with an increase in work-in-process and finished goods. Further, greater obsolescence risk exists with work-in process and finished goods due to major buildups. Raw materials have the best realizability because of greater universality and multipurpose.

Computation should be made of the turnover rate by each major inventory category and by department. A low turnover rate may be indicative of overstocking, obsolescence, or problems with the product line or marketing effectiveness. But there are cases where a low inventory rate is appropriate. For example, a higher inventory level may arise because of expected future increases in price.

A high inventory turnover rate may point to inadequate inventory possibly leading to a loss in business. At the "natural year-end" the turnover rate may be unusually high because at that time the inventory balance may be very low.

Computation should also be made of the number of days inventory is held. The age of inventory should be compared to industry averages and to prior years of the company.

High realization risk applies with specialized, technological, fad, luxurious, perishable, and price-sensitive merchandise. The credit analyst must be on guard that the company has not assigned values to unsalable and obsolete merchandise. If there is a sudden inventory write-off, the financial analyst may be suspicious of the firm's deferral policy. Low realization risk applies to standardized, staple, and necessity goods due to their better salability.

	19X5	19X4	19X3
Balance in sales returns account at year-end	$ 2,000	$ 3,800	$ 1,550
Sales	240,000	215,000	100,000
Percentage of sales returns to sales	0.0083	0.0177	0.0155

Collateralized inventory has greater risk because creditors can retain it in the event of nonpayment of an obligation. Also, inventory can have political risk associated with it. An example is increased gas prices due to a shortage situation making it unfeasible to purchase large cars.

Inventory may be overstated due to mistakes in quantities, costing, pricing, and valuation of work-in-process. The more technical the product and the more dependence on internally developed cost records, the greater is the susceptibility of the cost estimates to misstatement.

If adequate insurance cannot be obtained at reasonable rates due to an unfavorable geographic location of the merchandise (e.g., high crime area, flood susceptibility), a problem exists.

The investment analyst should note the appropriateness of a change in inventory. Is it required by a new FASB pronouncement, SEC release, or IRS tax ruling?

Investments

Are there any decreases in portfolio market values that have not been recognized in the accounts? An indication of the fair value of investments may be the revenue (dividend income, interest income) obtained from them. Higher realization risk exists where there is a declining trend in the percentage of earnings derived from investments to their carrying value. Also check subsequent event disclosures for unrealized losses in the portfolio occurring after year-end.

■ Example

Company X presents the following information:

	19X1	19X2
Investments	$50,000	$60,000
Investment income	7,000	5,000

The percentage of investment income to total investments decreased from 14% in 19X1 to 8.3% in 19X2, pointing to higher realization risk in the portfolio.

If a company is buying securities in other companies for diversification purposes, this will reduce overall risk. Risk in an investment portfolio can be ascertained by computing the standard deviation of its rate of return.

When an investment portfolio has a market value above cost, it constitutes an undervalued asset.

An investment portfolio of securities fluctuating widely in price is of higher realization risk than a portfolio that is diversified by industry and economic sector. But the former portfolio will show greater profitability in a bull market. The investment analyst should appraise the extent of diversification and stability of the investment portfolio. There is less risk when securities are negatively correlated (price goes in opposite directions) or not correlated, compared to a portfolio of positively correlated securities (price goes in same direction).

The financial analyst should be on guard against a dubious reclassification of a marketable security to long-term investment in order to avoid showing a future unrealized loss on the security portfolio in the income statement. The unrealized loss on a long-term portfolio is presented in the stockholders' equity section of the balance sheet.

The investment analyst should also note a case where debt securities have a cost in excess of market value.

Fixed Assets

Inadequate provision for the maintenance of property, plant, and equipment detracts from the long-term earning power of the firm. If obsolete assets are not replaced and repairs not properly made, breakdowns and detracted operational efficiency will result. Failure to write down obsolete fixed assets results in overstated earnings.

The financial analyst should determine the age and condition of each major asset along

with its replacement cost. The trend in fixed asset acquisitions to total gross assets should be reviewed. This trend is particularly revealing for a technological company that has to keep up to date. A decrease in the trend points to the failure to replace older assets on a timely basis. Inactive and unproductive asests put a drain on the firm. Asset efficiency may be reviewed by evaluating production levels, downtime, and discontinuances. Assets that have not been used for a long period of time may have to be written down.

Pollution-causing equipment may necessitate replacement or modification to meet governmental ecology requirements.

■ Example

Company T presents the following information regarding its fixed assets:

	19X1	19X2
Fixed assets	$120,000	$105,000
Repairs and maintenance	6,000	4,500
Replacement cost	205,000	250,000

The company has inadequately maintained its assets as indicated by (1) the reduction in the ratio of repairs and maintenance to fixed assets from 5% in 19X1 to 4.3% in 19X2; (2) the material variation between replacement cost and historical cost; and (3) the reduction in fixed assets over the year.

When a company's rate of return on assets (e.g., net income to fixed assets) is poor, the firm may be justified in not maintaining fixed assets. If there is a declining industry, fixed asset replacement and repairs may have been restricted.

The fixed asset turnover ratio (net sales to average fixed assets) aids in appraising a company's ability to use its asset base efficiently to obtain revenue. A low ratio may mean that investment in fixed assets is excessive relative to the output generated.

A company having specialized or risky fixed assets has greater vulnerability to asset obsolescence. Examples include machinery used to manufacture specialized products and fad items.

A depreciation method should be used that most realistically measures the expiration in asset usefulness. For example, the units-of-production method may result in a realistic charge for machinery. Unrealistic book depreciation may be indicated when depreciation for stockholder reporting is materially less than depreciation for tax return purposes.

The investment analyst should examine the trend in depreciation expense as a percentage of both fixed assets and net sales. A reduction in the trend may point to inadequate depreciation charges for the potential obsolescence of fixed assets. Another indication of inadequate depreciation charges is a concurrent moderate rise in depreciation coupled with a material increase in capital spending.

■ Example

The following information applies to X Company:

	19X1	19X2
Depreciation expense to fixed assets	5.3%	4.4%
Depreciation expense to sales	4.0%	3.3%

The previous declining ratios indicate improper provision for the deterioration of assets.

A change in classification of newly acquired fixed assets to different depreciation categories from the older assets (e.g., accelerated depreciation to straight-line) will result in lower earnings quality. A vacillating depreciation policy will distort continuity in earnings. Also, if there is a reduction in depreciation expense caused by an unrealistic change in the lives and salvage values of property, plant, and equipment, there will be overstated earnings.

An inconsistency exists when there is a material decline in revenue coupled with a major increase in capital expenditures. It may be indicative of overexpansion and later write-offs of fixed assets.

Intangibles

High realization risk is indicated when there are high ratios of (1) intangible assets to total assets and (2) intangible assets to net worth. Intangibles may be overstated compared to their market value or future earning potential. For example, a firm's goodwill may be overstated or worthless in a recessionary environment. A 40-year amortization period may be excessive. Also, intangibles acquired before 1970 may be retained on the books without amortization.

Leasehold improvements are improvements made to rented property, such as paneling and fixtures. Leasehold improvements are amortized over the life of the rented property or the life of the improvement, whichever is shorter. Leasehold improvements have no cash realizability.

A company's goodwill account should be appraised to ascertain whether the firm acquired has superior earning potential to justify the excess of cost over fair market value of net assets paid for it. If the acquired company does not have superior profit potential, the goodwill has no value because excess earnings do not exist relative to other companies in the industry. However, internally developed goodwill is expensed and not capitalized. It represents an undervalued asset, such as the good reputation of McDonald's.

Patents may be undervalued. Patents are recorded at the registration cost plus legal fees to defend them, which may be far below the present value of future cash flows to be derived from the patents. Patents are less valuable when they may easily be infringed upon by minor alteration or when they apply to high-technological-oriented items. Also considered is the financial condition of the company, because it may have to incur significant legal costs in defending patents. What is the expiration dates of the patents and the degree to which new patents are coming on stream?

The change in intangible assets to the change in net income should also be examined. A rising trend may mean this net income has been relieved of appropriate charges.

An unwarranted lengthening in the amortization period for intangibles overstates earnings. An example of an unjustified change is when the company's reputation has been worsened due to political bribes and environmental violations.

Deferred Charges

Deferred expenses depend to a greater extent on estimates of future probabilities than do other assets. The estimates may be overly optimistic. Is the company deferring an item having no future benefit just to defer costs so as not to burden net income? Deferred charges are not cash-realizable assets and cannot be used to meet creditor claims. Examples of questionable deferred charges are moving costs, start-up costs, plant rearrangement costs, merger expenses, and promotional costs.

A company may try to hide declining profitability by deferring costs that were expensed in prior years. The CPA should be on the outlook for such a situation.

The financial analyst should examine the trend in deferred charges to sales, deferred charges to net income, and deferred charges (e.g., deferred promotion costs) to total expenditures. Increasing trends may be indicative of a more liberal accounting policy.

■ Example

Company G presents the following information:

	19X1	19X2
Deferred charges	$ 70,000	$150,000
Total assets	500,000	590,000
Sales	800,000	845,000
Net income	200,000	215,000
Computed ratios are		
Deferred costs to total assets	14%	25.4%
Deferred costs to sales	8.8%	17.8%
Deferred costs to net income	35%	69.8%

The higher ratios of deferred charges to (1) total assets, (2) sales, and (3) net income indicate more realization risk in assets. Further, 19X2's earnings quality may be lower because deferred costs may include in it items that should have been expensed.

A high ratio of intangible assets and deferred charges to total assets points to an asset structure of greater realization risk. Overstated assets in terms of realizability may necessitate later write-off.

Unrecorded Assets

The investment analyst should note the existence of unrecorded assets representing resources of the business or items expected to have future economic benefit. Unrecorded assets are positive aspects of financial position even though they are not shown on the balance sheet. Examples of unrecorded assets are tax loss carry forward benefit and a purchase commitment where the company has a contract to buy an item at a price materially less than the going rate.

Liabilities

If liabilities are understated, net income is overstated because it does not include necessary charges to reflect the proper valuation of liabilities.

The credit analyst should examine trends in current liabilities to total liabilities, current liabilities to stockholders' equity, and current liabilities to sales. Rising trends may point to liquidity problems.

Are liabilities patient or pressing? A supplier with a long relationship may postpone or modify the debt payable for a financially troubled company. Pressing debts include taxes and loans payable. These have to be paid without excuse. A high ratio of pressing liabilities to patient liabilities points to greater liquidity risk.

▪ Example

Company A reports the following information shown in the table below.

The company has greater liquidity risk in 19X2, as reflected by the higher ratios of current liabilities to total liabilities, current liabilities to sales, and pressing current liabilities to patient current liabilities.

Arbitrary adjustments of estimated liabilities should be eliminated in deriving corporate earning power. For instance, profits derived from a recoupment of prior year reserves may necessitate elimination. If the credit analyst finds that reserves are used to manage earnings, he or she should add back the amounts charged to earnings and deduct the amounts credited to earnings. Estimated liability provisions should be realistic given the nature of the circumstances.

A firm having an unrealistically low provi-

Current Liabilities	19X1	19X2
Accounts payable	$ 30,000	$ 26,000
Short-term loans payable	50,000	80,000
Commercial paper	40,000	60,000
Total current liabilities	$ 120,000	$ 166,000
Total noncurrent liabilities	300,000	308,000
Total liabilities	$ 420,000	$ 468,000
Sales	$1,000,000	$1,030,000
Relevant ratios follow:		
Current liabilities to total liabilities	28.6%	35.5%
Current liabilities to sales	12.0%	16.1%
Pressing current liabilites to patient current liabilities (short-term loans payable plus commercial paper/accounts payable)	3.01	5.4

sion for future costs has understated earnings. For example, it is inconsistent for a company to have a lower warranty provision when prior experience points to a deficiency in product quality.

An overprovision in estimated liabilities is sometimes made when profits are too high and management wants to bring them down. In effect, the company is providing for a reserve for a rainy day.

Poor earnings quality is indicated when more operating expenses and losses are being charged to reserve accounts compared to prior years.

Unrecorded liabilities are not reported on the financial statements but do require future payment or services. Examples are lawsuits and noncapitalized leases.

Useful disclosures of long-term obligations is mandated by FASB 47. The credit analyst may want to review commitments applicable to unconditional purchase obligations and future payments on long-term debt and redeemable stock.

FASB Interpretation 34 requires disclosure of indirect guarantees of indebtedness. Included are contracts in which a company promises to advance funds to another if financial problems occur, as when sales drop below a stipulated level.

Preferred stock with a maturity date or subject to sinking fund requirements is more like debt than equity. However, convertible bonds with an attractive conversion feature are more like equity than debt since there is an expectation of conversion. *See also* Income Statement Analysis.

BANKRUPTCY This involves a discharge of the debtor's obligations through court order. The purpose of bankruptcy is to provide the debtor with a fresh start and to have an equitable distribution of the debtor's assets among creditors. A major federal law concerning bankruptcy is the Bankruptcy Reform Act of 1978. Chapter 7 deals with corporate bankruptcy; Chapter 9 provides procedures for municipal bankruptcy; and Chapter 13 pertains to individual bankruptcy. *See also* Business Failure.

BARRON'S CONFIDENCE INDEX This looks at the trading pattern of bond investors to determine the timing of buying or selling stocks. The index is based on the belief that bond traders are more sophisticated than stock traders and thus identify stock market trends sooner. *See also* Technical Analysis.

BARTER Many companies are turning to barter as a way of improving efficiency and increasing profits. But barter may not be for everyone. The substance of the arrangement must be evaluated to see if it is economically advantageous. Appropriate accounting measures are needed to ensure that the transaction conforms to financial and tax-reporting requirements. Financial management should study the pros and cons of entering into barter deals, weighing the possible effects on both the short- and long-term financial health of the business. On average, 8% of U.S. export sales are bartered. Counter trade is in excess of $100 billion a year.

What Is Barter?

Various kinds of barter arrangements are possible. The simplest is when two firms exchange services or products in a transaction involving no cash. There is a contract for a given quantity of items specifying what constitutes complete payment. When possible, it is recommended that two companies make an exchange *directly* to avoid the commission charged by a barter middleman. It may be best for the firm to make public a listing of the items it has available and a corresponding list describing what merchandise or services it needs.

Examples of bartering contracts are infinite. Only a few are cited here. An airline exchanges seats for advertising space and time. A manufacturer barters a product with a carrier in return for lower shipping rates.

Middlemen—act as intermediaries between companies. Often there is a barter club that prepares a catalog of commodities and services that are available among its members. There also may be a broker who can prepare a contract between companies entering into a barter arrangement.

When goods or services are transferred between members, there is a trade credit for the issuer and a trade charge for the receiver. Mainframe, minicomputer, or microcomputer systems may be used to keep abreast of dealings between parties.

When using a middleman, there are several factors to consider:
• What is the middleman charging and is it reasonable?
• Is there an initiation fee?
• What is the commission rate?
• How reliable is the middleman?

Accounts of member firms may be settled in cash from companies having goods not yet traded at period-end. Financial management should attempt cash-settlement arrangements so it does not have to accept unneeded merchandise or services.

Some barter firms where transaction information is available include Business Exchange Inc. and Universal Trading Exchange.

"You owe me." This is when one company delivers a product or service to another in return for the other company's promise to reciprocate later. Sometimes there is even a third company involved.

Buyback—when a United States entity provides goods or services to a foreign country to be paid back from the output generated from the plant it is helping to construct.

Counter trade—possible between both domestic or international companies. An example of such an arrangement is a business providing a machine in exchange for a certain commodity.

Bilateral clearing arrangements between central banks—used by certain countries. An even-netting effect occurs without the need for a company to use currency for settlement of a transaction with a company in a foreign country.

Favorable Bartering Conditions

Financial management may be more prone to employ bartering arrangements during the following circumstances:
• Difficulties with foreign currency
• Slow economic conditions
• High inflation
• Monetary problems in international markets or trade
• Rising interest rates
• A credit crunch
• High inventory balances
• The dollar is high priced
• A debt crisis exists in the world market

Advantages of Bartering

The reasons for opting to enter into barter arrangements are many. Barter can
• Attract cash customers who are satisfied with a product or service.
• Lessen cash flow problems by trading goods at wholesale for their full market value. For example, an accountant charges $3,000 for accounting work. He is paid by a company in merchandise having a market value of $3,000 but costing $2,500 wholesale. The accountant may not actually take the merchandise but instead obtains credits from a barter company.
• Minimize the production risk because it creates a greater market for a product or service.
• Get rid of excess inventory and do so at a higher price than in a liquidation.
• Improve the profit margin.
• Cover fixed costs in an idle-capacity situation.
• Generate new and sometimes innovative advertising channels.

• Help dispose of unattractive, discontinued, or surplus product lines without having to drastically lower prices.

• Help in starting new product lines, which is especially attractive for firms experiencing seasonal sales.

Limitations to Bartering

There are limitations and disadvantages to entering into barter arrangements, which financial management should carefully consider. Some disadvantages are

• The company giving the goods to another may not learn what the market for the product is really like and what manufacturing and marketing improvements can be made.

• Possible lower profitability on the bartered item compared to a normal sale.

• Unattractive or even unneeded items may be received in exchange (e.g., products lacking marketability).

• Commission fees may be high, often ranging from 2% to 12%.

• Merchandise received may be of inferior quality or lack marketability.

• A foreign government may restrict export of a good under a bartering contract.

• In the case of a firm with financial problems, the trader has a lien after secured creditors when the merchandise has been collateralized.

• Dumping bartered goods on the market may lower the selling price of goods in normal distribution channels, which may have a negative effect on overall earnings.

• Inefficiencies may be compounded by manufacturing excessive merchandise.

A Word of Caution

Before getting involved in a barter network, investigate the reliability of the broker, the companies involved, and the availability and desirability of the goods or services:

• Does the network or broker offer promises that can't be kept?

• What is the quality of the services or goods?

• What is the prior record of the broker or barter club you are considering?

• Is the barter network financially healthy to meet its commitments?

• Have club members withdrawn after receiving benefits but before reciprocating?

Financial management should get assurances that its company's products will not ultimately go into its own normal distribution channels, because that, in effect, will cause the company to be competing with itself. The bartered items often are sold at a lower price than nonbartered items. To protect itself, a legal contract with the broker or barter network should be entered into to restrict where the merchandise may be sold. For example, if a good is now sold only in New York, the contract might allow sales only to other states. The same holds true for sales in a given foreign geographic location. Similarly, merchandise currently distributed in the United States could be limited to bartering done overseas.

An accountant should advise his client that counter trade can be utilized for debt collection from a problem company. For example, assume an Italian company does not have sufficient dollars to pay a U.S. company. A trading company can be employed and the debt renegotiated in lira with the customer giving the lira to the trading company's Italian subsidiary. When the Italian subsidiary buys Italian commodities and sells them in the market, dollars can be transferred to the U.S.

The accountant should be involved in the selection process for an experienced barter middleman to handle barter arrangements for the client since financial aspects are crucial to the deal.

Authoritative Accounting Requirements

Accounting pronouncements are virtually silent regarding the accounting, financial reporting, and disclosures involving barter transactions. For such a growing area of business activity, clarification and mandates are necessary.

Some accounting guidelines in the area are APB 29 and FASB 63. According to APB 29, Accounting for Nonmonetary Transactions, barter transactions should be reported at the estimated fair market value of the product or service received. This requirement is consistent with the tax law that provides for each party to recognize as revenue the fair market value of the exchange.

FASB 63, Financial Reporting by Broadcasters, defines barter as the exchange of unsold advertising time for products or services. The broadcaster benefits (providing the exchange does not interfere with its cash sales) by exchanging unsold time for other products or services (i.e., fixed asset, merchandise, travel, and entertainment). Barter revenue is to be reported when commercials are broadcast. Merchandise or services received should be reported when received or used. If merchandise or services are received before the commercial is broadcast, a liability should be reported. Similarly, if the commercial is broadcast first, a receivable should be reported.

Recommended Accounting and Reporting

Accountants must assure themselves that their clients have reported all income from barter activities at their fair market value, in accordance with tax and financial reporting requirements. Is the fair market value assigned to the exchange realistic? Will the client be able to sell goods received at the price in the market or will a price cut be required? Has fair market value been manipulated to reduce the tax obligation?

The accountant must carefully determine the method used and relevant assumptions applicable to fair market value. Is it based on an objective appraisal, the present value of future cash flows, replacement cost, or some other approach?

Are there sham and unrealistically priced exchange transactions? Some swaps are not clear-cut and are subject to abuse. But the accountant must be assured the client is obtaining full tax benefits. For instance, a restaurant providing a meal for advertising space may recognize the revenue and the expense for the full amount since advertising is a business expense. Accountants must be assured the client never loses his tax benefit when rightfully due.

The accountant must watch out for unreported income through such means as examining inventory figures (an unexplained reduction in inventory may arise from bartering) because misrepresentation by the client may result in IRS attack. The IRS can trace unreported revenue from the other barter party who has reported it.

The accountant must assure himself that his client's counter trade party is not padding the price for the item in question by examining available price lists. Note that the fair market value of items to be exchanged may be less than current cash prices received due to excess supply on the market.

Audit difficulties occur because bartering may be abused. For example, a broadcaster may receive a credit card from a credit card company in exchange for broadcast time. The assumption is that the card will be used for proper travel and entertainment expenses to lower current cash flow problems. However, because the credit card company will be absorbing the charge in return for broadcast time, the audit trail is not clear. The possibility is present that the credit card will be used partly for nonbusiness purposes.

The accountant must evaluate situations where the terms of the barter are unrealistic.

■ Example

An exchange of a foreign product may be such that the foreign government demands an inflated price. This may cause both companies involved to appear as if they are going along with this by formulating a fictitious transaction to justify the outrageous price.

Assume two letters of credit are made up— one for the inflated value and one for the reasonable price. The letter of credit for the overstated amount is canceled by the exchange. The U.S. exporter obtains cash for the merchandise value from the bank, which obtains that cash by marketing the foreign country's product.

■ Example

Obsolete inventory may be given to a barter dealer for credit of $100,000. The credit is treated as a receivable on the company's books so a loss is not recognized. If television time is given in exchange for cash at a discount rate of 60% of the going price, the $100,000 credit is reduced by 40% of the spread between the price paid to the barter dealer and the normal price.

Hence, if the manufacturer draws down $30,000 worth of time, it pays $18,000 cash and has its credit reduced by the barter dealer for $12,000. When the receivable is totally eliminated, the manufacturer will have incurred $150,000 in cash for television time represented by the $100,000 credit. While the manufacturer has not had to show a write-down loss, it has unrealistically enhanced earnings and thus paid additional tax. The net effect has been detrimental to stockholders.

Conclusion

Financial management should take full advantage of all the positive aspects of the rapidly growing trend toward bartering. Bartering is especially advantageous to a firm that can dispose of surplus merchandise or services that cannot be sold on favorable terms via ordinary distribution channels.

Selecting the right bartering arrangement can lower risk, improve efficiency, and enhance the bottom line. If it is done correctly, it can satisfy the short- and long-term objectives of a business.

BASIC FORMS OF BUSINESS ORGANIZATION

The three basic forms are (1) the sole proprietorship, (2) the partnership, and (3) the corporation.

A *sole proprietorship* is a business owned by one individual. Of the three forms of business organizations, sole proprietorships are the greatest in number.

The advantages of this form are
• No formal charter required
• Minimal organizational costs
• Profits and control not shared with others
The disadvantages are
• Limited ability to raise large sums of money
• Unlimited liability for the owner
• Limited to the life of the owner

A *partnership* is similar to the sole proprietorship except that the business has more than one owner.

Its advantages are
• Minimal organizational effort and costs
• Free from governmental regulations
Its disadvantages are
• Unlimited liability for the individual partners
• Limited ability to raise large sums of money
• Dissolved upon the death or withdrawal of any of the partners
There is a special form of partnership, called *limited partnership,* where one or more partners but not all have limited liability up to their investment, to creditors in the event of failure of the business. The *general partner* manages the business. *Limited partners* are not involved in daily activities. The return to limited partners is in the form of income and capital gains. Often, tax benefits are involved. Examples of limited partnerships are in real estate and oil and gas exploration.

A *corporation* is a legal entity that exists apart from its owners, better known as stockholders. Ownership is evidenced by possession of shares of stock. In terms of types of businesses, the corporate form is not the greatest in number but is the most important in terms of total sales, assets, profits, and contribution to national income.

The advantages of a corporation are
• Unlimited life
• Limited liability for its owners
• Ease of transfer of ownership through transfer of stock
• Ability to raise large sums of capital

Its disadvantages are
• Difficult and costly to establish because a formal charter is required
• Subject to double taxation—on its earnings and dividends paid to stockholders

See also Going Public; Limited Partnership.

BAYESIAN PROBABILITY   This is revised prior estimates of probabilities, based on additional experience and information. An example of Bayesian probability applied to accounting is when the estimated bad debt percentage has to be revised because of such considerations as recent uncollectability experience of customer defaults, sales to more marginal customers, or poor economic conditions.

BETA COEFFICIENT   Many investors hold more than one financial asset. The portion of a security's risk, called *unsystematic risk*, can be controlled through diversification. This type of risk is unique to a given security. Business, liquidity, and default risks fall in this category. Nondiversifiable risk, more commonly referred to as *systematic risk,* results from forces outside of the firm's control and are therefore not unique to the given security. Purchasing power, interest rate, and market risks fall into this category. This type of risk is measured by *beta.* A particular stock's beta is useful in predicting how much the security will go up or down, provided that financial analysts and investors know which way the market will go. It does help them to figure out risk and expected return.

Most of the unsystematic risk affecting a security can be diversified away in an efficiently constructed portfolio. Therefore, this type of risk does not need to be compensated with a higher level of return. The only relevant risk is *systematic risk* or *beta risk* for which they can expect to receive compensation. Investors are compensated for taking this type of risk, which cannot be controlled.

In general, there is a relationship between a stock's expected (or required return) and its beta. The following formula, known as the Capital Asset Pricing Model (CAPM), is very helpful in determining a stock's expected return.

$$r_j = r_f + b\,(r_m - r_f)$$

where r_f = risk-free rate (the rate on a security such as a T-bill),

b = beta, the index of systematic risk,

r_m = expected market return (such as Standard & Poor's 500 Stock Composite Index),

$(r_m - r_f)$ = the market risk premium, the expected market return minus risk-free rate.

In words,

Expected return = risk-free rate + (beta × market risk premium)

The relevant measure of risk is the risk of the individual security, or its beta. The higher the beta for a security, the greater the return expected (or demanded) by the investor.

■ Example

Assume that r_f (the risk-free rate) = 6%, and r_m (the expected return for the market) = 10%. If a stock has a beta of 2.0, its risk premium $(r_m - r_f)$ should be 4% (10% − 6%). Therefore:

$$2.0 \times (10\% - 6\%) = 2.0 \times 4\% = 8\%$$

This means that an investor would expect (or demand) an extra 8% (risk premium) on this stock on top of the risk-free return of

6%. Therefore, the total expected (required) return on the stock should be 14%:

$$6\% + 8\% = 14\%$$

How to Read Beta

Beta measures a security's volatility relative to an average security. Put another way, it is a measure of a security's return over time to that of the overall market. For example, if Paine Webber's beta is 2.0, it means that if the stock market goes up 10%, Paine Webber's common stock goes up 20%; if the market goes down 10%, Paine Webber goes down 20%. Here is a guide for how to read betas:

Beta	What It Means
0	The security's return is independent of the market. An example is a risk-free security such as a T-bill.
0.5	The security is only half as responsive as the market.
1.0	The security has the same responsive, or risk, as the market (i.e., average risk). This is the beta value of the market portfolio such as Standard & Poor's 500 or Dow Jones 30 Industrials.
2.0	The security is twice as responsive, or risky, as the market.

How to Measure Beta

In measuring an asset's systematic risk, beta, an indication is needed of the relationship between the asset's returns and the market returns (such as returns on the Standard & Poor's 500 Stock Composite Index or Dow Jones 30 Industrials). This relationship can be statistically computed by determining the regression coefficient between asset and market returns. The equation is presented above.

$$b = \frac{Cov\,(r_j,\,r_m)}{\sigma_m^2}$$

where $Cov\,(r_j,\,r_m)$ is the covariance of the returns of the assets with the market returns, and σ_m^2 is the variance (standard deviation squared) of the market returns.

An easier way to compute beta is to determine the slope of the least-square's linear regression line $(r_j - r_f)$, where the excess return of the asset $(r_j - r_f)$ is regressed against the excess return of the market portfolio $(r_m - r_f)$. The formula for b is

$$b = \frac{\Sigma\,MK - n\,\bar{M}\bar{K}}{\Sigma\,M^2 - n\,\bar{M}^2}$$

where $M = (r_m - r_f)$,

$K = (r_j - r_f)$,

n = number of years,

$\bar{M}$ = average of M,

$\bar{K}$ = average of K.

■ Example

Compute the beta coefficient, b, using the following data for stock x and the market portfolio:

Historic Rates of Return

Year	r_j (%)	r_m (%)
19X5	−5	10
19X6	4	8
19X7	7	12
19X8	10	20
19X9	12	15

Assume that the risk-free rate is 6%. For easy computation, it is convenient to set up the following table:

Year	r_j	r_m	r_f	$(r_j - r_f) = K$	$(r_m - r_f) = M$	M^2	MK
19X5	−0.05	0.10	0.06	−0.11	0.04	0.0016	−0.0044
19X6	0.04	0.08	0.06	−0.02	0.02	0.0004	−0.0004
19X7	0.07	0.12	0.06	0.01	0.06	0.0036	0.0006
19X8	0.10	0.20	0.06	0.04	0.14	0.0196	0.0056
19X9	0.12	0.15	0.06	0.06	0.09	0.0081	0.0054
				−0.02	0.35	0.0333	0.0068

$$\bar{K} = -0.004 \quad \bar{M} = 0.07$$

Therefore, beta is

$$b = \frac{\Sigma MK - n\bar{M}\bar{K}}{\Sigma M^2 - n\bar{M}^2}$$

$$= \frac{0.0068 - (5)(-0.004)(0.07)}{0.0333 - (5)(0.07)^2}$$

$$= \frac{0.0082}{0.0088} = 0.93$$

See also Portfolio Theory; Capital Asset Pricing Model (CAPM).

BID AND ASKED This is the terminology used for a price quotation on an over-the-counter security. The highest price to be paid for a security by a prospective buyer is the bid price. The lowest price that a seller will accept for that security is the asked price. The differential between bid and asked is the spread that goes to the brokerage house, making a market in the security.

"BIG EIGHT" This refers to the eight largest CPA firms in the United States. In alphabetical order, they are Arthur Andersen & Co.; Coopers and Lybrand; Deloitte, Haskins and Sells; Ernst and Whinney; Peat, Marwick, Main and Co.; Price Waterhouse & Co.; Touche Ross & Co.; and Arthur Young & Co. Different bases exist to rank the CPA firms, such as by gross revenue, net income, number of staff, number of partners, and number of accounts. Also, firm ranking may change over time.

BLOCK SAMPLING This is a method of choosing sampling units (e.g., accounts, documents) in sequential sequence. Once the first item in the block is selected, the remainder of the block is automatically chosen. An example of a limited block, or cluster, from a given population is testing only a week of sales invoices for control deviations in April and May for the purpose of formulating a conclusion about the 6 months ended June 30. *See also* Sampling.

BOND ACCOUNTING The two methods of amortizing bond discount or bond premium are
* *Straight-line method*, which results in a constant dollar amount of amortization but a different effective rate each period.
* *Effective interest method*, which results in a constant rate of interest but different dollar amounts each period. This method is preferred over the straight-line method. The amortization entry is

Interest Expense (Yield × Carrying value of bond at the beginning of the year)
    Discount
    Cash (Nominal interest × Face value of bond)

In the early years, the amortization amount under the effective interest method is lower relative to the straight-line method (either for discount or premium).

■ Example

On 1/1/19X1, a $100,000 bond is issued at $95,624. The yield rate is 7% and the nominal interest rate is 6%. The schedule (shown below) is the basis for the journal entries to be made.

The entry on 12/31/19X1 is

Interest Expense   6,694
    Cash   6,000
    Discount   694

At maturity, the bond will be worth its face

Date	Debit Interest Expense	Credit Cash	Credit Discount	Carrying Value
1/1/19X1				$95,624
12/31/19X1	$6,694	$6,000	$694	96,318
12/31/19X2	6,742	6,000	742	97,060

value of $100,000. When bonds are issued between interest dates, the entry is

Cash
Bonds Payable
Premium (or debit Discount)
Interest Expense

■ Example

A $100,000, 5% bond having a life of 5 years is issued at 110 on 4/1/19X0. The bonds are dated 1/1/19X0. Interest is payable on 1/1 and 7/1. Straight-line amortization is used. The journal entries are

4/1/19X0	Cash (110,000 + 1,250)	111,250	
	Bonds Payable		100,000
	Premium on Bonds Payable		10,000
	Bond Interest Expense (100,000 × 5% × 3/12)		1,250
7/1/19X0	Bond Interest Expense	2,500	
	Cash		2,500
	100,000 × 5% × 6/12		
	Premium on Bonds Payable	526.50	
	Bond Interest Expense		526.50

4/1/19X0 −1/1/19X5   4 years, 9 months = 57 months

$$\frac{\$10,000}{57} = \$175.50 \text{ per month}$$

$175.50 × 3 months = $526.50

12/31/19X0	Bond Interest Expense	2,500	
	Interest Payable		2,500
	Premium on Bonds Payable	1,053	
	Bond Interest Expense		1,053
1/1/19X1	Interest Payable	2,500	
	Cash		2,500

Bonds Payable is shown on the balance sheet at its present value in the following manner:
- Bonds Payable
- Add: Premium
- Less: Discount
- Carrying Value

Bond issue costs are the expenditures incurred in issuing the bonds, such as legal, registration, and printing fees. Preferably, bond issue costs are deferred and amortized over the life of the bond. They are shown as a Deferred Charge.

In determining the price of a bond, the face amount is discounted using the present value of $1 table. The interest payments are discounted using the present value of annuity of $1 table. The yield rate is used as the discount rate.

■ Example

A $50,000, 10-year bond is issued with interest payable semiannually at an 8% nominal interest rate. The yield rate is 10%. The present value of $1 table factor for $n = 20$, $i = 5\%$ is 0.37689. The present value of annuity of $1 table factor for $n = 20$, $i = 5\%$ is 12.46221. The price of the bond should be

Present value of principal $50,000 × 0.37689	$18,844.50
Present value of interest payments $20,000 × 12.46221	24,924.42
	$43,768.92

In converting a bond into stock, there are three alternative methods that can be used: book value of bond, market value of bond, and market value of stock. Under the book value of bond method, no gain or loss on bond conversion will result because the book value of the bond is the basis to credit equity. Under the market value methods, gain or loss will result because the book value of the bond will be different from the market value of bond or market value of stock which is the basis to credit the equity accounts.

■ Example

A $100,000 bond with unamortized premium of $8,420.50 is converted to common stock.

There are 100 bonds ($100,000/$1,000). Each bond is converted into 50 shares of stock. Thus, 5,000 shares of common stock are involved. Par value is $15 per share. The market value of the stock is $25 per share. The market value of the bond is 120. Using the bond value method, the entry for the conversion is

Bonds Payable	100,000	
Premium on Bonds Payable	8,420.50	
Common Stock (5,000 × $15)		75,000
Premium on Common Stock		33,420.50

Using the market value of stock method, the entry is

Bonds Payable	100,000	
Premium on Bonds Payable	8,420.50	
Loss on Conversion	16,579.50	
Common Stock		75,000
Premium on Common Stock 5,000 × $25 = $125,000		50,000

Using the market value of the bond method, the entry is

Bonds Payable	100,000	
Premium on Bonds Payable	8,420.50	
Loss on Conversion	11,579.50	
Common Stock		75,000
Premium on Common Stock $100,000 × 120% = $120,000		45,000

BOND RATINGS These reflect the probability that a bond issue will go into default. They can influence investors' perceptions of risk and therefore have an impact on the interest rate. Bond investors tend to place more emphasis on independent analysis of quality than do common stock investors. Bond analysis and ratings are done, among others, by Stand-

ard & Poor's and Moody's. Below is an actual listing of the designations used by these well-known independent agencies. Descriptions on ratings are summarized. For original versions of descriptions, see Moody's *Bond Record* and Standard & Poor's *Bond Guide*.

Description of Bond Ratings		
Moody's	Standard & Poor's	Quality Indication
Aaa	AAA	Highest quality
Aa	AA	High quality
A	A	Upper medium grade
Baa	BBB	Medium grade
Ba	BB	Contains speculative elements
B	B	Outright speculative
Caa	CCC & CC	Default definitely possible
Ca	C	Default, only partial recovery likely
C	D	Default, little recovery likely

Bond investors pay careful attention to ratings because they can affect not only potential market behavior but relative *yields* as well. Specifically, the higher the rating, the lower the yield of a bond, other things being equal. It should be noted that the ratings do change over time and the rating agencies have "credit watch lists" of various types.

BOND REFUNDING Bonds may be refunded by the firm prior to maturity through either the issuance of a serial bond or exercising a call privilege on a straight bond. The issuance of serial bonds allows the company to refund the debt over the life of the issue. A call feature in a bond enables the issuer to retire it before the expiration date. The call feature is included in many corporate bond issues.

When future interest rates are expected to decline, a call provision in the bond issue is recommended. Such a provision enables the company to buy back the high-interest bond and issue a low-interest one. The timing for the refunding depends on expected future interest rates. A call price is usually established in excess of the face value of the bond. The resulting call *premium* equals the difference between the call price and the maturity value. The issuer pays the premium to the bondholder in order to acquire the outstanding bonds before the maturity date. The call premium is generally equal to one year's interest if the bond is called in the first year, and it declines at a constant rate each year thereafter. Also involved in selling a new issue are flotation costs. Both the call premium and flotation costs are tax-deductible expenses.

A bond with a call provision typically will be issued at an interest rate higher than one without the call provision. The investor prefers not to have a situation where the company can buy back the bonds early and issue lower interest bonds when interest rates de-

■ **Example**

Cypress Corporation is considering calling a $20 million, 30-year bond that was issued 10 years ago at 97 at a nominal interest rate of 14%. The call price on the bond is 104. The initial flotation cost was $200,000. The firm is considering issuing $20 million, 12%, 20-year bonds in order to net proceeds and retire the old bonds. The new bonds will be issued at 100. The flotation costs for the new issue are $225,000. The tax rate is 34%. The after-tax cost of new debt ignoring flotation costs is 7.92% (12% × 66%). With the flotation costs, the after-tax cost of new debt is anticipated to be 9%. There is a 2-month overlap in which interest must be paid on the old and new bonds. To determine whether refunding should take place, we need to compute the *net* initial cash outlay and net annual cash savings as follows:

The initial cash outlay is

Cost to call old bonds ($20,000,000 × 104%)	$20,800,000
Cost to issue new bond	225,000
Interest on old bonds for overlap period ($20,000,000 × 14% × 2/12)	466,667
Initial cash outlay	$21,491,667

The initial cash inflow is

Proceeds from selling new bond		$20,000,000
Tax-deductible items:		
Call premium	$ 800,000	
Unamortized discount ($600,000 × 20/30)	400,000	
Unamortized issue cost of old bond ($200,000 × 20/30)	133,333	
Overlap interest ($20,000,000 × 14% × 2/12)	466,667	
Total tax-deductible items	$1,800,000	
Tax rate	× 0.34	
Tax savings		612,000
Initial cash inflow		$20,612,000

cline. The investor would obviously want to hold onto a high-interest bond when prevailing rates are low.

The desirability of refunding a bond requires discount flow analysis.

The *net* initial cash outlay is therefore:

Initial cash outlay	$21,491,667
Inital cash inflow	20,612,000
Net initial cash outlay	$ 879,667

The annual cash flow for the old bond is

Interest (14% × $20,000,000)		$2,800,000
Less: Tax-deductible items		
Interest	$2,800,000	
Amortization of discount ($600,000/30)	20,000	
Amortization of issue cost ($200,000/30)	6,667	
Total tax-deductible items	$2,826,667	
Tax rate	× 0.34	
Tax savings		961,067
Annual cash outflow with old bond		$1,838,933

The annual cash flow for the new bond is

Interest (12% × $20,000,000)		$2,400,000
Less: Tax-deductible items		
Interest	$2,400,000	
Amortization of discount ($225,000/20)	11,250	
Total tax-deductible items	$2,411,250	
Tax rate	× 0.34	
Tax savings		819,825
Annual cash outflow with old bond		$1,580,175

The net annual cash savings with the new bond compared to the old bond is

Annual cash outflow with old bond	$1,838,933
Annual cash outflow with new bond	1,580,175
Net annual cash savings	$ 258,758

The net present value (NPV) with the refunding is

	Calculations	Present Value
Year 0	−$879,667 × 1	−$ 879,667
Year 1–20	$258,758 × 9.129*	+ 2,362,202
		$1,482,535

* PVIFA(9%, 20 years) = 9.129 from Table 4 in the Appendix.

Since a positive NPV exists, the refunding should take place.

BOND VALUATION   The process of determining security valuation involves finding the present value of an asset's expected future cash flows using the investor's required rate of return. Thus, the basic security valuation model can be defined mathematically as shown:

$$V = \sum_{t=1}^{n} \frac{C_t}{(1 + r)^t}$$

where V = intrinsic value or present value of an asset,

C_t = expected future cash flows in period $t = 1, \ldots, n$,

r = investor's required rate of return.

The valuation process for a bond requires a knowledge of three basic elements: (1) the amount of the cash flows to be received by the investor, which is equal to the periodic interest to be received and the par value to be paid at maturity; (2) the maturity date of the bond; and (3) the investor's required rate of return.

Incidentally, the periodic interest can be received annually or semiannually. The value of a bond is simply the present value of these cash flows. Two versions of the bond valuation model are presented below:

If the interest payments are made annually, then:

$$V = \sum_{t=1}^{n} \frac{I}{(1 + r)^t} + \frac{M}{(1 + r)^n}$$

$$= I(PVIFA_{r,n}) + M(PVIF_{r,n})$$

where I = interest payment each year = coupon interest rate × par value,

M = par value, or maturity value, typically $1,000,

r = investor's required rate of return,

n = number of years to maturity,

$PVIFA$ = present value interest factor of an annuity of $1 (which can be found in Table 4 in the Appendix)

$PVIF$ = present value interest factor of $1 (which can be found in Table 3 in the Appendix)

■ Example 1

Consider a bond maturing in 10 years and having a coupon rate of 8%. The par value is $1,000. Investors consider 10% to be an appropriate required rate of return in view of the risk level associated with this bond. The annual interest payment is $80 (8% × $1,000). The present value of this bond is

$$V = \sum_{t=1}^{n} \frac{I}{(1+r)^t} + \frac{M}{(1+r)^n} = I(PVIFA_{r,n})$$
$$+ M(PVIF_{r,n})$$

$$= \sum_{t=1}^{10} \frac{\$80}{(1+0.1)^t} + \frac{\$1,000}{(1+0.1)^{10}}$$

$$= \$80\,(PVIFA_{10\%,10}) + \$1,000\,(PVIF_{10\%,10})$$

$$= \$80\,(6.145) + \$1,000\,(0.386)$$

$$= \$491.60 + \$386.00 = \$877.60$$

If the interest is paid semiannually, then:

$$V = \sum_{t=1}^{2n} \frac{I/2}{(1+2/r)^t} + \frac{M}{(1+r/2)^{2n}}$$

$$= \frac{I}{2}(PVIFA_{r/2,2n}) + M(PVIF_{r/2,2n})$$

■ Example 2

Assume the same data as in Example 1, except the interest is paid semiannually.

$$V = \sum_{t=1}^{2n} \frac{I/2}{(1+r/2)^t} + \frac{M}{(1+r/2)^{2n}}$$

$$= \frac{I}{2}(PVIFA_{r/2,2n}) + M(PVIF_{r/2,2n})$$

$$= \sum_{t=1}^{20} \frac{\$40}{(1+0.05)^t} + \frac{\$1,000}{(1+0.05)^{20}}$$

$$= \$40(PVIFA_{5\%,20}) + \$1,000(PVIF_{5\%,20})$$

$$= \$40(12.462) + \$1,000(0.377)$$

$$= \$498.48 + \$377.00 = \$875.48$$

BOND YIELD—EFFECTIVE RATE OF RETURN ON A BOND

Bonds are evaluated on many different types of returns, including current yield, yield to maturity, yield to call, and realized yield.

Current Yield

The current yield is the annual interest payment divided by the current price of the bond. This is reported in *The Wall Street Journal*, among others.

■ Example 1

Assume a 12% coupon rate $1,000 par value bond is selling for $960. The current yield is

$$\$120/\$960 = 12.5\%$$

The problem with this measure of return is that it does not take into account the maturity date of the bond. A bond with 1 year to run and another with 15 years to run would have the same current yield quote if interest payments were $120 and the price were $960. Clearly, the 1-year bond would be preferable under this circumstance because you would not only get $120 in interest, but also a gain of $40 ($1,000 − $960) with a 1-year time period, and this amount could be reinvested.

Yield to Maturity

The yield to maturity takes into account the maturity date of the bond. It is the real return to be received from interest income plus capital gain, assuming the bond is held to maturity. There are two ways to calculate this measure: the exact method and the approximate method.

The Exact Method

Under the exact method, a bond's yield to maturity is the internal rate of return on investment in the bond. It is calculated by solving the bond valuation model for r:

$$V = \sum_{t=1}^{n} \frac{I}{(1 + r)^t} + \frac{M}{(1 + r)^n}$$
$$= I\ (PVIFA_{r,n}) + M(PVIF_{r,n})$$

where V is the market price of the bond, I is the interest payment, and M is the maturity value, usually $1,000. *PVIFA* and *PVIF* are found in Tables 4 and 3, respectively, in the Appendix.

Finding the bond's yield, r, involves trial and error. It is best explained by example.

■ Example 2

Suppose you are offered a 10-year, 8% coupon, $1,000 par value bond at a price of $877.60. What rate of return could you earn if you bought the bond and held it to maturity?

First, set up the bond valuation model:

$$V = \$877.60 = \sum_{t=1}^{10} \frac{\$80}{(1 + r)^t} + \frac{\$1,000}{(1 + r)^{10}}$$
$$= \$80(PVIFA_{r,10}) + \$1,000(PVIF_{r,10})$$

Since the bond is selling at a discount, the bond's yield is above the going coupon rate of 8%. Therefore, try a rate of 9%. Substituting factors for 9% in the equation, we obtain: $V = \$80(6.418) + \$1,000(0.422) = \$513.44 + \$422.00 = \$935.44$. The calculated bond value, $935.44, is above the actual market price of $877.60, so the yield is not 9%. To lower the calculated value, the rate must be raised. Trying 10%, we obtain: $V = \$80(6.145) + \$1,000(0.386) = \$491.60 + \$386.00 = \$877.60$. This calculated value is exactly equal to the market price of the bond; thus, 10% is the bond's yield to maturity.

The Approximate Method

$$\text{Yield} = \frac{I + (M - V)/n}{(M + V)/2}$$

here V = the market value of the bond,
          I = dollars of interest paid per year,
          M = maturity value, usually $1,000,
          n = number of years to maturity.

■ Example 3

Using the same data in Example 2,

$$\text{Yield} = \frac{\$80 + (\$1,000 - \$877.60)/10}{(\$1,000 + \$877.60)/2}$$
$$= \frac{\$80 + \$12.24}{\$938.80} = \frac{\$92.24}{\$938.80} = 9.8\%$$

which came out to very close to 10%.

Yield to Call

Not all bonds are held to maturity. If the bond may be called prior to maturity, the yield to maturity formula will have the call price in place of the par value ($1,000).

■ Example 4

Assume a 20-year bond was initially issued at a 13.5% coupon rate and after two years rates have dropped. Assume further that the bond is currently selling for $1,180, the yield to maturity on the bond is 11.15%, and the bond can be called in 5 years after issue at $1,090. Thus if you buy the bond two years after issue, your bond may be called back after 3 more years at $1,090. The yield to call can be calculated as follows:

$$\frac{\$135 + (\$1,090 - \$1,180)/3}{(\$1,090 + \$1,180)/2} = \frac{\$135 + (-90/3)}{\$1,135}$$
$$= \frac{\$105}{\$1,135} = 9.25\%$$

The yield to call figure of 9.25% is 190 basis points less than the yield to maturity of 11.15%. Clearly, you need to be aware of the differential because a lower return is earned.

Realized Yield

You may trade in and out of a bond long before it matures. You obviously need a measure of return to evaluate the investment appeal of any bonds you intend to buy and sell. Realized yield is used for this purpose. This measure is simply a variation of yield to maturity, as only two variables are changed in the yield to maturity formula. Future price is used in place of par value ($1,000), and the length of the holding period is substituted for the number of years to maturity.

■ Example 5

In Example 2, assume that you anticipate holding the bond only 3 years and that you have estimated interest rates will change in the future so that the price of the bond will move to about $925 from its present level of $877.60. Thus you will buy the bond today at a market price of $877.60 and sell the issue 3 years later at a price of $925. Given these assumptions, the realized yield of this bond would be

$$\text{Realized yield} = \frac{\$80 + (\$925 - \$877.70)/3}{(\$925 + \$877.70)/2}$$
$$= \frac{\$80 + \$15.80}{\$901.30} = \frac{\$95.80}{\$901.30} = 10.63\%$$

Fortunately, a bond table is available to find the value for various yield measures. A source is *Thorndike Encyclopedia of Banking and Financial Tables*, by Warren, Gorham & Lamont, Boston.

Equivalent Before-Tax Yield

Yield on a municipal bond needs to be looked at on an equivalent before-tax yield basis, because the interest received is not subject to federal income taxes. The formula used to equate interest on municipals to other investments is

Tax equivalent yield = Tax-exempt yield/(1 − tax rate)

■ Example 6

If you have a marginal tax rate of 28% and are evaluating a municipal bond paying 10% interest, the equivalent before-tax yield on a taxable investment would be

$$10\%/(1 - 0.28) = 13.9\%$$

Thus, you could choose between a taxable investment paying 13.9% and a tax-exempt bond paying 10% and be indifferent between the two.

BOOK VALUE PER SHARE The book value per share is the amount each share would obtain in the event the company was liquidated based on the historical cost valuation in the financial statements. However, the ratio has limited utility because the fair market value of the balance sheet accounts are not taken into account. Book value per share is computed for both preferred stock and common stock as follows. Book value per share for preferred stock equals:

$$\frac{\text{(Liquidation value of preferred stock} + \text{Preferred dividends in arrears)}}{\text{Preferred stock outstanding}}$$

Book value per share for common stock equals:

$$\frac{\text{Total stockholders' equity} - \text{(Liquidation value of preferred stock} + \text{Preferred dividends in arrears)}}{\text{Common stock outstanding}}$$
$$\frac{\text{Common stockholders' equity}}{\text{Common stock outstanding}}$$

■ Example

The stockholders' equity section of the balance sheet for XYZ Company is as follows:

Capital stock:	
Preferred stock, cumulative, 10,000 shares, $10 par value, liquidation value $12, 6% dividend rate	$100,000
Common stock, 20,000 shares, $15 par value	300,000
Total capital stock	$400,000
Paid-in-capital	150,000
Retained earnings	200,000
Total stockholders' equity	$750,000

Preferred dividends in arrears is $12,000. Book value per share for preferred stock:

$$\frac{(\$120,000 + \$12,000)}{10,000 \text{ shares}} = \frac{\$132,000}{10,000} = \$13.20$$

Book value per share for common stock:

$$\frac{(\$750,000 - \$132,000)}{20,000 \text{ shares}} = \frac{\$618,000}{20,000} = \$30.90$$

Excerpts From Bond Table
Four Years Interest Payable Semiannually

Percent Per Annum	Nominal Rate						
	3%	3½%	4%	4½%	5%	6%	7%
4.00	96.31	98.17	100.00	101.83	103.66	107.33	110.99
4.10	95.98	97.81	99.63	101.46	103.29	106.94	110.60
4.125	95.89	97.72	99.54	101.37	103.20	105.85	110.50
4.20	95.62	97.45	99.27	101.09	102.92	106.56	110.21
4.25	95.45	97.27	99.00	100.91	102.73	106.38	110.02
4.30	95.27	97.09	98.91	100.73	102.55	106.19	109.83
4.375	95.00	96.82	98.64	100.45	102.27	105.90	109.54
4.40	94.92	96.73	98.55	100.36	102.18	105.81	100.44
4.50	94.56	96.38	98.19	100.00	101.81	105.44	109.06
4.60	94.21	96.02	97.83	99.64	101.45	105.06	108.68
4.625	94.13	95.93	97.74	99.55	101.36	104.97	108.58
4.70	93.87	95.67	97.47	99.28	101.08	104.69	108.30
4.75	93.69	95.49	97.30	99.10	100.90	104.51	108.11
4.80	93.52	95.32	97.12	98.92	100.72	104.32	107.92
4.875	93.26	95.06	96.85	98.65	100.45	104.04	107.64
4.90	93.17	94.97	96.77	98.56	100.36	103.95	107.54
5.00	92.83	94.62	96.41	98.21	100.00	103.59	107.17
5.10	92.49	94.28	96.06	97.85	99.64	103.22	106.80
5.125	92.40	94.19	95.98	97.77	99.55	103.13	106.70
5.20	92.15	93.93	95.72	97.50	99.29	102.86	106.43
5.25	91.98	93.76	95.54	97.33	99.11	102.67	106.24
5.30	91.81	93.59	93.37	97.15	98.93	102.49	106.06
5.375	91.55	93.33	95.11	96.89	98.67	102.22	105.78
5.40	91.47	93.25	95.02	96.80	98.58	102.13	105.69
5.50	91.13	92.91	94.68	96.45	98.23	101.77	105.32
5.625	90.71	92.48	94.25	96.02	97.79	101.33	104.86
5.75	90.30	92.06	93.83	95.59	97.35	100.38	104.41
5.875	89.88	91.64	93.40	95.16	96.92	100.44	103.96
6.00	89.47	91.23	92.98	94.74	96.49	100.00	103.51

Effective Rate of Return (Yield)

Example: A $1,000, 4-year, 6% bond purchased at $104.69 (=$1,046.90) yields 4.70% effective interest. Interest is payable semiannually. To purchase this bond to yield 4.70% effective interest, an investor should pay $1,046.90.

BRANCH ACCOUNTING This is a separate accounting system for each branch of an organization. The home office opens an account in its general ledger entitled Branch, Branch Control, Investment in Branch, or some other similar name. Frequently, one account will be used to show the long-term investment in a branch while another account (such as Branch Current) will be used for more common accounts. In the home office ledger, this account or group of accounts is charged for everything sent to the branch or for services rendered to or for the branch, and it is credited for amounts received from the branch. In a similar manner, the branch ledger maintains an equity account entitled Home Office, Home Office Control, Home Office Current, or some other similar names. This account is credited for all assets received by the branch from the home office. It is also credited for all debts incurred for merchandise acquired or for services rendered by the home office for the branch. Such an account would also be credited as a result of expenses incurred by the home office for the benefit of the branch. It is debited for amounts sent by the branch to the home office. In operation, the branch account on the home office books will be debited when the home office account on the branch books is credited, and vice versa. Thus, the balance of each of such pair of accounts should be equal in dollar amount, but the balances should be the opposite sides of the respective accounts. Two accounts that have such relationship are often referred to as *reciprocal*.

BREADTH INDEX The Breadth Index computes each trading day the net advances or declines in stocks on the New York Stock Exchange. When there are net advances, a strong market exists. The magnitude of strength depends on the spread between the number of advancing and declining issues. The Breadth Index equals the number of net advances or declines in securities divided by the number of securities traded.

Advances and declines typically go in the same direction as a standard market average (e.g., Dow Jones Industrial Average). But they may go in the opposite direction at a market peak or bottom.

Change instead of level is emphasized in breadth analysis. The computed Breadth Index should be compared to popular market averages. Usually, consistency exists in their movement. In a bull market, the security analyst should watch out for an extended disparity of the two. An example is when the Breadth Index moves downward gradually to new lows while the Dow Jones Industrial Average goes to new highs. A comparison may also be made of the Breadth Index over a number of years.

■ Example

Net declining issues are 58. Securities traded are 1,475. The Breadth Index equals:

$$\frac{\text{Declining issues}}{\text{Number of issues traded}} = \frac{58}{1,475} = -3.9$$

The Breadth Index may be compared to a base year or included in a 150-day moving average.

Market strength is indicated when the Breadth Index and Dow Jones Industrial Av-

erage are increasing. Market weakness is pointed to when they are declining. *See also* Technical Analysis.

BREADTH OF MARKET INDICES Indices of market breadth apply to the dispersion of general price increases or decreases in the stock market. It acts as a valuable indicator of a major turn in stock prices. *See also* Technical Analysis.

BUDGETING FOR PROFIT PLANNING A comprehensive (master) budget is a formal statement of management's expectation regarding sales, expenses, volume, and other financial transactions of an organization for the coming period. Simply put, a budget is a set of *pro forma* (*projected* or *planned*) financial statements. It consists basically of a pro forma income statement, pro forma balance sheet, and cash budget.

A budget is a tool for both planning and control. At the beginning of the period, the budget is a plan or standard; at the end of the period it serves as a control device to help management measure its performance against the plan so that future performance may be improved.

The budget is classified broadly into two categories:
1. *Operating budget*, reflecting the results of operating decisions
2. *Financial budget*, reflecting the financial decisions of the firm

The operating budget consists of:
• Sales budget
• Production budget
• Direct materials budget
• Direct labor budget
• Factory overhead budget
• Selling and administrative expense budget
• Pro forma income statement

The financial budget consists of:
• Cash budget
• Pro forma balance sheet

The major steps in preparing the budget are

1. Prepare a sales forecast.
2. Determine expected production volume.
3. Estimate manufacturing costs and operating expenses.
4. Determine cash flow and other financial effects.
5. Formulate projected financial statements.

Figure 1 (p. 62) shows a simplified diagram of the various parts of the comprehensive budget, the master plan of the company.

Illustration

To illustrate how all these budgets are put together, we will focus on a manufacturing company called the Johnson Company, which produces and markets a single product. We will assume that the company develops the master budget in *contribution* format for 19B on a quarterly basis. We will highlight the variable cost-fixed cost breakdown throughout the illustration.

The Sales Budget

The sales budget is the starting point in preparing the master budget, since estimated sales volume influences nearly all other items

appearing throughout the master budget. The sales budget ordinarily indicates the quantity of each product expected to be sold. After sales volume has been estimated, the sales budget is constructed by multiplying the expected sales in units by the expected unit sales price. Generally, the sales budget includes a computation of expected cash collections from credit sales, which will be used later for cash budgeting.

▪ Example 1

Refer to table presented at bottom of the page.

The Production Budget

After sales are budgeted, the production budget can be determined. The number of units expected to be manufactured to meet budgeted sales and inventory requirements is set forth in the production budget. The expected volume of production is determined by subtracting the estimated inventory at the beginning of the period from the sum of the units expected to be sold and the desired inventory at the end of the period. The production budget is illustrated in Example 2, found on p. 63.

Example 1
The Johnson Company
Sales Budget for the Year Ending December 31, 19B

	Quarter				
	1	*2*	*3*	*4*	*Total*
Expected sales in units	800	700	900	800	3,200
Unit sales price	×$80	×$80	×$80	×$80	×$80
Total sales	$64,000	$56,000	$72,000	$64,000	$256,000

Schedule of Expected Cash Collections

	1	*2*	*3*	*4*	*Total*
Accounts receivable, 12/31/19A	$ 9,500[a]				$ 9,500
1st quarter sales ($64,000)	$44,800[b]	$17,920[c]			62,720
2nd quarter sales ($56,000)		39,200	$15,680		54,880
3rd quarter sales ($72,000)			50,400	$20,160	70,560
4th quarter sales ($64,000)				44,800	44,800
Total cash collections	$54,300	$57,120	$66,080	$64,960	$242,460

[a] All $9,500 accounts receivable balance is assumed to be collectable in the first quarter.
[b] 70% of a quarter's sales are collected in the quarter of sale.
[c] 28% of a quarter's sales are collected in the quarter following, and the remaining 2% are uncollectable.

Figure 1 Comprehensive Budget

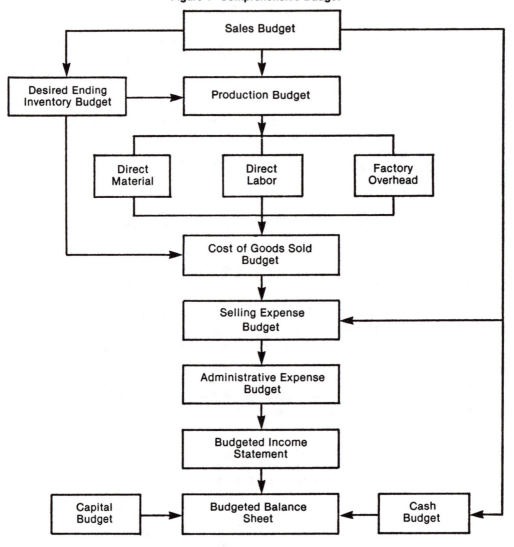

■ Example 2

Example 2
The Johnson Company
Production Budget for the Year Ending December 31, 19B

	Quarter				
	1	2	3	4	Total
Planned sales (Example 1)	800	700	900	800	3,200
Desired ending inventory[a]	70	90	80	100[b]	100
Total needs	870	790	980	900	3,300
Less: Beginning inventory[c]	80	70	90	80	80
Units to be produced	790	720	890	820	3,220

[a] 10% of the next quarter's sales
[b] Estimated
[c] The same as the previous quarter's ending inventory

The Direct Material Budget

When the level of production has been computed, a direct material budget should be constructed to show how much material will be required for production and how much material must be purchased to meet this production requirement. The purchase will depend on both expected usage of materials and inventory levels. The formula for computation of the purchase is

Purchase in units = Usage + Desired ending material inventory units − Beginning inventory units

The direct material budget is usually accompanied by a computation of expected cash payments for materials.

■ Example 3

Example 3
The Johnson Company
Direct Material Budget for the Year Ending December 31, 19B

	Quarter				
	1	2	3	4	Total
Units to be produced (Example 2)	790	720	890	820	3,220
Material needs per unit (lbs)	× 3	× 3	× 3	× 3	× 3
Material needs	2,370	2,160	2,670	2,460	9,660
Desired ending inventory of materials[a]	216	267	246	250[b]	250
Total needs	2,586	2,427	2,916	2,710	9,910
Less: Beginning inventory of materials[c]	237	216	267	246	237
Materials to be purchased	2,349	2,211	2,649	2,464	9,673
Unit price	× $2	× $2	× $2	× $2	× $2
Purchase cost	$4,698	$4,422	$5,298	$4,928	$19,346

Schedule of Expected Cash Disbursements

Accounts payable, 12/31/19A[a]	$2,200				$ 2,200
1st quarter purchases ($4,698)	2,349	$2,349[d]			4,698
2nd quarter purchases ($4,422)		2,211	$2,211		4,422
3rd quarter purchases ($5,298)			2,649	$2,649	5,298
4th quarter purchases ($4,928)				2,464	2,464
Total disbursements	$4,549	$4,560	$4,860	$5,113	$19,082

[a] 10% of the next quarter's units needed for production
[b] Estimated
[c] The same as the prior quarter's ending inventory.
[d] 50% of a quarter's purchases are paid for in the quarter of purchase; the remainder are paid for in the following quarter.

The Direct Labor Budget

The production requirements as set forth in the production budget also provide the starting point for the preparation of the direct labor budget. To compute direct labor requirements, expected production volume for each period is multiplied by the number of direct labor hours required to produce a single unit. The direct labor hours required to meet production requirements is then multiplied by the direct labor cost per hour to obtain budgeted total direct labor costs.

■ Example 4

See table below.

The Factory Overhead Budget

The factory overhead budget should provide a schedule of all manufacturing costs other than direct materials and direct labor. Using the contribution approach to budgeting requires the development of a predetermined overhead rate for the variable portion of the factory overhead. In developing the cash budget, we must remember that depreciation does not entail a cash outlay and therefore must

be deducted from the total factory overhead in computing cash disbursement for factory overhead.

■ Example 5

To illustrate the factory overhead budget, we will assume that
• Total factory overhead budgeted = $6,000 fixed (per quarter) plus $2 per hour of direct labor.
• Depreciation expenses are $3,250 each quarter.
• All overhead costs involving cash outlays are paid for in the quarter incurred.

See table below.

The Ending Inventory Budget

The desired ending inventory budget provides us with the information required for the construction of budgeted financial statements. Specifically, it will help compute the cost of goods sold on the budgeted income statement. Secondly, it will give the dollar value of the ending materials and finished goods inventory to appear on the budgeted balance sheet.

Example 4
The Johnson Company
Direct Labor Budget for the Year Ending December 31, 19B

	Quarter				
	1	2	3	4	Total
Units to be produced (Example 2)	790	720	890	820	3,220
Direct labor hours per unit	× 5	× 5	× 5	× 5	× 5
Total hours	3,950	3,600	4,450	4,100	16,100
Direct labor cost per hour	× $5	× $5	× $5	× $5	× $5
Total direct labor cost	$19,750	$18,000	$22,250	$20,500	$80,500

Example 5
The Johnson Company
Factory Overhead Budget for the Year Ending December 31, 19B

	Quarter				
	1	2	3	4	Total
Budgeted direct labor hours (Example 4)	3,950	3,600	4,450	4,100	16,100
Variable overhead rate	× $2	× $2	× $2	× $2	× $2
Variable overhead budgeted	7,900	7,200	8,900	8,200	32,200
Fixed overhead budgeted	6,000	6,000	6,000	6,000	24,000
Total budgeted overhead	13,900	13,200	14,900	14,200	56,200
Less: Depreciation	3,250	3,250	3,250	3,250	13,000
Cash disbursement for overhead	10,650	9,950	11,650	10,950	43,200

■ Example 6

Example 6
The Johnson Company
Ending Inventory Budget for the Year Ending December 31, 19B

	Ending Inventory Units	Unit Cost	Total
Direct materials	250 pounds (Example 3)	$2	$ 500
Finished goods	100 units (Example 2)	41[a]	4,100

[a] The unit variable cost of $41 is computed as follows:

	Unit Cost	Units	Total
Direct materials	$2	3 pounds	$ 6
Direct labor	5	5 hours	25
Variable overhead	2	5 hours	10
Total variable manufacturing cost			$41

The Selling and Administrative Expense Budget

The selling and administrative expense budget lists the operating expenses involved in selling the products and in managing the business. In order to complete the budgeted income statement in contribution format, variable selling and administrative expense per unit must be computed.

■ Example 7

See table presented below.

The Cash Budget

The cash budget is prepared for the purpose of cash planning and control. It presents the expected cash inflow and outflow for a designated time period. The cash budget helps management keep cash balances in reasonable relationship to its needs. It aids in avoiding unnecessary idle cash and possible cash shortages. The cash budget consists typically of four major sections:

1. The receipts section, which is the beginning cash balance, cash collections from customers, and other receipts

2. The disbursements section, which comprises all cash payments made by purpose

3. The cash surplus or deficit section, which simply shows the difference between the cash receipts section and the cash disbursements section

4. The financing section, which provides a detailed account of the borrowings and repayments expected during the budgeting period

Example 7
The Johnson Company
Selling and Administrative Expense Budget for the Year Ending December 31, 19B

	Quarter				
	1	2	3	4	Total
Expected sales in units	800	700	900	800	3,200
Variable selling and administrative expense per unit[a]	× $4	× $4	× $4	× $4	× $4
Budgeted variable expense	$ 3,200	$ 2,800	$ 3,600	$ 3,200	$12,800
Fixed selling and administrative expenses:					
Advertising	1,100	1,100	1,100	1,100	4,400
Insurance	2,800				2,800
Office salaries	8,500	8,500	8,500	8,500	34,000
Rent	350	350	350	350	1,400
Taxes			1,200		1,200
Total budgeted selling and administrative expenses[b]	$15,950	$12,750	$14,750	$13,150	$56,600

[a] Includes sales agents' commissions, shipping, and supplies
[b] Paid for in the quarter incurred

■ Example 8

To illustrate, we will make the following assumptions:

• The company desires to maintain a $5,000 minimum cash balance at the end of each quarter.

• All borrowing and repayment must be in multiples of $500 at an interest rate of 10% per annum. Interest is computed and paid as the principal is repaid. Borrowing takes place at the beginning of each quarter and repayment at the end of each quarter.

See table presented below.

The Budgeted Income Statement

The budgeted income statement summarizes the various component projections of revenue and expenses for the budgeting period. However, for control purposes the budget can be divided into quarters or even months, depending on the need.

See Example 9 on p. 67.

Example 8
The Johnson Company
Cash Budget for the Year Ending December 31, 19B

	Example	Quarter 1	2	3	4	Total
Cash balance, beginning	Given	$10,000	$ 9,401	$ 5,461	$ 9,106	$ 10,000
Add: Receipts—Collections from customers	1	54,300	57,120	66,080	64,960	242,460
Total cash available		64,300	66,521	71,541	74,066	252,460
Less: Disbursements						
Direct materials	3	4,549	4,560	4,860	5,113	19,082
Direct labor	4	19,750	18,000	22,250	20,500	80,500
Factory overhead	5	10,650	9,950	11,650	10,950	43,200
Selling and administration	7	15,950	12,750	14,750	13,150	56,600
Machinery purchase	Given	—	24,300	—	—	24,300
Income tax	Given	4,000	—	—	—	4,000
Total disbursements		54,899	69,560	53,510	49,713	227,682
Cash surplus (deficit)		9,401	(3,039)	18,031	24,353	24,778
Financing:						
Borrowing		—	8,500	—	—	8,500
Repayment		—	—	(8,500)	—	(8,500)
Interest		—	—	(425)	—	(425)
Total financing		—	8,500	(8,925)	—	(425)
Cash balance, ending		$ 9,401	$ 5,461	$ 9,106	$24,353	$ 24,353

■ Example 9

Example 9
The Johnson Company
Budgeted Income Statement for the Year Ending December 31, 19B

	Example No.		
Sales (3,200 units @ $80)	1		$256,000
Less: Variable expenses			
Variable cost of goods sold (3,200 units @ $41)	6	$131,200	
Variable selling and administration	7	12,800	144,000
Contribution margin			112,000
Less: Fixed expenses			
Factory overhead	5	24,000	
Selling and administration	7	43,800	67,800
Net operating income			44,200
Less: Interest expense	8		425
Income before taxes			43,775
Less: Income taxes (20%)			8,755
Net income			35,020

The Budgeted Balance Sheet

The budgeted balance sheet is developed by beginning with the balance sheet for the year just ended and adjusting it, using all the activities that are expected to take place during the budgeting period. Some of the reasons that the budgeted balance sheet must be prepared are

• It could disclose some unfavorable financial conditions that management might want to avoid.

• It serves as a final check on the mathematical accuracy of all the other schedules.

• It helps management perform a variety of ratio calculations.

• It highlights future resources and obligations.

■ Example 10

To illustrate, we will use the following balance sheet for the year 19A.

Example 10
The Johnson Company
Balance Sheet as of December 31, 19A

Assets		Liabilities and Stockholders' Equity	
Current assets:		Current liabilities:	
Cash	$10,000	Accounts payable	$ 2,200
Accounts receivable	9,500	Income tax payable	4,000
Material inventory	474	Total current liabilities	$ 6,200
Finished goods inventory	3,280	Stockholders' equity:	
Total current assets	$23,254	Common stock, no-par	70,000
Fixed assets:		Retained earnings	37,054
Land	$ 50,000		
Building and equipment	100,000		
Accumulated depreciation	(60,000)		
Total fixed assets	$ 90,000		
Total assets	$113,254	Total liabilities and stockholders' equity	$113,254

The Johnson Company
Budgeted Balance Sheet as of December 31, 19A

Assets			Liabilities and Stockholders' Equity		
Current assets:			Current Liabilities:		
Cash	$24,353	(a)	Accounts payable	$ 2,464	(h)
Accounts receivable	23,040	(b)	Income tax payable	8,755	(i)
Material inventory	500	(c)	Total current liabilities	$11,219	
Finished goods inventory	4,100	(d)	Stockholders' equity:		
Total current assets	$51,993		Common stock, no-par	70,000	(j)
Fixed assets:			Retained earnings	72,074	(k)
Land	$ 50,000	(e)			
Buildings and equipment	124,300	(f)			
Accumulated depreciation	(73,000)	(g)			
Total fixed assets	101,300				
Total assets	$153,293		Total liabilities and stockholders' equity	$153,293	

Computations:
- (a) From Example 8 (cash budget)
- (b) $9,500 + $256,000 sales − $242,460 receipts = $23,040
- (c) and (d) From Example 6 (ending inventory budget)
- (e) No change
- (f) $100,000 + $24,300 (from Example 8) = $124,300
- (g) $60,000 + $13,000 (from Example 5) = $73,000
- (h) $2,200 + $19,346 − $19,082 = $2,464 (all accounts payable relate to material purchases), or 50% of 4th quarter purchases = 50% ($4,928) = 2,464
- (i) From Example 9 (budgeted income statement)
- (j) No change
- (k) $37,054 + $35,020 net income = $72,074

A Shortcut Approach to Formulating the Budget

In actual practice use of a shortcut approach is very widely used in formulating a budget. The approach can be summarized as follows:

1. A *pro forma income statement* is developed using past percentage relationships between certain expense and cost items and the firm's sales and applying these percentages to the firm's projected sales. The income statement can be set up in a traditional or contribution format.

2. A *pro forma balance sheet* is estimated using the *percentage-of-sales method,* which involves the following steps:

   (a) Express balance sheet items that vary directly with sales as a percentage of sales. Any item that does not vary with sales (such as long-term debt) is designated not applicable (n.a.). Multiply these percentages by the sales projected to obtain the amounts for the future period.

   (b) Where no percentage applies (such as long-term debt, common stock, and paid-in-capital), simply insert the figures from the present balance sheet or their desired level in the column for the future period.

   (c) Compute the projected retained earnings as follows:

   Projected retained earnings = Present retained earnings + Projected net income − Cash dividend to be paid

   (d) Sum the asset accounts and the liability and equity accounts to see if there is any difference. The difference, if any, is a *shortfall,* which is the amount of financing the firm has to raise externally.

Computer-Based Models for Budgeting

More and more companies are developing computer-based models for financial planning and budgeting, using powerful yet easy-to-use financial modeling languages such as Execum's *Interactive Financial Planning System (IFPS)*™ and Social Systems' *SIMPLAN.*™ The models help not only to build a budget for profit planning but answer a variety of what-if scenarios. The resultant calculations provide a basis for choice among alternatives under conditions of uncertainty. Financial modeling can be accomplished using spreadsheet programs such as Lotus 1-2-3™ and SuperCalc.™ *See also* Budgeting Models; Financial Forecasting and the Percentage-of-Sales Method; Financial Models; Simulation Models.

BUDGETING MODELS   These are quantitative models that generate a budget. The models help accountants and budget analysts answer what-if questions. There are primarily two approaches to modeling in the corporate budgeting process: *simulation* and *optimization.* *See also* Financial Models; Simulation Models.

BUSINESS COMBINATIONS   A business combination occurs before a consolidation. Business combinations may be accounted for under the pooling-of-interests method and the purchase method. Criteria for pooling and purchase, accounting and reporting requirements, and disclosures are dealt with.

The purchase method is used when cash or other assets are given or liabilities incurred to effect the combination. An acquisition of a minority interest is always a purchase at a later date even if the original acquisition was accounted for as a pooling.

The pooling-of-interests method is used when there is an exchange of voting common stock and *all* the twelve criteria for a pooling

are satisfied. In a pooling, it is assumed for accounting purposes that both companies were always combined. No purchase or sale is assumed to have taken place. A pooling is a union of the ownership interests of the two previously separated groups of stockholders.

Pooling-of-Interests Method

The criteria for a pooling-of-interests deal with independence of the combining companies, time period for consummation of the combination, voting rights, consideration given in the exchange, purchase of treasury stock, ownership interests, and absence of planned transactions. The accounting for a pooling is based on recognizing net assets at book value with earnings recognized for the entire year. Footnote disclosure describes the terms of the agreement and accounting adjustments made.

Criteria for a Pooling

The twelve criteria, all of which must be met, for a pooling are indicated following. When more than one company is acquired in a combination plan, each pooling consideration must be met by each company.

1. The combining companies are autonomous, meaning that a combining company must not have been a subsidiary or division of any other combining company within 2 years before the initiation date. *Note:* A new company incorporated within 2 years qualifies unless it is in any respect a successor to a company not considered autonomous.

2. The combining companies are independent, meaning that a combining company does not own 10% or more of another combining company's voting common stock at the initiation or consummation dates or at any time in between. *Note:* A change in the exchange ratio results in a new initiation date.

The *consummation* date is the date when the net assets are transferred to the acquiring company. However, temporary assets (e.g., cash, marketable securities) may be held to settle liabilities and contingent items.

3. The combining companies come together in a single transaction or within 1 year after the initiation date. A delay is allowed for litigation or governmental action. For instance, if the combination took 15 months but 4 months involved a delay because of antitrust litigation, this criteria is still satisfied.

4. The acquiring company issues voting common stock in exchange for 90% or more of the voting common stock of the acquired company.

The following shares of the combiners are excluded from the 90% minimum.

• Shares owned by the issuing company or its subsidiaries prior to the initiation date

• Shares acquired by the initiating company other than by issuing its own common stock

• Shares outstanding subsequent to the consummation date

In determining if 90% of the stock of the combiner has been transferred to the issuing corporation, the number of shares transferred must be reduced by the equivalent number of shares of the issuing corporation owned by the combiner before combination. This reduced number of shares is then compared to 90% of the *total* outstanding shares of the combiner company, to determine if the requirement is satisfied.

An acquiring company may give cash or common stock for debt or preferred stock of an acquired business and qualify as a pooling, but only if the debt securities and preferred stock were not issued in an exchange for voting common stock of the acquired business within 2 years before the initiation date.

A combination plan may not provide for a pro rata cash distribution but may within certain restrictions have a cash distribution for fractional shares. Cash may also be used in a combination plan to retire or redeem callable debt and equity securities.

5. None of the combining companies alters the equity interest of voting common stock within 2 years before the combination in contemplation of it. The voting interest is deemed changed for abnormal dividends based on taking into account profits and prior dividends.

6. Treasury stock is acquired by a combining company for reasons other than the business combination between the initiation and consummation dates. Treasury stock may be acquired for purposes of a stock option plan, compensation plan, and similar recurring transactions.

7. The relative ownership percentage of each stockholder in the combined entity remains the same as before. For example, if Mr. A and Mr. B owned 2% of XYZ Company, they should still own the same percentage in the newly formed entity (e.g., 1.5%).

8. There is no restriction in voting rights among stockholders by the combined entity (e.g., delayed voting rights).

9. The combination is finalized at the consummation date with no pending provisions of any kind related to the combination. For instance, no contingently issuable shares or distribution of assets to the former stockholders of the combining companies are allowed.

There is an absence of planned or subsequent transactions related to the combination as follows:

10. Repurchase of stock issued to effect the combination.

11. Financial arrangements benefiting former stockholders of the combining companies. An example is guarantying loans secured by stock issued in the combination which in substance negates the exchange of equity securities.

12. Sale of a significant part of the combined entity's assets within two years subsequent

to the combination, such as the disposal of a division. However, the disposal of a duplicate warehouse would be in the ordinary course of business.

Accounting Under Pooling-of-Interests

• Net assets of the acquired company are brought forth at book value.

• Retained earnings and paid-in-capital of the acquired company are brought forth at book value. There is no change in *total* stockholders' equity, but the equity components do change. Any necessary adjustments are made to paid-in-capital. In the event that paid-in-capital is insufficient to absorb the difference, retained earnings would next be reduced. However, retained earnings could never be increased. If there is a deficit in retained earnings for a combining entity, it is continued in the combined entity.

• Net income of the acquired company is brought forth for the entire year regardless of the date of acquisition.

• Expenses of the pooling are charged against earnings as incurred. Examples are registration fees, finders' fees, and consultants' fees.

• A gain or loss from the sale of a major part of the assets of the acquired business within 2 years subsequent to combination is considered an extraordinary item.

■ Example

The mechanics of a pooling follow:

	Company X	Company Y	Combined
Assets	$300	$100	$200
Liabilities	50	20	30
Equity	250	80	*

* Addition of:
—Capital stock of Company X before
—Capital stock issued in the pooling
—Retained earnings of both
—Paid-in-capital absorbs the difference.

Note: There can be no new assets from a pooling. In the year of pooling, recurring intercompany transactions should be eliminated to the degree possible from the beginning of the period. But nonrecurring intercompany transactions relating to long-term assets and liabilities do not have to be eliminated.

An issuing company may effect a pooling by distributing treasury stock (acquired prior to 2 years before combination). The transfer of this stock is accounted for as if the stock had been *retired* and then reissued to effect the combination. The reissuance of this stock is accounted the same as the issuance of new shares.

Combining companies may hold investments in the common stock of each other. The accounting treatment follows:

• Investment of a combiner in the common stock of the *issuing* corporation. (The stock is in effect returned to the resulting combined entity and hence should be accounted for as treasury stock.)

• Investments in the common stock of the *other* combining companies. (This is an investment in the type of stock that is exchanged for the new shares issued. It should be accounted for as *retired* stock.)

Where one combining company employs a different GAAP than another (e.g., straight-line vs. double declining balance depreciation), the company is permitted to change to the GAAP used by the other combiner(s) and to record the cumulative effect of a change in accounting principle. Prior year financial statements when issued on a pooled basis should be restated for accounting principle changes.

Disclosures Under Pooling

Footnote disclosure of a pooling follows:

• Name and description of combined companies

• A statement that it is a pooling

• Description and number of shares issued to effect the pooling

• Net income of the previously separate companies

• Accounting method used for intercompany transactions

• Adjustments required to net assets so the combining companies are employing the same accounting methods and the related effects on earnings

• Particulars of changes in retained earnings due to a change in fiscal year of a combining company

• Reconciliation of profits previously reported by the issuing company

Advantages and Disadvantages of Pooling

An advantage of pooling is the retention of historical cost. A disadvantage from a financial reader's perspective is the possible overstated earnings (e.g., picking up net income for the whole year regardless of acquisition date, lower depreciation charges related to purchase method, and sale of low-cost basis assets at a gain).

Purchase Method

If any one of the 12 criteria is not satisfied for a pooling, the business combination is accounted for as a purchase. A purchase typically involves either the payment of assets or incurrence of liabilities for the other business. To effect a purchase, more than 50% of voting common stock has to be acquired.

Accounting Under Purchase Method

The accounting followed for a purchase is indicated below:

• Net assets of the acquired company are brought forth at fair market value.

Guidelines in assigning values to individual assets acquired and liabilities assumed (except goodwill) follow:

• *Marketable securities*—current net realizable values.

• *Receivables*—Present value of net receivables using present interest rates.

• *Inventories—finished goods* at estimated net realizable value less a reasonable profit allowance (lower limit). *Work-in-process* at estimated net realizable value of finished goods less costs to complete and profit allowance. *Raw materials* at current replacement cost.

• *Plant and equipment*—if to be employed in operations, show at replacement cost. If to be sold, reflect at net realizable value. If to be used temporarily, show at net realizable value recognizing depreciation for the period.

• *Identifiable intangibles*—at appraisal value.

• *Other assets* (including land and noncurrent securities)—at appraised values.

• *Payables*—at estimated present value.

• *Liabilities and accruals*—at estimated present value.

• *Other liabilities and commitments*—at estimated present value. However, a deferred income tax credit account of the acquired company is not brought forth.

• The excess of cost paid over book value of assets acquired is attributed to the identifiable net assets. The remaining balance not attributable to specific assets is of an unidentifiable nature and is assigned to goodwill. The identifiable assets are depreciated. Goodwill is amortized over the period benefited, not exceeding 40 years. Note that adjustments for fair value and amortization of goodwill are factors used just in preparing consolidated financial statements.

• Goodwill of the acquired company is not brought forth.

• None of the equity accounts of the acquired business (e.g., retained earnings) appear on the acquirer's books. Ownership interests of the acquired company stockholders are not continued subsequent to the merger.

• Net income of the acquired company is brought forth from the date of acquisition to year-end.

• Direct costs of the purchase are a deduction from the fair value of the securities issued, whereas indirect costs are expensed as incurred.

When stock is issued in a purchase transaction, quoted market price of stock is typically a clear indication of asset cost. Consideration should be given to price fluctuations, volume, and issue price of stock.

If liabilities are assumed in a purchase, the difference between the fixed rate of the debt securities and the present yield rate for comparable securities is reflected as a premium or discount.

Following is the step-by-step acquisition procedure:

• If control is not accomplished on the initial purchase, the subsidiary is not includable in consolidation until control has been accomplished.

• Once the parent owns in excess of 50% of the subsidiary, a retroactive restatement should be made including all of the subsidiary's earnings in consolidated retained earnings on a step-by-step fashion commencing with the initial investment.

• The subsidiary's earnings are included for the ownership years at the appropriate ownership percentage.

• After control is accomplished, fair value and adjustments for goodwill will be applied retroactively on a step-by-step basis. Each acquisition is separately determined.

The acquiring company cannot generally record a net operating loss carry forward of the acquired company since there is no assurance of realization. However, if realized in a later year, recognition will be a retroactive adjustment of the purchase transaction allocation, thus causing the residual purchase cost to be reallocated to the other assets acquired. In effect, there will be a reduction of a goodwill or the other assets.

FASB 38 provides guidelines for recording preacquisition contingencies during the allocation period as a part of allocating the cost of an investment in an enterprise acquired under the purchase method. A preacquisition contingency is a contingency of a business that is acquired with the purchase method and that exists prior to the consummation date. Examples of preacquisition contingencies are a contingent asset, a contingent liability, or a contingent impairment of an asset. The allocation period is the one required to identify and quantify the acquired assets and liabilities assumed. The allocation period ceases when the acquiring company no longer needs information it has arranged to obtain and that is known to be available. Hence, the existence of a preacquisition contingency for which an asset, a liability, or an impairment of an asset cannot be estimated does not, of itself, extend the allocation period. Although the time required depends on the circumstances, the *allocation period* typically is not greater than one year from the consummation date.

Preacquisition contingencies (except for tax benefits of NOL carry forwards) must be included in the allocation of purchase cost. The allocation basis is determined in the following manner:

• The *fair value* of the preacquisition contingency, assuming a fair value can be determined during the allocation period.

• If fair value is not determinable, the following criteria are used:

1. Information available before the termination of the allocation period indicates that it is probable that an asset existed, a liability had been incurred, or an asset had been impaired at the consummation date. It must be probable that one or more future events will occur confirming the existence of the asset, liability, or impairment.

2. The amount of the asset or liability can be reasonably estimated.

Adjustments necessitated from a preacquisition contingency occurring after the end of the allocation period must be included in income in the year the adjustment is made.

Disclosures Under Purchase

Footnote disclosures under the purchase method include:
• Name and description of companies combined.
• A statement that the purchase method is being used.
• The period in which earnings of the acquired company is included.
• Cost of the acquired company, including the number and value of shares issued, if any.
• Amortization period of goodwill.
• Contingencies arising under the acquisition agreement.
• Earnings for the current and prior periods as if the companies were combined at the beginning of the period. This pro forma disclosure is to make the purchase method comparable to that of pooling.

Advantages and Disadvantages of Purchase Method

An advantage of the purchase method is that fair value is used to recognize the acquired company's assets just as in the case of acquiring a separate asset. Disadvantages are the difficulty in determining fair value, the amortization period to use, and mixing fair value of acquired company's assets and historical cost for the acquiring company's assets.

BUSINESS CYCLE The business cycle is the regular pattern of expansion (recovery) and contraction (recession) in aggregate economic activity around the path of trend growth, with effects on growth, employment, and inflation. At the peak of the cycle, economic activity is high relative to trend, whereas at the trough (valley) of the cycle, the low point in economic activity is reached. The business cycle tends to have an impact on corporate earnings, cash flow, and expansion. *See also* Recession.

BUSINESS FAILURE In technical insolvency, the business is unable to meet current obligations even if total assets exceed total liabilities. In bankruptcy, liabilities exceed the fair market value of assets. A negative real net worth exists. According to law, business failure can be either technical insolvency or bankruptcy.

Voluntary Settlement

A voluntary settlement with creditors allows the company to save many of the costs that would exist in bankruptcy. The settlement is accomplished out of court. The voluntary settlement permits the company to either continue or be liquidated and is initiated to permit the debtor to recover some of its investment.

A creditor committee may allow the business to continue to operate if it is anticipated that the entity will recover. Creditors may also continue to do business with the company. In sustaining the firm's existence, there may be
• An extension
• A composition
• Creditor control
• Integration of each of the above

Extension

In an extension, creditors will receive the balances due but over a longer time period. Current purchases are made with cash. Creditors may also agree to subordinate their claims to suppliers giving credit to the company during the extension period. The creditors believe the debtor will be able to eventually handle the problems.

The creditor committee may require certain controls, including legal control over the entity's assets or common stock, getting a security interest in assets and approval of all cash payments.

Creditors objecting to the extension arrangement may be paid immediately to prevent them from having the business declared bankrupt.

Composition

In a composition, a voluntary reduction is made in the amount the debtor owes the creditor. The creditor receives a specified percentage of the balance owed in *full* settlement of the account. The creditor may try to work with the debtor in resolving financial difficulties. The advantages of a composition are the avoidance of court costs and the stigma of a bankrupt company.

If dissenting creditors exist, they may be paid in full or allowed to recover a higher percentage so they do not force the business to close.

In order that an extension or composition will work, the following should exist:

- The debtor is ethical so that company assets will not be used for personal use.
- The debtor is expected to recover.
- Current business conditions are favorable, enhancing the debtor's recovery.

Creditor Control

A creditor committee may decide to take control of the business if they are not pleased with current management. They will operate the business in order to satisfy their claims. Once paid, the creditors may recommend that new management replace the old before further credit is given. A drawback is the possibility of mismanagement lawsuits brought by stockholders against the creditors.

Integration

The creditors and the company negotiate a plan that involves a combination of extension, composition, and creditor control. For example, the agreement may provide for a 20% cash payment of the balance owed plus 5 future payments of 12%, typically in the form of notes. The total payment is thus 80%.

The advantages of negotiated settlements are that:

- They are less formal than bankruptcy proceedings.
- They cost less (thus reducing legal expenses).
- They are easier to implement than bankruptcy proceedings.
- They typically give creditors a better return.

The following disadvantages may arise:

- Although creditors implement controls, it is still possible that further decline in asset values may occur.
- Unrealistic small creditors may make the negotiating process difficult by demanding full payment.

Bankruptcy Reorganization

If there is no voluntary settlement, the creditors may place the firm into bankruptcy. The bankruptcy proceeding may either reorganize or liquidate the business.

Legal bankruptcy may be declared if the company cannot meet its bills or when liabilities exceed the fair market value of assets. A company may file for reorganization, under which it will develop a plan for continued existence.

Chapter 7 of the Bankruptcy Reform Act of 1978 outlines the steps in liquidation. This chapter is used when reorganization is not practical. Chapter 11 deals with reorganization. If reorganization is not possible under Chapter 11, the company will be liquidated under Chapter 7.

The two types of reorganization petitions are

- *Voluntary*—the company petitions for its own reorganization. The entity need not be insolvent to file for voluntary reorganization.
- *Involuntary*—creditors file for an involuntary reorganization of the entity. The petition must establish either that the debtor firm is not satisfying its debts when due or that a creditor or another party has taken control over the debtor's assets.

Reorganization involves the following steps:

- A reorganization petition is filed under Chapter 11 in court.
- A judge approves the petition and either appoints a trustee or allows the creditors to elect one to manage asset disposition.
- The trustee presents an equitable reorganization plan to the court.
- The plan is given to the creditors and stockholders for approval.
- The debtor pays the expenses associated with the reorganization.

The trustee in a reorganization values the company, recapitalizes it, and exchanges outstanding debts for new securities.

Valuation

In valuing the business, the trustee estimates its liquidation value relative to its value as a going concern. Liquidation is recommended when the liquidation value is greater than the continuity value. If the entity is more valuable when operating, reorganization is suggested. Future earnings must be estimated when determining the value of the reorganized company. The going concern value represents the present value of future earnings.

Recapitalization

A plan has to be formulated for the reorganization. The debts may be extended or equity securities may be issued in place of the obligations. Recapitalization is the process of exchanging liabilities for other types of liabilities or equity securities. In recapitalizing the business, the objective is to provide a combination of debt and equity that will allow the firm to satisfy its debt and provide reasonable earnings for the owners.

Exchange of Obligations

In exchanging obligations to derive the optimal capital structure, priorities are followed.

Senior claims come before junior claims. Senior debt holders must receive a claim on new capital equal to their prior claims. The last priority goes to common stockholders in receiving new securities. A debt holder typically receives a combination of different securities. Preferred and common stockholders may receive nothing. Typically, however, they keep some small ownership. Subsequent to the exchange, the debt holders may become the firm's new owners.

Liquidation Arising From Bankruptcy

If a company is declared bankrupt, creditors have to meet between 10 and 30 days after that declaration. A judge or referee presides over the meeting. The creditors appoint a trustee. The trustee manages the property of the defaulted company, liquidates the business, keeps suitable records, appraises the claims of creditors, makes payments, and gives applicable information about the liquidation process. Claim priority in bankruptcy follows:

1. *Secured claims.* Secured creditors receive the value of the secured assets in support of their claims. If the value of the secured assets is inadequate to meet their claims in full, the balance reverts to general creditor status.

2. *Bankruptcy administrative costs.* These costs include any expenses applicable to handling bankruptcy, such as legal and trustee expenses.

3. *Unsecured salaries and commissions.* These claims are limited to $2,000 per individual and must have been incurred within 90 days of the bankruptcy petition.

4. *Unsecured customer deposit claims.* The maximum per claim is $900.

5. *Taxes.* Tax claims relate to unpaid taxes due the government.

6. *General creditor claims.* General creditors have loaned the business money without

specific collateral. Included are debentures and accounts payable.

7. *Preferred stockholders.*

8. *Common stockholders.*

Usually, after creditor claims have been settled with the remaining assets, nothing is left for stockholders.

After the assets of the business are distributed in accordance with the priority order above, the business may be *discharged* from any legitimate debts still remaining (except for debts immune to discharge). Provided a debtor has not been discharged within the previous 6 years and was not bankrupt because of fraud, the debtor may begin a new business.

■ Example

The balance sheet of Ace Corporation for the year ended December 31, 19X4, follows:

The liquidation value is $625,000. Instead of liquidation, there could be a reorganization with an investment of an additional $320,000. The reorganization is anticipated to provide earnings of $115,000 each year. A multiplier of 7.5 is appropriate. If the $320,000 is obtained, long-term debt holders will obtain 40% of the common stock in the reorganized business in place of their present claims.

If the $320,000 of additional investment is made, the company's going concern value is $862,500 (7.5 × $115,000). The liquidation value is given at $625,000. Because the reorganization value is in excess of the liquidation value, reorganization is recommended.

■ Example

The balance sheet of the Oakhurst Company is presented below.

Balance Sheet of the Ace Corporation

Current assets	$400,000	Current liabilities	$475,000
Fixed assets	410,000	Long-term liabilities	250,000
		Common stock	175,000
		Retained earnings	(90,000)
Total assets	$810,000	Total liabilities and stockholders' equity	$810,000

Balance Sheet of the Oakhurst Company
Assets

Current assets		
Cash	$ 9,000	
Marketable securities	6,000	
Receivables	1,100,000	
Inventory	3,000,000	
Prepaid expenses	4,000	
Total current assets		$4,119,000
Noncurrent assets		
Land	1,800,000	
Fixed assets	2,000,000	
Total noncurrent assets		3,800,000
Total assets		$7,919,000

Balance Sheet of the Oakhurst Company—*Continued*
Liabilities and Stockholders' Equity

Current liabilities		
Accounts payable	$ 180,000	
Bank loan payable	900,000	
Accrued salaries	300,000[a]	
Employee benefits payable	70,000[b]	
Customer claims—unsecured	80,000[c]	
Taxes payable	350,000	
Total current liabilities		$1,880,000
Noncurrent liabilities		
First mortgage payable	$1,600,000	
Second mortgage payable	1,100,000	
Subordinated debentures	700,000	
Total noncurrent liabilities		3,400,000
Total liabilities		$5,280,000
Stockholders' equity		
Preferred stock (3,500 shares)	$ 350,000	
Common stock (8,000 shares)	480,000	
Paid-in-capital	1,600,000	
Retained earnings	209,000	
Total stockholders' equity		2,639,000
Total liabilities and stockholders' equity		$7,919,000

[a] The salary owed to each employee is less than $2,000 and was incurred within 90 days of the bankruptcy petition.
[b] Employee benefits payable have the same limitations as unsecured wages and are eligible in bankruptcy distribution.
No customer claim exceeds $900.

Additional data follows:

1. The mortgages relate to the firm's total noncurrent assets.

2. The subordinated debentures are subordinated to the bank loan payable. Thus, they come after the bank loan payable in liquidation.

3. The company's current assets and noncurrent assets have been sold for $2.1 million and $1.9 million, respectively.

Hence, the trustee received $4.0 million.

4. The company is bankrupt, since the total liabilities of $5.28 million exceed the $4 million of the fair value of the assets.

5. The administrative expense for handling the bankrupt company is $900,000. This liability is not reflected in the previous balance sheet.

The allocation of the $4 million to the creditors follows:

Proceeds		$4,000,000
Available to secured creditors		
First mortgage—payable from $1,900,000 proceeds of noncurrent assets	$1,600,000	
Second mortgage—payable from the balance of proceeds of noncurrent assets	300,000	1,900,000
Balance after secured creditors		$2,100,000
Next priority		
Administrative expenses	$ 900,000	
Accrued salaries	300,000	
Employee benefits payable	70,000	
Customer claims—unsecured	80,000	
Taxes payable	350,000	1,700,000
Proceeds available to general creditors		$ 400,000

Now that the claims on the proceeds from liquidation have been satisfied, general creditors receive the residual on a proportionate basis. The distribution of the $400,000 is shown below.

BYPRODUCT ACCOUNTING A byproduct is an incidental occurrence from the manufacturing process. The byproduct has little value relative to the main product. Byproduct income (selling price less completion and disposal costs) can be accounted for in any of the following ways:

• Reduce the cost of the main product
• Other revenue
• Reduce total costs

■ Example

Work-in-process has been charged with the cost of making furniture amounting to $60,000. Sawdust resulted, which was sold netting $200. The entry is

Cash	200	
Work-in-Process		200

See also Joint Product Accounting.

General Creditor	Amount	Pro Rata Allocation for Balance to Be Paid
Second-mortgage balance ($1,100,000–$300,000)	$ 800,000	$124,031
Accounts payable	180,000	27,907
Bank loan payable	900,000	248,062[a]
Subordinated debentures	700,000	0
Total	$2,580,000	$400,000

[a] Because the debentures are subordinated, the bank loan payable has to be met in full before any amount can be distributed to the subordinated debentures. The subordinated debenture holders thus receive nothing.

C

CALLABLE OBLIGATIONS BY THE CREDITOR

Included as a current liability is a long-term debt callable by the creditor because of the debtor's violation of the debt agreement except if one of the following conditions exist:

• The creditor waives or lost his right to require repayment for a period in excess of one year from the balance sheet date.

• There is a grace period in the terms of the long-term debt issue that the debtor may cure the violation, which makes it callable, and it is probable that the violation will be rectified within the grace period.

CAPITAL ASSET PRICING MODEL (CAPM) A

security risk consists of two components—diversifiable risk and nondiversifiable risk. Diversifiable risk, sometimes called controllable risk or *unsystematic* risk, represents the portion of a security's risk that can be controlled through diversification. This type of risk is unique to a given security. Business, liquidity, and default risks fall into this category. Nondiversifiable risk, sometimes referred to as noncontrollable risk or *systematic* risk, results from forces outside of the firm's control and is therefore not unique to the given security. Purchasing power, interest rate, and market risks fall into this category.

Nondiversifiable risk is assessed relative to the risk of a diversified portfolio of securities, or the market portfolio. This type of risk is measured by the beta coefficient.

The capital asset pricing model (CAPM) relates the risk measured by beta to the level of expected or required rate of return on a security. The model, also called the security market line (SML), is given as follows:

$$r_j = r_f + b\,(r_m - r_f)$$

where r_j = the expected (or required) return on security j,

r_f = the risk-free security (such as a T-bill),

r_m = the expected return on the market portfolio (such as Standard & Poor's 500 Stock Composite Index or Dow Jones 30 Industrials),

b = Beta, an index of nondiversifiable (noncontrollable, systematic) risk.

In words, the CAPM or (SML) equation shows that the required (expected) rate of return on a given security (r_j) is equal to the return required for securities that have no risk (r_f) plus a risk premium required by investors for assuming a given level of risk.

The higher the degree of systematic risk (b), the higher the return on a given security demanded by investors. *See also* Beta Coefficient; Capital Asset Pricing Model (CAPM); Portfolio Theory.

CAPITAL BUDGETING This is the process of deciding whether or not to commit resources to a project whose benefits will be spread over several time periods. There are typically two types of investments:

1. Selection decisions in terms of obtaining new facilities or expanding existing facilities. Examples include:
   (a) Investments in long-term assets such as property, plant, and equipment.
   (b) Resource commitments in the form of new product development, market research, refunding of long-term debt, introduction of a computer, and so on.
2. Replacement of decisions in terms of replacing existing facilities. Examples include replacing a manual bookkeeping system with a computerized system and replacing an inefficient lathe with one that is numerically controlled.

As such, capital budgeting decisions are a key factor in the long-term profitability of a firm. To make wise investment decisions, managers need tools at their disposal that will guide them in comparing the benefits and costs of various investment alternatives.

Capital Budgeting Techniques

Many techniques for evaluating investment proposals are widely available. They include:

1. Payback period
2. Accounting rate of return (ARR) (also called *simple rate of return*)
3. Net present value (NPV)
4. Internal rate of return (IRR) (also called *time-adjusted rate of return*)
5. Profitability index (also called the excess present value index)

The NPV method and the IRR method are called discounted cash flow (DCF) methods since they both recognize the time value of money and thus discount future cash flows. Each of the methods is discussed below.

Payback Period

Payback period measures the length of time required to recover the amount of initial investment. The payback period is determined by dividing the amount of initial investment by the cash inflow through increased revenues or cost savings.

■ Example 1

Assume:

Cost of investment	$18,000
Annual cash savings	3,000

Then, the payback period is

$$\frac{\$18,000}{\$3,000} = 6 \text{ years}$$

When cash inflows are not even, the payback period is determined by trial and error. When two or more projects are considered, the rule for making a selection decision is as follows:

Decision rule: Choose the project with the shorter payback period. The rationale behind this is: The shorter the payback period, the less risky the project and the greater the liquidity.

■ Example 2

Consider two projects whose cash inflows are not even. Assume each project costs $1,000.

Year	A	B
1	$100	$500
2	200	400
3	300	300
4	400	100
5	500	—
6	600	—

Based on trial and error, the payback period of project A is 4 years ($100 + $200 + $300 + $400 = $1,000 in 4 years). The payback period of project B is

$$2 \text{ years} + \frac{\$100}{\$300} = 2\frac{1}{3} \text{ years}$$

Therefore, according to this method, choose project B over project A.

Advantages of the payback period method:
1. It is simple to compute and easy to understand.
2. It handles investment risk effectively.

Shortcomings of the payback period method:
1. It does not recognize the time value of money.
2. It ignores the impact of cash inflows after the payback period which determines profitability of an investment.

Accounting (Simple) Rate of Return

Accounting rate of return (ARR) measures profitability from the conventional accounting standpoint by relating the required investment to the future annual net income. Sometimes the former is the average investment.

Decision rule: Under the ARR method, choose the project with the higher rate of return.

■ Example 3

Consider the investment:

Initial investment	$10,000
Estimated life	20 years
Cash inflows per year	$2,000
Depreciation by straight line	$ 500

then:

$$\text{ARR} = \frac{\$2,000 - \$500}{10,000} = 15.0\%$$

Using the average investment, which is usually assumed to be one half of the original investment, the resulting rate of return will be doubled:

$$\text{ARR} = \frac{\$2,000 - \$500}{\frac{1}{2}(\$10,000)} = \frac{\$1,500}{\$5,000} = 30.0\%$$

The justification for using the average investment is that each year the investment amount is decreased by $500 through depreciation, and therefore the average is computed as one half of the original cost.

Advantages: The method is easily understandable and simple to compute, and recognizes the profitability factor.

Shortcomings:
1. It fails to recognize the time value of money.
2. It uses accounting data instead of cash flow data.

Net Present Value

Net present value (NPV) is the excess of the present value (PV) of cash inflows generated by the project over the amount of the initial investment (I). Simply, $NPV = PV - I$. The present value of future cash flows is computed using the so-called *cost of capital* (or minimum required rate of return) as the discount rate.

Decision rule: If NPV is positive, accept the project. Otherwise, reject it.

■ Example 4

Initial investment	$4,356
Estimated life	6 years
Annual cash inflows	$1,000
Cost of capital (minimum required rate of return)	8%

Present value of cash inflows (*PV*):

$1,000 × PV of annuity of $1, 6 years and 8% $PVIFA_{8\%, 6 \text{ years}}$ [=$1,000(4.623)]	$4,623
Initial investment (*I*)	4,356
Net present value ($NPV = PV - I$)	$ 267

Since the investment's NPV is positive, the investment should be accepted.

Advantages: The NPV method obviously recognizes the time value of money and is easy to compute, whether the cash flows form an annuity or vary from period to period.

Disadvantage: It requires detailed long-term forecasts of incremental cash flow data.

Internal Rate of Return (or Time-Adjusted Rate of Return)

Internal rate of return (IRR) is defined as the rate of interest that equates I with the PV of future cash inflows. In other words, at IRR, $I = PV$, or $NPV = 0$.

Decision rule: Accept if IRR exceeds the cost of capital; otherwise, reject it.

■ Example 5

Assume the same data given in Example 4. We will set up the following equality ($I = PV$):

$$\$4,356 = \$1,000 \times PVIFA_{i,6}$$

$$PVIFA_{i,6} = \frac{\$4,356}{\$1,000} = 4.356$$

which gives exactly 10% in the 6-year line. (See Table 4 in the Appendix.) Since the investment's IRR (10%) is greater than the cost of capital (8%), the investment should be accepted.

Advantages: It considers the time value of money and is therefore more exact and realistic than ARR.

Shortcomings:
1. It is difficult to compute, especially when the cash inflows are not even.
2. It fails to recognize the varying size of investment in competing projects and their respective dollar profitability.

The trial-and-error method for computing IRR when cash inflows are not even is summarized, step by step, as follows:
1. Compute NPV at the cost of capital, denoted here as r_1.
2. See if NPV is positive or negative.
3. If NPV is positive, then pick another rate (r_2) much higher than r_1. If NPV is negative, then pick another rate (r_2) much smaller than r_1. The true IRR at which $NPV = 0$ must be somewhere in between these two rates.
4. Compute NPV using r_2.
5. Use interpolation for the exact rate.

■ Example 6

Consider the following investment whose cash flows are different from year to year:

Year	Cash Inflows
1	$1,000
2	2,500
3	1,500

Assume that the amount of initial investment is $3,000 and the cost of capital is 14%.

Step 1   NPV at 14%.

Year	Cash Inflows	$PVIF_{14\%,n}$ PV Factor at 14%	Total PV
1	$1,000	0.877	$ 877
2	2,500	0.769	1,923
3	1,500	0.675	1,013
			$3,813

Thus: $NPV = \$3,813 - \$3,000 = \$813$

Step 2   We see that $NPV = \$813$ is positive at $r_1 = 14\%$.

Step 3   Pick, say, 30% to play safe as r_2.

Step 4   Computing NPV at $r_2 = 30\%$:

Year	Cash Inflows	$PVIF_{30\%,n}$ PV Factor at 30%	Total PV
1	$1,000	0.769	$ 769
2	2,500	0.592	1,480
3	1,500	0.455	683
			$2,932

Thus: $NPV = \$2,932 - \$3,000 = \$(68)$

Step 5   Interpolate:

	NPV	
14%	$813	$813
IRR		0
30%	−68	
Difference	$881	$813

Therefore:

$$IRR = 14\% + \frac{\$813}{\$881}(30\% - 14\%)$$

$$= 14\% + 0.923(16\%)$$

$$= 14\% + 14.77\% = 28.77\%$$

Profitability Index (*Excess Present Value Index*)

The profitability index is the ratio of the total PV of future cash inflows to the initial investment, that is, PV/I. This index is used as a means of ranking projects in descending order of attractiveness. If the profitability index is greater than 1, then accept it.

■ Example 7

Using the data in Example 4, the profitability index, PV/I, is $4,623/\$4,356 = 1.06$. Since this project generates $1.06 for each dollar invested (or its profitability index is greater than 1), you should accept the project.

Income Tax Factors—Determining After-Tax Cash Flow

Income taxes make a difference in many capital budgeting decisions. In other words, the project that is attractive on a pre-tax basis may have to be rejected on an after-tax basis. Income taxes typically affect both the amount and the timing of cash flows. Since net income, not cash inflows, is subject to tax, after-tax cash inflows are not usually the same as after-tax net income.

Let us define: S = sales,
E = cash operating expenses,
d = depreciation,
t = tax rate.

Then, before-tax cash inflows = $S - E$, and net income = $S - E - d$. By definition,

After-tax cash inflow
= Before-tax cash inflow − Taxes

After-tax cash inflow
= $(S - E) - (S - E - d)(t)$

Rearranging, give the shortcut formula:

After-tax cash inflow = $(S - E)(1 - t) + (d)(t)$ [or after-tax cash inflow = $(S - E - d)(1 - t) + d$]

As can be seen, the deductibility of depreciation from sales in arriving at net income subject to taxes reduces income tax payments and thus serves as a tax shield.

Tax shield = Tax savings of depreciation = $(d)(t)$

■ Example 8

Assume: $S = \$12,000$,
$E = \$10,000$,
$d = \$500$/year by straight line,
$t = 40\%$.

Then:

After-tax cash inflow = $(\$12,000 - \$10,000)(1 - 0.4)$ + $(\$500)(0.4) = \$1,200 + \$200 = \$1,400$

Note that:

Tax shield = Tax savings on depreciation = $(d)(t)$
$= (\$500)(0.4) = \$200$.

After-tax cash outflow would be similarly computed by simply dropping S in the previous formula. Therefore:

After-tax cash outflow = $(-E)(1 - t) + (d)(t)$

■ Example 9

Assume: $E = \$6,000$,
$d = \$800$/year by straight line,
$t = 40\%$.

Then:

After-tax cash outflow = $(-\$6,000)(1 - 0.4) + (\$800)$ $(0.4) = -\$3,600 + \$320 = -\$3,280$, which is a cash outflow of $3,280.

Since the tax shield is $d \times t$, the higher the depreciation deduction, the higher the tax savings on depreciation.

■ Example 10

XYZ Corporation has provided its revenues and cash operating costs (excluding depreciation) for the old and the new machine, as follows:

	Revenue	Annual Cash Operating Costs	Net Profits Before Depreciation and Taxes
Old machine	$150,000	$70,000	$ 80,000
New machine	180,000	60,000	120,000

Assume that the annual depreciation of the old machine and the new machine will be $30,000 and $50,000, respectively. Assume further that the tax rate is 46%.

To arrive at net profits after taxes, we first have to deduct depreciation expenses from the net profits before depreciation and taxes, see below.

Subtracting the after-tax cash inflows of the old machine from the cash inflows of the new machine results in the relevant, or incremental, cash inflows for each year.

Therefore, in this example the relevant or incremental cash inflows for each year are $87,800 − $57,000 = $30,800.

Alternatively, the incremental cash inflows after taxes can be computed using the following simple formula:

After-tax incremental cash inflows = (Increase in revenues) (1 − Tax rate) − (Increase in cash charges) (1 − Tax rate) + (Increase in depreciation expenses) (Tax rate)

■ Example 11

Using the data in Example 10, after-tax incremental cash inflows for each year are

Increase in revenue × (1 − Tax rate): ($180,000 − $150,000) (1 − 0.46)	$16,200
−Increase in cash charges × (1 − Tax rate): ($60,000 − $70,000) (1 − 0.46)	−(−5,400)
+Increase in depreciation expense × Tax rate: ($50,000 − $30,000) (0.46)	9,200
	$30,800

CAPITAL BUDGETING AND INFLATION

The accuracy of capital budgeting decisions depends on the accuracy of the data regarding cash inflows and outflows. For example, failure to incorporate price-level changes due to inflation in capital budgeting situations can result in errors in the predicting of cash flows and thus in incorrect decisions. Typically, an analyst has two options dealing with a capital budgeting situation with inflation: Either restate the cash flows in nominal terms and discount them at a nominal *cost of capital* (minimum required rate of return) *or* restate both the cash flows and cost of capital in *constant* terms and discount the constant cash flows at a constant cost of capital. The two methods are basically equivalent.

■ Example

A company has the following projected cash flows estimated in real terms:

	Real Cash Flows (000s)			
Period	0	1	2	3
	−100	35	50	30

The nominal cost of capital is 15%. Assume that inflation is projected at 10% a year. Then the first cash flow for year 1, which is $35,000 in current dollars, will be $35,000 × 1.10 = $38,500 in year 1 dollars. Similarly, the cash flow for year 2 will be $50,000 × (1.10)^2 = $60,500 in year 2 dollars, and so on. If we discount these nominal cash flows at the 15% nominal cost of capital, we have the net present value (NPV) shown on p. 86:

	Net Profits After Taxes	Add Depreciation	After-Tax Cash Inflows
Old machine	($80,000 − $30,000) (1 − 0.46) = $27,000	$30,000	$57,000
New machine	($120,000 − $50,000) (1 − 0.46) = $37,800	50,000	87,800

Period	Cash Flows	PVIF (Table 3)	Present Values
0	−100	1.000	−100
1	38.5	0.870	33.50
2	60.5	0.756	45.74
3	39.9	0.658	26.25
		NPV =	5.49, or $5,490

Instead of converting the cash-flow forecasts into nominal terms, we could convert the cost of capital into real terms by using the following formula:

$$\text{Real cost of capital} = \frac{1 + \text{Nominal cost of capital}}{1 + \text{Inflation rate}} - 1$$

In the example, this gives

Real cost of capital = (1 + 0.15)/(1 + 0.10)
= 1.15/1.10 = 0.045 or 4.5%

We will obtain the same answer except for rounding errors ($5,490 vs. $5,580). Refer to table below.

CAPITAL EXPENDITURE   A capital expenditure is one that will benefit one year or more. It can increase the quantity or quality of services to be derived from an asset. It is charged to an asset account. An example is an addition to a fixed asset that is then depreciated. Rearrangement and relocation costs of existing assets may also be deferred if they have future benefit. *Note:* An *immaterial* expenditure even though benefiting more than one year (e.g., door knob) may be expensed.

In taxation, a capital expenditure has to be added to the cost basis of the asset. *See also* Revenue Expenditure.

CAPITAL INTENSIVE   This is a business with substantial investment in property, plant, and equipment. The auto industry, for instance, is capital intensive in nature. There is much downside risk with a capital intensive firm because if revenue declines, earnings will drastically fall since in the short run, fixed cost cannot be cut to adjust to reduction in demand. However, there does exist upside potential since an increase in revenue, with fixed costs being constant, results in a sharp increase in profits. The following diagram is revealing:

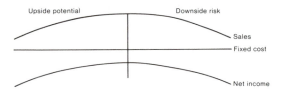

See also Labor Intensive.

CAPITALIZATION OF INTEREST   This refers to interest incurred on debt funds needed to self-construct an asset (e.g., machine) or to construct an asset intended for sale or lease that is a discrete project (e.g., real estate, ship). The interest is capitalized to the asset account involved and amortized over the life of the asset. Capitalized interest applies to the firm's actual borrowings and interest incurrence. The applicable interest rate for computational purposes is the interest on the particular borrowing for that asset. If not ascertainable, the weighted-average interest rate on the entity's obligations would be employed.

The capitalization period commences when *all* of the following are satisfied:

Period	Cash Flows	PVIF = $1/(1 + 0.045)^n$	Present Values
0	−100	1.000	−100
1	35	$1/(1 + 0.045) = 0.957$	33.50
2	50	$1/(1.045)^2 = 0.916$	45.80
3	30	$1/(1.045)^3 = 0.876$	26.28
		NPV =	5.58 or $5,580

• Expenditures have been made.
• Activities required to get the asset ready for intended use are in progress.
• Interest is being incurred.

■ Example

A company acquires land for the construction of a new facility through construction loans. The interest cost incurred on the loans would be capitalized for each accounting period as long as it does not exceed the total interest cost incurred by the enterprise in that period. Capitalization ceases when the facility is substantially complete and ready for use.

CAPITAL LEASE   Although the lessee does not legally own rental property, such property is theoretically acquired and recorded as an asset with the related liability. *See also* Leases.

CAPITAL MARKETS   These are the markets for long-term debt and corporate stocks. The New York Stock Exchange (NYSE), which trades the stocks of many of the larger corporations, is a prime example of a capital market. The American Stock Exchange and regional stock exchanges are also examples. In addition, securities are issued and traded through the thousands of brokers and dealers on the *over-the-counter* market. *See also* Financial Institutions and Markets.

CAPITAL RATIONING   Many firms specify a limit on the overall budget for capital spending. Capital rationing is concerned with the

problem of selecting the mix of acceptable projects that provides the highest overall NPV. The *profitability index* is used widely in ranking projects competing for limited funds.

■ Example

A company with a fixed budget of $250,000 needs to select a mix of acceptable projects from the table shown at bottom of the page.

The ranking resulting from the profitability index shows that the company should select projects A, B, and D.

	I	*PV*
A	$ 70,000	$112,000
B	100,000	145,000
D	60,000	79,000
	$230,000	$336,000

The overall profitability index for the best combination is

$$\$336,000/\$230,000 = 1.46$$

Therefore:

$$NPV = \$336,000 - \$230,000 = \$106,000$$

Unfortunately, the profitability index method has some limitations. One of the more serious is that it breaks down whenever more than one resource is rationed. In this case, the use of zero–one programming is suggested. *See also* Project Selection and Zero–One Programming.

CASH BASIS   This is an acceptable accounting method that recognizes revenue and expenses at the time of cash receipt or payment. The

Projects	*I*	*PV*	*NPV*	Profitability Index	Ranking
A	$ 70,000	$112,000	$42,000	1.6	1
B	100,000	145,000	45,000	1.45	2
C	110,000	126,500	16,500	1.15	5
D	60,000	79,000	19,000	1.32	3
E	40,000	38,000	−2,000	0.95	6
F	80,000	95,000	15,000	1.19	4

cash basis may be used in the case where a company deals in inventory *only* if there is an uncertain realization of the sale. If inventory is not involved, such as a service-oriented business, the cash basis may be chosen. In the preparation of a tax return for an individual, the cash basis is typically used. *See also* Accrual Basis.

CASH BREAK-EVEN POINT   If a firm has a minimum of available cash or the opportunity cost of holding excess cash is high, management may want to know the volume of sales that will cover all cash expenses during a period. This is known as the cash break-even point.

   Not all fixed operating costs involve cash payments. For example, depreciation expense is a noncash charge. To find the cash break-even point, the noncash charges must be subtracted from total fixed operating costs. Therefore, the cash break-even point is lower than the usual break-even point. The formula is

$$x = \frac{FC - d}{p - v}$$

where p = selling price per unit,
   v = unit variable cost,
   FC = fixed operating costs,
and d = depreciation expense.

■ **Example**

The XYZ Company manufactures and sells doors to home builders. The doors are sold for $25 each. Variable costs are $15 per door, and fixed operating costs total $50,000, which includes depreciation in the amount of $2,000. Then the company's cash break-even point is

$$x = \frac{FC - d}{p - v}$$

$$= \frac{\$50,000 - \$2,000}{\$25 - \$15} = \frac{\$48,000}{\$10} = 4,800 \text{ doors}$$

The company has to sell 4,800 doors to cover only the fixed costs involving cash payments

of $48,000 and to break even. *See also* Cost-Volume-Profit (CVP) and Break-Even Analysis; Leverage.

CASH BUDGET   This is a budget for cash planning and control presenting expected cash inflow and outflow for a designated time period. The cash budget helps management keep cash balances in reasonable relationship to its needs. It aids in avoiding idle cash and possible cash shortages. To meet its main objective, sound projections of cash collections from customers and cash expenditures are necessary. *See also* Budgeting for Profit Planning.

CASH MANAGEMENT   The purpose of cash management is to invest excess cash for a return and at the same time have adequate liquidity to meet future needs. The proper cash balance should exist, neither excessive nor deficient. Do you know how much cash you need, how much you have, and where the cash is? Proper cash forecasting is needed to determine (1) the optimal time to incur and pay back debt and (2) the amount to transfer daily between accounts. *Recommendation:* Analyze each bank account as to type, balance, and cost. Do not have an excessive cash balance because no return is earned. When quick liquidity is needed, invest in marketable securities.

Factors in Determining the Amount of Cash to Be Held

   • Your utility preferences regarding liquidity risk
   • Proper use of cash management
   • Expected future cash flows, considering the probabilities of different cash flows under alternative circumstances
   • Maturity period of debt
   • Your ability to borrow on short notice and on favorable terms
   • Probability of different cash flows under varying circumstances

What to Watch Out for: Having an "excessive" line of credit with the bank, which involves a commitment fee. Watch the amount of the compensating balance, since the portion of a loan that serves as collateral is restricted and unavailable for your use. Is cash unnecessarily tied up in other accounts (e.g., loans to employees, insurance deposits)? *Warning:* Liquid asset holdings are required during a downturn in a company's cycle, when funds from operations decline.

Recommendation: Do not seek to fund peak seasonal cash requirements internally. Rather, borrow on a short-term basis to enable internal funds to be used more profitably throughout the year, such as by investing in plant and equipment.

Acceleration of Cash Inflow

You should evaluate the causes and take corrective action for delays in having cash receipts deposited. *What to Do:* Ascertain how and where cash receipts come, how cash is transferred from outlying accounts to the main corporate account, and banking policy regarding availability of funds.

Types of Delays in Processing Checks

• *Mail float*—the time required for a check to move from debtor to creditor.

• *Processing float*—the time needed for the creditor to enter the payment.

• *Deposit collection float*—the time for a check to clear.

Means of Accelerating Cash Receipts

• Lockbox arrangement, where the collection point is placed near customers. Customer payments are mailed to strategic post office boxes geographically situated to hasten mailing and depositing time. Banks collect from these boxes several times a day and make deposits to the corporate account. *Recommendation:* Undertake a cost-benefit analysis to ensure that instituting a lockbox arrange-

ment will result in net savings. Determine the average face value of checks received, cost of operations eliminated, reducible overhead, reduction in mail float days, and per-item processing cost. *Tip:* Compare the returned earned on freed cash to the cost of the lockbox arrangement.

• Concentration banking, where funds are collected in local banks and transferred to a main concentration account.

• Transfer funds between banks by wire.

• Accelerate billing.

• Send customers preaddressed, stamped envelopes.

• Require deposits on large or custom orders or progress billings as the work progresses.

• Charge interest on accounts receivable after a certain amount of time.

• Use personal collection efforts.

• Offer discounts for each payment.

• Have postdated checks from customers.

• Have cash-on-delivery terms.

• Deposit checks immediately.

■ Example

You are determining whether to initiate a lockbox arrangement that will cost $150,000 annually. Its average daily collections are $700,000. The system will reduce mailing and processing time by 2 days. Your rate of return is 14%.

Return on freed cash (14% × 2 × $700,000)	$196,000
Annual cost	150,000
Net advantage of lockbox system	$ 46,000

■ Example

You presently have a lockbox arrangement with bank A in which it handles $5 million a day in return for an $800,000 compensating balance. You are thinking of canceling this arrangement and further dividing your western region by entering into contracts with two other banks. Bank B will handle $3 million a day in collections with a compensating balance of $700,000, and bank C will handle $2 million a day with a compensating balance of $600,000. Collections will be half a day quicker than the current situation. Your return rate is 12%.

Accelerated cash receipts ($5 million per day × 0.5 day)	$2,500,000
Increased compensating balance	500,000
Improved cash flow	$2,000,000
Rate of return	× 0.12
Net annual savings	$ 240,000

Delay of Cash Outlay

You should delay cash payments to earn a greater return on your money. Evaluate who your payees are and to what extent you can reasonably stretch time limits.

Ways of Delaying Cash Payments

• Centralize the payables operation so that debt may be paid at the most profitable time and so that the amount of disbursement float in the system may be ascertained.

• Make partial payments.

• Use payment drafts, where payment is *not* made on demand. Instead, the draft is presented for collection to the bank, which in turn goes to the issuer for acceptance. When approved, the company deposits the funds. *Net Result:* Less of a required checking balance.

• Draw checks on remote banks (e.g., a New York company can use a Texas bank).

• Mail from post offices with limited service or where mail has to go through numerous handling points. *Tip:* If you utilize float properly, you can maintain higher bank balances than the actual lower book balances. For instance, if you write checks averaging $200,000 per day and three days are necessary for them to clear, you will have a $600,000 checking balance less than the bank's records.

• Use probability analysis to determine the expected date for checks to clear. *Suggestion:* Have separate checking accounts (e.g., payroll, dividends) and monitor check-clearing dates. For example, payroll checks are not all cashed on the payroll date, so funds can be deposited later to earn a return.

• Use a computer terminal to transfer funds between various bank accounts at opportune times.

• Use a charge account to lengthen the time between buying goods and paying for them.

• Stretch payments as long as possible as long as there is no associated finance charge or impairment in credit rating.

• Do not pay bills before due dates.

• Utilize noncash compensation and remuneration methods (e.g., stock).

• Delay the frequency of your company payrolls.

• Disburse commissions on sales when the receivables are collected rather than when they are made.

■ Example

Every 2 weeks you disburse checks that average $500,000 and take 3 days to clear. You want to find out how much money you can save annually if you delay transfer of funds from an interest-bearing account that pays 0.0384% per day (annual rate of 14%) for those 3 days.

$$\$500,000 \times (0.000384 \times 3) = \$576$$

The savings per year is $576 × 26 (yearly payrolls) = $14,976.

Cash Models

William Baumol developed a model to determine the optimum amount of transaction cash under conditions of certainty. The objective is to minimize the sum of the fixed costs associated with transactions *and* the opportunity cost of holding cash balances. These costs are expressed as

$$F \cdot \left(\frac{T}{C}\right) + i \left(\frac{C}{2}\right)$$

where F = the fixed cost of a transaction,

T = the total cash needed for the time period involved,

i = the interest rate on marketable securities,

C = cash balance.

The optimal level of cash is determined using the following formula:

$$C^* = \sqrt{\frac{2FT}{i}}$$

A helpful graph follows:

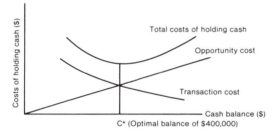

Costs of holding cash ($)

Total costs of holding cash

Opportunity cost

Transaction cost

Cash balance ($)

C* (Optimal balance of $400,000)

■ Example

You estimate a cash need for $4,000,000 over a 1-month period where the cash account is expected to be disbursed at a constant rate. The opportunity interest rate is 6% per annum, or 0.5% for a 1-month period. The transaction cost each time you borrow or withdraw is $100.

The optimal transaction size (the optimal borrowing or withdrawal lot size) and the number of transactions you should make during the month follow:

$$C^* = \sqrt{\frac{2FT}{i}} = \sqrt{\frac{2(100)(4,000,000)}{0.005}} = \$400,000$$

The optimal transaction size is $400,000.

The average cash balance is

$$\frac{C^*}{2} = \frac{\$400,000}{2} = \$200,000$$

The number of transactions required are

$$\frac{\$4,000,000}{\$400,000} = 10 \text{ transactions during the month}$$

You can use a stochastic model for cash management where major uncertainty exists regarding cash payments. The Miller-Orr model places an upper and lower limit for cash balances. When the upper limit is reached, a transfer of cash to marketable securities is made. When the lower limit is reached, a transfer from securities to cash takes place. A transaction will not occur as long as the cash balance falls within the limits.

Factors taken into account in the Miller-Orr model are the fixed costs of a securities transaction (F), assumed to be the same for buying as well as selling, the daily interest rate on marketable securities (i), and the variance of daily net cash flows (σ^2). The objective is to meet cash requirements at the lowest possible cost. A major assumption is the randomness of cash flows. The two control limits in the Miller-Orr model may be specified as d dollars as an upper limit and zero dollars at the lower limit. When the cash balance reaches the upper level, d less z dollars of securities are bought and the new balance becomes z dollars. When the cash balance equals zero, z dollars of securities are sold and the new balance again reaches z. Of course, practically speaking you should note that the minimum cash balance is established at an amount greater than zero due to delays in transfer as well as to having a safety buffer.

The optimal cash balance z is computed as follows:

$$z = \sqrt[3]{\frac{3F\sigma^2}{4i}}$$

The optimal value for d is computed as $3z$.

The average cash balance will approximate $\dfrac{(z + d)}{3}$.

■ Example

You wish to use the Miller-Orr model. The following information is supplied:

Fixed cost of a securities transaction	$10
Variance of daily net cash flows	50
Daily interest rate on securities (10%/360)	0.0003

The optimal cash balance, the upper limit of cash needed, and the average cash balance follow:

$$z = \sqrt[3]{\frac{3(10)(50)}{4(0.0003)}} = \sqrt[3]{\frac{3(10)(50)}{0.0012}}$$

$$= \sqrt[3]{\frac{1,500}{0.0012}} = \sqrt[3]{1,250,000} = \$102$$

The optimal cash balance is $102.
The upper limit is $306 (3 × $102).
The average cash balance is $136 $\dfrac{(\$102 + \$306)}{3}$.

A brief elaboration on these findings is needed for clarification. When the upper limit of $306 is reached, $204 of securities ($306 − $102) will be purchased to bring you to the optimal cash balance of $102. When the lower limit of zero dollars is reached, $102 of securities will be sold to again bring you to the optimal cash balance of $102.

An informative graph follows:

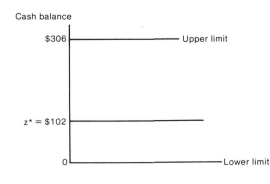

CASH SURRENDER VALUE OF LIFE INSURANCE This is the sum payable upon cancellation of the policy by the insured; the insured will of course receive less than the premiums paid in. Cash surrender value is classified under long-term investments. It applies to ordinary life and limited payment policies. It is *not* usually applicable to term insurance. The insurance premium payment consists of two elements—expense and cash surrender value.

■ Example

A premium of $6,000 is paid that increases the cash surrender value by $2,000. The appropriate entry is

Life Insurance Expense	4,000	
Cash Surrender Value of Life Insurance	2,000	
Cash		6,000

The gain on a life insurance policy is *not* typically considered an extraordinary item since it is in the ordinary course of business. *See also* Insurance Programs.

CASUALTY INSURANCE This covers such items as fire loss and water damage. The premiums are usually paid in advance and debited to Prepaid Insurance, which is then amortized over the policy period. Casualty insurance reimburses the holder for the fair market value of property lost. Insurance companies typically have a coinsurance clause so that the insured bears part of the loss. The insurance reimbursement formula follows (assumes an 80% coinsurance clause):

$$\frac{\text{Face of policy}}{0.8 \times \text{Fair market value}} \times \begin{array}{l}\text{Fair market value of loss} \\ = \text{Possible reimbursement}\end{array}$$
of insured property

Insurance reimbursement is based on the lower of the face of the policy, fair market value of loss, or possible reimbursement.

▪ Example

Case	Face of Policy	Fair Market Value of Property	Fair Market Value of Loss
A	$ 4,000	$10,000	$ 6,000
B	6,000	10,000	10,000
C	10,000	10,000	4,000

Insurance reimbursement follows:

Case A:

$$\frac{\$4,000}{0.8 \times \$10,000} \times \$6,000 = \boxed{\$\ 3,000}$$

Case B:

$$\frac{\boxed{\$6,000}}{0.8 \times \$10,000} \times \$10,000 = \$7,500$$

Case C:

$$\frac{\$10,000}{0.8 \times \$10,000} \times \boxed{\$4,000} = \$5,000$$

A blanket policy covers several items of property. The face of the policy is allocated based upon the fair market values of the insured assets.

▪ Example

A blanket policy of $15,000 applies to equipment I and equipment II. The fair values of equipment I and II are $30,000 and $15,000, respectively. Equipment II is partially destroyed, resulting in a fire loss of $3,000.

The policy allocation to equipment II is computed below:

	Fair Market Value	Policy
Equipment I	$30,000	$10,000
Equipment II	15,000	5,000
	$45,000	$15,000

The insurance reimbursement is

$$\frac{\$5,000}{0.8 \times \$15,000} \times \$3,000 = \boxed{\$1,500}$$

When a fire loss occurs, the asset destroyed has to be removed from the accounts, with the resulting fire loss recorded based on book value. The insurance reimbursement

reduces the fire loss. The fire loss is an extraordinary item (net of tax).

▪ Example

The following fire loss information exists for ABC Company. Merchandise costing $5,000 is fully destroyed. There is no insurance for it. Furniture costing $10,000 with accumulated depreciation of $1,000 and having a fair market value of $7,000 is entirely destroyed. The policy is for $10,000. Building costing $30,000 with accumulated depreciation of $3,000 and having a fair market value of $20,000 is 50% destroyed. The face of the policy is $15,000. The journal entries to record the book loss follow:

Fire Loss	5,000	
Inventory		5,000
Fire Loss	9,000	
Accumulated Depreciation	1,000	
Furniture		10,000
Fire Loss	13,500	
Accumulated Depreciation	1,500	
Building		15,000

Insurance reimbursement totals $16,375, computed as follows:

Furniture:

$$\frac{\$10,000}{0.8 \times \$7,000} \times \boxed{\$7,000} = \$12,500$$

Building:

$$\frac{\$15,000}{0.8 \times \$20,000} \times \$10,000 = \boxed{\$9,375}$$

The journal entry for the insurance reimbursement is

Cash	16,375	
Fire Loss		16,375

The net fire loss is $11,125 ($27,500 − $16,375), which will typically be shown as an extraordinary item. *See also* Insurance Programs.

CASUALTY LOSS

This is the loss due to fire, theft, or other casualty. The loss after insurance reimbursement is reported in the income statement as an extraordinary item (net of tax effect). The loss account is based on the book value of the assets destroyed. If insurance reimbursement, which is based on appraised value, exceeds the book value of assets destroyed or damaged, a net gain will occur. *See also* Insurance Programs.

CERTAINTY EQUIVALENTS

Certainty equivalent is the amount of cash (or rate of return) that a decision maker would require *with certainty* to make the recipient indifferent between this certain sum and a particular *uncertain*, *risky* sum. Multiplying the expected cash inflow by the certainty cash equivalent coefficient results in an *equivalent certain* cash inflow.

CHARTING

Investment analysts can use charts to appraise volume and price behavior of the overall market as well as individual securities. Charting information for many stocks may be gotten from Standard and Poor's *Trendline*. The interpretation of charts requires an evaluation of formations and identifying buy and sell signs. *Caution*: Analysts may differ somewhat in their interpretations even though they are looking at a particular chart pattern. *See also* Technical Analysis.

CHECK DIGIT

The check digit is appended to a number in order for the auditor to determine if that number is accurate when read or written. The digit involves a computation performed to that number. When the number is used in processing, a recalculation is made to assure that the computed check digit is identical to the original number. If the numbers do not match, there is an error indicated, perhaps arising from transposition or omission.

CLASSICAL VARIABLES SAMPLING

This is comprised of a family of three statistical techniques (mean per unit approach, difference sampling, and ratio sampling) that use normal distribution theory and are concerned with ascertaining whether account balances are properly stated. The method estimates the statistical range within which the true account balance being tested falls. It requires an estimate of population variability (population standard deviation) and necessitates the use of a computer. The technique predicts what the value of a particular variable in the population will be. Audit-related variables are usually the total population or the arithmetic mean. For example, an auditor may estimate the cost of a group of inventory components. The approach may also be used to estimate the dollar amount of error in a population. *See also* Probability Proportional to Size (PPS) Sampling; Sampling.

CLOSELY HELD CORPORATION

This is a corporation that has only a few stockholders. It contrasts with a privately held corporation in that a closely held corporation is public although most of the shares are not traded. The so-called corporate pocketbooks may become subject to the additional personal holding company tax on income not distributed. For example, deductions and losses in transactions between a major stockholder and the corporation may be disallowed under certain circumstances.

CLUSTER SAMPLING

Cluster sampling generally applies to samples of physical units in the case where a dollar-value estimate is needed. Groups (clusters) rather than individual items are selected at a random starting point in the population.

■ Example

Twenty-five groups of 10 consecutively numbered invoices are selected, starting with each of 15 randomly selected invoices.

Selection can be made of more than one item at a time. Each cluster becomes a sampling unit. Once the suitable number of clusters is chosen, the auditor may audit all items in the cluster (one-stage) or a random number of items in the cluster (two-stage). The mean for the individual sampling units is determined and is multiplied by the number of units in the population to arrive at the population's estimated value. A precision limit on this estimate must also be determined. With cluster sampling, there is a reduction in sampling cost because sample selection is facilitated. On the negative side, there is less statistical efficiency. Cluster sampling can be used to measure a variable (e.g., inventory value, accounts receivable balance). Attributes may also be measured. *See also* Sampling.

CODE OF PROFESSIONAL ETHICS The Code of Professional Ethics are the rules of conduct for certified public accountants in conducting their responsibilities to the public. Ethical regulations are published by the American Institute of CPAs and each state society. An example of an ethical violation is when a CPA issues an audit opinion even though he or she lacks independence. A lack of independence occurs, for example, when the CPA owns stock in the client or is associated with the company as a director. Another ethical violation is when the CPA fails to exercise due professional care in the audit engagement. GAAS must be followed in performing the attest function. Further, the CPA is not permitted to accept a contingent fee based on the findings of his or her services. If the accountant is in violation of an ethical standard, he or she faces disciplinary action.

COEFFICIENT OF DETERMINATION This is a statistical measure of how good the estimated regression equation is, designated as r^2 (read as *r*-squared). Simply put, it is a measure of "goodness of fit" in the regression. Therefore, the higher the *r*-squared, the more confi-

dence we have in our equation. Statistically, the coefficient of determination represents the proportion of the total variation in the dependent variable that is explained by the regression equation. It has the range of values between 0 and 1.

▪ **Example**

The statement "price/earnings ratio is a function of sales with $r^2 = 0.30$," can be interpreted as "only 30% of the total variation in the price/earnings ratio is explained by sales and the remaining 70% is still unexplained." This suggests inclusion of more explanatory variables (e.g., beta and asset size) in the regression equation in order to improve predictive power of the relationship. *See also* Regression Analysis.

COEFFICIENT OF VARIATION This is a measure of relative dispersion, or relative risk. It is computed by dividing the standard deviation (σ) by the expected value ($\bar{x}$). *See also* Decision Making Under Uncertainty.

COINCIDENT INDICATORS These are the types of economic indicator series that tend to move up and down in line with the aggregate economy and therefore are measures of current economic activity. Examples are gross national product (GNP), retail sales, and industrial production. *See also* Economic Indicators.

COLLECTIBLES These include art, rare stamps, valuable coins, antiques, and books. They provide profit potential and aesthetic enjoyment. To invest in collectibles, one must know well current market conditions and the factors affecting price. Purchase of collectibles may be made through dealers, auction, or directly from prior owners. Disadvantages to owning collectibles are high insurance costs, lack of immediate marketability, high transaction costs, and possible forgeries. Information regarding collectibles may be found in *Money*, *Collector/Investor*, and *Antique Monthly*.

COMMITMENT An expected expenditure supported by a purchase order or contract given to an external party. A commitment is not reflected in the accounting records. Footnote disclosure is required of the nature of the commitment and amount.

COMMODITIES FUTURES CONTRACTS The seller of a commodity contract guarantees to deliver a particular commodity by a specified date at a predetermined price. The contract indicates the item, price, expiration date (up to 1 year), and the standardized unit to be traded (e.g., 100,000 lbs). The investor has to closely monitor the financial impact of market price changes in the commodity as it affects the contract's value.

Assume one purchases a futures contract for delivery of 1,000 units of a commodity 6 months from now at $5 per unit. The seller of the contract need not take physical possession of the item, and the contract buyer does not have to take custody of the commodity at the "delivery" date. Usually, there is reversal of commodity contracts or termination before their consummation. For example, as an initial buyer of 1,000 bushels of corn, one may engage in a similar contract to sell the same quantity so that the position is effectively closed out.

The following table reveals the unit size of some commodity contracts:

Unit Size of Some Commodity Contracts

Contract	Contract Stated in
Cattle	40,000 lbs
Coffee	37,500 lbs
Cotton	50,000 lbs
Sugar	112,000 lbs
Wheat	5,000 bushels

The investor can directly acquire a commodity or have indirect ownership via a mutual fund. Another possibility is purchasing a limited partnership dealing in commodity investments. The more conservative approaches are mutual fund and partnership involvement because of diversification and management expertise.

An investor may undertake commodity trading to obtain high return or hedge against inflation. In inflation, commodities do well because they are tied into economic trends. *Warning*: There exists high risk and uncertainty due to the variability in commodity prices and the small down payment. *Caution*: The investor should have significant cash in reserve in case of a margin call to cover losses. Minimization of risk can be achieved by diversification. *Recommendation*: Be sure to ascertain the honesty and reliability of the commodities representatives (e.g., salespeople).

The purchaser of a commodity may terminate the contract or let it continue to obtain more profits. Alternatively, the investor may use profits earned to put up margin on another futures contract. The latter is termed an inverse pyramid in a futures contract.

Commodity futures exchanges permit buyers and sellers to negotiate cash (spot) prices. Cash is paid for immediately receiving physical possession of a commodity. Prices in the cash market are based to some extent on prices in the futures market. In fact, cash prices for commodities are close to prices in the short-term futures market. There may exist higher prices for the commodity over time, incorporating holding costs and expected inflation.

Commodity and financial futures are traded in the Chicago Board of Trade, which is the largest exchange. There exist other exchanges (e.g., Amex Commodities Exchange), some specializing in particular commodities. An example is the New York Cotton Exchange. Because of the possibility of significant gain and loss in commodities, there are exchange limitations on the highest price change for a commodity in a given day. The federal government's Commodity Futures Trading Commission regulates the commodities exchanges.

The financial pages of many newspapers (e.g., *The Wall Street Journal*) give the starting, high, low, and closing (settle) prices for the day, as well as the commodity's price change. In addition, the all-time high and low are given. Open interest refers to the number of outstanding futures contracts for the commodity and the expiration dates. An illustrative table is presented below.

The return on a futures contract is derived from capital gain (selling price less purchase price) because no current income is involved. There is significant capital gain potential because of price variability in the commodity and the effect of leverage arising from a low margin requirement. *Warning*: There also exists the possibility of losing all the margin put down quickly if commodity prices go against you. The return on investment equals:

$$\frac{\text{Selling price} - \text{Purchase price}}{\text{Margin deposit}}$$

■ Example

An investor buys a contract on a commodity for $70,000 giving an initial deposit of $7,000. The contract is subsequently sold for $75,000. The return equals:

$$\frac{\$75,000 - \$70,000}{\$7,000} = \frac{\$5,000}{\$7,000} = 71.4\%$$

Margin requirements for commodity contracts are relatively low, typically ranging from 5% to 10% of the contract's value. In commodities trading, no funds are being borrowed so there is no interest charge.

An initial margin is necessary as a deposit on the futures contract. The reason for the deposit is to cover a price decline on the contract. The amount of the deposit varies with the type of contract and the commodity exchange involved.

There is also a maintenance deposit that is lower than the initial deposit and provides the minimum margin that has to be kept in the account. It typically is about 80% of the initial margin.

■ Example

On July 1, an investor enters into a contract to purchase 37,500 pounds of coffee at $6 a pound to be delivered by October 1. The contract has a total value of $225,000. The initial margin requirement is 10%, or $22,500. The margin maintenance requirement is 60%, or $13,500. If a contract loss of $2,000 occurs, an additional $2,000 has to be remitted to cover the margin position. If not, the contract is terminated with the ensuing loss.

■ Example

An investor makes an initial deposit of $10,000 on a contract and a maintenance deposit of $7,500. If the market value of the contract does not decrease by more than $2,500, there is no problem. But if the market value of the contract declines by $4,500, the margin or deposit will go to $5,500, and the investor will have to deposit another $5,500 in order to keep the sum at the initial deposit level. If the investor does not come up with the additional $5,500, the contract will be canceled.

There are different forms of commodity

Commodity Quotes

					Lifetime		Open
Open	High	Low	Settle	Change	High	Low	Interest
Cotton (CTN)—50,000 lbs, cents per lb							
July 65.32	65.32	64.55	64.62	−0.64	79.85	63.86	5887
Oct. 63.80	63.80	63.51	63.53	−0.20	77.50	63.51	1555
Dec. 63.75	63.78	63.50	63.60	−0.15	73.00	63.50	6247

trading, including hedging, speculating, and spreading.

Hedging is used to protect a position in a commodity. For example, a fruit grower (seller) will hedge to obtain a higher price for his products, whereas a processor (or buyer) of the item will hedge to obtain a lower price. Although hedging is a conservative strategy that reduces the risk of loss, it also restricts gain potential.

■ Example

A commodity is presently selling for $120 a pound, but a potential buyer (manufacturer) anticipates a future price increase. To protect against higher prices, the buyer acquires a futures contract selling at $135 a pound. Six months later, the price of the commodity reaches $180 a pound. The futures contract price will similarly rise to, say $210. The buyer's profit is $75 a pound. If 5,000 pounds are involved, the total profit is $375,000. At the same time, the cost of the market increased by only $60 per pound, or $300,000. In effect, the manufacturer hedged his position, coming out with a profit of $75,000, and has controlled the increasing costs of the commodity.

Speculators also invest in commodities.

■ Example

An investor buys an October futures contract for 37,500 pounds of coffee at $5 a pound. If the price increases to $5.40, he will gain $0.40 a pound for a total gain of $15,000. The percentage gain, considering the initial margin requirement, is 80%. If the transactions occurred over a 2-month period, the annual gain would be 480%. This arose from only a 7.4% gain in the price of coffee.

In spreading, there is an attempt to profit from swings in price and at the same time limit loss exposure. The investor engages in two or more contracts to get some profit while restricting loss. The investor buys one contract and sells the other, expecting to ob-

tain a minimal but reasonable profit. In the worst case scenario, the spread will reduce the investor's loan.

■ Example

An investor buys Contract 1 for 10,000 pounds of Commodity Z at $500 a pound. At the same time, he sells short Contract 2 for 10,000 pounds of the same commodity at $535 a pound. Later, he sells Contract 1 for $520 a pound and buys Contract 2 for $543 a pound. Contract 1 yields a profit of $20 a pound, while Contract 2 involves a loss of $8 a pound. On net, however, the investor earns a profit of $12 a pound, so the total gain is $120,000.

COMMON-SIZE FINANCIAL STATEMENT A common-size financial statement is one expressed in percentages of a base, instead of in dollars. The base for the income statement is net sales, whereas for the balance sheet it is either total assets or total liabilities plus stockholders' equity. The percentages permit relative comparisons among companies of varying sizes. Also indicated are abnormal variations of a particular company's statistics to industry norms. *See also* Vertical Analysis.

COMMON STOCK EQUIVALENT A common stock equivalent is a security that can become common stock at a later date and as such is included in the computation of earnings per share. Examples are stock options, stock warrants, and convertible securities whose yield at the time of issuance is less than $66\frac{2}{3}\%$ of the Aa corporate bond yield. *See also* Earnings per Share.

COMMON STOCK VALUATION The process of determining security valuation involves finding the present value of an asset's expected future cash flows using the investor's required rate of return. Thus, the basic security valuation model can be defined mathematically as follows:

$$V = \sum_{t=1}^{n} \frac{C_t}{(1 + r)^t}$$

where V = intrinsic value or present value of an asset,

C_t = expected future cash flows in period $t = 1, \ldots, n,$

r = investor's required rate of return.

Like bonds, the value of a common stock is the present value of all future cash inflows expected to be received by the investor. The cash inflows expected to be received are dividends and the future selling price. For an investor holding a common stock for only 1 year, the value of the stock would be the present value of both the expected cash dividend to be received in 1 year (D_1) and the expected market price per share of the stock at year-end (P_1).

If r represents an investor's required rate of return, the value of common stock (P_o) would be:

$$P_o = \frac{D_1}{(1 + r)^1} + \frac{P_1}{(1 + r)^1}$$

▪ Example 1

Assume an investor is considering the purchase of stock A at the beginning of the year. The dividend at year-end is expected to be $1.50, and the market price by the end of the year is expected to be $40. If the investor's required rate of return is 15%, the value of the stock would be:

$$P_o = \frac{D_1}{(1 + r)^1} + \frac{P_1}{(1 + r)^1} = \frac{\$1.50}{(1 + 0.15)} + \frac{\$40}{(1 + 0.15)}$$

$= \$1.50(0.870) + \$40(0.870) = \$1.31 + \$34.80$

$= \$36.11$

Since common stock has no maturity date and is held for many years, a more general, multiperiod model is needed. The general common stock valuation model is defined as follows:

$$P_o = \sum_{t=1}^{\infty} \frac{D_1}{(1 + r)^t}$$

The model is based on the concept that a common stock is worth the present value of future dividends. However, future dividends may grow with three different patterns, as follows:

1. Zero growth
2. Constant growth
3. Nonconstant, or supernormal, growth

Zero growth. If dividends are expected to remain unchanged, i.e.,

$$D_o = D_1 = \ldots = D$$

then the above model reduces to the formula:

$$P_o = \frac{D}{r}$$

This is the case with a perpetuity. This model is most applicable to the valuation of preferred stocks or the common stocks of very mature companies such as big municipal utilities.

▪ Example 2

Assuming D equals $2.50 and r equals 10%, then the value of the stock is

$$P_o = \frac{\$2.50}{0.1} = \$25$$

Constant growth. If we assume that dividends grow at a constant rate of g every year [i.e., $D_t = D_o(1 + g)^t$], then the previous model is simplified to

$$P_o = \frac{D_1}{r - g}$$

This formula is known as the Gordon's growth model. This model is most applicable to the valuation of the common stock of very large or broadly diversified companies.

▪ Example 3

Consider a common stock that paid a $3 dividend per share at the end of the last year and is expected to pay a cash dividend every year at a growth rate of 10%. Assume the investor's required rate of return is 12%. The value of the stock would be

$$D_1 = D_o(1 + g) = \$3(1 + 0.10) = \$3.30$$

$$P_o = \frac{D_1}{r - g} = \frac{\$3.30}{0.12 - 0.10} = \$165$$

Nonconstant, or supernormal, growth. Firms typically go through life cycles, during part of which their growth is faster than that of the economy and then falls sharply.

The value of stock during such supernormal growth can be found by taking the following steps: (1) compute the dividends during the period of supernormal growth and find their present value; (2) find the price of the stock at the end of the supernormal growth period and compute its present value; and (3) add these two *PV* figures to find the value (P_o) of the common stock.

■ Example 4

Consider a common stock whose dividends are expected to grow at a rate of 25% for 2 years, after which the growth rate is expected to fall to 5%. The dividend paid last period was $2. The investor desires a 12% return. To find the value of this stock, take the following steps:

1. Compute the dividends during the supernormal growth period and find their present value. Assuming D_o is $2, g is 15%, and r is 12%:

$$D_1 = D_o(1 + g) = \$2(1 + 0.25) = \$2.50$$

$$D_2 = D_o(1 + g)^2 = \$2(1.563) = \$3.126$$

or $\quad D_2 = D_1(1 + g) = \$2.50(1.25) = \$3.126$

Therefore,

$$PV \text{ of dividends} = \frac{D_1}{(1 + r)^1} + \frac{D_2}{(1 + r)^2}$$

$$= \frac{\$2.50}{(1 + 0.12)^1} + \frac{\$3.125}{(1 + 0.12)^2}$$

$$= \$2.50(PVIF_{12\%,1})$$
$$+ \$3.125(PVIF_{12\%,2})$$

$$= \$2.50(0.893) + \$3.125(0.797)$$

$$= \$2.23 + \$2.49 = \$4.72$$

2. Find the price of the stock at the end of the supernormal growth period. The dividend for the third year is

$$D_3 = D_2(1 + g'), \text{ where } g' = 5\%$$

$$= \$3.125(1 + 0.05) = \$3.28$$

The price of the stock is therefore:

$$P_2 = \frac{D_3}{r - g'} = \frac{\$3.28}{0.12 - 0.05} = \$46.86$$

$$PV \text{ of stock price} = \$46.86$$
$$(PVIF_{12\%,2}) = \$46.86(0.797) = \$37.35$$

3. Add the two *PV* figures obtained in steps 1 and 2 to find the value of the stock.

$$P_o = \$4.72 + \$37.35 = \$42.07$$

Expected Rate of Return on Common Stock

The formula for computing the expected rate of return on common stock can be derived easily from the valuation models.

The single-period return formula is derived from

$$P_o = \frac{D_1}{(1 + r)} + \frac{P_1}{(1 + r)}$$

Solving for r gives:

$$r = \frac{D_1 + (P_1 - P_o)}{P_o}$$

In words,

$$\text{Rate of return} = \frac{\text{Dividends} + \text{Capital gain}}{\text{Beginning price}}$$

$$= \text{Dividend yield} + \text{Capital gain yield}$$

■ Example 5

Consider a stock that sells for $50. The company is expected to pay a $3 cash dividend at the end of the year, and the stock market price at the end of the year is expected to be $55 a share. Thus the expected return would be

$$r = \frac{D_1 + (P_1 - P_o)}{P_o} = \frac{\$3 + (\$55 - \$50)}{\$50}$$

$$= \frac{\$3 + \$5}{\$50} = 16\%$$

or:

$$\text{Dividend yield} = \frac{\$3}{\$50} = 6\%$$

$$\text{Capital gain yield} = \frac{\$5}{\$50} = 10\%$$

$$r = \text{Dividend yield} + \text{Capital gain yield}$$
$$= 6\% + 10\% = 16\%$$

Assuming a constant growth in dividend, the formula for the expected rate of return on an investment in stock can be derived as follows:

$$P_o = \frac{D_1}{r - g}$$

$$r = \frac{D_1}{P_o} + g$$

■ Example 6

Suppose that ABC Company's dividend per share was $4.50, expected to grow at a constant rate of 6%. The current market price of the stock is $30. Then the expected rate of return is

$$r = \frac{D_1}{P_o} + g = \frac{\$4.50}{\$30} + 6\% = 15\% + 6\% = 21\%$$

The Price-Earnings Ratio—A Pragmatic Approach

The dividend valuation models discussed so far are best suited for those companies that are at the expansion or maturity stage of their life cycle. A more pragmatic approach to valuing a common stock is to use the *P/E* ratio (or multiple). Many common stock analysts use the simple formula:

Forecasted price at the end of year
= Estimated *EPS* in year *t* × Estimated *P/E* ratio

■ Example 7

The XYZ Corporation had *EPS* of $5. The *EPS* is expected to grow at 20%. The company's normal *P/E* ratio is estimated to be 7, which is used as the multiplier. The value of the stock is

Estimated *EPS* = $5(1 + 0.20) = $6.00

Therefore, the expected price of the stock is $6 × 7 = $42.

Of course, for this method to be effective in forecasting the future value of a stock, earnings need to be correctly projected and the appropriate *P/E* multiple must be applied.

Forecasts of EPS

Forecasting *EPS* is not an easy task. Many security analysts use a simple method of forecasting *EPS*. They use a sales forecast combined with an after-tax profit margin, as follows:

Estimated earnings in year *t*
= Estimated sales in year *t*
× After-tax profit margin expected in year *t*

Estimated *EPS* in year *t*
= Estimated earnings in year *t*/
Number of common shares outstanding in year *t*

More sophisticated methods of forecasting sales and earnings, such as linear regression, are available.

■ Example 8

Assume that in the year just ended, the XYZ Corporation reported sales of $60 million, and it is estimated that revenues will grow at a 4% annual rate, while the after-tax profit margin should amount to about 8%, and the number of common shares outstanding is 400,000 shares. Then:

Estimated earnings in year *t*
= $60 million × 0.04 = $2.4 million

Estimated EPS in year *t*
= $2.4 million/400,000 shares = $6 per share

Determinants of the P/E Ratio

What determines the *P/E* multiple is very complex. Empirical evidence seems to suggest the following factors:
- Historical growth rate in earnings
- Forecasted earnings
- Average dividend payout ratio
- Beta coefficient measuring the firm's systematic risk

- Instability of earnings
- Financial leverage
- Other factors such as competitive position, management ability, and economic conditions

COMMUNICATION WITH AUDIT COMMITTEES

According to Statement on Auditing Standards No. 61, the auditor must bring to the attention of the client's audit committee certain results of the audit, such as problems with the internal control structure and the occurrence of illegal acts. The communication may be written or oral. In the case of the latter, the auditor must have documentation such as workpaper references or relevant memoranda. The following areas should be communicated to the audit committee:

- Internal control weaknesses
- Material misstatements in the financial statements
- Degree of audit responsibility assumed
- Audit tests conducted
- Accounting policies used and changes therein
- Method used to reflect unusual material transactions
- Approach management uses in deriving sensitive accounting estimates, and the auditor's opinion as to the reasonableness of the estimates
- Significant audit objectives required, impacting the company's financial reporting process
- Auditor responsibility for other data included in documents containing audited financial statements
- Audit procedures undertaken and results thereof
- Disagreements between the auditor and management, and whether they have been resolved

COMPENSATED ABSENCES These include sick leave, holiday, and vacation time. The employer shall accrue a liability for employee's

compensation for future absences when *all* of the following criteria are met:

- Employee services have already been performed.
- Employee rights to pay have vested.
- Probable payment exists.
- Amount of estimated liability can reasonably be determined.

If the criteria are satisfied except that the amount is not determinable, only a footnote can be made since an accrual is not possible.

Accrual for sick leave is required only when the employer permits employees to take accumulated sick leave days off irrespective of actual illness. But no accrual is required if employees can only take accumulated days off for actual illness, since losses for these are typically immaterial.

FASB 43 is not applicable to

- Severance or termination pay
- Deferred compensation
- Post retirement benefits
- Stock option plans
- Other long-term fringe benefits (e.g., insurance, disability)

■ Example

Estimated compensation for future absences is $30,000. The entry is

Expense	30,000	
Estimated Liability		30,000

If at a later date a payment of $28,000 is made, the entry is

Estimated Liability	28,000	
Cash		28,000

■ Example

Employees are entitled to 2 weeks vacation each year. Mr. X began work on July 1, 19X1. He is entitled to the equivalent of 1 week of vacation, which will be accrued on 12/31/19X1.

COMPILATION In a compilation, presented financial statement information is the representation of management or owners. There is

no audit opinion or other form of assurance given to the financial statements. As a result, the procedures conducted are very limited. In a compilation engagement, the practitioner should

• Obtain a letter of engagement.

• Obtain a knowledge of the accounting policies prevalent in the industry.

• Obtain an understanding of the nature of the client's transactions and accounting records.

• Evaluate the competency of client accounting personnel.

• Ascertain the basis of accounting used (e.g., accrual basis, cash basis).

• Determine if the client's books have to be adjusted.

• Obtain satisfaction regarding management representations that seem unsatisfactory and incorrect. *Note*: The practitioner does *not* have to verify management representations that appear logical.

• Modify the accountant's report if the client fails to prepare needed adjustments.

• Read the financial statements to assure that obvious errors do not exist, including departures from GAAP, insufficient footnotes, or mathematical errors.

The compilation report includes the following:

• Identification of the financial statements

• Statement that the compilation was conducted in accord with standards established by the AICPA

• Definition of a compilation, in that it is restricted to presenting in the form of financial statements information that is the representation of management (owners)

• Statement that the financial statements have *not* been audited or reviewed, and as such there is *no* opinion or any other form of assurance involved

• Date the compilation was completed

• Signature of accountant

Each page of the financial statements should be labeled, "See accountant's compilation report." If desired, the accountant may expand the label to include the footnotes to the financial statements. Further, to eliminate any possible misinterpretation, the practitioner may mark each page of the financial statements, "unaudited." *See also* Review.

COMPLIANCE AUDIT   A compliance audit examines specific activities for the purpose of ascertaining whether performance has been conducted as prescribed by a particular statute, contract, or specified purpose. An example is an audit of a physician's records to assure that proper charges have been made to the government.

COMPLIANCE TEST   Subsequent to the review of a client's system of internal control, compliance testing is performed, which is necessary so that the auditor is satisfied that prescribed internal controls are in proper operation. The results of compliance testing are obtained by inquiry, observation, and inspection. Compliance testing is necessary only for the internal controls that reliance is needed for. Often, attribute sampling is used to conduct compliance testing to result in economies of cost and time. The objective of the compliance test is to obtain reasonable assurance that a given control is performing properly. An example is verifying that the individual making out a check is different from the one who approves the payment after examining supplier invoices for accuracy. The auditor should be on the lookout for departures from prescribed controls. An example is the failure of a receiving department employee to verify that the quantity received agrees with the purchase order and, accordingly, failing to sign the receiving report. As a result of this departure in policy, an error may occur since substantiation has not taken place.

In appraising compliance-testing results, the auditor should take into account

• Potential and actual errors and irregularities.

• Controls and procedures to guard against errors and irregularities.

• Sufficiency of internal controls. A weakness in internal control exists when there does not exist reasonable reliance on a prescribed procedure to prevent or detect errors or irregularities.

Note: For audits of financial statements for periods beginning on or after January 1, 1990, the term *test of controls* will replace *compliance test*. *Test of controls* is a broader concept than *compliance tests*. Tests of controls is not only used to evaluate the effectiveness of policies and procedures in preventing or detecting material misstatements of assertions but is also used in obtaining an understanding of the client's internal control structure. Thus, *test of controls* relates to what SAS 1 previously referred to as review of the client's system, as well as test of compliance. *See also* Substantive Test.

COMPOSITE BREAK-EVEN POINT This is a break-even sales when a company sells more than one product or service. A break-even point for all the products or services combined can be determined, based on the expected *sales mix* and the composite or weighted average unit contribution margin. *See also* Cost-Volume-Profit (CVP); Break-Even Analysis.

COMPOSITION This is a voluntary reduction in the balance the debtor owes a creditor. *See also* Business Failure.

COMPREHENSIVE ANNUAL FINANCIAL REPORT (CAFR) CAFR is the annual report of a government. Financial reporting includes a combined, combining (showing information for all funds), and individual balance sheet. The following are shown as applicable on a combined, combining, and individual basis:

• Statement of revenues, expenditures, and changes in fund balance (all funds)

• Statement of revenues, expenditures, and changes in fund balance, budget and actual (general and special revenue funds)

• Statement of revenues, expenses, and changes in retained earnings (proprietary funds)

• Statement of changes in financial position (for proprietary funds)

See also Governmental Accounting.

COMPREHENSIVE INCOME This is the change in equity occurring from transactions and other events with nonowners. It excludes investment (disinvestment) by owners. Items included in comprehensive income but excluded from net income are

• Cumulative effect of a change in accounting principle

• Unrealized losses and gains on long-term investments

• Foreign currency translation gains and losses

Comprehensive income is subdivided into revenues and gains, as well as expenses and losses. These are further classified as either recurring or extraordinary.

COMPUTER CONFERENCING This occurs when financial executives located at distances apart are brought together for the purpose of giving and receiving information and to discuss corporate problems in order to develop strategy and solutions. Participants may become involved in discussions whenever desired through the use of their computers or terminals. Numerous on-line services exist, including GEnies's Business Real Time Conferencing and CompuServe. Computer conferencing allows for the quick dissemination and evaluation of corporate data to facilitate the decision-making process.

CONFIRMATION This is when the auditor makes a request in writing or orally asks a third party to a client to verify the existence and/or amount of a financial item. In a positive confirmation, the auditor seeks a reply even if the item is correct. In a negative confirmation, a reply is given only in the case of a disagreement.

■ Example

A company sends to its sampled customers a form on behalf of the CPA firm asking them to respond to the auditor if a discrepancy in the account balance exists.

Negative confirmations also may be used in confirming accounts payable and bank balances.

CONSIGNMENT   In a consignment, the consignor transfers goods to the consignee. The consignor retains legal title and includes the goods in his inventory. The consignee is acting as an agent in an attempt to sell the goods. Although the consignee is temporarily holding the goods, the inventory is not an asset on his books. If a sale occurs, the consignee deducts from the selling price his commission and related expenses, remitting the balance to the consignor. *See also* Inventory Valuation.

CONSOLIDATION   This occurs when the parent owns in excess of 50% of the voting common stock of the subsidiary. The major objective of consolidation is to present as one economic unit the financial position and operating results of a parent and subsidiaries. It shows the group as a single company (with one or more branches or divisions), rather than separate companies. It is an example of theoretical substance over legal form. The companies making up the consolidated group keep their individual legal identity. Adjustments and eliminations are for the sole purpose of financial statement reporting. Consolidation is still appropriate even if the subsidiary has a material amount of debt. Disclosure in footnotes or by explanatory headings should be made of the firm's consolidation policy.

A consolidation is negated, even if more than 50% of voting common stock is owned by the parent, in the following cases:

• Parent is not in actual control of subsidiary (e.g., subsidiary is in receivership, subsidiary is in a politically unstable foreign country).

• Parent has sold or contracted to sell subsidiary shortly after year-end. The subsidiary is a temporary investment.

• Minority interest is very large in comparison to the parent's interest, thus individual financial statements are more meaningful.

Intercompany eliminations include that for intercompany payables and receivables, advances, and profits. But for certain regulated companies, intercompany profit does not have to be eliminated to the extent the profit represents a reasonable return on investment. Subsidiary investment in the parent's shares is not consolidated outstanding stock in the consolidated balance sheet. Consolidated statements do not reflect capitalized earnings in the form of stock dividends by subsidiaries subsequent to acquisition.

Minority interest in a subsidiary is the stockholders' equity of those outside of the parent's controlling interest in the partially owned subsidiaries. Minority interest should be shown as a separate component of stockholders' equity. When losses applicable to the minority interest in a subsidiary exceed the minority interest's equity capital, the excess and any subsequent losses related to the minority interest are charged to the parent. If profit subsequently occurs, the parent's interest is credited to the degree of prior losses absorbed.

If a parent acquires a subsidiary in more than one block of stock, each purchase is on a step-by-step basis and consolidation does not occur until control exists.

In case the subsidiary is acquired within the year, the subsidiary should be included in consolidation as if it had been bought at the beginning of the year, with a subtraction for the preacquisition part of earnings applicable to each block of stock. An alternative, but less preferable, approach is to include in consolidation the subsidiary's earnings subsequent to the acquisition date.

The retained earnings of a subsidiary at the acquisition date is not included in the consolidated financial statements.

When the subsidiary is disposed of during the year, the parent should present its equity in the subsidiary's earnings prior to the sale date as a separate line item consistent with the equity method.

A subsidiary whose major business activity is leasing to a parent should always be consolidated.

Consolidation is still permissible without adjustments when the fiscal year-ends of the parent and subsidiary are 3 months or less apart. But footnote disclosure is needed of material events occurring during the intervening period.

The equity method of accounting is used for unconsolidated subsidiaries unless there is a foreign investment or a temporary investment. In a case where the equity method is not used, the cost method is followed. The cost method recognizes the difference between the cost of the subsidiary and the equity in net assets at the acquisition date. Depreciation is adjusted for the difference as if consolidation of the subsidiary was made. There is an elimination of intercompany gain or loss for unconsolidated subsidiaries to the extent the gain or loss exceeds the unrecorded equity in undistributed earnings. Unconsolidated subsidiaries accounted for with the cost method should have adequate disclosure of assets, liabilities, and earnings. Such disclosure may be in footnote or supplementary schedule form.

There may be instances when combined rather than consolidated financial statements are more meaningful, such as where a person owns a controlling interest in several related operating companies (brother-sister corporation).

There are cases where besides consolidated statements, parent company statements are required to properly provide information to creditors and preferred stockholders. In this event, *dual columns* are needed—one column for the parent and other columns for subsidiaries.

CONSTANT GROWTH MODEL The constant growth model for stock valuation, also called Gordon's model, is used to value the market price of a company's stock. It assumes dividends grow each year at a constant rate, g.

$$\text{Common stock value} = \frac{D_1}{r - g}$$

where D_1 = dividend in year 1,
r = required rate of return,
g = growth rate.

■ **Example**

Dividends per share for the current year is $10, required rate of return is 12%, and the constant growth rate in dividends is 2%. The value of the stock is

$$\frac{\$10}{0.12 - 0.02} = \frac{\$10}{0.10} = \$100$$

See also Common Stock Valuation.

CONSTRUCTION CONTRACT ACCOUNTING The two methods to account for construction contracts are the *completed contract method* and the *percentage of completion method*. Under the former method, profit on the contract is recognized in full in the year of completion, whereas under the latter method, profit on the contract is recognized gradually each year as work is performed. *See also* Revenue Recognition Methods.

CONSUMER PRICE INDEX (CPI) CPI is the measure of price level computed by the Bureau of Labor Statistics. It is the ratio of the cost of specific consumer items in any one year to the cost of those items in the base year, 1967. Because the CPI includes things consumers buy regularly, it is frequently called the *cost-of-living index*. The so-called market basket, covered by the index, includes items such as food, clothing, automobiles, homes, and doctor fees. *See also* Price Indices.

CONTRIBUTION APPROACH TO PRICING   This is an approach to pricing a special order. This situation occurs because a company often receives a nonroutine, special order for its products at lower prices than usual. In normal times, the company may refuse such as order since it will not yield a satisfactory profit. If times are bad or when there is idle capacity, an order should be accepted if the incremental revenue exceeds the incremental costs involved. Such a price, one lower than the regular price, is called a *contribution price*. This approach to pricing is called the contribution approach to pricing, also called the *variable pricing model*.

■ Example

Assume that a company with 100,000-unit capacity is currently producing and selling only 90,000 units of product each year with a regular price of $2. If the variable cost per unit is $1 and the annual fixed cost is $45,000, the income statement looks as follows:

		Per Unit
Sales (90,000 units)	$180,000	$2.00
Less: Variable cost	90,000	1.00
Contribution margin	$ 90,000	$1.00
Less: Fixed cost	45,000	0.50
Net income	$ 45,000	$0.50

The company has just received an order that calls for 10,000 units @ $1.20, for a total of $12,000. The acceptance of this special order will not affect regular sales. Management is reluctant to accept this order because the $1.20 price is below the $1.50 factory unit cost ($1.50 = $1.00 + $0.50). Is it advisable? The answer to this question is no. The company can add to total profits by accepting this special order even though the price offered is below the unit factory cost. At a price of $1.20, the order will contribute $0.20 (CM per unit = $1.20 − $1.00 = $0.20) toward fixed cost, and profit will increase by $2,000 (10,000 units × $0.20). Using the contribution approach to pricing, the variable cost of $1.00 will be a better guide than the full unit cost of $1.50. Note that the fixed costs will not increase because of the presence of idle capacity.

The same result can be seen using the *total project approach* shown below. *See also* Incremental Analysis; Relevant Costing; Total Project Approach.

CONTRIBUTION APPROACH VERSUS TRADITIONAL APPROACH TO THE INCOME STATEMENT   The traditional approach to the income statement shows the functional classification of costs; that is, manufacturing costs vs. nonmanufacturing expenses (or operating expenses). It is not organized according to cost behavior. The contribution approach, however, looks at cost behavior. That is, it shows the relationship of variable costs and fixed costs, regardless of the functions a given cost item is associated with. The contribution

	Per Unit	Without Special Order (90,000 Units)	With Special Order (100,000 Units)	Difference
Sales	$2.00	$180,000	$192,000	$12,000
Less: VC	1.00	90,000	100,000	10,000
CM	$1.00	$ 90,000	$ 92,000	$ 2,000
Less: FC	0.50	45,000	45,000	—
Net income	$0.50	$ 45,000	$ 47,000	$ 2,000

approach to income determination provides data that are useful for managerial planning and decision making. It is not acceptable, however, for income tax or external reporting purposes. A contribution income statement highlights the concept of *contribution margin*, which is the difference between sales and variable costs. The traditional format, on the other hand, emphasizes the concept of *gross margin*, which is the difference between sales and cost of goods sold. These two concepts are independent and have nothing to do with each other. Gross margin is available to cover nonmanufacturing expenses, whereas contribution margin is available to cover fixed costs. The concept of contribution margin has numerous applications for internal management. A comparison between the traditional format and the contribution format follows.

Traditional Format

Sales		$15,000
Less: Cost of goods sold		7,000
Gross margin		$ 8,000
Less: Operating expenses		
Selling	$2,100	
Administrative	1,500	3,600
Net income		$ 4,400

Contribution Format

Sales		$15,000
Less: Variable expenses		
Manufacturing	$4,000	
Selling	1,600	
Administrative	500	6,100
Contribution margin		$ 8,900
Less: Fixed expenses		
Manufacturing	$3,000	
Selling	500	
Administrative	1,000	4,500
Net income		$ 4,400

See also Contribution Income Statement.

CONTRIBUTION INCOME STATEMENT This is an income statement that organizes the cost by behavior. It shows the relationship of vari-

able costs and fixed costs, regardless of the functions a given cost item is associated with. A contribution income statement highlights the concept of *contribution margin (CM)*. This format provides data that are useful for internal management. An illustrative format of the contribution margin income statement follows:

- Sales
- Less: Variable Cost of Sales
     Variable selling and administrative expenses
- Contribution margin (CM)
- Less: Fixed overhead
     Fixed selling and administrative expenses
- Net income

Disadvantages of the contribution income statement are

1. It is not acceptable for external reporting purposes. It is only an internal measure.
2. It ignores fixed overhead as an inventoriable product cost.

See also Contribution Approach Versus Traditional Approach to the Income Statement; Contribution Margin.

CONTRIBUTION MARGIN (CM) Contribution margin, or marginal income, is the difference between sales and the variable costs of the product or service. It is the amount of money available to cover fixed costs and generate profits.

■ Example

If sales are $12,000 and variable costs are $5,000, contribution margin is $7,000 ($12,000 less $5,000).

The concept of contribution margin (CM) has many applications. A company can sell an item below the normal selling price when idle capacity exists as long as there is a contribution margin since it will help to cover the fixed costs or add to profits. The CM calculation requires the segregation of fixed and variable costs, which is needed in *break-even analysis*. Further, CM analysis is effective in evaluating the performance of the department as a whole and its manager. *See also* Contribution Income Statement.

CONTRIBUTION MARGIN (CM) VARIANCE

The CM variance is the difference between actual contribution margin per unit and the budgeted contribution margin per unit multiplied by the actual number of units sold. If the actual CM is greater than the budgeted CM per unit, a variance is favorable; otherwise, it is unfavorable.

CM variance = (Actual CM per unit
　　　　　　　− Budgeted CM per unit) × Actual sales

See also Contribution Margin; Profit Variance Analysis.

CORPORATE PLANNING MODELS

Today more and more companies are using, developing, or experimenting with some form of corporate planning model. This is primarily due to development of planning and modeling software packages that make it possible to develop the model without much knowledge of computer coding and programming. For the accountant and financial analyst, the attractive features of corporate modeling are the formulation of budgets, budgetary planning and control, and financial analyses that can be used to support management decision making. However, corporate modeling involves much more than the generation of financial statements and budgets. Depending on the structure and breadth of the modeling activity, a variety of capabilities, uses, and analyses are available. A corporate planning model is an integrated business planning model in which marketing and production models are linked to the financial model.

More specifically, a corporate model is a description, explanation, and interrelation of the functional areas of a firm (accounting, finance, marketing, production, and others) expressed in terms of a set of mathematical

and logical relationships so as to produce a variety of reports, including financial statements. The ultimate goals of a corporate planning model are to improve quality of planning and decision making; reduce decision risk; and, more importantly, influence or even shape the future environment favorably.

Generally speaking, a corporate model can be used to:

1. Simulate an alternative strategy by evaluating its impact on profits.
2. Help establish corporate and divisional goals.
3. Measure the interactive effect of parts within the firm.
4. Help management better understand the business and its functional relationships and help improve decision-making ability.
5. Link the firm's goals and strategies to its master budgets.
6. Assess critically the assumptions underlying environmental constraints.

Types of Analysis

The type of the corporate model that management is looking for would depend on what types of analysis it wishes to perform. There are typically three types of model investigations.

The first type of questions to be raised are "What is" or "What has been" questions, such as the relationship between variables of the firm and external macroeconomic variables such as GNP or inflation. The goal of this type of model investigation is to obtain a specific answer based on the stipulated relationship. For example, what is or has been the firm's profit when the price of raw material was $12.50?

The second type of investigation focuses on "What-if" questions. This is done through *simulation* or *sensitivity analysis*. This analysis often takes the following form: "What happens under a given set of assumptions if the decision variable(s) is changed in a prescribed manner?" For example,

''What is going to happen to the company's cash flow and net income if it is contemplating a reduction in price by 10% and an increase in advertising budget by 25%?

The third type of question that can be addressed by way of corporate-planning modeling takes the following form: ''What has to be done in order to achieve a particular objective?'' This type of analysis is often called *goal seeking*. It usually requires the use of optimization models such as linear programming and goal programming.

Typical Questions Addressed Via Corporate Modeling

The following is a list of questions management addresses itself using corporate modeling. (For greater detail, see F. Rosenkranz, *An Introduction to Corporate Modeling*, Duke University Press, Durham, NC, 1979.)

- What are the effects of different pricing policies?
- What is the effect of different interest rates and current exchange rates on the income statement and balance sheet of the firm?
- What will be the demand for the end products of the firm at various locations and different times?
- What is and will be the unit contribution margin for certain production, transportation, and sales allocations?
- What will the absence and turnover rates of the employees of the firm be and what effect will they have?
- What is the effect of advertising and distribution expenditures on sales?
- What marketing strategy can and should the firm follow?
- What do price-demand or supply relations on the output or input side of the firm look like? What are the effects of price/cost changes on sales?
- How do certain states of the national or world economy influence sales of the firm

on the one side and purchase price of the production factors on the other?
- What is the nature of the conditions that must be fulfilled if the total sales of the firm at a certain time are supposed to be higher than a certain budget value?
- Should the firm produce and sell a certain product, purchase and sell the product, or not get involved at all?
- What is the range of the return on investment on various projects and units?
- How will the income statement, the balance sheet, and the cash flow statement develop for several operating divisions? What will their contributions be?
- What effects with respect to the financial position of the firm could an acquisition or merger with another firm have?

Benefits derived from the corporate planning models include
- The ability to explore more alternatives
- Better quality decision making
- More effective planning
- A better understanding of the business
- Faster decision making
- More timely information
- More accurate forecasts
- Cost savings

Types of Models

Corporate planning models can be categorized according to two approaches: simulation and optimization. *Simulation models* are attempts to mathematically represent the operations of the company or of the conditions in the external economic environment. By adjusting the values of controllable variables and assumed external conditions, the future implications of present decision making can be estimated. Probabilistic simulation models incorporate probability estimates into the forecast sequence, whereas deterministic models do not. *Optimization models* are intended to identify the best decision, given specific constraints.

Current Trend in Corporate Modeling

Interactive computing facilities allow for faster and more meaningful input/output sequences for modelers; trial-and-error adjustments of inputs and analyses are possible while on-line to the central computer or to an outside time-sharing service. The advent of corporate simulation languages enables analysts with little experience to write modeling programs in an Englishlike programming language—for example, to name a few, IFPS™, SIMPLAN™, and XSIM™. In addition, a number of spreadsheet programs, such as Lotus 1–2–3™ and SuperCalc™, have become available for use by corporate planning modelers. By 1979, nearly every Fortune 1000 company was using a corporate simulation model. This statistic will definitely increase to cover small and medium-sized firms. *See also* Financial Models.

CORRELATION COEFFICIENT (*r*)

A measure of the degree of correlation between the two variables. The range of values it takes is between −1 and +1. A negative value of *r* indicates an inverse relationship; a positive value of *r* indicates a direct relationship; a zero value of *r* indicates that the two variables are independent of each other; an *r* of 1 indicates that the two variables are perfectly correlated; the closer *r* is to +1 or −1, the stronger the relationship between the two variables. *See also* Regression Analysis; Simple Regression.

COST BEHAVIOR ANALYSIS—ANALYSIS OF MIXED COSTS

Depending on how a cost will react or respond to changes in the level of activity, costs may be viewed as variable, fixed, or mixed (semivariable). (Reference should be made to Figure 1.) A mixed cost is one that contains both variable and fixed elements. For planning, control, and decision-making purposes, mixed costs need to be separated into their variable and fixed

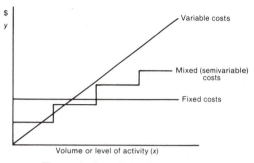

Figure 1   Cost Behavior Patterns

components, using such methods as the high-low method, the scattergraph method, and regression analysis. They are discussed following.

The High-Low Method

The high-low method, as the name indicates, uses two extreme data points to determine the values of a (the fixed cost portion) and b (the variable rate) in the equation $y = a + bx$. The extreme data points are the highest representative $x-y$ pair and the lowest representative $x-y$ pair. The activity level x, rather than the mixed cost item y, governs their selection.

The high-low method is explained, step by step, as follows:

• Step 1   Select the highest pair and the lowest pair.

• Step 2   Compute the variable rate, b, using the formula:

$$\text{Variable rate} = \frac{\text{Difference in cost } y}{\text{Difference in activity } x}$$

• Step 3   Compute the fixed cost portion as:

$$\text{Fixed cost portion} = \text{Total semivariable cost} - \text{Variable cost}$$

■ Example 1

Flexible Manufacturing Company decided to relate total factory overhead costs to direct labor hours (DLH) to develop a cost-volume formula in the form of $y' = a + bx$. Twelve

Table 1

Month	Direct Labor Hours (x) (000 omitted)	Factory Overhead (y) (000 omitted)
January	9 hours	$ 15
February	19	20
March	11	14
April	14	16
May	23	25
June	12	20
July	12	20
August	22	23
September	7	14
October	13	22
November	15	18
December	17	18
Total	174 hours	$225

monthly observations are collected. They are given in Table 1.

The high-low points selected from the monthly observations are

	x		y	
High	23	hours	$25	(May pair)
Low	7		14	(September pair)
Difference	16	hours	$11	

Thus:

Variable rate b

$$= \frac{\text{Difference in } y}{\text{Difference in } x} = \frac{\$11}{16 \text{ hours}}$$

$$= \$0.6875 \text{ per DLH}$$

The fixed cost portion is computed as

	High	Low
Factory overhead (y)	$25	$14
Variable expense ($0.6875/DLH)	(15.8125)	(4.8125)
	$ 9.1875	$ 9.1875

Therefore, the cost-volume formula for factory overhead is $9.1875 fixed, plus $0.6875 per DLH.

Or, alternatively:

$$y' = \$9.1875 + \$0.6875x$$

where y' = estimated factory overhead,

x = DLH.

Note that the reason for using a new symbol y' (read y-prime) is that the cost volume for-

mula just obtained gives an estimated value of y.

The high-low method is simple and easy to use. It has the disadvantage, however, of using two extreme data points, which may not be representative of normal conditions. The method may yield unreliable estimates of a and b in our formula. In such a case, it would be wise to drop them and choose two other points that are more representative of normal situations.

The Scattergraph Method

In this method, a semivariable expense is plotted on the vertical axis (or y axis) and activity measure is plotted on the horizontal axis (or x axis). Then a regression line is fitted by visual inspection of the plotted $x-y$ data. The method is best explained by the following example.

■ Example 2

For purposes of illustration, let us use the data in Example 1. The factory overhead and direct labor hours are plotted in Figure 2.

Since the regression line obtained by visual inspection strikes the factory overhead axis at the $6 point, that amount represents the fixed cost component. The variable cost component is computed as

Factory overhead at 23 hours of direct labor	$25
Less: Fixed cost component	6
Variable cost component	$19

Figure 2 The Scattergraph Method

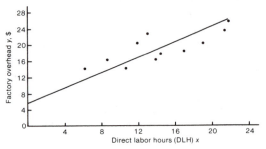

Therefore, the variable rate per hour is $19/23 hours = $0.8261 per DLH.

In summary, based on the scattergraph method, we obtain

$$y' = \$6 + \$0.8261x$$

where y' = estimated factory overhead,

$$x = \text{DLH}.$$

The scattergraph method is relatively easy to use and simple to understand. However, it should be used with extreme caution because it does not provide an objective test for assuring that the regression line drawn is the most accurate fit for the underlying observations.

Regression Analysis

One popularly used method for estimating the cost-volume formula is regression analysis. Regression analysis is a statistical procedure for estimating mathematically the average relationship between the dependent variables and the independent variable(s). Simple regression involves one independent variable (e.g., DLH or machine hours alone), whereas multiple regression involves two or more activity variables. We will assume simple linear regression, which means that we will maintain the $y = a + bx$ relationship.

Unlike the high-low method, in estimating the variable rate and the fixed cost portion, the regression method does include all the observed data and attempts to find a line of best fit. To find the line of best fit, a technique called the *method of least squares* is used.

To explain the least-squares method, we define the error as the difference between the observed value and the estimated value of some semivariable cost and denote it with u.

Symbolically,

$$u = y - y'$$

where y = observed value of a semivariable expense,

y' = estimated value based on $y' = a + bx$.

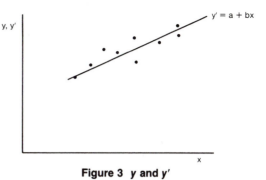

Figure 3 y and y′

The least-squares criterion requires that the line of best fit be such that the sum of the squares of the errors (or the vertical distance in Figure 3 from the observed data points to the line) is a minimum, that is,

minimum: $\Sigma u^2 = \Sigma(y - y')^2$

Using differential calculus we obtain the following equations, called normal equations:

$$\Sigma y = na + b\Sigma x$$
$$\Sigma xy = a\Sigma x + b\Sigma x^2$$

solving the equations for b and a yields

$$b = \frac{n\Sigma xy - (\Sigma x)(\Sigma y)}{n\Sigma x^2 - (\Sigma x)^2}$$

$$a = \bar{y} - b\bar{x}$$

where $\bar{y} = \Sigma y/n$ and $\bar{x} = \Sigma x/n$.

■ Example 3

To illustrate the computations of b and a, we will refer to the data in Table 1. All the sums required are computed and shown below.

Direct Labor Hours x	Factory Overhead y	xy	x^2	y^2
9 hours	$ 15	135	81	225
19	20	380	361	400
11	14	154	121	196
14	16	224	196	256
23	25	575	529	625
12	20	240	144	400
12	20	240	144	400
22	23	506	484	529
7	14	98	49	196
13	22	286	169	484
15	18	270	225	324
17	18	306	289	324
174 hours	$225	3,414	2,792	4,359

From the previous table:

$\Sigma x = 174$ $\Sigma y = 225$ $\Sigma xy = 3,414$ $\Sigma x^2 = 2,792$

$\bar{x} = \Sigma x/n = 174/12 = 14.5$

$\bar{y} = \Sigma y/n = 225/12 = 18.75$

Substituting these values into the formula for b first:

$$b = \frac{n\Sigma xy - (\Sigma x)(\Sigma y)}{n\Sigma x^2 - (\Sigma x)^2}$$

$$= \frac{(12)(3,414) - (174)(225)}{(12)(2,792) - (174)^2}$$

$$= \frac{1,818}{3,228} = 0.5632$$

$a = \bar{y} - b\bar{x} = 18.75 - (0.5632)(14.5)$

$= 18.75 - 8.1664 = 10.5836$

The cost formula then is:

$$y' = \$10.5836 + 0.5632x$$

Note that Σy^2 is not used here but rather is computed for future use.

Regression Statistics

Unlike the high-low method, regression analysis is a statistical method. It uses a variety of statistics that tell us about the accuracy and reliability of the regression results. They include:

1. Correlation coefficient (r) and coefficient of determination (r^2)
2. Standard error of the estimate (S_e)
3. Standard error of the regression coefficient (S_b) and t-statistic

Correlation Coefficient (r) and Coefficient of Determination (r²)

The correlation coefficient r measures the degree of correlation between y and x. The range of values it takes on is between -1 and $+1$. More widely used, however, is the coefficient of determination, designated r^2 (read as r-squared). Simply put, r^2 tells us how good the estimated regression equation is. In other words, it is a measure of "goodness of fit" in the regression. Therefore, the higher the r^2, the more confidence we can have in our estimated cost formula.

More specifically, the coefficient of determination represents the proportion of the total variation in y that is explained by the regression equation. It has the range of values between 0 and 1.

■ Example 4

The statement, "Factory overhead is a function of machine hours with $r^2 = 70\%$," can be interpreted as, "70% of the total variation of factory overhead is explained by the regression equation or the change in machine hours, and the remaining 30% is accounted for by something other than machine hours."

The coefficient of determination is computed as

$$r^2 = 1 - \frac{\Sigma(y - y')^2}{\Sigma(y - \bar{y})^2}$$

In a simple regression situation, however, there is a shortcut method available:

$$r^2 = \frac{[n\Sigma xy - (\Sigma x)(\Sigma y)]^2}{[n\Sigma x^2 - (\Sigma x)^2][n\Sigma y^2 - (\Sigma y)^2]}$$

Comparing this formula with the one for b in Example 3, we see that the only additional information we need to compute r^2 is Σy^2.

■ Example 5

From the table prepared in Example 3, $\Sigma y^2 = 4,359$. Using the shortcut method for r^2,

$$r^2 = \frac{(1,818)^2}{(3,228)[(12)(4,359) - (225)^2]}$$

$$= \frac{3,305,124}{(3,228)(52,308 - 50,625)} = \frac{3,305,124}{(3,228)(1,683)}$$

$$= \frac{3,305,124}{5,432,724} = 0.6084 = 60.84\%$$

This means that about 60.84% of the total variation in total factor overhead is explained by DLH and the remaining 39.16% is still unexplained. A relatively low r^2 indicates that there is a lot of room for improvement in our estimated cost-volume formula ($y' = \$10.5836 + \$0.5632x$). Machine hours or a combination of DLH and machine hours might improve r^2.

Standard Error of the Estimate (S_e)

The standard error of the estimate, designated S_e, is defined as the standard deviation of the regression. It is computed as

$$S\hat{e} = \sqrt{\frac{\Sigma(y - y')^2}{n - 2}} = \sqrt{\frac{\Sigma y^2 - a\Sigma y - b\Sigma xy}{n - 2}}$$

The statistics can be used to gain some idea of the accuracy of our predictions.

■ Example 6

Going back to our example data, S_e is calculated as

$$S_e = \sqrt{\frac{4,359 - (10.5836)(225) - (0.5632)(3,414)}{12 - 2}} = \sqrt{\frac{54.9252}{10}} = 2.3436$$

If a manager wants the prediction to be 95% confident, the confidence interval would be the estimated cost $\pm$ 2(2.3436).

Standard Error of the Regression Coefficient (S_b) and the t-Statistic

The standard error of the regression coefficient, designated S_b, and the *t*-statistic are closely related. S_b gives an estimate of the range where the true coefficient will ''actually'' fall. The *t*-statistic shows the statistical significance of an independent variable x in explaining the dependent variable y. It is determined by dividing the estimated regression coefficient b by its standard error S_b. Thus

the *t*-statistic measures how many standard errors the coefficient is away from zero. Generally, any *t* value greater than $+2$ or less than -2 is acceptable. The higher the *t* value, the greater the confidence we have in the coefficient as the predictor.

COST BEHAVIOR PATTERNS   Not all costs behave in the same way. There are certain costs that vary in proportion to change in activity, called *variable costs*. There are other costs that do not change regardless of the volume, called *fixed costs*. (See Figures 1 and 2 below.) An understanding of costs by behavior is very useful:

1. For break-even and cost-volume-profit (CVP) analysis
2. To analyze short-term, nonroutine decisions such as the make-or-buy decision and the sales mix decision
3. For appraisal of profit center performance by means of the contribution approach and for flexible capital budgeting

See also Cost Behavior Analysis.

COST-BENEFIT ANALYSIS   The cost-benefit, or benefit-cost, analysis is an analysis to determine whether the favorable results of an alternative are sufficient to justify the cost of taking that alternative. This analysis is widely used in connection with capital expend-

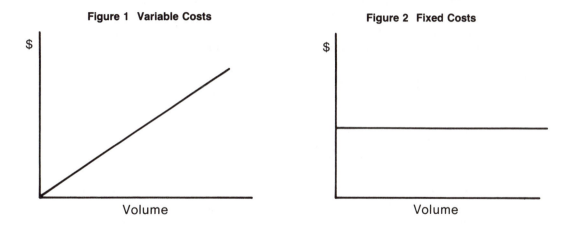

Figure 1 Variable Costs   **Figure 2 Fixed Costs**

iture projects. An example of cost-benefit analysis is where the cost incurred to uncover the reasons for a variance outweigh the benefit to be derived. Cost-benefit ratio or *profitability* index is widely used for capital expenditure decisions. *See also* Capital Rationing; Profitability Index.

COST FUNCTION This describes the relationship between cost and activity. A cost function may be either linear or nonlinear. A simple example of a cost function is a *cost-volume formula* which is in the form of $y = a + bx$, where y is the estimated value of a cost item for any specified value of x (activity). The constant a is the intercept; b is the slope. The fixed cost element is a, whereas b is the variable rate per unit of x. *See also* Cost Behavior Analysis—Analysis of Mixed Costs; Cost Behavior Patterns; Cost-Volume Formula.

COST METHOD FASB No. 12 covers accounting under the cost method. It does *not* apply to not-for-profit organizations, mutual life insurance companies, or employee benefit plans.

A security is usually classified as current if it is liquid and used for temporary excess cash. A security is usually classified as long term if the intent is to hold for one year or more, it is for capital appreciation purposes, dividend income is desired, possible eventual control is involved, there is a lack of market price quotations, and restricted marketability exists. "Restricted" stock is noncurrent except if it qualifies for sale within one year of the balance sheet date and there are readily available price quotations.

The cost method of accounting for investments is used when the holder owns less than 20% of the voting common stock of the company. However, the cost method could be used instead of the equity method when the holder owns between 20% to 50% of the voting common stock but *lacks* significant influence (effective control).

Significant influence may be indicated by one or more of the following:
• Involvement in decision making of owned company.
• Material intercompany transactions.
• Representation on the Board of Directors of the investee company.
• Investor owns a high percentage of investee's shares relative to other stockholders.
• Managerial personnel are interchanged between the investor and investee.
• Investor provides investee with technological expertise.

Indicators of a lack of significant influence follow:
• Concentration of majority ownership of investee among a limited number of stockholders, especially when the group operates the investee in disregard of the investor's viewpoints.
• Investor is unable to obtain the financial data needed from the investee to use the equity method.
• Investor and investee sign an agreement (called "standstill") in which the investor surrenders material shareholder rights. The standstill agreement is typically employed to settle disputes between the investor and investee.
• Investee opposes the investment (e.g., a lawsuit or complaint is filed).

The cost method must be used for equity securities. Although it is not required for debt securities, debt securities in practice are usually reflected in the entire investment portfolio at the lower of cost or market value. *Note:* The cost method is used to account for preferred stock since it is nonvoting irrespective of the percentage of shares owned.

The investment portfolio is broken down into current and noncurrent. Current securities are shown as marketable securities under current assets. Noncurrent securities are shown as noncurrent assets. The lower of cost or market value is applied to each portfolio separately.

If market value is in excess of cost, the securities are shown at cost with market value either disclosed in parentheses or in a footnote. If market value is less than cost, the securities portfolio is written down to market value, reflecting an unrealized loss due to conservatism. Thus, a temporary decline in value of the portfolio is reflected. The portfolio is shown on the balance sheet at the lower of total cost or total market value. The following entry is made at the end of the year:

> Unrealized Loss
> Allowance to Reduce Securities
>   from Cost to Market Value

For short-term securities, the unrealized loss is shown in the income statement. For long-term securities, the unrealized loss is shown as a separate item in the stockholders' equity section. The allowance account is a contra account to Investments to derive the net amount. The only time the allowance account is entered into is at the end of the year.

In the following year, if there is a partial or full recovery from cost to market value, the entry is

> Allowance to Reduce Securities
>   from Cost to Market Value
> Unrealized Gain

However, in recording the recovery from cost to market value, the portfolio can never be written up at an amount in excess of the original cost.

If securities are sold during the year, a realized loss or realized gain will occur. The realized loss or gain is shown in the income statement irrespective of whether the portfolio is current or noncurrent. The same realized loss or gain on sale is reflected for tax return preparation purposes.

The entry to record the sale of securities is

> Cash (proceeds received)
> Loss
>   Securities (at cost)
>   Gain

Either a loss or gain will be involved in the previous entry.

A security cannot be recorded at more than cost since that will lack conservatism. The only time market value can be used for valuation is the case of a *permanent* increase in value. However, accountants are very reluctant to state that a permanent increase has occurred because of legal liability exposure.

If a balance sheet is unclassified, the investment security portfolio is considered to be noncurrent.

A permanent decline in value of a particular security is immediately recognized with a realized loss being booked shown in the income statement even if it is a noncurrent portfolio. The investment account is credited directly. The new market value becomes the new cost basis, which means it cannot later be written up.

A permanent decline in market price of stock may be indicated when the company has several years of losses, is in a very weak financial condition, and has issued a liquidating dividend. For example, if the company sells some of its major divisions and distributes the proceeds to stockholders, a write-down of the investment may be appropriate.

■ Example

In a long-term investment portfolio, one stock in ABC Company has suffered a permanent decline in value from cost of $6,000 to market value of $5,000. The entry is

Realized Loss   1,000
  Long-term Investment   1,000

The new cost now becomes $5,000 (the market value). If in a later period the market value increased above $5,000, the stock would *not* be written up above $5,000.

If a particular stock is reclassified from noncurrent to current, or vice versa, it is transferred at the lower of cost or market value at the transfer date. If market value exceeds cost, it is transferred at cost intact, with no unrealized gain being recorded. If market value is below cost, a realized loss in the income statement is booked and the investment account is credited. The new cost basis becomes the market value, which means the portfolio cannot be written up above cost.

■ Example

XYZ stock is reclassified from noncurrent to current. If cost is $3,000 and market value is $2,700, the entry for the reclassification is

Short-term Securities	2,700	
Realized Loss	300	
Long-term Investment		3,000

If a later recovery occurs and market value becomes $2,900, no entry will be made.

If market value of a portfolio substantially drops below cost between year-end and the audit report date, subsequent event footnote disclosure is required.

Income tax allocation occurs with investments due to resulting temporary differences. A deferred tax credit will arise because unrealized losses and gains on securities are not reflected for tax return preparation purposes.

■ Example

On 1/1/19X1, Company X purchases long-term securities of $480,000 plus brokerage commissions of $20,000. On 5/12/19X1, a cash dividend of $15,000 is received. On 12/31/19X1, the market value of the portfolio is $490,000. On 2/6/19X2 securities costing $50,000 are sold for $54,000. On 12/31/19X2, the market value of the portfolio is $447,000. The journal entries follow:

1/1/19X1 Long-term Invest- ments	500,000	
Cash		500,000
5/12/19X1 Cash	15,000	
Dividend Revenue		15,000
12/31/19X1		
Unrealized Loss	10,000	
Allowance		10,000

The balance sheet presentation of the long-term investments is

Long-term Investments		$500,000
Less: Allowance		10,000
Net Balance		$490,000

If market value were $510,000 instead of $490,000, the securities portfolio would remain intact at $500,000 with the market value of $510,000 being disclosed.

2/2/19X2 Cash	54,000	
Long-term Investments		50,000
Gain		4,000
12/31/19X2		
Allowance	7,000	
Unrealized Loss		7,000

The balance sheet presentation of the long-term securities is

Long-term Investments		$450,000
Less: Allowance		3,000
Net Balance		$447,000

If instead the market value was $435,000, the entry would have been

Unrealized Loss	5,000	
Allowance		5,000

If instead the market value was $452,000, the entry would have been

Allowance	10,000	
Unrealized Loss		10,000

If two or more securities are purchased at one price, the cost is allocated among the securities based on their relative fair market value. In the exchange of one security for another, the new security received in the exchange is valued at its fair market value.

■ Example

Preferred stock costing $10,000 is exchanged for 1,000 shares of common stock having a market value of $15,000. The entry is

Investment in Common Stock	15,000	
Investment in Preferred Stock		10,000
Gain		5,000

A stock dividend involves a memo entry reflecting more shares at no additional cost. As a result, the cost per share decreases.

■ Example

Assume 50 shares at $12 per share for a total cost of $600 is owned. A 20% stock dividend is declared amounting to 10 shares. A memo entry is made reflecting the additional shares as follows:

Investment

50	$12	$600
10		0
60	($10)	$600

If 10 shares are later sold at $15, the entry is

Cash	150	
Long-term Investment		100
Gain		50

A stock split has the effect of increasing the shares and reducing the cost basis on a proportionate basis. A memo entry is made. Assume 100 shares costing $20 per share is owned. A 2 for 1 split would result in 200 shares at a cost per share of $10. Total cost remains at $2,000. *See also* Equity Method.

COST OF CAPITAL   This is defined as the rate of return that is necessary to maintain the market value of the firm (or price of the firm's stock). Financial managers must know the cost of capital (the minimum required rate of return) in (1) making capital budgeting decisions; (2) helping to establish the optimal capital structure; and (3) making decisions such as leasing, bond refunding, and working capital management. The cost of capital is computed as a weighted average of the various capital components, which are items on the right-hand side of the balance sheet, such as debt, preferred stock, common stock, and retained earnings.

Computing Individual Costs of Capital

Each element of capital has a component cost that is identified by the following:

k_i = before-tax cost of debt,

$k_d = K_i (1 - t)$ = after-tax cost of debt, where t = tax rate,

k_p = cost of preferred stock,

k_s = cost of retained earnings (or internal equity),

k_e = cost of external equity, or cost of issuing new common stock,

k_o = firm's overall cost of capital, or a weighted average cost of capital.

Cost of Debt

The before-tax cost of debt can be found by determining the internal rate of return (or yield to maturity) on the bond cash flows.

However, the following shortcut formula may be used for approximating the yield to maturity on a bond:

$$k_i = \frac{I + (M - V)/n}{(M + V)/2}$$

where I = annual interest payments in dollars,

M = par value, usually $1,000 per bond,

V = value or net proceeds from the sale of a bond,

n = term of the bond n years.

Since the interest payments are tax-deductible, the cost of debt must be stated on an after-tax basis. The after-tax cost of debt is

$$k_d = k_i (1 - t)$$

where t is the tax rate.

■ Example 1

Assume that the Carter company issues a $1,000, 8%, 20-year bond whose net proceeds are $940. The tax rate is 40%. Then, the before-tax cost of debt, k_i, is

$$k_i = \frac{I + (M - V)/n}{(M + V)/2}$$

$$= \frac{\$80 + (\$1,000 - \$940)/20}{(\$1,000 + \$940)/2}$$

$$= \frac{\$83}{\$970} = 8.56\%$$

Therefore, the after-tax cost of debt is

$$k_d = k_i(1 - t)$$
$$= 8.56\% (1 - 0.4) = 5.14\%$$

Cost of Preferred Stock

The cost of preferred stock, k_p, is found by dividing the annual preferred stock dividend, d_p, by the net proceeds from the sale of the preferred stock, p, as follows:

$$k_p = \frac{d_p}{p}$$

Since preferred stock dividends are not a tax-deductible expense, these dividends are paid out after taxes. Consequently, no tax adjustment is required.

■ Example 2

Suppose that the Carter company has preferred stock that pays a $13 dividend per share and sells for $100 per share in the market. The flotation (or underwriting) cost is 3% or $3 per share. Then the cost of preferred stock is

$$k_p = \frac{d_p}{p}$$
$$= \frac{\$13}{\$97} = 13.4\%$$

Cost of Equity Capital

The cost of common stock, k_e, is generally viewed as the rate of return investors require on a firm's common stock. Three techniques for measuring the cost of common stock equity capital are available: (1) the Gordon's growth model; (2) the capital asset pricing model (CAPM) approach; and (3) the bond plus approach.

The Gordon's Growth Model

The Gordon's model is

$$P_o = \frac{D_1}{r - g}$$

where P_o = value of common stock,
D_1 = dividend to be received in 1 year,
r = investor's required rate of return,
g = rate of growth (assumed to be constant over time).

Solving the model for r results in the formula for the cost of common stock:

$$r = \frac{D_1}{P_o} + g \quad \text{or} \quad k_e = \frac{D_1}{P_o} + g$$

Note that the symbol r is changed to k_e to show that it is used for the computation of cost of capital.

■ Example 3

Assume that the market price of the Carter Company's stock is $40. The dividend to be paid at the end of the coming year is $4 per share and is expected to grow at a constant annual rate of 6%. Then the cost of this common stock is

$$k_e = \frac{D_1}{P_o} + g = \frac{\$4}{\$40} + 6\% = 16\%$$

The cost of new common stock, or external equity capital, is higher than the cost of existing common stock because of the flotation costs involved in selling the *nw* common stock.

If f is flotation cost in percent, the formula for the cost of new common stock is

$$k_e = \frac{D_1}{P_o(1 - f)} + g$$

■ Example 4

Assume the same data as in Example 3, except the firm is trying to sell new issues of stock A and its flotation cost is 10%. Then:

$$k_e = \frac{D_1}{p_o(1 - f)} + g$$
$$= \frac{\$4}{\$40(1 - 0.1)} + 6\% = \frac{\$4}{\$36} + 6\%$$
$$= 11.11\% + 6\% = 17.11\%$$

The CAPM Approach

An alternative approach to measuring the cost of common stock is to use the CAPM, which involves the following steps:

1. Estimate the risk-free rate, r_f, generally taken to be the United States Treasury bill rate.
2. Estimate the stock's beta coefficient, b, which is an index of systematic (or nondiversifiable market) risk.
3. Estimate the rate of return on the market portfolio such as the Standard & Poor's 500 Stock Composite Index or Dow Jones 30 Industrials.
4. Estimate the required rate of return on the firm's stock, using the CAPM (or SML) equation:

$$k_e = r_f + b(r_m - r_f)$$

Again, note that the symbol r_j is changed to k_e.

■ Example 5

Assuming that r_f is 7%, b is 1.5, and r_m is 13%, then:

$$k_e = r_f + b(r_m - r_f) = 7\% + 1.5(13\% - 7\%) = 16\%$$

This 16% cost of common stock can be viewed as consisting of 7% risk-free rate plus a 9% risk premium, which indicates that the firm's stock price is 1.5 times more volatile than the market portfolio to the factors affecting nondiversifiable, or systematic, risk.

The Bond Plus Approach

Still another simple but useful approach to determining the cost of common stock is to add a risk premium to the firm's own cost of long-term debt, as follows:

$$k_e = \text{long-term bond rate} + \text{risk premium}$$
$$= k_i\,(1 - t) + \text{risk premium}$$

A risk premium of about 4% is commonly used with this approach.

■ Example 6

Using the data found in Example 1, the cost of common stock using the bond plus approach is

$$k_e = \text{long-term bond rate} + \text{risk premium}$$
$$= k_i\,(1 - t) + \text{risk premium}$$
$$= 5.14\% + 4\% = 9.14\%$$

Cost of Retained Earnings

The cost of retained earnings, k_s, is closely related to the cost of existing common stock, since the cost of equity obtained by retained earnings is the same as the rate of return investors require on the firm's common stock. Therefore:

$$k_e = k_s$$

Measuring the Overall Cost of Capital

The firm's overall cost of capital is the weighted average of the individual capital costs, with the weights being the proportions of each type of capital used. Let k_o be the overall cost of capital.

$$k_o = \sum \left(\begin{array}{c} \text{\% of total capital} \\ \text{structure supplied by} \\ \text{each type of capital} \end{array} \times \begin{array}{c} \text{Cost of capital} \\ \text{for each source} \\ \text{of capital} \end{array} \right)$$
$$= w_d \cdot k_d + w_p \cdot k_p + w_e \cdot k_e + w_s \cdot k_s$$

where w_d = % of total capital supplied by debt

w_p = % of total capital supplied by preferred stock.

w_e = % of total capital supplied by external equity,

w_s = % of total capital supplied by retained earnings (or internal equity).

The weights can be historical, target, or marginal.

Historical Weights

Historical weights are based on a firm's existing capital structure. The use of these weights is based on the assumption that the firm's existing capital structure is optimal and therefore should be maintained in the future. Two types of historical weights can be used—book value weights and market value weights.

Book Value Weights

The use of book value weights in calculating the firm's weighted cost of capital assumes that new financing will be raised using the same method the firm used for its present capital structure. The weights are determined by dividing the book value of each capital component by the sum of the book values of all the long-term capital sources. The computation of overall cost of capital is illustrated in the following example.

■ Example 7

Assume the following capital structure for the Carter Company:

Mortgage bonds ($1,000 par)	$20,000,000
Preferred stock ($100 par)	5,000,000
Common stock ($40 par)	20,000,000
Retained earnings	5,000,000
Total	$50,000,000

The book value weights and the overall cost of capital are computed as follows:

Source	Book Value	Weights	Cost	Weighted Cost
Debt	$20,000,000	40%	5.14%	2.06%
Preferred stock	5,000,000	10%	13.40%	1.34%
Common stock	20,000,000	40%	17.11%	6.84%
Retained earnings	5,000,000	10%	16.00%	1.60%
	$50,000,000	100%		11.84%

Overall cost of capital $= k_o = 11.84\%$

Market Value Weights

Market value weights are determined by dividing the market value of each source by the sum of the market values of all sources. The use of market value weights for computing a firm's weighted average cost of capital

is theoretically more appealing than the use of book value weights because the market values of the securities closely approximate the actual dollars to be received from their sale.

■ Example 8

In addition to the data from Example 7, assume that the security market prices are as follows:

$$\text{Mortgage bonds} = \$1,100 \text{ per bond}$$
$$\text{Preferred stock} = \$90 \text{ per share}$$
$$\text{Common stock} = \$80 \text{ per share}$$

The firm's number of securities in each category is

$$\text{Mortgage bonds} = \frac{\$20,000,000}{\$1,000} = 20,000$$

$$\text{Preferred stock} = \frac{\$5,000,000}{\$100} = 50,000$$

$$\text{Common stock} = \frac{\$20,000,000}{\$40} = 500,000$$

Therefore, the market value weights are

Source	Number of Securities	Price	Market Value
Debt	20,000	$1,100	$22,000,000
Preferred stock	50,000	90	4,500,000
Common stock	500,000.	80	40,000,000
			$66,500,000

The $40 million common stock value must be split in the ratio of 4 to 1 (the $20 million common stock versus the $5 million retained earnings in the original capital structure) since the market value of the retained earnings has been impounded into the common stock.

The firm's cost of capital is as follows:

Source	Market Value	Weights	Cost	Weighted Average
Debt	$22,000,000	33.08%	5.14%	1.70%
Preferred stock	4,500,000	6.77%	13.40%	0.91%
Common stock	32,000,000	48.12%	17.11%	8.23%
Retained earnings	8,000,000	12.03%	16.00%	1.92%
	$66,500,000	100.00%		12.76%

Overall cost of capital $= k_o = 12.76\%$

Target Weights

If the firm has determined the capital structure it believes most consistent with its goal, the use of that capital structure and associated weights is appropriate.

Marginal Weights

The use of marginal weights involves weighting the specific costs of various types of financing by the percentage of the total financing expected to be raised using each method. In using target weights, the firm is concerned with what it believes to be the optimal capital structure or target percentage. In using marginal weights, the firm is concerned with the actual dollar amounts of each type of financing to be needed for a given investment project.

▪ Example 9

The Carter Company is considering raising $8 million for plant expansion. Management

estimates using the following mix for financing this project:

Debt	$4,000,000	50%
Common stock	2,000,000	25%
Retained earnings	2,000,000	25%
	$8,000,000	100%

The company's cost of capital is computed as shown below.

Level of Financing and the Marginal Cost of Capital (MCC)

Because external equity capital has a higher cost than retained earnings due to flotation costs, the weighted cost of capital increases for each dollar of new financing. Therefore, the lower cost capital sources are used first. In fact, the firm's cost of capital is a function of the size of its total investment. A schedule or graph relating the firm's cost of capital to the level of new financing is called the weighted marginal cost of capital (MCC). Such a schedule is used to determine the

Source	Marginal Weights	Cost	Weighted Cost
Debt	50%	5.14%	2.57%
Common stock	25%	17.11%	4.28%
Retained earnings	25%	16.00%	4.00%
	100%		10.85%

Overall cost of capital $= k_o = 10.85\%$

discount rate to be used in the firm's capital budgeting process. The steps to be followed in calculating the firm's marginal cost of capital are summarized below.

1. Determine the cost and the percentage of financing to be used for each source of capital (debt, preferred stock, common stock equity).

2. Compute the break points on the MCC curve where the weighted cost will increase. The formula for computing the break points is

$$\text{Break point} = \frac{\begin{array}{c}\text{Maximum amount of the}\\ \text{lower cost source of capital}\end{array}}{\begin{array}{c}\text{Percentage of financing}\\ \text{provided by the source}\end{array}}$$

3. Calculate the weighted cost of capital over the range of total financing between break points.

4. Construct an MCC schedule or graph that shows the weighted cost of capital for each level of total new financing. This schedule will be used in conjunction with the firm's available investment opportunities schedule (IOS) in order to select the investments. As long as a project's IRR is greater than the marginal cost of new financing, the project should be accepted. Also, the point at which the IRR intersects the MCC gives the optimal capital budget.

■ Example 10

A firm is contemplating three investment projects, A, B, and C, whose initial cash outlays and expected IRR are shown below. IOS for these projects is

Project	Cash Outlay	IRR
A	$2,000,000	13%
B	$2,000,000	15%
C	$1,000,000	10%

If these projects are accepted, the financing will consist of 50% debt and 50% common stock. The firm should have $1.8 million in earnings available for reinvestment (internal common). The firm will consider only the effects of increases in the cost of common stock on its marginal cost of capital.

1. The costs of capital for each source of financing have been computed and are given following:

Source	Cost
Debt	5%
Common stock ($1.8 million)	15%
New common stock	19%

If the firm uses only internally generated common stock, the weighted cost of capital is

$k_o = \Sigma$ percentage of the total capital structure supplied by each source of capital $\times$ Cost of capital for each source

In this case the capital structure is composed of 50% debt and 50% internally generated common stock. Thus:

$$k_o = (0.5)5\% + (0.5)15\% = 10\%$$

If the firm uses only new common stock, the weighted cost of capital is

$$k_o = (0.5)5\% + (0.5)19\% = 12\%$$

Range of Total New Financing (in millions of dollars)	Type of Capital	Proportion	Cost	Weighted Cost
$0–$3.6	Debt	0.5	5%	2.5%
	Internal common	0.5	15%	7.5
				10.0%
$3.6 and up	Debt	0.5	5%	2.5%
	New common	0.5	19%	9.5
				12.0%

2. Next compute the break point, which is the level of financing at which the weighted cost of capital increases.

$$\text{Break point} = \frac{\text{Maximum amount of source of the lower cost source of capital}}{\text{Percentage financing provided by the source}}$$

$$= \frac{\$1,800,000}{0.5} = \$3,600,000$$

3. That is, the firm may be able to finance $3.6 million in new investments with internal common stock and debt without having to change the current mix of 50% debt and 50% common stock. Therefore, if the total financing is $3.6 million or less, the firm's cost of capital is 10%.

4. Construct the MCC schedule on the IOS graph to determine the discount rate to be used in order to decide in which project to invest and to show the firm's optimal capital budget. See Figure 1.

The firm should continue to invest up to the point where the IRR equals the MCC. From the graph in Figure 1, note that the firm should invest in projects B and A, since each IRR exceeds the marginal cost of capital. The firm should reject project C since its cost of capital is greater than the IRR. The optimal capital budget is $4 million,

since this is the sum of the cash outlay required for projects A and B.

COST OF PREDICTION ERRORS   There is always a cost involved with a failure to predict a certain variable accurately. For example, assume that a company has been selling a toy doll having a cost of $0.60 for $1.00 each. The fixed cost is $300. The company has no privilege of returning any unsold dolls. It has predicted sales of 2,000 units. However, unforeseen competition has reduced sales to 1,500 units. Then the cost of its prediction error—that is, its failure to predict demand accurately—would be calculated as follows:

1. Initial predicted sales = 2,000 units.
Optimal decision: purchase 2,000 units.
Expected net income = $500 [(2,000 units × $0.40 contribution) − $300 fixed costs]
2. Alternative parameter value = 1,500 units.
Optimal decision: purchase 1,500 units.
Expected net income = $300 [(1,500 units × $0.40 contribution) − $300 fixed costs]
3. Results of original decision under alternative parameter value.
Expected net income:
Revenue (1,500 units × $1.00) − Cost of dolls (2,000 units × $0.60) − $300 fixed costs = $1,500 − $1,200 − $300 = $0.
4. Cost of prediction error, (2) − (3) = $300.

COST-PLUS PRICING   This is a widely used pricing technique that involves: (1) defining an appropriate cost base and (2) adding the markup. There are two primary approaches to cost-plus pricing: the *absorption* or *full cost approach* and the *contribution approach*.

1. The absorption (or full) cost approach defines the cost base as the full unit manufacturing cost. Selling and administrative costs are provided for through the markup that is added

Figure 1 MCC Schedule and IOS Graph

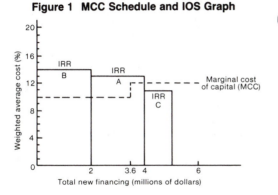

Total new financing (millions of dollars)

to the cost base. This approach is also called *full-cost-plus pricing*.

2. The contribution approach defines the cost base as the unit variable cost. Fixed costs are provided for through the markup that is added to this base. This approach is also called the *contribution approach to pricing*.

■ Example

XYZ Company has accumulated the following cost data on its regular product:

	Per Unit	Total
Direct materials	$6	
Direct labor	4	
Variable overhead	4	
Fixed overhead (based on 20,000 units)	6	$120,000
Variable selling and administrative expenses	1	
Fixed selling and administrative expenses (based on 20,000 units)	2	

Assume that in order to obtain its desired selling price, the company has a general policy of adding a markup equal to 50% of the full unit cost or 100% of the unit variable cost.

Under the absorption approach, the desired unit selling price is

Direct materials	$ 6	
Direct labor	4	
Factory overhead	10	($4 + $6)
Full (or absorption) cost per unit	$20	
Markup to cover selling and administrative expenses and desired profit —50% of full cost per unit	10	
Desired selling price	$30	

Using the contribution approach, the desired selling price is determined as follows:

Direct materials	$ 6
Direct labor	4
Variable costs (overhead, selling, and administration)	5
Variable cost per unit	$15
Markup to cover fixed costs and desired profit —100% of variable cost per unit	15
Desired selling price	$30

COST-VOLUME FORMULA   A cost-volume formula, also called a *flexible budget formula*, is a cost function in the form of

$$y = a + bx$$

where y = mixed (semivariable) costs to be broken up,

x = any given measure of activity such as machine or labor hours,

a = the fixed cost component,

b = the variable rate per unit of x.

For example, the cost-volume formula for factory overhead is $y = \$100 + \$5x$ where y = estimated factory overhead and x = direct labor hours, which means that the factory overhead is estimated to be $100 fixed, plus $5 per hour of direct labor. Cost accountants use the formula for *cost estimation* and *flexible budgeting* purposes. *See also* Cost Function; Flexible Budgets and Performance Reports.

COST-VOLUME-PROFIT (CVP) AND BREAK-EVEN ANALYSIS   CVP analysis, together with cost behavior information, helps managers perform many useful analyses. CVP analysis deals with how profit and costs change with a change in volume. More specifically, it looks at the effects on profits of changes in such factors as variable costs, fixed costs, selling prices, volume, and mix of products sold. By studying the relationships of costs, sales, and net income, management is better able to cope with many planning decisions. Break-even analysis, a branch of CVP analysis, determines the break-even sales, which is the level of sales where total costs equal total revenue.

Questions Answered by CVP Analysis

1. What sales volume is required to break even?
2. What sales volume is necessary in order to earn a desired profit?
3. What profit can be expected on a given sales volume?
4. How would changes in selling price, variable costs, fixed costs, and output affect profits?
5. How would a change in the mix of products sold affect the break-even and target income volume and profit potential?

Concepts of Contribution Margin (CM)

For accurate CVP analysis, a distinction must be made between costs as being either variable or fixed. Semivariable costs (or mixed costs) must be separated into their variable and fixed components.

In order to compute the break-even point and perform various CVP analyses, note the following important concepts.

Contribution margin (CM). The contribution margin is the excess of sales (S) over the variable costs (VC) of the product. It is the amount of money available to cover fixed costs (FC) and to generate profits. Symbolically, $CM = S - VC$.

Unit CM. The unit CM is the excess of the unit selling price (p) over the unit variable cost (v). Symbolically, unit $CM = p - v$.

CM ratio. The CM ratio is the contribution margin as a percentage of sales, that is

$$CM \text{ ratio} = \frac{CM}{S} = \frac{S - VC}{S} = 1 - \frac{VC}{S}$$

The *CM* ratio can also be computed using per-unit data as follows:

$$CM \text{ ratio} = \frac{\text{Unit } CM}{p} = \frac{p - v}{p} = 1 - \frac{v}{p}$$

Note that the *CM* ratio is 1 minus the variable cost ratio. For example, if variable costs account for 70% of the price, the *CM* ratio is 30%.

■ Example 1

To illustrate the various concepts of *CM*, consider the following data for Company Z:

	Per Unit	Total	Percentage
Sales (1,500 units)	$25	$37,500	100
Less: Variable costs	10	15,000	40
Contribution margin	$15	$22,500	60
Less: Fixed costs		15,000	
Net income		$ 7,500	

From the data just listed, *CM*, unit *CM*, and the *CM* ratio are computed as:

$$CM = S - VC = \$37,500 - \$15,000 = \$22,500$$
$$\text{Unit } CM = p - v = \$25 - \$10 = \$15$$
$$CM \text{ ratio} = \frac{CM}{S} = \frac{\$22,500}{\$37,500}$$
$$= 60\% \text{ or } 1 - \frac{VC}{S} = 1 - 0.4 = 0.6 = 60\%$$

Break-Even Analysis

The break-even point, the point of no profit and no loss, provides managers with insights into profit planning. It can be computed in three different ways:
1. The equation approach
2. The contribution approach
3. The graphical approach

The *equation approach* is based on the cost-volume equation, which shows the relationships among sales, variable and fixed costs, and net income: $S = VC + FC + $ Net income. At the break-even volume, $S = VC + FC + 0$.

Defining x = volume in units, this relationship can be rewritten in terms of x: $px = vx + FC$. To find the break-even point in units, simply solve the equation for x.

■ Example 2

In Example 1, $p = \$25$, $v = \$10$, and $FC = \$15,000$. Thus, the equation is

$$\$25x = \$10x + \$15,000$$
$$\$25x - \$10x = \$15,000$$
$$(\$25 - \$10)x = \$15,000$$
$$\$15x = \$15,000$$
$$x = \$15,000/\$15 = 1,000 \text{ units}$$

Therefore, Company Z breaks even at a sales volume of 1,000 units.

The *contribution margin approach*, another technique for computing the break-even point, is based on solving the cost-volume equation. Solving the equation $px = vx + FC$ for x yields:

$$x_{BE} = \frac{FC}{p - v}$$

where $p - v$ is the unit CM by definition, and x_{BE} = break-even unit sales volume. In words,

$$\text{Break-even point in units} = \frac{\text{Fixed costs}}{\text{Unit } CM}$$

If the break-even point is desired in terms of dollars, then:

Break-even point in dollars = Break-even point in units $\times$ unit sales price $= x_{BE} \cdot p$

Or, alternatively,

$$\text{Break-even point in dollars} = \frac{\text{Fixed costs}}{\text{CM ratio}}$$

■ Example 3

Using the same date given in Example 1, where unit $CM = \$25 - \$10 = \$15$ and CM ratio = 60%, we get:

Break-even point in units = $15,000/$15
  = 1,000 units

Break-even point in dollars = 1,000 units
  $\times \$25 = \$25,000$

or, alternatively:

$$\$15,000/0.6 = \$25,000$$

The *graphical approach* is based on the so-called break-even chart, as shown in Figure 1. Sales revenue, variable costs, and fixed costs are plotted on the horizontal axis. The break-even point is the point where the total sales revenue line intersects the total cost line. The chart can also effectively report profit potentials over a wide range of activity. The profit-volume $(P - V)$ chart, as shown in Figure 2, focuses more directly on how profits vary with changes in volume. Profits are plotted on the vertical axis, whereas units of output are shown on the horizontal axis. Note that the slope of the chart is the unit CM.

Figure 1 Break-Even Chart

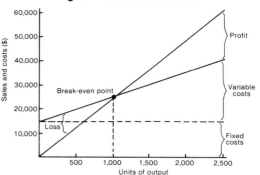

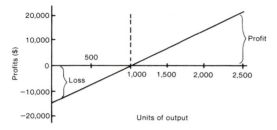

Figure 2　Profit-Volume (P/V) Chart

Determination Target Income Volume

Besides being able to determine the break-even point, *CVP* analysis determines the sales required to attain a particular income level or target net income. There are two ways target net income can be expressed:

　　Case 1—as a specific dollar amount.
　　Case 2—as a percentage of sales.

　　Case 1—as a specific dollar amount. The cost-volume equation specifying target net income is

$$px = vx + FC + \text{Target income}$$

Solving the equation for x yields:

$$x_{TI} = \frac{FC + \text{Target income}}{p - v}$$

where x_{TI} = sales volume required to achieve a given target income.

　　In words,

Target income sales volume
$$= \frac{\text{Fixed costs plus target income}}{\text{Unit } CM}$$

　　Case 2—specifying target income as a percentage of sales, the cost-volume equation is

$$px = vx + FC + \%(px)$$

Solving this for x yields:

$$x_{TI} = \frac{FC}{p - v - \%(p)}$$

In words,

Target income sales volume
$$= \frac{\text{Fixed costs}}{\text{Unit } CM - \% \text{ of unit sales price}}$$

■ Example 4

Using the same data given in Example 1, assume that Company Z wishes to attain:

　　• Case 1—a target income of $15,000 before tax
　　• Case 2—a target income of 20% sales

In Case 1, target income sales volume (in units) required would be

$$x_{TI} = \frac{FC + \text{Target income}}{p - v}$$
$$= \frac{\$15,000 + \$15,000}{\$25 - \$10} = 2,000 \text{ units}$$

In Case 2, the target income volume required would be

$$x_{TI} = \frac{FC}{p - v - \%(p)}$$
$$= \frac{\$15,000}{\$15 - (20\%)(\$25)}$$
$$= \frac{\$15,000}{\$15 - \$5} = 1,500 \text{ units}$$

To prove:

Sales (1,500 units)	$37,500	(100%)
VC (1,500 units)	−15,000	
CM	$22,500	(60%)
FC	−15,000	
Net income	$ 7,500	(20%)

Impact of Income Taxes

If target income is given on an after-tax basis, the target income volume formula becomes:

$$\text{Target income volume} = \frac{\text{Fixed costs} + [\text{Target after-tax income}/(1\text{-tax rate})]}{\text{Unit } CM}$$

■ Example 5

Assume in Example 1 that Company Z wants to achieve an after-tax income of $6,000. An income tax is levied at 40%. Then:

Target income volume

$$= \frac{\$15,000 + [\$6,000/(1 - 0.4)]}{\$15}$$

$$= \frac{\$15,000 + \$10,000}{\$15} = 1,667 \text{ units}$$

Margin of Safety

The margin of safety is a measure of difference between the budgeted level of sales and the break-even sales. It is the amount by which sales revenue may drop before losses begin, and is expressed as a percentage of budgeted sales:

Margin of safety

$$= \frac{\text{Budgeted sales} - \text{Break-even sales}}{\text{Budgeted sales}}$$

The margin of safety is often used as a measure of risk. The larger the ratio, the safer is the situation, since there is less risk of reaching the break-even point.

■ Example 6

Assume Company Z projects sales of $30,000 with a break-even sales level of $25,000. The expected margin of safety is

$$\frac{\$30,000 - \$25,000}{\$30,000} = 16.7\%$$

Some Applications of CVP Analysis and What-If Analysis

The concepts of contribution margin have many applications in profit planning and short-term decision making. Some applications are illustrated in Examples 7 to 11 using the same data as in Example 1.

■ Example 7

Recall from Example 1 that Company Z has a *CM* of 60% and fixed costs of $15,000 per period. Assume that the company expects sales to go up by $10,000 for the next period. How much will income increase?

Using the *CM* concepts, we can quickly compute the impact of a change in sales on profits. The formula for computing the impact is

Change in net income

$$= \text{Dollar change in sales} \times CM \text{ ratio}$$

Thus, in this question,

Increase in net income = $10,000 × 60% = $6,000

Therefore, the income will go up by $6,000, assuming there is no change in fixed costs.

If we are given the change in sales in units instead of dollars, then the formula becomes:

Change in net income

$$= \text{Change in unit sales} \times \text{Unit } CM$$

■ Example 8

What before-tax income is expected on sales of $47,500? The answer is the difference between the *CM* and the fixed costs:

CM: $47,500 × 60%	$28,500
Less: Fixed costs	15,000
Net income	$13,500

■ Example 9

Company Z is considering increasing the advertising budget by $5,000, which would increase sales revenue by $8,000. Should the advertising budget be increased?

The answer is no, since the increase in the *CM* is less than the increased cost:

Increase in *CM*: $8,000 × 60%	$4,800
Increase in advertising	5,000
Decrease in net income	$ (200)

■ Example 10

Company Z's sales manager is considering a $3,000 increase in sales salaries. What additional sales are required to cover the higher cost?

The increase in fixed cost must be matched by an equal increase in *CM*:

Increase in *CM* = Increase in fixed cost

0.60 sales = $3,000

Sales = $5,000

■ Example 11

Consider the original data. Assume again that Company Z is currently selling 1,500 units per period. In an effort to increase sales, management is considering cutting its unit price by $5 and increasing the advertising budget by $1,000. If these two steps are taken, management feels that unit sales will go up by 60%. Should the two steps be taken?

A $5 reduction in the selling price will cause the unit *CM* to decrease from $15 to $10. Thus:

Proposed *CM*: 2,400 units × $10	$24,000
Present *CM*: 1,500 units × $15	22,500
Increase in *CM*	$ 1,500
Increase in advertising outlay	1,000
Increase in net income	$ 500

The answer, therefore, is yes.

Sales Mix Analysis

Break-even and cost-volume-profit analysis require some additional computations and assumptions when a company produces and sells more than one product. Different selling prices and different variable costs result in different unit *CM* and *CM* ratios. As a result, break-even points vary with the relative proportions of the products sold, called the sales mix. In break-even and CVP analysis, it is necessary to predetermine the sales mix and then compute a weighted average *CM*. It is also necessary to assume that the sales mix does not change for a specified period. The break-even formula for the company as a whole is

$$\text{Company-wide break-even in units (or in dollars)} = \frac{\text{Fixed costs}}{\text{Average unit } CM \text{ (or average } CM \text{ ratio)}}$$

■ Example 12

Assume that Company X has two products with the following *CM* data:

	A	B
Selling price	$15	$10
Variable cost	12	5
Unit *CM*	$ 3	$ 5
Sales mix	60%	40%
Fixed costs	$76,000	

The weighted average unit *CM* = ($3)(0.6) + ($5)(0.4) = $3.80. Therefore, the company's break-even point in units is

$$\$76,000 \,/\, \$3.80 = 20,000 \text{ units}$$

which is divided as follows:

A: 20,000 units × 60% = 12,000 units
B: 20,000 units × 40% = 8,000
                                      20,000 units

■ Example 13

Assume that Company Y produces and sells three products with the following data:

	A	B	C	Total
Sales	$30,000	$60,000	$10,000	$100,000
Sales mix	30%	60%	10%	100%
Less: VC	24,000	40,000	5,000	69,000
CM	$ 6,000	$20,000	$ 5,000	$ 31,000
CM ratio	20%	33⅓%	50%	31%

Total fixed costs are $18,600.
The *CM* ratio for Company Y is $31,000/$100,000 = 31%. Therefore, the break-even point in dollars is

$$\$18,600/0.31 = \$60,000$$

which will be split in the mix ratio of 3:6:1 to give us the following break-even points for the individual products A, B, and C:

A: $60,000 × 30% = $18,000
B: $60,000 × 60% = 36,000
C: $60,000 × 10% =   6,000
                              $60,000

One of the most important assumptions underlying CVP analysis in a multiproduct firm is that the sales mix will not change during the planning period. But if the sales mix changes, the break-even point will also change.

■ Example 14

Assume that total sales from Example 13 remain unchanged at $100,000 but that a shift is expected in mix from product B to product C, as shown below.

Note that the shift in sales mix toward the more profitable line C has caused the *CM* ratio for the company as a whole to go up from 31% to 36%. The new break-even point will be $18,600/0.36 = $51,667. The break-even dollar volume has decreased from $60,000 to $51,667.

Break-Even and CVP Analysis Assumptions

The CVP models are subject to several limiting assumptions:
1. The behavior of both sales revenue and expenses is linear throughout the entire relevant range of activity.
2. There is only one product or a constant sales mix.
3. Volume is the only factor affecting variable costs.
4. Inventories do not change significantly from period to period.

CRITICAL PATH METHOD   CPM is a technique for project management that uses a single time estimate for each activity, rather than three time estimates (optimistic, most likely, and pessimistic). The primary objective of CPM is to identify the critical path for a project. *See also* Program Evaluation and Review Technique (PERT).

CURRENCY FUTURES CONTRACT   The holder of the contract has the right to a given amount of foreign currency at a later date. Standardized contracts exist, and there is a secondary market. The contract is expressed in terms of dollars or cents per unit of the related foreign currency. The delivery date is usually no more than 1 year.

Trading Units of Different Currencies

Currency	Trading Unit
British pound	25,000
Canadian dollar	100,000
Swiss franc	125,000
West German mark	125,000

Currency futures may be used for hedging or speculation purposes. A banker might hedge in a currency to lock in the best money exchange possible.

■ Example

A financial manager agrees to obtain pounds in 6 months. If the pound declines relative to the dollar, there is less value to the manager. To hedge his exposure, the manager can sell a futures contract in pounds by going short. If the pound declines in value, there will be a gain in the futures contract offsetting the loss when the manager receives the pounds.

	A	B	C	Total
Sales	$30,000	$30,000	$40,000	$100,000
Sales mix	30%	30%	40%	100%
Less: VC	24,000	20,000*	20,000	64,000
CM	$ 6,000	$10,000	$20,000	$ 36,000
CM ratio	20%	33⅓%	50%	36%

* $20,000 = $30,000 × 66⅔%

■ Example

There is a standardized contract of 50,000 pounds. In April, a currency futures contract is bought for delivery in August. The contract price is $1 equals 2.5 pounds. The contract's value is $20,000, and the margin requirement is $3,000. The pound becomes more valuable in the currency market equaling 2 pounds to $1. Thus, the value of the contract increases to $25,000, providing a return of 167%. In the event of a weakening pound, a loss would have been incurred.

CURRENT SERVICE COST   This is the actuarial present value of benefits derived from the pension benefit formula for employee services rendered in the current year. It is a component of pension expense. *See also* Pension Plans.

CURTAILMENT IN PENSION PLAN   An occurrence significantly *reducing* employees' future service years or eliminating for many the accrual of benefits for future services. *See also* Pension Plans.

D

DATA BASE MANAGEMENT SYSTEMS (DBMS)

A data base package is an organized collection of readily accessible related information used on a recurring basis by the financial manager and/or accounting practitioner. There are numerous examples where this package can be used (e.g., accounts receivable and inventory monitoring). DBMS acts as an administration aid by enabling the accessing of data items in many different, logically related files (e.g., a master file contains permanent information updated by transactional file data). Data base systems also provide answers to numerous questions from the same data file. The DBMS integrates data in one place so that it can be shared by all systems. Thus, any change automatically can impact all relevant and interrelated systems. It also allows cross-referencing of data among files to eliminate data repetition.

Data base programs allow practitioners to enter, manipulate, retrieve, display, extract, select, sort, edit, and index data. DBMS packages define the structure of collected data, design screen formats for input information, handle files, and generate reports. In creating a data base, the user has to name the fields and describe the type of data in each field. DBMS permits the creation of

financial statement formats and the performance of numerical calculations. In essence, it is an electronic filing cabinet providing a common core of information accessible by a program. DBMS allows the accountant or auditor to formulate custom programs and applications by stipulating what data must be entered into the microcomputer and what should be done to it to accomplish the desired output.

Data base packages can be used for specific purposes and general applications. The first may only be utilized for the particular objective for which it was designed (e.g., accounting module for accounts receivable). The second type lets the CPA set up the objective and design of the data base. The types of general application data base programs include file managers and relational data base systems. Differences primarily exist in the capacity to use information from more than one file concurrently. File managers can support many individual files, but only one file may be accessed and manipulated at a time. A File Management System is software permitting the user to describe file, processing, and report formats to produce a data processing system without the need to write computer programs. Relational

Exhibit 1 Hierarchical Data Base Model for Staff Assignments

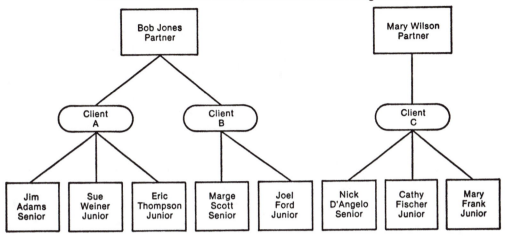

data bases can access data from two or more files concurrently. This ability varies depending on the particular program.

Data Base Models

Data bases relate data sets into one of three models comprising hierarchical, network, and relational.

In a hierarchical data base manager (tree-structured), one data set is subservient to another (i.e., parent–child relationship). For example, data may be put in a standard input form and then taken from that form to prepare reports. The finalized reports represent modifications of data included in one master information form. A filer puts data in any order desired. Here, data are stored in discrete records. A real-life example is a "tree" model for staff assignments for audit engagements. As can be seen in Exhibit 1, a one-to-one relationship exists. That is one path is followed by the individual data elements.

Modification of the hierarchical data base to include multipath relationships converts

Exhibit 2 Network Data Base Model for Staff Assignments

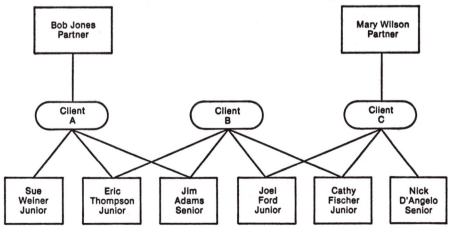

Exhibit 3 Partial Relational Data Base Model for Staff Assignments

COLUMNS

	Partner	Client	Staff Member
	Bob Jones	A	Jim Adams
	Bob Jones	B	Jim Adams
	Bob Jones	C	Jim Adams
	Mary Wilson	A	Jim Adams
R	Mary Wilson	B	Jim Adams
O	Mary Wilson	C	Jim Adams
W	Bob Jones	A	Sue Weiner
S	Bob Jones	B	Sue Weiner
	Bob Jones	C	Sue Weiner
	Mary Wilson	A	Sue Weiner
	Mary Wilson	B	Sue Weiner
	Mary Wilson	C	Sue Weiner
	, ,	,	, ,
	, ,	,	, ,
	, ,	,	, ,

the DBMS into a network data base. Such a relationship exists in Exhibit 2.

A relational data base manager has data sets of information in a table of rows and columns (matrix) with no parent–child relationship. Information is stored in two-dimensional data sets or tables similar to a traditional file-processing system, and there is an integration of several different files. The reports produced from this can have greater complexity and they could be more useful than is the case with a hierarchical system. A relational data base allows for the access of data fields by enabling the accountant to ignore the traditional one-to-one relationship by permitting access to a particular grid or cell. For example, if a relational data base includes first and last names of clients as well as their area codes, telephone numbers, street address, city, state, and zip code, data can be accessed by stipulating any one of the parameters for selection. Exhibit 3 illustrates a partial relational data base system for staff assignments.

dBASE III+ ™, by Ashton-Tate, is one of the more powerful and popular data base models that makes use of this type of system.

Features

An appraisal should be made by the accountant or financial person of a particular DBMS package in terms of

• Compatibility with other packages and applications in terms of ascertaining whether data formatted with other data base packages can be imported and translated into the format your program utilizes. Also, how many other programs can the DBMS package exchange data with?

• Commands that make sense in describing the operation to be performed.

• Search capabilities.

• The number of fields that can be edited at a time.

• Permitting an enumerated field that allows for specifying all of a field's possible values.

• Flexibility in field type and record structure (i.e., adding or deleting fields even subsequent to entering information on records).

• Types and limitations of data field. It

is crucial that the program have the ability to handle the types of fields the practitioner requires and that the fields are sufficient to permit expansion should the need arise.

• Ability to hide selected facts.

• Ability to generate derived or computed fields. A derived field is one that performs mathematical calculations on data sorted in other fields.

• Processing of multiple files simultaneously.

• Available formats for reporting purposes.

• Report features in terms of graphics and formatting.

• Reformatting ease (allowing for changing a format at any time).

• Error-catching ability (i.e., existence of unique fields to prevent erroneous duplication of records).

• Error messages along with an indexed listing of all errors at the end of the manual.

• Number and size of records that can be contained in one file, including maximum records to be accommodated. Care must be exercised in selection to ensure that the program is capable of handling more records than your present needs mandate. For instance, if the DBMS is to be used for billing, the maximum number of records capable of being accommodated should be greatly in excess of your present client or customer list.

• Linkage of files, where a change in one automatically changes another.

• Creation of a new data base representing a subset of a parent file.

• Ability to peek into unopened files of the data base. For example, while looking at the inventory file, a view command allows for the calling of an unrelated file onto the screen.

• Capability to sort data. Sorting can be on the basis of numeric or alphabetic relationships. More sophisticated programs like dBASE III+™ have the ability to sort data utilizing a "conditional sort" command. For example, client customers can be selected

for accounts receivable confirmations "if" their balances exceed a prescribed limit. Sorting based on "multiple key fields" is a further extension of the capabilities of many DBMS. Thus, telephone numbers can be arranged in ascending or descending order, firstly by area code and then by the first three digits of the number.

• Calculational ability, including present value, future value, growth rate, log, exponential notation, square root, and absolute value. If a derivation is changed, the program automatically recomputes the data throughout the data base.

• Ability to work with many files at once.

• Available templates for different applications. A template is a preformatted setup that comes ready for use. The practitioner merely inputs data relevant to a specific application. For example, a template may exist for the maintenance of perpetual inventory records relevant to fixed asset additions and deletions.

• Window features. This enables the accountant to simultaneously use and view different files and/or programs. This is especially useful for integrating data base files with word processing applications.

Applications

Financial managers and accountants may utilize DMBS for the following applications:

• Retrieving information based on varied criteria. In a general ledger formatted data base, the accountant has the ability to recall or retrieve information based upon varied criteria; that is, based upon (a) the date a check was issued, (b) the payee, (c) the amount paid, or (d) the account to which an amount was posted. If the "payee" criteria is selected, a listing may be generated of all checks written over a specified period. This assists in the audit attest function.

• Searching for accounting records having a key word or amount such as listing accounts that are 90 days past due.

• Establishing upper and lower limits. This may be utilized by clients in establishing credit limits. From the accountant's point of view, this can assist in the selection of accounts receivable to be confirmed positively and negatively. Similarly, assistance is available for the confirmation of other accounts, such as accounts payable.

• Field calculations. A client's DBMS with this ability facilitates the footings and extensions of inventory listings. Further, in applying the lower-of-cost-or-market rule, field calculations can prove most useful.

• Existence of utility functions to assist accountants in conducting common functions. A good data base program should provide the more common utility functions so as to enable the practitioner to (a) rename existing files without destroying its contents, (b) copy or transport the contents of a particular file to another file, and (c) erase files permanently.

• Asking what-if questions and their effect on client financial data. This feature, most commonly found in spreadsheets, enables the practitioner to recalculate the effects of changing one or more variables. One application is in the use of forecasting.

• Audit aspects such as performing entry validation procedures. Also, it can be used in analytical review in terms of performing ratio analysis of selected accounts of interest to the auditor. A data base showing a schedule of expenses and revenue by type and data may be made for audit analysis, where warranted. Further, asset listings may be made to evaluate the adequacy of insurance coverage.

• Preparation of listings by client, customer, supplier, and so on. The tax practitioner utilizing a relational data base can format and generate schedules and reports to control the preparation of client tax returns by fiscal year-end, initial due date, and due date after any extensions. Tax returns may be for federal and local reporting, including payroll tax returns.

• Client mailing list along with telephone numbers.

• Payroll. Users of DBMS may keep track of all payroll information required by both federal and state governments.

• Inventory management. Keeping track of individual items by description, vendor, or price is no longer an involved process. Determination of reorder points, possibly using the economic order quantity (EOQ), can be built into data base application. Obsolescence can be determined when the inventory control system generates lists of items based upon given criteria.

• General ledger. Perhaps the most useful application of DBMS programs for the accountant is the preparation of client general ledgers.

• Tax preparation and planning. A data base may be established for tax information of a repetitive nature that will be used for several years. An example is the management of a stock portfolio involving acquisition dates and cost. Tax projections may be used to minimize the overall tax liability of the client considering different variables. For example, projections may be made for oil and gas shelters and the timing of the sale of securities.

DEBT FINANCING This may be short-term, intermediate-term, and long-term. Short-term and intermediate-term financing sources include trade credit, bank loan, finance company loan, commercial paper, inventory financing, and leasing. Long-term financing includes the issuance of mortgages and bonds.

Trade Credit

Trade credit is the amount owed to suppliers on account. Advantages are easy to obtain, no collateral is required, there is little or no interest, and trade creditors are more lenient than other creditors. However, trade credit is limited to certain types of items. Further, the opportunity cost of not taking a discount on early payment should be determined, since it may be very costly.

■ Example

A $10,000 purchase is made on terms of 2/20, net/60. The opportunity cost of not taking the discount is

$$\frac{\text{Discount foregone}}{\text{Proceeds from use of}} \times \frac{360}{\text{Days use of the money}}$$

$$\frac{\$200}{\$9,800} \times \frac{360}{40} = 18.37\%$$

You could most likely borrow at a lower rate than 18.37% in order to take advantage of the discount.

Bank Loan

Types of Bank Credit

• *Unsecured loans*—recommended for financing projects that have immediate cash flow or for interim financing for a long-term project. *Suggestion*: Use for seasonal cash shortfalls, desired inventory buildups, or any situation in which you need immediate cash flow and can repay the loan quickly or shortly obtain longer term financing. Disadvantages are its short term, higher interest rate, and the fact that it is repaid in a lump sum.

• *Line of credit*—a continuing agreement for loans up to a specified amount. *Recommendation*: Use if you work on large individual projects for a long time period and obtain minimal or no payments until the job is completed. Advantages are easy access to funds in tight money periods and ability to borrow only when needed, with quick repayment possibility. Disadvantages are that collateral is required and there are greater limitations (e.g., restrictions on capital expenditures). Determine whether your line of credit is adequate for your present and immediate future needs.

• *Revolving credit*—notes are short term (typically 90 days). You may renew the loan or borrow additional funds up to a maximum amount. Advantages are readily available credit and fewer restrictions relative to the line-of-credit agreement. A disadvantage is the bank restrictions.

• *Intermediate-term loans*—recommended for financing fixed assets, acquiring another business, and to retire long-term debt. An advantage is that they may be adjusted more easily than a bond indenture or a preferred stock agreement. Disadvantages are possible collateral requirements, restrictive covenants (e.g., dividend restrictions), and periodic submission of financial reports.

• *Installment loans*—necessitate monthly payments. As the loan principal is lowered, refinancing may take place at lower interest rates. *Suggestion*: Tailor the loan to satisfy seasonal financing requirements.

The cost of a short-term loan equals

$$\frac{\text{Interest}}{\text{Proceeds Received}}$$

A bank typically discounts a loan, meaning that interest is deducted from the face of the loan to obtain the proceeds. A compensating balance also reduces the proceeds. As a result, the effective (real) interest rate on the loan exceeds the face interest, since the proceeds received are less than the face of the loan.

■ Example

You take out a $320,000, 1-year, 11% loan with a compensating balance of 15%. The loan is made on a discount basis. The effective interest rate is

$$\frac{11\% \times \$320,000}{\$236,800^*} = \frac{\$35,200}{\$236,800} = 14.9\%$$

* Proceeds received equals

Face of loan	$320,000
Less:	
Interest	(35,200)
Compensating balance (15% × $320,000)	(48,000)
Proceeds	$236,800

Vital Question: If your bank chose to call your demand loans, could you obtain alternative financing without impairing your business?

Finance Company Loan

If you cannot obtain bank financing because of credit risks, you may be able to borrow from a finance company. Such borrowings are secured (collateral usually exceeds the loan balance) and they have higher interest rates than bank loans.

Commercial Paper

Commercial paper is unsecured and represents short-term notes issued by the highest quality companies. Advantages are that the interest rate is lower than the bank borrowing rate and no security is required.

■ Example

You need $300,000 for the month of November. Your options are
1. A 1-year line of credit for $300,000 with a bank. The commitment fee is 0.5%, and the interest charge on the used funds is 12%.
2. Issue 2-month commercial paper at 10% interest. Because the funds are required for only 1 month, the excess funds ($300,000) can be invested in 8% marketable securities for December. The total transaction fee for the marketable securities is 0.3%.
1. The line of credit costs:

Commitment fee for unused period	
(0.005) (300,000) (11/12)	$1,375
Interest for 1 month	
(0.12) (300,000) (1/12)	3,000
Total cost	$4,375

2. The commercial paper costs:

Interest charge (0.10) (300,000) (2/12)	$5,000
Transaction fee (0.003) (300,000)	900
Less:	
Interest earned on marketable securities	
(0.08) (300,000) (1/12)	(2,000)
Total cost	$3,900

Note: The commerical paper arrangement is less costly.

Inventory Financing

Inventory financing usually occurs when you have already made full use of your ability to borrow on receivables. It requires that inventory be marketable, have a high turnover rate, not be perishable, and not be subject to rapid obsolescence. Raw materials and finished goods will typically be financed at about 75% of their value. The interest rate is typically several points in excess of the prime interest rate.

■ Example

You need $500,000 for a 3-month period. An insurance company has agreed to lend you the money at an 8% per annum interest rate using the inventory as collateral. A field warehouse agreement would be used, costing $1,300 per month.

For 3 months:

$$\text{Effective interest rate} =$$

$$\frac{(3 \times 1,300) + (0.08 \times 500,000 \times 3/12)}{500,000}$$

$$\frac{13,900}{500,000} = 0.028$$

For 1 year:

$$0.028 \ (3 \text{ months}) \times 4 = 0.112$$

Leasing

Advantages of leasing are the absence of an immediate substantial cash payment, the possibility of a bargain purchase option, the availability of the lessor's service capability, fewer financing restrictions, protection from technological obsolescence, and the fact that the obligation to pay does not necessarily have to be reported as a liability on the balance sheet. Disadvantages of leasing are higher cost than outright purchase, the necessity of paying current prices at lease termination to enter into a new lease or acquire property, and having to use property no longer usable or suitable.

Comparing Short-term to Long-term Financing

Short-term financing is easier to arrange, has lower cost, and is more flexible than long-term financing. However, short-term financing makes the borrower more susceptible to interest rate changes, requires refinancing more quickly, and is more difficult to repay. *Recommendation*: Use short-term financing as additional working capital, to finance short-lived assets, or as interim financing on long-term projects. Long-term financing is more suitable to finance long-term assets or construction projects.

Advice: If there are financial problems, attempt to refinance short-term loans on a long-term basis, such as by extending the maturity date.

Mortgages

Mortgages are notes payable to banks, which are secured by real property and are used to finance long-term requirements (e.g., buying fixed assets, plant construction and renovation). Positive aspects are attractive interest rates, less financing restrictions than other long-term sources, long payment schedules, and availability. On the negative side, there is a collateral requirement.

Bonds

In a private placement, bonds are issued to a few investors (typically institutional investors) without a public offering. Advantages are the elimination of underwriter fees and no need for SEC registration.

Reasons to issue debt rather than equity securities are the tax deductibility of interest and the fact that you will be paying back in cheaper dollars during inflation, there is no dilution of voting control, and flexibility in financing is possible due to a call provision

in the bond indenture. Drawbacks are the required repayment of principal and fixed interest charges and indenture restrictions.

Factors Favoring Long-Term Debt Issuance

- High profits
- Stability in revenue and earnings
- Low debt to equity ratio
- Presently depressed market price of stock

Financial leverage should be employed when the entity's profits are sufficient to meet preferred stock dividends. However, when the debt position is high, the business should attempt to reduce other risks (e.g., product risk). A bond issue usually requires the establishment of a sinking fund. *Recommendation*: If you expect declining interest rates in the future, it is advisable to include a call provision.

Convertible bonds offer several positive aspects including marketability, lower interest rates, and nonrepayment because of conversion to stock.

Warning: If the maturity structure of debt requires large repayments to be due, stock issuance is recommended.

DECISION MAKING UNDER CERTAINTY A management accountant or financial manager is often faced with a decision situation where for each decision alternative there is only one event and therefore only one outcome for each action.

■ Example

Assume there is only one possible event for the two possible actions: "Buy" a facility at a future cost of $5 per unit for 10,000 units, or "lease" it at a future cost of $4.80 for the same number of units. We can set up the following table:

Actions	Possible Outcome With Certainty
Buy	$50,000 (10,000 units × $5)
Lease	48,000 (10,000 units × $4.80)

Since there is only one possible outcome for each action (with certainty) the decision is obviously to choose the action that will result in the most desirable outcome (least cost); that is, to "lease."

DECISION MAKING UNDER UNCERTAINTY

When decisions are made in a world of uncertainty, it is often helpful to make the following computations:

1. Expected value
2. Standard deviation
3. Coefficient of variation

Expected Value

Expected value is a weighted average using the probabilities as weights. For decisions involving *uncertainty*, the concept of expected value provides a rational means for selecting the best course of action. The expected value ($E(x)$) is found by multiplying the probability of each outcome by its *payoff*.

$$E(x) = \sum_{i=1} x_i p_i$$

where x_i is the outcome for ith possible event and p_i is the probability of occurrence of that outcome.

■ Example 1

Consider two investment proposals, A and B, with the following probability distribution of cash flows in each of the next 5 years:

Cash Inflows

Probability	(0.2)	(0.3)	(0.4)	(0.1)
A	$50	200	300	400
B	$100	150	250	850

The expected value of the cash inflow in proposal A is

$50(0.2) + 200(0.3) + 300(0.4) + 400(0.1) = $230

The expected value of the cash inflow in proposal B is

$100(0.2) + 150(0.3) + 250(0.4) + 850(0.1) = $250

Standard Deviation

Standard deviation is a measure of the dispersion of a probability distribution. It is the square root of the mean of the squared deviations from the *expected value E(x)*.

$$\sigma = \sqrt{\Sigma (x_i - E(x))^2 p_i}$$

It is commonly used as an absolute measure of risk. The higher the standard deviation, the higher the risk.

■ Example 2

Consider the two investment proposals, A and B, in Example 1.

The standard deviations of proposals A and B are computed as follows:

$$\text{For A:} = \sqrt{\begin{array}{l}(\$50 - 230)^2 (0.2) + (200 - 230)^2 (0.3) \\ + (300 - 230)^2 (0.4) + (400 - 230)^2 \\ (0.1) = \$107.70\end{array}}$$

$$\text{For B:} = \sqrt{\begin{array}{l}(\$100 - 250)^2 (0.2) + (150 - 250)^2 (0.3) \\ + (250 - 250)^2 (0.4) + (850 - 250)^2 \\ (0.1) = \$208.57\end{array}}$$

Proposal B is more risky than proposal A, since its standard deviation is greater.

Coefficient of Variation

Coefficient of variation is a measure of relative dispersion, or relative risk. It is computed by dividing the standard deviation (σ) by the expected value $E(x)$.

■ Example 3

From Examples 1 and 2, we note:

Proposal	Expected Value	Standard Deviation
A	$230	$107.70
B	250	208.57

The coefficient of variation for each proposal is

For A: $107.70/$230 = 0.47

For B: $208.57/$250 = 0.83.

Therefore, because the coefficient is a relative measure of risk, B is considered more risky than A.

DECISION SUPPORT SYSTEMS (DSS) DSS software furnishes support to the accountant in the decision-making processes. They analyze a specific situation and can be modified as the practitioner wishes. Models are constructed and decisions analyzed. Planning and forecasting are facilitated.

Financial modeling systems such as Execum's IFPS™ (Interactive Financial Planning System) and Social Systems' SIMPLAN™ are widely used for decision support. They have a column and row format similar to a spreadsheet, but they are really multifile systems. It is important to note that financial modeling software is superior to spreadsheets because they can carry out complex modeling and evaluation. More specifically, they are designed to

• Perform what-if analysis. That is, they provide a picture of the current financial position and allow the accountant to see the effect of changes in variables upon outcome.

• Perform goal seeking (opposite of what-if) to calculate the effect required to generate a specific outcome in another variable (e.g., how much should service A be billed out to earn a certain net income?).

• Evaluate risk of the alternatives being considered.

• Perform statistical functions, including regression analysis, trend analysis, and econometrics.

• Generate graphics to illustrate accounting and financial matters.

There are special purpose packages that are widely used for decision support. They include

• Infordata Systems' INQUIRE™ for query, data retrieval, and report generation.

• SPSS™ (Statistical Package for Social Scientists) and SAS™ (Statistical Analysis

System) for extensive statistical analysis and forecasting.

• Various packages handling inventory planning, material requirement planning (MRP), project management, and linear programming. *See also* Management Information System.

DECISION THEORY Although the statistics such as expected value and standard deviation are essential for choosing the best course of action under uncertainty, the decision problem can best be approached using what is called decision theory. Decision theory is a systematic approach to making decisions especially under uncertainty. Decision theory utilizes an organized approach such as a *decision matrix (payoff table)*, which is characterized by: (1) the *row* representing a set of alternative *courses of action* available to the decision maker; (2) the *column* representing the *state of nature* or conditions that are likely to occur that the decision maker has no control over; and (3) the *entries* in the body of the table representing the outcome of the decision, known as *payoffs*, which may be in the form of costs, revenues, profits, or cash flows. By computing expected value of each action, we will be able to pick the best one.

■ **Example 1**

Assume the following probability distribution of daily demand for strawberries:

Daily demand	0	1	2	3
Probability	0.2	0.3	0.3	0.2

Also assume that unit cost = \$3, selling price = \$5 (i.e., profit on sold unit = \$2), and salvage value on unsold units = \$2 (i.e., loss on unsold units = \$1). We can stock either 0, 1, 2, or 3 units. The question is, How many units should be stocked each day? Assume that units from one day cannot be sold the next day. Then the payoff table can be constructed as follows:

	State of Nature					
Demand		0	1	2	3	Expected value
Stock (probability)		(0.2)	(0.3)	(0.3)	(0.2)	
	0	$0	0	0	0	$0
Actions	1	−1	2	2	2	1.40
	2	−2	1[a]	4	4	1.90[b]
	3	−3	0	3	6	1.50

[a] Profit for (stock 2, demand 1) equals (no. of units sold) (profit per unit) − (no. of units unsold) (loss per unit) = (1) ($5 − 3) − (1) ($3 − 2) = $1

[b] Expected value for (stock 2) is −2 (0.2) + 1 (0.3) + 4 (0.3) + 4 (0.2) = $1.90.

The optimal stock action is the one with the highest *expected monetary value*; that is, stock 2 units.

Expected Value of Perfect Information

Suppose the decision maker can obtain a perfect prediction of which event (state of nature) will occur. The *expected value with perfect information* would be the total expected value of actions selected on the assumption of a perfect forecast. The *expected value of perfect information* can then be computed as: expected value with perfect information *minus* the expected value with existing information.

■ Example 2

From the payoff table in Example 1 above, the analysis at the bottom of the page yields the expected value *with* perfect information. Alternatively:

$0 (0.2) + 2 (0.3) + 4 (0.3) + 6 (0.2) = $3.00

With existing information, the best that the decision maker could obtain was select stock 2 and obtain $1.90. With perfect information (forecast), the decision maker could make as much as $3. Therefore, the expected value of perfect information is $3.00 − $1.90 = $1.10. This is the maximum price the decision maker is willing to pay for additional information.

DECISION TREE This is another approach used in *decision making under uncertainty*. It is a pictorial representation of a decision situation. As in the case of the *decision matrix* (*payoff table*) approach, it shows decision alternatives, states of nature, probabilities attached to the state of nature, and conditional benefits and losses. The decision tree approach is most useful in a sequential decision situation.

■ Example

Assume ABC Corporation wishes to introduce one of two products to the market this year. The probabilities and present values (PV) of projected cash inflows are given on the following page:

		State of Nature					
	Demand	0	1	2	3	Expected value
	Stock	(0.2)	(0.3)	(0.3)	(0.2)	
	0	$0				$0
Actions	1		2			0.6
	2			4		1.2
	3				6	1.2
						$3.00

Products	Initial Investment	PV of Cash Inflows	Probabilities
A	$225,000		1.00
		$450,000	0.40
		200,000	0.50
		−100,000	0.10
B	80,000		1.00
		320,000	0.20
		100,000	0.60
		−150,000	0.20

A decision tree analyzing the two products follows.

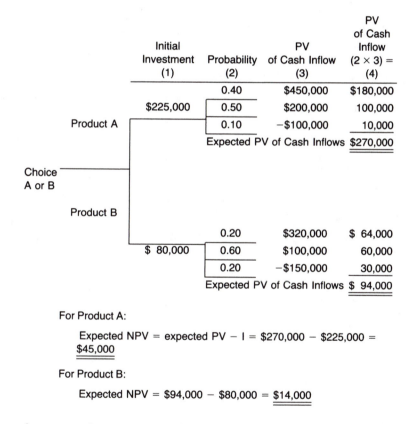

	Initial Investment (1)	Probability (2)	PV of Cash Inflow (3)	PV of Cash Inflow (2 × 3) = (4)
Product A	$225,000	0.40	$450,000	$180,000
		0.50	$200,000	100,000
		0.10	−$100,000	10,000
			Expected PV of Cash Inflows	$270,000
Product B	$ 80,000	0.20	$320,000	$ 64,000
		0.60	$100,000	60,000
		0.20	−$150,000	30,000
			Expected PV of Cash Inflows	$ 94,000

Choice A or B

For Product A:

Expected NPV = expected PV − I = $270,000 − $225,000 = $45,000

For Product B:

Expected NPV = $94,000 − $80,000 = $14,000

Based on the expected net present value, the company should choose product A over product B.

DEFICIT FINANCING AND CROWDING OUT

Deficit financing refers to borrowing by a government to cover a revenue shortfall. This can stimulate the economy for a time but dampen the economy in the long run by putting upward pressure on interest rates. Government borrowing can create the situation of "crowding out" consumers and businesses out of credit markets. *Crowding out* means that large increases in government spending and the resultant deficit financing are likely to reduce personal consumption and business investment spending for the following reasons:

1. Financial resources that may otherwise be used by the consumer and business sectors are diverted to public use.

2. Interest rates may be pushed up due to competition between the private and public sectors, which increases the costs of borrowing by the private sector and drives it out of their financial markets.

For these reasons, private incentives to work and invest may be diminished, thereby dampening the economy.

DEFLATION This is a general decrease in prices. It is the opposite of *inflation* and distinguished from *disinflation*, which is a reduction in the rate of price increases. Deflation is caused by a reduction in the money stock of the economy. *See also* Inflation.

DEPLETION This is the physical exhaustion of a natural resource (wasting asset). Examples of wasting assets are minerals, petroleum, and timber. Natural resources are consumed physically over the years of use and do not keep their physical characteristics. Typically, depletion expense is determined using the units of production method.

■ Example

A coal mine costs $150,000. Estimated salvage value is $30,000. The estimated total tons to be extracted are 10,000. In the first year, 1,500 tons are extracted. Depletion expense is

$$\frac{\text{Cost} - \text{Salvage value}}{\text{Estimated total tons}} = \frac{\$150,000 - \$30,000}{10,000}$$

$$= \frac{\$120,000}{10,000}$$

$$= \$12 \text{ per ton}$$

Depletion equals: 1,500 tons × $12 per ton = $18,000

The entry is

Depletion Expense	18,000	
Accumulated Depletion		18,000

DEPRECIATION This is the allocation of the historical cost of a fixed asset into expense over the period benefited to result in matching expense against revenue.

Fractional year depreciation is computing depreciation when the asset is acquired during the year. A proration is required.

■ Example

On 10/1/19X7, a fixed asset costing $10,000 with a salvage value of $1,000 and a life of 5 years is acquired.

Depreciation expense for 19X8 using the sum-of-the-years' digits method is

1/1/19X8 − 9/30/19X8	5/15 × $9,000 × 9/12	$2,250
10/1/19X8 − 12/31/19X8	4/15 × $9,000 × 3/12	600
		$2,850

Depreciation expense for 19X8 using double declining balance is shown in the table at the bottom of this page.

Group and composite depreciation methods involve similar accounting. The group method is used for similar assets, whereas the composite method is used for dissimilar assets. Both methods are generally accepted. There is one accumulated depreciation account for the entire group. The depreciation rate equals

$$\frac{\text{Depreciation}}{\text{Gross cost}}$$

Depreciation expense for a period equals:

$$\text{Depreciation rate} \times \text{Gross cost}$$

The depreciable life equals:

$$\frac{\text{Depreciable cost}}{\text{Depreciation}}$$

Year	Computation	Depreciation	Book Value
0			$10,000
10/1/19X7 − 12/31/19X7	3/12 × $10,000 × 40%	$1,000	9,000
1/1/19X8 − 12/31/19X8	$9,000 × 40%	3,600	5,400

When an asset is sold in the group, the entry is

Cash (proceeds received)
Accumulated Depreciation (plug figure)
Fixed Asset (cost)

Note that upon sale of a fixed asset in the group the difference between the proceeds received and the cost of the fixed asset is plugged to accumulated depreciation. No gain or loss is recognized upon the sale. The only time a gain or loss would be recognized is if the entire assets were sold.

■ Example

Calculations for composite depreciation appear in the table at the bottom of this page.
Composite rate:

$$\frac{\$17,600}{\$117,000} = 15.04\%$$

Composite life:

$$\frac{\$106,000}{\$17,600} = 6.02 \text{ years}$$

The entry to record depreciation is

Depreciation   17,600
  Accumulated Depreciation   17,600

The entry to sell asset B for $36,000 is

Cash   36,000
Accumulated Depreciation   4,000
  Fixed Asset   40,000

DEPRESSION This represents a bottom phase of a business cycle in which the economy is operating with substantial unemployment of its resources (such as labor) and a depressed rate of business investment and con-

sumer spending. *See also* Business Cycle; Recession.

DESKTOP SOFTWARE In an attempt to get rid of the clutter on the accountant's or financial executive's desk, organizer software exists. Desktop software operates in windows that overlay the accountant's main application. When a desk accessory is called up, the practitioner is temporarily exiting the main program. Some accessories let the user transfer information to and from the main application. Applications cover almost all office activities. An evaluation must be made of the compatibility of the desk software to the main programs being used.

Features of Desktop Software

• Appointment calendar. When an appointment time occurs, a beep sounds.
• Telling and setting time.
• Recording time spent with specific files.
• Notepad, including a place for memos and reminders.
• Directory for mail and telephone, including names, addresses, and telephone numbers.
• Telephone dialing as well as keeping track of important calls.
• Card filing.
• Performing calculator functions.
• Dating stamps.
• Preparation of custom forms.
• Voice and modem communications.
• Ability to access and execute major DOS commands. There should also be commands to customize screens and windows.

Disk organization software enables the practitioner who has many different things

Asset	Cost	Salvage	Depreciable Cost	Life	Depreciation
A	$ 25,000	$ 5,000	$ 20,000	10	$ 2,000
B	40,000	2,000	38,000	5	7,600
C	52,000	4,000	48,000	6	8,000
	$117,000	$11,000	$106,000		$17,600

to do at one time to press some keys and become familiar with a given situation. The micro in effect can handle paperwork difficulties that come up.

■ Example

Borland International's Sidekick™ is designed to complement a word processor, data base, or spreadsheet. The windows include notepad for typing comments and memos and taking notes of telephone conversations, calculator, appointment calendar, automatic telephone dialer, and on-screen help. The windows can be moved around the screen, enlarged, and contracted. Multiple windows overlay each other, but you can change the order at any time. It has a report generator.

DEVELOPMENT STAGE ENTERPRISE A development stage entity is one concentrating on establishing a new business and either major operations have not begun or principal operations have started but no significant revenue has been derived. Some types of activities of a development stage enterprise are establishing sources of supply, developing markets, obtaining financing, financial and production planning, research and development, buying capital assets, and recruiting staff. The *same* generally accepted accounting principles for an established company must be followed by a development stage enterprise. A balance sheet, income statement, and statement of cash flows are prepared. The balance sheet shows the accumulated net losses as a deficit. The income statement presents cumulative amounts of revenues and expenses since inception of the business. Similarly, the Statement of Cash Flows presents the cumulative amount of cash. The stockholders' equity statement shows for each equity security from inception: (1) date and number of shares issued and (2) dollar figures per share applicable to cash and non-

cash consideration. The nature and basis to determine amounts for noncash consideration must also be provided.

Financial statements must be headed "Development Stage Enterprise." A footnote should describe the development stage activities. In the first year that the entity is no longer in the development stage, it should disclose that in previous years it was.

DIF (DATA INTERCHANGE FORMAT) FILE In a computer system, the DIF feature allows for the transfer of files among programs. An example is the transfer of files from a data base management system to a spreadsheet. DIF is the suffix to the file name. The accountant can import files generated on other systems (e.g., client) into the practitioner's spreadsheet or data base. Many spreadsheet and data base programs allow for the DIF format. Numerous accounting packages (e.g., BPI) enable the creation of DIF files. A financial manager can take a Lotus 1–2–3™ spreadsheet and place it into another spreadsheet or word processing program. A drawback, however, is that a DIF file requires extra storage space.

DIRECT COSTING VERSUS ABSORPTION COSTING Direct costing is a costing method where the costs to be inventoried include only the *variable* manufacturing costs. The fixed factory overhead is treated as a period cost—it is deducted along with the selling and administrative expenses in the period incurred. That is,

Direct materials	$xx
Direct labor	xx
Variable factory overhead	xx
Product cost	$xx

Under *absorption costing*, the cost to be inventoried includes all manufacturing costs, both variable and fixed. Nonmanufacturing (operating) expenses—that is, selling and administrative expenses—are treated as period expenses and thus are charged against the current revenue.

Direct materials	$xx
Direct labor	xx
Variable factory overhead	xx
Fixed factory overhead	xx
Product cost	$xx

Two important facts are noted:

1. Effects of the two costing methods on net income:

   a. When production exceeds sales, a larger net income will be reported under absorption costing.

   b. When sales exceed production, a larger net income will be reported under direct costing.

   c. When sales and production are equal, net income will be the same under both methods.

2. Reconciliation of the direct and absorption costing net income figures:

   a. The difference in net income can be reconciled as follows:

$$\frac{\text{Difference in}}{\text{net income}} = \frac{\text{Change in}}{\text{inventory}} \times \frac{\text{Fixed factory}}{\text{overhead rate}}$$

   b. The previous formula works only if the fixed overhead rate per unit does not change between the periods.

■ Example

Given:

19x1

Inventory	
Beginning balance	0
Production	10,000
Available for sale	10,000
Units sold	6,500
Ending balance	3,500

Other data	
Sales (6,500 × @ $2)	$13,000
Variable manufacturing costs	
(10,000 × @ $0.75)	7,500
Fixed manufacturing costs	5,000
Selling and administrative expenses	4,500

Assuming that selling and administrative expenses are 50% variable and 50% fixed, income statements for 19x1 using both *direct costing* and *absorption costing* can be constructed as shown in Figure 1 below.

We can prove:

1. Difference in net income: $375 − ($1,375) = $1,750. Absorption costing shows a larger net income.

2. Reconciliation of difference in net income:

$$\frac{\text{Change in}}{\text{inventory}} \times \frac{\text{Fixed factory}}{\text{overhead rate}} = \frac{\text{Difference in}}{\text{net income}}$$

$$3,500 \times \$0.5\ (\$5,000/10,000) = \$1,750$$

It is important to realize that direct costing is used for internal management only. It highlights the concept of *contribution margin* and focuses on the costs by behavior rather than by function. Its managerial uses include:

Figure 1

19x1

Direct		Absorption	
Sales	$13,000	Sales	$13,000
Less: VC		Less: CGS	
VMC (6,500 × $0.75)	4,875	VMC (6,500 × $0.75)	4,875
VS&A (4,500 × 0.5)	2,250	FMC (6,500 × $0.5)	3,250
CM	$ 5,875	Gross margin	$ 4,875
Less: FC		Less:	
FMC	5,000	VS&A	2,250
FS&A	2,250	FS&A	2,250
Net income (loss)	($ 1,375)	Net income	$ 375

1. Relevant cost analysis
2. Break-even and cost-volume-profit (CVP) analyses
3. Short-term decision making

Direct costing is, however, not acceptable for external reporting or income tax reporting. Companies that use direct costing for internal reporting must convert to absorption costing for external reporting. *See also* Contribution Income Statement; Contribution Margin (CM); Relevant Costing.

DIRECT FINANCING LEASE The lessor is *not* a manufacturer or dealer in the rented property. The lessor records interest revenue over the life of the lease. *See also* Leases.

DISCLOSURE This is required for any information that if not disclosed would mislead a reader of the financial statements. Disclosure may be made in the footnotes, a separate schedule, or body to the financial statements. Examples of disclosures are accounting policies employed, litigation, lease information, and pension plan particulars.

According to AICPA Statement on Auditing Standards No. 32, if the auditor concludes that audited financial statements omit information required by GAAP, the auditor should express either an "except for" qualified opinion or an adverse opinion. If practical, the auditor should provide the omitted information in a middle explanatory paragraph of the audit report. Practical means in this context that the data is obtainable from the client's records and that the auditor is not put in the position of a preparer of the information.

DISCLOSURE OF LONG-TERM OBLIGATIONS An unconditional purchase obligation is an obligation to provide funds for goods or services at a determinable future date. An example is a take-or-pay contract making the buyer obligated to pay specified periodic amounts for products or services. Even in the case where the buyer does not take delivery of the goods, periodic payments must still be made.

When unconditional purchase obligations are recorded in the balance sheet, disclosure is still made of the following:

• Payments made for recorded unconditional purchase obligations
• Maturities and sinking fund requirements for long-term borrowings

Unconditional purchase obligations that are not reflected in the balance sheet should usually be disclosed if they meet the following criteria:

• Noncancellable but may be cancellable upon a remote contingency
• Negotiated to arrange financing to provide contracted goods or services
• A term in excess of one year

The disclosure needed for unconditional purchase obligations when not recorded in the accounts are

• Nature and term
• Fixed and variable amounts
• Total amount for the current year and for the next 5 years
• Purchases made under the obligation for each year presented

Optional disclosure exists of the amount of imputed interest required to reduce the unconditional purchase obligation to present value.

DISCONTINUED OPERATION A discontinued operation is a business segment that has ceased operation or will shortly be liquidated after year-end. Income from discontinued operations are shown separately in the income statement. *See also* Income Statement Format.

DISCOUNTED PAYBACK PERIOD This is the length of time required to recover the initial cash outflow from the discounted future cash inflows. This is obtained at the point where the present values of cash inflows are accumulated until they equal the initial investment.

■ Example

Assume a machine purchased for $18,000 yields cash inflows of $4,000, $5,000, $6,000, $6,000, and $8,000. The cost of capital is 10%. Then we have

Year	Cash Flow	$PVIF_{10\%,n}$	PV of Cash Flow
1	$4,000	0.909	$3,636
2	5,000	0.826	4,130
3	6,000	0.751	4,506
4	6,000	0.683	4,098
5	8,000	0.621	4,968

The number of years required to recoup the $18,000 investment is

Year 1	$ 3,636
2	4,130
3	4,506
4	4,098
	$16,370

Balance in year 5: ($18,000 − $16,370) = $1,630

Therefore, the discounted payback period is 4 years + $1,630/$4,968 = 4 + 0.33 = 4.33 years. *See also* Payback Period.

DISCOVERY SAMPLING This is usually used in a search for critical deviations such as when the audit suggests the existence of irregularities. This sampling technique may be employed when the auditor wants to determine if an acceptable error rate in the population has been exceeded. If the error rate is not excessive, no additional audit testing is required. If it is exceeded, alternative audit procedures are necessary. An attribute estimate may also be required. In discovery sampling, there is a minimum sample size that would include at least one error if the population errors are greater than a given rate. Hence, if one error is found in the sample, the test is resolved. Because discovery sampling is based on a minimum sample size to uncover only one error, the sample size has to be increased in the event a useful attribute estimate is needed, such as the real error rate in the population.

In using discovery sampling, a determination has to be made regarding population size, minimum unacceptable error rate, and confidence level. Sample size is determined from a sampling table. In the event that none of the random samples show an error, it is concluded that the actual error rate is less than the minimum unacceptable error rate at the desired confidence level. Typically, the technique is used to spot groups of documents needing thorough testing.

■ Example

The auditor wants to assure the accuracy of pricing documents from 15 branches. Discovery sampling can be used to identify those batches having, for instance, a 95% probability of an error rate less than 1%. The auditor accepts those batches as satisfactory and appraises fully the remaining batches.

Discovery sampling is a sound approach in testing the correctness of clerical work. When there is not much time available in the final couple of months at the end of the reporting year, discovery sampling can provide the auditor with confidence that error incidence is below a specified percentage using a small sample size. Another benefit of this sampling method is to test auditor reliability.

■ Example

Even though the auditor used a random sample, an error was not uncovered. But once the error has been identified, the auditor can arrive at the probability of having found this error. The auditor may have examined n random units furnishing a 95% confidence level that the error rate in the population was less than 1%. Assume the incorrect units are, say 0.1% of the population. Thus, the method and assumptions employed were appropriate.

■ Example

The auditor wants to examine for inventory items, quantity, unit cost, and total cost. Cost/benefit makes it not practical for the CPA to verify all pricings and extensions for the inventory listing. Discovery sampling can be used to obtain a 90% confidence level that the error rate in pricing and extension is less than 1%. According to the sampling table, for 2,000 inventory items, a random sample size of 220 is needed. If no mistakes exist in the sample, it is concluded that all inventory items are correct. In the event a single error is found, the CPA stops sampling and examines extensions for all inventory items.

Discovery sampling has a pitfall in the possible rejection of some acceptable batches. Using a level of significance of 0.05, one is willing to reject on acceptable batch 5% of the time. It is appropriate for use by the internal auditor as a final check. But the external auditor should employ it only as a *preliminary* scanning procedure in examining the quality of population data. *See also* Sampling.

DIVIDENDS These represent distributions paid out by the company to stockholders. After the date of declaration of a dividend is the date of record. In order to qualify to receive a dividend, a person must be registered as the owner of the stock on the date of record. Several days prior to the date of record, the stock will be selling "ex-dividend." This is done to alert investors that those owning the stock before the record date are eligible to receive the dividend, and that those selling the stock before the record date will lose their rights to the dividend.

A dividend is usually in the form of cash or stock. A dividend is based on the outstanding shares (issued shares less treasury shares).

■ Example

Issued shares are 5,000, treasury shares are 1,000, and outstanding shares are therefore 4,000. The par value of the stock is $10 per share. If a $0.30 dividend per share is declared, the dividend is

$$4,000 \times \$.30 = \$1,200$$

If the dividend rate is 6%, the dividend is

$$4,000 \text{ shares} \times \$10 \text{ par value} = \$40,000$$
$$\times .06$$
$$\$ 2,400$$

Assuming a cash dividend of $2,400 is declared, the entry is

Retained Earnings	2,400	
Cash Dividend Payable		2,400

No entry is made at the record date. The entry at the payment date is

Cash Dividend Payable	2,400	
Cash		2,400

In the case of a property dividend, the entry at the declaration date at the fair market value of the asset is

Retained Earnings	
Asset	

Gain or loss arising between the carrying value and fair market value of the asset is recorded at the time of declaration.

A stock dividend is issued in the form of stock. Stock dividend distributable is shown in the capital stock section of stockholders' equity. It is *not* a liability. If the stock dividend is less than 20% to 25% of outstanding shares at the declaration date, retained earnings is reduced at the market price of the shares. If the stock dividend is in excess of 20% to 25% of outstanding shares, retained earnings is charged at par value. Between 20% to 25% is a gray area.

■ Example

A stock dividend of 10% is declared on 5,000 shares of $10 par value common stock having a market price of $12. The entry at the declaration and issuance dates follow:

Retained Earnings (500 shares × $12)	6,000	
Stock Dividend Distributable		
(500 shares × $10)		5,000
Paid-in-capital		1,000
Stock Dividend Distributable	5,000	
Common Stock		5,000

Assume instead that the stock dividend was 30%. The entries would be

Retained Earnings (500 × $10)	5,000	
Stock Dividend Distributable		5,000
Stock Dividend Distributable	5,000	
Common Stock		5,000

A liability dividend (scrip dividend) is payable in the form of a liability (e.g., notes payable). A liability dividend sometimes occurs when a company has financial problems.

■ Example

On 1/1/19X2, a liability dividend of $20,000 is declared in the form of a 1-year, 8% note. The entry at the declaration date is

Retained Earnings	20,000	
Scrip Dividend Payable		20,000

When the scrip dividend is paid, the entry is

Scrip Dividend Payable	20,000	
Interest Expense	1,600	
Cash		21,600

A liquidating dividend can be deceptive because it is not actually a dividend. It is a return of capital and not a distribution of earnings. The entry is to debit paid-in-capital and credit dividends payable. The recipient of a liquidating dividend pays no tax on it.

DIVISIONAL PERFORMANCE EVALUATION

The ability to measure performance is essential in developing management incentives and controlling the operation toward the achievement of organizational goals. A typical de-centralized subunit is an *investment center* that is responsible for an organization's invested capital (operating assets) and the related operating income. There are two widely used measurements of performance for the investment center: the rate of return on investment (ROI) and residual income (RI).

Rate of Return on Investment (ROI)

ROI relates net income to invested capital. Specifically,

$$\text{ROI} = \frac{\text{Operating income}}{\text{Operating assets}}$$

■ Example 1

Consider the following financial data for a division:

Operating assets	$100,000
Operating income	18,000

ROI = $18,000/$100,000 = 18%

Residual Income (RI)

Another approach to measuring performance in an investment center is residual income (RI). RI is the operating income that an investment center is able to earn above some minimum rate of return on its operating assets. RI, unlike ROI, is an absolute amount of income rather than a specific rate of return. When RI is used to evaluate divisional performance, the objective is to maximize the total amount of residual income, not to maximize the overall ROI figure.

RI = Operating income
    − (Minimum required rate of return
                × Operating assets)

■ Example 2

In Example 1, assume the minimum required rate of return is 13%. Then the residual income of the division is

$18,000 − (13% × $100,000)
              = $18,000 − $13,000 = $5,000

RI is regarded as a better measure of performance than ROI because it encourages investment in projects that would be rejected under ROI. A major disadvantage of RI, however, is that it cannot be used to compare divisions of different sizes. RI tends to favor the larger divisions due to the larger amount of dollars involved.

Investment Decisions Under ROI and RI

The decision whether to use ROI or RI as a measure of divisional performance affects financial managers' investment decisions. Under the ROI method, division managers tend to accept only the investments whose returns exceed the division's ROI; otherwise, the division's overall ROI would decrease. Under the RI method, on the other hand, division managers would accept an investment as long as it earns a rate in excess of the minimum required rate of return. The addition of such an investment will increase the division's overall RI.

▪ Example 3

Consider the same data given in Examples 1 and 2:

Operating assets	$100,000
Operating income	18,000
Minimum required rate of return	13%
ROI = 18% and RI = $5,000	

Assume that the division is presented with a project that would yield 15% on a $10,000 investment. The division manager would not accept this project under the ROI approach since the division is already earning 18%. Acquiring this project will bring down the present ROI to 17.73%, as shown below:

	Present	New Project	Overall
Operating assets (a)	$100,000	$10,000	$110,000
Operating income (b)	18,000	1,500*	19,500
ROI (b / a)	18%	15%	17.73%

* $10,000 × 15% = $1,500

Under the RI approach, the manager would accept the new project since it provides a higher rate than the minimum required rate of return (15% vs. 13%). Accepting the new project will increase the overall residual income to $5,200, as shown following:

	Present	New Project	Overall
Operating assets (a)	$100,000	$10,000	$110,000
Operating income (b)	18,000	1,500	19,500
Minimum required income at 13% (c)	13,000	1,300*	14,300
RI (b − c)	$ 5,000	$ 200	$ 5,200

* $10,000 × 13% = $1,300

See also Du Pont Formula.

DOLLAR-COST AVERAGING This may be used for stock deemed to be a good long-term investment. A constant dollar amount of stock or stocks is bought at regularly spaced intervals. The strategy represents time diversification. By investing a fixed amount each time, more shares are purchased at a low price and less shares are bought at a high price. It typically results in a lower average cost per share because the investor buys more shares of stock with the same dollars. The technique is advantageous when a stock price moves within a narrow range. If there is a decrease in stock price, the investor will incur less of a loss than ordinarily. If there is an increase in stock price, the investor will gain, but less than usual. Drawbacks to dollar-cost averaging are (1) higher transaction costs and (2) it will not work when stock prices are in a continuous downward direction. *Tip*: Dollar-cost averaging is a conservative investment strategy since it avoids whims when the investor may be tempted to buy when the market is high or sell when the market is low. A conservative stock may be acquired with relatively little risk benefiting from long-term price appreciation. Further, the investor is not stuck with too many shares at high prices. In addition, in a bear market many shares are purchased at very depressed prices.

▪ Example

An investor makes a $100,000 investment per month in ABC Company and engages in the following transactions:

Date	Investment	Market Price Per Share	Shares Purchased
6/1	$100,000	$40	2,500
7/1	100,000	35	2,857
8/1	100,000	34	2,941
9/1	100,000	38	2,632
10/1	100,000	50	2,000

The investor has purchased fewer shares at the higher price and more shares at the lower price. The average price per share is

$$\frac{\$197}{5} = \$39.40$$

However, with the $500,000 investment, 12,930 shares have been bought, resulting in a cost per share of $38.67. At 10/1, the market price of the stock of $50 exceeded the average cost of $38.67, reflecting an attractive gain.

DOLLAR UNIT SAMPLING (DUS)   DUS is useful when the auditor wishes to confirm if a population value is materially correct. Under dollar unit sampling, an examination is made of sample units of $1 to ascertain whether an error exists. Random samples of monetary units not physical units are involved. An estimate is made of the maximum proportion or amount of dollars in error in the population.

There is a separate analysis for understatement and overstatement errors. When sample errors are uncovered, various analytical methods may be used (e.g., combined attributes-variables) to adjust the simple attribute result to take into account the magnitude of the errors. But as additional errors are uncovered, the estimates become overly conservative, thus, it is recommended to use dollar-unit sampling only for cases where few or no errors are anticipated. In other words, there is a low error rate. A possible statistical statement to use is, There are overstatement errors not exceeding $300,000 in the population at a particular confidence level. Another statement might be, The population is overstated not in excess of $150,000 and understated by no more than $100,000.

▪ Example

A maximum error rate of 4% in a population of $200,000 results in a maximum error of $8,000 (4% × $200,000).

Dollar unit sampling is a probability proportionate to size sampling of audit units having an upper precision level of possible error based on dollar mistakes found in the sample combined with an attribute resulting from a probability determination. For instance, a supplier account with a carrying value of $500 represents 500 *dollar units*. The auditor performs a random sample of the dollar units with probabilities proportionate to size. The auditor then audits the sample dollar units. In the event a dollar error is found in a sampled item, it is converted on a "per dollar" basis. Sample results are projected to the population. In essence, this sampling approach converts into dollars the conclusion that a given attribute has been exceeded. *See also* Sampling.

DOLLAR VALUE LIFO   This is an acceptable method in which price indices are used in determining the value of ending inventory. Inventory is restated in base dollars. The change in inventory for the period in base dollars is then multiplied by the price index for the current year. *See also* Inventory Valuation.

DOW THEORY   The Dow Theory applies to specific stocks and the overall market. It is based on the movements in the Dow Jones Industrial

Average and the Dow Jones Transporation Average. Stock market direction has to be substantiated by both averages. *See also* Technical Analysis.

DU PONT FORMULA The Du Pont formula combines the income statement and balance sheet into either of two summary measures of performance, *return on investment* (ROI) and *return on equity* (ROE).

The first version of the Du Pont formula breaks down the return on investment (ROI) into *net profit margin* and *total asset turnover*, as shown below.

$$\text{ROI} = \frac{\text{Net profit after taxes}}{\text{Total assets}}$$

$$= \frac{\text{Net profit after taxes}}{\text{Sales}} \times \frac{\text{Sales}}{\text{Total assets}}$$

$$= \text{Net profit margin} \quad \times \text{Total asset turnover}$$

■ Example 1

Consider the following financial data:

Total assets	$200,000
Net profit after taxes	20,000
Sales	$400,000

Then;

ROI = $20,000/$200,000 = 10%

Net profit margin = $20,000/$400,000 = 5%

Total asset turnover = $400,000/$200,000 = 2 times

Therefore:

$$\text{ROI} = 10\% = 5\% \times 2 \text{ times} = 10\%$$

The breakdown provides a lot of insights to financial managers on how to improve profitability of the company and investment strategy. Specifically, it has several advantages over the original formula (i.e., net profits after taxes/total asset) for profit planning. They are

1. The importance of turnover as a key to overall return on investment is emphasized in the breakdown. In fact, turnover is just as important as profit margin in enhancing overall return.

2. The importance of sales is explicitly rec-

ognized, which is not there in the original formula.

3. The breakdown stresses the possibility of trading one off for the other. The margin and turnover complement each other. In other words, a low turnover can be made up for by a high margin and vice versa.

The breakdown of ROI into its two components shows that a number of combinations of margin and turnover can yield the same rate of return, as shown below:

	Margin	×	Turnover	=	ROI
(1)	5%	×	2 times	=	10%
(2)	4	×	2.5	=	10
(3)	3	×	3.33	=	10
(4)	2	×	5	=	10
(5)	1	×	10	=	10

The turnover-margin relationship and its resulting ROI follow.

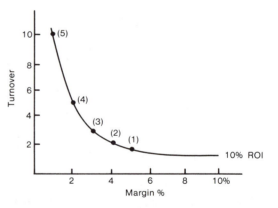

The previous figure indicates that the total asset turnover and net profit margin factors complement each other. Weak margin can be complemented by a strong turnover, and vice versa. It also shows how important turnover is as a key to profit making. In effect, these two factors are equally important in overall profit performance.

4. The formula indicates where your weaknesses are: margin or turnover, or both. Various actions can be taken to enhance ROI. They include:

   a. Reduce expenses (e.g., improve productivity, automate, or cut down on discretionary expenses), thereby increasing net profit.

b. Reduce assets (e.g., improve inventory control, speed up receivable collections, etc.) without decreasing sales.

c. Increase sales while maintaining profit margin.

The second version of the Du Pont formula, also called the *modified Du Pont formula*, ties together the ROI and the degree of financial leverage as measured using the *equity multiplier*, which is the ratio of total assets to stockholders' equity to determine the *return on equity* (ROE):

$$ROE = \frac{\text{Net profit after taxes}}{\text{Stockholders' equity}}$$

$$= \frac{\text{Net profit after taxes}}{\text{Total assets}} \times \frac{\text{Total assets}}{\text{Stockholders' equity}}$$

$$= \quad\text{ROI}\quad \times \quad\text{Equity multiplier}$$

The use of the equity multiplier to convert the ROI to the ROE reflects the impact of the leverage (use of debt) on stockholders' return.

■ Example 2

In Example 1, assume stockholders' equity of $90,000. Then, equity multiplier = $200,000/$90,000 = 2.22

ROE = $20,000/$90,000 = 22.2%, or

ROE = ROI × Equity multiplier
$$= 10\% \times 2.22 = 22.2\%$$

If the company used only equity, the 10% ROI would equal ROE. However, 55% of the firm's capital is supplied by creditors ($90,000/$200,000 = 45% is the equity-to-asset ratio). Since the 10% ROI all goes to stockholders, who put up only 45% of the capital, the ROE is higher than 10%. This example indicates the company was using the leverage (debt) positively (favorably). (If the assets in which the funds are invested are able to earn a return greater than the fixed rate of return required by the creditors, the leverage is positive and the common stockholders benefit.)

The advantage of this formula is that it enables the company to break its ROE into a profit margin portion (net profit margin), an efficiency-of-asset-utilization portion (total asset turnover), and a use-of-leverage portion (equity multiplier). Financial managers have the task of determining just what combination of asset return and leverage will work best in its competitive environment. Most companies try to keep at least a level equal to what is considered to be "normal" within the industry.

The Du Pont and Modified Du Pont Formulas

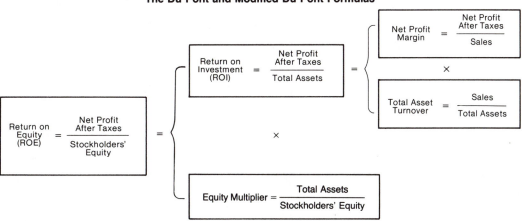

DURBIN-WATSON STATISTIC This is a summary measure of the amount of *autocorrelation* in the error terms of the *regression*. Roughly speaking, if the statistic approaches a value of 2, there is no autocorrelation. If the error terms are highly positively correlated, the statistic would be less than 1 and could get near 0. If the error terms are highly negatively correlated, the statistic would be greater than 3 and could get near the upper limit of 4. *See also* Autocorrelation; Regression Analysis.

DYNAMIC PROGRAMMING This is a form of mathematical programming. It is a programming technique that divides the problem to be solved into a number of subproblems and then solves each subproblem in such a way that the overall solution is optimal to the original problem. For example, a firm may wish to make a series of accounting and financial decisions over time that will provide it with the highest possible cash inflow. *See also* Mathematical Programming.

E

EARLY EXTINGUISHMENT OF DEBT Long-term debt may be called back early when new debt can be issued at a lower interest rate. It can also occur when the company has excess cash and wants to avoid paying interest charges and having the debt on its balance sheet. The gain or loss on the early extinguishment of debt is an extraordinary item shown net of tax. Extraordinary classification occurs whether the extinguishment is early, at scheduled maturity, or later. An exception exists in that the gain or loss on extinguishment is an ordinary item if it satisfies a sinking fund requirement that has to be met within one year of the date of extinguishment. But serial bonds do not have characteristics of sinking fund requirements.

Debt may be construed as being extinguished in the case where the debtor is relieved of the principal liability and it is probable the debtor will not have to make future payments.

■ Example

A $100,000 bond payable with an unamortized premium of $10,000 is called at 85. The entry is

Bonds Payable	100,000	
Premium on Bonds Payable	10,000	
Cash (85% × 100,000)		85,000
Extraordinary Gain		25,000

Footnote disclosures regarding extinguishment of debt follow:

• Description of extinguishment transaction including the source of funds used

• Per share gain or loss net of tax

If convertible debt is converted to stock in connection with an "inducement offer" where the debtor alters conversion privileges, the debtor recognizes an expense rather than an extraordinary item. The amount is the fair value of the securities transferred in excess of the fair value of securities issuable according to the original conversion terms. This fair market value is measured at the earlier of the conversion date or date of the agreement. An inducement offer may be accomplished by giving debt holders a higher conversion ratio, payment of additional consideration, or other favorable changes in terms.

According to FASB 76, if the debtor puts cash or other assets in a trust to be utilized only for paying interest and principal on debt on an irrevocable basis, disclosure should be made of the particulars, including a description of the transaction and the amount of debt considered to be extinguished. *See also* Bond Accounting.

EARNINGS PER SHARE

APB 15 requires that earnings per share must be computed by publicly held companies. It is not required for nonpublic companies. In a simple capital structure, no potentially dilutive securities exist. (Potentially dilutive means the security will be converted into common stock at a later date reducing EPS). Thus, only one EPS figure is necessary. In a complex capital structure, dilutive securities exist requiring dual presentation. The dual presentation of EPS for all periods presented is

$$\text{Primary EPS} = \frac{\text{Net income} - \text{Preferred dividend}}{\substack{\text{Weighted} - \text{average common stock} \\ \text{outstanding} + \text{Common} \\ \text{stock equivalents}}}$$

$$\text{Fully diluted EPS} = \frac{\text{Net income} - \text{Preferred dividend}}{\substack{\text{Weighted-average common stock} \\ \text{outstanding} + \text{Common stock} \\ \text{equivalents} + \text{Other fully} \\ \text{diluted securities}}}$$

Fully diluted EPS reflects the *maximum* potential dilution per share on a prospective basis.

Weighted-average common stock shares outstanding takes into account the number of months in which those shares were outstanding.

■ Example

On 1/1/19X1, 10,000 shares were issued. On 4/1/19X1, 2,000 of those shares were bought back by the company. The weighted-average common stock outstanding is

$$(10{,}000 \times 3/12) + (8{,}000 \times 9/12) = 8{,}500 \text{ shares}$$

The inclusion of common stock equivalents in determining EPS is an example of theoretical substance over legal form. Although the common stock equivalent (e.g., stock option) is not legally common stock, it is treated as such since in theoretical substance the common stock equivalent is common stock. Common stock equivalents are securities that can become common stock at a later date and are shown in both primary EPS and fully diluted EPS.

Common stock equivalents include
• Stock options.
• Stock warrants.
• Subscribed stock.
• Two-class common stock.
• Contingent shares only related to the passage of time.
• Convertible securities (convertible bonds, convertible preferred stock) when the yield at the time of issuance is less than $2/3$ of the average Aa bond yield at the time of issuance. Once a convertible security is defined as a common stock equivalent, it continues as such. Aa bonds are defined by Standard and Poor's and Moody's as of the highest quality. For zero-coupon bonds, the effective yield is the interest rate necessary to discount the maturity value of the bond to its present value. This rate is then used to determine common stock equivalent by company by comparing it to the $2/3$ average yield. In the situation where convertible securities are issued in a foreign country, we use the most comparable long-term yield in that country in performing the cash yield test.

Note: Although stock options are *always* deemed a common stock equivalent, they are only included in computing EPS if the market price of common stock is greater than the option price for substantially all of the last 3 months of the year. In this case, we assume the stock options were exercised at the *beginning* of the year (or at time of issuance, if later). Although convertible securities are classified as common stock equivalents based on the circumstances at time of issue, warrants are classified according to the conditions at each period.

In computing EPS, common stock equivalents are included if they have a dilutive effect. Dilutive effect means that the inclusion of a common stock equivalent reduced EPS by 3% or more in the aggregate and is applied by type of security. The 3% dilution also applies to presenting fully diluted EPS. Fully diluted EPS is also shown if it reduces primary EPS by 3% or more. Antidilutive securities that increase EPS are not shown in the EPS computation because they will increase EPS, which violates conservatism.

When shares are issued because of a stock dividend or stock split, the computation of weighted-average common stock shares outstanding mandates retroactive adjustment as if the shares were outstanding at the beginning of the year.

In computing the common stock equivalent in shares of options and warrants, the *treasury stock method* is used. Options and warrants are assumed to have been exercised at the beginning of the year (or at time of issuance, if later). The proceeds received from the options and warrants are assumed to:

• First, buy back common stock at the average market price for the period not exceeding 20% of common stock outstanding at year-end.

• Second, reduce long- or short-term borrowing.

• Third, invest in U.S. government securities or commerical paper.

Assumption of exercise of options exists only when market price of stock is greater than exercise price for 3 consecutive months ending with the year-end month.

In computing fully diluted EPS, the treasury stock method is modified in that the market price at the end of the accounting period is used if it is higher than the average market price for the period.

■ Example

Assume 100 shares are under option at an option price of $10. The average market price of stock is $25. The common stock equivalent is 60 shares, as calculated below:

Issued shares from option 100 shares × $10 = $1,000
Less: Treasury shares　　　 40 shares × $25 = $1,000
Common stock equivalent 60 shares

Convertible securities are accounted for using the "if converted method." The convertible securities are assumed converted at the beginning of the earliest year presented or date of security issuance. Interest or dividends on them are added back to net income since the securities are considered part of equity in the denominator of the EPS calculation.

Other fully diluted securities are defined as convertible securities that did not meet the ⅔ test. They are included only in the calculation of fully diluted EPS. Thus, fully diluted EPS will be a lower figure than primay EPS because of the greater shares in the denominator. Contingent issuance of shares in computing fully diluted EPS is assumed to have occurred at the beginning of the year or at the time of issuance if later. Fully diluted EPS is a pro forma presentation showing what EPS would be if *all* potential contingencies of common stock issuances having a dilutive effect took place.

To accomplish the fullest dilution in arriving at fully diluted EPS, an assumption is made that all common stock issuances on exercise of options or warrants during the period were made at the start of the year. The *higher* of the closing price or the average price of common stock is used in determining the number of shares of treasury stock to be purchased from the proceeds received upon issuance of the options. If the ending market price exceeds the average market price, the assumed treasury shares acquired will be lessened, resulting in higher assumed outstanding shares with the resulting decrease in EPS.

Net income less preferred dividends is in the numerator of the EPS fraction, representing earnings available to common stockholders. On cumulative preferred stock, preferred dividends for the current year are subtracted out whether or not paid. Further, preferred dividends are only subtracted out for the current year. Thus, if preferred dividends in arrears were for 5 years all of which were paid plus the sixth year dividend, only the sixth year dividend (current year) is deducted. Note that preferred dividends for each of the prior years would have been deducted in those years.

In computing EPS, preferred dividends are only subtracted out on preferred stock that was not included as a common stock equivalent. If the preferred stock is a common stock equivalent, the preferred dividend would *not* be subtracted out since the equivalency of preferred shares into common shares are included in the denominator.

If convertible bonds are included in the denominator of EPS, they are considered as equivalent to common shares. Thus, interest expense (net of tax) has to be added back in the numerator.

Disclosure of EPS should include information on the capital structure, explanation of the computation of EPS, identification of common stock equivalents, assumptions made, and number of shares converted. Rights and privileges of the securities should also be disclosed. Such disclosure includes dividend and participation rights, call prices, conversion ratios, and sinking fund requirements.

A stock conversion occurring during the year or between year-end and the audit report date may have materially affected EPS if it had taken place at the beginning of the year. Thus, supplementary footnote disclosure should be made reflecting on an "as-if" basis what the effects of these conversions would have had on EPS if they were made at the start of the accounting period.

If a subsidiary has been acquired under the *purchase accounting method* during the year, the weighted-average shares outstanding for the year is used from the purchase date. But if a *pooling of interests* occurred, the weighted-average shares outstanding for all the years are presented.

If common stock or a common stock equivalent are sold during the year and the monies obtained to buy back debt or retire preferred stock, there should be a presentation of supplemental EPS figures.

When comparative financial statements are presented, there is a retroactive adjustment for stock splits and stock dividends. Assume in 19X5 a 10% stock dividend occurs. The weighted-average shares used for previous years' computations has to be increased by 10% to make EPS data comparable.

When a prior period adjustment occurs that causes a restatement of previous years' earnings, EPS should also be restated.

■ Example

The stockholders' equity section of ABC Company's balance sheet as of 12/31/19X3 appears at the bottom of the page.

On 5/1/19X3, ABC Company acquired XYZ Company in a pooling-of-interest. For each of XYZ Company's 800,000 shares, ABC issued one of its own shares in the exchange.

On 4/1/19X3, ABC Company issued 500,000 shares of convertible preferred stock at $38 per share. The preferred stock is con-

$1.20 cumulative preferred stock (par value of $10 per share, issued 1,200,000 shares of which 500,000 were converted to common stock and 700,000 shares are outstanding)	$ 7,000,000
Common stock (par value of $2.50 issued and outstanding 6,000,000 shares)	15,000,000
Paid-in-capital	20,000,000
Retained earnings	32,000,000
Total stockholders' equity	$74,000,000

vertible to common stock at the exchange rate of 2 shares of common for each share of preferred. On 9/1/19X3, 300,000 shares and on 11/1/19X3, 200,000 shares of preferred stock were converted into common stock. The market price of the convertible preferred stock is $38 per share.

During August, ABC Company granted stock options to executives to buy 100,000 shares of common stock at an option price of $15 per share. The market price of stock at year-end was $20.

ABC Company has 8%, $10,000,000 convertible bonds payable issued at fair value in 19X1. The conversion rate is 4 shares of

common stock for each $100 bond. No conversions have occurred yet.

The Aa corporate bond yield is 10%. The tax rate is 34%. Net income for the year is $12,000,000.

The convertible bonds are not common stock equivalents because the interest rate of 8% is more than ⅔ of the Aa bond yield of 10%.

The convertible preferred stock is a common stock equivalent because its yield of 3.16% ($1.20/$38.00) is less than ⅔ of the Aa bond yield of 10%.

Stock options are always considered common stock equivalents.

Shares outstanding from 1/1/19X3 (including 800,000 shares issued upon acquisition of XYZ Company):		
6,000,000 − 1,000,000		5,000,000
Shares issued upon conversion of 500,000 shares of preferred stock to common stock:		
Issued 9/1/19X3 600,000 × 4/12	200,000	
Issued 11/1/19X3 400,000 × 2/12	66,667	266,667
Total shares of common stock		5,266,667
Common stock equivalents:		
Convertible preferred stock:		
500,000 shares of convertible preferred issued on 4/1/19X3		
500,000 × 2 × 9/12	750,000	
Less: Common shares applicable to 500,000 preferred shares converted during the year	266,667	
Common stock equivalents of convertible preferred stock		483,333

Common stock equivalents of stock options:		
Option	100,000 × $15 = $1,500,000	
Less: Treasury stock	75,000 × $20 = 1,500,000	
Common stock equivalent of stock options	25,000	25,000
Weighted-average common stock outstanding plus common stock equivalents for primary EPS		5,775,000
Convertible bonds payable assumed converted at 1/1/19X3 ($10,000,000/$100) = 100,000 bonds		
100,000 bonds × 4 shares per bond		400,000
Weighted-average common stock outstanding plus common stock equivalents plus other fully diluted securities for fully diluted EPS		6,175,000

Primary EPS equals:

$$\frac{\$12,000,000}{5,775,000 \text{ shares}} = \$2.08$$

Fully diluted EPS equals:

$$\frac{\$12,000,000 + \$528,000^*}{6,175,000 \text{ shares}} = \$2.03$$

* $10,000,000 × 8% = $800,000 × 66% = $528,000

EBIT—EPS APPROACH TO CAPITAL STRUCTURE

This is a practical tool for use by financial managers in order to evaluate alternative financing plans. This is a practical effort to move toward achieving an optimal capital structure that results in the lowest overall cost of capital.

The use of financial leverage has two effects on the earnings that go to the firm's common stockholders: (1) an increased risk in earnings per share (EPS) due to the use of fixed financial obligations and (2) a change in the level of EPS at a given EBIT associated with a specific capital structure.

The first effect is measured by the degree of financial leverage. The second effect is analyzed by means of EBIT-EPS analysis. This analysis is a practical approach that enables the financial manager to evaluate alternative financing plans by investigating their effect on EPS over a range of EBIT levels. Its primary objective is to determine the *EBIT break-even, or indifference, points* between the various alternative financing plans. The indifference points between any two methods of financing can be determined by solving for EBIT in the following equality:

$$\frac{(EBIT - I)(1 - t) - PD}{S_1} = \frac{(EBIT - I)(1 - t) - PD}{S_2}$$

where t = tax rate,

PD = preferred stock dividends,

S_1 and S_2 = number of shares of common stock outstanding after financing for plan 1 and plan 2, respectively.

■ Example

Assume that ABC Company, with long-term capitalization consisting entirely of $5 million in stock, wants to raise $2 million for the acquisition of special equipment by (1) selling 40,000 shares of common stock at $50 each; (2) selling bonds, at 10% interest; or (3) issuing preferred stock with an 8% dividend. The present EBIT is $8 million, the income tax rate is 50%, and 100,000 shares of common stock are now outstanding. In order to compute the indifference points, we begin by calculating EPS at a projected EBIT level of $1 million as shown in the table below.

Now connect the EPS at the level of EBIT of $1 million with the EBIT for each financing alternative on the horizontal axis to obtain the EPS-EBIT graphs. We plot the EBIT necessary to cover all fixed financial costs for each financing alternative on the horizontal axis. For the common stock plan, there are no fixed costs, so the intercept on the horizontal axis is zero. For the debt plan, there must be an EBIT of $200,000 to cover interest charges. For the preferred stock plan, there must be an EBIT of $320,000 [$160,000/(1 − 0.5)] to cover $160,000 in preferred stock dividends at a 50% income tax rate; so $320,000 becomes the horizontal axis intercept. See Figure 1.

	All Common	All Debt	All Preferred
EBIT	$1,000,000	$1,000,000	$1,000,000
Interest		200,000	
Earnings before taxes (EBT)	$1,000,000	$ 800,000	$1,000,000
Taxes	500,000	400,000	500,000
Earnings after taxes (EAT)	$ 500,000	$ 400,000	$ 500,000
Preferred stock dividend			$ 160,000
EAC	$ 500,000	$ 400,000	$ 340,000
Number of shares	140,000	100,000	100,000
EPS	$3.57	$4.00	$3.40

Figure 1 EBIT/EPS Graph

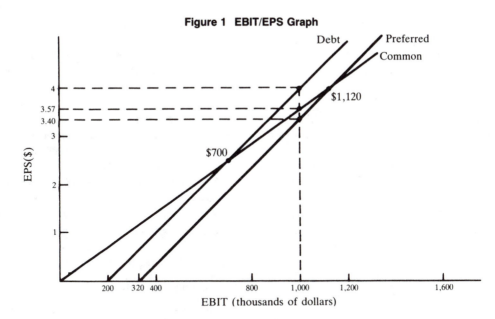

EBIT (thousands of dollars)

In this example, the indifference point between all common and all debt is:

$$\frac{(EBIT - I)(1 - t) - PD}{S_1} = \frac{(EBIT - I)(1 - t) - PD}{S_2}$$

$$\frac{(EBIT - 0)(1 - 0.5) - 0}{140,000}$$

$$= \frac{(EBIT - 200,000)(1 - 0.5) - 0}{100,000}$$

Rearranging yields:

$$0.5\ (EBIT)\ (100,000) = 0.5\ (EBIT)\ (140,000)$$
$$- 0.5\ (200,000)(140,000)$$
$$20,000\ EBIT = 14,000,000,000$$
$$EBIT = \$700,000$$

Similarly, the indifference point between all common and all preferred would be

$$\frac{(EBIT - I)(1 - t) - PD}{S_1} = \frac{(EBIT - I)(1 - t) - PD}{S_2}$$

$$\frac{(EBIT - 0)(1 - 0.5) - 0}{140,000}$$

$$= \frac{(EBIT - 0)(1 - 0.5) - 160,000}{100,000}$$

Rearranging yields:

$$0.5(EBIT)(100,000) = 0.5(EBIT)(140,000)$$
$$- 160,000(140,000)$$
$$20,000\ EBIT = 22,400,000,000$$
$$EBIT = \$1,120,000$$

Based on the previous computations, we can draw the following conclusions:
1. At any level of EBIT, debt is better than preferred stock.
2. At a level of EBIT above $700,000, debt is better than common stock. If EBIT is below $700,000, the reverse is true.
3. At a level of EBIT above $1,120,000, preferred stock is better than common. At or below that point, the reverse is true.
   See also Cost of Capital; Leverage.

ECONOMETRICS This is concerned with empirical testing of economic theory using various statistical methods such as *regression analysis*. Econometric analysis involves four basic phases:
1. Specification of the model, which utilizes economic theory and economic reality
2. Estimation of the model, using statistical methods such as regression analysis

3. Verification of the model, which involves economic interpretation and statistical tests

4. Applications, which include testing economic theorems and forecasting economic variables

Econometrics have been used widely both by accountants and financial analysts for forecasting purposes. Examples include projection of earnings and analysis of mixed costs. *See also* Cost Behavior Analysis; Regression Analysis.

ECONOMIC INDICATORS These attempt to size up where the economy seems to be headed and where it's been. Each month government agencies, including the Federal Reserve, and several economic institutions publish economic indicators. These may be broken down into six broad categories:

1. *Measures of overall economic performance*—include gross national product (GNP), personal income, plant and equipment expenditures, corporate profits, and inventories.

2. *Price indices*—designed to measure the rate of inflation of the economy. The Consumer Price Index (CPI), the most well-known inflation gauge, is used as the cost-of-living index, to which labor contracts and social security are tied. The Producer Price Index (PPI) covers raw materials and semifinished goods and measures prices at the early stage of the distribution system. It is the one that signals changes in the general price level, or the CPI, some time before they actually materialize. The GNP *implicit deflator* is the third index of inflation that is used to separate price changes in GNP calculations from real change in economic activity.

3. *Indices of labor market conditions*—unemployment rate, average workweek of production workers, applications for unemployment compensation, and hourly wage rates.

4. *Money and credit market indicators*—most widely reported in the media are money supply, consumer credit, the Dow Jones industrial average, and the Treasury bill rate.

5. *Index of leading indicators*—most widely publicized signal caller made up of 12 data series. They are money supply, business formation, stock prices, vendor performance, average workweek, new orders, contracts, building permits, inventory change, layoff rate, change in sensitive prices, and change in total liquid assets. They monitor certain business activities that can signal a change in the economy.

6. *Measures for major product markets*—designed to be indicators for segments of the economy such as housing, retail sales, steel, and automobile. Examples are 10-day auto sales, advance retail sales, housing starts, and construction permits.

How to Use Economic Indicators

It is important to note that indicators are only signals. They tell you something about the economic conditions in the country, a particular area, an industry, and, over time, the trends that seem to be shaping up. Here are some tips for using the indicators:

1. Choose indicators closely related to the line of business, its specific aspects, and the geographical area. Home insurance business should monitor building permits as an indicator of future demand for homeowners' policies. Suppliers to the auto industry should closely watch average workweek and new orders as indicators appropriate to their business, rather than looking at money supply or stock prices.

2. Systematically trace the movement of the indicators chosen and assess their appropriateness for the business.

3. Use combinations of important economic indicators for best results—to avoid overreliance on one indicator.

4. Select a price index related to a specific business activity. Effective business planning and budgeting require selecting appropriate price indices. Remember there is no one all-purpose price index. Review separate price indices for products and markets, unit labor costs, raw material costs, and energy costs.

See also Index of Leading Economic Indicators.

ECONOMIC ORDER QUANTITY (EOQ)

The economic order quantity (EOQ) model determines the order size that minimizes the sum of carrying and ordering costs. EOQ is computed as follows:

$$EOQ = \sqrt{\frac{2(\text{Annual demand})\,(\text{Ordering cost})}{\text{Carrying cost per unit}}}$$

See also Inventory Planning and Control.

ECONOMIC PRODUCTION RUN SIZE

This is an optimum production run quantity that minimizes the sum of carrying and setup costs. The way it is computed is exactly the same as economic order quantity (EOQ), except that the ordering cost in the EOQ formula is replaced by the setup cost. The setup cost is the cost incurred each time a batch is produced. It includes the engineering cost of setting up the production runs or machines, paperwork cost of processing the work order, and ordering cost to provide raw materals for the batch. *See also* Economic order Quantity (EOQ); Inventory Planning and Control.

EFFECTIVE INTEREST RATE

1. The true (real) interest rate on a loan computed as:

$$\frac{\text{Nominal interest}}{\text{Loan proceeds}}$$

■ Example

A borrower took out a $30,000 1-year 12% discounted loan (interest is subtracted at the time of loan in deriving loan proceeds). A compensating balance of 6% is also required. The effective interest rate is

$$\frac{\$3,600}{\$30,000 - \$3,600 - \$1,800} = \frac{\$3,600}{\$24,600} = 14.6\%$$

Note: A discounted loan and compensating balance both act to increase the real interest rate.

2. Yield to maturity.
See also Yield.

EFFICIENT MARKET

An efficient market is one in which the market price of a stock is identical to its real (intrinsic) value. In an efficient market, all data are fully and immediately reflected in price. A price change is equally possible to be positive or negative. The hypothesis applies most directly to large companies trading on the New York and American Stock Exchanges. An efficient market may be of the weak, semistrong, or strong type.

In the weak form, no relationship exists between prior and future stock prices. Independence exists over time between prices. The value of historical information already lies in the current price. Therefore, there is no importance associated with reviewing past prices. This puts into question the very nature of technical analysis.

In the semistrong type, stock prices immediately reflect new information. Therefore, action after a known event produces random results. All public information is incorporated in a stock's value. Therefore, fundamental analysis is not helpful in ascertaining whether a stock is over- or undervalued. Investors quickly consider information.

The storng form suggests that stock prices reflect *all* information, whether it be public or private (insider). A perfect market exists. There is no individual who has sole access to information. Hence, a superior return cannot be earned by one individual or group of individuals. *See also* Random Walk Theory.

EFFICIENT PORTFOLIO

This combines assets so as to minimize the risk for a given level of return. *See also* Portfolio Theory and Capital Asset Pricing Model (CAPM).

ELASTICITY OF DEMAND

One of the most important concepts in demand is elasticity, which is the sensitivity of change in quantity demanded to a change in a factor in the demand function. The principal variables involved with demand elasticity are

1. The price of the good (in the case of price elasticity)

2. Income (in the case of income elasticity)
3. The price of a substitute-product (in the case of cross elasticity)
4. Advertising (in the case of promotional elasticity)

We discuss only the price elasticity here in detail since other elasticity concepts are much the same with respect to their calculations and implications.

Price Elasticity of Demand

Price elasticity, denoted with e_p, is the ratio of a percentage change in quantity demanded (Q) to a percentage change in price (p).

$$e_p = \frac{dQ/Q}{dp/p} = dQ/dp \cdot p/Q$$

where dQ/dp is simply the slope of the demand function $Q = (p)$. We classify the price elasticity demand into three categories:

If $e_p = 1$, elastic

$e_p = 1$, unitary

$e_p < 1$, inelastic

■ Example

The demand function is given as $Q = 200 - 6p$. The price elasticity at $p = 4$ is computed as follows:

First, $Q = 200 - 6(4) = 176$

Since $dQ/dp = -6$, the e_p at $p = 4$ is

$$e_p = -6 \times (4/176) = -0.136$$

which means that a 1% change in price will bring about a 0.14% change in demand. The product under study is considered price inelastic, since the e_p is less than 1 in absolute value.

Economists have established the following relationships between price elasticity (e_p) and total revenue (TR), which can aid a firm in setting its price.

Price	$e_p > 1$	$e_p = 1$	$e_p < 1$
Price rises	TR falls	No change	TR rises
Price falls	TR rises	No change	TR falls

Firms need to be aware of the eleasticity of their own demand curves when they set product prices.

■ Example

A profit maximizing firm would never choose to lower its price in the inelastic range of its demand curve—such a price decrease would only decrease total revenue (see the previous chart) and at the same time increase costs, since output would be rising. The result would be a drastic decrease in profits. In fact, when costs are rising and the product is inelastic, the firm would have no difficulty passing on the increases by raising the price to the customer.

On the other hand, when there are many substitutes and demand is quite elastic, increasing prices may lead to a reduction in total revenue rather than an increase. The result may be lower profits rather than higher profits.

Similarly, managers are sometimes surprised by a lack of success of price reductions, this merely being a reflection of the fact that demand is relatively inelastic. In such a case, they may have to rely on other marketing efforts such as advertising and sales promotion in an effort to increase their market share.

ELECTRONIC MAIL   This is a document transmitted electronically from the user's computer or terminal to an on-line data base or other information service. Examples of transmitted documents are spreadsheets, records, reports, letters, and memos. Accountants and financial executives use electronic mail to send and receive timely and important messages from or to clients or others within the organization. There is a "mailbox" for each individual within the system, where messages are received, held, and sent to others. Many services exist, including AT&T and MCI.

ELIMINATIONS Transactions that occur between a parent and its subsidiaries are not considered to reflect arms-length actions; thus, the resulting account balances have to be eliminated in consolidation. An example of an item that would be eliminated in consolidation is the unrealized intercompany profit on the sale of inventory. This would result from the sale of products between parent and subsidiary at a price that is higher than the cost to the transferor. At the end of the reporting period a determination has to be made of the inventory on hand that was bought in this manner. An elimination in the consolidation process is then made for the amount of profit on the company's books applicable to the remaining inventory. Other items that have to be eliminated include profit related to the intercompany sale of fixed assets, the elimination of bonds issued by one company and purchased by another member of the consolidated group, along with related interest expense and income and the shifting of a subsidiary's retained earnings to its common stock account in consolidation in a year when a subsidiary declares a stock dividend on its common stock which is payable in the same class of stock. This entry would take place even though the stock dividend does not affect relative ownership interests and only requires a memo entry on the parent's books. *See also* Consolidation.

EMBEZZLEMENT This occurs when an employee of an entity is involved with theft of money or assets of that business over which he has been given responsibility. For example, an employee who has custody of inventory steals some merchandise. A sound internal control system is needed to guard against improprieties. *See also* Internal Control Structure.

EMPLOYEE STOCK OWNERSHIP PLAN (ESOP)

An ESOP is a stock bonus plan that encourages employees to invest in the employer's stock. Employees may participate in the management of a company and even take control of the company, which would otherwise go bankrupt. The ESOP, however, is an inappropriate instrument for retirement savings. Because most of the funds are concentrated in the stock of one company, it does not provide any safety through diversification.

ENCUMBRANCE

1. In the case of accounting for governmental funds, encumbrances are contractual commitments or purchase orders for merchandise or goods. An encumbrance is established to prevent additional expenditures from being made so that adequate funds exist to meet the commitments that have already been made. When a contractual commitment occurs, encumbrances is debited and reserve for encumbrances credited for the estimated amount. (Reserve for encumbrances represents a reservation of fund equity.) When the actual amount of the encumbered item is known, the initial entry is reversed. A second entry is made, debiting expenditures and crediting vouchers payable.

■ Example

On 6/2/19X1, a contractual commitment is made for an estimated $10,000. The items are received on 7/1/1X1, and the actual cost is $10,200. The entries are

6/2/19X1	Encumbrances	10,000	
	Reserve for Encumbrances		10,000
7/1/19X1	Reserve for Encumbrances	10,000	
	Encumbrances		10,000
	Expenditures	10,200	
	Vouchers Payable		10,200

Since encumbrances is a nominal account, it is credited and fund balance debited at the end of the budget year.

2. An obligation collateralized by a lien on assets.

See also Governmental Accounting.

EQUATION OF EXCHANGE Basically, this is a statement of the fundamental principle that the aggregate amount spent by buyers is equal to the total value of the goods and services sold. Mathematically, the equation is an identity, expressed as follows:

$$MV = PQ$$

where M = money supply,
V = income velocity of money,
P = average price of final goods and services produced during the year,
Q = physical quantity of those goods and services.

■ Example

If the supply of money is $300 billion and each of these dollars on the average is spent five times a year for currently produced goods and services, total expenditures for currently produced goods and services will be $1,500 billion. If producers turn out 750 billion "units" of goods and services and these are subsequently sold at an average price of $2 per unit, then the value of these currently produced goods and services, or GNP, is $1,500 billion. In other words,

$$MV = PQ$$
$$(\$300 \text{ billion}) (5) = (\$2) (750 \text{ billion units})$$
$$\$1,500 \text{ billion} = \$1,500 \text{ billion}$$

The equation of exchange is very important because it provides insights into what will happen to output (Q) and prices (P) when the money supply (M) changes. For example, assume that the velocity of money (V) is constant. If M increases, then either P or Q or both must increase. The effects of P and Q will depend on the state of the economy.

1. If the economy is operating well below the full employment level, Q will tend to rise relatively more than P as unemployed resources are reemployed.

2. If the economy is at full employment, P will tend to rise more than Q; that is, the increase in M will be purely inflationary.

If it is assumed that both V and Q remain

constant, then P depends directly on M. This theory is called the *quantity theory of money*. The theory states, for example, that a 5% increase in money supply will cause a 5% increase in P. Similarly, a 5% decrease in M will cause a 5% decrease in P.

EQUILIBRIUM PRICE AND QUANTITY Equilibrium is a state of balance between opposing forces. *Equilibrium price* is the price of a commodity (good and service) determined by the intersection of the market forces of demand and supply (Figure 1). It is also the price that maximizes a firm's profit (Figure 2). *Equilibrium quantity* is the quantity that corresponds to the equilibrium price. The *Capital Asset Pricing Model* (*CAPM*) provides an equilibrium price on capital assets (Figure 3).

Figure 1 Demand and Supply

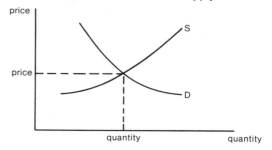

Figure 2 Profit Maximization

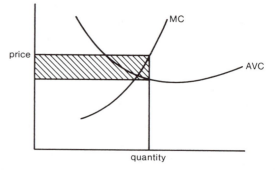

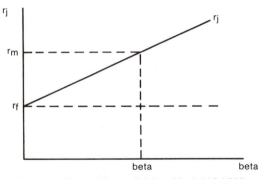

Figure 3 Capital Asset Pricing Model (CAPM)

See also Capital Asset Pricing Model (CAPM).

EQUITY FINANCING Equity issuance may be in the form of common stock or preferred stock. The company obtains cash, other assets, or services. When debt levels are excessive, equity financing is preferred. *Suggestion*: If you are materially affected by outside forces, you need more stability and reliability in your financing.

If stock price is *temporarily low* (e.g., after a stock market crash such as October 1987), funds should be obtained on a short-term debt basis. After stock prices rebound, equity financing may be made and the debt repaid.

Small businesses can obtain equity financing economically by going to venture capital groups that take a position in a small business. A ''finder'' may act as an intermediary between the company and investing group. Alternatively, an ad may be placed in a newspaper. Another possibility is direct private placement to an institutional investor or a key customer or supplier. *Warning*: Avoid stringent restrictions that will curtail your freedom (e.g., minimum working capital requirement).

Common stock is the real ownership interest in the company, since it carries voting rights. Advantages are that there are no fixed charge payments, no maturity date, no sinking fund requirements, no dividends to pay in times of financial distress, and they improve the debt-equity ratio. Disadvantages are that you give up voting rights, ownership interest is diluted, there are higher flotation costs, investors receive dividends after preferred stockholders, investors come after preferred stockholders in the event of liquidation, dividend payments are not tax deductible (unlike interest), and the cost is higher because greater risk exists with common stock than with preferred stocks and bonds.

Preferred stock comes after debt but before common stock in liquidation and in the distribution of earnings. With cumulative preferred stock, preferred dividends in arrears must be paid before any dividends can be paid to common stockholders. *Suggestion*: To avoid SEC disclosures and reduce issuance costs, private placement may be made.

The advantages of preferred stock relative to bonds are that you can omit a dividend but not interest and there is no maturity date and no sinking fund requirement. Compared to common stock, there is no ownership dilution with preferred stock. Disadvantages of preferred stock relative to debt are that dividends are not tax deductible and there is a higher yield because of the greater risk to the holder. *Recommendation*: Issue preferred stock where debt is already excessive and issuing common stock will result in control problems for the ownership group.

The cost of preferred stock usually follows changes in interest rates. Hence, the cost of preferred stock will most likely be low when interest rates are low. When the cost of common stock is high, preferred stock issuance may be achieved at a lower cost.

Suggestion: If you want to issue preferred stock at a lower cost with fewer restrictions, warrants may be given as ''sweeteners.'' Warrants are rights to buy common stock at a certain price at a later date.

EQUITY METHOD The investor company is the owner and the investee company is being owned. If an investor owns between 20%–50% of the voting common stock of an investee, the equity method is used. The equity method would also be employed if the holder owned less than 20% of the voting common stock but possessed significant influence (effective control). The equity method is also used if more than 50% of the voting common stock is owned but one of the negating factors for consolidation exists. Investments in joint ventures have to be accounted for under the equity method.

The accounting under the equity method can be illustrated by examining the following ''T-accounts,'' which will be described in more detail shortly:

Investment in Investee

Cost	Dividends
Ordinary profit	Amortization expense on goodwill
Extraordinary gain	Depreciation on excess of fair market value less book value of specific assets
	Permanent decline

Equity in Earnings of Investee

Amortization expense	Ordinary profit
Depreciation	

Loss

Permanent decline	

Extraordinary Gain

	Extraordinary gain

The cost of the investment includes brokerage fees. The investor recognizes his percentage ownership interest in the ordinary profit of the investee by debiting investment in investee and crediting equity in earnings of investee. The investor's share in investee's earnings is computed after deducting cumulative preferred dividends, whether or not declared. Investor's share of investee's profit should be based on the investee's most recent income statement applied on a consistent basis. Extraordinary gains or losses as well as prior period adjustments are also picked up as shown on the investee's books. Dividends reduce the carrying value of the investment account.

The excess paid by the investor for the investee's net assets is first assigned to the specific assets and liabilities and depreciated. The unidentifiable portion of the excess is considered goodwill, which is amortized over the period benefited, not exceeding 40 years. The amortization expense on goodwill and depreciation on excess value of assets reduce the investment account and are charged to equity in earnings. Temporary decline in price of the investment in the investee is ignored. Permanent decline in value of the investment is reflected by debiting loss and crediting investment in investee.

When the investor's share of the investee's losses is greater than the balance in the investment account, the equity method should be discontinued at the zero amount unless the investor has guaranteed the investee's obligations or where immediate profitability is assured. A return to the equity method is made only after offsetting subsequent profits against losses not recorded.

When the investee's stock is sold, a realized gain or loss will arise for the difference between selling price and the cost of the investment account.

The mechanics of consolidation essentially apply with the equity method. For example, intercompany profits and losses are eliminated. Investee capital transactions impacting the investor's share of equity should be accounted for as in a consolidation. Investee's capital transactions should be accounted for as if the investee were a consolidated subsidiary. For example, when the investee issues its common stock to third parties at a price in excess of book value, there will be an increase in the value of the investment and a related increase in the investor's paid-in-capital.

Interperiod income tax allocation will occur because the investor shows the investee's profits for book reporting but dividends for tax reporting. This results in a deferred income tax credit account.

If the ownership goes below 20% or the investor for some reason is unable to control the investee, the investor should cease recognizing the investee's earnings. The equity method is discontinued but the balance in the investment account is maintained. The cost method should then be applied.

If the investor increases his ownership in the investee to 20% or more, the equity method should be used for current and future years. Further, the effect of using the equity method rather than the cost method on prior years at the old percentage (e.g., 15%) should be recognized as an adjustment to retained earnings and other accounts so affected, such as investment in investee. The retroactive adjustment on the investment, earnings, and retained earnings should be applied in the same manner as a step-by-step acquisition of a subsidiary.

Disclosures should be made by the investor in footnotes, separate schedules, or parenthetically of the following: percent owned, name of investee, investor's accounting policies employed, material effects of possible conversions and exercises of investee common stock, and quoted market price (for investees not qualifying as subsidiaries). Further, summarized financial data as to assets, liabilities, and earnings should be given in footnotes or separate schedules for material investments in unconsolidated subsidiaries. Material realized and unrealized gains and losses relating to the subsidiary's portfolio occurring between the dates of the financial statements of the subsidiary and parent must also be disclosed.

■ **Example**

On 1/1/19X5, X Company bought 30,000 shares at $25 per share for a 40% interest in the common stock of AB Company. Bro-

kerage commissions were $10,000. During 19X5, AB's net income was $140,000 and dividends received were $30,000. On 1/1/19X6, X Company received 15,000 shares of common stock as a result of a stock split by AB Company. On 1/4/19X6, X Company sold 2,000 shares of AB stock at $16 per share. The journal entries follow:

1/1/19X5	Investment in Investee	760,000	
	Cash		760,000
12/31/19X5	Investment in Investee	56,000	
	Equity in Earnings of Investee 40% × $140,000 = $56,000		56,000
	Cash	30,000	
	Investment in Investee		30,000
1/1/19X6	Memo entry for stock split		
1/4/19X6	Cash (2,000 × $16)	32,000	
	Loss on Sale of Investment	2,940	
	Investment in Investee (2,000 × $17.47)		34,940

$$\frac{\$786,000}{45,000} = \$17.47 \text{ per share}$$

Investment in Investee

1/1/19X5	760,000	12/31/19X5	30,000
12/31/19X5	56,000		
	816,000		
	786,000		

■ **Example**

On 1/1/19X6, the investor purchased 100,000 shares of investee's 400,000 shares outstanding for $3,000,000. The book value of net assets acquired was $2,500,000. Of the $500,000 excess paid over book value, $300,000 is attributable to undervalued tangible assets and the remainder is attributable to unidentifiable assets. The depreciation period is 20 years and the maximum period is used to amortize goodwill. In 19X6, investee's net income was $800,000, including an extraordinary loss of $200,000. Dividends of $75,000 were paid on June 1, 19X6. The following journal entries are necessary for the acquisition of investee by investor accounted for under the equity method.

1/1/19X6	Investment in In-		
	vestee	3,000,000	
	Cash		3,000,000
6/1/19X6	Cash	18,750	
	Investment in In-vestee 25% × $75,000		18,750
12/31/19X6	Investment in In-vestee	250,000	
	Equity in Earnings of Investee $1,000,000 × 25% = $250,000		250,000
	Extraordinary Loss from Investment	50,000	
	Investment in In-vestee $200,000 × 25% = $50,000		50,000
	Equity in Earnings of Investee	20,000	
	Investment in In-vestee		20,000

Computation follows:

Undervalued depreciable as-sets $300,000/20 years	$15,000
Unrecorded goodwill $200,000/ 40 years	5,000
	$20,000

See also Cost Method.

EQUIVALENT TAXABLE YIELD

This is what the return would be on a nontaxable security if it were taxable given the individual's tax rate.

■ Example

A client owns a municipal bond that pays an interest rate of 7%. The client's tax rate is 28%. The equivalent rate on a taxable instrument is

$$\frac{0.07}{1-0.28} = \frac{0.07}{0.72} = 9.7\%$$

See also Bond Yield—Effective Rate of Return on a Bond.

ERRORS AND IRREGULARITIES

The AICPAs' Statement on Auditing Standard No. 53 titled ''The Auditor's Responsibility to Detect and Report Errors and Irregularities'' specifies the auditor's responsibility to uncover material misstatements (material errors and irregularities). The auditor must evaluate the risk that errors and irregularities may result in the material misstatement of the financial statements. Based on his evaluation, the auditor has to design the audit to obtain reasonable assurance of uncovering significant errors. However, certain irregularities (e.g., forgery, collusion) may reasonably go undetected by the auditor even with a properly designed and executed audit.

ESTATE

An estate consists of the real and personal assets of an individual at the time of death. The distribution of the assets to the heirs is based on the will. If no will exists, the distribution is in accordance with a court order. It is a liquidation process. Court-supervised probate achieves the following purposes:

• Determine ownership of property
• Ascertain who is to receive benefits
• Assure the proper transfer of property
• Provide for the payment of debts and taxes

The executor of a will is the individual chosen by the decedent during his lifetime to fulfill the terms of the will. Some activities of the executor are

• Collect estate assets
• Manage property
• Pay creditors
• Distribute remaining property

In general, expenses applicable to settle a decedent's estate reduce principal. Expenses to operate, preserve, and manage income-producing property are charged against income.

Accounting for a fiduciary to the court is in the form of Charge-and-Discharge Statements showing the fiduciary's activities relating to principal and income.

The following table shows an illustrative Charge-and-Discharge Statement as to Principal.

Mr. X, Executor
Estate of Mr. A
Charge-and-Discharge Statement as to Principal
Feb. 1, 19X1, to June 30, 19X1

I charge myself with:		
Assets per inventory	$200,000	
Assets discovered	10,000	
Total charges		$210,000
I credit myself with:		
Debts paid	$ 35,000	
Legacies paid or delivered	100,000	
Loss on realization of principal assets	1,000	
Administration expenses	20,000	
Funeral expenses	4,000	
Devise distributed	30,000	
Total credits		190,000
Balance as to principal		$ 20,000
Consisting of:		
Principal cash		$ 5,000
Savings accounts		11,000
Securities		4,000
Total		$ 20,000

The "I charge myself with" section shows the assets the fiduciary is accountable for. The "I credit myself with" section reveals the way in which the fiduciary conducted his responsibilities.

ESTATE PLANNING This involves deriving the most favorable tax consequences for wealth that has been accumulated. This would assume that any inheritance is passed on to the beneficiaries with the least amount given over to taxes.

The tax-planning aspects for estates include:

• Determining what financial strategy could be developed, taking into account the particular assets being considered.

• The transfer of assets before the taxpayer's death. For example, title to property should be transferred to those who would benefit the most from their lower income tax brackets. *Note*: When property will ultimately be transferred to children, it's best to start with gradual transfers at an early age through judicious use of the $10,000 gift tax annual exclusion.

• The attorney should draft a will considering the tax and asset transfer ramifications. For instance, property can be transferred between spouses without any tax because of the unlimited marital deduction.

• Consideration must be given to the terms of any life insurance policies. Will the proceeds go to the estate? If so, how much will it be? Did the insured possess any incidents of ownership? With some policies, the insured will collect if he or she outlives the life expectancy. However, if the insured then dies, the size of the taxable estate will increase, thus increasing the amount of the estate tax.

Estate tax planning begins with the calculation of the consequences of shifting property at some point in the future. Estate tax rates are graduated—the higher the incremental value of the estate, the higher is the incremental tax. To calculate the estate tax, start with determining the gross estate (generally, the taxable estate plus adjusted taxable gifts). Subtract from that figure the allowable deductions, such as administrative expenses, debts, and the marital and charitable deductions. Then compute the tax. Subtract from the tax any credits allowable. Perhaps the most valuable credit is the unified credit. Like other credits, it's a direct reduction of the computed tax. However, because of its size ($192,800), it can allow some estates (those up to $600,000) to pass tax free. Note that the effect of the full unified credit may be diminished if lifetime gifts were made by the decedent that exceeded the $10,000 annual gift tax exclusion.

On-line data bases can provide accurate and cost-effective estate data to the tax accountant or attorneys. Examples are Lexis™, Westlaw™, and PHINet™. The practitioner enters key words for the estate-planning item and the relevant information is downloaded.

ESTIMATED LIABILITIES (CONTINGENCIES)   A loss contingency should be accrued if *both* of the following criteria exist:

• At year-end, it is *probable* (likely to occur) that an asset was impaired or a liability was incurred.

• The amount of loss is subject to reasonable estimation.

The loss contingency is booked because of the principle of conservatism. The entry for a probable loss is

Expense (Loss)
  Estimated Liability

A probable loss that cannot be estimated should be footnoted.

■ Example

On 12/31/19X6, warranty expenses are estimated at $20,000. On 3/15/19X7, actual warranty costs paid for were $16,000. The journal entries are

12/31/19X6 Warranty Expense	20,000	
Estimated Liability		20,000
3/15/19X7 Estimated Liability	16,000	
Cash		16,000

If a loss contingency exists at year-end but no asset impairment or liability incurrence exists (e.g., uninsured equipment), footnote disclosure may be made.

A probable loss occurring after year-end but before the audit report date only requires subsequent event disclosure.

Examples of probable loss contingencies may be

• Warranties
• Lawsuits
• Claims and assessments
• Expropriation of property by a foreign government
• Casualties and catastrophes (e.g., fire)

If the amount of loss is within a range, the accrual is based on the best estimate within that range. However, if no amount within the range is better than any other amount, the *minimum amount* (not maximum amount) of the range is booked. The exposure to additional losses should be disclosed.

In the case of a reasonably possible loss (more than remote but less than likely), no accrual is made but rather footnote disclosure is required. The disclosure includes the nature of the contingency and the estimate of probable loss or range of loss. If an estimate of loss is not possible, that fact should be stated.

A remote contingency (slight chance of occurring) is usually ignored and no disclosure is made. There are exceptions when a remote contingency would be disclosed in the case of guarantees of indebtedness, standby letters of credit, and agreements to repurchase receivables or properties.

General (unspecified) contingencies are not accrued. Examples are self-insurance and possible hurricane losses. Disclosure and/or an appropriation of retained earnings can be made for general contingencies. To be booked as an estimated liability, the future loan must be *specific* and *measurable*, such as parcel post and freight losses.

Gain contingencies cannot be booked because it violates conservatism. However, footnote disclosure can be made.

ESTIMATING CASH COLLECTION RATES (PAYMENT PROPORTIONS) FOR CASH BUDGETING   A forecast of cash collections and potential write-offs of accounts receivable is essential in cash budgeting and in judging the appropriateness of current credit and discount policies.

The critical step in making such a forecast is estimating the cash collection rates (or payment proportions) to be applied to sales or accounts receivable. Two methods are discussed following. They are the probability matrix approach and the lagged regression approach.

The Probability Approach

The probability matrix (or Markov) approach has been around for a long time. This approach has been successfully applied by Cyert and others to accounts receivable analysis, specifically to the estimation of that portion of the accounts receivable that will eventually become uncollectable. The method requires classification of outstanding accounts receivable according to age categories that reflect the stage of account delinquency; for example, current accounts, accounts 1 month past due, accounts 2 months past due, and so forth.

■ Example

XYZ department store divides its accounts receivable into two classifications: 0–60 days old and 61–120 days old. Accounts that are more than 120 days old are declared uncollectable by XYZ. XYZ currently has $10,000 in accounts receivable: $7,000 from the 0–60 day-old category and $3,000 from the 61–120 day-old category. Based on an analysis of its past records, we can formulate with what is known as the matrix of transition probabilities. The matrix is given, as shown in Table 1.

Transition probabilities are nothing more than the probabilities that an account receivable moves from one age stage category to another. We will note three basic features of this matrix. First, notice the squared element, 0 in the matrix. This indicates that $1 in the 0–60 day-old category *cannot* become a bad debt in 1 month's time. Now look at the two circled elements; each of these is 1, indicating that, in time, all the accounts receivable dollars will either be paid

or become uncollectable. Eventually, all the dollars do wind up either as collected or uncollected, but XYZ is interested in knowing the probability that a dollar of 0–60 day-old or 61–120 day-old receivable would eventually find its way into either paid bills or bad debts. It is convenient to partition the matrix of transition probabilities into four submatrices as follows:

$$\left[\begin{array}{c|c} I & O \\ \hline R & Q \end{array}\right]$$

so that

$$I = \begin{bmatrix} 1 & 0 \\ 0 & 1 \end{bmatrix} \quad O = \begin{bmatrix} 0 & 0 \\ 0 & 0 \end{bmatrix}$$

$$R = \begin{bmatrix} 0.3 & 0 \\ 0.5 & 0.1 \end{bmatrix} \quad Q = \begin{bmatrix} 0.5 & 0.2 \\ 0.3 & 0.1 \end{bmatrix}$$

Now we are in a position to illustrate the procedure used to determine
1. Estimated collection and bad debt percentages by age category
2. Estimated allowance for doubtful accounts

Step by step, the procedure is as follows:

Step 1. Set up the matrix $[I - Q]$.

$$[I - Q] = \begin{bmatrix} 1 & 0 \\ 0 & 1 \end{bmatrix} - \begin{bmatrix} 0.5 & 0.2 \\ 0.3 & 0.1 \end{bmatrix} = \begin{bmatrix} 0.5 & -0.2 \\ -0.3 & 0.9 \end{bmatrix}$$

Step 2. Find the inverse of this matrix, denoted by N.

$$N = [I - Q]^{-1} = \begin{bmatrix} 2.31 & 0.51 \\ 0.77 & 1.28 \end{bmatrix}$$

Step 3. Multiply this inverse by matrix R.

Table 1

From \ To	Collected	Uncollectable	0–60 days old	61–120 days old
Collected	①	0	0	0
Uncollectable	0	①	0	0
0–60 days old	0.3	⓪	0.5	0.2
61–120 days old	0.5	0.1	0.3	0.1

$$NR = \begin{bmatrix} 2.31 & 0.51 \\ 0.77 & 1.28 \end{bmatrix} \begin{bmatrix} 0.3 & 0 \\ 0.5 & 0.1 \end{bmatrix} = \begin{bmatrix} 0.95 & 0.05 \\ 0.87 & 0.13 \end{bmatrix}$$

NR gives us the probabilities that an account will eventually be collected or become a bad debt. Specifically, the top row in the answer is the probability that $1 of XYZ's accounts receivable in the 0–60 day-old category will end up in the collected and bad debt categories. There is a 0.95 probability that $1 currently in the 0–60 day-old category will be paid, and a 0.05 probability that it will eventually become a bad debt. Turning to the second row, the two entries represent the probabilities that $1 now in the 61–120 day-old category will end up in the collected and bad debt categories. We can see from this row that there is a 0.87 probability that $1 currently in the 61–120 day-old category will be collected and a 0.13 probability that it will eventually become uncollectable.

If XYZ wants to estimate the future of its $10,000 accounts receivable, it must set up the following matrix multiplication:

$$[7,000 \quad 3,000] \begin{bmatrix} 0.95 & 0.05 \\ 0.87 & 0.13 \end{bmatrix} = [9,260 \quad 740]$$

Hence, of the $10,000 accounts receivable, it expects to collect $9,260 and to lose $740 to bad debts. Therefore, the estimated allowances for uncollectable accounts is $740.

The variance of each component is equal to

$$A = be(cNR - (cNR)_{sq})$$

where $c_i = b_i \Big/ \sum_{i=1}^{2} b_i$ and e is the unit vector.

In our example, $b = (7,000 \quad 3,000)$, $c = (0.7 \quad 0.3)$.

Therefore:

$$A = [7,000 \quad 3,000] \begin{bmatrix} 1 \\ 1 \end{bmatrix} \left[[0.7 \quad 0.3] \begin{bmatrix} 0.95 & 0.05 \\ 0.87 & 0.13 \end{bmatrix} \right.$$

$$- [0.7 \quad 0.3] \begin{bmatrix} 0.95 & 0.05 \\ 0.87 & 0.13 \end{bmatrix}_{sq} \right]$$

$$= 10,000 \big[[0.926 \quad 0.074]$$

$$- [0.857476 \quad 0.005476] \big] = [685.24 \quad 685.24]$$

which makes the standard deviation equal to $26.18 ($\sqrt{685.24}$). If we want to be 95% confident about our estimate of collections, we would set the interval estimate at $9,260 $\pm$ 2(26.18), or $9,207.64 – $9,312.36, assuming $t = 2$ as a rule of thumb. We would also be able to set the allowance to cover the bad debts at $740 + 2(26.18), or $792.36.

The Lagged Regression Approach

Credit sales affect cash collections with time lags. In other words, there is a time lag between the point of credit sale and realization of cash. More specifically, the lagged effect of credit sales and cash inflows is distributed over a number of periods as follows:

$$C_t = b_1 S_{t-1} + b_2 S_{t-2} + \cdots + b_i S_{t-i}$$

where C_t = cash collections,
S_t = credit sales made in period t,
$b_1, b_2, \ldots b_i$ = collection percentages,
i = number of periods lagged.

By using the regression method, we will be able to estimate these collection rates (or payment proportions). We can utilize /Data Regression of Lotus 1–2–3™ or special packages such as STATPACK™ and SAS™.

It should be noted that the cash collection percentages, $(b_1, b_2, \ldots, b_i)$ may not add up to 100% because of the possibility of bad debts. Once we estimate these percentages by using the method, we should be able to compute the bad debt percentage with no difficulty.

Table 2 shows the regression results using actual monthly data on credit sales and cash inflows for a real company. Equation I can be written as follows:

$$C_t = 60.6\%(S_{t-1}) + 24.3\%(S_{t-2}) + 8.8\%(S_{t-3})$$

This result indicates that the receivables generated by the credit sales are collected at the following rates: first month after sale, 60.6%; second month after sale, 24.3%; and third month after sale, 8.8%. The bad debt

Table 2   Regression Results for Cash Collection (C_t)

Independent Variables	Equation I	Equation II
S_{t-1}	0.606[a]	0.596[a]
	(0.062)[b]	(0.097)
S_{t-2}	0.243[a]	0.142
	(0.085)	(0.120)
S_{t-3}	0.088	0.043
	(0.157)	(0.191)
S_{t-4}		0.136
		(0.800)
$\bar{R}^2$	0.754	0.753
Durbin-Watson	2.52[c]	2.48[c]
Standard error of the estimate	11.63	16.05
# of monthly observations	21	20
Bad debt percentages	0.063	0.083

[a] Statistically significant at the 5% significance level
[b] The figure in the parentheses is the standard error of the estimate for the coefficient.
[c] No autocorrelation present at the 5% significance level

percentage is computed as 6.3% (100% − 93.7%).

It is very important to note, however, that these collection and bad debt percentages are probabilistic variables; that is, variables whose values cannot be known with precision. However, the standard error of the regression coefficient and the t-value permit us to assess a probability that the true percentage is between specified limits. The confidence interval takes the following form:

$$b \pm t \text{ (standard error)}$$

■ Example

To illustrate, assuming $t = 2$ as a rule of thumb at the 95% confidence level, the true collection percentage from the prior month's sales will be

$$60.6\% \pm 2(6.2\%)$$
$$= 60.6\% \pm 12.4\%$$

Turning to the estimation of cash collections and allowance for doubtful accounts, we will use the following values for illustrative purposes:

$S_{t-1} = \$77.6, S_{t-2} = \$58.5, S_{t-3} = \$76.4,$
and forecast average monthly net credit sales = \$75.2

Then, (i) the forecast cash collection for period t would be

$$C_t = 60.6\%(77.6) + 19.3\%(58.5)$$
$$+ 8.8\%(76.4) = \$65.04$$

If the financial planner wants to be 95% confident about this forecast value, then he or she would set the interval as follows:

$$C_t \pm t(\text{standard error of the estimate})$$

To illustrate, using $t = 2$ as a rule of thumb at the 95% confidence level, the true value for cash collections in period t will be

$$\$65.04 \pm 2(11.63)$$
$$= \$65.04 \pm 23.26$$

See also Budgeting for Profit Planning; Cash Budget.

EXPECTED VALUE   The expected value ($E(x)$) is found by multiplying the probability of each outcome by its *payoff*.

$$E(x) = x_i \, p_i$$

where x_i is the outcome for ith possible event and p_i is the probability of occurrence of that outcome. *See also* Decision Making Under Uncertainty.

EXPERT SYSTEM   An expert system refers to a computer-oriented information system employing knowledge about a difficult area to serve as an advisor to you. The expert system includes a knowledge base and software modules that carry out logical inferences on the knowledge and give appropriate answers to problems faced. The software is also able to explain the reasons for answers. Knowledge refiner programs reduce significant amounts of data to more meaningful knowledge. The result can then be transferred to an expert system in helping you solve a problem.

Special Note: Expert systems simulate the human reasoning process. They codify the knowledge and guidelines used to derive conclusions. Knowledge is used to answer complex questions. The system has programmed in it rules for reasoning (inference or logical functions). Information received is compared to the stored knowledge base and a recommended solution offered along with supporting rationale. There is an interface representing interaction between the user and expert system. The system can be used for financial and managerial decision making such as portfolio management. The knowledge base must be updated for new information and trends and hence will have to be tied into an on-line data base.

What goes on? The computer ascertains what data are necessary for a decision and asks appropriate sequential questions. It then searches, retrieves, and derives relevant data to make that decision. For example, in an acquisition and merger setting, the program determines the appropriate information from the data base and communicates the information in quantitative terms, including analysis.

Many practitioner benefits exist with the use of expert systems, including:
- Reduction of CPA firm staff time.
- Use of ''real-situation'' simulation for the instruction of accounting, audit, and tax staff.
- Transmittal of knowledge from the partners to lower staff levels, including associated reasoning. It can provide a confirming opinion to that initially selected by the partner or manager for a particular problem.

■ Example

Human Edge Software's Expert Ease™ induces rules and a knowledge base based on the expert information including examples given to it. The rules permit decisions and diagnoses via an inquiry interface. It appraises a range of factors relative to a particular objective and ignores irrelevant variables.

It can perform complicated financial analysis models.

■ Example

Applied Expert Systems' Planpower™ provides expert assistance to professional financial planners. It emulates the knowledge of planning experts in the firm, evaluates and plans, and prepares the actual plan, including recommendations. It has many decision rules in its knowledge base. Reasoning behind recommendations is given and recommendations are tested against all alternatives.

■ Example

Unitek Technologies' Expert Strategist™ interprets financial statements transferred from a conventional accounting package. In effect, financial statement analysis is performed. It also reveals the impact of different management actions on the financial ratios.

EXPONENTIAL SMOOTHING This is a popular technique for short-run forecasting by financial managers. It uses a weighted average of past data as the basis for a forecast. The procedure gives heaviest weight to more recent information and lesser weights to observations in the more distant past. The reason for this is that the future is more dependent upon the recent past than on the distant past. In connection with sales forecasting, the method is known to be effective when there is random demand and no seasonal fluctuations in the sales data. One disadvantage of the method, however, is that it does not include industrial or economic factors such as market conditions, prices, or the effects of competitors' actions.

The Model

The formula for exponential smoothing is

$$\hat{y}_{t+1} = \alpha \, y_t + (1 - \alpha) \, \hat{y}_t$$

or in words,

$$\hat{y}_{new} = \alpha\, y_{old} + (1 - \alpha)\, \hat{y}_{old}$$

where $\hat{y}_{new}$ = exponentially smoothed aver-
              age to be used as the forecast,
         y_{old} = most recent actual data,
         $\hat{y}_{old}$ = most recent smoothed forecast,
         α = smoothing constant.

The higher the α, the higher the weight given to the more recent information.
Data on sales follow.

Time Period (t)	Actual Sales (000) (y_t)
1	$60.0
2	64.0
3	58.0
4	66.0
5	70.0
6	60.0
7	70.0
8	74.0
9	62.0
10	74.0
11	68.0
12	66.0
13	60.0
14	66.0
15	62.0

To initialize the exponential smoothing process, we must have the initial forecast. The first smoothed forecast to be used can be
1. First actual observations.
2. An average of the actual data for a few periods.
For illustrative purposes, let us use a six-period average as the initial forecast ($\hat{y}_7$) with a smoothing constant of $\alpha = 0.40$.

Then $\hat{y}_7 = (y_1 + y_2 + y_3 + y_4 + y_5 + y_6)/6$
$$= (60 + 64 + 58 + 66 + 70 + 60)/$$
$$6 = 63$$

Note that $y_7 = 70$. Then $\hat{y}_8$ is computed as follows:

$$\hat{y}_8 = \alpha\, y_7 + (1 - \alpha)\, \hat{y}_7$$
$$= (0.40)\,(70) + (0.60)\,(63)$$
$$= 28.0 + 37.80 = 65.80$$

Similarly:

$$\hat{y}_9 = \alpha\, y_8 + (1 - \alpha)\, \hat{y}_8$$
$$= (0.40)\,(74) + (0.60)\,(65.80)$$
$$= 29.60 + 39.48 = 69.08$$

and:

$$\hat{y}_{10} = \alpha\, y_9 + (1 - \alpha)\, \hat{y}_9$$
$$= (0.40)\,(62) + (0.60)\,(69.08)$$
$$= 24.80 + 41.45 = 66.25$$

By using the same procedure, the values of $\hat{y}_{11}$, $\hat{y}_{12}$, $\hat{y}_{13}$, $\hat{y}_{14}$, and $\hat{y}_{15}$ can be calculated. The table on page 182 shows a comparison between the actual sales and predicted sales by the exponential smoothing method.

Due to the negative and positive differences between actual sales and predicted sales, the forecaster can use a higher or lower smoothing constant α, in order to adjust his/her prediction as quickly as possible to large fluctuations in the data series. For example, if the forecast is slow in reacting to increased sales, (that is to say, if the difference is negative), he/she might want to try a higher value. For practical purposes, the *optimal* α may be picked by minimizing what is known as the *mean squared error* (MSE).

$$\text{MSE} = \sum_{t=1}^{n} (y_t - \hat{y}_t)^2/(n - i)$$

where i = the number of observations used to determine the initial forecast (in our example, $i = 6$).
In our example,

$$\text{MSE} = 307.27/(15 - 6) = 307.27/9 = 34.14$$

The idea is to select the α that minimizes MSE, which is the average sum of the variations between the historical sales data and the forecast values for the corresponding periods.

Comparison of Actual Sales and Predicted Sales

Time Period (t)	Actual Sales (y_t)	Predicted Sales ($\hat{y}_t$)	Difference ($y_t - \hat{y}_t$)	Difference^2 ($y_t - \hat{y}_t)^2$
1	$60.0			
2	64.0			
3	58.0			
4	66.0			
5	70.0			
6	60.0			
7	70.0	63.00	7.00	49.00
8	74.0	65.80	8.20	67.24
9	62.0	69.08	−7.08	50.13
10	74.0	66.25	7.75	60.06
11	68.0	69.35	−1.35	1.82
12	66.0	68.81	−2.81	7.90
13	60.0	67.69	−7.69	59.14
14	66.0	64.61	1.39	1.93
15	62.0	65.17	−3.17	10.05
				307.27

EXTRAORDINARY ITEMS These items are *both* unusual in nature and infrequent in occurrence. They are presented net of tax separately in the income statement. *See also* Income Statement Format.

F

FACTORING OF ACCOUNTS RECEIVABLE *See* Accounts Receivable Financing.

FACTORY OVERHEAD APPLICATION Regardless of the cost accumulation system used (i.e., job order, process, or standard costing), factory overhead is applied to a job or process using a *predetermined overhead rate*, which is determined based on budgeted factory overhead cost and budgeted activity. The rate is calculated as follows:

Predetermined overhead rate =

$$\frac{\text{Budgeted yearly total factory overhead costs}}{\text{Budgeted yearly activity (direct labor hours, etc.)}}$$

Budgeted activity units used in the denominator of the formula, more often called the *denominator level*, are measured in direct labor hours, machine hours, direct labor costs, production units, or any other representative surrogate of production activity.

■ **Example**

Assume that two companies have prepared the budgeted data shown in the table at the bottom of this page for the year 19A. Now assume that actual overhead costs and the actual level of activity for 19A for each firm are shown as follows:

	Company X	Company Y
Actual overhead costs	$198,000	$256,000
Actual machine hours	96,000	
Actual direct labor cost		176,000

Note that for each company the actual cost and activity data differ from the budgeted figures used in calculating the predetermined overhead rate. The computation of the resulting *underapplied* and *overapplied* overhead for each company follows on page 184.

	Company X	Company Y
Predetermined rate based on	Machine hours	Direct labor cost
Budgeted overhead	$200,000 (1)	$240,000 (1)
Budgeted machine hours	100,000 (2)	
Budgeted direct labor cost		$160,000(2)
Predetermined overhead rate (1)/(2)	$2 per machine hours	150% of direct labor cost

	Company X	Company Y
Actual overhead costs	$198,000	$256,000
Factory overhead applied to work-in-process		
during 19A:		
96,000 actual machine hours × $2	192,000	
$176,000 actual direct labor cost × 150%		264,000
Underapplied (overapplied) factory overhead	$ 6,000	($ 8,000)

See also Job Order Cost Accounting.

FEDERAL FUNDS   These are unsecured loans that commercial banks make to one another, usually overnight and over-the-counter by telephone or telegraph, out of their excessive reserve. The *federal fund market* is one in which commercial banks trade deposit balances at the Federal Reserve banks. Banks that are deficient to meet the Federal Reserve requirements borrow or "buy" federal funds. Banks that have more than enough to meet requirements lend or "sell" federal funds. The interest rate involved—the *federal fund rate*—is a highly sensitive and widely quoted money market yield. In general, the lower the volume of excess reserves, the higher will be the rate. Therefore, the federal fund rate is an important indicator that the Fed watches to decide whether it should add to banks' reserves or take them away. As part of its policy-making function, the Fed attempts to maintain a federal fund rate that is consistent with other monetary goals. *See also* Monetary Policy; Money Supply.

FEDERAL RESERVE SYSTEM   This is the system, created by an act of Congress in 1913, that is made up of 12 *Federal Reserve District Banks*, their 25 branches, and all national and state banks (about 5,700 member banks) that are part of the system scattered throughout the nation. It is headed by a seven-member Board of Governors. (see Figure 1.) The primary function of the Board is to establish and conduct the nation's monetary policy. The system manages the nation's monetary policy by exercising control over the money stock. (See Figure 2.) It controls the money

supply primarily in three ways: (1) by raising or lowering the reserve requirement; (2) by setting the *discount rate* for loans to commercial banks; and (3) by purchasing and selling the government securities, mainly 3-month bills and notes issued by the U.S. Treasury. The system also serves as the central bank of the United States and a banker's bank that offers banks many of the same services that banks provide their customers. It performs many other functions. It sets margin requirements, regulates member banks, and acts as fiscal agent in the issuance of U.S. Treasury and U.S. government agency securities. *See also* Monetary Policy.

FIDUCIARY   A fiduciary is an individual who holds something in trust for another. The fiduciary is typically responsible for investing money prudently for the benefit of the beneficiary. Examples of fiduciaries are executors of estates, administrators of trusts, and receivers in bankruptcy. Fiduciaries are very often restricted as to what they are allowed to do with a beneficiary's assets. The term is also used to refer to corporate directors, trustees of nonprofit entities, and agencies. *See also* Estate; Trust.

FINANCIAL ANALYSIS   This involves the use and transformation of financial data into a form that can be used to monitor and evaluate the firm's financial position, to plan future financing, and to designate the size of the firm and its rate of growth. Financial analysis includes the use of *financial statement analysis* and *cash flow analysis*. *See also* Financial Statement Analysis; Z Scores.

Figure 1 Organization and Map of the Federal Reserve System

FINANCIAL FORECASTING AND THE PERCENTAGE-OF-SALES METHOD

Financial forecasting, an essential element of planning, is the basis for budgeting activities. It is also needed where future financing needs are being estimated. Basically, forecasts of future sales and their related expenses provide the firm with the information needed to project its future needs for financing.

The basic steps involved in projecting those financing needs are

1. Project the firm's sales. The sales forecast is the initial most important step. Most other forecasts (budgets) follow the sales forecast.
2. Project additional variables such as expenses.
3. Estimate the level of investment in current and fixed assets that are required to support the projected sales.
4. Calculate the firm's financing needs.

The most widely used method for projecting the company's financing needs is the *per-*

Figure 2 Flow of Federal Reserve System Influence

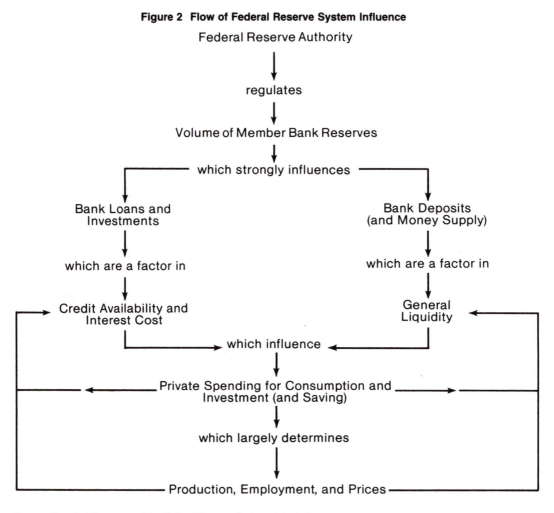

Federal Reserve Authority

↓

regulates

↓

Volume of Member Bank Reserves

↓

which strongly influences

Bank Loans and Investments

which are a factor in

Credit Availability and Interest Cost

Bank Deposits (and Money Supply)

which are a factor in

General Liquidity

which influence

Private Spending for Consumption and Investment (and Saving)

which largely determines

Production, Employment, and Prices

Source: Board of Governors of the Federal Reserve System. Adapted.

cent-of-sales method. This method involves estimating the various expenses, assets, and liabilities for a future period as a percentage of the sales forecast and then using these percentages, together with the projected sales, to construct *pro forma* balance sheets. The following example illustrates how to develop a pro forma balance sheet and determine the amount of external financing needed.

■ Example 1

Assume that sales for 19x1 = $20, projected sales for 19x2 = $24, net income = 5% of sales, and the dividend payout ratio = 40%.

The steps for the computations are outlined as follows:

Step 1. Express those balance sheet items *that vary directly with sales* as a percentage of sales. Any item such as long-term debt that does not vary directly with sales is designated "n.a.," or "not applicable."

Step 2. Multiply these percentages by the 19x2 projected sales = $2.4 to obtain the projected amounts, as shown in the last column.

Step 3. Simply insert figures for long-term debt, common stock, and paid-in capital from the 19x1 balance sheet.

Step 4. Compute 19x2 retained earnings as shown in (b).

Step 5. Sum the asset accounts, obtaining a total projected assets of $7.2, and also add the projected liabilities and equity to obtain $7.12, the total financing provided. Since liabilities and equity must total $7.2 but only $7.12 is projected, we have a shortfall of $0.08 "external financing needed."

Although the forecast of additional funds required can be made by setting up pro forma balance sheets, as described previously, it is often easier to use the following formula:

$$\begin{matrix} \text{External} & \text{Required} & \text{Spontaneous} & \text{Increase in} \\ \text{funds} & = \text{increase} & - \text{increase in} & - \text{retained} \\ \text{needed} & \text{in assets} & \text{liabilities} & \text{earnings} \\ \text{(EFN)} & & & \end{matrix}$$

$$\text{EFN} = (A/S)\,\Delta S - (L/S)\,\Delta S - (PM)\,(PS)\,(1 - d)$$

where A/S = assets that increase spontaneously with sales as a percentage of sales,

L/S = liabilities that increase spontaneously with sales as a percentage of sales,

ΔS = change in sales,

PM = profit margin on sales,

PS = projected sales,

d = dividend payout ratio.

Figure 1   Projecting Balance Sheet Using Percentage-of-Sales Method

Pro Forma Balance Sheet
(in millions of dollars)

	Present (19x1)	% of Sales (19x1 sales = $20)	Projected (19x2 sales = $24)	
Assets				
Current assets	2	10	2.4	
Fixed assets	4	20	4.8	
Total assets	6		7.2	
Liabilities and stockholder's equity				
Current liabilities	2	10	2.4	
Long-term debt	2.5	n.a.	2.5	
Total liabilities	4.5		4.9	
Common stock	0.1	n.a.	0.1	
Paid-in-capital	0.2	n.a.	0.2	
Retained earnings	1.2		1.92[a]	
Total equity	1.5		2.22	
Total liabilities and stockholders' equity	6		7.12	Total financing provided
			0.08[b]	External financing needed
			7.2	Total

[a] 19x2 retained earnings = 19x1 retained earnings + projected net income − cash dividends paid = $1.2 + 5%($24) − 40%[5%($24)] = $1.2 + $1.2 − $0.48 = $2.4 − $0.48 = $1.92
[b] External financing needed = projected total assets − (projected total liabilities + projected equity) = $7.2 − ($4.9 + $2.22) = $7.2 − $7.12 = $0.08

■ Example 2

In Example 1, $A/S = \$6/\$20 = 30\%$,
$L/S = \$2/\$20 = 10\%$,
$\Delta S = (\$24 - \$20) = \$4$,
$PM = 5\%$ on sales,
$PS = \$24$,
$d = 40\%$.

Plugging these figures into the formula yields:

$$EFN = 0.3(\$4) - 0.1(\$4) - (0.05)\,(\$24)\,(1 - 0.4)$$
$$= \$1.2 - \$0.4 - \$0.72 = \$0.08$$

Thus, the amount of external financing needed is $800,000, which can be raised by issuing notes payable, bonds, stocks, or any combination of these financing sources.

The major advantage of the precent-of-sales method of financial forecasting is that it is simple and inexpensive to use. To obtain a more precise projection of the firm's future financing needs, however, the preparation of a *cash budget* is required. One important assumption behind the use of the method is that the firm is operating at full capacity. This means that the company has no sufficient productive capacity to absorb a projected increase in sales and thus requires additional investment in assets. *See also* Cash Budget.

FINANCIAL FUTURES   These may be utilized to hedge for the variability in interest and exchange rates. They may also be employed as speculative investments due to the potential for significant price fluctuation. Further, financial futures involve a lower margin requirement than commodities. For instance, the margin on a U.S. Treasury bill may be as low as 2%. Some places where financial futures may be traded are the New York Futures Exchange and the Chicago Board of Trade. Financial futures are mostly for fixed income debt securities designed to hedge or speculate on changes in interest rates or foreign currency. *See also* Interest Rate Futures Contract; Currency Futures Contract.

FINANCIAL GAMES   These focus on middle management decisions and emphasize particular areas of the firm. Financial games deal with the finance function of the firm. For example, a popular financial game, known as *FINANSIM: A Financial Management Simulation*™ (by Greenlaw and Frey), is a computerized functional game that emphasizes capital cost and budgeting, cash utilization and acquisition, and the asset structure of the firm. Marketing decisions are excluded; demand and price are considered exogeneous factors. Typically, there is no interaction in many functional games between player decisions. They bear strong resemblance to *simulation models*. *See also* Management Games; Simulation Models.

FINANCIAL INFORMATION SYSTEM   The financial information system is a subsystem of a *management information system (MIS)*. The financial information system is concerned with the financial resources of the firm and their acquisition, management, and expenditure in line with the overall objectives of the firm. Its primary objective is to meet the firm's financial obligations as they become due, using the minimum amount of minimum resources consistent with an established margin of safety. The financial information system typically has two input subsystems and four output systems. Internal accounting data and external sources such as information on the firm's stockholders and money and credit markets are fed into the input subsystems—*the accounting information system (AIS)* and the financial intelligence subsystem. The four output subsystems—the forecasting subsystem, funds management subsystem, financial control subsystem, and financial decision support system—are concerned with forecasting the future financial condition of the firm, managing the flow of funds in and out of the firm, controlling disbursements, and facilitating financial decision making. *See also* Account-

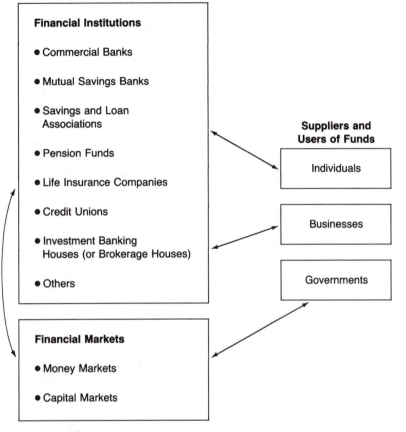

Figure 1   General Flow of Funds Among Financial Institutions and Financial Markets

ing Information System (AIS); Decision Support System (DSS); Financial Model; Management Information System (MIS).

FINANCIAL INSTITUTIONS AND MARKETS   A
healthy economy depends heavily on efficient transfer of funds from savers to the individuals, businesses, and governments who need capital. Most transfers occur through specialized *financial institutions* (see Figure 1) that serve as intermediaries between suppliers and users of funds. *Financial intermediaries* are firms that serve as middlemen between lenders and borrowers. In general, they are wholesalers and retailers of funds. It is in the *financial markets* that entities demanding funds are brought together with those having

surplus funds. Financial markets provide a mechanism through which the financial manager may obtain funds from a wide range of sources, including financial institutions. Figure 1 depicts the general flow of funds among financial institutions and financial markets.

The financial markets are composed of money markets and capital markets. *Money markets* (credit markets) are the markets for short-term (less than 1 year) debt securities. Examples of money market securities include U.S. Treasury bills, federal agency securities, bankers' acceptances, commercial paper, and negotiable certificates of deposit issued by government, business, and financial institutions. The money market securities are characterized by their highly liquid nature and a relatively low default risk.

Capital markets are the markets in which long-term securities issued by the government and corporations are traded. Unlike the money market, both debt instruments (bonds) and equities (common and preferred stocks) are traded. Relative to money market instruments, those of the capital market often carry greater default and market risks but return a relatively high yield in compensation for the higher risks. The New York Stock Exchange, which handles the stock of many of the larger corporations, is a prime example of a capital market. The American Stock Exchange and the regional stock exchanges are still another example. These exchanges are organized markets. In addition, securities are traded through the thousands of brokers and dealers on the *over-the-counter* (*or unlisted*) *market*, a term used to denote an informal system of telephone contacts among brokers and dealers. There are other markets that include (1) the commodity markets, which handle various commodity futures; (2) the foreign exchange market, which involves international financial transactions between the U.S. and other countries; and (3) the insurance, shipping, and other markets handling short-term credit accommodations in their operations. A *primary market* refers to the market for new issues, whereas a *secondary market* is a market in which previously issued, "secondhand" securities are exchanged. The New York Stock Exchange is an example of a secondary market.

FINANCIAL LEVERAGE This is a portion of a firm's assets financed with debt instead of equity and therefore involves contractual interest and principal obligations. Financial leverage benefits common stockholders as long as the borrowed funds generate a return in excess of the cost of borrowing, although the increased risk can offset the general cost of capital. For this reason, financial leverage

is popularly called *trading on equity. See also* Leverage; Trading on Equity.

FINANCIAL MODELS A financial model is a system of mathematical equations, logic, and data that describe the relationships among financial and operating variables. A financial model can be viewed as a subset of broadly defined *corporate planning models* or a stand-alone functional system that is essentially used to generate *pro forma* financial statements and financial ratios. It is the basic tool for budgeting and profit planning. Also, the financial model is a technique for risk analysis and what-if experiments. In the face of uncertainty about the future, financial management is particularly interested in obtaining the best possible course of action under a given circumstance. The model is used as a tool to help minimize risk and uncertainty and develop the best corporate strategy. For example, a company is able to examine the effects of proposed mergers and acquisitions with much less uncertainty and to estimate with more confidence the potential profits from new markets. The financial model is also needed for day-to-day operational and tactical decisions for immediate planning problems. A financial model is one in which:
1. One or more financial variables appear (expenses, revenues, investment, cash flow, taxes, earnings, and so on).
2. The model user can manipulate (set and alter) the value of one or more financial variables.
3. The purpose of the model is to influence strategic decisions by revealing to the decision maker the implications of alternative values of these financial variables.

Financial models fall into two types: *simulation*, better known as *what-if*, models and *optimization* models. *What-if models* are models that attempt to simulate the effects of alternative management policies and assumptions about the firm's external environment. They are basically a tool for management's laboratory. *Optimization models* are those in which the goal is to maximize or minimize an objective such as present value of profit or cost. Multiobjective techniques such as *goal programming* are being experimented.

Models can be deterministic or probabilistic. Deterministic models do not include any random or probabilistic variables, whereas probabilistic models incorporate random numbers and/or one or more probability distributions for variables such as sales, costs, and so on.

Financial models can be solved and manipulated computationally to derive from them the current and projected future implications and consequences. Due to technological advances in computers (such as spreadsheets, financial modeling languages, graphics, data base management systems, and networking), more and more companies are using modeling.

Applications and Uses of Financial Models

Basically, a financial model is used to generate projected financial statements such as the income statement, balance sheet, and cash flow statement. Such a model can be called a budgeting model, since we are essentially developing a master budget with such a model. Applications and uses of the model are numerous. They include:

- Projection of financial statements or development of budgets
  - Financial forecasting and analysis
  - Cash budgeting
  - Capital expenditure analysis
  - Tax planning
  - Exchange rate analysis
  - Analysis for mergers and acquisitions
  - Labor contract negotiations
  - Capacity planning
  - Cost-volume-profit analysis
  - New venture analysis
  - Lease/purchase analysis

- Evaluation of performance by segments
- Market analysis
- New product analysis
- Development of long-term strategy
- Planning for financial requirements
- Risk analysis
- Cash flow analysis
- Cost and price projections

Development of Financial Models

Development of financial models essentially involves two steps: (1) definition of variables and input parameters and (2) model specification. As far as model specification goes, we will explain only the simulation-type model here.

Generally speaking, the model consists of three important ingredients:
- Variables
- Input parameter values
- Definitional and/or functional relationships

Definition of Variables and Input Parameters

Fundamental to the specification of a financial model is the definition of the variables to be included in the model. There are basically three types of variables: policy variables (Z), external variables (X), and performance variables (Y).

Policy variables—the variables over which financial management can exert some degree of control. The policy variables are often called control variables. Among these we may list, in the area of finance, such variables as cash management policy, working capital policy, debt management policy, depreciation policy, tax policy, merger-acquisition decisions, the rate and direction of the firm's capital investment programs, the extent of its equity and external debt financing and the financial leverage represented thereby, and the size of its cash balances and liquid assets position. Policy variables are denoted by the symbol Z in Figure 1.

Figure 1 Variables in a Financial Model

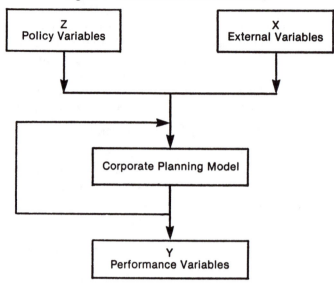

External variables—the environmental variables that are external to the company and that influence the firm's decisions from outside of the firm, generally exogeneous in nature. Generally speaking, the firm is embedded in an industry environment. This industry environment, in turn, is influenced by overall general business conditions. General business conditions exert influences upon particular industries in several ways. Total volume of demand, product prices, labor costs, material costs, money rates, and general expectations are among the industry variables affected by the general business conditions. The symbol X represents the external variables in the figure.

Performance variables—measure the firm's economic and financial performance, which are usually endogenous. We use the symbol Y in the diagram. The Y's are often called output variables. The output variables of a financial model would be the line items of the balance sheet, cash budget, income statement, or statement of cash flows. How to define the output variables of the firm will depend on the goals and objectives of

financial management. They basically indicate how financial officers measure the performance of the organization or some segments of it. Financial management is likely to be concerned with: (1) the firm's level of earnings; (2) growth in earnings; (3) projected earnings; (4) growth in sales; and (5) cash flow.

Frequently when we attempt to set up a financial model we face risk or uncertainty associated with particular projections. In a case such as this, we treat some of these variables such as sales as *random* variables with given probability distributions. The inclusion of random variables in the model transforms it from a *deterministic* model to a *risk analysis* model. However, the use of the risk analysis model in practice is rare because of the difficulty involved in modeling and computation.

Input parameter values—the model as a major part includes various input parameter values. For example, in order to generate the balance sheet, the model needs to input beginning balances of various asset, liability, and equity accounts. These input and parameter values are supplied by management. The ratio between accounts receivable and sales and financial decision variables such as the maximum desired debt-equity ratio would be good examples of parameters.

Model Specification—Functional Relationships

Once we define various variables and input parameters for our financial model, we must then specify a set of mathematical and logical relationships linking the input variables to the performance variables. The relationships usually fall into two types of equations: definition equations and behavioral equations. Definitional equations take the form of accounting identities. Behavioral equations involve theories or hypotheses about the behavior of certain economic and financial events. They must be empirically tested and validated before they are incorporated into the financial model.

Definitional Equations

Definitional equations are exactly what the term refers to—mathematical or accounting definitions. For example,

$$\text{Assets} = \text{Liabilities} + \text{Equity}$$
$$\text{Net income} = \text{Revenues} - \text{Expenses}$$

These definitional equations are fundamental definitions in accounting for the balance sheet and income statement, respectively. Two more examples follow:

$$CASH = CASH(-1) + CC$$
$$+ OCR + DEBT - CD - LP$$

This equation is a typical cash equation in a financial model. It states that ending cash balance (CASH) is equal to the beginning cash balance (CASH(-1)) plus cash collections from customers (CC) plus other cash receipts (OCR) plus borrowings (DEBT) minus cash disbursements (CD) minus loan payments (LP).

$$INV = INV(-1) + MAT + DL + OVER - CGS$$

This equation states that ending inventory (INV) is equal to the beginning inventory (INV(-1)) plus cost of materials used (MAT) plus cost of direct labor (DL) plus manufacturing overhead (OVER) minus the cost of goods sold (CGS).

Behavioral Equations

Behavioral equations describe the behavior of the firm regarding the specific activities that are subject to empirical testing and validation. The classical demand function in economics is

$$Q = f(P) \text{ or more specifically } Q = a - bP$$

It simply says that the quantity demanded is negatively related to the price. That is to say, the higher the price, the lower the demand. However, the firm's sales are more realistically described as follows:

$$SALES = f(P, ADV., I, GNP, Pc, \text{etc.}) \text{ or}$$

assuming linear relationship among these variables, we can specify the model as follows:

$$SALES = a + bP + cADV + dI + eGNP + fPc + u$$

which says that the sales are affected by such factors as price (P), advertising expenditures (ADV), consumer income (I), gross national product (GNP), prices of competitive goods (Pc), and so on. The error term is u. With the data on SALES, P, ADV, I, GNP, and Pc, we will be able to estimate parameter values a, b, c, d, e, and f, using linear regression. We can test the statistical significance of each of the parameter estimates and evaluate the overall explanatory power of the model, measured by the t-statistic and r-squared, respectively. This way we will be able to identify most influential factors that affect the sales of a particular product. With the best model chosen, financial management can simulate the effects on sales of alternative pricing and advertising strategies. We can also experiment with alternative assumptions regarding the external economic factors such as GNP, consumer income, and prices of competitive goods.

Model Structure

A majority of financial models that have been in use are recursive and/or simultaneous models. *Recursive* models are the ones in which each equation can be solved one at a time by substituting the solution values of the preceding equations into the right-hand side of each equation. An example of a financial model of recursive type follows.

(1) SALES   = $A - B*$PRICE + $C*$ADV
(2) REVENUE = SALES*PRICE
(3) CGS   = 0.70*REVENUE
(4) GM   = SALES − CGS
(5) OE   = \$10,000 + 0.2*SALES
(6) EBT   = GM − OE
(7) TAX   = 0.46*EBT
(8) EAT   = EBT − TAX

In this example, the selling price (PRICE) and advertising expenses (ADV) are given. A, B, and C are parameters to be estimated and

SALES = sales volume in units
REVENUE = sales revenue
CGS = cost of goods sold
GM = gross margin
OE = operating expenses
EBT = earnings before taxes
TAX = income taxes
EAT = earnings after taxes

Simultaneous models are frequently found in econometric models which require a higher level of computational methods such as matrix inversion. An example of a financial model of this type follows:

(1) INT   = 0.10*DEBT
(2) EARN = REVENUE − CGS − OE
                − INT − TAX − DIV
(3) DEBT = DEBT(−1) + BOW
(4) CASH = CASH(−1) + CC + BOW
                + EARN − CD − LP
(5) BOW = MBAL − CASH

Note that earnings (EARN) in Equation (2) is defined as sales revenue minus CGS, OE, interest expense (INT), TAX, and dividend payment (DIV). But INT is a percentage interest rate on total debt in Equation (1). Total debt in Equation (3) is equal to the previous period's debt (DEBT(−1)) plus new borrowings (BOW). New debt is the difference between a minimum cash balance (MBAL) minus cash. Finally, the ending cash balance in Equation (5) is defined as the sum of the beginning balance (CASH(−1)), cash collection, new borrowings and earnings *minus* cash disbursements and loan payments of the existing debt (LP). Even though the model presented here is a simple variety, it is still simultaneous in nature, which requires the use of a method capable of solving simultaneous equations. Very few of the financial modeling languages have the capability to solve this kind of system.

Decision Rules

The financial model may, in addition to those previously discussed—that is, definitional equations and behavioral equations—include basic decision rules specified in a very general form. The decision rules are not written in the form of conventional equations. They are described algebraically using *conditional operations*, consisting of statements of the type: "IF . . . THEN . . . ELSE." For example, suppose that we wish to express the following decision rule: "If X is greater than 0, then Y is set equal to O."

Then we can express the rule as follows:

Y = IF X GT O THEN X*5 ELSE 0

Suppose the company wishes to develop the financing decision problem, which is based upon alternative sales scenarios. To attempt to determine an optimal financing alternative, financial managers might want to incorporate some decision rules into the model for a what-if or sensitivity analysis. Some examples of these decision rules are as follows:

• The amount of dividends paid are determined on the basis of targeted earnings available to common stockholders and a maximum dividend payout ratio as specified by financial management.

• After calculating the external funds needed to meet changes in assets as a result of increased sales, dividends, and maturing debt, the amount of long-term debt to be floated is selected on the basis of a prespecified leverage ratio.

• The amount of equity financing to be raised is chosen on the basis of funds needed, which are not financed by new long-term debt but are constrained by the responsibility to meet minimum dividend payments.

In the model just described, *simultaneity* is quite evident. A sales figure is used to generate earnings, and this in turn leads to, among other items, the level of long-term debt required. Yet the level of debt affects the interest expense incurred within the current period and, therefore, earnings. Furthermore, as earnings are affected, so is the price at which new shares are issued, the number of shares to be sold, and thus earnings per share. Earnings per share then "feeds back" into the stock price calculation.

Lagged Model Structure

Lagged model structure is common in financial modeling. Virtually all balance sheet equations or identities are of this type. For example,

$$\text{Capital} = \text{Capital}(-1) + \text{Net income}$$
$$+ \text{Contributions} - \text{Cash dividends}$$

More interestingly,

$$CC = a*\text{SALES} + b*\text{SALES}(-1) + c*\text{SALES}(-2)$$

where CC = cash collections from customers,

a = percentage received within the current period,

b = percentage received with one period lag,

c = percentage received with two period lag.

Figure 2 (page 196) shows the basic structure of a corporate financial model. *See also* Corporate Planning Models.

FINANCIAL PLANNER A financial planner is the one who is engaged in providing *personal financial planning* service to individuals. He or she may be an independent professional or may be affiliated with a large investment, insurance, accounting, or other institution. Financial planners come from a variety of backgrounds and, therefore, may hold a variety of degrees and licenses. Currently, there are no state or federal regulations for the financial planning industry. However, some take specialized training in financial planning and earn credentials such as Certified Financial Planner (CFP) or Chartered Financial Consultant (ChFC). Others may hold degrees or registrations such as attorney (JD), Chartered Life Underwriter (CLU), or, of course, Certified Public Accountant (CPA).

To become a CFP conferred by the Institute of Certified Financial Planners (ICFP), a candidate must take a two year course that consists of six parts, each capped by a three-hour test: introduction to financial planning; risk management (insurance); investments; tax planning and management; retirement planning and employee benefits; and estate planning. To become a CLU or ChFC, designations granted by the American College of the American Society of Chartered Life Underwriters, a person must pass a ten-course program and have three years' professional experience.

A handful of colleges award degrees and certificates in financial planning or "family financial counseling." Adelphi University offers a certificate in financial planning. Golden Gate University offers master degrees in both financial planning and services. The American College also grants a master's degree in financial services. Baylor, Brigham Young, Drake, Georgia State, San Diego State, University of California extensions,

Figure 2 Corporate Financial Model

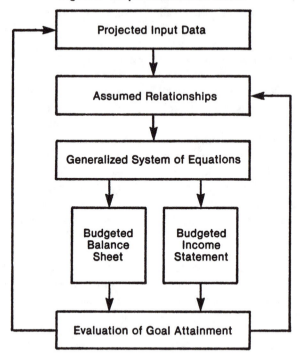

Sarasota, and other colleges offer certificates or degree programs with either a concentration or major in financial planning.

A financial planner should assist the client in the following ways:

1. Assess the client's financial history, such as tax returns, investments, retirement plans, wills, and insurance policies.
2. Help the client decide on a financial plan based on his or her personal and financial goals, history, and preferences.
3. Identify financial areas where the client may need help, such as building up retirement income or improving investment returns.
4. Prepare a financial plan based upon the client's individual situation and discuss it thoroughly with the client in plain English.
5. Help the client implement the financial plan, including referring the client to specialists such as attorneys, investment counselors, bankers, and certified financial planners, if necessary.

6. Review the client's situation and financial plan periodically and suggest changes in the program when needed.

See also Personal Financial Planning.

FINANCIAL RATIO A financial ratio is the relationship of one account or category to another account or category. Financial statement analysis involves the computation of ratios to evaluate a company's financial position and results of operations. Examples of major classifications of ratios are

•*Liquidity ratios*—evaluate short-term ability to meet maturing debt.

•*Activity ratios*—determine effectiveness of the company to use assets in generating revenue.

•*Profitability ratios*—appraise a company's earning power ability.

•*Coverage ratios*—look at the extent long-term creditors and investors are protected.

A ratio should be examined over time to evaluate direction. The ratio should also be compared to that of competing companies and industry averages. *See also* Balance Sheet Analysis; Income Statement Analysis; Financial Statement Analysis.

FINANCIAL STATEMENT ANALYSIS This involves appraising the financial statements and related footnotes of an entity. This may be done by accountants, investment analysts, credit analysts, management, and other interested parties. The financial statements to be evaluated are the balance sheet, income statement, and statement of cash flows. Financial statement analysis includes an appraisal of a company's previous financial performance and its future potential.

The CPA analyzes financial statements of clients for a number of important reasons, including:

• They indicate areas requiring audit attention. The CPA can look at the percentage change in an account over the years or relative to some base year to identify inconsistencies. For example, if promotion and entertainment expense to sales last year was 2% and this year shot up to 16%, the auditor would want to uncover the reasons. This would be especially disturbing if other companies in the industry still have a percentage relationship of 2%. The auditor would be quite suspicious that the promotion and entertainment expense account may contain some personal rather than business charges. Supporting documentation for the charges would be requested and carefully reviewed by the CPA.

• They indicate the financial health of the client, which is of interest to the CPA for the following reasons:

• A determination has to be made if the client is financially sound to pay the accounting fees.

• The CPA wants to ascertain whether poor financial condition exists regarding a qualified audit opinion as to a going-concern problem.

• The CPA wants to know his potential legal exposure. If the client has a poor financial condition, corporate failure may occur, resulting in lawsuits by creditors and others. If financial problems exist, the auditor would have to take proper audit and reporting steps, including suitable references in the audit report.

• They provide vital information to be included in the management letter.

• They assist in identifying areas of financial problems and means of corrective action for the client.

• They aid the client in determining appropriateness of mergers and acquisitions.

The investor evaluates financial statements to see if the company would be a good investment. The investor is interested in earning a good return in the form of dividends and appreciation in market price of stock. Emphasis is focused on corporate profitability and utility ratios (return on assets, return on sales, and so on).

Creditors are primarily concerned with getting their money from the company. Therefore, emphasis is placed on the company's liquidity position as a basis to pay off the account balance. Cash flow analysis is important.

Management analyzes the financial statements to see how the company looks to the financial community and what corrective steps can be made to minimize liquidity and solvency problems. Areas of risk are identified. Means to efficiently utilize assets and earn greater returns are concentrated on.

A company's financial health has a bearing upon its price-earnings ratio, bond rating, cost of financing, and availability of financing. Financial analysts should especially watch out for the "high accounting risk" companies, including

• "Glamour" companies known for earnings growth

• Companies in the public eye

• Companies having difficulty obtaining future financing

• Companies whose management previously committed dishonest acts

To obtain worthwhile conclusions from financial ratios, the financial analyst has to make two comparisons:

1. *Industry comparison*—the financial analyst should compare the company's ratios to those of competing companies in the industry or with industry standards. Industry norms can be obtained from such services as Dun and Bradstreet, Robert Morris Associates, Standard and Poor, and Value Line. For example, Dun and Bradstreet computes 14 ratios for each of 125 lines of business. They are published annually in *Dun's Review* and *Key Business Ratios*. Robert Morris Associates publishes *Annual Statement Studies*. Sixteen ratios are computed for more than 300 lines of business, as well as a percentage distribution of items, on the balance sheet and income statement (common size financial statements). In analyzing a company, the CPA should appraise the trends in the particular industry. What is the pattern of expansion or contraction in the industry? The profit dollar is worth more if earned in a healthy, expanding industry than a declining one.

2. *Trend analysis*—a company's ratio may be compared over several years to identify direction of financial health or operational performance.

The optimum value for any given ratio usually varies across industry lines, through time, and even within different companies in the same industry. In other words, a ratio deemed optimum for one company may be inadequate for another. A particular ratio is typically deemed optimum within a given range of values, and an increase or decrease beyond this range points to weakness or inefficiency. For instance, while a low current ratio may indicate poor liquidity, a very high current ratio may indicate inefficient utilization of assets (e.g., excessive inventory) or

inability to use short-term credit to the firm's advantage.

In appraising a seasonal business, the financial analyst may find that year-end financial data are not representative. Thus, averages based on quarterly or monthly information may be used to level out seasonality effects.

FLEXIBLE BUDGETS AND PERFORMANCE REPORTS
A flexible budget is a tool that is extremely useful in cost control. In contrast to a *static budget*, the flexible budget is characterized as follows:

1. It is geared toward a range of activity rather than a single level of activity.

2. It is dynamic in nature rather than static. By using the *cost-volume formula* (or *flexible budget formula*), a series of budgets can easily be developed for various levels of activity.

The static (*fixed*) budget is geared for only one level of activity and has problems in cost control. Flexible budgeting distinguishes between fixed and variable costs, thus allowing for a budget that can be automatically adjusted (via changes in variable cost totals) to the particular level of activity *actually* attained. Thus, variances between actual costs and budgeted costs are adjusted for volume ups and downs before differences due to price and quantity factors are computed.

The primary use of the flexible budget is for accurate measure of performance by comparing actual costs for a given output with the budgeted costs for the *same level of output*.

■ Example 1

To illustrate the difference between the static budget and the flexible budget, assume that the Assembly Department of Company Y is budgeted to produce 6,000 units during June. Assume further that the company was able to produce only 5,800 units. The budget for direct labor and variable overhead costs is as follows:

Company Y
The Direct Labor and Variable Overhead Budget
Assembly Department
for the Month of June

Budgeted production	6,000 units
Actual production	5,800 units
Direct labor	$39,000
Variable overhead costs:	
Indirect labor	6,000
Supplies	900
Repairs	300
	$46,200

If a static budget approach is used, the performance report will appear as follows:

Company Y
The Direct Labor and Variable Overhead Budget
Assembly Department
for the Month of June

	Budget	Actual	Variance (U or F)*
Production in units	6,000	5,800	200 U
Direct labor	$39,000	$38,500	$500 F
Variable overhead costs:			
Indirect labor	6,000	5,950	50 F
Supplies	900	870	30 F
Repairs	300	295	5 F
	$46,200	$45,615	$585 F

* A variance represents the deviation of actual cost from the standard or budgeted cost. U and F stand for "unfavorable" and "favorable," respectively.

These cost variances are useless in that they are comparing oranges with apples. The problem is that the budget costs are based on an activity level of 6,000 units, whereas the actual costs were incurred at an activity level below this (5,800 units). From a control standpoint, it makes no sense to try to compare costs at one activity level with costs at a different activity level. Such comparisons would make a production manager look good as long as the actual production is less than the budgeted production. Using the cost-volume formula and generating the budget based on the 5,800 actual units gives the performance report appearing at the bottom of the page. Notice that all cost variances are unfavorable (U), as compared to the favorable cost variances on the performance report based on the static budget approach.

FORECASTING EARNINGS PER SHARE Dividends and market price of stock depend upon future earnings per share.

Estimated earnings at the end of the year = Estimated sales at the end of the year × After-tax profit margin

$$\frac{\text{Estimated earnings at the end of the year}}{\text{Estimated outstanding shares at the end of the year}}$$

Company Y
Peformance Report
Assembly Department
For the Month of June

Budgeted production		6,000 units		
Actual production		5,800 units		
	Cost-volume formula	Budget 5,800 units	Actual 5,800 units	Variance (U or F)
Direct labor	$6.50 per unit	$37,700	$38,500	$800 U
Variable overhead:				
Indirect labor	1.00	5,800	5,950	150 U
Supplies	.15	870	870	0
Repairs	.05	290	295	5 U
	$7.70	$44,660	$45,615	$955 U

■ Example

You expect the sales for ABC Company to be $2,000,000 based on financial projections you read in a brokerage report and/or reading management's discussion in the annual report. The company's tax rate is 34%. After-tax profit is therefore:

$$\$2,000,000 \times 66\% = \$1,320,000$$

Assume expected shares outstanding are 1,000,000.

Estimated earnings per share

$$= \frac{\$1,320,000}{1,000,000 \text{ shares}} = \$1.32$$

If the price/earnings ratio is 10, the estimated market price of stock is

Estimated EPS × Estimated P/E ratio
$$= \$1.32 \times 10 = \$13.20$$

FOREIGN CORRUPT PRACTICES ACT According to the act, management and independent auditors for publicly held companies must maintain internal controls to assure the reliability of accounting records. Further, it is a crime to offer a bribe to a foreign official to obtain business. *See also* Internal Control.

FOREIGN CURRENCY TRANSLATION AND TRANSACTIONS FASB 52 applies to foreign currency transactions such as exports and imports denominated in other than a company's functional currency. It also relates to foreign currency financial statements of branches, divisions, and other investees incorporated in the financial statements of a U.S. company by combination, consolidation, or the equity method.

A purpose of translation is to furnish data of expected impacts of rate changes on cash flow and equity. Also, it provides data in consolidated financial statements relative to the financial results of each individual foreign consolidated entity.

Covered in FASB 52 are the translation of foreign currency statements and gains and losses on foreign currency transactions. Translation of foreign currency statements is typically needed when the statements of a foreign subsidiary or equity-method investee having a functional currency other than the U.S. dollar are to be included in the financial statements of a domestic enterprise (e.g., through consolidation or using the equity method). Generally, the foreign currency statements should be translated using the exchange rate at the end of the reporting year. Resulting translation gains and losses are shown as a separate item in the stockholders' equity section.

Also important is the accounting treatment of gains and losses emanating from transactions denominated in a foreign currency. These are presented in the current year's income statement.

Foreign Currency Terminology

Key definitions to be understood by the practitioner follow:

• *Conversion*—an exchange of one currency for another.

• *Currency swap*—an exchange between two companies of the currencies of two different countries as per an agreement to re-exchange the two currencies at the same rate of exchange at a specified future date.

• *Denominate*—pay or receive in that *same* foreign currency. It can only be denominated in one currency (e.g., pounds). It is a real account (asset or liability) fixed in terms of a foreign currency irrespective of exchange rate.

• *Exchange rate*—ratio between a unit of one currency and that of another at a particular time. If there is a *temporary lack of exchangeability* between two currencies at the transaction date or balance sheet date, the *first rate available* thereafter at which exchanges could be made is used.

• *Foreign currency*—a currency other than the functional currency of the business (for instance, the dollar could be a foreign currency for a foreign entity).

• *Foreign currency statements*—financial statements using as the unit of measure a functional currency that is not the reporting currency of the business.

• *Foreign currency transactions*—transactions whose terms are denominated in a currency other than the entity's functional currency. Foreign currency transactions take place when a business (a) buys or sells on credit goods or services whose prices are denominated in foreign currency; (b) borrows or lends funds, and the amounts payable or receivable are denominated in foreign currency; (c) is a party to an unperformed forward exchange contract; or (d) acquires or disposes of assets, or incurs or settles liabilities denominated in foreign currency.

• *Foreign currency translation*—expressing in the reporting currency of the company those amounts that are denominated or measured in a different currency.

• *Foreign entity*—an operation (e.g., subsidiary, division, branch, joint venture) whose financial statements are prepared in a currency other than the reporting currency of the reporting entity.

• *Functional currency*—an entity's functional currency is the currency of the *primary economic environment* in which the business operates. It is typically the currency of the environment in which the business primarily obtains and uses cash. This is usually the foreign country. The functional currency of a foreign operation may be the same as a related affiliate in the case where the foreign activity is an essential component or extension of the related affiliate.

Prior to translation, the foreign country figures are remeasured in the functional currency. For instance, if a company in Italy is an independent entity and received cash and incurred expenses in Italy, the Italian currency is the functional currency. However, in the event the Italian company was an extension of a Canadian parent, the functional currency is the Canadian currency. The functional currency should be consistently used except if material economic changes necessitate a change. However, previously issued financial statements are not restated for an alteration in the functional currency.

If a company's books are *not* kept in its functional currency, remeasurement into the functional currency is mandated. The remeasurement process occurs before translation into the reporting currency takes place. When a foreign entity's functional currency is the reporting currency, remeasurement into the reporting currency obviates translation. The remeasurement process is intended to generate the same result as if the entity's books had been kept in the functional currency.

Guidelines are referred to in determining the functional currency of a foreign operation. The benchmarks apply to selling price, market, cash flow, financing, expense, and intercompany transactions. A detailed discussion follows:

1. *Selling price.* The functional currency is the foreign currency when the foreign operation's selling price of products or services are primarily because of local factors such as government law and competition. It is *not* due to changes in exchange rate. The functional currency is the parent's currency when foreign operation's sales prices mostly apply in the short-run to fluctuation in the exchange rate resulting from international factors (e.g., worldwide competition).

2. *Market.* The functional currency is the foreign currency when the foreign activity has a strong local sales market for products or services, even though a significant amount of exports may exist. The functional currency is the parent's currency when the foreign operation's sales market is mostly in the parent's country.

3. *Cash flow.* The functional currency is the foreign currency when the foreign operation's cash flows are primarily in foreign currency not directly affecting the parent's cash flow. The functional currency is the parent's currency when the foreign operation's cash flows directly impact the parent's cash flows. They

are usually available for remittance via intercompany accounting settlement.

4. *Financing*. The functional currency is the foreign currency if financing the foreign activity is in foreign currency and funds obtained by the foreign activity are sufficient to meet debt obligations. The functional currency is the parent's currency when financing foreign activity is provided by the parent or occurs in U.S. dollars. Funds obtained by the foreign activity are insufficient to satisfy debt requirements.

5. *Expenses*. The functional currency is the foreign currency when foreign operation's production costs or services are usually incurred locally. However, some foreign imports may exist. The functional currency is the parent's currency when the foreign operation's production and service costs are primarily component costs obtained from the parent's country.

6. *Intercompany transactions*. The functional currency is the foreign currency when minor interrelationship occurs between the activities of the foreign entity and parent except for competitive advantages (e.g., patents). There is a restricted number of intercompany transactions. The functional currency is the parent's currency when material interrelationship exists between the foreign entity and parent. Many intercompany transactions exist.

Consistent use of the functional currency of the foreign entity must exist over the years except if there are changes in circumstances warranting a change. If a change in the functional currency takes place, it is accounted for as a change in estimate.

• *Local currency*—the currency of the particular foreign country.

• *Measure*—translation into a currency other than the original reporting currency. Foreign financial statements are measured in U.S. dollars by using the applicable exchange rate.

• *Reporting currency*—the currency the business prepares its financial statements in. It is usually U.S. dollars.

• *Spot rate*—exchange rate for immediate delivery of currencies exchanged.

• *Transaction gain or loss*—occur due to a change in exchange rates between the functional currency and the currency in which a foreign currency transaction is denominated. They represent an increase or decrease in (a) the actual functional currency cash flows realized upon settlement of foreign currency transactions and (b) the expected functional currency cash flows on unsettled foreign currency transactions.

• *Translation adjustments*—arise from translating financial statements from the entity's functional currency into the reporting one.

Translation Process

Translation of Foreign Currency Statements When the U.S. Dollar Is the Functional Currency

The foreign entity's financial statements in a highly *inflationary* economy is not stable enough and should be remeasured as if the functional currency were the reporting currency. Thus, the financial statements of those entities should be remeasured into the reporting currency (the U.S. dollar becomes the functional currency). In effect, the reporting currency is used directly.

A *highly inflationary environment* is one that has cumulative inflation of about *100% or more over a 3-year period*. In other words, the inflation rate must be increasing at a rate of about 35% a year for 3 consecutive years. *Tip*: The International Monetary Fund of Washington, DC, publishes monthly figures on international inflation rates.

Translation of Foreign Currency Statements When the Foreign Currency Is the Functional Currency

Balance sheet items are translated via the *current exchange rate*. For assets and liabilities, use the rate at the balance sheet date.

If a current exchange rate is not available at the balance sheet date, use the first exchange rate available after that date. The *current exchange rate* is also used to translate the *Statement of Cash Flows* except for those items found in the Income Statement, which are translated using the weighted-average rate. For income statement items (revenues, expenses, gains, and losses), use the exchange rate at the dates those items are recognized. Since translation at the exchange rates at the dates the many revenues, expenses, gains, and losses are recognized is almost always impractical, use a *weighted-average exchange rate* for the period in translating *income statement items*.

A material change occurring between the date of the financial statements and the audit report date should be disclosed as a subsequent event. Disclosure should also be made of the effects on unsettled balances pertaining to foreign currency transactions.

Translation Adjustments

There are several steps in translating the foreign country's financial statements into U.S. reporting requirements. They are

1. Conform the foreign country's financial statements to U.S. GAAP.
2. Determine the functional currency of the foreign entity.
3. Remeasure the financial statements in the functional currency, if necessary. Gains or losses from remeasuremnt are includable in remeasured current net income.
4. Convert from the foreign currency into U.S. dollars (reporting currency).

If a company's functional currency is a foreign currency, *translation adjustments* arise from translating that company's financial statements into the reporting currency. Translation adjustments are unrealized and should not be included in the income statement but should be reported separately and accumulated in a *separate component of equity*. However, if remeasurement from the

recording currency to the functional currency is required before translation, the gain or loss is reflected in the income statement.

Upon sale or liquidation of an investment in a foreign entity, the amount attributable to that entity and accumulated in the translation adjustment component of equity is removed from the stockholders' equity section and considered a part of the gain or loss on sale or liquidation of the investment in the income statement for the period during which the sale or liquidation occurs.

As per Interpretation 37, a sale of an investment in a foreign entity may include a partial sale of an ownership interest. In that case, a pro rata amount of the cumulative translation adjustment reflected as a stockholders' equity component is includable in arriving at the gain or loss on sale. For example, if a business sells a 40% ownership interest in a foreign investment, 40% of the translation adjustment applicable to it is included in calculating gain or loss on sale of that ownership interest.

Foreign Currency Transactions

Foreign currency transactions are those denominated in a currency other than the company's functional currency. Foreign currency transactions may result in receivables or payables fixed in terms of the amount of foreign currency to be received or paid.

A foreign currency transaction requires settlement in a currency other than the functional currency: A change in exchange rates between the functional currency and the currency in which a transaction is denominated increases or decreases the expected amount of functional currency cash flows upon settlement of the transaction. This change in expected functional currency cash flows is a *foreign currency transaction gain or loss* that typically is included in arriving at earnings in the *income statement* for the period in which the exchange rate is altered. An example of a transaction gain or loss is when a

British subsidiary has a receivable denominated in pounds from a French customer.

Similarly, a transaction gain or loss (measured from the *transaction date* or the most recent intervening balance sheet date, whichever is later) realized upon settlement of a foreign currency transaction usually should be included in determining net income for the period in which the transaction is settled.

■ Example

An exchange gain or loss occurs when the exchange rate changes between the purchase date and sale date.

Merchandise is bought for 100,000 pounds. The exchange rate is 4 pounds to 1 dollar. The journal entry is

Purchases	$25,000	
Accounts Payable		$25,000

100,000/4 = $25,000

When the merchandise is paid for, the exchange rate is 5 to 1. The journal entry is

Accounts Payable	$25,000	
Cash		$20,000
Foreign Exchange Gain		$5,000

100,000/5 = $20,000

The $20,000 using an exchange rate of 5 to 1 can buy 100,000 pounds. The transaction gain is the difference between the cash required of $20,000 and the initial liability of $25,000.

Note that a foreign transaction gain or loss has to be determined at each balance sheet date on all recorded foreign transactions that have not been settled.

■ Example

A U.S. company sells goods to a customer in England on 11/15/X7 for 10,000 pounds. The exchange rate is 1 pound to 75 cents. Thus, the transaction is worth $7,500 (10,000 pounds × 0.75). Payment is due 2 months later. The entry on 11/15/X7 is

Accounts Receivable—England	$7,500	
Sales		$7,500

Accounts receivable and sales are measured in U.S. dollars at the transaction date employing the spot rate. Even though the accounts receivable is measured and reported in U.S. dollars, the receivable is fixed in pounds. Thus, there can occur a transaction gain or loss if the exchange rate changes between the transaction date (11/15/X7) and the settlement date (1/15/X8).

Since the financial statements are prepared between the transaction date and settlement date, receivables that are denominated in a currency other than the functional currency (U.S. dollar) have to be restated to reflect the spot rate on the balance sheet date. On December 31, 19X7, the exchange rate is 1 pound equals 80 cents. Hence, the 10,000 pounds are now valued at $8,000 (10,000 × $0.80). Therefore, the accounts receivable denominated in pounds should be upwardly adjusted by $500. The required journal entry on 12/31/X7 is

Accounts Receivable—England	$500	
Foreign Exchange Gain		$500

The income statement for the year-ended 12/31/X7 shows an exchange gain of $500. Note that sales is not affected by the exchange gain since sales relates to operational activity.

On 1/15/X8, the spot rate is 1 pound = 78 cents. The journal entry is

Cash	$7,800	
Foreign Exchange Loss	200	
Accounts Receivable—England		$8,000

The 19X8 income statement shows an exchange loss of $200.

Transaction Gains and Losses to be Excluded from Determination of Net Income

Gains and losses on the following foreign currency transactions are not included in earnings but rather reported as translation adjustments:

• Foreign currency transactions designated as *economic hedges* of a net investment in a foreign entity, beginning as of the designation date

• Intercompany foreign currency transactions of a *long-term investment* nature (settlement is not planned or expected in the foreseeable future), when the entities to the transaction are consolidated, combined, or accounted for by the equity method in the reporting company's financial statements

A gain or loss on a forward contract or other foreign currency transaction that is intended to *hedge* an identifiable foreign currency commitment (e.g., an agreement to buy or sell machinery) should be deferred and included in the measurement of the related foreign currency transaction. Losses should *not* be deferred if it is anticipated that deferral would cause recognizing losses in subsequent periods. A foreign currency transaction is considered a hedge of an identifiable foreign currency commitment provided both of the following criteria are satisfied:
1. The foreign currency transaction is designated as a hedge of a foreign currency commitment.
2. The foreign currency commitment is firm.

Forward Exchange Contracts

A forward exchange contract is an agreement to exchange different currencies at a given future date and at a specified rate (forward rate). A forward contract is a foreign currency transaction. A gain or loss on a forward contract that does not meet the conditions described following are includable in net income. *Note*: Currency swaps are accounted for in a similar fashion.

A gain or loss (whether or not deferred) on a forward contract, except a speculative forward contract, should be computed by multiplying the foreign currency amount of the forward contract by the difference between the *spot rate* at the balance sheet date

and the spot rate at the date of inception of the forward contract.

The *discount or premium on a forward contract* (i.e., the foreign currency amount of the contract multiplied by the difference between the contracted forward rate and the spot rate at the date of inception of the contract) should be accounted for separately from the gain or loss on the contract and typically should be included in computing net income over the life of the forward contract.

A gain or loss on a *speculative forward contract* (a contract that does not hedge an exposure) should be computed by multiplying the foreign currency amount of the forward contract by the difference between the forward rate available from the remaining maturity of the contract and the contracted forward rate (or the forward rate last used to measure a gain or loss on that contract for an earlier period). *No separate accounting recognition is given to the discount or premium on a speculative forward contract.*

Hedging

Foreign currency transactions gains and losses on assets and liabilities denominated in a currency other than the functional currency can be hedged if the U.S. company engages into a forward exchange contract.

A hedge can occur even if there does not exist a forward exchange contract. For instance, a foreign currency transaction can serve as an economic hedge offsetting a parent's net investment in a foreign entity when the transaction is entered into for hedging purposes and is effective.

■ Example

A U.S. parent completely owns a French subsidiary having net assets of $3 million in francs. The U.S. parent can borrow $3 million francs to hedge its net investment in the French subsidiary. Also assume the French franc is the functional currency and the $3 million obligation is denominated in francs. Variability in the exchange rate for francs does *not* have a net impact on the parent's consolidated balance sheet since increases in the translation adjustments balance arising from translation of the net investment will be netted against decreases in this balance emanating from the adjustment of the liability denominated in francs.

FOREIGN EXCHANGE RATES

Foreign exchange is the instrument used for international payments. Such instruments consist not only of currency, but also of checks, drafts, and bills of exchange. A *foreign exchange market* is available for trading foreign exchanges. A *foreign exchange rate* is the price of one currency in terms of another. For example, 1 American dollar is 125 yens in Japanese currency. Foreign exchange rates are determined in various ways:

1. *Fixed exchange rates*—an international financial arrangement in which governments directly intervene in the foreign exchange market to prevent exchange rates from deviating more than a very small margin from some central or parity value.

2. *Flexible (floating exchange) rates*—an arrangement by which exchange rate levels are allowed to change daily in response to market demand and supply. Arrangements may vary from *free float* (i.e., absolutely no government intervention) to *managed float* (i.e., limited but sometimes aggressive government intervention in the foreign exchange market).

3. *Forward exchange rate*—the exchange rate in contract for receipt of and payment for foreign currency at a specified date, usually 30 days, 90 days, or 180 days in the future, at a stipulated current or "spot" price. By buying and selling forward exchange, importers and exporters can protect themselves against the risks of fluctuations in the current exchange market.

See also Financial Institutions and Markets.

401 (K) PLAN

This is a company-sponsored retirement plan that allows an employee to defer up to $7,000, under the new tax law, of the employee's gross salary withheld and invested in stocks, bonds, or money market funds, also called *salary reduction plan*. This amount is indexed for inflation using the Consumer Price Index, beginning in 1988. The employee's contributions and all earnings arising therefrom go tax free until withdrawn at the request of the employee or until the employee retires or leaves the company. Usually the employer provides a choice of investment vehicles into which the funds may be placed while earning tax-deferred returns. Furthermore, many employers offer matching contributions. The $7,000 limitation of annual deferrals to 401(k) plans applies only to an employee's elective deferrals—not the employer's matching funds. The employee's contributions plus the employer's may total, annually, the lesser of $30,000 or 25% of earnings. These contributions plus the current reduction in income taxes typically make 401(k) salary reduction plans an excellent long-term investment. *See also* Retirement and Pension Planning.

FRACTIONAL SHARE WARRANTS

These may be issued when less than a full share is involved.

■ Example

There are 1,000 shares of $10 par value common stock. The common stock has a market price of $15. A 20% dividend is declared, resulting in 200 shares (20% × 1,000). Included in the 200 shares are fractional share warrants. Each warrant equals 1/5 of a share of stock. There are 100 warrants resulting in 20 shares of stock (100/5). Thus, 180 regular snares and 20 fractional shares are involved.

The journal entries follow:

At the declaration date:

Retained Earnings (200 shares × $15	3,000	
Stock Dividends Distributable (180 shares × $10)		1,800
Fractional Share Warrants (20 shares × $10)		200
Paid-in-Capital		1,000

At time of issuance:

Stock Dividend Distributable	1,800	
Common Stock		1,800
Fractional Share Warrants	200	
Common Stock		200

If instead of all the fractional share warrants being turned in, only 80% were turned in the entry is

Fractional Share Warrants	200	
Common Stock		160
Paid-in-Capital		40

FRANCHISE FEE REVENUE According to FASB 45, the franchisor can record revenue only from the initial sale of the franchise when all significant services and obligations applicable to the sale have been substantially performed. Substantial performance is indicated by

• Absence of intent to give cash refunds or relieve the accounts receivable due from the franchisee.

• Nothing material remains to be done by the franchisor.

• Initial services have been rendered.

The earliest date that substantial performance can occur is the franchisee's commencement of operations unless special circumstances can be shown to exist. In the case where it is probable that the franchisor will ultimately repurchase the franchise, the initial fee must be deferred and treated as a reduction of the repurchase price.

If revenue is deferred, the related expenses must be deferred for later matching in the year in which the revenue is recognized. This is illustrated following.

Year of initial fee:

Cash
  Deferred Revenue
Deferred Expenses
  Cash

Year when substantial performance takes place:

Deferred Revenue
  Revenue
Expenses
  Deferred Expenses

In case the initial fee includes both initial services and property (real or personal), there should be an appropriate allocation based on fair market values.

When part of the initial franchise fee applies to *tangible property* (e.g., equipment, signs, inventory), revenue recognition is based on the fair value of the assets. Revenue recognition may take place prior to or after recognizing the portion of the fee related to initial services. For instance, part of the fee for equipment may be recognized at the time title passes, with the balance of the fee being recorded as revenue when future services are performed.

Recurring franchise fees are recognized as earned and receivable. Related costs are expensed. An exception does exist to this revenue recognition practice. If the price charged for the continuing services or goods to the franchisee is below the price charged to third parties, it indicates that the initial franchise fee was in essence a partial *prepayment* for the recurring franchise fee. In this situation, part of the initial fee has to be deferred and recognized as an adjustment of the revenue from the sale of goods and services at bargain prices.

When probability exists that continuing franchise fees will not cover the cost of the continuing services and provide for a reasonable profit to the franchisor, the part of the initial franchise fee should be deferred to satisfy the deficiency and amortized over the life of the franchise. The deferred amount should be adequate to meet future costs and generate an adequate profit on the recurring services. This situation may occur if the continuing fees are minimal relative to services provided or the franchisee has the privilege of making bargain purchases for a particular time period.

Unearned franchise fees are recorded at present value. Where a part of the initial fee constitutes a nonrefundable amount for services already performed, revenue should be recognized accordingly.

The initial franchise fee is *not* typically allocated to specific franchisor services before all services are performed. This practice can be done only if actual transaction prices are available for individual services.

If the franchisor sells equipment and inventory to the franchisee at no profit, a receivable and payable is recorded. *No* revenue or expense recognition is given.

In the case of a repossessed franchise, refunded amounts to the franchisee reduce current revenue. If there is no refund, the franchisor books additional revenue for the consideration retained that was not previously recorded. In either situation, *prospective* accounting treatment is given for the repossession. *Warning*: Do *not* adjust previously recorded revenue for the repossession.

Indirect costs of an operating and recurring nature are expensed immediately. Future costs to be incurred are accrued no later than the period in which related revenue is recognized. Bad debts applicable to expected uncollectability of franchise fees should be recorded in the year of revenue recognition.

Installment or cost recovery accounting may be employed to account for franchisee fee revenue *only* if a long collection period is involved and future uncollectability of receivables cannot be accurately predicted.

Footnote disclosure is required of
• Outstanding obligations under agreement
• Segregation of franchise fee revenue between initial and continuing. *See also* Revenue Recognition Methods.

FRAUD The auditor should distinguish between negligence (belief in the absence of adequate basis), constructive fraud (not believing in a position), and fraud (known to be wrong). Fraud is a legal concept, in which the person falsifies with knowledge and intent to deceive. Fraud can occur through a false representation of a material fact that results in damage to a party relying on that information. An example of fraud is the theft of corporate assets while falsifying records.

Management fraud relates to employing improper practices to overstate net income or to prevent insolvency. Fraud may be perpetrated by engaging in fictitious transactions, transactions lacking substance, and purposely not applying GAAP. Employee fraud typically involves theft.

The auditor is obligated to uncover fraud, including intentional errors and irregularities, by exercising due professional care.

The auditor must examine significant transactions to ascertain if management is involved in fraudulent activities. He or she should withdraw from an engagement if confidence in management's integrity is lacking. Investigation of fraud should take into account the following:
• Special audit engagements are less likely to detect fraud than audits.
• A standard audit procedure may not in all cases detect fraud, such as where customers returning confirmations are in collusion with management.
• A prospective or existing client may be dishonest.
• Extent to which internal control prevents the detetion of fraud.
• The nature of the client's business and the industry to which it is a part.
• Clients with severe financial problems are more desperate and as a result more prone to engage in fraudulent activity.

Tax fraud may either be civil or criminal. In civil fraud, the IRS can charge a penalty of 50% of a tax underpayment. In criminal fraud, fines and/or imprisonment can be involved, depending upon the nature of the fraud. Conviction requires that the taxpayer intended to *evade* the tax payment through the preparation of an intentional misstatement of the tax return. The burden of proof is on the IRS. *See also* Internal Control.

FUNDAMENTAL ANALYSIS This appraises a company's stock based on an examination of the financial statements. It considers overall financial health, economic and political conditions, industry factors, and future outlook of the company. The analysis attempts to determine if a security is overpriced, underpriced, or priced in proportion to its market value. A stock is valuable only if one can predict the future financial performance of the business. Financial statement analysis provides much data needed to predict earnings and dividends. *See also* Balance Sheet Analysis; Income Statement Analysis; Financial Ratios; Financial Statement Analysis.

FUTURES CONTRACT Futures trading can relate to commodities and financial instruments. A future is a contract to buy or sell a specified amount of an item for a certain price by a given date. The seller of a futures contract agrees to deliver the item to the buyer of the contract, who agrees to purchase the item. The contract stipulates an amount, valuation, method, quality, month, means of delivery, and exchange to be traded on. The expiration date is the month of delivery of the commodity or financial instrument. *Commodity contracts* are assurances by a seller to deliver a commodity. *Financial contracts* are commitments by sellers to deliver a financial instrument (e.g., a Treasury bill) or a specified amount of foreign currency. *Beware*: Futures contracts are a risky investment.

A *long position* is buying a contract expecting the price to rise. A *short position* is selling the contract anticipating the price to decrease. The position may be terminated by reversing the transaction. For example, the long buyer can subsequently take a short position of the same amount of the commodity or financial instrument. Most futures contracts are canceled out prior to delivery. Rarely does delivery settle the future contract.

Futures trading may be performed by hedgers and speculators. Hedgers protect themselves with futures contracts in the commodity they produce or in the financial instrument they own. For example, if a cotton producer expects a drop in price, he can sell a futures contract to assure a higher current price. Then at the time of the future delivery he will obtain a higher price. Speculators employ futures contracts to get capital gain on price increases of the commodity, financial instrument, or currency.

Commodity futures trading may be done by auction. A futures contract can be traded in the futures market. Trading is accomplished through specialized brokers and some commodity firms dealing only in futures. Fees for futures contracts depend on the amount of the contract and the price of the item. There is a varying commission based on the amount and nature of the contract. An investor has to have a commodity trading account. Contracts are typically bought on margin. The investor can buy or sell a contract with specified terms.

A futures contract assists in keeping pace with inflation. But futures contracts are a high-risk specialized area due to the many variables involved (e.g., international economic instability). Further, there may be wide vacillation in contract prices. *See also* Commodities Futures Contracts; Financial Futures Contracts.

FUTURES CONTRACTS ACCOUNTING A futures contract is a legal arrangement entered into by the purchaser or seller and a regulated futures exchange in the U.S. or overseas.

However, FASB 80 does not apply to foreign currencies futures, which are dealt with in FASB 82. Futures contracts involve

• A buyer or seller receiving or making a delivery of a commodity or financial instrument (e.g., stocks, bonds, commercial paper, mortgages) at a given date. Cash settlement rather than delivery often exists (e.g., stock index future).

• A futures contract may be eliminated prior to the delivery date by engaging in an offsetting contract for the particular commodity or financial instrument involved. For instance, a futures contract to buy 100,000 pounds of a commodity by December 31, 19X1, may be canceled by entering into another contract to sell 100,000 pounds of that same commodity on December 31, 19X1.

• Changes in value of open contracts are settled regularly (e.g., daily). The usual contract provides that when a decrease in the contract value occurs, the contract holder has to make a cash deposit for such decline with the clearinghouse. If the contract increases in value, the holder may withdraw the increased value.

The change in market value of a futures contract involves a gain or loss that should be recognized in earnings. An exception exists that for certain contracts the timing of income statement recognition relates to the accounting for the applicable asset, liability, commitment, or transaction. This accounting exception applies when the contract is designed as a hedge against price and interest rate fluctuation. When the criteria noted following are satisfied, the accounting for the contract relates to the accounting for the hedged item. Thus, a change in market value is recognized in the same accounting period that the effects of the related changes in price or interest rate of the hedged item is reflected in income.

The *hedge* exists when both of the following criteria are met:

• The hedged item places price and interest rate risk on the firm. Risk means the sensitivity of corporate earnings to market price changes or rates of return of existing assets, liabilities, commitments, and expected transactions. This criteria is *not* met in the case where other assets, liabilities, commitments, and anticipated transactions *already* offset the risk.

• The contract lowers risk exposure and is entered into as a hedge. High correlation exists between the change in market value of the contract and the fair value of the hedged item. In effect, the market price change of the contract offsets the price and interest rate changes on the exposed item. An example is when there exists a futures contract to sell silver that offsets the changes in the price of silver.

A change in market value of a futures contract that meets the hedging criteria of the related asset or liability should adjust the carrying value of the hedge item. For instance, a company has an investment in a government bond that it anticipates to sell at a later date. The company can reduce its susceptibility to changes in fair value of the bonds by engaging in a futures contract. The changes in the market value of the futures contract adjusts the book value of the bonds.

A change in market value of a futures contract that is for the purpose of hedging a firm commitment is included in measuring the transaction satisfying the commitment. An example is when the company hedges a firm purchase commitment by using a futures contract. When the acquisition takes place thus satisfying the purchase commitment, the gain or loss on the futures contract is an element of the cost of the acquired item. Assume ABC Company has a purchase commitment for 30,000 pounds of a commodity at $2 per pound, totaling $60,000. At the time of the consummation of the transaction, the $60,000 cost is *decreased* by any gain (e.g., $5,000) arising from the "hedged" futures contract. The net cost is shown as the carrying value (e.g., $55,000).

A futures contract may apply to transactions the company *expects* to conduct in the ordinary course of business. It is not obligated to do so. These expected transactions do not involve existing assets or liabilities, or transactions applicable to *existing* firm commitments. For instance, a company may *anticipate* buying a certain commodity in the future but has not made a formal purchase commitment. The company may minimize risk exposure to price changes by entering into a futures contract. The change in market value of this "anticipatory hedge contract" is included in measuring the subsequent transaction. The change in market value of the futures contract adjusts the cost of the acquired item. The following criteria must be met for "anticipatory hedge accounting":

1. and 2. are the same as the criteria for regular hedge contracts related to *existing* assets, liabilities, or firm commitments.

3. Identification exists of the major terms of the contemplated transaction. Included are the type of commodity or financial instrument, quantity, and expected transaction date. If the financial instrument carries interest, the maturity date should be given.

4. It is probable that the expected transaction will take place.

Probability of occurrence depends on the following:

• Time period involved
• Monetary commitment for the activity
• Financial capability to conduct the transaction

• Frequency of previous transactions of a similar nature
• Possibility that other types of transactions may be undertaken to accomplish the desired goal
• Adverse operational effects of not engaging in the transaction

The accounting applicable for a "hedge type" futures contract related to an expected asset acquisition or liability incurrence should be consistent with the company's accounting method employed for those assets and liabilities. For instance, the firm should book a loss for a futures contract that is a hedge of an expected inventory acquisition if the amount will not be recovered from the sale of inventory.

If a "hedged" futures contract is closed prior to the expected transaction, the accumulated value change in the contract should be carried forward to be included in measuring the related transaction. If it is probable that the quantity of an expected transaction will be less than the amount initially hedged, recognize a gain or loss for a pro rata portion of futures results that would have been included in the measurement of the subsequent transaction.

A "hedged" futures contract requires disclosure of

• Firm commitments
• Nature of assets and liabilities
• Accounting method used for the contract, including a description of events or transactions resulting in recognized changes in contract values
• Expected transactions that are hedged with futures contracts

G

GAIN CONTINGENCY A gain contingency is the future possibility that the business will obtain a favorable financial development. Examples are winning a lawsuit, or contract renegotiation with another company or government. Due to conservatism, a gain contingency cannot be recorded in the accounts. Instead, footnote disclosure is made.

GAME THEORY This is an *operations research* technique that deals with competitive situations where two or more participants pursue conflicting objectives. The theory attempts to provide optimal strategies for the participants. In games, the participants are competitors; the success of one is usually at the expense of the other. Each person selects and executes those strategies that he believes will result in winning the game. There are many different types of games that reflect different conflict situations. A two-person, zero sum game is an example.

GOAL PROGRAMMING (GP) GP is a special case of *linear programming* (*LP*), that attempts to find a solution to resource allocation. LP, however, has one important drawback in that it is limited primarily to solving problems where the objectives of manage-

ment can be stated in a single goal such as profit maximization or cost minimization. But financial management must now deal with multiple goals, which are often incompatible and conflict with each other. GP gets around this difficulty. In GP, unlike LP, the objective function may consist of multiple, incommensurable, and conflicting goals. Rather than maximizing or minimizing the objective criterion, the deviations from these set goals are minimized, often based on the priority factors assigned to each goal. The fact that financial management will have multiple goals that are in conflict with each other means that instead of maximizing or minimizing financial executives attempt to *satisfice*. In other words, they will look for a satisfactory solution rather than an optimal solution.

Examples of Multiple Conflicting Goals

For example, consider an investor who desires investments that will have a maximum return and minimum risk. These goals are generally incompatible and therefore unachievable. Other examples of multiple conflicting goals can be found in businesses that want to

1. Maximize profits and increase wages paid to employees

2. Upgrade product quality and reduce product costs

3. Pay larger dividends to shareholders and retain earnings for growth

4. Increase control of channels of distribution and reduce working capital requirements

5. Reduce credit losses and increase sales

GOING CONCERN QUALIFICATION AICPAs' Statement on Auditing Standards No. 59 applies to the auditor's consideration of an entity's ability to continue as a going concern. The auditor must appraise the client's going concern potential, and if a substantial doubt exists, the auditor must provide an explanatory paragraph in the audit report. The auditor looks at the client's "going concern" ability for a reasonable time period, not to exceed one year beyond the date of the audited financial statements. An example follows:

> The accompanying financial statements have been prepared assuming that Company Y will continue as a going concern. As discussed in Note X to the financial statements, Company Y has suffered recurring losses from operations and has a net capital deficiency that raises substantial doubt about the entity's ability to continue as a going concern. Management's plans in regard to these matters are also described in Note X. The financial statements do not include any adjustments that might result from the outcome of this uncertainty.

Note that the absence of a reference of substantial doubt in the audit report cannot be construed as providing assurance of continued existence.

GOING PUBLIC This refers to selling formerly privately held shares to new investors on the over-the-counter market for the first time. For the individual company, going public marks a historic moment. It often is the springboard for greater growth and success. There are the advantages and disadvantages of raising capital through a public offering.

The Pros of Going Public

• Going public raises money. If it is common stock, it does not have to be repaid.

• The use of proceeds from the sale of the issue is generally unrestricted.

• Management often experiences an increase in prestige and reputation.

• Public companies can acquire other businesses with stock without depleting cash reserves.

• Other financing alternatives may improve.

The Cons of Going Public

• Much jealously guarded information must be disclosed. The guarded items include management salaries, competitive position, transactions between the company and its management, and the identity of significant customers and suppliers.

• Corporate decision making becomes more cumbersome as the company attempts to move from a tightly controlled entrepreneurially oriented company to a professionally managed one where ownership and management are divorced. Any decision, long-term or short-term, may be manifested promptly in the company's stock price. The company may worry constantly about improving quarterly earnings (and stock prices) instead of trying to take a longer perspective in developing its strategy.

• Since the number of shares outstanding increases when the company goes public, greater earnings must be achieved to avoid reducing earnings per share.

• If the market price declines, many problems may result: management is usually personally blamed; the flexibility of issuing stock to make acquisitions may be hampered; if the decline occurs soon after the offering, litigation against everyone involved may take place; and other financing alternatives may evaporate.

• Preparation of various reports and financial statements may be costly.

How to Avoid the Drawbacks of Going Public

Here are some tips for avoiding the pitfalls of going public.

• Assemble the proper team. This involves selecting an underwriter, accountant, counsel, and perhaps some new directors.

• When choosing an underwriter, distribution capacity is important. An underwriter appropriate for one company or one industry may be inappropriate for another. In addition to technical ability, personalities and confidence in each also should be considered.

• The selection of accountants and lawyers need careful examination. The registration process is complex, coupled with absolute liability for the company for material misstatements or omissions—regardless of good faith or motive. It is important to remember that malpractice insurance in the securities field is the most expensive of any specialty. That carries a message. It is good to hire a ''Big Eight'' or nationally prominent accounting firm for the reasons that it enhances marketability and may be viewed by the underwriter as insurance in the event of litigation. *See also* Private Placement.

GOLDEN PARACHUTE   A golden parachute is an agreement giving very significant financial benefit to corporate officers in terms of money (e.g., severance pay, bonus), stock options, and so on in the event the firm is bought out by another and the officers are not retained in the new entity. This is particularly done when the business is a target of acquisition.

GOVERNMENTAL ACCOUNTING   This is the accounting policies, reporting requirements, and disclosures required for government units. There is an absence of private ownership. The government provides goods and services to the public without a profit motive. According to the fund theory, assets equal restrictions on assets. The purpose of financial reporting is accountability to the public.

Funds assure accountability and expenditure for specified purposes. Revenues are obtained and used in accordance with special regulations and restrictions. They should be classified by source. Expenditures should be classified by function, activity, character, and principal classes of objectives. Depreciation is not recorded in governmental funds (except for proprietary funds and certain trust funds). Budgets are adopted and recorded in the accounts of the applicable fund. Recording both the budget and actual transactions aid in identifying responsibility and maintaining control. The journal entry to record the budget at the beginning of the year is

Estimated Revenue (authorization to raise funds)
Fund Balance
   Appropriation (authorization to spend)

The journal entry to close the budget at the end of the reporting period is

Appropriations
Revenue
   Estimated Revenue
   Expenditures
   Encumbrances
   Fund Balance

Fund balance is the difference between assets and liabilities and reserve for encumbrances. Fund balance is affected by budgetary (nominal) accounts and actual accounts. Nominal accounts of governmental units relate to controlling accounts that support detailed (subsidiary) ledgers. Nominal accounts are closed out at the end of the accounting period. Examples are appropriations, estimated revenues, expenditures, and encumbrances.

Some funds follow GAAP employing accrual accounting just as commercial enterprises. They include the proprietary funds (enterprise fund and internal service fund) since their operations are similar to those of profit-oriented organizations. The users of the services pay for them. Thus, proprietary funds have profit and loss attributes. Examples of enterprise funds are utilities, airports, transportation systems, hospitals, and port authority. An internal service fund provides services or goods to other funds on a cost reimbursement basis. Examples are maintenance and data processing. Proprietary funds record depreciation.

A fund is a fiscal and accounting entity with a self-balancing set of accounts recording assets, liabilities, and fund balance. Each fund has its own self-contained double-entry set of accounts.

The various types of governmental funds that follow the modified accrual basis of accounting include

• *General fund*—accounts for all financial resources, except those accounted for in another fund.

• *Special revenue fund*—accounts for the proceeds of specific revenue sources that are restricted to expenditure for specified projects. Examples are financing libraries, schools, and parks.

• *Capital projects fund*—accounts for resources used to buy or construct capital facilities. There has to be a capital projects fund for each authorized project to assure that the proceeds of a bond issue are expended only as authorized.

• *Debt service fund*—accounts for the accumulation of resources for and the payment of principal and interest on long-term debt. Three types of long-term debt are term or sinking fund bonds, serial bonds, and note or time warrants having a maturity of more than one year.

Fiduciary funds relate to trust and agency funds, which account for assets held by the governmental body acting as trustee or agent for individuals, organizations, or other governmental units. The funds do *not* own the assets held. The difference between agency and trust is that agency transactions cancel out while trust transactions reflect custody over assets in a more permanent sense. All agency fund assets are owed to another party. Fiduciary funds may be nonexpendable (can-

not expend principal) and expendable (can use principal). Nonexpendable fiduciary funds use accrual accounting, while those that are expendable use modified accrual. An example of a nonexpendable fund is a loan fund in which the original amount must remain intact. Examples of expendable funds are pension and retirement funds.

There are also account groups that are *not* funds but are accounting entities. Account groups are presented in the balance sheet only. There are *no* revenue or expenditures for account groups. They are self-balancing sets of accounts. They furnish double-entry control in memorandum form. The two types are

• *General fixed asset account group*—accounts for all fixed assets that are not shown in another fund. The funds that do show fixed assets are proprietary and trust. The fixed assets are maintained at original cost. Property records are kept for each piece of property and equipment held.

• *General long-term debt account group*—accounts for principal on long-term debt except that payable from a proprietary or trust fund. Under GAAP the proper valuation for the long-term liability is the sum of the discounted value of the principal and interest payments. At maturity, funds are transferred to the debt service fund. There is multiple recording of transactions where two or more funds record that transaction.

■ Example

The general fund expends $1,000,000 to buy fixed assets. The entry in the general fund is

Expenditures	1,000,000	
Vouchers Payable		1,000,000

A memo is made of the $1,000,000 fixed assets being held in the general fixed asset account group.

Interfund transactions may be loans and advances. They are temporary shifts of resources that will be repaid later. They are recorded in "due to" and "due from" accounts.

The name of the annual report for a government is "comprehensive annual financial report." The basic financial statements are prepared in conformity with GAAP as applied to governmental units. The reporting standards are provided in Statement No. 1, "Governmental Accounting and Financial Reporting Principles," of the National Council on Governmental Accounting.

While legal provisions come before accounting principles, there should exist adequate records to allow for GAAP-based reporting. Differences between legal provisions and governmental accounting principles should be disclosed in the footnotes to the financial statements.

There is a combined financial statement with columns for each fund and a total column for all funds. In addition, to a combined, combining (assembling data for all funds within a type), and individual balance sheet, the following is also shown:

• Statement of revenues, Expenditures, and Changes in fund balance (all funds)

• Statement of revenues, Expenditures, and Changes in fund balance, Budget and actual (General and special revenue funds)

See also Encumbrance; Modified Accrual; Not-for-Profit Accounting, Other Than Governmental.

GRAPHICAL METHOD OF LP The graphical method in *linear programming* (LP) is a solution procedure used when an LP problem has usually no more than two decision variables. The graphical method follows the steps:

1. Change inequalities to equalities.
2. Graph the equalities.
3. Identify the correct side for the original inequalities.
4. After all this, determine the *feasible region*, the area of feasible solutions.

5. Evaluate the *corner points* (*basic feasible solution*) of the feasible region.
6. Pick the one that maximizes (or minimizes) the objective function, which is an *optimal solution*.

See also Linear Programming; Simplex Method of LP.

GRAPHIC SOFTWARE Graphic software put numeric data in graphic form, including charts, diagrams, and signs. Graphs can be turned into photographic slides, overhead transparencies, and images on paper. Absolute amounts (i.e., totals, increases), percentages, dollars, and units can be of multiple color. Software that allows free-style drawing is more beneficial for imaginative enhancements. Structured programs clarify a simple chart. *Note:* Better quality can be gotten with stand-alone graphic packages rather than programs that are part of an integrated package.

Accounting graphics can capture complex data collection, show relationships between different numbers, and present them dramatically. Graphics can be used by financial executives to appraise trends and make superior managerial decisions. Presentation graphic packages can produce slides, transparencies, and hard-copy output to accompany presentations and reports at meetings. Audit uses of graphic software include analytical review, reports, and proposals.

Graphic hardware and software are able to accommodate both standard charts and special charts. IBM's Enhanced Graphics Adapter™ card is a graphic interface. Graphic boards provide high resolution and hundreds of colors.

Types of graphics include bar charts (stacked, horizontal, and three-dimensional), line graphs, area graphs, pie shapes, high-low-close charts, bubble charts (depict the relative values of items by size and position of circles in a coordinate range), surface area charts, scatter diagrams, and spherical diagrams.

Graphics may display the following accounting and financial applications:

• Charting revenue and/or costs by product line, market share, and customer

• Break-even analysis

• Trends in major expense categories such as promotion and entertainment expense

• Depicting the variance between actual and budget costs and sales

• Backlog information on orders

• Trends in capital expenditures

• Showing personnel statistics, such as number of employees, sales per employee, and productivity measures

In looking at graphic programs under consideration, the following should be taken into account:

• Compatibility with other packages and applications

• Maximum number of actions and symbols

• Maximum number of columns and rows in chart, automatic overlapped column specifications, and three-dimensional columns

• Maximum number of bars

• Image libraries, which let the financial person merge a picture with a chart or with another image

• Formatting aspects, such as screen resolution display and multiple graph sizes

• Ability to modify predefined or drawn images

• Editing abilities, such as titles, labels, and modification of graph type

• Ability to adjust plot orientation and page size

• Ability to generate graphs with different *y* axes

• Printing features such as bold type, pattern handling, and multiple copies

• Availability of chart legends

• Degree of color selection

• Ability of a graphics enhancement program to accept charts from a standardized business graphics package

Remember: Often, graphics come after data are gotten from an integrated spreadsheet. For example, a chart may depict alternative earnings derived from altering the sales base.

In the case of project management, Gantt charts may be utilized. These are boxes that "float," showing the starting and ending dates of some activity. Haven Tree Software's Interactive Easy Flow™ is a graphics program dedicated to flow charts and organization charts.

■ Example

IBM's PC Storyboard™ is a graphics program having four separate elements. It gives the financial manager the ability to create, edit, and combine business graphics and freehand drawings. Whatever is on the screen can be put into the final design.

■ Example

Software Publishing's Harvard Presentation Graphics™ integrates text, graphs, and charts into a full feature package.

GREENMAIL This refers to "pay-off" payments made by a targeted takeover company to the suitor (prospective acquiring company) so as to cease the takeover attempt. Usually, the targeted company purchases its shares of stock back from the acquirer at materially higher than the current market price. In exchange, the prospective acquirer stops the takeover effort. Existing stockholders in the targeted company may suffer since the company is paying more than the prevailing price for the stock, which ultimately comes out of the stockholders' pockets.

GRETHAM'S LAW This law is popularly phrased as "bad money drives good money out of circulation." More accurately, the law asserts that when an item has a use as both a commodity and money, it will be used where its value is greater. The rapid disappearance of silver certificates is an example of Gretham's law. If a one dollar silver certificate entitles the holder to more than a dollar's worth of silver, the certificate will be hoarded, melted down, exported, or exchanged for silver bullion, thereby disppearing from circulation.

GROSS NATIONAL PRODUCT (GNP) GNP is the current market value in dollars of all final goods and services produced in the economy in a given period. It is normally stated in annual terms, though data are compiled and released quarterly. GNP consists of personal consumption expenditures, gross private domestic investment, government spending, and net exports (exports minus imports).

H

HASH TOTAL   This is adding numbers without practical meaning but done for audit control, mainly in computer applications. The objective is to uncover a lost or omitted file during processing.

■ Example

A hash total may be made of sales invoice numbers. A lack of agreement between processed sales invoices and the hash total indicates an error mandating investigation. *See also* Internal Control.

HEDGING

1. Financing assets with liabilities of similar maturity. In this way, there are sufficient funds to satisfy debt when due. For example, permanent assets should be financed with long-term debt rather than short-term debt. 2. Entering into a futures contract to buy or sell an item at a future date at the *current* price. This strategy is recommended when price increases are anticipated, such as that due to inflation or expected shortage situations.

■ Example

A company wants to buy 1,000 units of an item having a current price of $25 each but does not need the goods until 3 months from now. By entering into a futures contract to take delivery 3 months later at $25 each, the company has protected itself from possible price increases (e.g., $40 price).

HIGH-LOW METHOD   The high-low method is an algebraic procedure used to separate a *mixed (semivariable) cost* into the fixed and the variable portion. The high-low method, as the name indicates, uses two extreme data points to determine the values of *a* (the fixed-cost portion) and *b* (the variable rate) in the *cost-volume formula y = a + bx*. The extreme data points are the highest and lowest cost-volume pairs. The high-low method is simple and easy to use. It has the disadvantage, however, of using two extreme data points, which may not be representative of normal conditions. The method may yield unreliable estimates of *a* and *b* in the formula. In such a case, it would be wise to drop them and choose two other points that are more representative of normal situations. *See also* Cost Behavior Analysis.

HOLDING COMPANY   A holding company has the sole objective of owning the stock of other firms. A holding company can buy a small percentage of another business (e.g., 10%), which may be enough to get effective control over the other, particularly if stock ownership is widely disbursed. A holding company that desires to obtain voting control of a business may make a direct market purchase or a tender offer to obtain additional shares. What would encourage the officers of a company to turn it into a holding company? A company in a declining industry, for instance, may decide to move out of its basic operations by liquidating assets and use the funds obtained to invest in other companies that have good growth potential.

Because the operating companies held by the holding company are distinct legal entities, the obligations of any one are isolated from the others. If one of them goes bankrupt, there is no claim on the assets of another. However, a loan officer that lends to one company may require a guarantee by the other companies. This will, in effect, join the assets of the companies. In any event, a major financial setback involving one company is not the responsibility of the others.

Advantages of Holding Company Arrangement

• The ability of the holding company to buy a large amount of assets with a small investment. In effect, the holding company can control more assets than it could acquire through a merger.

• Risk protection since the failure of one of the companies does not cause the failure of the holding company. The most the holding company would lose is its investment in the failed business.

• Easy to obtain control of another firm because all that is required is purchasing enough stock. Unlike a merger in which stockholder or management approval is required, no approval is needed for a holding company.

Disadvantages of Holding Company Arrangement

• Multiple taxation exists because the income of the holding company that it receives from subsidiaries is in the form of cash. Before paying dividends, the subsidiary must pay taxes on its earnings. When the earnings are distributed to the holding company as dividends, it must pay tax on the dividends received less the 80% dividend exclusion. But if the holding company owns 80% or more of the subsidiary's stock, there will be a 100% dividend exemption. There is no multiple taxation for a subsidiary that is part of a merged company.

• Usually more costly to administer than a single company resulting from a merger. The increased costs result since economies of scale accomplished from a merger do not typically occur.

• The U.S. Department of Justice may construe the holding company as a monopoly and force dissolution.

• By acquiring stock ownership in other companies with debt, a deterioration in financial leverage ratios may occur, as well as magnifying earnings changes. A greater debt position means more risk, with the resulting effect of fluctuating earnings.

A holding company can get a large amount of control for a small investment by obtaining voting control in a company for a minimal amount and then using that firm to gain voting control in another, and so on.

HOME EQUITY LOAN   The home equity loan comes in two forms: a second trust deed (mortgage) and an equity line of credit.
1. *Second trust deed*—similar to a first trust deed (mortgage) except that in the event of foreclosure, the holder of the first mortgage has priority in payment over the holder of the second mortgage.
2. *Line of credit*—under the line of credit provision, a check may be written whenever funds are needed. Interest is charged only on the amount borrowed. Under the Tax Reform Act of 1986, interest incurred on the first and second homes is deductible for tax purposes. However, limitations exist on the deductibility of other types of interest—especially interest on consumer loans. As a result,

it is a good idea to convert your consumer loan interest to interest on a home equity loan in order to continue the full tax-deductibility of interest expense.

Advantages of Home Equity Loan

1. Low interest rates because (a) the loan is secured by a house and (b) it usually bears variable rates.
2. No loan-processing fees. There is no need to go through a loan application and incur fees each time money is borrowed.
3. Convenience. A check may be written only when money is needed. Interest is charged only on the amount borrowed.

Pitfalls of Home Equity Loan

1. *High points.* Points imposed on an equity loan are based on the amount of the credit line, not on the amount actually borrowed. Many home equity loans have no caps on interest rates.
2. *Long payback period.* It is convenient to have to pay a small minimum amount each month, but stretching out the loan payback period usually means higher interest rates over the period.
3. *High balloon payments.* Some loans require a large balloon payment of the principal at the end of the loan period.
4. *Risk of home loss.* Unlike other loans, there is risk in losing a home. It may be difficult to sell the home fast enough and at fair market price to be able to meet the balloon.
5. *Frivolous spending habit.* One may get into the habit of spending on unnecessary things.

HOMOSCEDASTICITY   (or constant variance)

This is one of the assumptions required in a *regression* in order to make valid statistical inferences about population relationships. Homoscedasticity requires that the standard deviation and variance of the error terms be constant for all x's and that the error terms are drawn from the same population. This indicates that there is a uniform scatter or dispersion of data points about the regression line (see figures below). If the assumption does not hold, the accuracy of the regression coefficient(s) is open to question. *See also* Regression Analysis.

HUMAN RESOURCE ACCOUNTING (HRA)   A

positive relationship exists between an entity's success and the quality of its employees. Companies' annual reports often state that their employees are their most valuable assets. Why, then, if the employees are valuable assets, is their value not seen on the accompanying financial statements?

Acceptance of human resource accounting involves a decision to accept the notion that

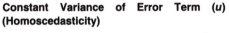

Constant Variance of Error Term (u) (Homoscedasticity)

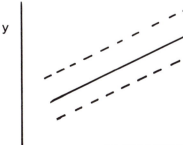

y

x

Nonconstant Variance of Error Term (u)

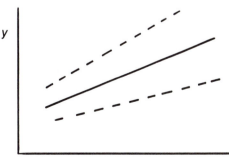

y

x

employees are assets and have a value in monetary terms to the firm's future performance. Employee valuation should be considered in management decisions. HRA can provide data that gives the relative value of employee groups and can relate employees to their effects on the long-term performance of the entity. Human resources can be accounted for much like intangible prepaid expenses.

The objectives of HRA are to provide

• Quantitative information on an entity's human resources that management and investors can utilize in their decision-making process

• Methods of appraising management's utilization of its human resources such as the funds spent on personnel turnover

• Methods to value people, identify relevant variables, and develop models for the management of human resources

The two major valuation approaches are recording human resource expenditures as assets and recording human resources at their value (i.e., present value or future value). The advantage of the former approach is that expenditures (costs) are how assets are measured under GAAP.

The cost approach to human resource valuation is perhaps the most acceptable to traditional accountants, but it is a diluted form of the basic premise of human resource accounting; namely, what are the entity's human resources worth? Worth is a value and not a cost, but value judgments are not acceptable by GAAP.

Historical cost valuation is probably the most widely accepted approach. Costs includable in the human resource asset account would be the actual costs incurred to hire, train, and develop employees. These costs are capitalized and amortized for each employee over the employee's expected period of working with the firm. If the employee leaves earlier than expected, the unamortized balance in the assets would be immediately written off as a loss.

Another cost approach is to use replacement cost, where the employee is valued according to the expense that would be incurred to replace him or her. The costs would include the costs of recruiting and training a replacement. An advantage of this approach is that the replacement cost will be adjusted to price changes in the labor market and hence better approximate the employee's worth to the business.

The economic value approach is in conflict with GAAP but may come up with a more realistic measure. A calculation is made of the present value of the contribution to future profits and the amount is capitalized. This discounted value of future earnings provided by the employee is debited to human resources (asset account) and credited to stockholders' equity.

A macro-economic model may be used employing the discounted value of future salary payments for 5 years. This is multiplied by the efficiency ratio, which is the entity's rate of return relative to industry norms. The final outcome is the present value of the human resources.

Another approach is unpurchased goodwill. The nonhuman assets are valued, net income determined (using assets' market values), and the net income is then compared to the industry average. Differences are then capitalized. Such differences presumably reflect corporate earning power.

For a large number of service organizations, the only product being offered is the professional talents (an intangible product) of their human resources (e.g., law firms with lawyers, hospitals with doctors and nurses).

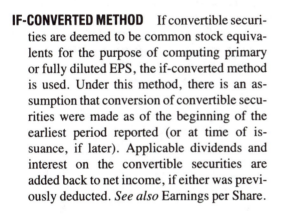

IF-CONVERTED METHOD   If convertible securities are deemed to be common stock equivalents for the purpose of computing primary or fully diluted EPS, the if-converted method is used. Under this method, there is an assumption that conversion of convertible securities were made as of the beginning of the earliest period reported (or at time of issuance, if later). Applicable dividends and interest on the convertible securities are added back to net income, if either was previously deducted. *See also* Earnings per Share.

ILLEGAL ACTS   Under Statement on Auditing Standard No. 54, an illegal act is the violation of a governmental regulation or law. The illegal act may be perpetrated by management or the employees representing it. The following audit procedures and analysis of findings may indicate that an illegal act has occurred.

• Questionable disbursements to employees, outside parties, and government representatives

• Absence of the filing of government forms (e.g., tax returns, compliance reports)

• Unusually high payments for services that have not been documented (e.g., consulting fees)

• Unusual penalties and fines assessed by federal or local authorities

• Government investigation of corporate activities

• Enforcement proceedings against the entity

• Documented violations of regulations and laws

• Excessive commissions and finders' fees

• Material payments in cash

• Significant checks payable to bearer

• Improperly executed and recorded transactions

• Excessive time delays in record keeping or exercising controls

The auditor should attempt to comprehend the nature of the illegal act, the circumstances surrounding it, and its impact upon the financial statements. Inquiry should be made of one level of management above that committing the illegal act. In the event that management does not furnish acceptable assurance that an illegal act has not occurred, the auditor should ask the client's legal counsel about applicable laws and regulations, and the impact the illegal act will have upon the financial statements. The meeting between the auditor and the client's attorney should be made by the client.

The auditor should extend his audit procedures to gather additional relevant information, including

• Ascertaining the proper authorization of transactions

• Obtaining confirmations of essential data from external parties (e.g., attorneys, banks)

• Reviewing documentation in support of the transaction (e.g., canceled checks, invoices, freight bills)

• Comparing how similar transactions were accounted for in the past

The auditor must appraise the impact of an illegal act on financial statement figures, including contingent monetary amounts (e.g., damages, penalties). Contingencies that may occur because of illegality are expropriations, litigation, and bankruptcy. Disclosure of significant revenue obtained from illegal activities is needed. Further, the additional risks forthcoming from illegal acts and relationships should be mentioned.

If a material act has taken place that has not been satisfactorily reflected in the body or notes to the financial statements, a qualified or adverse opinion is necessitated based on the significance of the act or the financial statements.

The auditor should disclaim an opinion when the client prevents the auditor from obtaining competent evidential matter regarding the materiality of the illegal act on the client's financial position.

IMPUTING INTEREST ON NOTES In the case where the face amount of a note does not represent the present value of the consideration given or received in the exchange, imputation of interest is needed to avoid the misstatement of profit. Interest is imputed on noninterest-bearing notes, notes that provide for an unrealistically low interest rate, and notes for which the face value is significantly different from the "going" selling price of the property or market value of the note.

If a note is issued only for cash, the note should be recorded at the cash exchanged, irrespective of whether the interest rate is reasonable or the amount of the face value of the note. The note has a present value at issuance equal to the cash transacted. When a note is exchanged for property, goods, or services, a presumption exists that the interest rate is fair and reasonable. Where the stipulated interest rate is not fair and adequate, the note has to be recorded at the fair value of the merchandise or services or at an amount that approximates fair value. If fair value is not determinable for the goods or services, the discounted present value of the note has to be used.

The imputed interest rate is one that would have resulted if an independent borrower or lender had negotiated a similar transaction. For example, it is the prevailing interest rate the borrower would have paid for financing. The interest rate is based on economic circumstances and events.

Factors to be considered in deriving an appropriate discount rate include

• Prime interest rate

• "Going" market rate for similar quality instruments

• Issuer's credit standing

• Collateral

• Restrictive convenants and other terms in the note agreement

• Tax effects of the arrangement

APB 21 applies to long-term payables and receivables. Short-term payables and receivables are typically recorded at face value since the extra work of amortizing a discount or premium on a short-term note is not worth the information benefit obtained. APB 21 is *not* applicable to

• Security deposits

• Usual lending activities of banks

• Amounts that do not mandate repayment

• Receivables or payables occurring within the ordinary course of business

• Transactions between parent and subsidiary

The difference between the face value of the note and the present value of the note represents discount or premium that has to be accounted for as an element of interest over the life of the note. Present value of the payments of the note is based on an imputed interest rate.

The interest method is used to amortize the discount or premium on the note. The interest method results in a constant rate of interest. Under the method, amortization equals

Interest rate × Present value of the liability/
                      Receivable at the beginning of the year

Interest expense is recorded for the borrower, whereas interest revenue is recorded for the lender. Issuance costs are treated as a deferred charge.

The note payable and note receivable are presented in the balance sheet as follows:

Notes payable (principal plus interest)
Less: Discount (interest)
Present value (principal)

Notes receivable (principal plus interest)
Less: Premium (interest)
Present value (principal)

■ Example

On 1/1/19X1, equipment is acquired in exchange for a 1-year note payable of $1,000 maturing on 12/31/19X1. The imputed interest rate is 10%, resulting in the present value factor for $n = 1$, $i = 10\%$ of 0.91. Relevant journal entries follow:

1/1/19X1	Equipment	910	
	Discount	90	
	Notes payable		1,000
12/31/19X1	Interest Expense	90	
	Discount		90
	Notes Payable	1,000	
	Cash		1,000

■ Example

On 1/1/19X1, a machine is bought for cash of $10,000 and the incurrence of a $30,000, 5-year, noninterest-bearing note payable. The imputed interest rate is 10%. The present value factor for $n = 5$, $i = 10\%$ is 0.62. Appropriate journal entries follow:

1/1/19X1		
Machine ($10,000 + $18,600)	28,600	
Discount	11,400	
Notes Payable		30,000
Cash		10,000

Present value of note equals $30,000 × 0.62 = $18,600. On 1/1/19X1, the balance sheet shows:

Notes payable	$30,000
Less: Discount	11,400
Present value	$18,600
12/31/19X1	
Interest Expense	1,860
Discount	1,860
10% × $18,600 = $1,860	
1/1/19X2	
Notes payable	$30,000
Less: Discount (11,400 − 1,860)	9,540
Present value	$20,460
12/31/19X2	
Interest Expense	2,046
Discount	2,046
10% × $20,460 = $2,046	

INCOME SMOOTHING   This is a form of income manipulation that results in earnings that do not reflect economic reality but rather what the company desires them to be. This masks the inherent cyclical irregularities that are part of the reality of the entity's experience and, thus, detracts from the quality of earnings. Additionally, a firm's taking a "financial bath" causes a lowering in current period earnings while relieving future income of these charges. Improper revenue recognition, either belatedly or prematurely, lowers earnings quality. For instance, the recognition of revenue before it is reasonably assured to be collected may cause the reporting of earnings in one year and its reversal, and an ensuing loss, in a later year. Net income is improperly stated for both periods.

The financial analyst should restate net income for profit increases or decreases arising from income-smoothing attempts.

The quality of earnings depends on the extent to which profits stand on their own for the current period, as well as on the degree to which they borrow from the future or benefit from the past. Earnings are of lower quality if they do not portray the economic performance of the business entity for the period.

INCOME STATEMENT ANALYSIS

The analysis of the income statement indicates a company's earning power, quality of earnings, and operating performance. Net income backed up by cash is important for corporate liquidity. The accounting policies employed should be realistic in reflecting the substance of the transactions. Accounting changes should be made only for proper reasons. Further, a high degree of estimation in the income measurement process results in uncertainty in reported figures. Earnings stability enhances the predictability of future results based on currently reported profits.

Cash Flow From Operations

Cash flow from operations equals net income plus noncash expenses less noncash revenue. Net income is of higher quality if it is backed up by cash. The trend in the ratio of cash flow from operations to net income should be evaluated.

The closer a transaction is to cash, the more objective is the evidence supporting revenue and expense recognition. As the proximity to cash becomes less, the less objective is the transaction and the more subjective are the interpretations. Higher earnings quality relates to recording transactions close to cash realization.

In appraising the cash adequacy of a company, the CPA should compute the following:
• Cash flow generated from operations before interest expense
• Cash flow generated from operations less cash payments to meet debt principal, dividends, and capital expenditures

■ Example

A condensed income statement for Company A follows:

Sales		$1,000,000
Less: Cost of sales		300,000
Gross margin		$ 700,000
Less: Operating expenses		
Salary	$100,000	
Rent	200,000	
Telephone	50,000	
Depreciation	80,000	
Amortization expense	60,000	
Total operating expenses		490,000
Income before other items		$ 210,000
Other revenue and expense		
Interest expense	$ 70,000	
Amortization of deferred credit	40,000	
Total other revenue and expense		30,000
Net income		$ 180,000

The ratio of cash flow from operations to net income is 1.55, calculated as follows:

Cash flow from operations		$180,000
Add: Noncash expenses		
Depreciation	$80,000	
Amortization expense	60,000	140,000
Less: Noncash revenues		
Amortization of deferred credit		(40,000)
Cash flow from operations		$280,000

$$\frac{\text{Cash flow from operations}}{\text{Net income}} = \frac{\$280,000}{\$180,000} = 1.55$$

Discretionary Costs

Discretionary costs may easily be changed by management decision. They include advertising, repairs and maintenance, and research and development. Discretionary costs may be decreased when a company is having problems or wants to show a stable earnings trend. A pullback in discretionary costs results in overstated earnings and a long-term negative effect because management is starving the company of needed expenses. Cost reduction programs may lower earnings quality when material cutbacks are made in discretionary costs. However, the CPA cannot always conclude that any reduction in discretionary costs is improper. The reduction may be necessary when the prior corporate strategy is deficient and ill-conceived.

The CPA should determine if the present level of discretionary costs is in conformity with the company's prior trends and with current and future requirements. Index numbers may be utilized to make a comparison of current discretionary expenditures with base year expenditures. A vacillating trend in discretionary costs to revenue may indicate the company is smoothing earnings by altering its discretionary costs. A substantial increase in discretionary costs may have a positive impact on corporate earning power and future growth.

A declining trend in discretionary costs to net sales may indicate lower earnings quality. Also to be reviewed is the relationship of discretionary costs to the assets to which they apply.

■ Example

The following relationship exists between advertising and sales:

	19X1	19X2	19X3
Sales	$120,000	$150,000	$100,000
Advertising	11,000	16,000	8,000

19X1 is the most typical year.
Increasing competition is expected in 19X4.
Advertising to sales equals:

19X1	19X2	19X3
9.2%	10.7%	8%

In terms of base dollars, 19X1 is assigned 100. In 19X2, the index number is 145.5 ($16,000/$11,000) and in 19X3 it is 72.7 ($8,000/$11,000).

The indicators regarding 19X3 are negative. Advertising is of a lower level than in previous years. In fact, advertising should have risen due to expected increased competition.

Accounting Policies

Conservatively determined net income is of higher quality than liberally determined net income. Conservatism applies to the accounting methods and estimates used. A comparison should be made between the company's accounting policies and the prevailing accounting policies in the industry. If the firm's policies are more liberal, earnings quality may be lower. The CPA should take into account the company's timing of revenue recognition and the deferral of costs relative to prevailing industry practices.

The accounting policies employed should be realistic in reflecting the economic substance of the firm's transactions. The underlying business and financial realities of the company and industry have to be taken into account. For example, the depreciation method should most approximately measure the decline in usefulness of the asset. The CPA may question the reasonableness of a company's accounting estimates when prior estimates have been materially different from what actually occurred. Examples of realistic accounting policies are cited in AICPA Industry Audit Guides and in accounting policy guides published by various CPA firms. If the use of realistic policies would have resulted in substantially lower earnings than the policies used, earnings quality is lower.

The artificial shifting of earnings from one year to another results in poor earnings quality. This encompasses bringing future revenue into the current year (or its converse), shifting earnings from good years to bad years, or shifting expenses and losses among the years.

It is questionable when a company immediately recognizes revenue even though services still have to be performed. An example is a magazine publisher recognizing subscription income immediately when payment is received even though the subscription period may be for 3 years.

The unrealistic deferral of revenue recognition results in poor earnings quality because profits are unjustifiably understated. When there is a reversal of previously recorded profits, the CPA may question the company's revenue recognition policies.

If expenses are underaccrued or overaccrued, lower earnings quality results. An example of an underaccrued expense is the failure of a computer manufacturer to provide for normal maintenance service for rented computers because they are being used by lessees. An example of an overaccrued expense is when a company with high earnings decides to accrue for possible sales returns that are highly unlikely to materialize. The CPA should try to ascertain what these normal charges are and adjust reported earnings accordingly.

Accounting changes made to conform with new FASB Statements, AICPA Industry Audit Guides, and IRS Regulations are justifiable. However, an unjustified accounting change causes an earnings increment of low quality. Unwarranted changes may be made in accounting principles, estimates, and assumptions.

Are accounting changes being made to create artificial earnings growth? If there are numerous accounting changes, it will be more difficult to use current profits as a predictor for future earnings.

Degree of Certainty in Accounting Estimates

The more subjective accounting estimates and judgments are in arriving at earnings, the more uncertain is the net income figure. For example, a firm engaged in long-term activity (e.g., a shipbuilder using the percentage of completion contract method) has more uncertainty regarding earnings due to the material estimates involved. A higher percentage of assets subject to accounting estimates (intangibles) to total assets means uncertain earnings.

The CPA may want to determine the difference between estimated reserves and actual losses for previous years. A significant difference between the two may point to lower earnings quality. Further, substantial gains and losses on the sale of assets may point to inaccurate depreciation estimates being originally used.

The CPA should segregate cash expenses versus estimated expenses. Trends should be determined in
- Cash expenses to net sales
- Estimated expenses to net sales
- Estimated expenses to total expenses
- Estimated expenses to net income

■ Example

The CPA assembles the following information for Company B for the period 19X1 and 19X2:

	19X1	19X2
Cash and near-cash (conversion period to cash is short) revenue items	$100,000	$110,000
Noncash revenue items (long-term receivables arising from credit sales to the government, revenue recognized under the precentage of completion method)	150,000	200,000
Total revenue	$250,000	$310,000
Cash and near-cash expenses (salaries, rent, telephone)	$ 40,000	$ 60,000
Noncash expenses (depreciation, depletion, amortization, bad debts)	70,000	120,000
Total expenses	$110,000	$180,000
Net income	$140,000	$130,000

Estimated revenue items to total revenue was 60% ($150,000/$250,000) in 19X1 and 65% ($200,000/$310,000) in 19X2. Estimated revenue to net income was 107% ($150,000/$140,000) in 19X1 and 154% ($200,000/$130,000) in 19X2.

Estimated expense items to total expenses was 64% ($70,000/$110,000) in 19X1 and 67% ($120,000/$180,000) in 19X2. Estimated expenses to total revenue was 28% ($70,000/$250,000) in 19X1 and 39% ($120,000/$310,000) in 19X2. Estimated expenses to net income was 50% ($70,000/$140,000) in 19X1 and 92% ($120,000/$130,000) in 19X2.

Uncertainty exists with respect to the earnings of 19X1 and 19X2 arising from the high percentages of estimated income statement items. Also, a greater degree of estimation exists with regard to 19X2's income measurement process.

Residual Income

An increasing trend in residual income to net income points to a strong degree of corporate profitability because the company is earning enough to meet its imputed cost of capital.

Taxable Income

If a company reports significant stockholder earnings and a substantial tax loss, the CPA may want to evaluate the quality of reported results.

A company having a significant deferred income tax credit account will have book profits in excess of taxable earnings. An increase in the deferred tax credit account may indicate the company is moving toward more liberal accounting policies. This is because a widening gap in the deferred tax credit account indicates a greater disparity between book earnings and taxable earnings.

A decline in the effective tax rate because of a nonrecurring source (e.g., a loss carry forward that will shortly expire) results in an earnings increment of low quality. The tax benefits will not continue in the future. However, the effective tax rate may be stable when it results from a recurring source (e.g., foreign tax credit, interest on municipal bonds).

Lower earnings quality exists if there is a high percentage of foreign earnings that will not be repatriated to the U.S. for a long time.

Foreign Operations

The CPA should consider the following in evaluating the effect of foreign operations on the company's financial health:

- Degree of intercountry transactions
- Different year-ends of foreign subsidiaries
- Foreign restrictions on the transfer of funds
- Tax structure of the foreign country
- Economic and political stability of the foreign country

An erratic foreign exchange rate results in instability. The CPA can measure the degree of vacillation of the foreign exchange rate by determining its percentage change over time and/or its standard deviation. The CPA should look at the trend in the ratio of foreign translation gains and losses (reported in the stockholders' equity section) to net income to evaluate the degree of stability.

Discontinued Operations

Income from discontinued operations is usually of a one-time nature and should be ignored when forecasting future earnings. Further, a discontinued operation implies a company is in a state of decline or that a poor management decision is the cause for the firm's entering the discontinued line of business in the first place. *See also* Balance Sheet Analysis.

INCOME STATEMENT FORMAT

The format of the income statement starting with income from continuing operations follows:

Income from continuing operations before tax
Less: Taxes
Income from continuing operations after tax
Discontinued operations:
 Income from discontinued operations (net of tax)
 Loss or gain on disposal of a division (net of tax)
Income before extraordinary items
Extraordinary items (net of tax)
Cumulative effect of a change in accounting principle
 (net of tax)
Net income

Note that earnings per share is shown on the previous items as well.

Extraordinary Items

Extraordinary items are those that are *both* unusual in nature and infrequent in occurrence. Unusual in nature means the event is abnormal and not related to the typical operations of the entity. The environment of a company includes consideration of industry characteristics, geographic location of operations, and extent of government regulation. Infrequent in occurrence means the transaction is not anticipated to take place in the foreseeable future, taking into account the corporate environment. Materiality is considered by judging the items individually and not in the aggregate. However, if arising from a single specific event or plan they should be aggregated. Extraordinary items are shown net of tax between income from discontinued operations and cumulative effect of a change in accounting principle. Extraordinary items include

 • Casualty losses
 • Losses on expropriation of property by a foreign government
 • Gain on life insurance proceeds

 • Loss or gain on the early extinguishment of debt
 • Gain on troubled debt restructuring
 • Loss from prohibition under a newly enacted law or regulation
 • Gain or loss on disposal of a major part of the assets of a previously separate company in a business combination when sale is made within 2 years subsequent to the combination date

Losses on receivables and inventory occur in the normal course of business and therefore are not extraordinary. There is an exception, however, that losses on receivables and inventory are extraordinary if they relate to a casualty loss (e.g., earthquake) or governmental expropriation (e.g., banning of a product because of a health hazard).

Nonrecurring Items

Nonrecurring items are items that are *either* unusual in nature or infrequent in occurrence. They are shown as a separate line item before tax in arriving at income from continuing operations. An example is the gain or loss on the sale of a fixed asset.

Discontinued Operations

A business segment is a major line of business or customer class. A discontinued operation is an operation that has been discontinued during the year or will be discontinued shortly after year-end. A discontinued operation may be a segment that has been sold, abandoned, or spun off. Even though it may be operating, there exists a formal plan to dispose. Footnote disclosure regarding the discontinued operation should include an identification of the segment, disposal date, the manner of disposal, and description of remaining net assets of the segment at year-end.

The two components of discontinued operations are (1) income or loss from operations and (2) loss or gain on disposal of division.

Income or Loss From Operations. In a year that includes the measurement date, it is the income from the beginning of the year to the measurement date. The measurement date is the one on which management commits itself to a formal plan of action. Applicable estimates may be required.

If comparative financial statements are presented, including periods before the measurement date, discontinued operations should be separately shown from continuing operations.

Loss or Gain on Disposal of Division. Income or loss from activities subsequent to the measurement date and before the disposal date is an element of the gain or loss on disposal. The disposal date is the date of closing by sale or the date activities cease because of abandonment. The gain or loss is shown in the disposal year. However, if losses are expected, such losses are recorded in the year of the measurement date even if disposal is not completed in that year. Loss or gain should include estimated net losses from operations between the measurement date and the disposal date. If the loss cannot be estimated, a footnote is required. Loss on disposal includes the costs directly associated with the disposal decision. On the other hand, if a gain is expected, it should be recognized at the disposal date. The estimated gain or loss is determined at the measurement date and includes consideration of the net realizable value of the segment's assets. Also, loss or gain on disposal includes costs and expenses *directly* applicable to the disposal decision. These costs include severance pay, additional pension costs, employment relocation, and future rentals on long-term leases where subrentals are not possible. *Note*: Normal business adjustments (e.g., routinely writing down accounts receivable) are not includable in the loss on disposal. These ordinary adjustments apply to the discontinued segment's operation rather than

to the disposal of the segment. Typically, disposal is expected within one year of the measurement date. *See also* Accounting Changes.

INCOME TAX ACCOUNTING   FASB No. 96 provides that income taxes should be allocated to financial periods using the *liability method*. Tax allocation is required when *temporary differences* rather than permanent differences exist.

The deferred tax liability or asset is measured at the tax rate under existing law that will be in effect when the temporary difference reverses itself. Further, the deferred tax liability or asset must be adjusted for changes in tax law or in tax rate. The liability method is balance sheet oriented since emphasis is placed on asset and liability recognition.

Comprehensive deferred tax accounting is followed where tax expense equals taxes payable plus the tax effects of all temporary differences.

Income tax is accounted for on the *accrual basis*.

Interperiod tax allocation is employed to recognize current (or deferred) tax liability or asset for the current (or deferred) tax effect of events that have taken place at year-end. Tax effects of future events should be reflected in the year they take place.

Temporary Differences

Temporary differences are differences between periods in which transactions affect taxable income and accounting income. They originate in one period and subsequently reverse in another. Temporary differences are created by four types of transactions, the nature of which (and examples) are as follows:

1. Income included in taxable income after being included in accounting income (e.g., installment sales)

2. Expenses deducted for taxable income after being deducted for accounting income (e.g., warranty provision)

3. Income included in taxable income before being included in accounting income (e.g., rents received in advance)

4. Expenses deducted for taxable income before being deducted for accounting income (e.g., accelerated depreciation)

A temporary difference may result from increases in the tax basis of assets because of indexing for inflation.

If tax rates are graduated based on taxable income, aggregate calculations may be made using an estimated average rate.

Permanent Differences

Permanent differences do not reverse (turn around) and as such do not require tax allocation. Examples of nontax-deductible expenses are goodwill amortization, premiums on officers' life insurance, and fines. An example of income that is not taxable is interest on municipal bonds.

Financial Statement Presentation

In the balance sheet, deferred charges and credits are netted against each other and shown net current and net noncurrent. However, offset is not permitted for deferred tax liabilities or assets that apply to different tax jurisdictions.

Deferred taxes are classified as current or noncurrent based on the expected reversal dates of the temporary differences. Temporary differences reversing within one year are current, whereas those reversing in greater than one year are noncurrent.

In the income statement, disclosure is made of (1) income tax expense currently payable (the liability) and (2) the *deferred portion* of the expense (the portion of the expense based on temporary differences). (The total expense provision is based on financial reporting income, excluding permanent differences.)

Presentation of these two expense portions (with numbers and a 40% tax rate assumed) would be as follows:

Income before income taxes		$200
Income tax expense:		
Amount currently payable	$400	
Deferred portion	(320)	80
Net income		$120

Intraperiod tax allocation is when tax expense is shown in different parts of the financial statements for the current year. The income statement shows the tax allocated to (1) income from continuing operations; (2) income from discontinued operations; (3) extraordinary items; and (4) cumulative effect of a change in accounting principle. Note that in the retained earnings statement, prior period adjustments are shown net of tax.

Loss Carry Backs and Loss Carry Forwards

The tax effects of net operating *loss carry backs* should be allocated to the loss period. An entity may carry back a net operating loss 3 years and obtain a refund for taxes paid in those years. The loss is first applied to the earliest year. Any residual loss is carried forward up to 15 years.

Presentation of *loss carry back* with recognition of refund during loss year:

Loss before refundable income taxes	$1,000
Refund of prior year's income taxes arising from carry back of operating loss	485
Net loss	$ 515

(*Note*: The refund should be computed at the amount actually refundable, regardless of current tax rates).

The tax effects of net operating *loss carry forwards* and tax credits (e.g., alternative minimum tax credit) generally cannot be recognized until the year realized (the year in which the tax liability is reduced). A journal entry typically *cannot* be made in the loss year for any possible tax benefits because of the uncertainty of future earnings. Recognition is given only in the year realized.

When the tax benefit of a loss carry forward is recognized when realized in a later year, it is classified in the same way as the income enabling recognition (typically reducing tax expense).

Presentation of the loss carry forward with recognition of benefit in year realized (numbers and 50% rate assumed):

Income before income taxes		$1,000
Income tax expense:		
Without carry forward	$500	
Reduction of income taxes arising from carry forward of prior year's operating losses	(300)	200
Net income		$800

An exception exists to the general rule of not permitting the recognition of a net operating loss carry forward in the current year. The net operating loss carry forward may be recognized to the extent of net taxable amounts in the carry forward period (deferred tax liabilities now exist to absorb them).

Disclosure should be made of the amounts and expiration dates of operating loss carry forwards.

Deferred Tax Liability vs. Deferred Tax Asset

If book income exceeds taxable income, tax expense exceeds tax payable so a deferred tax liability results. If book income is less than taxable income, tax expense is less than tax payable so a deferred tax asset results.

Deferred Tax Liability

■ Example

Assume book income and taxable income are $1,000. Depreciation for book purposes is $50 based on the straight-line method and $100 for tax purposes based on the accelerated cost recovery system. Assuming a tax rate of 34%, the entry is

Income Tax Expense ($950 × 34%)	323	
Income Tax Payable ($900 × 34%)		306
Deferred Tax Liability		17

At the end of the asset's life, the deferred tax liability of $17 will be fully reversed.

■ Example*

At the end of year 1, future recovery of the reported amount of an enterprise's installment receivables will result in taxable amounts totaling $240,000 in years 2–4. Also, a $20,000 liability for estimated expenses has been recognized in the financial statements in year 1, and those expenses will be deductible for tax purposes in year 4 when the liability is expected to be paid. Those temporary differences are estimated to result in net taxable amounts in future years as presented at bottom of this page.

This example assumes that the enacted tax rates for years 2–4 are 20% for the first $50,000 of taxable income, 30% for the next $50,000, and 40% for taxable income over $100,000. The liability for deferred tax consequences is measured at top of page 234.

	Year 2	Year 3	Year 4
Taxable amounts	$70,000	$110,000	$60,000
Deductible amount	—	—	(20,000)
Net taxable amounts	$70,000	$110,000	$40,000

* *Source*: Financial Accounting Standards Board, FASB No. 96, "Accounting for Income Taxes," Stamford, CT, December 1987, p. 32.

	Year 2	Year 3	Year 4
20% tax on first $50,000	$10,000	$10,000	$8,000
30% tax on next $50,000	6,000	15,000	—
40% tax on over $100,000	—	4,000	—
	$16,000	$29,000	$8,000

A deferred tax liability is recognized for $53,000 (the total of the taxes payable for years 2–4) at the end of year 1.

Deferred Tax Asset

A deferred tax asset results in a future deductible amount (for tax purposes) that can only be recognized as an asset in the current year if the entity is certain to have taxable income in the future. Thus, a deferred tax asset can be booked only for the amount of the certain future deductibility of the item for tax purposes (e.g., resulting from temporary differences due to deferred tax liabilities already existing).

■ Example

In 19X8, a company sold a fixed asset reporting a gain of $70,000 for book purposes which was deferred for tax purposes (installment method) until 19X9. In addition, in 19X8, $40,000 of subscription income was received in advance. The income was recognized for tax purposes in 19X8 but was deferred for book purposes until 19X9.

The deferred tax asset may be recorded because the deductible amount in the future ($40,000) offsets the taxable amount ($70,000). Assuming a 34% tax rate and income taxes payable of $100,000, the entry in 19X8 is

Income Tax Expense	110,200	
Deferred Tax Asset ($40,000 × 34%)	13,600	
Deferred Tax Liability ($70,000 × 34%)		23,800
Income Taxes Payable		100,000

Note: The deferred tax asset can be recognized only up to the later years' deferred tax liabilities caused from temporary differences. Thus, if the gain on the sale of fixed assets was $25,000, the maximum amount of deferred revenue that could be recognized as a deferred tax asset would be $25,000. In this case, the entry is

Income Tax Expense	100,000	
Deferred Tax Asset (maximum up to deferred liability)	8,500	
Deferred Tax Liability ($25,000 × 34%)		8,500
Income Taxes Payable		100,000

A deferred tax asset can also be recognized for the tax benefit of deductible amounts realizable by carrying back a loss from future years to reduce taxes paid in the current or a prior year.

The restrictions on the recording of the deferred tax asset is based on *conservatism*.

Tax Rates

Tax rates in later years may be different. Further, a change in tax law may occur.

Different Tax Rates in the Future

Deferred taxes are reflected at the amounts of settlement when the temporary differences reverse.

■ Example

Assume in 19X3 a cumulative temporary difference of $200,000 that will reverse in the future generating the following taxable amounts and tax rate:

	19X4	19X5	19X6	Total
Reversals	$60,000	$90,000	$50,000	$200,000
Tax rate	×0.34	×0.30	×0.25	
Deferred tax liability	$20,400	$27,000	$12,500	$ 59,900

On December 31, 19X3, the deferred tax liability is recorded at $59,900.

A future tax rate can be used *only* if it has been enacted by law.

While there may be graduated tax rates, the highest tax rate may be used when the difference is not material.

Change in Tax Rate

Immediately reflect the impact of a change in tax rate on the accounts. Tax expense and deferred tax are appropriately adjusted in the year of change.

■ Example

Assume at the end of 19X2, a law is passed reducing the tax rate from 34% to 30% starting in 19X4. In 19X2, there was deferred profit of $100,000, showing a deferred tax liability of $34,000 as of 19X2. The gross profit is to be reflected equally in 19X3, 19X4, 19X5, and 19X6. Thus, the deferred tax liability at the end of 19X2 is $31,000, as shown at the bottom of this page.

The appropriate entry in 19X2 is

Deferred Tax Liability	3,000	
Income Tax Expense		3,000

Purchase Combination

In a purchase combination, the net assets acquired are reflected at their gross fair values with a separate deferred tax balance for the applicable tax effects. Further, a temporary difference will occur for the difference between the financial reporting and tax basis of assets and liabilities acquired. If the acquired company has an operating loss or tax credit carry forward, it may be used to reduce the deferred tax liability of the acquired company.

Disclosures

Disclosure should be made of the types of temporary differences that have occurred causing a material deferred tax liability or asset. An example is the disclosure that ACRS is used for tax and straight-line depreciation is used for books.

If a deferred tax liability is *not* recognized, disclosure should be made of the following:

• Description of the kinds of temporary differences for which *no* recognition has been given to a deferred tax liability and the types of events that would result in tax recognition of the temporary differences

• Cumulative amount of each kind of temporary difference

A reconciliation should exist between the reported amount of tax expense and the tax expense that would have occurred using federal statutory tax rates. The reconciliation should be in terms of percentages or dollar amounts. If statutory tax rates do not exist, use the regular tax rates for alternative tax systems. Disclosure should be given of the estimated amount and the nature of each material reconciling item.

Disclosure should be made of the provisions of intercorporate tax-sharing arrangements and tax-related balances due to or from affiliates.

Extensions of Tax Allocation

In accordance with APB Opinions No. 23 and 24, undistributed earnings (parent/investor share of subsidiary/investee income less dividends received) are considered to be temporary differences.

The rationale for this treatment is based on the basic presumption that such earnings will eventually be transferred.

	19X3	19X4	19X5	19X6	Total
Reversals	$25,000	$25,000	$25,000	$25,000	
Tax rate	×0.34	×0.30	×0.30	×0.30	
Deferred tax liability	$ 8,500	$ 7,500	$ 7,500	$ 7,500	$31,000

Temporary Difference

Income taxes related to temporary differences should be accounted for in accordance with FASB No. 96. In the case of investee income arising from the application of APB No. 18, if evidence indicates eventual realization by disposition of investment, income taxes should be determined at capital gains or other appropriate rates.

Indefinite Reversal

There is no interperiod tax allocation in the case of indefinite reversal. Indefinite reversal is when undistributed earnings in a foreign subsidiary will indefinitely be postponed or when earnings will be remitted in a tax-free liquidation.

If there is a change in circumstances and the presumption of indefinite reversal no longer holds, there should be an adjustment to tax expense.

Disclosure should be made of the declaration to reinvest indefinitely or to remit tax free, and the cumulative amount of undistributed earnings.

Amount of Temporary Difference

Of the dividends received from affiliated corporations 80% are generally exempt from tax. Consequently, the temporary difference is equal to 20% of the undistributed earnings (parent/investor interest less dividends received).

INCREMENTAL ANALYSIS   Incremental (differential) analysis is an approach to choosing the best decision alternative that utilizes the concept of *relevant* costs. Under this approach, the decision involves the following steps:

1. Gather all revenue and cost data for each decision alternative.
2. Drop the *sunk* costs, since they are past costs and therefore are irrelevant to the decision.

3. Drop those costs that do not differ between alternatives. Only consider incremental revenue and cost data.
4. Select the best alternative based on the remaining data.

■ Example

A company produces three products, X, Y, and Z, from a joint process. Joint manufacturing costs for the year were $100,000. Product Z may be sold at the point of separation, called the *split-off point*, or processed further for more revenue. Specific data for product Z are as follows:

Units Produced	Sales Value at Split-off	Additional Cost and Sales Value After Further Processing	
		Sales	Cost
50,000	$250,000	$300,000	$25,500

The decision as to whether product Z should be sold at split-off or processed further can be analyzed using the incremental approach, under which incremental revenue is compared with incremental cost, as shown following.

Incremental sales revenue	$50,000 ($300,000 − $250,000)
Incremental costs, additional processing	25,500
Incremental gain	$24,500

The analysis shows that it pays to extend processing. Note that the joint production cost of $100,000 is not included in the analysis, since it is a sunk cost and therefore irrelevant to the decision. *See also* Relevant Costing; Sell-or-Process-Further Decision.

INDEXATION   This refers to the assignment of escalator clauses to long-term contracts where wages, incomes, social security payments, and even the tax system can be readjusted automatically in order to prevent inflation from distorting real income or other real values. This way an individual's gains are not taxed away, thereby reducing real income. *Escalator clause* is a provision in a long-term contract whereby these payments are tied to a comprehensive measure of price-level and cost-of-living changes. The consumer price index (CPI) and GNP deflator (implicit price index) are the measures most commonly used for indexation. Indexation may be partial or comprehensive in nature.

■ Example

Assume an employee's income goes up by 5% while prices go up by 5%. That means he/she has no more purchasing power than before, although the income tax will rise because a higher income will push one into a higher tax bracket. Indexation can avoid this situation by correcting the income for inflation. *See also* Inflation; Price Indices.

INDEX OF LEADING ECONOMIC INDICATORS
The index of leading economic indicators (economic indicator series) are the economic series of indicators that tend to predict future changes in economic activity; officially called *Composite Index of 12 Leading Indicators*. This series is the government's main barometer for forecasting business trends. Each of the series has shown a tendency to change before the economy makes a major turn—hence, the term "leading indicators." This series is published monthly by the U.S. Department of Commerce, consisting of:

•*Average workweek of production workers in manufacturing*

Employers find it a lot easier to increase the number of hours worked in a week than to hire more employees.

•*Initial claims for unemployment insurance*

The number of people who sign up for unemployment benefits signals changes in present and future economic activity.

•*Vendor performance*

Vendor performance represents the percentage of companies reporting slower deliveries. As the economy grows, firms have more trouble filling orders.

•*Change in total liquid assets*

This indicates changes in the amount of buying power readily available.

•*Percentage change in prices of sensitive crude materials*

Rises in prices of such critical materials as steel and iron usually mean factory demands are going up, which means factories plan to step up production.

•*Contracts and orders for plant and equipment*

Heavier contracting and ordering usually lead economic upswings.

•*Net business formation*

More businesses are created in anticipation of profit prospects. This usually leads rebounds by several months.

•*Stock prices*

A rise in the common stock index indicates expected profits and lower interest rates. Stock market advances usually precede business upturns by 3 to 8 months.

•*Money supply*

A rising money supply means easy money that sparks brisk economic activity. This usually leads recoveries by as much as 14 months.

•*New orders for manufacturers of consumer goods and materials*

New orders mean more workers hired, more materials and supplies purchased, and increased output. Gains in this series usually lead recoveries by as much as 4 months.

•*Residential building permits for private housing*

Gains in building permits signal business upturns.

•*Change in inventories*

Expected higher sales means the building up of inventories on the part of companies. Rises usually lead upswings by up to 8 months.

These 12 components of the index are adjusted for inflation. Rarely do these components of the index all go in the same direction at once. Each factor is weighted. The composite figure is designed to tell only in which direction business will go. It is not intended to forecast the magnitude of future ups and downs.

INFLATION This means a general rise in the price level. When inflation is present, a dollar today can buy more than a dollar in the future. Although the causes of inflation are diverse, a frequent source of inflationary pressures is the excess demand for goods and services which pulls product prices upward—*demand-pull inflation*. Rising wages and material costs may lead to the upward pressure on prices—*cost-push inflation*. Furthermore, excessive spending and/or heavy borrowing due to a budget deficit by the federal government can be inflationary. All of these sources may be intermingled at a particular point in time, making it difficult to pinpoint the cause for inflation.

There are numerous ways in which financial management can counteract the adverse effects of inflation upon the business, including:

1. *Selling price considerations*. Inflation risks can be passed on to consumers, as by increasing selling prices at short intervals (e.g., monthly). Further, the company can swiftly modify price catalogs and sales literature. Price quotations should be held only for short periods of time (e.g., 2 months).

Sales pricing policy should be determined on a next-in, first-out basis so that replacement costing is taken into account. Pricing ahead of inflation is a key weapon.

In sales agreements, a provision should exist that prices may be increased up to the point of actual shipment when a long lead time exists between the time an order is received and the goods are shipped. Further, in such cases, progress billings should be received as work is performed. Long-term contracts should include a ''cost plus'' provision, possibly tied into a Consumer Price Index.

2. *Control over costs*. Product components that typically experience excessive increases should be deemphasized. The company should contract for long-term purchase agreements and encourage suppliers to quote firm prices. A change in suppliers may be advisable if they give more liberal credit or easier terms.

When inflation is anticipated to worsen, the company should engage in future contracts in order to lock itself into buying raw materials at current lower prices.

It is recommended that competitive bids from insurance companies be periodically received and carriers changed when costs are beneficial.

A redesign of truck logistics may be made to accomplish economies of petroleum products.

3. *Marketing aspects*. Deemphasis should be on products significantly impacted by inflation (production, promotion). Inflation-resistant product substitutes should be emphasized.

4. *Labor implications*. Companies with automated facilities and a minimal labor force do better during inflation.

5. *Financial matters*. A good hedge against inflation is a tangible asset such as gold, silver, or real estate. Another is to borrow from insurance companies against the cash surrender value of life insurance. The rates provided for the policies are most likely less than the prevailing interest rate.

See also Price Indices.

INSTABILITY INDEX OF EARNINGS This is a measure of the variation between actual earnings and trend earnings. It equals:

$$I = \sqrt{\frac{\Sigma(y - y^T)^2}{n}}$$

where y = net income,
$\quad y^T$ = trend earnings,
$\quad n$ = number of periods.

Trend earnings is computed through the use of a trend equation solved by the computer. A low index indicates stability in the entity's profitability. A high index points to unstable earnings.

INSURANCE PROGRAMS provide a vital means of meeting the financial objectives of individuals. The type and amount of insurance depends on the age, assets, income, and needs of an individual. Insurance is basically replacement: life insurance provides income lost at the death of the wage earner; disability insurance assures income when the insured is not able to work full time; health insurance covers medical bills; and homeowners/casualty policies pay most of the costs of theft, accident, or fire.

Life Insurance

Life insurance is the most important tool of estate planning and one of the most valuable aids to financial planning. There are two basic types of life insurance policies—term insurance and whole life insurance. All other kinds of policies are variations on one or more of the two basic types.

1. *Term insurance*—protection for the client for a specified period of time. It pays a benefit only if the insured dies during the period covered by the policy. It provides for a level premium rate for a set period, after which the policy ceases and becomes void, except when renewed or changed to some other form of policy. It is the cheapest form of life insurance because it provides the most coverage for the least money.

2. *Whole life insurance* (cash value insurance or straight life insurance)—provides insurance protection by the payment of a fixed premium throughout the lifetime of the insured. However, in addition to death protec-tion, whole life insurance has a savings element called "cash value." As the policies mature, they develop cash values representing the early surplus plus investment earnings. There are many variations of whole life insurance: universal life, variable life, single-premium whole life, adjustable life, and adjustable-premium life.

Aspects of term insurance:
- Protection for a specified period of time.
- Low initial premium.
- May be renewable and/or convertible.
- Premium rises with each new term.
- You or your dependents get nothing back if you survive the term.

Aspects of whole life insurance:
- Protection for life.
- Fixed premium.
- Growing cash value.
- Higher initial premium than term.
- You or your dependents always receive benefits.
- Available as universal, variable, single-premium whole life, adjustable life, and adjustable-premium life.
- Should be purchased with the intention of keeping for life or for a long period of time.

Disability Insurance

This insurance provides a regular cash income when an insured person is unable to work as a result of a covered illness, injury, or disease. Most disability payments are tax exempt as long as the individual policyholder pays the premium.

Health Insurance

For most people, health insurance is provided by the employer as a major fringe benefit. Otherwise, individual policies can be purchased. There are three kinds of medical or health insurance: basic hospitalization, basic medical/surgical, and major medical.

Property and Liability Insurance

Property and liability insurance is important to an individual's personal financial security. He or she can be successful in the job, investments, and the like, and yet be almost destroyed financially by an accident, disaster, or lawsuit for which there is not adequate property and liability insurance. It is wise to carry such insurance to protect family assets and future income from a catastrophic event. *See also* Personal Financial Planning.

INTANGIBLE ASSETS These are assets having a life of one year or more and lack physical substance (e.g., goodwill) or represent a right granted by the government (e.g., patent) or another company (e.g., franchise fee). APB 17 covers accounting for intangible assets, whether purchased or internally developed. The costs of intangibles *acquired* from others should be reported as assets. The cost equals the cash or fair market value of the consideration given. The individual intangibles that can be separately identified must be costed separately. If not separately identified, the intangibles are assigned a cost equal to the difference between the total purchase price and the cost of identifiable tangible and intangible assets. *Note*: Goodwill does not include identifiable assets.

The cost of developing and maintaining intangibles should be charged against earnings if the assets are not specifically identifiable, have indeterminate lives, or are inherent in the continuing business (e.g., goodwill). An example of internally developed goodwill that is expensed are the costs incurred in developing a name (e.g., Burger King).

All intangible assets are amortized over the period benefited using the straight-line method not exceeding a 40-year life. Factors in estimating useful lives include
• Legal, contractual, and regulatory provisions.
• Renewal or extension provisions. If a renewal occurs, the life of the intangible may be increased.
• Obsolescence and competitive factors.
• Product demand.
• Service lives of essential employees within the organization.
For example, an intangible may be enhanced because of good public relations staff.

Intangibles on the books before 1970 need *not* be amortized.

Footnote disclosure is made of the amortization period and method.

If a firm buys, on a step-by-step basis, an investment using the equity method, the fair value of the acquired assets and the goodwill for each step purchased must be separately identified.

When the purchase of assets results in goodwill, later sale of a separable portion of the entity acquired mandate a proportionate reduction of the goodwill account. A portion of the unamortized goodwill is included in the cost of assets sold.

Goodwill is recorded only in a business combination accounted for under the purchase method when the cost to the acquirer exceeds the fair market value of the net identifiable assets acquired. Goodwill may be determined by an individual appraiser, a purchase audit done by the acquiring company's public accounting firm, and so on. Goodwill is then amortized using the straight-line method over the period benefited, not exceeding 40 years. If the cost to the acquirer is less than the fair market value of the net identifiable assets acquired, a credit arises which reduces the noncurrent assets acquired on a proportionate basis (excluding long-term investments). If a credit still remains, it is treated as a deferred credit not to be amortized over more than 40 years under the straight-line method.

Goodwill is theoretically equal to the present value of future excess earnings of a company over other companies in the industry. However, it is difficult to predict the length of time superior earnings will occur. Some factors involved in the makeup of goodwill are superior salesforce, outstanding management talent, effective advertising, strategic location, and dependable suppliers.

In buying a new business, a determination must often be made as to the estimated value of the goodwill. Two possible methods that can be used are (1) capitalization of earnings and (2) capitalization of excess earnings.

■ Example

The following information is available for a business that we are contemplating acquiring:

Expected average annual earnings	$10,000
Expected future value of net assets exclusive of goodwill	$45,000
Normal rate of return	20%

Using the capitalization-of-earnings approach, goodwill is estimated at:

Total asset value implied ($10,000/20%)	$50,000
Estimated fair value of assets	45,000
Estimated goodwill	$ 5,000

Assuming the same facts except a capitalization rate of excess earnings of 22% and using the capitalization of excess earnings method, goodwill is estimated at:

Expected average annual earnings	$10,000
Return on expected average assets ($45,000 × 20%)	9,000
Excess earnings	$ 1,000

Goodwill ($1,000/0.22) = $4,545

■ Example

The net worth of ABC Company excluding goodwill is $800,000, and profits for the last 4 years were $750,000. Included in the later figure are extraordinary gains of $50,000 and nonrecurring losses of $30,000. It is desired to determine a selling price of the business. A 12% return on net worth is deemed typical for the industry. The capitalization of excess earnings is 45% in determining goodwill.

Net income for 4 years	$750,000
Less: Extraordinary gains	50,000
Add: Nonrecurring losses	30,000
Adjusted 4-year earnings	$730,000
Average earnings ($730,000/4)	$182,500
Normal earnings ($800,000 × 0.12)	96,000
Excess annual earnings	$ 86,500

Excess earnings capitalized at 45%:

$$\frac{\$86,500}{0.45} = \$192,222$$

The determination of goodwill and its amortization can have a large impact on the balance sheet and financial position of a company. A good example of this is when Turner Broadcasting attempted to take over CBS. Turner assigned the difference of what he would pay for CBS and its book value entirely to goodwill and amortized this amount over 40 years. CBS claimed a smaller amount should be assigned to goodwill and their assets revalued, which would have lowered the net income of the combined Turner–CBS Company. Here, the valuation of goodwill was extremely important in this takeover battle.

Internally generated costs to derive a patented product are expensed such as R&D incurred in developing a new product. The patent is recorded at the registration fees to secure and register it, legal fees in successfully defending it in court, and the cost of acquiring competing patents from outsiders. The patent account is amortized over its useful life, not exceeding 17 years. If an intangible asset is deemed worthless, it should be written off, recognizing an extraordinary item.

Organization costs are the costs incurred to incorporate a business (e.g., legal fees). They are deferred and amortized.

Leaseholds are rent paid in advance and are amortized over the life of the lease.

If the amortization expense of an intangible is not tax deductible (e.g., amortization of goodwill), a permanent difference arises. Thus, no interperiod tax allocation is involved.

INTEGER PROGRAMMING This is a form of mathematical programming. It is really a special case of *linear programming* where all (or some) variables are restricted to being integers (whole numbers). For example, quantities like 5.25 cars, 32.75 tables, and 1½ persons may be unrealistic. Simply rounding off the linear programming solution to the nearest whole numbers may not produce a feasible solution. The integer programming method allows managers to find the optimal *integer* solution to a problem without violating any of the constraints. *See also* Linear Programming; Mathematical Programming.

INTEGRATED SOFTWARE Integrated software comprises two or more modules that perform together. Integrated packages permit moving data between several programs. *Remember*: They utilize common, comprehendable commands (instructions) and file structures for all applications. In effect, you have multiple applications in memory simultaneously.

Integrated software may combine functions like word processing, spreadsheets, data base management, telecommunications, and graphics. In effect, different processing tasks are carried out with the same data file. For example, data derived from spreadsheets or data base management files may be graphed. Word processing software can merge text with data from other records. From a data base of client names you could print labels for mailing of overdue balance letters.

When should an integrated package be used? If identical source information is to be used for varying purposes and activities, an integrated package is recommended. It is superior to an individual package, which requires the practitioner to load each program and data file each time another package is required. With integrated software, a sequence of applications is accomplished without the need to go from separate, distinct programs. Also, some canned software will not perform with files derived from other programs.

Questions to Ask When Selecting an Integrated Package

• Are all applications in the package necessary?

• What is the quality of individual tasks within each program that will be used the most?

• Does the integration work satisfactorily?

• Does one of the programs in the integrated package duplicate already existing software?

• Is there a possibility of modifying applications?

• Does the integrated package run well on the present computer? If not, what additional hardware must be acquired?

With an integrated package, one function is transferred to another. Windows depict the contents of each on the monitor.

■ Example

ABC Company's integrated software:

• Generates an accounting file via data base management systems

• Has an electronic worksheet perform what-if calculations

• Graphs the options with a graphics package

• Prints out a report, schedule, and management letter with the word processing program

• Sends the letter by electronic mail to the client via a data communications package

You can use integrated software to accomplish the following accounting applications:

• Develop a model to test various scenarios (e.g., effect of tax law changes on the operations and accounts)

• Prepare consolidated worksheets and statements

• Prepare reports and related graphical information

• Make an appraisal of business segments

• Prepare and analyze financial data
• Evaluate trends

■ Example

Ashton-Tate's Framework™ is an integrated package of word processing, spreadsheet, graphics, data base management, and communications.

INTEREST METHOD OF AMORTIZATION (SCIENTIFIC AMORTIZATION)

Interest expense (or interest revenue) equals the interest rate times the carrying value of the liability (or receivable) at the beginning of the period. It is the preferred method of amortizing bond discount or bond premium. *See also* Bond Accounting.

INTEREST RATE FUTURES CONTRACT

This contract gives the holder the right to a specified amount of the related debt security at a future time (typically, no more than 3 years). It may cover Treasury bills, commercial paper, GNMA certificates, and certificates of deposit.

Interest rate futures are stated in percentage terms of the par value of the related obligation. The contract's value is directly related to interest rates. For example, contract value will increase when interest rates decrease, and vice versa. As the contract's price increases, the buyer of the contract profits while the seller loses. A change of one basis point in interest rates results in a price change. A basis point equals $\frac{1}{100}$ of 1%.

The buyer of the contract will not typically take possession of the financial instrument. The contract is basically employed either for hedging or speculation purposes on future interest rates and security prices. For instance, the banker may utilize the contract to hedge the bank's position in financial instruments.

■ Example

Company XYZ will issue bonds in 4 months. Terms of the underwriting are now being made up. There is an anticipation that interest rates will increase in the next 4 months. Investors can hedge by selling short the Treasury bills. An increase in interest rates will cause a lower price to reacquire the interest rate future with the resulting profit. This profit reduces the higher interest cost of the debt.

Financial futures may attract speculators due to the significant return possible on a small investment. With a large contract (e.g., $500,000 Treasury bill), a small change in the contract's price may generate a substantial profit. *Caution*: Do not forget the risk involved. Volatile securities may exist, resulting in substantial loss. A speculator anticipating rising interest rates will desire to sell an interest rate future because it will shortly decline in value.

INTERIM REPORTING

Interim periods are essential parts of the annual period. Interim reports may be issued at appropriate reporting intervals, such as quarterly or monthly. Complete financial statements or summarized data may be given. Interim financial statements do not have to be certified. It is recommended that interim balance sheets and funds flow data be provided. If not presented, material changes in liquid assets, working capital, long-term debt, and stockholders' equity should be disclosed.

Usually, interim reports include results of the current interim period and the cumulative year-to-date figures. Typically, comparisons are made to results of comparable interim periods for the prior year.

Interim results should be based on the accounting principles used in the last year's annual report unless a change has been made in the current year.

A gain or loss cannot be deferred to a later interim period except if such deferral would have been permissible for annual reporting.

Revenue from merchandise sold and services performed should be accounted for as earned in the interim period in the same way as accounted for in annual reporting. If an advance is received in the first quarter and benefits the entire year, it should be allocated ratably to the interim periods affected.

Costs and expenses should be matched to related revenue in the interim period. If a cost cannot be associated with revenue in a future interim period, it should be expensed in the current period. Yearly expenses such as administrative salaries, insurance, pension plan expense, and year-end bonuses should be allocated to the quarters. The allocation basis may be based on such factors as time expired, benefit obtained, and activity.

The gross profit method can be used to estimate interim inventory and cost of sales. Disclosure should be made of the method, assumptions made, and material adjustments by reconciliations with the annual physical inventory.

A permanent inventory loss should be reflected in the interim period it occurs. A subsequent recovery is treated as a gain in the later interim period. However, if the change in inventory value is temporary, no recognition is given in the accounts.

When there is a temporary liquidation of the LIFO base with replacement expected by year-end, cost of sales should be based on replacement cost.

■ Example

The historical cost of an inventory item is $10,000 with replacement cost expected at $15,000. The entry is

Cost of Sales	15,000	
Inventory		10,000
Reserve for Liquidation of LIFO Base		5,000

Note the Reserve for Liquidation of LIFO Base account is shown as a current liability.

When replenishment is made at year-end the entry is

Reserve for Liquidation of LIFO Base	5,000	
Inventory	10,000	
Cash		15,000

Volume discounts given to customers tied into annual purchases should be apportioned to the interim period based on the ratio of:

$$\frac{\text{Purchases for the interim period}}{\text{Total estimated purchases for the year}}$$

When a standard cost system is used, variances expected to be reversed by year-end may be deferred to an asset or liability account.

With regard to income taxes, the income tax provision includes current and deferred taxes. Federal and local taxes are provided for. The tax provision for an interim period should be cumulative (e.g., total tax expense for a 9-month period is shown in the third quarter based on a 9-month income). The tax expense for the 3-month period based on 3 months of revenue may also be presented (e.g., third quarter tax expense based on only the third quarter). In computing tax expense, the estimated annual effective tax rate should be used. The effective tax rate should be based on income from continuing operations. If a reliable estimate is not practical, the actual year-to-date effective tax rate should be used.

At the end of each interim period, a revision to the effective tax rate may be necessary, employing the best current estimates of the annual effective tax rate. The projected tax rate includes adjustment for net deferred credits. Adjustments should be contained in deriving the maximum tax benefit for year-to-date figures.

The estimated effective tax rate should incorporate all available tax credits (e.g., foreign tax credit) and available alternative tax methods in determining ordinary earnings. A change in tax legislation is reflected only in the interim period affected.

Income statement items after income from continuing operations (e.g., income from discontinued operations, extraordinary items, cumulative effect of a change in accounting principle) should be presented net of the tax effect. The tax effect on these unusual line items should be reflected only in the interim period in which they actually occur. For example, we should not predict items before they occur. Prior period adjustments in the retained earnings statement are also shown net of tax when they take place.

The tax implication of an interim loss is recognized *only* when realization of the tax benefit is assured beyond reasonable doubt. If a loss is expected for the remainder of the year and carry back is not possible, the tax benefits typically should not be recognized.

The tax benefit of a previous year operating loss carry forward is recognized as an extraordinary item in each interim period to the extent that income is available to offset the loss carry forward.

When a change in principle is made in the first interim period, the cumulative effect of a change-in-principle account should be shown net of tax in the first interim period. If a change in principle is made in a quarter other than the first (e.g., third quarter), we assume the change was made at the beginning of the first quarter, showing the cumulative effect in the first quarter. The interim periods will have to be *restated* using the new principle (e.g., first, second, and third quarters).

When interim data for previous years is presented for comparative purposes, data should be restated to conform with newly adopted policies. Alternatively, disclosure can be made of the effect on prior data had the new practice been applied to that period.

For a change in principle, disclosure should be made of the nature and justification in the interim period of change. The effect of the change on per share amounts should be given.

Disclosure should be made of seasonality aspects affecting interim results. Also disclose contingencies. When a change in the estimated effective tax rate occurs, it should be disclosed. Further, if a fourth quarter is not presented, any material adjustments to that quarter must be commented upon in the footnotes to the annual report. If an event is immaterial on an annual basis but material in the interim period, it should be disclosed. Purchase or pooling transactions should be noted.

The financial statement presentation for prior period adjustments follow:
- Include in net income for the current period the portion of the effect related to current operations.
- Restate earnings of impacted prior interim periods of the current year to include the portion related thereto.
- If the prior period adjustment affects prior years, include it in the earnings of the first interim period of the current year.

The criteria to be met for prior period adjustments in interim periods follow:
- Materiality
- Estimable
- Identified to a prior interim period

Examples of prior period adjustments for interim reporting are
- Error corrections
- Settlement of litigation or claims
- Adjustment of income taxes
- Renegotiation proceedings
- Utility revenue under rate-making processes

Earnings per share are computed for interim purposes the same way as for annual purposes.

Segmental disposal is separaely shown in the interim period it occurs.

INTERNAL AUDIT An internal audit is performed by auditors working for the business entity itself. They independently perform an audit review and appraisal of the firm's accounting records, controls, and operations. In addition, a determination is made as to whether assets are being properly safeguarded. It is also ascertained whether management policies and procedures are being followed throughout the entity. Often, the internal auditors report directly to the Audit Committee of the Board of Directors so that they may objectively provide their viewpoints of management's performance. Recommendations for improvement in the accounting system are made.

INTERNAL CONTROL STRUCTURE Probably, this is the most important aspect of the auditor's examination. As per Statement on Auditing Standards No. 55, the auditor must consider the internal control structure when planning the audit and incorporate internal control considerations in gathering audit evidence. The major elements of internal control are the control environment, accounting system, and control procedures. All must be understood by the auditor to plan the audit. The CPA must be familiar with relevant policies, procedures, and records, and whether they have been put into operation. Control risk should be appraised in relation to financial statement assertions. This evaluation at the assertion level should be at the maximum (highest control risk) when an inadequate internal control structure exists.

The internal control system of a client is comprised of an organizational plan, accounting records, procedures, and controls to reasonably assure that the entity's assets are safeguarded and reliability exists in the financial records to fairly present financial position and opeating results.

An adequate internal control system should have the following attributes:

• Restricted access to assets
• Proper authorization of transaction
• Agreement between the amount per the books and the physical existence of the assets
• Segregation of duties, including a separation between individuals resonsible for keeping the books and those having physical custody of assets
• Technically competent individuals performing accounting tasks

• Recording transactions so that they reflect their substance

An examination of internal controls is necessary so that the auditor can determine his or her reliance on it in order to formulate the degree and timing of necessary substantive tests. Under the second fieldwork standard of GAAS, the auditor must perform an adequate evaluation of the client's internal control structure. In conducting the internal control analysis, the auditor should use the cycle approach, involving the selection of broad areas of activity so that specific transactions may be tested. The major cycles are for revenue (e.g., credit approval, invoicing, cash receipts), expenditure (e.g., purchasing, receiving, and cash payments), production (e.g., inventories and fixed assets), financing (e.g., notes receivable, leases), and external reporting (e.g., GAAP, financial statement preparation).

The preliminary review of internal control structure gives the auditor an overall understanding of the client's control environment, transaction flow, and means of data processing. This review encompasses the following aspects:

• Prior experience with the client and inquiry of client personnel
• Observing client activities
• Referring to previous years' workpapers
• Evaluation of relevant client material such as accounting manuals

In completing the review, documentation must exist, such as in the form of flow charts and questionnaires.

When the internal control structure may be relied upon, compliance tests will be performed and results evaluated.

As per AICPA Statement on Auditing Standards No. 60, the auditor must report deficiencies in the control environment, accounting system, and control procedures to the audit committee of the company. To be reported are matters representing material deficiencies in the design or operation of the

internal control structure that could negatively impact the company's ability to record,
process, summarize, and report financial data
in the financial statements. *See also* Compliance Test; Substantive Test.

INTERNAL RATE OF RETURN (IRR) IRR, also
called time adjusted rate of return (TARR),
is the rate of interest that equates the initial
investment (I) with the present value (PV)
of future cash inflows. That is, at *IRR*, *I* =
PV, or *NPV* (net present value) = 0. Under
the internal rate of return method, the decision rule is: Accept the project if IRR exceeds
the cost of capital; otherwise, reject the proposal.

■ **Example**

Consider the following data:

Initial investment	$12,950
Estimated life	10 years
Annual cash inflows	$ 3,000
Cost of capital (minimum required return)	12%

We will set up the following equality (*I* =
PV):

$$\$12,950 = \$3,000 \times PVIFA$$

Then *PVIFA* = $12,950/$3,000 = 4.317,
which stands somewhere between 18% and
20% in the 10-year line of Table. The interpolation follows:

	PV Factor	
18%	4.494	4.494
IRR		4.317
20%	4.192	
Difference	0.302	0.177

Therefore, *IRR* = 18% + (0.177/0.302)
                      (20% − 18%)
            = 18% + 0.586(2%)
            = 18% + 1.17% = 19.17%

Since the investment's IRR (19.17%) is
greater than the cost of capital (12%), the
investment should be accepted.

The IRR method is easy to use as long
as cash inflows are even from year to year.
Where the cash flows are uneven, the IRR
must be determined by trial and error. Assume, for example, that a company is considering an investment project that promises
cash inflows of $400,000, $600,000, and
$1,000,000 for each of the next 3 years for
a given investment of $800,000. The IRR
is found by selecting a rate and discounting
the cash inflows. If the PV is greater than
I, select a higher rate until one is found that
equates the PV of the cash inflows with I.
In this example, the IRR is approximately
20%, determined as follows:

Present Values (Based on Table 3) = PVIF

Annual Cash Inflows	20%	22%
$ 400,000	$333,200	$328,000
600,000	416,400	403,200
1,000,000	57,900	55,100
	$807,500	$786,300

An advantage of the IRR method is that it
considers the *time value of money* and is
therefore more exact and realistic than *the
simple (or accounting) rate of return*. Disadvantages are (1) it fails to recognize the varying size of investment in competing projects
and their respective dollar profitabilities; and
(2) in limited cases, where there are multiple
reversals in the cash-flow streams, the project
could yield more than one internal rate of
return.

INVENTORY CONTROL AND MANAGEMENT
This is maintaining the optimum inventory
level through inventory records. This is done
to maximize profits by creating a good balance between inventory investment and
smooth, continuous production, for a profit-
oriented firm. For a nonprofit entity, this
means minimizing costs.

Maintaining excessive inventories may
mean risk of carrying obsolete items and high
carrying costs. Maintaining inadequate in-

ventories may mean losing sales and poor production control. Maintaining adequate inventory means some hedge against sudden price increases and being able to serve customers promptly, in order to satisfy their needs. By maintaining a functional inventory supply, a company will be able to protect itself against unplanned changes in supply and demand.

An optimal safety stock level should exist. It requires a balancing of expected costs of stockouts against the costs of carrying the additional inventory.

Good internal control over inventory is necessary to guard against theft and other irregularities. A surprise inventory count should periodically occur to assure agreement between the book inventory and physical inventory.

Major shortages may take place and go unnoticed for a long time period if satisfactory control is lacking. Inventory is an area in which many frauds take place. Good control is needed in the acquisition and handling phases. Segregation should exist in purchasing, receiving, storing, and shipping of inventories. There should be a separation of the accounting for and the custody of merchandise.

An inventory control system should accomplish the following objectives: (1) proper record keeping; (2) implementing inventory decision models; (3) reporting exceptions; (4) aiding in forecasting usage and needs; and (5) maintaining proper safeguards to prevent misuse. *See also* ABC Inventory Method; Economic Order Quantity (EOQ); Inventory Planning and Control.

INVENTORY PLANNING AND CONTROL One of the most common problems that faces managerial accountants is that of inventory planning and control. This is understandable because inventory usually represents a sizable portion of a firm's total assets. Excess funds tied up in inventory is a drag on profitability.

The purpose of inventory planning and control is to develop policies that will achieve an optimal investment in inventory. This objective is achieved by determining the optimal level of inventory necessary to minimize inventory-related costs.

Inventory costs fall into three categories:
1. Order costs include all costs associated with preparing a purchase order.
2. Carrying costs include storage costs for inventory items plus opportunity cost (i.e., the cost incurred by investing in inventory).
3. Shortage (stockout) costs include those costs incurred when an item is out of stock. These include the lost contribution margin on sales plus lost customer goodwill.

There are many inventory planning and control models available that try to answer basically the following questions:
1. How much to order?
2. When to order?

They include the basic economic order quantity (EOQ) model, the reorder point, and the determination of safety stock.

Economic Order Quantity (EOQ)

The economic order quantity (EOQ) model determines the order size that minimizes the sum of carrying and ordering costs. Demand is assumed to be constant throughout the year. EOQ is computed as

$$EOQ = \sqrt{2OD/C}$$

where O = cost of placing an order.

D = annual demand (usage) in units,

and C = cost of carrying one unit in stock. If the carrying cost is expressed as a percentage of average inventory value (say, 12% per year to hold inventory), then the denominator value in the EOQ formula would be 12% times the price of an item.

▪ Example 1

Assume ABC store buys sets of steel at $40 per set from an outside vendor. ABC will sell 6,400 sets evenly throughout the year.

ABC desires a 16% return (cost of borrowed money) on its inventory investment. In addition, rent, taxes, and so on for each set in inventory is $1.60. The ordering cost is $100 per order. Then the carrying cost per dozen is 16%($40) + $1.60 = $8.00.
Therefore:

$$\text{EOQ} = \sqrt{\frac{2(6,400)(\$100)}{\$8.00}} = \sqrt{160,000} = 400 \text{ sets}$$

Total inventory costs = Carrying cost per unit $\times \dfrac{\text{EOQ}}{2}$

$$+ \text{ Ordering cost per order}$$
$$\times \frac{\text{Annual demand}}{\text{EOQ}}$$

$$= (\$8.00)(400/2)$$
$$+ (\$100)(6,400/400)$$
$$= \$1,600 + \$1,600 = \$3,200$$

Total number of orders per year
$$= \text{Annual demand/EOQ} = 6,400/400$$
$$= 16 \text{ orders}$$

The EOQ model is depicted graphically in Figure 1.

There are some basic assumptions underlying the EOQ model. They are

1. Demand is constant and known with certainty.
2. Depletion of stock is linear and constant.
3. No discount is allowed for quantity purchases.
4. *Lead time*, which is the time interval between placing an order and receiving delivery, is a constant (i.e., stockout is not possible).

Reorder Point (ROP)

Reorder point (economic order point), which answers *when* to place a new order, requires a knowledge about the lead time. Reorder point (ROP) can be calculated as follows:

Reorder point = Average usage per unit of lead time
$$\times \text{ Lead time + Safety stock}$$

First, multiply average daily (or weekly) usage by the lead time in days (or weeks) yielding the lead time demand. Then add safety stock to this to provide for the variation in lead time demand to determine the reorder point. If average usage and lead time are both certain, no safety stock is necessary and should be dropped from the formula.

■ Example 2

Assume in Example 1, lead time is constant at 1 week and there are 50 working weeks in a year. Then reorder point is 128 sets = (6,400 sets/50 weeks) × 1 week. Therefore, when the inventory level drops to 128 sets, the new order should be placed. Figure 2 shows this inventory system when the order quantity is 400 sets and the reorder point is 128 sets.

Figure 1

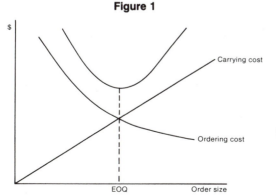

Figure 2 Basic Inventory System With EOQ and Reorder Point

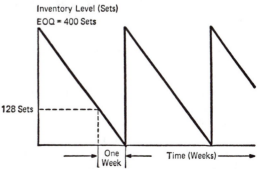

Computation of Safety Stock

Safety Stock Levels in Units	Stockout and Probability	Average Stockout in Units	Average Stockout Costs	No. of Orders	Total Annual Stockout Cost	Carrying Costs	Total
0	50 with 0.2 100 with 0.1 150 with 0.1	35[a]	$420[b]	16	$6,720[c]	0	$7,140
50	50 with 0.1 100 with 0.1	15	180	16	2,880	400[d]	3,280
100	50 with 0.1	5	60	16	960	800	1,760
150	0	0	0	16	0	1,200	1,200

[a] $50(.2) + 100(.1) + 150(.1) = 10 + 10 + 15 = 35$ units
[b] 35 units $\times$ $\$12 = \$420$
[c] $\$420 \times 16$ times $= \$6,720$
[d] 50 units $\times$ $\$8 = \$400$

Assumptions and Applications

The EOQ model described here is appropriate for a pure inventory system; that is, for single-item, single-stage inventory decisions for which joint costs and constraints can be ignored. They assume that both lead time and demand rates are constant and known with certainty. This may be unrealistic; however, these models have proved to be useful in inventory planning for many firms.

Many situations exist where such an assumption holds or nearly holds. Subcontractors who must supply parts on a regular basis to a primary contractor face a constant demand. Even where demand varies, the assumption of uniform usage is not unrealistic. Demand for automobiles, for example, varies from week to week but, over a season, the weekly fluctuations tend to cancel each other out so that seasonal demand can be assumed constant.

Safety Stock and Reorder Point

When lead time and demand are not certain, the firm must carry extra units of inventory, called *safety stock*, as protection against possible stockouts. Stockouts can be quite expensive. Lost sales and disgruntled customers are examples of external costs. Idle machines and disrupted production scheduling are ex-

amples of internal costs. We will illustrate the probability approach to show how the optimal size of safety stock can be determined in the presence of stockout costs.

■ Example 3

Recall from Example 2 that the reorder point is 128 sets. If either lead time or demand is variable, the store needs to carry an extra stock as safety. Suppose that the total usage over a 1-week period is expected to be

Total Usage	Probability
78	0.2
128	0.4
178	0.2
228	0.1
278	0.1
	1.00

Suppose further that a stockout cost is estimated at $12 per set. Recall that the carrying cost is $8 per set. The computation at the top of the page shows that the total costs are minimized at $1,200, when a safety stock of 150 sets is maintained. Therefore, the reorder point is 128 sets + 150 sets = 278 sets.

INVENTORY VALUATION   Inventory may be valued at the lower of cost or market value. Specialized inventory methods may be used such as retail, retail lower of cost or market, retail LIFO, and dollar value LIFO. Losses on purchase commitments should be recognized in the accounts.

If ending inventory is overstated, cost of sales is understated, and net income is overstated. If beginning inventory is overstated, cost of sales is overstated and net income is understated.

Lower of cost or market value method— inventories are recorded at the lower of cost or market value for conservatism purposes applied on a total basis, category basis, or individual basis. The method used must be consistently applied.

If cost is below market value (replacement cost), cost is taken. If market value is below cost, we start with market value. However, market value cannot exceed the ceiling, which is net realizable value (selling price less costs to complete and dispose). If it does, the cost is chosen. Further, market value cannot be less than the floor, which is net realizable value less a normal profit margin. If market value is less than the floor, the floor value is used. Of course, market value is used when it lies between the ceiling and floor. The following diagram may be helpful:

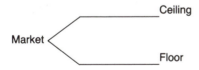

■ Example

The lower of cost or market value method is being applied on an item-by-item basis. The circled figure is the appropriate valuation.

Product	Cost	Market	Ceiling	Floor
A	($5)	$7	$9	$6
B	14	12	(11)	7
C	18	(15)	16	12
D	20	12	18	(16)
E	(6)	5	12	7

Note that in case E, market value of $5 was originally selected. The market value of $5 exceeded the floor of $7, so the floor value would be used. However, if after applying the lower of cost or market value rule the valuation derived ($7) exceeds the cost ($6), the cost figure is more conservative and thus is used.

Note that if market (replacement cost) is below the original cost but the selling price has not likewise declined, no loss should be recognized. To do so would create an abnormal profit margin in the future period.

The lower of cost or market value method is not used with LIFO, since under LIFO current revenue is matched against current costs.

Retail method—used by department stores and other large retail businesses. These businesses usually carry inventory items at retail selling price. The retail method is used to estimate the ending inventory at cost by employing a cost to retail (selling price) ratio. The ending inventory is first determined at selling price and then converted to cost. Markups and markdowns are both considered in arriving at the cost to retail ratio resulting in a higher ending inventory than the retail lower of cost or market value method.

Retail lower of cost or market value method (conventional retail)—a modification of the retail method and preferable to it. In computing the cost to retail ratio, markups but not markdowns are considered, resulting in a lower inventory figure.

The following example illustrates the accounting difference between the retail method and the retail lower of cost or market value method.

■ Example Retail Method vs. Retail Lower of Cost or Market Value Method

	Cost	Retail	
Inventory—1/1	16,000	30,000	
Purchases	30,000	60,000	
Purchase returns	(5,000)	(10,000)	
Purchase discount	(2,000)		
Freight in	1,000		
Markups	25,000		
Markup cancellations	5,000		
Net markups		20,000	
Total	40,000	100,000	(40%)
Markdowns	22,000		
Markdown cancellations	2,000		
Net markdowns		20,000	
Cost of goods available	40,000	80,000	(50%)
Deduct:			
Sales	55,000		
Sales returns	5,000		
		50,000	
Inventory—retail		30,000	
Retail method:			
At cost 50% × 30,000		15,000	
Retail lower of cost or market method:			
40% × 30,000		12,000	

Retail LIFO—in computing ending inventory, the mechanics of the retail method are basically followed. Beginning inventory is *excluded* and both markups and markdowns are *included* in computing the cost to retail ratio. A decrease in inventory during the period is deducted from the most recently added layer and then subtracted from layers in the inverse order of addition. A retail price index is used in restating inventory.

■ Example

Retail LIFO

Retail price indices follow:

19X7	100
19X8	104
19X9	110

19×8	Cost	Retail	
Inventory—Jan. 1 (base inv.)	80,000	130,000	
Purchases	240,000	410,000	
Markups		10,000	
Markdowns		(20,000)	
Total (exclude beg. inv.)	240,000	400,000	60%
Total (include beg. inv.)	320,000	530,000	
Sales		389,600	
19X8 inv.—end—retail		140,400	

Cost Basis	Cost	Retail		
19X8 Inventory in forms of				
19X7 prices 140,400 ÷ 1.04		135,000		
19X7 Base	80,000	130,000	130,000 × 1.04	135,200
19X8 Layer in 19X7 prices		5,000		
19X8 Layer in 19X8 prices		5,200	5,000 × 1.04	5,200
				140,400
19X8 LIFO cost 60% × 5,200	3,120			
	83,120	140,400		

19X9	Cost	Retail		
Inventory—Jan. 1	83,120	140,400		
Purchases	260,400	430,000		
Markups		20,000		
Markdowns		(30,000)		
Total (exclude beg. inv.)	260,400	420,000	62%	
Total (include beg. inv.)	343,520	560,400		
Sales		408,600		
19X9 Inventory—end of retail		151,800		

Cost Basis	Cost	Retail		
19X9 Inventory in 19X7 prices 151,800 ÷ 1.10		138,000		
19X7 base	80,000	130,000	130,000 × 1.10	143,000
Excess over base year		8,000		
19X8 layer in 19X8 prices	3,120	5,000	5,000 × 1.10	5,500
19X9 layer in 19X7 prices		3,000		
19X9 layer in 19X9 prices		3,300	3,000 × 1.10	3,300
19X9 Increase in 19X9 prices				
LIFO cost 62% × 3,300	2,046			
	85,166	151,800		151,800

Dollar value LIFO—an extension of the historical cost principle. The method aggregates dollars instead of units into homogeneous groupings. The method assumes that an inventory decrease came from the last year.

The procedures under dollar value LIFO follow:

1. Restate ending inventory in the current year into base dollars by applying a price index.
2. Subtract the year 0 inventory in base dollars from the current year's inventory in base dollars.
3. Multiply the incremental inventory in the current year in base dollars by the price index to obtain the incremental inventory in current dollars.
4. Obtain the reportable inventory for the current year by adding to the year 0 inventory in base dollars the incremental inventory for the current year in current dollars.

■ Example

At 12/31/19X1, the ending inventory is $130,000 and the price index is 1.30. The base inventory on 1/1/19X1 was $80,000. The 12/31/19X1 inventory is computed following:

12/31/19X1 inventory in base dollars	
$130,000/1.30	$100,000
1/1/19X1 beginning base inventory	80,000
19X1 Increment in base dollars	$ 20,000
19X1 Increment in current year dollars	× 1.3
	$ 26,000
Inventory in base dollars	$ 80,000
Increment in current year dollars	26,000
Reportable inventory	$106,000

Losses on purchase commitments—significant net losses on purchase commitments should be recognized at the end of the reporting period.

■ Example

In 19X8, ABC Company committed itself to buy raw materials at $1.20 per pound. At the end of the year, before fulfilling the purchase commitment, the price of the materials dropped to $1 per pound. Conservatism dictates that a loss on purchase commitment of $0.20 per pound be recognized in 19X8. Loss on Purchase Commitment is debited and Allowance for Purchase Commitment Loss is credited.

Inventory valuation difficulties—while the basics of inventory cost measurement is easily stated, difficulties arise because of cost allocation problems. For example, idle capacity costs and abnormal spoilage costs may have to be written off immediately in the current year instead of being allocated as an element of inventory valuation. Furthermore, general and administrative expenses are inventoriable when they specifically relate to production activity.

Inventory stated at market value in excess of cost—in unusual circumstances, inventories may be stated in excess of cost. This may occur when there is no basis for cost apportionment (e.g., meat-packing industry). Market value may also be used when immediate marketability exists at quoted prices (e.g., certain precious metals or agricultural prod-

ucts). Disclosure is necessary when inventory is stated above cost.

INVESTMENT BANKING involves public flotation, or sale, of a security issue. The investment banker acts as the intermediary between the issuing company and the security purchaser. Investment bankers conduct the following activities.

• *Underwriting*—the investment banker purchases a new security issue, pays the issuer, and markets the securities. The underwriter's compensation is the difference between the price at which the securities are sold to the public and the price paid to the issuing company.

• *Distributing*—the investment banker markets the security issue.

• *Giving advice*—the investment banker provides advice to the company regarding the optimal means of raising funds. The investment banker is knowledgeable regarding the alternative sources of long-term funds, debt and equity markets, and SEC regulations.

• *Providing funds*—the investment banker provides funds to the issuing company during the distribution period.

A *syndicate* is a group of investment bankers dealing with a particular issue. One investment banker among the group will be the manager, called *originating house*. The originating house underwrites the major amount of the issue. One bid price for the issue is made on behalf of the group, but the terms and features of the issue are set by the company.

Two kinds of underwriting syndicates are *divided* and *undivided*. In a *divided account*, each member's liability is limited in terms of participation. Once a member sells the securities assigned, that investment banker has no further obligation, regardless of whether the other members are able to sell their part of the security issue. In an *undivided account*, each member is obligated for unsold securities up to the amount of the percentage participation, regardless of the number of securities that investment banker has sold. Most syndicates are of the undivided type.

In another approach to investment banking, the investment banker contracts to sell securities on a best-efforts basis, or as an agent for the issuer. The investment banker is not acting as an underwriter but instead sells the stock and obtains a commission on the sale. The investment banker may opt for this arrangement when he or she is not sure about the successful issuance of that security in the marketplace. *See also* Going Public.

INVESTMENT CENTER An investment center is a responsibility center within an organization that has control over revenue, cost, and investment funds. It is a *profit center* whose performance is evaluated on the basis of the return earned on invested capital. The corporate headquarters or division in a large decentralized organization would be an example of an investment center. *Return on investment* and *residual income* are two key performance measures of an investment center. *See also* Divisional Performance Evaluation; Profit Center; Responsibility Accounting.

INVESTMENT MANAGEMENT The maturity dates of investment should be staggered. For instance, if all the securities mature on one date, reinvestment may be subject to low returns if interest rates are low at the time.

Risk should be examined. You should analyze the degree of diversification and stability of the portfolio. It is best if securities are negatively correlated with each other. In this way, as one security goes up in price, another decreases in price. Positively correlated securities are risky since they all move in the same direction. Examples are auto, steel, and tire stocks.

Note whether declines in portfolio market values have been reflected in the accounts.

Use the ratio of revenue (dividend revenue, interest income) to the book value as a clue. The footnotes should be examined for subsequent event disclosure regarding any unrealized losses that have taken place in the portfolio. You may wish to adjust downward the extent to which an investment account can be realized in the event of such declines. You should also evaluate the riskiness of the portfolio by computing the standard deviation of its rate of return.

■ Example

Travis Company reports the following data for year-ends 19X1 and 19X2:

	19X1	19X2
Investments	$30,000	$33,000
Income from investments	4,000	3,200

The 19X2 annual report has a footnote titled "Subsequent Events," which indicates a $5,000 decline in the portfolio as of March 5, 19X3. The ratio of investment income to total investments went from 0.133 in 19X1 to 0.097 in 19X2, indicating a higher realization risk in the portfolio. Further, the post balance sheet disclosure of a $5,000 decline in value should prompt you to adjust downward the amount to which the year-end portfolio can be realized.

When formulating an optimal investment strategy, tax aspects must be taken into account. For instance, interest income on bonds is fully taxable, whereas dividend income has an 80% tax exclusion.

An investment portfolio that has a market value in excess of cost represents an undervalued asset.

By scrutinizing the investment portfolio, one may see signs of a company's attempt to gain a controlling interest in another. Such expansion may have positive or negative implications, depending on the reader's viewpoint. For example, expansion for diversification purposes tends to curtail operating risk.

INVESTMENT PLANNING This involves formulating an investment strategy based on an individual's goals and financial characteristics. Investment planning should be aimed at arriving at a good mix of risk and reward. It should first outline the types of investments available, including their return potential and riskiness. It should take into account the general risks of investing, including those related to stock market price variability, inflation, and money market conditions. Investing is an integral part of all personal financial planning. Realistically, it can be done only with money left over after paying expenses, having proper insurance, and making pension contributions. The person with capital has a wide choice of investments.

Types of Investments

Investments can be classified into two forms: fixed dollar and variable dollar. Simply stated, fixed-income investments promise the investor a stated amount of income periodically. These include corporate bonds and preferred stocks, U.S. government securities, municipal bonds, and other savings instruments (savings accounts, certificates of deposit). On the other hand, variable-dollar investments are those where neither the principal nor the income is contractually set in advance in terms of dollars. That is, both the value and income of variable-dollar investments can change in dollar amount, either up or down, with changes in internal or external economic conditions. These include common stocks, mutual funds, real estate, variable annuities, and other tax-sheltered investments.

Factors to Be Considered in Investment-Planning Decisions

Consideration should be given to safety, return rate, stability of income and dividends, and liquidity.

Security of principal—the degree of risk involved in a particular investment. There should not be a loss of part or all of the initial investment.

Rate of return—the primary purpose of investing is to earn a return on the investor's capital in the form of interest, dividends, rental income, and capital appreciation. However, increasing total investment returns would entail greater investment risks. Thus, yield and degree of risk are directly related. An investor has to choose the priority that fits his or her circumstances and objectives.

Stability of income—when steady income is an important consideration, bond interest or stock dividends should be emphasized. This might be the situation for retired people or individuals who need to supplement their earned income on a regular basis with income from their outside investment.

Marketability and liquidity—the ability of an investor to find a ready market to dispose of the investment at the right price. *See also* Personal Financial Planning.

INVESTMENT SOFTWARE The investment analyst is called upon to render investment advice to clients. Included are the tax ramifications of buy-and-sell decisions, selection of securities based on the client's tax rate and risk preferences, and keeping track of portfolio performance. Familiarity is required with available software so the analyst can best help the client in deriving the right portfolio and accurately monitoring security performance.

How Is the Portfolio? Investment maintenance software keeps track of investments in terms of shares, cost, and revenue. Some programs also include the price and dividend history of securities. Comparisons can be made with major market indicators.

Dow Jones Market Analyzer™ uses information from Dow Jones News/Retrieval to construct price and volume charts of securities, moving averages, and support and resistance lines.

Dow Jones Market Manager™ accesses Dow Jones News/Retrieval and enables the immediate valuation of a portfolio. There is a Tax Lot™ accounting system that records all transactions and assists in matching sell transactions with existing positions to lower the tax liability. Dow Jones Market Manager Plus™ handles all security types, stock splits, dividend distributions, and fractional shares. It separately totals federal, state, and municipal exempt funds.

Dow Jones Market Microscope™ uses fundamental analysis techniques. It obtains fundamental data from Media General Financial Services and Corporate Earnings Estimator available on line from Dow Jones News/ Retrieval. By preestablishing financial indicators, you can employ the data to generate screening reports and warnings. The program identifies securities meeting criteria standards and improves the timing of buys and sells.

Dow Jones Investment Evaluator™ is a basic portfolio management product. It permits the formulation of multiple portfolios comprising stocks, bonds, mutual funds, options, and other securities. It automatically values issue positions in terms of current value, unrealized gain or loss, and daily price change.

Value Line's Value Pac™ provides financial data and ratios on companies.

The Winning on Wall Street™ program by Samna Software permits the maintenance of a data base of securities, allows for technical analysis, and keeps track of the investment portfolio. It produces charts and graphs, allowing for technical analysis to properly time buys and sells. It shows points where a stock price exceeds or goes below price trend lines.

Standard and Poor's Stockpac II™ allows for the screening of takeover candidates for investment purposes.

Lotsoff Systems™ has several packages designed for financial institutions to keep track of commodity future transactions and to assist investors in hedging.

Option Strategy Calculation and Reporting™ software by ATS Software allows traders to analyze option trading strategies using price data. The program enables traders to appraise strategies on every object or combination. It prescreens trades based on the user's trading criteria and ranks them.

Software Option's Portfolio™ keeps track of foreign exchange positions. It handles forward contacts and options simultaneously.

A detailed listing of investment management and financial analysis software appears in the American Association of Individual Investor's newsletter.

Regarding real estate investment, HowardSoft's Real Estate Analyzer™ allows you to make projections considering changes in interest rates, rental payments, and inflation. There is an after-tax analysis of cash flows and profitability. Taft Cameron Company's Real Estate and Financial Software™ series determines property worth, compares different offers, amortization schedule, present value and internal rate of return analysis, and considers IRS compliance rules. Some real estate management programs include Realty Software Company's Property Management Plus™ and Yardi's Systems' Property Management™

Datext Inc. offers corporate financial information on compact disks, including financial statements, SEC documents, and investment analysts' reports for many companies.

INVOLUNTARY CONVERSION   There may exist an involuntary conversion of nonmonetary assets into monetary assets and the later replacement of the involuntarily converted assets. For example, a warehouse destroyed by a fire and the insurance proceeds received are used to purchase a similar warehouse.

As per Interpretation 30, gain or loss is recognized for the difference between the insurance recovery and the book value of the destroyed asset. The new warehouse is recorded at its purchase price.

A contingency results if the old fixed asset is damaged in one period but the insurance recovery is not received until a later period. A contingent gain or loss is reported in the period the old fixed asset was damaged. The gain or loss may be recognized for book and tax purposes in different years, causing a temporary difference requiring interperiod income tax allocation.

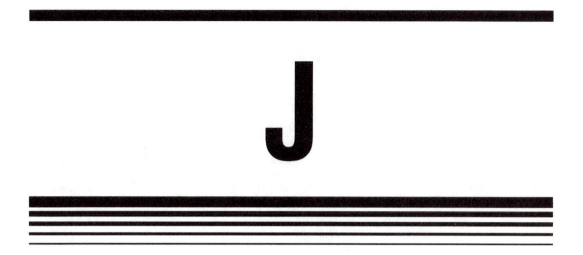

JOB ORDER COST ACCOUNTING is the cost accumulation system under which costs are accumulated by specific jobs, contracts, or orders. This costing method is appropriate when direct costs can be identified with specific units of production. Job order costing is widely used by custom manufacturers such as printing, aircraft, construction, auto repair, and professional services. Job order costing keeps track of costs as follows: direct material and direct labor are traced to a particular job. Costs not directly traceable—factory overhead—are applied to individual jobs using a *predetermined overhead (application) rate*. The overhead rate is determined as follows:

Overhead rate = Budgeted annual overhead/
Budgeted annual activity units
(direct labor hours, machine hours, etc.)

At the end of the year, the difference between actual overhead and overhead applied is closed to cost of goods sold, if an immaterial difference. On the other hand, if a material difference exists, work-in-process, finished goods, and cost of goods sold are adjusted on a proportionate basis based on units or dollars at year-end for the deviation between actual and applied overhead.

A job cost sheet is used to record various production costs for work-in-process inventory. A separate cost sheet is kept for each identifiable job, accumulating the direct materials, direct labor, and factory overhead assigned to that job as it moves through production. The form varies according to the needs of the company. A sample job cost sheet follows on page 260.

Job Cost Sheet
XYZ Company

Job No. _____

For Stock _____ Customer _____
Product _____ Date Started _____ Date Completed _____

	Direct Material			Direct Labor			Overhead
Date	Reference	Amount	Date	Reference	Amount	Date	Amount
	(Stores requisition number)			(work ticket number)			(based on predetermined overhead rate)

Summary of Costs

Direct materials	xx
Direct labor	xx
Factory overhead applied	xx
Total	xxx

Typical journal entries required to account for job order costing transactions are as follows:

1. To apply direct material and direct labor to, say, job X

Work-in-process (WIP)—job X	xx	
Stores Control		xx
Accrued Payroll		xx

2. To *apply* overhead to the job in process

WIP—job X	xx	
Overhead Applied		xx

3. To record *actual* overhead

Overhead Control	xx	
Stores Control, Accrued Payroll, Other Sundries		xx

4. To transfer completed goods

Finished Goods—job X	xx	
WIP—job X		xx

5. To record sale of finished goods

Cost of Goods Sold	xx	
Finished Goods		xx
Accounts Receivable	xx	
Sales		xx

JOINT PRODUCT ACCOUNTING Joint products are two or more products manufactured simultaneously by a common processing operation. The joint cost is allocated to the joint products based on sales values or physical measures (e.g., pounds, feet, units). Commonly used sales value methods are

• Relative sales value at the split-off point.
• Relative sales value attached to all production, whether or not sold. Any costs incurred after the split-off point (called separable costs) are subtracted from the sales value.
• Total sales price.

■ **Example**

The joint cost to manufacture products X and Y was $63,000. The following information relates to both products:

	Product X	Product Y
Production	10,000 units	50,000 units
Selling price	$3.00	$1.20
Separable costs	$2,000	$5,000

The relative sales value method is used. The joint cost allocations are

Product	Sales Value	− Separable Costs	= Sales Value	Joint Cost
X	$30,000	$2,000	$28,000	$21,253
Y	60,000	5,000	55,000	41,747
Total	$90,000	$7,000	$83,000	$63,000

If instead the allocation was based on volume, the joint cost assigned to each product would be

Product X 10,000/60,000 × $63,000 = $10,500
Product Y 50,000/60,000 × $63,000 = 52,500
                                                            $63,000

See also Byproduct Accounting.

JOINT VENTURE A joint venture occurs when two or more entities join together for a particular purpose. A joint venture is typically restricted to one project. An example is when IBM and Intel had a joint undertaking with regard to computer activities. The objectives of a joint venture may be to
 • Reduce risk applicable to an activity
 • Limit liabilities
 • Obtain capital
 • Add management talent
 • Attract investors
 • Accomplish synergistic effects
The equity method is typically used to account for joint ventures. *See also* Equity Method.

JUDGMENT SAMPLING This occurs when an auditor uses his prior experience and knowledge with a particular client and industry to compute the number of sampling units and specific items to be studied from the population. The sample takes into account the nature of the business and the unique characteristics that may exist. The CPA must be objective in carrying out the sample and performing a detailed analysis to assure the sampled units are correct. This approach may be advisable when a particular area of the population is being carefully examined or immediate results and feedback are needed. *Note*: A judgment sample does *not* involve random selection. There is no computation made of sampling error, precision, or confidence level. Thus, there is an absence of statistical techniques and conclusions. *See also* Sampling.

K

KEYNESIAN ECONOMICS This is a body of economic thought and principles that originated with the British economist John Maynard Keynes (1882–1946) in the 1930s. It has since been modified, extended, and empirically tested to the point where many of its basic prescriptions, ideas, and tools are now an integral part of general economic theory and governmental economic policy. Through his book *The General Theory of Employment, Interest and Money* (1936), he contends that an economy may be in equilibrium at any level of employment, not necessarily at full employment, and therefore active fiscal and monetary policies are needed to seek full employment and economic growth with price stability. In addition, Keynesian economics focuses on stimulating aggregate demand and thus has been referred to as demand-side economics. Features of Keynesian economics include

1. The dependency of consumption on income, called the consumption function
2. The *multiplier* effect of an autonomous spending on GNP
3. The marginal efficiency of investment as a measure of business demand for investment

See also Multipliers; Supply-Side Economics vs. Demand-Side Economics.

KITING This is a form of fraud that conceals a poor cash position and overstates cash receipts. The company keeps the bank from uncovering an overdraft in the account by exploiting the time needed for check clearance.

■ Example

Travis Company's main office is in Stamford and a branch office is in Dallas. The firm has a bank account with banks in both cities. A shortage of $80,000 exists in the Stamford bank. The bookkeeper covers up the cash deficiency by preparing a check on December 30, 19X4, on the Dallas bank that is deposited in the Stamford bank on December 30th. The check is listed as a cash payment in the cash disbursements book on January 2, 19X5. On January 4, 19X5, the check clears the Dallas bank. Note that the balance per bank and balance per book of the Stamford bank will be in agreement on December 31, 19X4, but not on January 2, 19X5. This impropriety may be detected by the auditor through an examination of bank transfers before and subsequent to December 31, 19X4, to assure that a book entry has been made in the same year that the check was dated and the deposit in the Stamford bank was made.

When transfers exist between bank accounts, a schedule should be prepared of interbank transfers showing data of withdrawal and deposit as per bank and books. The auditor must trace transfer checks in transit at the year-end date to outstanding checks and deposits in transit when examining bank reconciliations. The deposit date of a transfer may be substantiated by tracing the deposit to the cutoff bank statements for the receiving bank. *See also* Internal Control.

LABOR INTENSIVE Labor intensive describes an industry or business entity that primarily employs labor in its activities. Relative to capital intensive businesses, those that are labor intensive have more stability in profit due to the greater emphasis on variable costs to total costs. Labor cost is a variable cost that changes with production activity. Thus, if a downturn in business occurs, variable costs may be slashed. However, the fixed cost emphasis of capital intensive companies prevents reducing costs for business downturns since by definition fixed costs remain constant regardless of production activity. For example, you cannot fire a machine. A problem, however, with labor intensive companies is more vulnerability to union actions, such as strikes and slowdowns. Further, during inflationary periods employees will demand greater wage increases. This problem is acute if the company is unable to pass along higher wage rates by raising selling prices due to competitive factors. *See also* Capital Intensive.

LAFFER CURVE The Laffer curve shows a hypothetical relationship between the marginal tax rate and tax revenues. As Figure 1 indicates, as the tax rate increases from 0 to 100%, tax revenues rise from 0 to some maximum level and then declines to 0. The optimum tax rate is of course the one that reaches the maximum revenue. Rates that are lower than optimum are regarded "normal" since tax revenues can be increased by raising the rate. Rates that are above optimum are viewed as prohibitive because they dampen incentives on the part of businesses and individuals and are thus counterproductive. Therefore, when the rate is in the prohibitive range, reductions in tax are needed to provide *incentives*, stimulate production, and bring higher, not lower, tax revenues. There is no empirical evidence to support this relationship and it still remains a hypothesis. Profes-

Figure 1 Laffer Curve

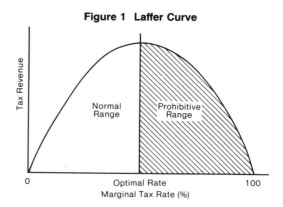

sor Laffer, who originated this curve, is considered the principal advocate of the controversial *supply-side economics*. *See also* Supply-Side Economics vs. Demand-Side Economics.

LAGGING INDICATORS These are the economic series of indicators that follow or trail behind aggregate economic activity. There are currently six lagging indicators published by the government, comprising unemployment rate, business expenditures, labor cost per unit, loans outstanding, bank interest rates, and book value of manufacturing and trade inventories. *See also* Index of Leading Economic Indicators.

LAPPING This is a form of fraud in which a customer's payment is misappropriated. A customer's account is credited when cash is received from another customer at a later date. It involves repeated misappropriations and posting delays to customer accounts. It is also possible that the cashier may transfer shortages to other accounts (i.e., inventory) for temporary concealment. Lapping may occur if a bookkeeper who receives customer collections also records transactions to customer accounts. Lapping may be prevented by having a separation of the handling of cash receipts and the posting to accounts. The auditor should also be on guard against the alteration of duplicate deposit tickets. A comparison should be made between the duplicate copy and the original one retained at the bank. The auditor should compare the entries in the cash receipts journal, postings to accounts receivable, listing of cash receipts from the mailroom, and deposit slips for the bank. *See also* Internal Control.

LEARNING CURVE The learning curve is based on the proposition that labor hours decrease in a definite pattern as labor operations are repeated. More specifically, it is based on the statistical findings that as the cumulative output doubles, the cumulative average labor

input time required per unit will be reduced by some constraint percentage, ranging between 10 and 40%. The curve is usually designated by its complement. If the rate of reduction is 20%, the curve is referred to as an *80% learning curve*.

The following data illustrate the 80% learning curve relationship:

| Quantity (*In Units*) | | Time (*In Hours*) | |
Per Lot	Cumulative	Total Cumulative	Average Time Per Unit
15	15	600	40.0
15	30	960	32.0(40.0 × 0.8)
30	60	1,536	25.6(32.0 × 0.8)
60	120	2,460	20.5(25.6 × 0.8)
120	240	3,936	16.4(20.5 × 0.8)

As can be seen, as production quantities double, the average time it takes per unit goes down by 20% of its immediate previous time. Figure 1 depicts a learning curve.

■ Example

Stanley Electronics Products, Inc., finds that new-product production is affected by an 80% learning effect. The company has just produced 50 units of output at 100 hours per unit. Costs were as follows:

Materials @ $20	$1,000
Labor and labor-related costs:	
Direct labor—100 hrs @ $8	800
Variable overhead—100 hrs @ $2	200
	$2,000

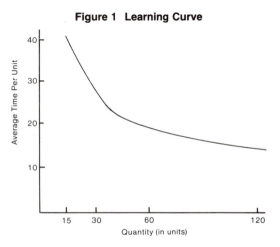

Figure 1 Learning Curve

The company has just received a contract calling for another 50 units of production. It wants to add a 50% markup to the cost of materials and labor and labor-related costs. Let us determine the price for this job.

Building up the table yields:

Quantity	Total Time (In Hours)	Average Time (Per Unit)
50 units	100 hours	2 hours
100	160	1.6 (80% × 2 hrs)

Thus, for the new 50-unit job, it takes 60 hours total.

Materials @ $20	$1,000
Labor and labor-related costs:	
Direct labor—60 hrs @ $8	480
Variable overhead—60 hrs @ $2	120
	$1,600
50% markup	800
Contract price	$2,400

Other applications of learning curve theory include

1. Scheduling labor requirements
2. Capital budgeting decisions
3. Setting incentive wage rates

LEASE-PURCHASE DECISION The lease-purchase decision is one commonly confronting firms considering the acquisition of new assets. It is a hybrid *capital budgeting* decision which forces a company to compare the leasing and purchasing alternatives. To make an intelligent decision, an after-tax, cash outflow, present value comparison is needed. There are special steps to take when making this comparison. When considering a lease, take the following steps:

1. *Find the annual lease payment.* Since the annual lease payment is typically made in advance, the formula to be used is

Amount of lease
$$= A + A(PVIFA_{i,n-1}) \text{ or}$$
$$A = \frac{\text{Amount of lease}}{1 + PVIFA_{i,n-1}}$$

Notice we use $n - 1$ rather than n.

2. Find the after-tax cash outflows.
3. Find the present value of the after-tax cash outflows.

When considering a purchase, take the following steps:

1. Find the annual loan amortization by using:

$$A = \frac{\text{Amount of loan for the purchase}}{PVIFA_{i,n}}$$

This step may not be necessary since this amount is usually available.

2. *Calculate the interest.* The interest is segregated from the principal in each of the annual loan payments because only the interest is tax deductible.

3. Find the cash outflows by adding interest and depreciation (plus any maintenance costs) and then compute the after-tax outflows.

4. Find the present value of the after-tax cash outflows.

■ Example

A firm has decided to acquire an asset costing $100,000 that has an expected life of 5 years, after which the asset is not expected to have any residual value. The asset can be purchased by borrowing or it can be leased. If leasing is used, the lessor requires a 12% return. As is customary, lease payments are to be made in advance, that is, at the end of the year prior to each of the 10 years. The tax rate is 50% and the firm's cost of capital, or after-tax cost of borrowing, is 8%.

First compute the present value of the after-tax cash outflows associated with the leasing alternative.

1. Find the annual lease payment:

$$A = \frac{\text{Amount of lease}}{1 + PVIFA_{i,n-1}}$$
$$= \frac{\$100,000}{1 + PVIFA_{12\%,4 \text{ years}}} = \frac{\$100,000}{1 + 3.3073}$$
$$= \frac{\$100,000}{4.3073} = \$23,216 \text{ (rounded)}$$

Steps 2 and 3 can be done in the same schedule, as follows:

(1)	(2)	(3) = (1) − (2)	(4)	(5) = (3) × (4)
Lease	Tax	After-Tax	PV	PV of Cash Out-
Year Payment ($)	Savings($)	Cash Outflow ($)	at 8%	flow ($, Rounded)
0	23,216		23,216	1.000	23,216
1–4	23,216	11,608[a]	11,608	3.312[b]	38,445
5		11,608	(11,608)	0.681[c]	(7,905)
					53,756

[a] $23,216 × 50%
[b] From Table 4 in the Appendix
[c] From Table 3 in the Appendix

If the asset is purchased, the firm is assumed to finance it entirely with a 10% unsecured term loan. Straight-line depreciation is used with no salvage value. Therefore, the annual depreciation is $20,000 ($100,000/5 years). In this alternative, first find the annual loan payment by using:

$$A = \frac{\text{Amount of loan}}{PVIFA_{i,n}}$$

$$A = \frac{\$100,000}{PVIFA_{10\%,5 \text{ years}}}$$

$$= \frac{\$100,000}{3.7906} = \$26,381 \text{ (rounded)}$$

2. Calculate the interest by setting up a loan amortization schedule.

The sum of the present values of the cash outflows for leasing and purchasing by borrowing shows that purchasing is preferable because the *PV* of borrowing is less than the *PV* of leasing ($52,090 versus $53,756). The incremental savings is $1,664.

LEASES   These are typically long-term noncancelable commitments. In a lease, the lessee acquires the right to use property owned by the lessor. Even though no legal transfer of title occurs, many leases transfer substantially all the risks and ownership benefits. Theoretical substance governs over legal form in accounting resulting in the lessee

(1)	(2)	(3) = (2)(10%)	(4) = (1) − (3)	(5) = (2) − (4)
Loan	Beginning-of-Year			End-of-Year
Year Payment ($)	Principal ($)	Interest ($)	Principal ($)	Principal
1	26,381	100,000	10,000	16,381	83,619
2	26,381	83,619	8,362	18,019	65,600
3	26,381	65,600	6,560	19,821	45,779
4	26,381	45,779	4,578	21,803	23,976
5	26,381	23,976[a]	2,398	23,983[a]	

[a] Because of rounding errors, there is a slight difference between (2) and (4)

Steps 3 (cash outflows) and 4 (present values of those outflows) can be done as follows:

recording an asset and liability for a capital lease.

A lease may be between related parties.

(1)	(2)	(3)	(4) = (2) + (3)	(5) = (4) × 40%	(6) = (1) − (5)	(7)	(8) = (6) × (7)
Loan			Total	Tax	Cash	PV at	PV of
Year Payment ($)	Interest ($)	Depreciation ($)	Deductions ($)	Savings ($)	Outflow ($)	8%	Cash Outflow
1	26,381	10,000	20,000	30,000	15,000	11,381	0.926	10,538
2	26,381	8,362	20,000	28,362	14,181	12,200	0.857	10,455
3	26,381	6,560	20,000	26,560	13,280	13,101	0.794	10,402
4	26,381	4,578	20,000	24,578	12,289	14,092	0.735	10,357
5	26,381	2,398	20,000	22,398	11,199	15,182	0.681	10,338
							$52,090

This occurs when an entity has significant influence over operating and financial policies of another entity.

The *date of inception* of a lease is the time of lease *agreement or commitment*, if earlier. A commitment has to be in writing, signed, and provide principal provisions. If any major provisions are to be negotiated later, there is *no* committed agreement.

Lessee

The two methods to account for a lease by the lessee are the operating method and capital method.

Operating lease—a regular rental of property. As rental payments become payable, rent expense is debited and cash and/or payables credited. The lessee does not show anything on the balance sheet. Rent expense is reflected on a straight-line basis unless another method is more appropriate under the circumstances. Accrual basis accounting is followed.

Capital lease—the lessee uses the capital lease method if any *one* of the following four criteria are met:

• The lessee obtains ownership to the property at the end of the lease term.

• There is a bargain purchase option where either the lessee can acquire the property at a nominal amount or renew the lease at nominal rental payments.

• The life of the lease is 75% or more of the life of the property.

• The present value of minimum lease payments at the inception of the lease equals or is greater than 90% of the fair market value of the property. Minimum lease payments exclude executory costs to be paid by the lessor, such as maintenance, insurance, and property taxes.

If criteria 1 or 2 are met, the depreciation period is the life of the property. If criteria 3 or 4 are satisfied, the depreciation period is the life of the lease.

It should be noted that the third and fourth criteria do not apply when the beginning of the lease term falls within the last 25% of the total economic life of the property, including earlier years of use.

The asset and liability are recorded at the present value of the minimum lease payments plus the present value of the bargain purchase option. The expectation is that the lessee will take advantage of the nominal purchase price. If the present value of the minimum lease payments plus the bargain purchase option is greater than the fair value of the leased property at the time of lease inception, the asset should be capitalized at the fair market value of the property. The discount rate used by the lessee is the *lower* of the lessee's incremental borrowing rate (the rate at which the lessee would have to borrow to be able to buy the asset) or the lessor's implicit interest rate. The lessor's implicit interest rate is the one implicit in the recovery of the fair value of the property at lease inception through the present value of minimum lease payments, including the lessee's guarantee of salvage value. The liability is broken down between current and noncurrent.

The lessee's minimum lease payments (MLP) usually include MLP over the lease term plus any residual value guaranteed by the lessee. The guarantee is the determinable amount for which the lessor has the right to require the lessee to buy the property at the lease termination. It is the stated amount when the lessee agrees to satisfy any dollar deficiency below a stated amount in the lessor's realization of the residual value. MLP also includes any payment lessee must pay due to failure to extend or renew the lease at expiration. If there exists a bargain purchase option, MLP includes *only* MLP over the lease term and exercise option payment. MLP does *not* include contingent rentals, lessee's guarantee of lessor's debt, and lessee's obligation for executory costs.

Each minimum lease payment is allocated as a reduction of principal (debiting the liability) and as interest (debiting interest expense). The interest method is used to result in a constant periodic rate of interest. Interest expense equals the interest rate times the carrying value of the liability at the beginning of the year.

The balance sheet shows the Asset under lease less Accumulated depreciation. The income statement shows interest expense and depreciation expense. In the first year, the expenses under a capital lease (interest expense and depreciation) are greater than the expenses under an operating lease (rent expense).

As per Interpretation 26, when a lessee buys a leased asset during the lease term that has been originally capitalized, the transaction is considered an *extension* of a capital lease rather than a termination. Thus, the difference between the purchase price and the carrying amount of the lease obligation recorded is an *adjustment* of the carrying amount of the asset. *No loss recognition* is required on an *extension* of a capital lease.

■ Example

On 1/1/19X1, the lessee enters into a capital lease for property. The minimum rental payment is $20,000 a year for 6 years to be made at the end of the year. The interest rate is 5%. The present value of an ordinary annuity factor for $n = 6$, $i = 5\%$ is 5.0757. The journal entries for the first 2 years follow:

1/1/19X1 Asset	101,514	
Liability		101,514
12/31/19X1		
Interest Expense	5,076	
Liability	14,924	
Cash		20,000
5% × $101,514 = $5,076		
Depreciation	16,919	
Accumulated Depreciation		16,919

$$\frac{\$101,514}{6} = \$16,919$$

The liability as of 12/31/19X1 follows:

Liability			
12/31/19X1	14,924	1/1/19X1	101,514
		12/31/19X1	86,590

12/31/19X2		
Interest Expense	4,330	
Liability	15,670	
Cash		20,000
5% × $86,590 = $4,330		
Depreciation	16,919	
Accumulated Depreciation		16,919

Footnote disclosures under a capital lease include

• Assets under lease by class
• Future minimum lease payments in total and for each of the next five years
• Contingent rentals (rentals based on other than time, such as based on sales)
• Total future sublease rentals
• Description of leasing arrangements, including renewal terms, purchase options, escalation options, and restrictions in the lease agreement

Lessor

The three methods of accounting for leases by the lessor are the operating, direct-financing, and sales-type methods.

Operating method—a regular rental by the lessor. An example is Avis renting automobiles. Under the operating method, the lessor records rental revenue less related expenses, including depreciation and maintenance expense. The income statement shows rental revenue less expenses to obtain profit. The balance sheet presents the asset under lease less accumulated depreciation to derive book value.

Rental income is recognized as earned using the straight-line basis over the lease term except if there is another preferable method. Initial direct costs are deferred and amortized over the lease term on a pro rata basis based on rental income recognized. However, if immaterial relative to the allocation amount, the initial direct costs may be expensed.

■ Example

Hall Corporation produced machinery costing $5,000,000 which it held for resale from January 1, 19X1, to June 30, 19X1, at a price to Travis Company under an operating lease. The lease is for 4 years with equal monthly payments of $85,000 due on the first of the month. The initial payment was made on July 1, 19X1. The depreciation period is 10 years, with no salvage value.

Lessee's rental expense for 19X1:

$85,000 × 6	$510,000

Lessor's income before taxes for 19X1:

Rental income	$510,000
Less: Depreciation $\dfrac{\$5,000,000}{10} \times \dfrac{6}{12}$	250,000
Income before taxes	$260,000

Direct-financing method—satisfies one of the four criteria for a capital lease by the lessee plus both of the following two criteria for the lessor:

• Collectibility of lease payments is assured.

• No important uncertainties exist regarding future costs to be incurred.

The lessor is *not* a manufacturer or dealer. The lessor acquires the property for the sole purpose of leasing it out. An example is a bank leasing computers. The carrying value and fair value of the leased property are the same at the inception of the lease.

The lessor uses as the discount rate the interest rate implicit in the lease.

Interest income is only recognized in the financial statements over the life of the lease using the interest method. Unearned interest income is amortized as income over the lease term to result in a constant rate of interest. Interest revenue equals the interest rate times the carrying value of the receivable at the beginning of the year.

Contingent rentals are recognized in earnings as earned.

The lessor's MLP includes the (1) MLP made by the lessee (net of any executory costs together with any profit thereon) and (2) any guarantee of the salvage value of the leased property or of rental payments after the lease term made by a third party unrelated to either party in the lease provided the third party is financially able to satisfy the commitment. A guarantee by a third party related to the lessor makes the residual value unguaranteed. A guarantee by a third party related to the lessee infers a guaranteed residual value by the lessee.

A change in lease provisions, which would have resulted in a different classification had they taken place at the beginning of the lease, mandate that the lease be considered a new agreement and classified under the new terms. However, exercise of existing renewal options are not deemed lease changes. A change in estimate does not result in a new lease.

A provision for escalation of the MLP during a construction or preacquisition period may exist. The resulting increase in MLP is considered in determining the fair value of the leased property at the lease inception. There may also exist a salvage value increase that takes place from an escalation clause.

Initial direct costs are incurred by the lessor and are directly applicable with negotiating and consummating *completed* leasing transactions such as legal fees, commissions, document preparation and processing for new leases, credit investigation, and the relevant portion of salespersons' and other employees' compensation. It does *not* include costs for *leases not consummated* nor supervisory, administrative, or other indirect expenses. Initial direct costs of the lease are expensed as incurred. A portion of the unearned income equal to the initial direct costs shall be recognized as income in the same accounting period.

If the lease agreement contains a penalty for failure to renew and becomes inoperative due to lease renewal or other extension of time, the unearned interest income account must be adjusted for the difference between the present values of the old and revised agreements. The present value of the future minimum lease payments under the new agreement should be computed employing the original rate used for the initial lease.

Lease termination is accounted for by the lessor through eliminating the net investment, recording the leased property at the lower of cost or fair value, and charging the net adjustment against earnings.

The lessor shows on his balance sheet as the gross investment in the lease the total minimum lease payments plus salvage value of the property accruing to the lessor. This represents lease payments receivable. Deducted from lease payments receivable is unearned interest revenue. The balance sheet presentation follows:

• Lease payments receivable (principal + interest)
• Less: Unearned interest revenue (interest)
• Net receivable balance (principal)

The income statement shows:
• Interest revenue
• Less: Initial direct costs
• Less: Executory costs
• Net income

Footnote disclosure should include assets leased out by category, future lease payments in total and for each of the next 5 years, contingent rentals, and the terms of the lease.

Sales-type method—must satisfy the same criteria as the direct-financing method. The only difference is that the sales-type method involves a lessor who is a manufacturer or dealer in the leased item. Thus, a manufacturer or dealer profit results. Although legally there is no sale of the item, theoretical substance governs over legal form and a sale is assumed to have taken place. *Note*: The distinction between a sales-type lease and a direct-financing lease affects only the lessor; as to lessee, either type would be a capital lease.

If there is a renewal or extension of an existing sales-type or financing lease, it shall *not* be classified as a sales-type lease. There is an *exception* which may exist when the renewal occurs toward the end of the lease term.

In a sales-type lease, profit on the assumed sale of the item is recognized in the year of lease as well as interest income over the life of the lease. The cost and fair value of the leased property are different at the inception of the lease.

An annual appraisal should be made of the salvage value and where necessary reduce the net investment and recognize a loss but do not adjust the salvage value.

The cost of the leased property is matched against the selling price in determining the assumed profit in the year of lease. Initial direct costs of the lease are expensed.

Except for the initial entry to record the lease, the entries are the same for the direct-financing and sales-type methods.

■ Example

Assume the same facts as in the capital lease example. The accounting by the lessor assuming a direct-financing lease and a sales-type lease appear on the top of page 272.

Direct-Financing Lease			Sales-Type Lease		
1/1/19X1					
Receivable	120,000		Receivable	120,000	
Asset		101,514	Cost of Sales	85,000	
Unearned Interest			Inventory		85,000
Revenue		18,486			
			Sales		101,514
			Unearned Interest		
			Revenue		18,486
12/31/19X1					
Cash	20,000				
Receivable		20,000			
Unearned Interest					
Revenue	5,076				
Interest Revenue		5,076	Same entries		
12/31/19X2					
Cash	20,000		The income statement for 19X1 presents:		
Receivable		20,000			
Unearned Interest			Interest		
Revenue	4,330		revenue $5,076	Sales	$101,514
Interest Revenue		4,330		Less: Cost of	
				sales	85,000
				Gross profit	$ 16,514
				Interest revenue	5,076

■ Example

Jones leased equipment to Tape Company on October 1, 19X1. It is a capital lease to the lessee and a sales-type lease to the lessor. The lease is for 8 years, with equal annual payments of $500,000 due on October 1 each period. The first payment was made on October 1, 19X1. The cost of the equipment to Tape Company is $2,500,000. The equipment has a life of 10 years with no salvage value. The appropriate interest rate is 10%.

Tape reports the following in its income statement for 19X1:

Asset cost ($500,000 × 5.868 = $2,934,000)

Depreciation $\left(\dfrac{\$2,934,000}{10} \times \dfrac{3}{12} \right)$ $73,350

Interest expense:

Present value of lease payments	$2,934,000
Less: Initial payment	500,000
Balance	$2,434,000

Interest expense $2,434,000 × 10% × $\dfrac{3}{12}$ 60,850

Total expenses $134,200

Jones' income before tax is

Interest revenue		$ 60,850
Gross profit on assumed sale of property:		
Selling price	$2,934,000	
Less: Cost	2,500,000	
Gross profit		434,000
Income before tax		$494,850

Sales-Leaseback Arrangement

A sales-leaseback is when the lessor sells the property and then leases it back. The lessor may do this when he is in need of funds.

The profit or loss on the sale is deferred and amortized as an adjustment on a proportionate basis to depreciation expense in the case of a capital lease or in proportion to rental expense in the case of an operating lease. However, if the fair value of the property at the time of the sales-leaseback is below its book value, a loss is immediately recognized for the difference between book value and fair value.

■ Example

The deferred profit on a sales-leaseback is $50,000. An operating lease is involved where rental expense in the current year is $10,000 and total rental expense is $150,000. Rental expense is adjusted as follows:

Rental expense	$10,000
Less: Amortization of deferred gross profit	
$50,000 \times \dfrac{\$10,000}{\$150,000}$	3,333
	$6,667

Subleases and Similar Transactions

There are three types of transactions. In a *sublease*, the original lessee leases the property to a third party. The lease agreement of the original parties remains intact. Another possibility is where a new lessee is substituted under the original agreement. The original lessee may still be secondarily liable. Finally, the new lessee is substituted in a new agreement. There is a cancellation of the original lease.

In accounting by the original lessor, he continues his present accounting method if the original lessee subleases or sells to a third party. If the original lease is replaced by a new agreement with a new lessee, the lessor terminates the initial lease and accounts for the new lease in a separate transaction.

In accounting by the original lessee, if the original lessee is relieved of primary obligation by a transaction other than a sublease, terminate the original lease:

• If original lease was a capital lease remove the asset and liability; recognize a gain or loss for the difference, including any additional consideration paid or received; and

accrue a loss contingency where secondary liability exists.

• If the original lease was an operating one and the initial lessee is secondarily liable, recognize a loss contingency accrual.

If the original lessee is not relieved of *primary* obligation under a sublease, the original lessee (now sublessor) accounts in the following manner:

• If original lease met lessee criteria 1 or 2, classify the new lease per normal classification criteria by lessor. If sublease is sales-type or direct-financing lease, the unamortized asset balance becomes the cost of the leased property. Otherwise, it is an operating lease. Continue to account for the original lease obligation as before.

• If original lease met only lessee criteria 3 or 4, classify the new lease using lessee criteria 3 and lessor criteria 1 and 2. Classify as a direct-financing lease. The unamortized balance of the asset becomes the cost of the leased property. Otherwise, it is an operating lease. Continue to account for the original lease obligation as before.

If the original lease was an *operating lease,* account for old and new leases as operating leases.

Leveraged Leases

A leveraged lease occurs when the lessor (equity participant) finances a small part of the acquisition (retaining total equity ownership) while a third party (debt participant) finances the balance. The lessor maximizes his leveraged return by recognizing lease revenue and income tax shelter (e.g., interest deduction, rapid depreciation).

A leveraged lease meets *all* of the following:

• It satisfies the tests for a direct-financing lease. Sales-type leases are not leveraged leases.

• It involves at least three parties: lessee, long-term creditor (debt participant), and lessor (equity participant).

• The long-term creditor provides nonrecourse financing as to the general credit of the lessor. The financing is adequate to give the lessor significant leverage.

• The lessor's net investment (see following) decreases during the initial lease years, then increases in the subsequent years just before its liquidation by sale. These increases and decreases in the net investment balance may take place more than once during the lease life.

The lessee classifies and accounts for leveraged leases in the same way as nonleveraged leases.

The lessor records investment in the leveraged lease net of the nonrecourse debt. The net of the following balances represent the initial and continuing investment: rentals receivable (net of the amount applicable to principal and interest on the nonrecourse debt), estimated residual value, and unearned and deferred income. The initial entry to record the leveraged lease is

> Lease receivable
> Residual value of asset
> Cash investment in asset
> Unearned income

The lessor's net investment in the leveraged lease for computing net income is the investment in the leveraged lease less deferred income taxes. *Periodic net income* is determined in the following manner employing the net investment in the leveraged lease:

• Determine annual cash flow equal to the following:

Gross lease rental (plus residual value of asset in last year of lease term)
Less: Loan interest payments
Less: Income tax charges (or add income tax credits)
Less: Loan principal payments
Annual cash flow

• Determine the return rate on the net investment in the leveraged lease. The rate of return is the one when applied to the net investment in the years when it is positive

will distribute the net income (cash flow) to those positive years. The net investment will be positive (but declining rapidly due to accelerated depreciation and interest expense) in the early years; it will be negative during the middle years; and it will again be positive in the later years (because of the declining tax shelter).

LEAST-SQUARES METHOD The least-squares method is a technique of developing a regression equation that relates the dependent variable (such as a company's price-earnings ratio) to one or more independent (explanatory) variables (such as growth in earnings, dividend payout ratio, beta, and so on). This method is mathematically contrived in such a way that the resulting combination of explanatory variables produces the smallest error between the observed values and those fitted by the regression. *See also* Regression Analysis.

LEGAL LIABILITY This refers to litigation against an accountant because he or she is guilty of an improper act, including fraud or gross negligence. Significant monetary damages may be assessed to plaintiffs who suffered losses as a result of relying upon the accountant's work. These parties may include investors, stockholders, and creditors. In addition, the accountant may be faced with disciplinary action by the American Institute of CPAs. The accountant may not have complied with GAAS, GAAP, or other professional standards. An ethical violation may have occurred, such as the expression of an audit opinion when a lack of independence existed. As a result of increased lawsuits against accounting firms, the premiums for malpractice insurance have skyrocketed.

LEVERAGE This is the portion of the fixed costs that represents a risk to the firm. *Operating leverage*, a measure of operating risk, refers to the fixed operating costs found in the firm's income statement. *Financial leverage*, a measure of financial risk, refers to financing a portion of the firm's assets, bearing fixed financing charges in hopes of increasing the return to the common stockholders. The higher the financial leverage, the higher the financial risk, and the higher the cost of capital. Cost of capital rises because it costs more to raise funds for a risky business. *Total leverage* is a measure of total risk.

To determine the degrees of operating, financial, and total leverage, let us define:

$$x = \text{sales volume in units,}$$
$$p = \text{selling price per unit,}$$
$$v = \text{unit variable cost,}$$
$$FC = \text{fixed operating costs.}$$

Operating Leverage

Operating leverage is a measure of operating risk and arises from fixed operating costs. A simple indication of operating leverage is the effect that a change in sales has on earnings. The formula is

Operating leverage at a given level of sales (x)

$$= \frac{\text{Percentage change in EBIT}}{\text{Percentage change in sales}} = \frac{(p - v)x}{(p - v)x - FC}$$

where:

$$EBIT = \text{earnings before interest and taxes}$$
$$= (p - v)x - FC$$

■ Example 1

The Wayne Company manufactures and sells doors to home builders. The doors are sold for $25 each. Variable costs are $15 per door, and fixed operating costs total $50,000. Assume further that the Wayne Company is currently selling 6,000 doors per year. Its operating leverage is

$$\frac{(p - v)x}{(p - v)x - FC}$$
$$= \frac{(\$25 - \$15)(6,000)}{(\$25 - \$15)(6,000) - \$50,000}$$
$$= \frac{\$60,000}{\$10,000} = 6$$

which means if sales increase by 10%, the company can expect its EBIT to increase by six times that amount, or 60%.

Financial Leverage

Financial leverage is a measure of financial risk and arises from fixed financial costs. One way to measure financial leverage is to determine how earnings per share are affected by a change in EBIT (or operating income).

Financial leverage at a given level of sales (x)

$$= \frac{\text{Percentage in change in EPS}}{\text{Percentage in change in EBIT}}$$
$$= \frac{(p - v)x - FC}{(p - v)x - FC - IC}$$

where EPS is earnings per share, and IC is fixed finance charges; that is, interest expense or preferred stock dividends. [Preferred stock dividend must be adjusted for taxes; that is, preferred stock dividend/$(1 - t)$.]

■ Example 2

Using the data in Example 1, the Wayne Company has total financial charges of $2,000, half in interest expense and half in preferred stock dividend. The corporate tax rate is 40%. First, the fixed financial charges are

$$IC = \$1,000 + \frac{1,000}{(1 - 0.4)}$$
$$= \$1,000 + \$1,667 = \$2,667$$

Therefore, Wayne's financial leverage is computed as follows:

$$\frac{(p - v)x - FC}{(p - v)x - FC - IC}$$
$$= \frac{(\$25 - \$15)(6,000) - \$50,000}{(\$25 - \$15)(6,000) - \$50,000 - \$2,667}$$
$$= \frac{\$10,000}{\$7,333} = 1.36$$

which means that if EBIT increases by 10%, Wayne can expect its EPS to increase by 1.36 times, or by 13.6%.

Total Leverage

Total leverage is a measure of total risk. The way to measure total leverage is to determine how EPS is affected by a change in sales.

Total leverage at a given
level of sales (X)

$$= \frac{\text{Percentage in change in EPS}}{\text{Percentage in change in sales}}$$

$$= \text{Operating leverage} \times \text{Financial leverage}$$

$$= \frac{(p - v)x}{(p - v)x - FC} \cdot \frac{(p - v)x - FC}{(p - v)x - FC - IC}$$

$$= \frac{(p - v)x}{(p - v)x - FC - IC}$$

■ Example 3

From Examples 1 and 2, the total leverage for Wayne company is

Operating leverage $\times$ financial leverage $= 6 \times 1.36$
$$= 8.16$$

or

$$\frac{(p - v)X}{(p - v)x - FC - IC}$$

$$= \frac{(\$25 - \$15)(6,000)}{(\$25 - \$15)(6,000) - \$50,000 - \$2,667}$$

$$= \frac{\$60,000}{\$7,333} = 8.18 \text{ (due to rounding error)}$$

See also Cost-Volume-Profit (CVP); Break-Even Analysis.

LEVERAGED BUYOUT A leveraged buyout occurs when an entity primarily borrows money in order to buy another company. Typically, the acquiring company uses as collateral the assets of the acquired business. Generally, repayment of the debt will be made from the funds flow of the acquired company. A leveraged buyout may also be made when the acquiring company uses its own assets as security for the loan. It may also be used if a firm wishes to go *private*. In most cases, the stockholders of the acquired company will receive an amount greater than the current market price of the stock. A leveraged buyout involves more risk than an acquisition done through the issuance of equity securities. *See also* Going Public.

LEVERAGED LEASES In a leveraged lease, the lessor finances part of the purchase of property with a third party financing the balance. *See also* Leases.

LEVERAGE IN REAL ESTATE INVESTING Leverage means use of other people's money (OPM) in an effort to increase the reward for investing. To a lot of people, it means risk. The fact of the matter is, using leverage in real estate investing is an exciting way to earn big yields on small dollars. When building real estate wealth, leverage will help one grow quickly without involving too much risk. High-leveraged investing in real estate is especially powerful when inflation is in full swing. High-leverage investors have numbers going for them because property values rise faster than the interest charges on their borrowed money. To see the full power of high-leverage investing, an example is given below.

■ Example 1

You pay a seller $100,000 cash for a piece of property. During the next 12 months, the property appreciates 5% and grows in resale value to $105,000. The $5,000 gain equals a 5% yield on your investment. But suppose you had put down only 10% ($10,000) on the property and mortgaged the balance. Now, your return on investment leaps to an astonishing 50% ($5,000/$10,000)! Another way of looking at the result is: Since you only put down $10,000 on $100,000 worth of property, you actually control the asset ten times the value of your actual cash outlay. This means 5% × 10 times = 50%. (In this example, for simplicity, we've omitted mortgage interest costs as well as the return on the $10,000 you would have invested somewhere else plus any rental income you would have earned from the property.)

■ Example 2

Instead of putting 100% down ($100,000), you put down 10% ($10,000) and bought nine more pieces of property, each costing $100,000, and each bought with 10% down ($10,000). Again assume that they appreciate at the rate of 5%. Therefore, your wealth increases: $5,000 a piece × 10 pieces = $50,000. All that in one year. Tying up your wealth in one property ($100,000) cost you $45,000 ($50,000 − $5,000). Conversely, by spreading your funds over more properties and leveraging the balance, you would multiply your earnings ten times.

The lower the amount of cash invested, the higher your return (from value appreciation and/or rental income). On the other hand, the larger your cash investment, the lower your return. Also, a higher appreciation will greatly increase earnings on your leveraged investment.

Pitfalls of High-Leverage Real Estate Investing

High-leverage real estate investing sounds really good as long as an investor watches out for some of the pitfalls. They are

• Property values can go down as well as up. Some types of real estate in some parts of the country are experiencing value declines.

• Select the property carefully.

• Anticipate a rising market due to a lower mortgage rate or a high inflation rate before jumping in a high-leverage world.

• Look out for negative cash flow. Income from highly leveraged property may be insufficient to cover operating expenses and debt payments. Do not overpay for property and underestimate costs. Buying for little or nothing down is easy. The difficult part is making the payments. Try to avoid negative cash flow (losses are tax deductible, however).

• Watch out for deferred maintenance. Deferred maintenance can create lots of prob-lems down the road. One can avoid hidden costs and potential future expenditure by bargaining for a fair (or less than market) price and reasonable terms. In any case, overrepair is poison to the high-leverage investor.

See also Leverage.

LIABILITY MANAGEMENT OF BANKS Traditionally, banks have taken the liability side of the balance sheet pretty much as outside of their control in the short run. They have taken liabilities as given and have been concerned with *asset management. Liability management* involves actions taken by banks and other depositary institutions to actively obtain funds at their own initiative by issuing negotiable certificates of deposit (CDs), borrowing federal funds, and other procedures. It means altering the bank's liability structure (mix of demand deposits, time deposits, and so on) by changing the interest paid on nontransaction liabilities (such as CDs). The technique of liability management is certainly an important discretionary source of bank funds. However, the excessive use of the technique would make them vulnerable in future liquidity crises. The example of the Continental Illinois Bank is a case in point. *See also* Asset Management of Banks.

LIMIT ORDER   *See* Stock Orders.

LIMITED AUDIT

1. Audit covering all accounts for a short time period
2. Audit restricted to specific accounts or transactions
3. Audit in which an agreement is reached to exclude specified typical features

LIMITED PARTNERSHIP   A limited partnership is one in which one or more partners but not all have limited liability up to their investment to creditors in the event of the failure of the business or activity. The general partner manages the business. Limited partners are not involved in daily activities. The return to limited partners is in the form of income and capital gains. Often, tax benefits are involved. Examples of limited partnerships are in real estate and oil and gas exploration. In general, public limited partnerships are sold by brokerage firms in $5,000 minimums. Typically, private limited partnerships consist of less than 35 limited partners. *See also* Basic Forms of Business Organization; Real Estate Syndicate.

LINEAR PROGRAMMING (LP) LP concerns itself with the problem of allocating limited resources among competing activities in an optimal manner. Specifically, it is a technique used to maximize a revenue, contribution margin, or profit function, or minimize a cost function subject to constraints. Linear programming consists of two important ingredients:
1. Objective function
2. Constraints (including nonnegativity constraints), which are typically inequalities

■ Example 1

A firm wishes to find an optimal product mix so as to maximize its total contribution without violating restrictions imposed upon the availability of resources. Or it may want to determine a least cost combination of input materials while satisfying production requirements, maintaining required inventory levels, staying within production capacities, and using available employees. The objective function is to minimize production cost, and the constraints are production requirements, inventory levels, production capacity, and available employees.

Applications

Other managerial applications include
- Selecting an investment mix
- Blending chemical products
- Scheduling flight crews
- Assigning jobs to machines

- Determining transportation routes
- Determining distribution or allocation pattern

Formulation of Linear Programming

To formulate the LP problem, the first step is to define what are called *decision variables* for which you are trying to solve. The next step is to express the objective function and constraints in terms of these decision variables. Notice, however, that, as in the name of *linear* programming, all the expressions must be of *linear* form.

■ Example 2

A firm produces two products, A and B. Both products require time in two processing departments, Assembly Department and Finishing Department. Data on the two products are as follows:

Processing	Products A	B	Available Hours
Assembly	2	4	100
Finishing	3	2	90
Contribution margin per unit	$25	$40	

The firm wants to find the most profitable mix of these two products. First, define the decision variables as follows:

A = the number of units of product A to be produced.

B = the number of units of product B to be produced.

Then, the objective function that is to minimize total contribution margin (CM) is expressed as:

$$\text{Total } CM = \$25A + \$40B$$

Then formulate the constraints as inequalities:

$$2A + 4B \leqq 100 \quad \text{(Assembly constraint)}$$
$$3A + 2B \leqq 90 \quad \text{(Finishing constraint)}$$

and do not forget to add the nonnegativity constraints:

$$A, B \geqq 0$$

Our LP model is

$$\text{maximize} \quad \text{Total } CM = 25A + 40B$$
$$\text{subject to} \quad 2A + 4B \leqq 100$$
$$3A + 2B \leqq 90$$
$$A, B \geqq 0$$

Computational Methods of LP

There are several solution methods available to solve LP problems. They include (1) the simplex method and (2) the graphical method.

The *simplex* method is the technique most commonly used to solve LP problems. It is an algorithm, which is an iteration method of computation, to move from one solution to another until it reaches the best solution. The graphical solution is easier to use but limited to the LP problems involving two (or at most three) decision variables. The graphical method follows the steps:
1. Change inequalities to equalities.
2. Graph the equalities.
3. Identify the correct side for the original inequalities.
4. After all this, identify the feasible region, the area of feasible solutions. *Feasible solutions* are values of decision variables that satisfy all the restrictions simultaneously.
5. Determine the contribution margin at all of the corners in the feasible region.

■ Example 3

In Example 2, after having gone through steps 1 to 4, we obtain the following feasible region (shaded area):

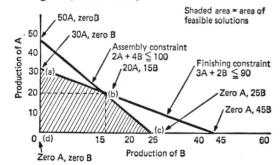

Then we evaluate all of the corner points in the feasible region in terms of their CM, as follows:

Corner Points		Contribution Margin
A	B	$25A + $40B$
(a) 30	0	$25(30) + $40(0) = $ 750
(b) 20	15	25(20) + 40(15) = 1,100
(c) 0	25	25(0) + 40(25) = 1,000
(d) 0	0	25(0) + 40(0) = 0

The corner, 20A, 15B produces the most profitable solution.

Shadow Prices (Opportunity Costs)

A decision maker who has solved an LP problem might wish to know whether it pays to add capacity in hours in a particular department. He or she would be interested in the monetary value to the firm of adding, say, an hour per week of assembly time. This monetary value is the additional contribution margin that could be earned. This amount is called the *shadow price* of the given resource. A shadow price is in a way an opportunity cost—the contribution margin that would be lost by not adding an additional hour of capacity. To justify a decision in favor of a short-term capacity expansion, the decision maker must be sure that the shadow price (or opportunity cost) exceeds the actual price of that expansion. Shadow prices are computed, step by step, as follows:
1. Add 1 hour (preferably, more than 1 hour to make it easier to show graphically) to the constraint under consideration.
2. Resolve the problem and find the maximum CM.
3. Compute the difference between the CM of the original LP problem and the CM determined in step 2, which is the shadow price.

Other methods, such as using the dual problem, are available to compute shadow prices.

■ Example 4

Using the data in Example 3, we shall compute the shadow price of the assembly capacity. To make it easier to show graphically, we shall add 8 hours of capacity to the assembly department, rather than 1 hour. The new assembly constraint is shown in the graph that follows.

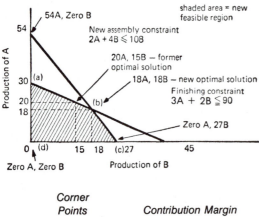

	Corner Points		Contribution Margin	
	A	B	$25A + $40B	
(a)	30	0	$25(30) + $40(0) =	$ 750
(b)	18	18	25(18) + 40(18) =	1,170
(c)	0	27	25(0) + 40(27) =	1,080
(d)	0	0	25(0) + 40(0) =	0

The new optimal solution of 18A, and 18B has a total CM of $1,170 per week. Therefore, the shadow price of the assembly capacity is $70 ($1,170 − $1,100 = $70). The firm would be willing to pay up to $70 to obtain an additional 8 hours per week, or $8.75 *per hour* per week.

LIQUIDATION *Corporation*: An insolvent corporation decides to liquidate under Chapter 7 of the Bankruptcy Reform Act of 1978. The objective of the liquidation is to sell assets and pay off liabilities in order to cease activities rather than remaining in business as a reorganization. Proceeds remaining are distributed to creditors in priority order. A discharge of the unsatisfied debts is received by the debtor.

Partnership: A partnership liquidates its assets and settles partnership affairs. After assets are sold and liabilities are paid, the residual left over is distributed to the partners.

See also Business Failure.

LIQUIDITY This is the ability of a company to meet short-term debt out of current assets. A company's liquidity is primarily of interest to short-term creditors. In analyzing liquidity, funds flow is a major consideration. Liquidity measures include:

• *Current ratio*—equal current assets divided by current liabilities.

• *Quick ratio*—equals cash plus marketable securities plus receivables divided by current liabilities. It is a stringent test of liquidity.

• *Working capital*—equals current assets less current liabilities. A high working capital is needed when the company may have difficulty borrowing on short notice. Working capital should be compared to other financial statement items such as sales and total assets. For example, working capital to sales indicates if the company is optimally employing its liquid balance. To identify changes in the composition of working capital, the financial analyst should ascertain the trend in the percentage of each current asset to total current assets. A movement from cash to inventory, for instance, points to less liquidity.

• *Sales to current assets*—a high turnover rate indicates inadequate working capital. Maybe current liabilities will be due prior to inventories and receivables turning into cash.

• *Working capital provided from operations* (net income plus nonworking capital expenses minus nonworking capital revenue) *to net income*—liquidity is enhanced when net income is backed up by liquid funds.

• *Working capital provided from operations to total liabilities*—indicates the extent internally generated working capital is available to meet debt.

• *Cash plus marketable securities to current liabilities*—indicates the immediate amount of cash available to satisfy short-term obligations.

• *Cost of sales, operating expenses, and taxes to average total current assets*—the trend in this ratio indicates the adequacy of current assets in meeting ongoing business-related expenses.

• *Quick assets to year's cash expenses*—indicates the days of expenses the highly liquid assets could support.

• *Sales to short-term trade liabilities*—indicates whether the firm can partly finance by cost-free funds. A decline in trade credit means creditors have less faith in the financial strength of the business.

• *Net income to sales*—a decline in the profit margin of the business indicates financial deterioration.

• *Fixed assets to short-term debt*—a company financing long-term assets with short-term obligations has a problem satisfying debt when due because the return and proceeds from the fixed asset will not be realized prior to the maturity date of the current liabilities.

• *Short-term debt to long-term debt*—a higher ratio points to greater liquidity risk because debt is of a current nature.

• *Accounts payable to average daily purchases*—indicates the number of days required for the company to pay creditors.

• *Liquidity index*—indicates the days in which current assets are removed from cash.

■ Example

	Amount	Days Removed From Cash	Total
Cash	$10,000 ×	—	—
Accounts receivable	40,000 ×	25	$1,000,000
Inventory	60,000 ×	40	2,400,000
	$110,000		$3,400,000

$$\text{Index} = \frac{\$3,400,000}{\$110,000} = 30.9 \text{ days}$$

■ Example

Company B provides the following financial information:

Current assets	$ 400,000
Fixed assets	800,000
Current liabilities	500,000
Noncurrent liabilities	600,000
Sales	5,000,000
Working capital provided from operations	100,000
Industry norms are	
Fixed assets to current liabilities	4.0 times
Current liabilities to noncurrent liabilities	45.0%
Sales to current assets	8.3 times
Working capital provided from operations to total liabilities	30.5%
Company B's ratios are	
Fixed assets to current liabilities	1.6 times
Current liabilities to noncurrent liabilities	83.3%
Sales to current assets	12.5 times
Working capital provided from operations to total liabilities	9.1%

Company B's liquidity ratios are all unfavorable compared to industry standards. There is a high level of short-term debt as well as deficiency in current assets. Also, working capital provided from operations to satisfy total debt is inadequate.

A company's failure to take cash discounts raises a question as to management's financial astuteness because a high opportunity cost is involved.

■ Example

Company C bought goods for $300,000 on terms of 2/10, net/60. It failed to take advantage of the discount. The opportunity cost is

$$\frac{\text{Discount foregone}}{\text{Proceeds use of}} \times \frac{360}{\text{Days delayed}}$$

$$\frac{\$6,000}{\$294,000} \times \frac{360}{50} = 14.7\%$$

The firm would have been better off financially paying within the discount period by taking out a loan since the prime interest rate is below 14.7%.

LOCAL AREA NETWORKS   One of the more recent innovations in the area of data communications systems is the concept of local area networking. The overall objective of a local area network, known as a LAN, is to link computer devices and systems in the same geographical area, typically in a building. Local area networking (LAN) consists of a collection of microcomputers and expensive peripherals such as hard disk drives and laser printers linked together by connections that provide a cost effective means of sharing data and hardware among all linked users. This concept not only permits a centralizing control over policies and processing, but also provides for the flexibility of decentralization. In addition, they permit the sharing of information in an office building in an efficient and timely manner. LANs are fast, flexible, and provide ease of informational flow. One micro, for example, may easily communicate with another to transfer data among locations.

In its most basic form, the LAN, physically speaking, is nothing more than a group of microcomputers, printers, and other peripherals connected by twisted-pair wires or coaxial cables. However, fiber optics—the up and coming technology—is quickly replacing these more traditional connecting media. An important part of the LAN technology is the server, which can be a microcomputer or a peripheral that handles all the requests of the interconnected microcomputers making up the network. The server usually takes the form of a hard disk drive that is available to all participating PCs. Frequently, it is partitioned so that each computer can access a specific, private storage area. However, many systems allow certain areas to be accessed by all computer work stations. Thus, data files, such as data bases and spreadsheets, can be shared by all users making up the network. Optimally, the LAN should allow any user access to any computer resource that he or she is authorized to access

within the system, irrespective of its location. More will be said on this topic later.

In general, LANs provide the practitioner with immeasurable benefits enhancing profitability, accuracy and timeliness. In addition, they are relatively easy to install, expandable, and overall not expensive.

LAN Configurations

There are three basic LAN configurations, consisting of star, ring, and bus (tree). A description of each of these follows.

Star Network

In a star network, there is a linking of subsidiary micros or terminals to a central (host) computer whose task is to link all system micros together and route data and transmission among terminals and satellite micros. Clearly, all micros must be wired to the central controller. It is this resulting pattern of connecting micros to the central computer that produces the starlike shape that gives this configuration its name.

In this system, all information must pass through the central controller for direction to their final destination. This centralization predicates the performance of this network system on the performance of the central controller. In fact, failure of the central computer impairs the entire network. This is a major weakness of this configuration. The central controller, which regulates all communication in the system, should have adequate controls that are reviewed and tested periodically.

A star network is best utilized when it is necessary to enter and process data at many locations with distributions to different remote users, for example, shared data bases. Star networks are most frequently designed with a polling technology to communicate to all introcomponental PCs. In this technology the central controller waits for a signal from one of the microcomputers and then processes it. Another star communications technology, called reservation, permits the transmission of signals at preset times. These reservations occur several times per second.

Ring Networks

The ring network configuration was developed as a result of attempting to eliminate the dependence of the central controller in the star network. A ring network has multiple computers connected together through a continuous communications cable. The network frequency does not involve a central computer. It does, however, offer the fastest response time of any LAN configuration. In this system the sending PC originates a message with the address of the intended receiver PC. The message is then passed on to the next PC in the ring. If this PC determines that this message was not intended for it (incorrect address), it passes the message along to the next PC. This process continues in an orderly sequential fashion until the message is accepted by the correct PC.

The ring network basically represents a communications system in which all stations constantly monitor the system. For example, the ring configuration is frequently used when several users at different locations have to access updated information on a continual basis. In this situation, more than one data transmission occurs simultaneously, keeping the system current on an ongoing basis. A ring network, for example, permits accountants within the firm to create and update shared data bases (e.g., general ledger, accounts receivable, accounts payable).

Given the fact that data are accessed or processed by many users in a ring configuration, it is important that controls be established to ensure that all messages and information have been communicated correctly. One such control requires that a message that has been delivered to a receiver continues on to the sender PC so that it may be determined that the data has remained intact. Another control requires that the receiving PC

remove the message from the ring and replace it with a verification that the message has been delivered.

In general, although a ring network is reliable, it is difficult to service and expand. In addition, loss of one station may cause the entire system to crash.

Bus Networks

A bus network consists of a series of microcomputers or peripherals at different locations attached to a central cable. The PCs and peripherals tap directly to the main cable, which may be installed over floors in an office building with drop cables running to the micros. As a result of this configuration, it is very easy to expand the system by just tapping into the central line. In addition, if a single PC work station malfunctions, the LAN will continue to operate.

One of two types of communication technologies may be utilized in most bus networks. Each is based on a first come, first serve assumption. The first, termed Common Sense Multiple Access/Carrier Avoidance, has the sending micro first determine whether any other station is sending. If not, it starts to transmit. However, if two stations transmit at the same time, the signals are sent garbled, preventing the sending stations from receiving a verification that the messages were received. As a result, retransmission occurs. Another related technology, called the Common Sense Multiple Access/Collision Detection, is comparable to the first technology except that when two micros transmit at the same time, they both immediately stop and will singularly start to retransmit again only after waiting for a short period of time.

Which Network Should Be Acquired?

In deciding which network is best given the particular circumstances of the accountant's office or that of the client, the following questions must be answered. How many users are involved, and what is the nature of their work? What kind of accounting and internal controls exist? How often must data be updated, and what processing speed is required? Is the cost/benefit relationship attractive? Does the ''right'' software exist for desired network applications? What is the maximum data storage possible? Can the system be maintained in an efficient and cost-effective manner?

It should be noted that a network can consist of multivendor equipment where a proper protocol is used. An example is Sytek's Local Net™.

It is possible to combine two networks to enhance performance and obtain desirable features.

Be careful! IBMs DOS 3.1 NETBIOS™ operating system appears to be the standard for LANs. You are taking a risk if you select another operating system.

Software Considerations

Currently the choice of network software is limited by the network system purchased. However, it is hoped that this incompatibility restrictiveness will diminish in the future. Network software consists of data communications packages typically termed communications monitors or teleprocessing monitors. Included are communications access programs formulating a connection between terminals and computer systems, and the link between application programs and the network. Also involved are network control programs managing the communications network functions.

Communications monitors perform many processing and controlling activities that accounting practitioners should be aware of. These include such activities as establishing the amount of waiting in the system for transfer and processing; connecting and disconnecting links; polling terminals; establishing the direction for message transfer; identifying, keeping track, and correcting errors in the network process; and editing and executing of programs and varied data base activities.

Of course, the practicing accountant should carefully examine and review all network-related software to make sure that the network activity will run reasonably with adequate controls. He or she should make sure that there are proper communications links and transfers, that the terminals and micros work correctly, that reasonable waiting time exists to send and receive data, and that all system errors that occur are capable of being identified, documented, corrected, and disposed of.

For several networks, there exist multiuser packages. Examples of software for networking systems include dBASE PLUS™, Lotus' Symphony™, and IBM's Business Management Series™. A specialist in networking software is Torus Systems of England. Accounting software for LANs is also available.

Internal Control Considerations That Must Be Evaluated by the Accountant

The accountant must consider important internal control considerations related to a networking system to assure that data integrity and security exist. Clearly, errors must be minimized since the reliability and communicability of the financial reporting system is effected.

The accountant must make sure that the proposed network system is viable, especially when different types of computers are used, to assure there is appropriate data communication. Standard protocols, communications hardware and software interfaces should exist. In addition, there should be a uniform multilevel interface between the central system and users.

To ensure the overall quality of the proposed system the CPA should compare the network to the International Standards Organization's Open System Interconnection reference model for quality control design in seven categories. The areas covered by the model include data routing and transmissions and user applications.

Parity checking provides the system with a means of controlling errors in transmitting and routing. In this control, the system ascertains whether there exists an odd or even number of digits in a character of information being sent. Communications control units should be used to control errors in data transmissions.

As was previously noted, the server is that part of the LAN (a microcomputer or peripheral) that handles all information requests of the member work station. It usually takes the form of a hard disk drive that is available to all participating PCs. As was noted, this hard disk drive should be partitioned so that each micro has its own storage segment. From a control point of view, this provides for segregation to isolate the responsibility for specific processing. Also, it is clear from this segregation that one micro will not improperly effect information going to others. Where segments of the hard disk are accessed equally by all network micros, only one work station may do the accessing at a time.

For data files that contain more confidential information, good internal control dictates that there be higher level security measures in effect to prevent unauthorized access of information. For example, determination must be made of the specific people who have the authority to access and update files. Logs should be kept of who altered and used files as well as the amount of time spent in the system. Additional control considerations include

• Making sure that adjacent work stations are properly connected, both physically and electrically.

• Safeguards should be established to make sure that unauthorized personnel have not accessed data transferred over communication lines. Passwords and voice recognition may be used.

• Checks should be made of information stored in the storage areas and devices within the network system. This includes assurance that data have not been lost in processing or tampered with.

• The adequacy of network communications should be reviewed. The quality of the protocol management scheme to gain access to the network, uniform rules, and procedures should be periodically reviewed.

• Data sent between adjacent micro work stations should be monitored for accuracy.

• Procedures should exist for avoiding and detecting signal collisions immediately. The effect of the collision on the network should be ascertained.

• Volume locking should be available so that when an accountant uses a file, client personnel are unable to access it.

• "Read-only" configurations should enable the reading of a file but not writing to it.

• "Redundant" cables should be used to prevent a break in the network link.

• Encryption, which is a form of difficult coding, should be used for data transmission. Data are decoded when received. National Data Encryption Standards exist.

• Use of a polynomial equation instead of an arithmetic addition should be used to obtain a check answer for transmission reliability.

• Block coding should exist for putting bytes in a matrix.

• Security controls should be enhanced as files become more confidential.

LONG-FORM REPORT   This is a detailed audit report by the independent CPA. It is addressed to management or the board of directors. It may be prepared in addition to or in substitution of the short-form report. Typically, the long-form report includes information regarding the audit scope, comments on financial condition, operating results and cash flow statement, trends over the years, and recommendations.

M

MAKE-OR-BUY DECISION   This is a decision whether to produce a component part internally or to buy it externally from an outside supplier. This decision involves both quantitative and qualitative factors. The qualitative considerations include ensuring product quality and the necessity for long-run business relationships with the subcontractors. The quantitative factors deal with cost. The quantitative effects of the make-or-buy decision are best seen through *incremental analysis*.

■ Example

Assume a firm has prepared the cost estimates (above right) for the manufacture of a subassembly component based on an annual production of 8,000 units:

	Per Unit	Total
Direct materials	$ 5	$ 40,000
Direct labor	4	32,000
Variable overhead applied	4	32,000
Fixed overhead applied (150% of direct labor cost)	6	48,000
Total cost	$19	$152,000

The supplier has offered to provide the subassembly at a price of $16 each. Two thirds of fixed factory overhead—which represents executive salaries, rent, depreciation, and taxes—continue regardless of the decision. Should the company buy or make the product? The key to the decision lies in the investigation of those relevant costs that change between the make-or-buy alternatives. Assuming that the productive capacity will be idle if not used to produce the subassembly, the analysis takes the following form:

	Per Unit		Total of 8,000 units	
	Make	Buy	Make	Buy
Purchase price		$16		$128,000
Direct materials	$ 5		$40,000	
Direct labor	4		32,000	
Variable overhead	4		32,000	
Fixed overhead that can be avoided by *not* making	2	—	16,000	
Total relevant costs	$15	$16	$120,000	$128,000
Difference in favor of making		$1		$8,000

The make-or-buy decision must be investigated in the broader perspective of available facilities. The alternatives are

1. Leaving facilities idle
2. Buying the parts and renting out idle facilities
3. Buying the parts and using unused facilities for other products

MANAGEMENT ADVISORY SERVICES (MAS)

MAS are performed by accountants to aid the management of a company. Types of services performed can be to assist in computer use, budgeting, controls, operations, planning, personnel, and other management decision-making purposes. The objective is to enhance a company's financial posture and operating performance as well as to reduce corporate risk. There exist standards to be followed in conducting MAS engagements. Independence must be maintained by CPAs involved in MAS activities. Reference should be made to the AICPA Statements for Management Advisory Services (SSMAS).

MANAGEMENT AUDIT   In a management audit, an evaluation is done of the ability of management to conduct operational activities. An appraisal is made of the nature and quality of management decisions in generating profit and controlling risk. *See also* Operational Audit.

MANAGEMENT GAMES   These offer a unique means of teaching business managers and financial executives financial and managerial concepts and developing strategic abilities. More and more companies as well as virtually all MBA programs across the nation are using management games as a basic teaching tool for industrial training programs.

     The management game is a form of simulation. The distinction between a game and a simulation is a subtle one. Both are mathematical models, but they differ in purpose and mode of use. *Simulation models* are designed to simulate a system and to generate a series of quantitative and financial results regarding system operations. Games are also a form of simulation, except that in games human beings play a significant part. In games, participants make decisions at various stages; thus, games are distinguished by the idea of play. The major goals of the game play can be summarized as follows:

1. Improve decision-making and analytical skills
2. Facilitate an understanding of the external environment simulated on the part of the participants
3. Integratively apply the knowledge, concepts, and skills acquired in various business courses
4. Develop awareness of the need to make decisions lacking complete information
5. Improvise appropriately and adapt constructively from previously learned concepts, theories, and techniques
6. Develop ability to recognize the need for additional factual material
7. Develop an understanding of the interrelationships of the various functions within the firm and how these interactions affect overall performance
8. Learn about the effects of present decisions on future decisions
9. Develop an understanding of the fact of uncertainty and the impact of competitive environment on the firm
10. Have an understanding of the necessity for good communications, teamwork, leadership, and the organization
11. Develop ability to function cooperatively and effectively in a group situation

     The basic structure of a typical executive management game is given in Figure 1 (page 288).

Executive Games Versus Functional Games

Management games generally fall into two categories: executive games and functional games. *Executive games* are general management games and cover all functional areas

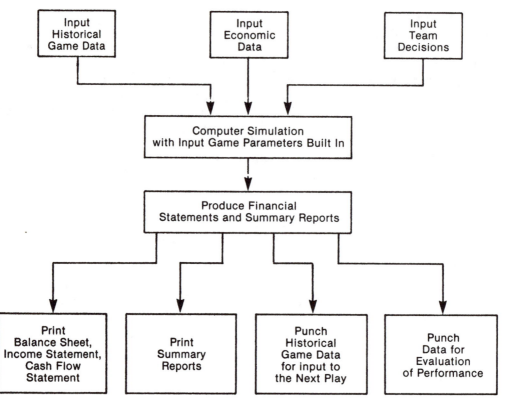

Figure 1 Structure of a Typical Executive Game

of business and theory interactions and dynamics. Executive games are designed to train general executives.

Following is a partial list of some well-known executive management games.

- XGAME™ by Jackson and Henshaw
- The IMAGINIT MANAGEMENT GAME™ by R. Barton
- COGITATE™ by Carnegie Mellon University
- The Business Policy Game™ by Cotter and Fritzsche
- Top Management Decision Game™ by Schrieber
- Harvard Business Game™ by Harvard University
- Management Accounting Game™ by K. Goosen

Functional games, on the other hand, focus on middle management decisions and emphasize particular functional areas of the firm. They cover such areas as:

- Resource allocation in general
- Production planning and scheduling
- Manpower requirements and allocation
- Logistics systems
- Material management
- Maintenance scheduling
- Sales management
- Advertising and promotion
- Stock transactions
- Investment analysis
- Research and development management

The objective in the play of functional games is usually to minimize cost by achieving efficient operations or to maximize revenues by allocating limited resources efficiently. With emphasis on efficiency in specific functional areas rather than competition in a marketplace, found in executive management games, there is little or no interaction in many functional games between player decisions. From that standpoint, functional games are very similar to simulation models. Here is a partial list of some well-known functional games:

Name of Functional Game	Area(s) They Cover
• The Westinghouse Plant Scheduling™ Warehouse Simulation Exercise™	Distribution and logistics
• Greene and Sisson's Materials™ Inventory Management Game™	Inventory planning
• Greene and Sisson's Production™ Scheduling Management Game™	Production scheduling
• X-Otol™	Distribution
• IBM Production Manpower Decision Model™	Production and manpower scheduling decisions
• MARKSIM™	Marketing decision simulation
• FINASIM™	Financial management simulation
• PERT-SIM™	Project planning and control

See also Corporate Planning Models; Financial Games; Financial Models.

MANAGEMENT INFORMATION SYSTEM (MIS)

MIS is a manual or a computer-based system that transforms data into information useful in the support of planning, control, and decision making. MIS can be classified as performing three functions:

1. MIS that generates reports. These reports can be financial statements, inventory status reports, performance reports, or financial analysis reports that are needed for routine and nonroutine purposes. *Accounting infor-*

mation system (AIS) and *financial information system* are two subsystems of MIS.

2. MIS that answer what-if kinds of questions asked by financial management. For example, questions such as "What would happen to cash flow if the company grants a lenient cash discount term?" can be answered by MIS. This type of MIS can be called *simulation.*

3. MIS that supports decision making. This type of MIS is appropriately called *Decision Support System (DSS)*. DSS attempts to integrate the decision maker, the data base, and the quantitative models being used. Financial modeling packages such as *IFPS* can be used for this kind of purpose.

See also Accounting Information System (AIS); Decision Support System (DSS); Financial Information System; Simulation.

MARGIN TRADING
This involves buying securities on credit. An investor opening a margin account signs a margin agreement, similar to an agreement signed to obtain a bank loan. This document states the annual rate of interest, its method of computation, and specific conditions under which interest rates can be changed. The Federal Reserve Board sets rules specifying the minimum percentage of the purchase price that a margin customer must pay in cash, known as a margin requirement. This requirement is currently for at least 50% of the current market value of the security. (Some securities may not be purchased on margin.) A 60% margin requirement means that 100 shares of a stock selling for $200 a share can be purchased by putting up, in cash, only 60% of the total purchase price; that is, $12,000 and borrowing the remaining $8,000. The stockbroker lends the margin purchaser the money, retaining custody of the stock as collateral. This is a form of leverage that, whether used in a long position or a short position, magnifies the gains and losses from a given percentage of price fluctuation in securities.

MARGINAL ANALYSIS

This is a key principle of microeconomics that can be applied to financial and investment decisions. The analysis suggests that financial and investment decisions should be made and actions taken only when *marginal revenues* exceed *marginal costs*. If this condition exists, a given decision should maximize the firm's profits.

MARGINAL COST (MC)

MC is the change in total cost associated with a unit change in quantity. For example, the marginal cost of the five hundredth unit of output can be calculated by finding the difference in total cost at 499 units of output and total cost at 500 units of output. MC is thus the additional cost of one more unit of output. It is calculated as:

$$MC = \text{change in total cost/change in quantity}$$

MC is also the change in total variable cost associated with a unit change in output. This is because total cost changes, whereas total fixed cost remains unchanged. MC may also be thought of as the rate of change in total cost as the quantity (Q) of output changes and is simply the first derivative of the total cost (TC) function.
Thus:

$$MC = dTC/dQ$$

In *accounting* and actual applications of this concept, MC is viewed as being equivalent to *incremental cost*, which is the increment in cost between the two alternatives or two discrete volumes of output. *See also* Marginal Revenue.

MARGINAL REVENUE

This is the rate of change of total revenue with respect to quantity sold. Marginal revenue indicates to a firm how total sales revenues will change if there is a change in the quantity of a firm's product sold. In economics, marginal revenue must equal marginal cost in order for profit to be maximized. In a discrete range of activity, marginal revenue is equivalent to incremental revenue.

MARKET (STOCK) INDEXES AND AVERAGES

These are market gauges used to track performance for stocks and bonds. At least in theory, an average is the simple arithmetic mean, whereas an index is an average expressed relative to a preestablished market value. In practice, the distinction is not all that clear. There are many stock market indexes and averages available. Each market has several indexes published by Dow Jones, Standard & Poor's, and other financial services. Different investors prefer different indexes. Indexes and averages are also used as the underlying value of index futures and index options.

Dow Jones Averages

Dow Jones averages are the most widely used and watched market indexes published by *The Wall Street Journal*. The *Dow Jones Industrial Average (DJIA)* is one of the four stock averages compiled by the *Journal*. This average consists of 30 large companies and is considered a blue chip index (stocks of very high quality). There are three other Dow Jones averages: the transportation (composed of 20 transportation issues), the 15 utilities, and a composite of the total 65 stocks. The DJIA would be a simple average of 30 blue chip stocks, but when a firm splits its stock price, the average has to be adjusted in some manner. In fact, the divisor is changed from time to time to maintain continuity of the average. The Dow Jones averages are designed to serve as indicators of broad movements in the securities markets. The *Dow Jones Composite*, also called *65 Stock Average*, combines all three Dow Jones averages.

Barron's Indexes

Barron's, which is also a publication of Dow Jones, compiles *Barron's 50 Stock Average* and an index of low-priced securities that meets the needs of small investors. Barron's also publishes a weekly average called *Barron's Group Stock Averages*, covering 32 industry groups.

Standard & Poor's Indexes

Standard & Poor's Corporation publishes several indexes, including two most widely used indexes—the *S&P 400 Industrials* and the *S&P 500 Stock Index*. The S&P 400 is composed of 400 industrial common stocks of companies listed on the New York Stock Exchange, and the S&P 500 Stock Index consists of the 400 industrials and utilities and transportation stocks. They are used as broad measures of the market direction. They are also frequently used as proxies for market return when computing the systematic risk measure (*"beta"*) of individual stocks and portfolios. The S&P 500 Stock Index is one of the U.S. Commerce Department's 12 leading economic indicators. This index represents some 80% of the market value of all issues traded on the NYSE.

The *Standard & Poor's 100 Stock Index* consists of stocks for which options are listed on the Chicago Board Option Exchange (CBOE).

Value Line Average

The Value Line average is a simple average of 1,685 companies from the NYSE, AMEX, and the over-the-counter market.

Other Market Indexes

Different exchanges publish their market indexes. The NYSE publishes a composite index as well as industrial, utility, transportation, and financial indexes. The American Stock Exchange (AMEX) compiles two major indexes—the *AMEX Market Value Index* (*AMVI*) and the *AMEX Major Market Index*. The National Association of Securities Dealers also publishes several indexes to represent the companies in the over-the-counter mar-

ket. It publishes the *NASDAQ OTC* composite, insurance, industrial, and banking indexes. *Wilshire 5000 Equity Index*, published by the Wilshire Associates of Santa Monica, California, represents the market value of 5,000 NYSE, AMEX, and over-the-counter issues.

Bond Averages

Barron's publishes an index of 20 bonds, 10 utility bonds, and 10 industrial bonds as an average of the bond market. Dow Jones publishes two major bond averages—the *Dow Jones 40 Bond Average*, representative of six different bond groups, and the *Dow Jones Municipal Bond Yield Average*.

Mutual Fund Averages

Lipper Analytical Services compiles the Lipper Mutual Fund Investment Performance Averages. It publishes three basic fund indexes for growth funds, growth income funds, and balanced funds. *See also* Beta Coefficient; Index of Leading Economic Indicators.

MARKOV ANALYSIS   This is an *operations research* technique. It is a technique that attempts to analyze the current behavior of some variable to predict the future behavior of that variable. It can be used to estimate the percentages of cash collections (payment proportions) from customers for cash-budgeting purposes. It can also be used to estimate the amount of bad debt allowance required. *See also* Budgeting Models.

MATERIALITY   An item is material if the absence to disclose it would mislead readers of the financial statements. Disclosure may be made in the body of the financial statements, footnotes, or separate schedule. Materiality is difficult to measure. In SEC Accounting Series Release No. 159, the SEC requires disclosure by management of a change in a revenue or expense item by 10% or more than the prior year. Some CPA firms have a more stringent requirement to guard against possible litigation. Some use a conservative 5% figure. In APB Opinion No. 15, a common stock equivalent is only included in the EPS calculation if it decreases EPS by 3% or more.

MATHEMATICAL PROGRAMMING
This is a branch of *Operations Research/Management Science* whose primary objective is to search for an optimal solution to a decision problem. It is an optimization model. It typically consists of two ingredients in its model formulation: objective function and constraints. Mathematical programming covers a wide range of techniques, including linear programming, integer programming, dynamic programming, zero–one programming, quadratic programming, and other forms of nonlinear programming. *See also* Operations Research/Management Science; Optimization Models.

MATURITY VALUE
1. The face amount of an obligation payable on the maturity date. The maturity value will differ from the issuance price if a security is sold at a discount (below face value) or premium (above face value). Maturity value equals issuance price only if the security was issued at par.

■ Example 1

A $100,000 bond is issued at 97%, or $97,000. The bond was issued at a discount. At maturity, the company will retire the bond by paying its maturity value of $100,000.

2. On a note receivable that is discounted at the bank before the maturity date, maturity value equals

> Face value of note
> Plus: Interest to maturity
> Maturity value

■ Example 2

A $10,000, 6%, 90-day note is received from a customer. It is discounted at the bank with 60 days still remaining. The bank discount rate is 7%.

Face value of note	$10,000
Interest to maturity ($10,000 × 6% × 90/360)	150
Maturity value	$10,150
Bank discount ($10,150 × 7% × 60/360)	118
Proceeds	$10,032

MEAN
The mean gives us the average, or central value, of our data. Typically, there are three measures of central tendency: (1) arithmetic mean, (2) weighted mean, and (3) geometric mean. Each of these means is described following.

1. Arithmetic Mean($\bar{x}$)

The arithmetic mean is a simple average. To find it, we sum the value in our data and divide by the number of observations. Symbolically:

$$\bar{x} = \frac{\Sigma x}{n}$$

where n = number of observations.

■ Example 1

John Jay Lamp Company has a revolving credit agreement with a local bank. The loan showed the following ending monthly balances last year:

Jan	$18,500
Feb	21,000
Mar	17,600
Apr	23,200
May	18,600
Jun	24,500
Jul	60,000
Aug	40,000
Sep	25,850
Oct	33,100
Nov	41,000
Dec	28,400

Then the mean monthly balance for the loan last year is computed as follows:

Arithmetic mean balance

$$= \frac{\begin{matrix} \$18,500 + \$21,000 + \$17,600 + \$23,200 \\ + \$18,600 + \$24,500 + \$60,000 \\ + \$40,000 + \$25,850 + \$33,100 + \$41,000 + \$28,400 \end{matrix}}{12}$$

$$= \frac{\$351,750}{12} = \$29,312.50$$

2. Weighted Mean

The arithmetic mean is an unweighted average. It assumes equal likelihood of each value in one data. When our observations have different degrees of importance or frequency, we use the *weighted mean*. The weighted average enables us to take into account the importance of each value in the overall total. Symbolically, the formula for calculating the weighted average is

$$\text{Weighted mean} = \Sigma \ w \cdot x$$

where w = weight (in percentage or in relative frequency) assigned to each observation.

■ Example 2

Consider the company that uses three grades of labor to produce a finished product. The company wants to know the average cost of labor per hour for this product.

Grade of Labor	Labor Hours per Unit of Output	Hourly Wages (x)
Skilled	6	$10
Semiskilled	3	8
Unskilled	1	6

Using the arithmetic mean, the labor wage rates would be

$$\text{Arithmetic mean} = \frac{\$10 + \$8 + \$6}{3} = \frac{\$24}{3}$$
$$= \$8/\text{hour}$$

which implicitly assumes that the same amounts of each grade of labor were used to produce the output. More specifically,

$$\frac{\$10 + \$8 + \$6}{3} = \$10(\frac{1}{3}) + \$8(\frac{1}{3}) + \$6(\frac{1}{3})$$
$$= \$8/\text{hour}$$

This is simply not true. We have to consider different amounts of each grade of labor in calculating the average cost of labor per hour. The correct way is to take a weighted average, as follows:

$$\begin{aligned} \text{Weighted mean} &= \$10(\frac{6}{10}) + \$8(\frac{3}{10}) \\ &\quad + \$6(\frac{1}{10}) \\ &= \$9/\text{hour} \end{aligned}$$

Note that we weight the hourly wage for each grade by its proportion of the total labor required to produce the product.

3. Geometric Mean

Sometimes we are dealing with quantities that change over a period of time. In such a case, we need to know an average rate of change, such as an average rate of return on investment or an average rate of growth in earnings over a period of several years. The formula for finding the geometric mean over n periods is

$$\begin{aligned} \text{Geometric mean} \\ = \sqrt[n]{(1 + x_1)(1 + x_2) \ldots \ldots (1 + x_n)} - 1 \end{aligned}$$

where x's represent the percentage rate of change or percentage return on investment. Since it is cumbersome to calculate the nth root (although most scientific calculators have a key to compute this), we will illustrate only the two-period return calculation ($n = 2$).

■ Example 3

Consider the following, which shows the inadequacy of the arithmetic mean return when the price of a stock doubles in one period and then depreciates back to the original price.

	Time Periods		
	$t = 0$	$t = 1$	$t = 2$
Price (end of period)	$80	$160	$80
Rate of return	—	100%	−50%

The rate of return for periods 1 and 2 are computed as follows:

$$\text{Period 1 } (t=1) \frac{(\$160 - \$80)}{\$80} = \frac{\$80}{\$80} = 100\%$$

$$\text{Period 2 } (t=2) \frac{(\$80 - \$160)}{\$160} = \frac{-\$80}{\$160} = -50\%$$

Therefore, the arithmetic mean return over the two periods is the average of 100% and −50%, which is 25%, as shown following:

$$\frac{100\% + (-50\%)}{2} = 25\%$$

As can be easily seen, the stock purchased for $80 and sold for the same price two periods later did not earn 25%; it clearly earned a *zero* return. This can be shown by computing the geometric mean return, as follows:

Note that $n = 2$, $x_1 = 100\% = 1$, and $x_2 = -50\% = -0.5$

Geometric mean return

$$= \sqrt[2]{(1+1)(1-0.5)} - 1$$
$$= \sqrt[2]{(2)(0.5)} - 1$$
$$= \sqrt{1} - 1 = 1 - 1 = 0\%$$

MICROECONOMICS VERSUS MACROECO-NOMICS

Microeconomics is the study of the individual units of the economy—individuals, households, firms, and industries, whereas macroeconomics is concerned with the workings of the whole economy or large sectors of it. Microeconomics zeros in on such economic variables as the prices and outputs of specific firms and industries, the expenditures of consumers, wage rates, competition, and markets. The focus is on the trees, not the forest. Questions that can be addressed by microeconomics include

• What determines the price and output of individual goods and services?

• What are the factors that determine supply and demand of a particular good?

• How can government policies such as price controls, subsidies, and excise taxes affect the price and output levels of individual markets?

Macroeconomics is the study of the national economy as a whole, or of its major sectors. It deals with national price, output, unemployment, inflation, and international trade. It looks at the forest, not the trees. Typical macroeconomic questions include

• What determines national income and employment levels?

• What determines the general price level or rate of inflation?

• What are the policies that combat typical economic problems such as inflation, unemployment, and recession?

MINIMUM PENSION LIABILITY

The minimum pension liability equals the excess of the accumulated benefit obligation over the fair value of pension plan assets. *See also* Pension Plans.

MINORITY INTEREST

Minority interest in a subsidiary, whether acquired in a purchase or pooling-of-interests, refers to the equity of the shareholders outside the parent's controlling interest in partially owned subsidiaries. The preferable presentation in the balance sheet is to show the minority interest as a separate item in stockholders' equity. If two or more subsidiaries exist, a supplementary schedule may be prepared summarizing the external ownership equities.

■ Example

An external group owns 7% of the voting common stock of a subsidiary company that is controlled by a parent. The outside group represents a minority interest. *See also* Consolidation.

MODIFIED ACCRUAL

This is the accounting method used by most funds in government. Under it there is recognition given to revenue when it is available and measurable. An example would be property taxes delayed beyond the normal time of receipt. Expenditures are usually reflected in the accounting period in which the liability is incurred, with the expectation that: (1) encumbrances are recorded; (2) interest on long-term debt is booked on the due date; (3) inventories of materials and supplies may be deemed expenditures when bought or consumed; and (4) prepaid items are immediately shown as expenditures.

Note: Proprietary governmental funds (e.g., enterprise, internal service) follow accrual accounting since they have profit and loss attributes.

MONETARY POLICY This is a deliberate exercise of the Federal Reserve's power to induce changes in the money supply in order to achieve price stability, to help smooth out business cycles, and to bring the economy's employment and output to desired levels. Monetary policy is essentially directed at regulating the economy's overall money supply; credit availability; and, to a lesser degree, the level of interest rates by the Federal Reserve System. The Federal Reserve System has three major devices that it can use to control the money supply: (1) changes in the required reserve ratio; (2) changes in the discount rate; and (3) open market operations—that is, purchase and sale of government securities.

MONEY MARKETS (CREDIT MARKETS) The money markets are for short-term debt instruments, such as certificates of deposit, commercial paper, Treasury bills, and bankers' acceptances. Also included are bank loans, trade credit, federal funds borrowing between banks, and bank borrowings from the Federal Reserve. Money market instruments are liquid and secure. *See also* Capital Markets; Financial Institutions and Markets.

MONEY SUPPLY This is the level of funds available at a given time for conducting transactions in an economy. The Federal Reserve System can influence the money supply through its monetary policy measures. There are many definitions of the money supply. For example, $M1$, a broadly used measure of money supply, currency in circulation, demand deposits, traveler's checks, and those in interest-bearing NOW accounts. Other definitions of money supply, that is, $M2$, $M3$, and L are given below.

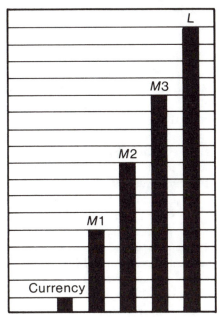

$L = M3$ + LIQUID AND NEAR-LIQUID ASSETS
Treasury obligations, including bills and bonds
Term Eurodollars, high-grade commercial paper, and banker's acceptances

$M3 = M2$ + WIDE-RANGE MONEY
Large-denomination time deposits
Term repurchase agreements

$M2 = M1$ + MEDIUM-RANGE MONEY
Savings (time) deposits
Repurchase agreements (overnight)
Money market mutual fund shares
Eurodollars (overnight)

$M1 =$ NARROW-TRANSACTIONS MONEY, BASIC MONEY SUPPLY
Traveler's checks
Other checkable deposits
(NOW, share draft, and other accounts)
Demand deposits
Currency

Other checkable deposits
Demand deposits
Currency

See also Federal Reserve System; Monetary Policy.

MONTE CARLO SIMULATION

This is a special type of *simulation* in which the variables of a given system are subject to uncertainty. The technique gets its name from the famous Mediterranean resort associated with games of chance. In fact, the chance element is an important aspect of Monte Carlo simulation. The method can be used only when a system has a *random*, or chance, component. Under this approach, a probability distribution is developed that reflects the random component of the system under study. Random samples taken from this distribution are analogous to observations made on the system itself. As the number of observations increases, the results of the simulation will tend to more closely approximate the random behavior of the real system, provided a proper model has been developed. Sampling is done by the use of random numbers. Business applications of simulation include testing alternative credit policies and inventory policies. *See also* Simulation.

MORTGAGES

These are liens securing notes payable that have as collateral real assets and require periodic payments. For personal property, such as machines or equipment, the lien is called a *chattel mortgage*. Mortgages can be issued to finance the acquisition of assets, construction of plants, and modernization of facilities. The bank will require that the value of the property exceed the mortgage on that property. Mortgages have a number of advantages over other debt instruments, including favorable interest rates, less financing restrictions, and extended maturity date for loan repayment.

MOVING AVERAGE

A moving average is an average that is updated as new information is received. With the moving average, an accountant employs the most recent observa- tions to calculate an average, which is used as the forecast for the next period. For example, assume that the accountant has the following cash inflow data.

Month	Cash Collections (000)
May	20
June	24
July	22
August	26
September	25

Using a four-period moving average, predicted cash collection for October is computed as follows:

$$(24 + 22 + 26 + 25)/4 = 97/4 = 24.25, \text{ or } \$24,250$$

MULTICOLLINEARITY

This is the condition that exists when the independent variables are highly correlated with each other. In the presence of multicollinearity, the estimated regression coefficients may be unreliable. The presence of multicollinearity can be tested by investigating the correlation between the independent variables. One way to correct for multicollinearity is to keep one variable and drop the rest of the variables that are highly correlated. *See also* Regression Analysis.

MULTIPLE DISCRIMINANT ANALYSIS (MDA)

MDA is a statistical classificatory technique, similar to *regression analysis*, that has a wide number of applications in financial analysis. In general, MDA uses any quantifiable factor to help classify populations. For example, in the case of consumer credit, loan applicants may be divided into those with a high probability of becoming default and those unlikely to default, based on such factors as annual income, job security, and the like. This is referred to as *a credit scoring system*. Lenders, mortgage companies, credit card service companies, and retailers use MDA to make a credit-granting decision. MDA is used to classify firms into two groups; those with a high chance of experiencing failure and those that are unlikely to go bankrupt, based on each firm's characteristics as measured by its financial ratios. Altman's Z score model (bankruptcy prediction model) is a classic use of MDA. MDA is also used to develop a bond-rating scheme.

MDA involves the following three steps:
1. Estimate the discriminant function.
2. Select the cutoff point for the discriminant function.
3. Investigate the predictive capability of the model on the validation sample.

There are two MDA methods: *linear* discriminant analysis and *quadratic* discriminant analysis. *See also* Bond Ratings; Regression Analysis; Z Scores; Forecasting Business Failures.

MULTIPLE REGRESSION   This attempts to estimate statistically the average relationship between the dependent variable (e.g., sales) and two or more independent variables (e.g., price, advertising, income, and so on). It takes the following form:

$$y = b_0 + b_1x_1 + b_2x_2 \ldots b_kx_k + u$$

where y = dependent variable,
     x's = independent (explanatory) variables,
     b's = regression coefficients,
     u = error term.
See also Regression Analysis.

MULTIPLIERS   These generally refer to the fact that changes in an economic variable can bring about magnified changes in another performance-related economic variable. There are various multipliers in economics, depending on what we try to measure. They are

1. *Expenditure (simple or investment) multiplier*—refers to the fact that any change in spending—whether by households, businesses, or government and whether for consumption or for investment—can have a mag-

nified effect on income. The expenditure multiplier is calculated as:

$$\text{Multiplier} = 1/ (1 - \text{MPC}) = 1/\text{MPS}$$

where MPC = the marginal propensity to consume and MPS = the marginal propensity to save.

■ **Example**

Assume that MPC = 4/5 and hence MPS = 1/5. Then the multiplier is 5. An increase in business investment (or government spending) of $5 billion will bring about an increase in income of $25 billion, as shown following.

Change in income (or GNP)
    = Multiplier × Change in Spending
    $25 billion = 5 × $5 billion

2. *Tax multiplier*—shows the relationship between a change in income taxes and the change in GNP. It is computed as:

$$\text{MPC} \times (1/\text{MPS})$$

■ **Example**

Assume that MPC = 4/5 and MPS = 1/5. Then the tax multiplier is 4. A $1 increase in taxes will reduce GNP by $4.

3. *Balanced-budget multiplier*—under this principle, if government spending and taxes are changed simultaneously by equal amounts, income (or GNP) will be changed by the same amount.

■ **Example**

An equal increase (decrease) in government spending and taxes of $10 billion will raise (lower) GNP by 1 × $10 billion = $10 billion.

4. *Foreign-trade multiplier*—a principle that states that fluctuations in net exports (exports − imports) can generate magnified changes in GNP. It is calculated as:

$$1/(\text{MPS} + \text{MPM})$$

where MPM = the fraction of any increase in income that "leaks" into imports.

▪ Example

Assume MPS = 0.2 and MPM = 0.05. The foreign-trade multiplier is $1/(0.2 + 0.05) = 1/0.25 = 4$.

5. *Deposit multiplier*—tries to determine the maximum multiple by which the banking system's deposits can expand as a result of an initial increase in excess reserve. It is the reciprocal of the required-reserve ratio $(1/r)$.

▪ Example

If $r = 10\%$, or $1/10$, the deposit multiplier is 10. For example, excess reserves of, say, $5,000 can generate a new increase in newly created money of as much as $50,000 (10 × $5,000).

6. *Money multiplier*—implies that the money supply, such as $M1$, is some multiple, m, of the monetary base, B. That is $M1 = mB$, where m = the money multiplier (m can be derived from regularly published data from $M1$ and B).

▪ Example

If in a given year $M1 = \$850$ billion and $B = \$400$ billion, then $m = 2.25$. Over the long run, m has ranged between 2 and 3 in value.

MULTISTAGE SAMPLING This consists of sampling at multilevels where an estimate of the total dollars of the population that is in groups over a wide area is required. For example, if an estimate of the total dollar value of inventory of a chain store with widely distributed outlets is required, the multistage technique would be appropriate. Selections at any level may be accomplished using alternative sampling methods (e.g., random, stratified, systematic).

Multistage sampling will necessitate a larger sample size and more sophisticated evaluation formulas than is the case with simple or stratified sampling methods. *See also* Sampling.

MUTUAL FUNDS These are popular investment vehicles that represent ownership in a professionally managed portfolio of securities. Major advantages of investing in mutual funds are

1. *Diversification*—each share of a fund gives an investor an interest in a cross section of stocks, bonds, or other investments.
2. *Small minimum investment*—an investor with a small amount of money (as little as $50) can achieve diversification through the large number of securities in the portfolio. A handful of funds have no minimums.
3. *Automatic reinvestment*—most funds allow investors to automatically reinvest dividends and any capital gains that may arise from the fund's buying and selling activities. Funds typically do not charge a sales fee on automatic reinvestments.
4. *Automatic withdrawals*—most funds will allow shareholders to withdraw money on a regular basis.
5. *Liquidity*—an investor is allowed to redeem the shares owned.
6. *Switching*—an investor may want to make changes in his investments. His long-term goals may remain the same, but the investment climate does not. To facilitate switching among funds, such companies as Fidelity and Vanguard have introduced ''families'' of funds. The investor may move among them with relative freedom, usually at no fee.

Net Asset Value (NAV)

The value of a mutual fund share is measured by net asset value (NAV), which equals

$$\frac{\text{Fund's total assets} - \text{Liabilities}}{\text{Number of shares outstanding in the fund}}$$

▪ Example

For simplicity, assume that a fund owns 100 shares each of GM, Xerox, and IBM. Assume also that on a particular day, the following market values existed. Then NAV of the fund is calculated as follows (assume the fund has no liabilities):

(a) GM—$90 per share × 100 shares = $ 9,000
(b) Xerox—$100 per share × 100 shares = 10,000
(c) IBM—$160 per share × 100 shares = 16,000
(d) Value of the fund's portfolio $35,000
(e) Number of shares outstanding in the fund 1,000
(f) Net asset value (NAV) per share
    = (d)/(e) $ 35

If an investor owns 5% of the fund's outstanding shares, or 50 shares (5% × 1,000 shares), then the value of the investment is $1,750 ($35 × 50).

It is important to note at this point that there are three ways to make money in mutual funds. NAV is only one of the three. NAV only indicates the current market value of the underlying portfolio. An investor also receives capital gains and dividends. Therefore, the performance of a mutual fund must be judged on the basis of these three, which will be discussed later.

Types of Mutual Funds

Mutual funds may be classified into different types, according to organization, the fees charged, methods of trading funds, and their investment objectives. In *open-end* funds, investors buy from and sell their shares back to the fund itself. On the other hand, *closed-end* funds operate with a fixed number of shares outstanding, which trade among individuals in secondary markets like common stocks. All open- and closed-end funds charge management fees. A major point of closed-end funds is the size of discount or premium, which is the difference between their market prices and their net asset values (NAVs). Many funds of this type sell at discounts, which enhances their investment appeal. Funds that charge sales commissions are called *load* funds. *No-load funds* do not charge sales commissions.

Load funds perform no better than no-loads. Many experts believe investors should buy only no-load or low-load funds. They should have no trouble finding such funds that meet their investment requirements. The prospectus contains such information as the fund's investment objective, method of selecting securities, performance figures, sales charges, and other expenses.

Depending on their investment philosophies, mutual funds generally fall into ten major categories:

1. *Money market funds*—mutual funds that invest exclusively in debt securities maturing within 1 year, such as government securities, commercial paper, and certificates of deposit. These funds provide a safety valve for many investors because the price never changes. They are known as dollar funds, which means investors always buy and sell shares at $1.00 each.

2. *Aggressive growth funds*—go for big future capital gains instead of current dividend income. They invest in the stocks of upstart and high-tech-oriented companies. Return can be great but so can risk. These funds are suited for investors who are not particularly concerned with short-term fluctuations in return but with long-term gains. Aggressive growth funds are also called *maximum capital gain, capital appreciation,* and *small company growth funds.*

3. *Growth funds*—seek long-term gains by investing in the stocks of established companies that are expected to rise in value faster than inflation. These stocks are best for investors who wish steady growth over a long-term period but feel little need for income in the meantime.

4. *Income funds*—best suited for investors who seek a high level of dividend income. Income funds usually invest in high-quality bonds and stocks with consistently high dividends.

5. *Growth and income funds*—seek both current dividend income and capital gains. The goal of these funds is to provide long-term

growth without much variation in share value.

6. *Balanced funds*—combine investments in common stock and bonds and often preferred stock, and attempt to provide income and some capital appreciation. Balanced funds tend to underperform all-stock funds in strong bull markets.

7. *Bond and preferred stock funds*—invest in both bonds and preferred stock, with the emphasis on income rather than growth. The funds that invest exclusively in bonds are called *bond funds*. There are two types of bond funds: bond funds that invest in corporate bonds and *municipal bond funds* that provide tax-free income and a diversified portfolio of municipal securities. In periods of volatile interest rates, bond funds are subject to price fluctuations. The value of the shares will fall when interest rates rise.

8. *Index funds*—invest in a portfolio of corporate stocks, the composition of which is determined by the Standard & Poor's 500 or some other market index.

9. *Sector funds*—funds that invest in one or two fields or industries. These funds are risky in that they rise and fall depending on how the individual fields or industries do. They are also called *specialized funds*.

10. *International funds*—invest in the stocks and bonds of corporations traded on foreign exchanges. These funds make significant gains when the dollar is falling and foreign stock prices are rising.

How to Read Mutual Fund Quotations

The following are quotations of mutual funds shown in a newspaper.

Funds	NAV	Offer Price	NAV Chg.
Acorn Fund	30.95	N.L.	+0.38
.....	....	......	...
American Growth	8.52	9.31	+0.05

In a *load fund*, the price you pay for a share is called the *offer price*, and it is higher than net asset value (NAV), the difference being

the commission. American Growth is a load fund. As shown, American Growth has a load of $0.79 ($9.31 − $8.52), or 8.49% ($0.79/$9.31). Acorn Fund is a *no-load* fund, as "N.L." indicates. In a no-load fund, the price you pay is NAV.

In the case of a *closed-end* fund, the following is a typical listing shown in a newspaper.

Funds	NAV	Strike Price	% Diff
Claremont	35.92	29⅜	−18.2
......	....	....	...
Nautilus	34.41	34½	+0.2

In the "% Diff" column, negative difference means the shares sell at a discount; positive difference means they sell at a premium.

Performance of Mutual Funds

Generally, mutual funds provide returns to investors in the form of (1) change in share value (or net asset value); (2) dividend income; and (3) capital gain distribution. The return for mutual funds is calculated as follows:

$$\frac{\begin{array}{c}(\text{Dividends} + \text{Capital gain distributions}) \\ + (\text{Ending NAV} - \text{Beginning NAV})\end{array}}{\text{Beginning NAV}}$$

▪ Example

Assume XYZ mutual fund paid dividends of $0.50 and capital gain distributions of $0.25 per share over the course of the year and had a price (NAV) at the beginning of the year of $8.50 that rose to $9.50 per share by the end of the year. The return is

$$\frac{(\$0.50 + \$0.25) + (\$9.50 - \$8.50)}{\$8.50} = \frac{\$1.75}{\$8.50} = 20.59\%$$

In assessing fund performance, investors must also resort to the published *beta* of the funds being considered in order to determine the amount of risk involved. Beta is a measure of risk. It is based on the price swings of a fund compared with the market as a whole, measured by the Standard & Poor's 500 Stock

Index. The higher the beta, the greater the risk.

Beta	What It Means
1.0	A fund moves up and down just as much as the market.
>1.0	The fund tends to climb higher in bull markets and dip lower in bear markets than the S&P index.
<1.0	The fund is less volatile (risky) than the market.

Betas for individual funds are widely available in many investment newsletters and directories. An example is *Value Line Investment Survey*.

Mutual Fund Ratings

Investors can get help in selecting mutual funds from a number of sources, including investment advisory services that charge fees. More readily available sources, however, include *Money*, *Forbes*, *Barron's*, and *Personal Finance*. *Money* has a "Fund Watch" column appearing in each monthly issue. In addition, it ranks about 450 funds twice a year in terms of fund performance and risk. *Forbes* has an annual report covering each fund's performance in both up and down markets. *Value Line Investment Survey* shows the makeup of the fund's portfolio *beta* values. Information about no-load funds is contained in *The Individual Investor's Guide to No Load Mutual Funds* (American Association of Individual Investors, 612 N. Michigan Ave., Chicago, IL 60611).

In summary, investors should not choose a fund only on the basis of its performance rating. They should consider *both performance and risk (beta)*.

How to Choose a Mutual Fund

What mutual fund to choose is not an easy question and there is no sure answer. It will be advisable to take the following steps:
1. Develop a list of funds that appear to meet investment goals.

2. Obtain a prospectus. The prospectus contains the fund's investment objectives. Read the statement of objectives as well as risk factors and investment limitations. Also request the Statement of Additional Information, which includes the details of fees and lists the investments; a copy of the annual report; and the most recent quarterly report.
3. Make sure the fund's investment objectives and investment policies meet investment goals.
4. Analyze the fund's past performance in view of its set objectives, in both *good* markets and *bad* markets. The quarterly and annual statements issued by the fund will show results for the previous year and probably a comparison with the S&P 500. Look at historical performance over a 5- or 10-year period. Look for *beta* figures in investment newsletters and directories. Also, read the prospectus summary section for per-share and capital changes. *Money*, *Forbes*, and other investment periodicals publish semiannual or annual performance data on mutual funds.
5. From the prospectus, try to determine some clues to management's ability to accomplish the fund's investment objectives. Emphasize the record, experience, and capability of the management company.
6. Note what securities comprise the fund's portfolio to see how they look to you. Not all mutual funds are fully diversified. Not all mutual funds invest in high-quality companies.
7. Compare various fees (such as redemption, management, and sales charges, if any) and various shareholder services offered by the funds being considered (such as the right of accumulation, any switch privilege within fund families, available investment plans, and a systematic withdrawal plan).
See also Beta Coefficient.

MUTUALLY EXCLUSIVE INVESTMENTS A project is said to be mutually exclusive if the acceptance of one project automatically

excludes the acceptance of one or more other projects. In the case where one must choose between mutually exclusive investments, the NPV and IRR methods may result in contradictory indications. The conditions under which contradictory rankings can occur are
1. Projects that have different life expectancies.
2. Projects that have different sizes of investment.
3. Projects whose cash flows differ over time. For example, the cash flows of one project increase over time, while those of another decrease.

The contradictions result from different assumptions with respect to the reinvestment rate on cash flows from the projects.
1. The NPV method discounts all cash flows at the cost of capital, thus implicitly assuming that these cash flows can be reinvested at this rate.
2. The IRR method implies a reinvestment rate at IRR. Thus, the implied reinvestment rate will differ from project to project.

The NPV method generally gives correct ranking, since the cost of capital is a more realistic reinvestment rate.

■ Example

Assume the following:

			Cash Flows			
	0	1	2	3	4	5
A	(100)	120	–	–	–	–
B	(100)	–	–	–	–	201.14

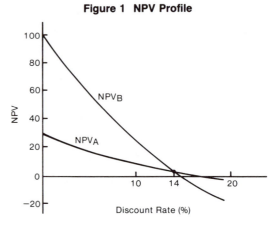

Figure 1 NPV Profile

Computing IRR and NPV at 10% gives the following different rankings:

	IRR	NPV at 10%
A	20%	9.01
B	15%	24.90

The NPVs plotted against the appropriate discount rates form a graph called an NPV profile (Figure 1).

At a discount rate larger than 14%, A has a higher NPV than B. Therefore, A should be selected. At a discount rate less than 14%, B has the higher NPV than A and thus should be selected. The correct decision is to select the project with the higher NPV, since the NPV method assumes a more realistic reinvestment rate, that is, the cost of capital.

NATIONAL INCOME ACCOUNTING This is the accounting system for macroeconomics. It is a necessary step in learning how macroeconomic variables—such as the economy's total output, the price level, the level of employment, interest rates, and others—are determined. The national income accounts give us regular estimates of gross national product (GNP), the basic measure of the performance of the economy in producing goods and services. They are also useful because they provide us with a conceptual framework for describing the relationships among three key macroeconomic variables: output, income, and spending.

NEGATIVE ASSURANCE This is when the CPA indicates to financial statement users (usually underwriters and bankers) that nothing came to his or her attention that has a detrimental effect upon the financial statements and related data. Negative assurance is typically requested by investment bankers in connection with an equity or debt issuance. It may also be expressed if the CPA is requested to comment on financial statements that were audited in a prior year and for which an audit opinion was given. Negative assurance cannot be given if a certifying audit in con-

formity with GAAS has been made. It may also not be given unless an examination has been made in accordance with GAAP for the prior year. An expression of negative assurance gives confidence to the user that nothing was found by the auditor to give the opinion that the financial statements do not fairly present financial position in conformity with GAAP consistently applied.

■ Example

If a company wants to issue securities to the public, it has to file a registration statement with the SEC that typically includes unaudited financial statements besides the audited statements. Usually, the underwriters will ask the independent CPA to furnish a *comfort letter* covering the accountant's independence, compliance of the format of audited financial statements with SEC requirements, unaudited financial statements, material subsequent events after the date of the financial statements, and other financial data. The CPA will state in giving negative assurance that nothing was found in the course of applying procedures that would make him or her believe that the statements are in violation of accounting requirements.

NEGLIGENCE   This refers to the auditor's failure to exercise due care in the performance of the attest function. *Ordinary negligence*, which is unintentional, occurs from judgmental mistakes due to such factors as inexperience, inadequate training, or poor supervision. *Gross negligence* arises from reckless disregard for promulgated accounting, reporting, and auditing standards. Legal liability exists to a greater degree for gross negligence.

NEGOTIATED PRICE   The negotiated price is the *transfer* price that is established through meetings between the buying and supplying divisions. Negotiated transfer prices, like *market price*-based transfer prices, are believed to preserve divisional autonomy. In case divisions cannot agree on a transfer price, some companies establish arbitrary procedures to help settle disputes between divisions. However, an intervention by an arbitrator reduces divisional autonomy. *See also* Transfer Pricing.

NET PRESENT VALUE METHOD (NPV)   This is a method widely used for evaluating investment projects. Under the NPV method, the present value (PV) of all cash inflows from the project is compared against the initial investment (I). The net present value (NPV), which is the difference between the present value and the initial investment (i.e., NPV = PV − I), determines whether or not the project is an acceptable investment. Under the method, if the net present value is positive (NPV > 0 or PV > I), the project should be accepted. *See also* Capital Budgeting.

NONMONETARY EXCHANGE OF ASSETS   Nonmonetary transactions covered under APB Opinion 29 primarily deal with exchanges or distributions of fixed assets.

In an exchange of similar assets (e.g., truck for truck), the new asset received is recorded at the book value of the old asset plus the cash paid. Since book value of the old asset is the basis to charge the new asset, no gain is possible. However, a loss is possible because in no case can the new asset exceed the fair market value of the new asset.

In an exchange of dissimilar assets (e.g., truck for machine), the new asset is recorded at the fair market value of the old asset plus the cash paid. Thus, a gain or loss may arise because the fair market value of the old asset will be different from the book value of the old asset. However, the new asset cannot be shown at more than its fair market value. Fair market value in a nonmonetary exchange may be based upon

- Quoted market price
- Appraisal
- Cash transaction for similar items

■ **Example**

An old fixed asset costing $10,000 with accumulated depreciation of $2,000 is traded in for a new fixed asset having a fair market value of $22,000. Cash paid on the exchange is $4,000. The fair market value of the old asset is $5,000.

If a similar exchange is involved, the entry is

Fixed Asset ($8,000 + $4,000)	12,000	
Accumulated Depreciation	2,000	
Fixed Asset		10,000
Cash		4,000

Assume instead that the fair market value of the new asset was $11,000, resulting in the exception where the new fixed asset must be recorded at $11,000. Note the new fixed asset cannot be shown at more than its fair market value. In this case, the entry is

Fixed Asset	11,000	
Accumulated Depreciation	2,000	
Loss	1,000	
Fixed Asset		10,000
Cash		4,000

Assume the original facts except that a dissimilar exchange is involved. The entry is

Fixed Asset ($5,000 + $4,000)	9,000	
Accumulated Depreciation	2,000	
Fixed Asset		10,000
Gain		1,000

In a nonmonetary exchange, the entity receiving the monetary payment (boot) recognizes a gain to the degree the monetary receipt is greater than the proportionate share of the book value of the asset given up.

$$\text{Gain} = \frac{\text{Monetary}}{\text{receipt}} - \left(\frac{\text{Monetary receipt}}{\begin{array}{c}\text{Fair market value of}\\\text{total consideration}\\\text{received}\end{array}} \right)$$

$$\times \left(\begin{array}{c}\text{Book value of asset}\\\text{given up}\end{array} \right)$$

The company receiving the boot records the asset acquired at the carrying value of the asset surrendered minus the portion considered sold.

The company paying the boot records the asset purchased at the carrying value of the asset surrendered plus the boot paid.

NONROUTINE DECISIONS These are usually short-term, nonrecurring types of decisions such as the following:
1. Acceptance or rejection of a special order
2. Make or buy a certain subassembly
3. Sell or process further
4. Keep or drop a certain business segment
In these types of decisions, a choice is typically made considering *relevant costs* and *contribution margin. See also* Contribution Margin (CM); Relevant Costing.

NONSTATISTICAL SAMPLING Nonstatistical sampling occurs when an auditor uses his prior experience and knowledge with a particular client and industry to compute the number of sampling units and specific items to be studied from the population. The sample takes into account the nature of the business and unique characteristics that may exist. The CPA must be objective in carrying out the sample and perform detailed analysis to assure the sampled units are correct. This approach may be advisable when a particular area of the population is being carefully examined or immediate results and feedback are needed. *Note*: A nonstatistical sample does *not* involve random selection. There is no computation made of sampling error, precision, or confidence level. Thus, there is an absence of statistical techniques and conclusions.

The auditor in using nonstatistical sampling considers the same factors in determining sample size and in evaluating sample results as in statistical sampling. The difference is that in nonstatistical sampling, the auditor does not quantify or explicitly enumerate values for these factors. In statistical sampling, however, they are explicitly quantified. That is, in nonstatistical sampling, the auditor determines the sample size, selects a sample, and evaluates the sample results entirely on the basis of subjective criteria and his own experience, that is, judgment. In addition, it is important to note that a properly designed nonstatistical sample may be just as effective as a statistical sample. *See also* Sampling.

NORMAL DISTRIBUTION This is the most popular probability distribution that is used for statistical decision making in business. It has the following important characteristics:
1. The curve has a single peak.
2. It is bell-shaped.
3. The mean (average) lies at the center of the distribution and the distribution is symmetrical around the mean.
4. The two tails of the distribution extend indefinitely and never touch the horizontal axis.
5. The shape of the distribution is determined by its *mean* (μ) and *standard deviation* (σ).

Normal distribution is pictured in Figure 1. Since it is a symmetric distribution, it has the nice property that a known percentage

Figure 1   Normal Distribution

$$z = \frac{(\chi = \mu)}{\sigma}$$

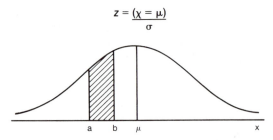

Figure 3   Standard Normal Variate

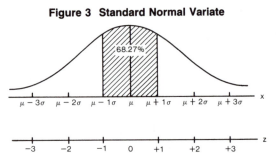

of all possible values of x lie within $\pm$ a certain number of standard deviations of the mean, as illustrated by Figure 2. For example, 68.27% of the values of any normally distributed variable lie within the interval $(\mu - 1\sigma, \mu + 1\sigma)$.

Figure 2   Area Under the Curve

%	99.73%	99%	95.45%	95%	90%	68.27%
No. of $\pm\sigma$'s	3.00	2.58	2.00	1.96	1.645	1.00

The probability of the normal distribution, as just given, is difficult to work with in determining areas under the curve, and each set of x values generates another curve (as long as the means and standard deviations are different). To facilitate computations, every set of x values is translated to a new axis, a z axis, with the translation defined as

$$z = \frac{x - \mu}{\sigma}$$

The resulting values, called z-values, are the values of a new variable called the *standard normal variate*, z. The translation process is depicted in Figure 3.

The new variable z is normally distributed with a mean of zero and a standard deviation of 1. Tables of areas (See Table 5 in the Appendix) under this standard normal distribution have been compiled and widely published so that areas under any normal distribution can be found by translating the x values

to z values and then using the tables for the standardized normal.

▪ Example

Assume the total book value of an inventory is normally distributed with $\mu = \$5,000$ and $\sigma = \$1,000$. What percentage of the population lies between $3,000 and $7,000? To answer, we first translate these two x-values to z-values using the z formula:

$$z_1 = (\$3,000 - \$5,000)/\$1,000 = -2$$
$$z_2 = (\$7,000 - \$5,000)/\$1,000 = +2$$

Referring to Figure 2, we see that 95.45% of the population lies between these two values. This means that total book value will lie between $3,000 and $7,000 with 95.45% chance.

Applications of a normal distribution in accounting and finance are numerous, including

1. Capital budgeting under risk
2. Probability of meeting a delivery date
3. Determination of safety stock

NOT-FOR-PROFIT ACCOUNTING, OTHER THAN GOVERNMENTAL   This applies to universities, voluntary hospitals, and voluntary health and welfare organizations. The *accrual basis* of accounting is required. There exists segregation of activities by fund. A fund is an accounting entity established with the objective of accounting for resources considered to meet specified activities in conformity with legal restrictions and regulations. Funds may be restricted or unrestricted. Restricted funds are limited in activity by outside parties (e.g., agencies). Unrestricted funds are not limited through external restrictions or terms of activity. Fund balance is the residual of assets over liabilities. Budgetary accounting and encumbrance accounting are *not* followed. Fixed assets are reported in the balance sheet and depreciated. Investments may be valued at lower of cost or market, or just market value. Pledges are reflected as receivables and income when they are received. Donations of service, materials, and facilities are recorded at their fair market value. There is a functional reporting of expenses, meaning that expenses are accumulated by pro-

gram purpose instead of by object of expenditure.

The not-for-profit institutions present a balance sheet with a distinction between restricted and unrestricted resources by type of fund. The activity statement shows the results of support, revenue, expenses, and expenditures. The activity statement is referred to differently depending upon the type of organization. For instance, it is termed "statement of current funds revenue and expenditures" by colleges and universities. The statement of changes in fund balance is prepared by all entities, either by itself or as a part of the activity statement. *See also* Governmental Accounting.

O

OBSERVATION TEST An observation test is performed by the auditor who *visually* evaluates operations occurring at the client. A substantive test would be observing the quantity and quality of inventory. A compliance procedure would be to see if the person who has physical custody over inventory records is someone different from the one who has responsibility for physical custody.

ODD LOT An odd-lot transaction is one involving less than 100 shares of a stock. *See also* Stock Orders.

ODD-LOT THEORY In odd-lot trading, the investment analyst can see popular opinion. According to the theory, the rule of contrary opinion holds that whatever small investors are doing, the opposite is the correct choice. *See also* Technical Analysis.

OFF-BALANCE SHEET ASSET An unrecorded asset is a financial resource of the company for which future benefit may be received. Although it is not listed on the balance sheet as an asset, it represents a favorable attribute of financial position. For analytical purposes, the credit or investment analyst may consider it as an asset in evaluating a company. Exam-

ples are a tax loss carryforward benefit, purchase commitment where the price to be paid for the contract is currently less than its market value, value of human resources, worth of a mailing list, expected rebate, a contingent asset in which payment will be received in the event a certain occurrence takes place, and a long-term lease at low rental payments. *See also* Off-Balance Sheet Liability.

OFF-BALANCE SHEET LIABILITY An unrecorded obligation is not shown on the balance sheet as a liability, but it may require later payment or the rendering of services. For analytical purposes, the analyst may consider it as a liability of the entity. Examples are many, including a lawsuit, tax dispute, co-signing of a loan for a problem borrower, dispute under a government contract, long-term lease at a higher rental in an undesirable location (e.g., warehouse located in a high crime area), projected benefit obligation exceeds the accumulated benefit obligation in a pension plan, and unrecognized health insurance benefits to be paid in the future for retired employees. *See also* Off-Balance Sheet Asset.

OKUN'S LAW This describes the relationship between changes in the rate of economic growth (measured by changes in GNP) and changes in the unemployment rate. This law is attributed to Arthur Okun, chairman of the Council of Economic Advisors under President Johnson. The law states that for every 2½ percentage points of growth in real GNP above the trend rate that is sustained for a year, the unemployment rate declines by 1 percentage point.

It means that the economy must continue to grow considerably faster than its trend (long-term average) rate in order to achieve a substantial reduction in the unemployment rate.

■ Example

Suppose that the trend rate of growth is 3% per year and the unemployment rate is currently 9%. How many years would it take to return to a target rate of, say, 6% unemployment? The answer depends on how fast the economy grows in the recovery. Assume that the growth rate of potential output is 3% per year. One possible path to achieve the target is for output to grow at 5½% per year for 3 years. On this path, each year the economy is growing 2½% above trend, and thus each year it takes 1 percentage point off the unemployment rate.

ON-LINE DATA BASES An accountant or financial manager must know the existing data bases and what they contain to obtain relevant accounting, audit, tax, financial, and legal information. A listing of data bases is provided in the *Directory of On-Line Data Bases* and *Data Pro Directory of On-Line Services*. Also, reference can be made to Mike Cane's books on on-line services (e.g., *The Computer Phone Book*: *Directory of On-Line Systems* published by New American Library).

Before using a new data base, you should ask the following questions:

• Is a data base demonstration available?

• Will the data base meet your information needs?

• Is the data base updated on a regular basis and at what cost?

• Is the data base easy to use?

• Is there an index of terms to facilitate data base use?

• Does the data base provide numeric codes for industries or geographic locations?

When using an on-line data base, there may be several ways to search in order to obtain an answer to a question, including by key word or phrase, code section, citation or case name, and document type.

In using an accounting data base, a search may be made by key word or phrase, Financial Accounting Standards Board Number, Statement on Auditing Standards Number, and Securities and Exchange Commission Release Number.

When accessing a legal data base for a legislative item or document, the search may be made by bill number, public law number, tax act, or originating committee.

After the search is completed and the information found, the result may be output in various ways, such as (1) sorting the documents in order (e.g., chronologically), ranking documents by relevance, displaying the documents, listing the items, and printing the output.

Dialog Information Services' Dialoglink Communications Manager™ is communications software that saves the tax practitioner money by reducing the connect time when accessing on-line data bases. It facilitates the data base search for tax-related items.

Available data bases for accounting and tax needs are cited in *Computers in Accounting* and the *The CPA Journal*.

Easy Net™ allows the accountant and tax practitioner without special software to use an 800 telephone number to access 600 data bases. For information, call (800) 841-9553. Compuserve Information Service™ allows the attorney and accountant to access up to

700 domestic and international data bases through the Iquest on-line search and retrieve.

Lockheed's Dialog™ contains over 150 different data bases covering areas of interest to accountants and attorneys as Securities and Exchange Commission filings. The American Institute of CPA's time-sharing library has accounting and tax information, including Internal Revenue Service codes and regulations, proposed regulations, and Supreme Court decisions.

On-line data bases of interest to accountants and tax practitioners are

• *Prentice Hall's Information Network (PHINet)*—contains tax information included in Prentice Hall's looseleaf tax services. Included in the data base are Prentice Hall's daily tax update, articles written by tax experts, tax court case rulings, editorial explanations of tax requirements, annotations, announcements, Internal Revenue Code sections, tax regulations, new legislation, committee reports, revenue rulings and procedures, news releases, and private letter rulings. Covered in the data base are federal income tax, estate tax, gift tax, and excise tax questions. There is a pension and profit sharing service as well. The data base also contains selected Internal Revenue Service numbered publications that interpret code sections, regulations, and court decisions. Documents related to tax shelters are also provided.

• *American Institute of CPAs' NAARS*—contains recommended accounting practices and footnote references, answers practice questions, and furnishes proper accounting for a transaction or event. NAARS has about 4,200 companies in each annual report file.

• *West's Westlaw*—contains legal cases and information for attorneys. It comes in handy for the tax attorney who wants to search for legal precedents relating to a tax case.

• *Mead Data Central's Legal Exchange Information Service (Lexis)*—covers diverse areas of law such as tax and bankruptcy.

• *Legal Source*—contains federal and state court procedures along with a full text data base manager for lawyers.

• *Mead Data Central's News Exchange Information Service (Nexis)*—covers authoritative pronouncements, preferred practice, and industry information. Data are presented regarding different types of business situations, including litigation, acquisitions, and bankruptcy.

• *Source Telecomputing's The Source*—provides answers to tax questions and the option of reading IRS publications.

• *Business/Professional Software Data Base*—describes software packages for accounting functions, including inventory control.

• *Western Union's InfoMaster*—includes corporate descriptions, legal references, and financial statements and analysis.

• *Predicasts*—contains acquisition/merger information.

• *American Institute of CPAs' Accountant's Index*— lists accounting and tax articles and books.

See also Electronic Mail.

OPERATING LEASE   This is a lease accounted for by the lessee or lessor as a regular rental of property. The lessee charges rental expense while the lessor credits rental revenue. *See also* Leases.

OPERATING LEVERAGE   This is a measure of *operating risk* and arises from fixed operating costs. A simple indication of operating leverage is the effect that a change in sales has an operating income. The formula is

$$\text{Operating leverage at a given level of sales} = \frac{\text{Percentage change in EBIT (or operating income)}}{\text{Percentage change in sales}}$$

Another measure of operating leverage (risk) is the ratio of fixed costs to total costs. High fixed costs in a company's cost structure is indicative of risk because fixed costs cannot be slashed in the short run to meet declining demand for the product or service. *See also* Leverage.

OPERATIONAL AUDIT   An operational audit is conducted on a recurring basis by internal auditors of the business entity. A review is made of the efficiency and appropriateness of the company's operations and organization in meeting goals. Additionally, irregularities and errors are searched out. Management's performance and ability to conform to stated procedures and budgets are examined. Areas evaluated include policies, processes, structure, and controls. The subject of an operational audit may be a business segment (e.g., division, product line) and specific task (activity). Management is the major user of the operational audit results. The typical operational audit report specifies the success in which functions are being carried out, deficiencies in the process, recommendations for improvement, and overall conclusions. *See also* Internal Audit.

OPERATIONS RESEARCH/MANAGEMENT SCIENCE   Operations research (OR), which is very often used interchangeably with management science, is a scientific method of providing the decision maker with a quantitative basis for decisions regarding the operations under his or her control. It is divided broadly into two categories of techniques (models): optimization models (mathematical programming) and simulation models. *Optimization models* attempt to provide an optimal solution (or prescriptive solution) to a problem, whereas *simulation models* produce a descriptive (or what-if type of) solution. Operations research, for example, covers such quantitative techniques as inventory models, linear programming, queuing theory, program evaluation and review technique (PERT), and Monte Carlo simulation. *See also* Mathematical Programming; Optimization Models.

OPPORTUNITY COST APPROACH   This is where the concept of *opportunity cost* is applied to solve a decision problem. Opportunity cost represents the net benefit lost by rejecting some alternative course of action. Its significance in decision making is that the best decision is always sought, since it considers the cost of the best available alternative *not* taken. The opportunity cost does not appear on formal accounting statements.

■ **Example**

If $1 million can be invested in a CD earning 9%, the opportunity cost of using that money for a particular business venture would be computed to be $90,000 ($1 million × 0.09). *See also* Incremental Analysis; Total Project Approach.

OPTIMAL REORDER POINT   This is the inventory level at which it is appropriate to replenish stock. Reorder point is calculated as follows:

Reorder point = Average usage per unit of lead time
        × Lead time + Safety stock

First, multiply average daily (or weekly) usage by the lead time in days (or weeks), yielding the lead time demand. Then add safety stock to this to provide for the variation in lead time demand to determine the reorder point. If aveage usage and lead time are both certain, no safety stock is necessary and should be dropped from the formula. *See also* Inventory Planning and Control.

OPTIMIZATION MODELS   These are quantitative models (such as operations research/ management science) that attempt to provide an optimal (profit-maximizing or cost-minimizing) solution to a resource allocation problem. They typically consist of two important ingredients in their formulation: (1) objective function to be maximized or minimized and (2) constraints. Optimization models include *linear programming (LP)*, *integer programming*, *quadratic programming*, and *dynamic programming*. *See also* Mathematical Programming; Simulation Models.

OPTIONS: CALLS AND PUTS Options provide the investor with the right to buy a security at a given price for a specified time period. Options have their own inherent value and are traded in secondary markets. Option prices are tied into the market price of the common stock to which they apply. High risk is involved when investing in options.

Calls and puts are types of stock options. They are bought and sold in 100-share denominations.

When a *call* is bought, the investor has the right to purchase a stock at a stated price for a given time frame. The expectation is that the company's market price of stock will increase. There is an opportunity for a substantial gain from a small investment, but significant risk exists because if the market price does not increase sufficiently, the entire investment will be lost.

When a *put* is bought, the investor has the right to sell stock at a given price for a stated time horizon. A put is bought when there is an expectation of a declining stock price. There is an opportunity for substantial gain from a small investment, but significant risk exists because the entire investment will be lost if stock price does not fall sufficiently.

Calls and puts are in bearer negotiable form with a life ranging between 1 month to 9 months. They are usually written for widely held, actively traded companies. Brokerage fees are based on the amount and value of the option contract.

Calls do *not* give the holder ownership rights in the stock and thus dividend and voting rights do not exist. But options are adjusted for stock dividends and stock splits.

The life of calls and puts is longer than for stock rights but shorter than for stock warrants. Calls and puts are speculative and provide leverage. They are an alternative to investments in common stock.

Calls and puts are not issued by the company with the common stock but rather by option writers. The option writer receives the price paid for the call or put less commission costs. Options are traded on the open market. Calls and puts are written and can be bought through brokers and dealers. The writer buys or delivers the stock when requested.

To earn a return, the holder of a call or put does not have to exercise it. The option can be sold in the secondary market for its market price. The value of a call rises as the related common stock increases. The call may be sold prior to its expiration date.

Calls and puts are traded on listed option exchanges (e.g., Chicago Board Options Exchange, American Stock Exchange, Philadelphia Stock Exchange). They are also traded on the over-the-counter market. Option exchanges deal solely with the buying and selling of calls and puts. *Listed options* are traded on organized exchanges. *Conventional options* are traded in the over-the-counter market.

The Options Clearing Corporation issues calls listed on the options exchanges. Orders are placed with this corporation, which then issues the calls or closes the position. When a call is exercised, the holder goes through the Clearing Corporation, which picks at random a writer from member accounts. A call writer must sell 100 shares of common stock at the exercise price.

The price per share for 100 shares, which the buyer may buy at, is called the *striking price* (exercise price). For a put, it is the price at which the stock may be sold. The purchase or sale of the stock is to the writer of the option. The striking price is fixed for the life of the option. When a change in stock price occurs, new strike prices may be introduced for trading to reflect new value.

In the case of conventional calls, there are *no* restrictions as to what the striking price should be. But it is typically near the market price of the stock to which it applies. For listed calls, stocks having a price below $50 per share must have striking prices in $5 increments, stocks between $50 and $100 have striking prices in $10 increments, and stocks selling at more than $100 per share have striking prices in $20 increments.

The expiration date of an option is the last day it can be exercised. In the case of conventional options, it can be any business day. A listed option has a standardized expiration date.

Premium is the term used to connote the cost of the option. It is the price the buyer of the call or put pays the option writer.

Factors Determining the Premium

- Trading volume of the option. The greater the trading volume, the greater the price.
- Direction of the stock market and the particular security itself. An upward market usually means a higher premium for a call.
- Dividend trend of the security.
- Fluctuation in stock price of the company. Wider vacillation in price means a higher premium since there is more speculative appeal to the option.
- Exchange on which the option is listed. A more reputable exchange means a higher premium for a call.
- Going interest rates.
- Change in market price of the underlying security.
- The spread between the market price of

the stock and the option's exercise price. A greater differential means a higher price.
- The period still left before expiration of the option. A longer period justifies a higher premium.

A call is *in-the-money* when market price is greater than the strike price. A call is *out-of-the-money* when market price is less than the strike price. Call options in-the-money have intrinsic value equal to:

Value of call = (Market price of stock
$$- \text{Exercise price of call}) \times 100$$

■ Example

The market price of stock is $30 and the strike price is $27. The value of the call is

$$(\$30 - \$27) \times 100 = \$300$$

There is no intrinsic value to out-of-the-money calls. Typically, the investor can earn a higher return at lower risk with out-of-the-money calls. A problem however is that the price consists only of the investment premium which is lost if the stock price does not increase.

If the total premium (option price) of an option is $8 and the intrinsic value is $5, the difference of $3 is for other factors. The amount of the premium equals the intrinsic value plus speculative premium (time value), considering such items as variability, risk, expected future prices, leverage, expiration date, and dividend.

Total premium = Intrinsic value
$$+ \text{Speculative premium}$$

The meaning of in-the-money and out-of-the-money is different for puts since they allow the owner to sell stock at the strike price. When strike price is greater than market price of stock, an in-the-money put option exists. Its value equals:

Value of put = (Exercise price of put
$$- \text{Market price of stock}) \times 100$$

■ Example

The market price of a stock is $60 and the strike price of the put is $67. The value of the put equals:

$$(\$67 - \$60) \times 100 = \$700$$

An out-of-the-money put exists when the market price of stock is greater than the strike price. Since a stock owner can sell it for a greater amount in the market than he could obtain by exercising the put, no intrinsic value exists for an out-of-the-money put.

	ABC Calls at $70 Strike Price	ABC Puts at $70 Strike Price
	Stock Price	Stock Price
In the money	over $70	under $70
At the money	$70	$70
Out of the money	under $70	over $70

The theoretical value for calls and puts indicates the price at which the options should be traded. However, they are usually traded at prices in excess of true value when a long expiration period exists. This difference is termed the investment premium.

Investment premium

$$= \frac{\text{Option premium} - \text{Option value}}{\text{Option value}}$$

■ Example

A put has a theoretical value of $2,000 and a price of $2,400. The investment premium equals:

$$\frac{\$2,400 - \$2,000}{\$2,000} = \frac{\$400}{\$2,000} = 20\%$$

Calls

The call purchaser gains if the market price of the stock increases.

■ Example

An investor buys a 3-month call option to purchase 1,000 shares of ABC Company at $15 per share. When the stock price reaches $22, the option is exercised. The gain is

$$\$7 \times 1,000 \text{ shares} = \$7,000$$

If the market price had declined below $15, the cost of the option would be lost.

The advantage of a call is that the investor owns common stock for a fraction of the cost of purchasing regular shares. Leverage exists since a little change in the price of the common stock can cause a significant change in the option price of the call.

■ Example

The market price of stock is $40. A call can be bought for $350, permitting the acquisition of 100 shares at $40 each. The market price of the stock rises to $58. The gain is $18 per share, or a total of $1,800 on an investment of $350. This translates to a 414% return after considering the cost of the option:

$$\frac{\text{Gain} - \text{Cost of option}}{\text{Cost of option}} = \frac{\$1,800 - \$350}{\$350}$$

$$= \frac{\$1,450}{\$350} = 414\%$$

In effect, when the investor exercises the call at $40, he can sell the stock at $58. *Note*: The investor could have earned the same gain of $1,800 but would have had to invest $4,000 so the rate of return would have been only 45% ($1,800/$4,000).

■ Example

A call gives an investor the right to buy 100 shares of $30 stock at $27. The call will trade at a price of about $3 a share. The call option may be used if the investor believes the stock price will increase in the future but has a cash flow problem and is unable to buy the stock. However, the investor will have adequate cash to do so later. In this case, the investor can buy a call so as not to lose a good investment opportunity. For instance, on February 6, the investor purchases a $32 June call option for $3 a share. If the stock price is $34½, the speculative premium is $½. In June, the investor exercises the call option when the stock price is $37. The cost of the 100 shares of stock for tax reporting is the strike price ($32) plus the option premium ($3), or $35.

Puts

A put holder may sell 100 shares at the strike price to a put writer prior to the expiration date.

■ Example

The market price of a stock is $45 per share. A put is bought at $45 per share. The cost of the put is $400. When the market price of the stock reaches $30, the put is exercised, realizing a profit of $15 per share, or a total of $1,500. You buy on the market 100 shares at $30 and sell them to the writer of the put for $45. The net gain equals:

$$\text{Gain} - \text{Cost of put} = \text{Net gain}$$
$$\$1,500 - \$400 = \$1,100$$

This translates into a percentage gain of 275% computed as follows:

$$\frac{\text{Gain} - \text{Cost of put}}{\text{Cost of put}} = \frac{\$1,500 - \$400}{\$400}$$
$$= \frac{\$1,100}{\$400} = 275\%$$

If the put is not exercised, a loss of $400 equal to the cost of the put is lost.

■ Example

A company's stock price was $55 on March 2. An investor buys a $56 June put for $4. The speculative premium is therefore $3. On June 7, the stock price falls to $47 and the price of the June $56 put to $8. The intrinsic value is $9 and the speculative premium is $1. As the put holder, the investor has a gain of $4.

Hedging

An owner of a call and put option may *hedge* by holding on to two or more securities to reduce risk and at the same time to earn a

profit. It may relate to buying a stock and subsequently purchasing an option on it. For instance, a stock may be acquired along with writing a call on it. Further, a holder of stock that has increased in price may buy a put in order to obtain downside risk protection.

■ Example

An investor buys 100 shares of ABC Company at $25 each and a put for $175 with a strike price of $25. If the stock remains static, a $175 loss is incurred. If the price decreases, the loss on the stock is offset by the gain on the put. If stock price rises, there is a gain on the stock and a loss on the put. In effect, to accomplish the benefit of a hedge, a loss on the put has to be incurred. *Careful*: At the expiration of the put, a loss is incurred with no further hedge.

A put may also be bought to hedge a position after earning a profit on the stock. Assume you buy 100 shares of ABC Company at $70 per share. The stock is now at $85, for a profit of $15 per share. To assure a profit, a put costing $250 is purchased with an $85 strike price. Regardless of what transpires in the future, there is a minimum gain of $1,250 ($1,500 − $250).

If the stock price drops, the minimum profit of $1,700 will be earned. If the stock price increases, an additional profit will be earned.

A call may be bought to protect a short sale from the risk of an increasing stock price. In this hedging strategy, the short seller will not incur a loss above a stated amount. But profit will be decreased by the cost of the call.

Speculation

Calls and puts may be employed as an alternative to investing in the common stock itself. While a higher return is possible from the leverage effect, speculation is involved, since all the invested funds may be lost.

■ Example

A speculator purchases an option contract to buy 100 shares at $25 a share. The option costs $150. Assume a rise in stock price to $33 a share. The speculator exercises the option and sells the shares in the market, realizing a gain of $650 ($33 − $25 − $1.50 = $6.50 × 100 shares). Now the speculator can sell the option in the market and make a profit because of its increased value. However, if there is a decline in stock price, the loss to the holder is limited to $150 (the option's cost). Of course, brokerage fees are involved. In effect, this call option permitted the speculator to purchase 100 shares worth $2,500 for $150 for a short period. *See also* Stock Right; Stock Warrant.

OPTION WRITING The writer of a call agrees to sell shares at the strike price paid for the call option. Call option writers do the opposite of what buyers do. An option is written because it is believed that a price increase in the stock will be less than what the call purchaser expects. The writer may even anticipate a static or decreasing price in the security. Option writers receive the option premium less related transaction costs. If the option is not exercised, the writer earns the price paid for it. If the option is exercised, the writer incurs a loss, which may be substantial.

If the writer of the option decides to sell shares, he has to come up with stock at the agreed-upon price if the option is exercised. In either case, the option writer receives income from the premium. The option is in 100-share denominations. The writer sells the option because he feels it will not be exercised. The risk of option writing is that the writer if uncovered has to buy the stock or if covered loses the gain.

The writer can elect to buy back the option to eliminate his exposure.

■ Example

There is a strike price of $30 and the premium for the option is $4. If the stock is at less than $30, the call will not be exercised and the writer earns the $4 premium. If the stock goes above $30, the call may be exercised and the writer will have to come up with 100 shares at $30. But the call writer only incurs a loss if the stock goes beyond $34.

Options may be naked (uncovered) or covered. In a naked option, the writer does not own the underlying stock. The investor writes the call or put for the premium and will retain it if the price change is in his favor or insignificant in amount. However, there is unlimited loss exposure to the writer. In a covered option, the writer already owns the underlying stock and thus less risk is involved. For example, a call can be written for stock the writer owns or a put can be written for stock sold short. This is a conservative strategy to obtain positive returns. The goal is to write an out-of-the-money option, keep the premium paid, and have the market price of the stock be equal but not greater than the option exercise price. Writing a covered call option is similar to hedging a position, since if stock price drops, the writer's loss on the stock is in part netted against the option premium.

OVER-THE-COUNTER MARKET The over-the-counter market is not a specific institution but instead a means of trading securities. Although it is not an auction market, it furnishes a forum where new unlisted issues are traded. Traders (dealers) utilize a telecommunications network referred to as the National Association of Security Dealers Automated Quotation System (NASDAQ) for transactions in these securities. The NASDAQ index is comprised of about 2,300 companies. The over-the-counter market trades a higher dollar volume of securities than the national and regional exchanges.

Each over-the-counter trader makes a market in specified securities by offering to buy or sell them at specified prices. Dealers are the second party to a transaction. The *bid price* is the maximum price the dealer offers for a security. The *ask price* is the lowest price at which the dealer will sell the security. The dealer's profit is the spread between the bid price and the ask price.

Advantages of Buying Stocks in the Over-the-Counter Market

• Some securities are traded only in this market.

• Some securities have potential for substantial return but possess high risk.

• Through the NASDAQ communications network, there is much marketability for stocks and a good reflection of accurate stock price.

A disadvantage of buying over-the-counter stocks is that the companies whose stocks are sold there are often lower quality firms than those listed on the organized exchanges.

P

PARALLEL PROCESSING This applies to the simultaneous performance of two or more activities in a computer. For example, one task may be running at the same time another task is being read from memory.

PARITY CHECK A parity check is a test performed by checking a unit of information (i.e., word, byte) for even or odd parity to determine if an error has occurred in reading, writing, or transferring data. For example, if information is written, the computed parity bit is compared to the parity bit already appended to that information. Correctness exists if the parity bits agree. Otherwise, a mistake has occurred.

PARTNERSHIP ACCOUNTING According to the Uniform Partnership Act, a partnership is an association of two or more individuals as co-owners carrying on a business for profit. There are separate capital and drawing accounts for each partner. When a noncash asset is invested, it should be recorded at its fair market value at the date of transfer to the partnership. An obligation assumed by the partnership is credited to the specific liability account involved. If it is a long-term liability, it is recorded at the present value of future payments.

■ Example

Enright and Geller form a partnership. Enright, who was previously the sole proprietor, brings the following into the partnership:

	Book Value	Fair Market Value
Cash	$12,000	$12,000
Accounts receivable	7,000	7,000
Inventory	20,000	18,000
Auto	7,000	
Accumulated depreciation, auto	2,000	
Accounts payable	9,000	9,000
Allowance for uncollectible accounts	600	600

The following entry is made to record Enright's initial investment:

Cash	12,000	
Accounts receivable	7,000	
Inventory	18,000	
Auto	5,500	
Allowance for uncollectible accounts		600
Accounts payable		9,000
Enright, Capital		32,900

Depreciation on the auto on the partnership books will be based on the assigned value of $5,500.

Allocating Net Income or Loss to Partners

Partnership profit or loss is allocated according to the partnership agreement. Typically, the division is based upon the proportionate capital interest of each partner.

Division Based on Capital Interest

In this approach, profit is assigned based upon the ratio of the partners' capital balances.

■ Example

Nelson and Loft have capital balances of $40,000 and $10,000, respectively. The profit is $5,000. The entry is

Income Summary	5,000	
Nelson, Capital		4,000
Loft, Capital		1,000

Division Based Equally

In the absence of a stipulation in the partnership agreement, profits are assigned equally to the partners. Assuming the same facts as the previous example, each partner would receive $2,500.

Division Partially Based on Salary

Under this approach, partners are given credit for work performed and the remaining profit is allocated on some specific basis.

■ Example

Nelson and Loft have capital balances of $40,000 and $10,000, respectively. The net income is $5,000. Nelson and Loft are given salary allowances of $2,000 and $8,000, respectively. The remaining net income is to be allocated based on their capital balances.

The computation is

	Nelson	Loft	Total
Salary	$2,000	$ 800	$2,800
Balance	1,760[a]	440[b]	2,200
Total	$3,760	$1,240	$5,000

[a] $\frac{\$40,000}{\$50,000} \times \$2,200 = \$1,760$

[b] $\frac{\$10,000}{\$50,000} \times \$2,200 = \$440$

Division Partially Based on Interest

In this case, each partner receives interest on his or her capital balance and the remaining net income is allocated on some specified basis.

■ Example

Nelson and Loft have capital balances of $40,000 and $10,000, respectively. The net income for the year is $5,000. Each partner is to receive 8% interest on his or her capital balance and the remaining earnings are to be divided equally. The computation is

	Nelson	Loft	Total
Interest on capital balance	$3,200	$ 800	$4,000
Balance	500	500	1,000
Total	$3,700	$1,300	$5,000

Division Partially Based on Salary and Interest

Each partner may get a salary, interest on the capital balance, and the remainder of the profit on some basis.

■ Example

Nelson and Loft have capital balances of $40,000 and $10,000, respectively. The net income for the year is $5,000. Nelson and Loft receive salaries of $1,000 and $600, respectively, receive 5% interest on capital, and divide the remainder of the profit equally. The computation is

	Nelson	Loft	Total
Salary	$1,000	$ 600	$1,600
Interest	2,000	500	2,500
Balance	450	450	900
Total	$3,450	$1,550	$5,000

If the net income is less than the salary and/or interest allowances for the partners, the remaining negative balance should be allocated to the partners as if it were a loss.

Admitting a New Partner

According to the Uniform Partnership Act, a partner has the option to sell all or a portion of his or her interest without the consent of the others. The person buying the selling partner's interest obtains the right to share in profits. However, unless admitted to the firm, the individual cannot vote or participate in partnership affairs.

Admission by Acquiring an Interest

A new partner who purchases an interest from an old partner pays the purchase price directly to the old partner. An entry is made on the partnership books to transfer only the capital from the old partner to the new one. All other accounts remain intact.

■ Example

Simon and Davis have capital balances of $60,000 and $40,000, respectively. Smith buys half of Simon's interest for $33,000. The entry to transfer the capital balances is

Simon, Capital	30,000	
Smith, Capital		30,000

Note that $30,000, half of Simon's capital, has been transferred to Smith. The extra $3,000 paid by Smith to Simon is not reflected in the partnership books. Instead the $3,000 is in the nature of a *personal* benefit to Simon.

Admission by Contributing Assets

If the new partner contributes assets to the firm, the entry is to debit assets and credit capital.

■ Example

Assume the same facts as the prior example except that Smith contributes $25,000 for a one-fifth interest in the new partnership. The entry is

Cash	25,000	
Smith, Capital		25,000

Smith now has a one-fifth interest ($25,000/$125,000).

In the previous two examples, we assumed that the book value of the assets of the partnership reflected their fair market value when Smith was admitted. Thus, no adjustments to the recorded values were needed. But, in many instances, partnership assets must be revalued or goodwill recognized before the admission of a new partner.

Asset revaluation—before admitting a new partner, certain assets of the partnership have to be adjusted from book value to fair market value. The net effect of this revaluation is allocated to the existing partners based on the profit-sharing ratio.

■ Example

Simon and Davis share profits equally. Prior to the admission of Smith, it is decided that equipment having a book value of $6,000 is worth $7,500. The entry for the revaluation is

Equipment	1,500	
Simon, Capital		750
Davis, Capital		750

Recording goodwill—if a partnership earns excess earnings over other similar firms, there exists goodwill. When a new partner is admitted, he or she may have to pay for that goodwill. The goodwill account is debited and the capital accounts of the old partners credited based on the profit-and-loss ratio.

■ Example

Smith and Davis have capital balances of $60,000 and $40,000, respectively. Net income is shared equally. Smith gains admission to the partnership by contributing $30,000 for a one-fifth interest. Although the total capital of the partnership before Smith's admission is $100,000, the parties agree that the firm is worth $120,000. The $20,000 excess constitutes goodwill that has to be divided equally between the old partners. The journal entry to record goodwill is

Goodwill	20,000	
Simon, Capital		10,000
Davis, Capital		10,000

The entry to admit the new partner is

Cash	30,000	
Smith, Capital		30,000

Note that Smith now has a one-fifth interest in the partnership ($30,000/$150,000).

Goodwill may be associated with the incoming partner. If the old partners agree to give the new partner recognition for his or her goodwill, the goodwill account is debited and the new partner's capital account is credited.

■ Example

Simon and Davis have capital balances of $60,000 and $40,000, respectively. Smith obtains admittance by making an investment of $40,000. Smith is granted goodwill recognition of $10,000. The entry is

Cash	40,000	
Goodwill	10,000	
Smith, Capital		50,000

Liquidating a Partnership

In liquidating a partnership, the following steps are involved: (1) the accounts are adjusted and closed; (2) assets are sold; (3)

liabilities are paid; and (4) the remaining cash is distributed to the partners based on their remaining capital balances.

■ Example

Tyler, Simpson, and White discontinue their partnership. The partnership books have been adjusted and all the accounts have been closed. The following is the post-closing trial balance:

Cash	$40,000	
Noncash assets	25,000	
Liabilities		$15,000
Tyler, capital		5,000
Simpson, capital		10,000
White, capital		35,000
	$65,000	$65,000

The partners share net income equally. Noncash assets are sold for $40,000. Appropriate journal entries follow:

(a) For the sale of assets

Cash	40,000	
Noncash Assets		25,000
Tyler, Capital		5,000
Simpson, Capital		5,000
White, Capital		5,000

(b) For the payment to creditors

Liabilities	15,000	
Cash		15,000

(c) For the cash distribution

Tyler, Capital	10,000	
Simpson, Capital	15,000	
White, Capital	40,000	
Cash		65,000

Note that the final cash distribution is based on the partners' ending capital balances.

PAYBACK PERIOD   This is the length of time required to recover the initial amount of a capital investment. If the cash inflows occur at a uniform rate, it is the ratio of the amount of initial investment over expected annual cash inflows, or

$$\text{Payback period} = \text{Initial investment/Annual cash inflows}$$

■ Example

Assume projected annual cash inflows are expected to be $4,500 a year for 5 years from an investment of $18,000. The payback period on this proposal is 4 years, which is calculated as follows:

$$\text{Payback period} = \$18,000/\$4,500 = 4 \text{ years}$$

If annual cash inflows are not even, the payback period would have to be determined by trial and error. Assume instead that the cash inflows are $4,000 in the first year, $5,000 in the second year, $6,000 in the third year, $6,000 in the fourth year, and $8,000 in the fifth year. The payback period would then be 3.5 years. In 3 years, all but $3,000 has been recovered. It takes one-half year ($3,000/$6,000) to recover the balance. When two or more projects are considered, the rule for making a selection decision is as follows: Choose the project with the shorter payback period. The rationale behind this is that the shorter the payback period, the greater the liquidity and the less risky the project. Advantages of the method include (1) it is simple to compute and easy to understand and (2) it handles investment risk effectively. Disadvantages of the method include (1) it ignores profitability of an investment and (2) it does not recognize the *time value of money*. To take into account the time value of money, the discounted payback period may be used. *See also* Discounted Payback Period.

PAYBACK RECIPROCAL

Payback reciprocal is the reciprocal of the payback time. This often gives a quick, accurate estimate of the *internal rate of return* (*IRR*) on an investment when the project life is more than twice the payback period and the cash inflows are uniform every period.

■ Example

ABC Company is contemplating three projects, each of which would require an initial investment of $10,000 and each of which is expected to generate a cash inflow of $2,000 per year. The payback period is 5 years ($10,000/$2,000), and the payback reciprocal is 1/5, or 20%. The table of the present value of an annuity of $1 (see Table 4 in the Appendix) shows that the factor of 5.00 applies to the following useful lives and internal rates of return:

Useful Life	IRR
10 years	15%
15	18
20	19

It can be observed that the payback reciprocal is 20% as compared with the IRR of 18% when the life is 15 years and 20% as compared with the IRR of 19% when the life is 20 years. This shows that the payback reciprocal gives a reasonable approximation of the IRR if the useful life of the project is at least twice the payback period.

PEER REVIEW This is an analysis conducted by one CPA firm of the quality of another CPA firm's performance in the accounting and auditing processes. At a minimum, the review takes place every 3 years. An objective is to make certain that quality controls exist in accord with AICPA Quality Control Standards. Included in the review is an appraisal of the quality of working papers and accounting procedures employed. Peer review includes consideration of (1) firm organization; (2) administrative and personnel files; (3) quality of issued reports and statements; and (4) existence of appropriate documentation for findings. Once peer review has been completed, the reviewer and reviewee discuss the findings and an evaluation report is prepared. Poor quality work by the CPA firm may necessitate additional training, fines, censures, and in an extreme case suspension.

A typical peer review would be performed in the following manner. An accounting firm is usually chosen to do the review from among the members of the Division for CPA Firms. When a firm review is to be performed, the Public Oversight Board must be appointed to meet SEC standards. The board oversees the review process. This board was enacted in response to criticisms by the SEC, which felt that it would be difficult for a CPA firm to give another firm a bad review. The audit team chosen to do the review must be independent of the firm to be reviewed. Any information obtained during the review is confidential and should not be communicated to anyone not involved with the review. The firm supplies the review team with documents of the firm's quality control policies and procedures. With these documents the review team does a study and evaluation of the firm's quality control system. They test to see whether the firm is complying with its quality control policies and procedures. The review team then communicates its conclusions to the firm. At this time the review team will often make recommendations for improvement of the firm's controls. A written report is then prepared, stating the findings of the review. If the review team finds no irregularities in the firm's quality controls, a standard unqualified report will be issued. If the firm did not comply with quality control policies and procedures, a qualified report will be issued.

PENSION PLANS A company does not have to have a pension plan. If it does, the firm must conform to FASB and governmental rules regarding the accounting and reporting for the pension plan. FASB 87 requires ac-counting for pension costs on the accrual basis. Pension expense is reflected in the service periods using a method that considers the benefit formula of the plan. On the income statement, pension expense is presented as a single amount. The pension plan relationship between the employer, trustee, and employee is diagramed below.

The two types of pension plans are

• *Defined contribution*—the annual contribution amount by the employer is specified instead of the benefits to be paid.

• *Defined benefit*—the determinable pension benefit to be received by participants upon retirement is specified. In determining amounts, consideration is given to such factors as age, salary, and service years. The employer has to provide plan contributions so that sufficient assets are accumulated to pay for the benefits when due. Typically, an annuity of payments is made. Pension expense applicable to administrative staff is expensed. Pension expense related to factory personnel is inventoriable.

The following pension plan terminology should be understood:

• *Actuarial assumptions*—actuaries make assumptions as to variables in determining pension expense and related funding. Examples of estimates are mortality rate, employee turnover, compensation levels, and rate of return.

• *Actuarial cost (funding) method*—the method used by actuaries in determining the employer contribution to assure sufficient funds will be available at employee retirement. The method used determines the pension expense and related liability.

Figure 1 Pension Plan Relationship

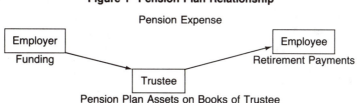

Pension Plan Assets on Books of Trustee

• *Actuarial present value of accumulated plan benefits*—the discounted amount of money that would be required to satisfy retirement obligations for active and retired employees.

• *Benefit information date*—the date the actuarial present value of accumulated benefits is presented.

• *Vested benefits*—employee vests when he or she has accumulated pension rights to receive benefits upon retirement. The employee no longer has to remain in the company to receive pension benefits.

• *Projected benefit obligation*—the year-end pension obligation based on *future* salaries. It is the actuarial present value of vested and nonvested benefits for services performed before a particular actuarial valuation date based on expected future salaries.

• *Accumulated benefit obligation*—the year-end obligation based on *current* salaries. It is the actuarial present value of benefits (vested and nonvested) attributable to the pension plan based on services performed before a specified date based on current salary levels.

The accumulated and projected benefit obligation figures will be the same in the case of plans having flat-benefit or nonpay-related pension benefit formulas.

• *Net assets available for pension benefits*—represent plan assets less plan liabilities. The plan's liabilities exclude participants' accumulated benefits.

Defined Contribution Pension Plan

Pension expense equals the employer's cash contribution for the year. There is no deferred charge or deferred credit arising. If the defined contribution plan stipulates contributions are to be made for years subsequent to an employee's rendering of services (e.g., after retirement), there should be an accrual of costs during the employee's service period.

Footnote disclosure includes

• Description of plan, including employee groups covered

• Basis of determining contributions
• Nature and effect of items affecting interperiod comparability
• Cost recognized for the period

Defined Benefit Pension Plan

The components of pension expense in a defined benefit pension plan follow:
• Service cost
• Prior service cost
• Expected return on plan assets (reduces pension expense)
• Interest on projected benefit obligation
• Actuarial gain or loss

Service cost is based on the present value of future payments under the benefit formula for employee services of the current period. It is recognized in full in the current year. The calculation involves actuarial assumptions.

Prior service cost is the pension expense applicable to services rendered before the adoption or amendment date of a pension plan. The cost of the retroactive benefits is the increase in the projected benefit obligation at the date of amendment. It involves the allocation of amounts of cost to future service years. Prior service cost determination involves actuarial considerations. The total pension cost is *not* booked but rather there are periodic charges based on actuarial determinations. Amortization is accomplished by assigning at the amendment date an equal amount to each service year of these active employees who are expected to receive plan benefits. The amortization of prior service cost may take into account future service years, change in the projected benefit obligation, the period in which employees will receive benefits, and decrement in employees receiving benefits each year.

■ Example

X Company changes its pension formula from 2% to 5% of the last 3 years of pay multiplied by the service years on January 1, 19X1. This results in the projected benefit obligation being increased by $500,000. Employees are anticipated to receive benefits over the next 10 years.

Total future service years equals:

$$\frac{n(n + 1)}{2} \times P$$

where n = the number of years services are to be made,

P = the population decrement each year.

$$\frac{10(10 + 1)}{2} \times 9 = 495$$

Amortization of prior service cost in 19X1 equals:

$$\$500,000 \times \frac{10 \times 9}{495} = \$90,909$$

The expected return on plan assets (e.g., stocks, bonds) reduces pension expense. Plan assets are valued at the moving average of asset values for the accounting period.

Interest is on the projected benefit obligation at the beginning of the year. The settlement rate is employed representing the rate for which pension benefits could be settled. Interest equals:

Interest rate $\times$ Projected benefit obligation
at the beginning of the year

Actuarial gains and losses are the difference between estimates and actual experience. For example, if the assumed interest rate is 10% and the actual interest rate is 12%, an actuarial gain results. There may also be a change in actuarial assumptions regarding the future. Actuarial gains and losses are deferred and amortized as an adjustment to pension expense over future years. Actuarial gains and losses related to a single event *not* related to the pension plan and not in the ordinary course of business are immediately recognized in the current year's income statement. Examples are plant closing and segment disposal.

Pension expense will not usually equal the employer's funding amount. Pension expense is typically based on the unit credit method. Under this approach, pension expense and related liability is based on estimating future salaries for total benefits to be paid.

If Pension expense > Cash paid
= Deferred pension liability

If Pension expense < Cash paid
= Deferred pension charge

Interest on the deferred pension liability reduces future pension expense. On the other hand, interest on the deferred pension charge increases pension expense.

Note: The "unit credit" method is used for flat-benefit plans (benefits are stated as a constant amount per year of service). In the case of final-pay plans, the projected unit credit method is used.

Minimum pension liability—must be recognized when the accumulated benefit obligation exceeds the fair value of pension plan assets. However, no minimum pension assets are recognized because it violates conservatism. When there is an accrued pension liability, an additional liability is booked up to the minimum pension liability.

When an additional liability is recorded, the debit is to an intangible asset under the pension plan. However, the intangible asset cannot exceed the unamortized prior service cost. If it does, the excess is reported as a separate component of stockholders' equity shown net of tax. While these items may be adjusted periodically, they are not amortized.

■ Example

Accumulated benefit obligation	$500,000
Less: Fair value of pension plan assets	200,000
Minimum pension liability	$300,000
Less: Accrued pension liability	120,000
Additional liability	$180,000

Note that if instead of there being an accrued pension liability there was an accrued pension asset of $120,000, the additional liability would have been $420,000.

Assume unamortized prior service cost is $100,000. The entry is

New Intangible Asset Under		
Pension Plan	100,000	
Stockholders' Equity	80,000	
Additional Liability		180,000

■ Example

Mr. A has 6 years prior to retirement. The estimated salary at retirement is $50,000. The pension benefit is 3% of final salary for each service year payable at retirement. The retirement benefit is computed below:

Final annual salary	$50,000
Formula rate	× 3%
	$ 1,500
Years of service	× 6
Retirement benefit	$ 9,000

■ Example

On 1/1/19X1, a company adopts a defined benefit pension plan. Expected return and interest rate are both 10%. Service cost for 19X1 and 19X2 are $100,000 and $120,000, respectively. The funding amount for 19X1 and 19X2 are $80,000 and $110,000, respectively.

The entry for 19X1 is

Pension Expense	100,000	
Cash		80,000
Pension Liability		20,000

The entry in 19X2 is

Pension Expense	122,000	
Cash		110,000
Pension Liability		12,000

Computation:

Service cost	$120,000
Interest on projected benefit obligation 10% × $100,000	10,000
Expected return on plan assets 10% × $80,000	(8,000)
	$122,000

At 12/31/19X2:

Projected benefit obligation $230,000 ($100,000 + $120,000 + $10,000).
Pension plan assets $198,000 ($80,000 + $110,000 + $8,000).

■ Example

Company X has a defined benefit pension plan for its 100 employees. On 1/1/19X1, pension plan assets have a fair value of $230,000, accumulated benefit obligation is $285,000, and the projected benefit obligation is $420,000. Ten employees are expected to resign each year for the next 10 years. They will be eligible to receive benefits. Service cost for 19X1 is $40,000. On 12/31/19X1, the projected benefit obligation is $490,000, fair value of plan assets is $265,000, and accumulated benefit obligation is $340,000. The expected return on plan assets and the interest rate are both 8%. No actuarial gains or losses occurred during the year. Cash funded for the year is $75,000.

Pension expense equals:

Service cost	$40,000
Interest on projected benefit obligation 8% × $420,000	33,600
Expected return on plan assets 8% × $230,000	(18,400)
Amortization of actuarial gains and losses	—
Amortization of unrecognized transition amount	34,545[a]
Pension expense	$89,745

[a] Projected benefit obligation	$420,000
Fair value of pension plan assets	230,000
Initial net obligation	$190,000

$$\text{Amortization } \frac{\$190,000}{5.5 \text{ years}^b} = \$34,545$$

$$^b \frac{n(n+1)}{2} \times P = \frac{10(10+1)}{2} \times 10 = 550$$

$$\frac{550}{100} = 5.5 \text{ years (average remaining service period)}$$

The journal entries at 12/31/19X1 follow:

Pension Expense	89,745	
Cash		75,000
Deferred Pension Liability		14,745
Intangible Asset—Pension Plan	60,255	
Additional Pension Liability		60,255

Computation follows:

Accumulated benefit obligation—	
12/31/19X1	$340,000
Fair value of plan assets—12/31/19X1	265,000
Minimum liability	$ 75,000
Deferred pension liability	14,745
Additional pension liability	$ 60,255

Disclosures—footnote disclosure for a pension plan follow:

• Describing the plan, including benefit formula, funding policy, employee groups covered, and retirement age

• Components of pension expense

• Pension assumptions (e.g., interest rate, mortality rate, employee turnover)

• Reconciling funded status of plan with employer amounts recognized on the balance sheet, including fair value of plan assets, projected benefit obligation, and unrecognized prior service cost

• Present value of vested and nonvested benefits

• Weighted-average assumed discount rate involved in measuring the projected benefit obligation

• Weighted-average expected return rate on pension plan assets

• Amounts and types of securities included in pension plan assets

• Amount of approximate annuity benefits to employees

Settlement in a Pension Plan

As per FASB 88, a settlement is discharging some or all of the employer's pension benefit obligation. Excess plan assets can revert to the employer. A settlement must satisfy *all* of the following criteria:

• Irrevocable

• Relieves pension benefit responsibility

• Materially curtails risk related to the pension obligation

The amount of gain or loss recognized in the income statement when a pension obligation is settled is limited to the unrecognized net gain or loss from realized or unrealized changes in either the pension benefit obligation or plan assets caused from actual experiences being different from original assumptions. All or a pro rata share of the unrecognized gain or loss is recognized when a plan is settled. If full settlement occurs, all unrecognized gains or losses are recognized. If only a part of the plan is settled, a pro rata share of the unrecognized net gain or loss is recognized.

An example of a settlement is when the employer furnishes employees with a lump-sum amount to give up pension rights. The gain or loss resulting is included in the current year's income statement.

Curtailment in a Pension Plan

As per FASB 88, a curtailment occurs when an event significantly reduces future service years of present employees or eliminates for most employees the accumulation of defined benefits for future services. An example is a plant closing that ends employee services prior to pension plan expectations. The gain or loss is recognized in the current year's income statement and contains the following elements:

• Unamortized prior service cost attributable to employee services no longer needed

• Change in pension benefit obligation due to the curtailment

Termination in a Pension Plan

When termination benefits are offered by the employer, accepted by employees, and the amount can reasonably be determined, an expense and liability are recognized. The amount of the accrual equals the down payment plus the present value of future payments to be made by the employer. The entry is to debit loss and credit cash (down payment) and liability (future payments). Footnote disclosure of the arrangement should be given.

Trustee Reporting for a Defined Benefit Pension Plan

FASB 35 deals with the reporting and disclosures of the trustee of a defined benefit pension plan. Generally accepted accounting principles must be followed. Financial statements are *not* required to be issued by the plan. If they are issued, reporting guidelines have to be followed. The prime objective is to assess the plan's capability to meet retirement benefits.

The balance sheet presents pension assets and liabilities as an offset. Operating assets are at book value. In determining net assets available, accrual accounting is followed. An example is accruing for interest earned but not received. Investments are shown at fair market value. An asset shown is "contributions receivable due from employer." In computing pension plan liability, participants' accumulated benefits are *excluded*. In effect, plan participants are equity holders rather than creditors of the plan.

Disclosure is required of:

• Net assets available for benefits.

• Changes in net assets available for benefits, including net appreciation in fair value of each major class of investments.

• Actuarial present value of accumulated plan benefits. Accumulated plan benefits include benefits anticipated to be paid to retired employees, beneficiaries, and present employees.

• Changes in actuarial present value of accumulated plan benefits.

• Description of the plan, including amendments.

• Accounting and funding policies.

There may exist an annuity contract in which an insurance company agrees to give specified pension benefits in return for receiving a premium.

PERMANENT DIFFERENCE

A permanent difference is an item that affects either book income or taxable income but never both. It does *not* reverse itself. Interperiod tax allocation is *not* applicable to permanent differences. Examples of permanent differences are

• Amortization expense on goodwill is not tax deductible.

• Premium on life insurance for executives is not tax deductible.

• Interest income on municipal securities is not taxable.

• Difference between percentage depletion and cost depletion.

• Special deductions under the tax law for domestic dividends received.

• Depreciation for book and tax differ due to different bases of carrying the related asset. The different bases arise from a business combination treated as a purchase for book purposes and a tax-free exchange for tax purposes.

See also Income Tax Accounting.

PERSONAL FINANCIAL PLANNING

This is a process for arriving at comprehensive solutions to an individual's personal, business, and financial problems and concerns. It therefore involves the development and implementation of total coordinated plans for the achievement of his or her overall financial objectives. Each individual will have different financial objectives, depending on the circumstances, goals, attitudes, and needs. But the total objectives of most people can be classified as follows:

1. Protection against personal risks such as death, disability, or unemployment
2. Capital accumulation for family purposes in case of emergency
3. Provision for retirement income
4. Reduction of tax burden
5. Estate planning
6. Investment and property management

Personal financial planning covers a wide variety of financial services and products:

1. Tax planning and management
2. Investments

3. Insurance
4. Retirement planning
5. Estate planning

Our economic growth, the tax structure, and the changes that have taken place in our social framework have created complexity in financial planning. The following events should be noted:

• Increasingly complex tax laws.

• A complex economy and proliferation of available financial products.

• The difficulty of saving for retirement.

• Middle-class individuals are now in higher income tax brackets.

• Inflationary pressures create artificial increases in income and losses in purchasing power.

Most people are not trained to deal with these complex factors. Financial planning has emerged as an important new profession in recent years. Personal financial planning can address money matters and help find ways to ensure a client's secure financial future.

PERSONAL FINANCIAL PLANNING SOFTWARE

Computer software in personal financial planning enables the individual to accumulate and evaluate sources of income and expenses. An analysis of the deviation between actual and budget figures may be made. Personal assets and liabilities are determined and valued in order to derive net worth. The person's objectives may be quantified and appraised over time. Some packages keep track of the investment portfolio and analyze it. Financial planning may be done, including that for tax, retirement, insurance, and estate. In essence, personal financial planning enables the strategic management of a person's financial affairs. A good planning package is Andrew Tobias's *Managing Your Money*™. Additionally, templates exist that may be used along with a spreadsheet program.

Financial management programs enable basic functions such as budgeting, checkbook management, analysis of cash flow, and fi-

nancial calculations. With regard to checkbook management, the program will combine check writing, allocations, and recording. The program will write and print out the check, update the check balance, and post expenditures to the appropriate budget category.

Financial calculation software aids in capital needs analysis and in determining effects of compounding and inflation. The person inputs the beginning amount, growth rate, and period, and then the computer performs the calculations. By using a growth formula, one can see the impact of different growth assumptions on varying beginning amounts. If there is a goal-seeking formula, one can work backward to see what kind of growth or how much capital is needed to start with to accomplish a desired sum of money at a particular date.

Financial calculations can also be involved with life expectancy analysis. Life expectancy calculations take personal data—such as age, sex, height, weight, and behavioral information (e.g., eating habits, fitness)—and translate them into a life expectancy estimate.

PERSONAL FINANCIAL STATEMENTS These
may be prepared for an individual or family to show financial status. The accrual basis is followed. Some uses include computation of net worth, obtaining credit, retirement planning, estate planning, tax planning, and to meet disclosure requirements (e.g., public figures). AICPA's Statement of Position No. 82–1 titled "Accounting and Financial Reporting for Personal Financial Statements" presents the accounting and disclosure requirements, including valuation approaches in arriving at current value amounts. Further guidance on accounting and reporting are offered in Statements on Standards for Accounting and Review Services 1 and 6 as well as the AICPA's "Personal Financial Statements Guide."

In the Statement of Financial Condition, assets are reflected at the estimated current value and are listed in the order of liquidity (maturity). Current value may be determined based on recent transactions of similar items, appraisals, present value of future cash flows from the asset, adjusting historical cost for inflation, and so on. In determining current value of assets, a deduction should be made for relevant selling costs. Historical cost may be provided as supplementary information. There is no breakdown between current and noncurrent classifications in the balance sheet.

Investments should be shown by major category, such as real estate. Significant investments in a sole proprietorship or partnership should be segregated. For instance, a material interest in a closely held company should be shown separately from the equity investment in other companies. Ownership of property (e.g., community property) should be ascertained under the applicable state law. If assets are jointly owned, only the individual's beneficial interest should be reported.

Asset valuation guidelines exist. Receivables should be reported at the discounted value of future cash receipts. The discount rate is the interest rate the debtor would typically incur for financing. Marketable securities, including stocks and bonds, are recorded at current quoted market prices. In the event a stock is not traded on the financial statement date, the bid price should preferably be used. When valuation difficulty exists with a particular security, a reputable brokerage firm may be consulted. Precious metals should be shown at current value. Life insurance should be reported at cash surrender value after deducting any loans against it. Documentation exists in the form of insurance company reports. With regard to retirement accounts, the current balance in IRA and Keogh plans should be listed. Also included are the current value of vested benefits in company profit-sharing and pension plans. The amounts shown are the proceeds to be received today. The investment in a closely held business can be valued by a qualified appraiser, such as one affiliated with the Institute of Business Appraisers. The practitioner should refrain from valuing the business, since an appearance of lack of independence (and even knowledge) may present a legal problem. Real estate should be at anticipated selling price using a licensed appraiser's report. Personal property should be valued at appraised value derived from a specialist's opinion or reference to a guide indicating valuation of personal items (e.g., blue book for auto values). Wholesale value rather than retail value should be used because the former would be received upon sale of the item by the individual. Intangible assets should be at appraisal value. If not possible, value can be based on anticipated sale proceeds or discounted value of future receipts from the asset. However, historical cost can be used if current value is not objectively determinable. Do not spend much time estimating the value of household items, since an approximation is usually sufficient. A listing of assets may take the following form:

Asset	Description	Current Value	Percentage of Total Assets

The accountant must be assured that current value figures are accurate. Legal liability problems may arise if unreasonable amounts are used. It is best to retain independent appraisers to derive current values. The practitioner must also insist on adequate documentation to support the figures, especially if possible litigation may arise.

Liabilities are reported at current value by payment date, without distinction between current and noncurrent. Guidelines exist in the valuation of liabilities. Payables should be at the discounted value of future payments, utilizing the interest rate implicit in the transaction. In the event debt may be settled at an amount less than the discounted value of the payments, the lower amount should be used. Usually, the liability equals the principal and accrued interest due. A noncancelable commitment should be reflected at the present value of future payments, such as alimony payments. Separately listed should be personal, investment, and business liabilities. Excluded from liabilities is nonrecourse debt that was subtracted in the determination of investment values. The current balance of the mortgage should be listed. Include loans for business or investment purposes, including margin accounts. Debt should not be included if it was considered in the valuation of a closely held firm. Include obligations with respect to limited partnership investments if a personal liability exists for those debts.

Income taxes are estimated on the difference between assets and liabilities and their tax bases. Taxes are based *as if* assets have been sold. Disclosure should be given of the methods and assumptions employed in the computation of income taxes. In making tax estimates, the effect of previous year's unpaid tax obligations and the current year's estimates should be taken into account. Also considered are withholding tax payments.

■ Example

An individual owns ABC stock that was bought 5 years ago for $8,000. The stock is currently worth $17,000. The individual is in the 38% tax bracket. If the individual sold the stock today, there would be a $9,000 gain, which would result in $3,420 in taxes. The $3,420 should be included in the "provision for estimated taxes on the difference between carrying amounts and tax bases of assets and liabilities." Since the $3,420 constitutes an amount of taxes that would be payable upon sale of the stock, it should be presented as a credit in the Statement of Financial Condition reducing the individual's net worth.

An illustrative Statement of Financial Condition follows:

Mr. and Mrs. J. Smith
Statement of Financial Condition
December 31, 19X2

Assets

Cash	$ 5,000
Interest and dividends receivable	200
Marketable securities	10,000
Interest in closely held company	6,000
Cash surrender value of life insurance	1,000
Real estate	100,000
Personal property	30,000
Total	$152,200

Liabilities

Credit cards	$ 6,000
Income taxes payable	3,000
Loans payable	10,000
Mortgage payable	60,000
	$ 79,000
Estimated taxes on the differences between the estimated current values of assets, the current amounts of liabilities, and their tax bases	40,000
Net worth	33,200
Total	$152,200

As an option, a Statement of Changes in Net Worth may be prepared. It is useful in showing the mix of business and personal items in personal financial statements. The statement should be broken down into realized and unrealized portions. Increases and decreases in net worth are shown. Examples of items increasing net worth are income, increases in current value of assets, decreases in the current amounts of liabilities, and decreases in estimated taxes on the difference between estimated current asset values and liability amounts and their tax bases. Items decreasing net worth are expenses, decreases in current values of assets, increases in current amounts of liabilities, and increases in estimated taxes.

Also optional are comparative financial statements.

An income statement is *not* prepared.

Disclosures are recommended to better appraise an individual's or family's financial health. Disclosures include

• Individuals covered by the statement

• Methods used in determining current values

• Change in method or assumption from a prior year

• Nature of joint ownership of property

• Identification of specific industries and companies where a material percentage of total assets are invested

• Percentage of ownership in an identified closely held business, including the nature of business activities consummated, basis of accounting, and summarized financial data

• Identification of intangibles, including estimated lives

• Face value of life insurance

• Vested rights in pension and stock ownership plans

• Methods and estimates employed in computing income taxes

• Particulars of receivables and payables such as interest rates, pledged items, and maturities

• Noncapitalized commitments such as rental agreements

If you see a client's assets are concentrated in one category, you should recommend a move toward diversification. If there is a high concentration of illiquid assets but yet significant impending debt exists, you should point out this precarious financial situation to the client. An evaluation should be made of which assets are being financed by debt and the reasonableness of the interest rate. Is debt being incurred for personal assets or investment assets? Is the repayment schedule of debt comfortable for the client? What are the sources of repaying that debt? Do client goals match actual results? Projections should be made to determine whether the client is going in the direction of meeting obligations. If not, corrective action should be taken.

PHILLIPS CURVE Economic history indicates that the twin objectives of price stability and full employment (such as 4% unemployment rate) have been extremely difficult to achieve. Many economists believe that there is an apparent conflict between maintaining stable prices and achieving low employment throughout the economy due to the strong tendency for the general price level to begin to rise before full employment is reached. The relationship between inflation and the unemployment rate is described by a Phillip's curve—named after A. W. Phillips, a British economist who proposed it in the late 1950s. Figure 1 illustrates a conventional Phillips curve and indicates the nature of the trade-off between lower unemployment and high rates of inflation. Every point on the curve denotes a different combination of unemployment and inflation. A movement along the curve reflects the reduction in one at the expense of a gain in the other. The dilemma posed by the curve is that the economy must accept inflation in order to achieve full employment or to accept a high unemployment rate to control inflation. To the extent that a Phillips curve phenomenon actually exists, economic policy makers are confronted with a difficult choice of finding a fiscal-monetary mix. Figure 2 shows statistical evidence on the trade-off. Ideally, policy makers wish

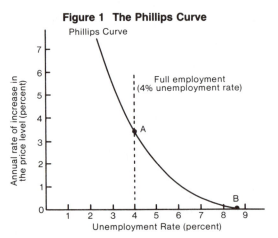

Figure 1 The Phillips Curve

Figure 2 U.S. Unemployment and Inflation Rates 1963–1984

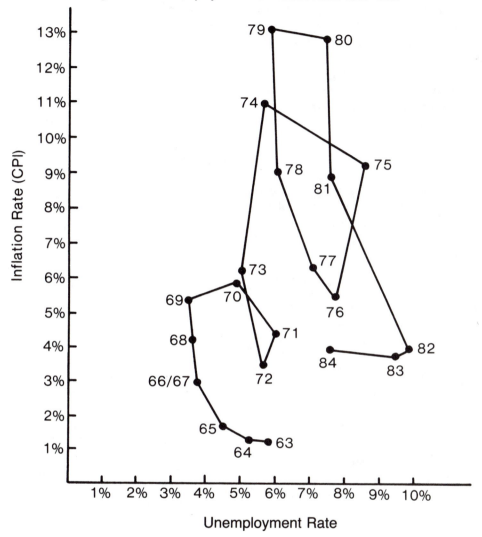

to find a policy mix that would shift the Phillips curve downward and to the left, thus making price stability and full employment more compatible and bearable. Unfortunately, in the recent past, experiencing "stagflation" shows the curve shifting outward to the right.

POOLING-OF-INTERESTS METHOD The pooling method is used to account for the acquisition of another company when the acquiring company exchanges its voting common stock for the voting common stock of the acquired company and all of twelve criteria are met. *See also* Business Combinations.

PORTFOLIO THEORY AND CAPITAL ASSET PRICING MODEL (CAPM)

Most financial assets are not held in isolation; rather, they are held as parts of portfolios. Therefore, risk-return analysis should not be confined to single assets only. It is important to look at portfolios and the gains from diversification. What is important is the return on the portfolio, not just the return on one asset, and the portfolio's risk.

Portfolio Return

The expected return on a portfolio (r_p) is simply the weighted average return of the individual sets in the portfolio, the weights being the fraction of the total funds invested in each asset:

$$r_p = w_1 r_1 + w_2 r_2 + \cdots + w_n r_n = \sum_{j=1}^{n} w_j r_j$$

where r_j = expected return on each individual asset,

w_j = fraction for each respective asset investment,

n = number of assets in the portfolio.

$$\sum_{j=1}^{n} w_j = 1.0$$

■ Example 1

A portfolio consists of assets A and B. Asset A makes up one third of the portfolio and has an expected return of 18%. Asset B makes up the other two thirds of the portfolio and is expected to earn 9%. What is the expected return on the portfolio?

Asset	Return(r_j)	Fraction (w_j)	$w_j r_j$	
A	18%	⅓	⅓ × 18% =	6%
B	9%	⅔	⅔ × 9% =	6%
			r_p =	12%

Portfolio Risk

Unlike returns, the risk of a portfolio (σp) is not simply the weighted average of the standard deviations of the individual as-

sets in the contribution, for a portfolio's risk is also dependent on the correlation coefficients of its assets. The correlation coefficient is a measure of the degree to which two variables "move" together. It has a numerical value that ranges from -1.0 to 1.0. In a two-asset (A and B) portfolio, the portfolio risk is defined as:

$$\sigma_p = \sqrt{w_A^2 \sigma_A^2 + w_B^2 \sigma_B^2 + 2 w_A w_B \cdot p_{AB} \sigma_A \sigma_B}$$

where $\sigma - A$ and $\sigma - B$ = standard deviations of assets A and B, respectively.

w_A and w_B = weights, or fractions, of total funds invested in assets A and B

p_{AB} = the correlation coefficient between assets A and B.

Incidentally, the correlation coefficient is the measurement of joint movement between two securities.

Diversification

As can be seen in the previous formula, the portfolio risk, measured in terms of σp is not the weighted average of the individual asset risks in the portfolio. We have in the formula of the third term (ρ), which makes a significant contribution to the overall portfolio risk. What the formula basically shows is that portfolio risk can be minimized or completely eliminated by *diversification*. The degree of reduction in portfolio risk depends upon the correlation between the assets being combined. Generally speaking, by combining two perfectly negatively correlated assets $(P = -1.0)$, we are able to eliminate the risk completely. In the real world, however, most securities are negatively but not perfectly correlated. In fact, most assets are positively correlated. We could still reduce the portfolio risk by combining even positively correlated assets. An example of the latter might be ownership of two automobile stocks or two housing stocks.

■ Example 2

Assume the following:

Asset	σ	w
A	20%	⅓
B	10%	⅔

The portfolio risk then is

$$\sigma_p = \sqrt{w_A^2\sigma_A^2 + w_B^2\sigma_B^2 + 2\,w_Aw_B \cdot \rho_{AB}\sigma_A\sigma_B}$$
$$= \sqrt{(\tfrac{1}{3})^2(0.2)^2 + (\tfrac{2}{3})^2(0.1)^2 + 2\rho_{AB}(\tfrac{1}{3})(\tfrac{2}{3})(0.2)(0.1)}$$
$$= \sqrt{0.0089 + 0.0089\rho_{AB}}$$

(a) Now assume that the correlation coefficient between A and B is +1 (a perfectly positive correlation). This means that when the value of asset A increases in response to market conditions, so does the value of asset B, and it does so at exactly the same rate as A. The portfolio risk when $\rho = +1$ then becomes:

$$\sigma_p = \sqrt{0.0089 + 0.0089\rho_{AB}} = \sqrt{0.0089 + 0.0089(1)}$$
$$= \sqrt{0.0178} = 0.1334 = 13.34\%$$

(b) If $\rho = 0$, the assets lack correlation and the portfolio risk is simply the risk of the expected returns on the assets, that is, the weighted average of the standard deviations of the individual assets in the portfolio. Therefore, when $\rho_{AB} = 0$, the portfolio risk for this example is:

$$\sigma_p = \sqrt{0.0089 + 0.0089\rho_{AB}}$$
$$= \sqrt{0.0089 + 0.0089(0)}$$
$$= \sqrt{0.0089} = 0.0943 = 9.43\%$$

(c) If $\rho = -1$ (a perfectly negative correlation coefficient), then as the price of A rises, the price of B declines at the very same rate. In such a case, risk would be completely eliminated. Therefore, when $\rho_{AB} = -1$, the portfolio risk is

$$\sigma_p = \sqrt{0.0089 + 0.0089\rho_{AB}}$$
$$= \sqrt{0.0089 + 0.0089(-1)}$$
$$= \sqrt{0.0089 - 0.0089} = 0 = 0$$

When we compare the results of (a), (b), and (c), we see that a positive correlation between assets increases a portfolio's risk above the level found at zero correlation, whereas a perfectly negative correlation eliminates that risk.

■ Example 3

To illustrate the point of diversification, assume data on the following three securities are as follows:

Year	Security X (%)	Security Y (%)	Security Z (%)
19X1	10	50	10
19X2	20	40	20
19X3	30	30	30
19X4	40	20	40
19X5	50	10	50
r_j	30	30	30
σ_p	14.14	14.14	14.14

Note here that securities X and Y have a perfectly negative correlation, and securities X and Z have a perfectly positive correlation. Notice what happens to the portfolio risk when X and Y, and X and Z are combined. Assume that funds are split equally between the two securities in each portfolio.

Year	Portfolio XY (50% – 50%)	Portfolio XZ (50% – 50%)
19X1	30	10
19X2	30	20
19X3	30	30
19X4	30	40
19X5	30	50
r_p	30	30
σ_p	0	14.14

Again, see that the two perfectly negative correlated securities (XY) result in a zero overall risk.

Markowitz's Efficient Portfolio

Dr. Harry Markowitz, in the early 1950s, provided a theoretical framework for the systematic composition of optimum portfolios. Using a technique called "quadratic programming," he attempted to select from

Figure 1   Efficient Frontier

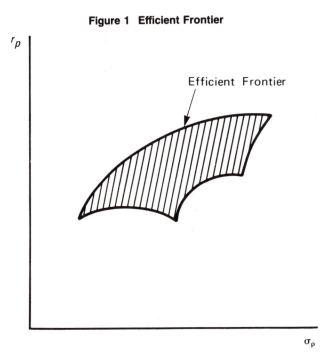

among hundreds of individual securities, given certain basic information supplied by portfolio managers and security analysts. He also weighted these selections in composing portfolios.

The central theme of Markowitz's work is that rational investors behave in a way that reflects their aversion to taking increased risk without being compensated by an adequate increase in expected return. Also, for any given expected return, most investors will prefer a lower risk and for any given level of risk, prefer a higher return to a lower return. Markowitz showed how quadratic programming could be used to calculate a set of "efficient" portfolios such as illustrated by the curve in Figure 1. In Figure 2, an efficient set of portfolios that lie along the ABC line, called "efficient frontier" is noted. Along this frontier, the investor can receive a maximum return for a given level of risk or a minimum risk for a given level of return. Specifically, comparing three port-

folios—A, B, and D—portfolios A and B are clearly more efficient than D because portfolio A could produce the same expected return but at a lower risk level, whereas portfolio B would have the same degree of risk as D but would afford a higher return.

Figure 2   Efficient Portfolio

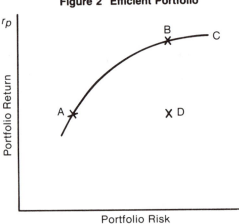

Figure 3　Risk-Return Indifference Curves

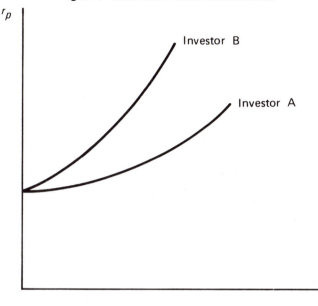

To see how the investor tries to find the optimum portfolio, we first introduce the *indifference curve*, which shows the investor's trade-off between risk and return. Figure 3 shows the two different indifference curves for two investors. The steeper the slope of the curve, the more risk averse the investor is. For example, investor B's curve has a steeper slope than investor A's. This means that investor B will want more incremental return for each additional unit of risk. Figure 4 depicts a family of indifference curves for investor A. The objective is to maximize his or her satisfaction by attaining the highest curve possible.

By matching the indifference curve showing the risk-return trade-off with the best investments available in the market as represented by points on the efficient frontier, investors are able to find an optimum portfolio. According to Markowitz, investor A will achieve the highest possible curve at point B along the efficient frontier. Point B is thus the optimum portfolio for this investor.

Portfolio Selection as a Quadratic Programming Problem

A portfolio selection problem was formulated by Markowitz as a quadratic programming model as follows:

$$\text{Min } E(r_p) - \lambda V(r_p)$$

subject to

$$\Sigma x_i = 1$$
$$x_i \geqq 0$$

where $E(r_p)$ = the expected return,
$V(r_p)$ = the variance or covariance of any given portfolio,
x_i = proportion of the investor's total investment in security i,
n = number of securities.

Especially, λ(Lambda) is called the coefficient of risk aversion. It represents the rate at which a particular investor is just willing to exchange expected rate of return for risk. $\lambda = 0$ indicates the investor is a risk lover, whereas $\lambda = 1$ means he or she is a risk averter.

Figure 4 Matching the Efficient Frontier and Indifference Curves

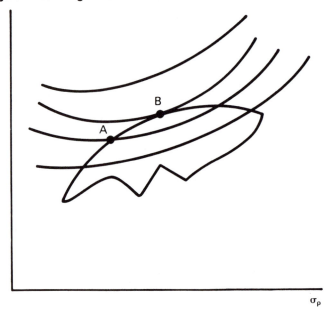

The resulting solution to the problem would identify a portfolio that lies on the *efficient* portfolio. If one knows the coefficient of risk aversion, λ, for a particular investor, the model will be able to find the *optimal* portfolio for that investor.

The Market Index Model

For even a moderately sized portfolio, the formulas for portfolio return and risk require estimation of a large number of input data. Concerned with the computational burden in deriving these estimates led to the development of the following *market index model:*

$$r_j = a + b\, r_m$$

where r_j = return on security j.
r_m = return on the market portfolio,
b = the beta, or systematic risk, of a security.
What this model attempts to do is measure the systematic or uncontrollable risk of a security. The beta is measured as follows:

$$b = \mathrm{Cov}\,(r_j, r_m)/\sigma^2_m$$

where $\mathrm{Cov}(r_j, r_m)$ = the covariance of the returns of the securities with the market return.
σ^2_m = the variance (standard deviation squared) of the market return.

The market return is the return on the Standard & Poor's 500 or Dow Jones 30 Industrials.

An easier way to compute beta is to determine the slope of the least-squares linear regression line $(r_j - r_f)$, where the excess return of the security $(r_j - r_f)$ is regressed against the excess return of the market portfolio $(r_m - r_f)$. The formula for beta is

$$b = \Sigma MK - n\,\bar{M}\bar{K}/(\Sigma M^2 - n\,\bar{M}^2)$$

where $M = (r_m - r_f)$,
$K = (r_j - r_f)$,
n = the number of periods,
$\bar{M}$ = the average of M,
$\bar{K}$ = the average of K.

The market index model was initially proposed to reduce the number of inputs required in portfolio analysis. It can also be justified in the context of the *capital asset pricing model*.

The Capital Asset Pricing Model (CAPM)

The CAPM takes off where the efficient frontier concluded with an assumption that there exists a risk-free security with a single rate at which investors can borrow and lend. By combining the risk-free asset and the efficient frontier, we create a whole new set of investment opportunities that will allow us to reach higher indifference curves than would be possible simply along the efficient frontier. The $r_f mx$ line in Figure 5 shows this possibility. This line is called the capital market line (CML) and the formula for this line is

$$r_p = r_f + (r_m - r_f/\sigma_m - 0)\sigma_p$$

$$\left(r_p = r_f + \left(\frac{r_m - r_f}{\sigma_m - 0}\right)\sigma_p\right)$$

which indicates the expected return on any portfolio (r_p) is equal to the risk-free return (r_f) plus the slope of the line times a value

along the horizontal axis (σ_p) indicating the amount of risk undertaken.

The Security Market Line

We can establish the trade-off between risk and return for an *individual security* through the security market line (SML) in Figure 6. SML is a general relationship to show the risk-return trade-off for an *individual security*, whereas CML achieves the same objective for a *portfolio*.

The formula for SML is

$$r_j = r_f + b (r_m - r_f)$$

where r_j = the expected (or required) return on security j,

r_f = the risk-free security (such as a T-bill),

r_m = the expected return on the market portfolio (such as Standard & Poor's 500 Stock Composite Index or Dow Jones 30 Industrials),

b = beta, an index of nondiversifiable (noncontrollable, systematic) risk.

Figure 5 Graph of CAPM

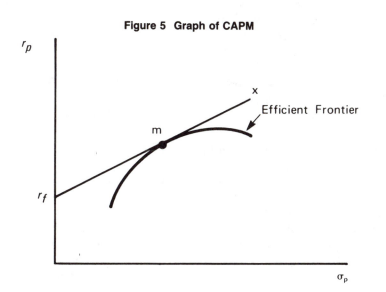

Figure 6 The Security Market Line (SML)

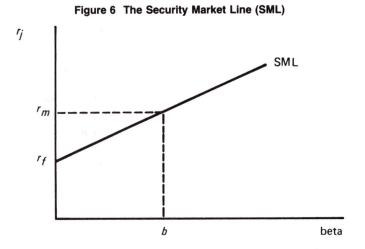

This formula is called the *Capital Asset Pricing Model* (*CAPM*). The model shows that investors in individual securities are only assumed to be rewarded for systematic, uncontrollable, market-related risk, known as the beta (*b*) risk. All other risk is assumed to be diversified away and thus is not rewarded.

The key component in the CAPM, beta (*b*), is a measure of the security's volatility relative to that of an average security. For example: $b = 0.5$ means the security is only half as volatile, or risky, as the average security; $b = 1.0$ means the security is of average risk; and $b = 2.0$ means the security is twice as risky as the average risk.

The whole term $b(r_m - r_f)$ represents the risk premium, the additional return required to compensate investors for assuming a given level of risk.

Thus, in words, the CAPM or (SML) equation shows that the required (expected) rate of return on a given security (r_j) is equal to the return required for securities that have no risk (r_f) plus a risk premium required by investors for assuming a given level of risk. The higher the degree of systematic risk (*b*), the higher the return on a given security demanded by investors.

■ Example 4

Assuming that the risk-free rate (r_f) is 8% and the expected return for the market (r_m) is 12%, then if

$b = 0$ (risk-free $r_j = 8\% + 0(12\% - 8\%)$ = 8%
 security)
$b = 0.5$ $r_j = 8\% + 0.5(12\% - 8\%) = 10\%$
$b = 1.0$ (market $r_j = 8\% + 1.0(12\% - 8\%) = 12\%$
 portfolio)
$b = 2.0$ $r_j = 8\% + 2.0(12\% - 8\%) = 16\%$

See also Beta Coefficient.

POST AUDIT A post audit occurs subsequent to the time a transaction took place. For example, the independent auditor examines the validity of the record keeping of an item by looking at documentation after the occurrence of the event.

PRECIOUS METALS These include gold and silver. Advantages of precious metals are liquidity, international markets, and hedge against inflation. But instability in price exists. The prices usually rise in difficult times and decline in stable periods. There is no periodic tax, such as with real estate.

Gold

Gold is a valuable commodity constituting a private store of value. The measurement is in troy ounces. It is an attractive investment in times of depreciating paper currency and when low interest rates exist. Low interest rates encourage gold investment since other types of investment provide low returns. Gold investment may be in the form of bullion, coins, shares of a mining company, certificates, jewelry, and futures.

Gold typically performs contrary to common stock. As common stock decreases in price, gold increases in price. Thus, gold can be used to diversify an investment portfolio. Transaction costs change depending upon the kind of gold involved. However, the percentage commission drops as the quantity bought increases.

Gold coins can be bought from post offices, banks, and gold dealers. Gold coins vary in price based on quality and content. Commissions usually vary from 2% to 4%. Coins are easily marketable and movable.

Gold bullion may be purchased from banks and dealers. Dealer markups and commissions range from 3% to 10%, depending upon the quantity transacted. *Tip*: Assaying to test for gold content may be needed. A gold certificate may also be bought, showing ownership in a specified number of gold ounces stored at the bank. Advantages of gold certificates are that they may not be subject to state sales tax applicable to bullion and there is no need to be concerned with loss from theft since they are held in a bank vault.

Indirect ownership may be gotten by acquiring shares in a gold mine. But market price of the stock may not always go in the same direction as the physical gold. Gold mining companies are listed on the major exchanges and in the over-the-counter market. Most gold mines are located in South Africa.

Mutual funds solely investing in gold stocks and gold bullion also exist (e.g., Fidelity Select Gold and Lexington Gold). Diversification is achieved through mutual fund ownership. Gold futures may be gotten on some commodities exchanges. A down payment as little as 10% of the contract's value can be made to buy the contract. The low margin requirement furnishes a leveraging opportunity. Commissions are usually below 1% of the value of the contract. Gold futures are traded in some U.S. and foreign exchanges.

Disadvantages With Physical Gold Ownership

• High transaction and storage costs.

• Price variability resulting in high risk. Volatility in price partly arises from changes in the international market caused usually from speculation.

• No dividends are received.

• Bearer form for some types of gold investment (e.g., bullion and coins). If lost or stolen, there is no protection from registration.

Silver

Silver may be in the form of bars, coins, jewelry, or flatware. There are also futures contracts traded on some commodities exchanges. Return is in the form of appreciation in the value of the silver. Silver is substantially less in price relative to gold. Carrying costs are quite high.

Market prices of silver mining companies depend both on the price of physical silver and the financial position of the firms themselves.

PREFERRED STOCK Although participating preferred stock rarely exists, if it does, it may be partially or fully participating. In the case of partially participating, preferred stockholders participate in excess dividends over the preferred dividend rate proportionately with common stockholders, but there is a maximum additional rate. For example, an 8% preferred stock issue may permit participating up to 12%, so that an extra 4% dividend may be tacked on. In the case of fully participating preferred stock, there is a distribution for the current year at the preference rate plus any cumulative preference. Further, the preferred stockholders share in dividend distributions in excess of the preferred stock rate on a proportionate basis, using the total par value of the preferred stock and common stock. For instance, a 10% fully participating preferred stock will get the 10% preference rate plus a proportionate share based on the total par value of the common and preferred stock of excess dividends once common stockholders have obtained their matching 10% of par of the common stock.

■ Example

Assume 5% preferred stock, $20 par, 5,000 shares. The preferred stock is partially participating up to an additional 2%. Common stock is $10 par, 30,000 shares. A $40,000 dividend is declared. Dividends are distributed as follows:

	Preferred	Common
Preferred stock, current year ($100,000 × 5%)	$5,000	
Common stock, current year ($300,000 × 5%)		$15,000
Preferred stock, partial ($100,000 × 2%)	2,000	
Common stock, matching ($300,000 × 2%)		6,000
Balance to common stock		12,000
Total	$7,000	$33,000

Cumulative preferred stock means that if no dividends are paid in a given year, the dividends accumulate and must be paid before any dividends can be paid to noncumulative stock.

The liquidation value of preferred stock means that in corporate liquidation, preferred stockholders will receive the liquidation value (sometimes stated as par value) before

any funds may be distributed to common stockholders.

Disclosure for preferred stock includes liquidation preferences, call prices, and cumulative dividends in arrears.

When preferred stock is converted to common stock, the preferred stock and paid-in-capital account are eliminated and the common stock and paid-in-capital account are credited. If a deficit results, retained earnings would be charged.

■ Example

Preferred stock shares having a par value of $300,000 and paid-in-capital (preferred stock) of $20,000 are converted into common stock. There are 30,000 preferred shares having a $10 par value per share. Common stock shares issued are 10,000 shares having a par value of $25.

The journal entry is

Preferred stock	300,000	
Paid-in-Capital (preferred stock)	20,000	
Common Stock (10,000 × $25)		250,000
Paid-in-Capital (common stock)		70,000

PRELIMINARY AUDIT

1. An initial engagement requiring an appraisal of the entire business and accounting system of the client. The adequacy of internal control is a prime consideration so that a proper auditing plan may be formulated.

2. Audit work conducted before year-end so that less audit testing is required at the close of the year. A preliminary audit tests transactions and accounting records to assure that the accounts are properly stated.

PRICE/BOOK VALUE RATIO The price/book value ratio equals:

$$\frac{\text{Market price per share}}{\text{Book value per share}}$$

Market price per share should generally be higher than book value per share due to inflation and good corporate performance over the years. Market price is based on current prices, whereas book value is based on historical prices. The higher the ratio, the more desirable, since it shows the stock market places a higher value on the company. It should be noted that in some cases, the book value per share may in fact be higher than the market price per share. This is the case for many banks, for example.

■ Example

A company's market price per share is $20 and its book value per share is $25. The price/book value ratio equals:

$$\frac{\$20}{\$25} = 0.8$$

The analytical implication may be that the company has not been performing well since market price is below book value. Perhaps the company has financial and operating problems.

It should be noted, however, that some analysts view a buying situation to exist when book value is above market price because the stock may be undervalued. *See also* Book Value per Share.

PRICE-EARNINGS RATIO (P/E RATIO)

The price-earnings ratio equals market price of stock divided by earnings per share. It is used by potential investors in deciding whether to invest in the company. A high P/E ratio is desirable because it indicates that investors highly value a company's earnings by applying to it a higher multiple. The P/E ratio of a company is dependent upon several factors, including quality of earnings, stability of earnings, risk trend in earnings, cash flow, liquidity position, solvency status, and growth potential, among others. Financial analysts who are of the opinion that the firm will generate future profit at higher levels than present may value the stock higher than its current earnings may justify.

■ Example

A company's earnings per share is $5 and the market price per share is $50. The P/E multiple is 10.

PRICE INDICES

There are various price indices that are used to measure living costs, price-level changes, and inflation. They are

1. *Consumer Price Index (CPI)*—measures the cost of buying a fixed bundle of goods (some 400 consumer goods and services), representative of the purchases of the typical working-class urban family. The fixed basket is divided into the following categories: food and beverages, housing, apparel, transportation, medical care, entertainment, and other. Generally referred to as a "cost-of-living index," it is published by the Bureau of Labor Statistics of the U.S. Department of Labor. The CPI is widely used for *escalation clauses*. The base year for the CPI index was 1967, at which time it was assigned 100.

2. *Producer Price Index (PPI)*—like the CPI, the PPI is a measure of the cost of a given basket of goods priced in wholesale markets, including raw materials, semifinished goods, and finished goods. The PPI is published monthly by the Bureau of Labor Statistics of the Department of Commerce. The PPI signals changes in the general price level, or the CPI, some time before they actually materialize. (Since the PPI does not include services, caution should be exercised when the principal cause of inflation is service prices.) For this reason, the PPI and especially some of its subindexes, such as the *index of sensitive materials*, serve as one of the *leading indicators* that are closely watched by policy makers.

3. *GNP Deflator (Implicit Price Index)*—a weighted average of the price indexes used to deflate the components of GNP. Thus, it reflects price changes for goods and services bought by consumers, businesses, and gov-

ernments. The GNP deflator is found by dividing current GNP in a given year by constant (real) GNP. Because it covers a broader group of goods and services than the CPI and PPI, the GNP Deflator is a very widely used price index that is frequently used to measure inflation. The GNP deflator, unlike the CPI and PPI, is available only *quarterly*, not monthly. It too is published by the U.S. Department of Commerce.

See also Economic Indicators; Indexation; Index of Leading Economic Indicators.

PRICE-LEVEL ACCOUNTING Price-level information is *optional* by a company. At one time, disclosure was required. If presented, certain guidelines exist.

Historical cost is first stated in terms of current cost. Current cost is then adjusted to constant purchasing power using the average consumer price index (CPI) for the current year as follows:

$$\text{Replacement cost} \times \frac{\text{Average CPI for current year}}{\text{CPI at time of transaction}}$$

In terms of general inflation, the following two types of accounts exist:

• *Monetary accounts.* 1. Monetary assets include cash and claims to cash (e.g., receivables). Monetary assets remain intact in the price-level balance sheet because they are stated in current dollars. During a period of inflation, holding monetary assets results in a purchasing power loss shown in the price-level income statement. 2. Monetary liabilities are obligations payable in dollars (e.g., accounts payable, notes payable, bonds payable, and advances to unconsolidated subsidiaries). Monetary liabilities remain intact in the price-level balance sheet. During a period of inflation, owing money results in a purchasing power gain shown in the price-level income statement.

• *Nonmonetary accounts.* 1. Nonmonetary assets are in older dollars and require adjustment to current dollars in the price-level balance sheet. Examples are land, equipment, machinery, and goodwill. 2. Nonmonetary

liabilities are those payable in *services*, not dollars. An example is warranty payable. 3. Stockholders' equity representing equity securities that were issued in older dollars.

Purchasing power gain or loss on monetary items has to be considered.

■ Example

On 1/1/19X1, monetary assets were $70,000 and monetary liabilities were $20,000. During the year, net monetary assets (monetary assets less monetary liabilities) increased by $40,000. The CPI indices for 19X1 were

1/1/19X1	200
Average for 19X1	215
12/31/19X1	220

	Historical Cost		Conversion Factor	Average CPI Dollars
1/1/19X1 Net monetary assets	$50000	×	215/200	$53750
Increase in net monetary assets	40000	×	215/215	40000
				$93750
12/31/19X1 Net monetary assets	$90000	×	220/215	92093
Purchasing power loss				$ 1657

Inflationary disclosures include the following items in terms of their inflation adjusted amounts: sales, income from continuing operations, net income, cash dividends, market price of stock, inventory, fixed assets, intangible assets, cost of sales, depreciation, amortization, and purchasing power gain or loss. *See also* Inflation.

PRICING A SPECIAL ORDER Pricing of a special order is a short-term and nonroutine decision such as whether to accept a production order at an offered price that is below the normal selling price or what price to charge for a product that could be produced with otherwise idle facilities.

■ Example

Assume product X normally sells for $20 per unit. The unit variable cost is $12. Total fixed costs are $100,000 for the currently produced 20,000 units. Thus, fixed cost per unit is currently $5. Idle capacity is assumed to exist. A prospective customer offers to buy 100 units at $15. The $15 offered price is of course less than the current selling price of $20. However, in this special order decision, the company should sell at the $15 price because profitability results, as indicated following:

Sales	100 × $15	$1,500
Less: Variable costs	100 × $12	1,200
Contribution margin		$ 300
Less: Fixed costs		0*
Net income		$ 300

* At idle capacity, total fixed cost does not increase with an additional order.

See also Contribution Approach to Pricing.

PRIOR PERIOD ADJUSTMENT

The two types of prior period adjustments are (1) correction of an error that was made in a prior year and (2) recognition of a tax loss carry forward benefit arising from a purchased subsidiary (curtailed by the 1986 Tax Reform Act).

When a single year is presented, prior period adjustments adjust the beginning balance of retained earnings. The presentation follows:

• Retained earnings—1/1 unadjusted
• Prior period adjustments (net of tax)
• Retained earnings—1/1 adjusted
• Add: Net income
• Less: Dividends
• Retained earnings—12/31

Errors may be due to mathematical mistakes, incorrect application of accounting principles, or misuse of the facts existing when the financial statements were prepared. Further, a change in principle from one that is not GAAP to one that is GAAP is an error correction. Disclosure should be made of the nature of the error and the effect of correction on earnings.

When comparative statements are prepared, a retroactive adjustment for the error

is made as it effects the prior years. The retroactive adjustment is disclosed by showing the effects of the adjustment on previous years' earnings and component items of net income.

■ Example

In 19X1, a company incorrectly charged furniture for promotion expense amounting to $30,000. The error was discovered in 19X2. The correcting journal entry is

Retained Earnings	30,000	
Furniture		30,000

■ Example

X Company acquired Y Company on 1/1/19X3 recording goodwill of $60,000. Goodwill was not amortized. The correcting entry on 12/31/19X5 follows:

Amortization Expense (1500 × 1 for 19X5)	1,500	
Retained Earnings (1500 × 2 for 19X3 and 19X4)	3,000	
Goodwill		4,500

■ Example

At the end of 19X2, a company failed to accrue telephone expense that was paid at the beginning of 19X3. The correcting entry on 12/31/19X3 is

Retained Earnings	16,000	
Telephone Expense		16,000

■ Example

On 1/1/19X2, an advance retainer fee of $50,000 was received covering a 5-year period. In error, revenue was credited for the full amount. The error was discovered on 12/31/19X4 before closing the books. The correcting entry is

12/31/19X4 Retained Earnings	30,000	
Revenue		10,000
Deferred Revenue		20,000

■ Example

A company bought a machine on January 1, 19X4, for $32,000 with a $2,000 salvage value and a 5-year life. By mistake repairs expense was charged. The error was discovered on December 31, 19X7, before closing the books. The correcting entry follows:

Depreciation Expense	6,000	
Machine	32,000	
Accumulated Depreciation		24,000
Retained Earnings		14,000

Accumulated depreciation of $24,000 is calculated following:

$$\frac{\$32,000 - \$2,000}{5} = \$6,000 \text{ per year} \times 4 \text{ years}$$
$$= \$24,000$$

The credit to retained earnings reflects the difference between the erroneous repairs expense of $32,000 in 19X4 versus showing depreciation expense of $18,000 for 3 years (19X4–19X6).

■ Example

At the beginning of 19X5, a company bought equipment for $300,000 with a salvage value of $20,000 and an expected life of 10 years. Straight-line depreciation is used. In error, salvage value was not deducted in computing depreciation. The correcting journal entries on 12/31/19X7 follow:

	19X5 and 19X6
Depreciation taken $300,000/10 × 2 years	$60,000
Depreciation correctly stated $280,000/10 × 2 years	56,000
	$ 4,000

Depreciation	28,000	
Accumulated Depreciation		28,000
Depreciation for current year		
Accumulated Depreciation	4,000	
Retained Earnings		4,000
Correct prior year depreciation misstatement		

PRIOR SERVICE COST This is the retroactive cost for employee services performed before the date of adoption or amendment to the pension plan. As a result, the projected benefit obligation will increase. *See also* Pension Plans.

PRIVATE PLACEMENT In a private placement, a company issues equity and debt securities directly to either one or a few large investors. The large investors are financial institutions such as insurance companies, pension plans, and commercial banks.

Advantages of Private Placement Versus Public Issuance

• The flotation cost is less. Flotation cost is the expense of registering and selling the stock issue. Examples are brokerage commissions and underwriting fees. The flotation cost for common stock exceeds that for preferred stock. Flotation cost expressed as a percentage of gross proceeds is higher for smaller issues than for larger ones.

• It avoids SEC filing requirements.

• It avoids the disclosure of information to the public at large.

• There is less time involved to obtain funds.

• It may not be practical to issue securities in the public market when a company is so small that an investment banker would not find it profitable.

• The company's credit rating may be low and as a consequence, investors may not be interested in buying securities when the money supply is limited.

Disadvantages of Private Placement Versus Public Issuance

• It is more difficult to obtain significant amounts of money privately.

• Large investors usually employ stringent credit standards requiring the company to be in a strong financial position.

• Large institutional investors may watch more closely the company's activities.

• Large institutional investors are more capable of obtaining voting control of the company.

PRIVILEGED COMMUNICATION This is a confidential relationship between parties for which the recipient of the information is legally allowed to withhold disclosure of it. An example is the relationship between client and lawyer. There is *no* such common law relationship between client and CPA. However, some states have passed statutes recognizing this relationship.

PROBABILITY PROPORTIONAL TO SIZE (PPS) SAMPLING PPS sampling estimates the maximum amount of dollar value error that probably exists in an account. PPS sampling involves defining the sampling unit, selecting the sample, computing sample size, and appraising sample results (no sample errors, occurrence of sample errors, and significance thereof).

In PPS sampling, the sampling unit is the individual dollar. Thus, the population is the total dollars involved. Each individual dollar in the population has the same probability of being chosen. However, the auditor does *not* select and audit individual dollars in the population. Instead, the CPA will examine the customer accounts or transactions (referred to as logical units) associated with the specific dollars that are selected for sampling.

■ **Example**

The auditor wishes to test the reasonableness of a client's recorded accounts receivable. Confirmations are mailed to a random sample of customers. Each customer's account is a logical unit. The total of all logical units subject to audit is the sample.

The more dollars associated with a logical unit, the greater is the chance for selection. A drawback, however, is the PPS is not best suitable to test an account for understatement.

■ **Example**

A client's accounts receivable is $1,000,000. A required sample size of 2,000 is computed. The sampling interval is computed to be $500 ($1,000,000/2,000). The auditor selects a random start that has to be a number between one and the sampling interval ($500). This is necessary so the auditor may select the first logical unit from the first interval. The first logical unit is the one containing the dollar amount corresponding to the random start. After selecting the logical unit containing the random start dollar, the auditor then proceeds to select each logical unit associated with every xth dollar thereafter (x being the sampling interval size). Assume the auditor chooses a random start derived from a random number table of $26. The auditor would then select the logical unit associated with the 26th dollar as the first sample item and would proceed to choose the logical units associated with the 526th dollar ($26 and $500), the 1,026th dollar ($26 and $500 and $500), the 1,526th dollar ($26 and $500 and $500 and $500), and so on until all 2,000 logical units are chosen. In effect, the auditor has segregated the $1,000,000 of accounts receivable into 2,000 intervals of $500 each.

Because of the selection of logical units associated with every xth dollar (x equals the computed sampling interval), all logical units with dollar amounts equal to or in excess of the sampling interval will be selected for the sample with 100% certainty. This assures that customer accounts of greater magnitude (amounts equal to or greater than the sampling interval) will be included in the sample for testing.

PPS is appropriate when the auditor's purpose is to ascertain the existence of overstatement errors. Therefore, it is a good approach for examining asset balances, such as receivables, securities, and inventory.

PPS is best appropriate when the population contains debit balances. If the auditor finds zero or credit balances in the population, special design considerations are required. Also, design modification is needed in the event the audited amount of the sampling unit exceeds the recorded amount (causing the book value to be understated) or less than zero (making the overstatement error to be greater than the recorded book value).

PPS sampling should be employed only if a few errors of overstatement are anticipated. If there are many overstatement errors that are uncovered, there is a higher probability that the auditor will reject an acceptable recorded amount. *Recommendation*: If many overstatement or understatement errors are expected, a sampling method other than PPS should be used, such as classical variables sampling. *See also* Classical Variables Sampling; Sampling.

PROCESS COSTING This is a cost accumulation system that aggregates manufacturing costs by departments or by production processes. Total manufacturing costs are accumulated by two major categories—direct materials and conversion costs (the sum of direct labor and factory overhead applied). Unit cost is determined by dividing the total costs charged to a cost center by the output of that cost center. Process costing is appropriate for companies that produce a continuous mass of like units through a series of operations or processes. Process costing is generally used in such industries as petroleum, chemicals, oil refinery, textiles, and food processing.

The process-costing method uses what is called the *cost of production report,* which summarizes the total cost charged to a department and the allocation between the ending work-in-process inventory and the units completed and transferred to the next department or finished goods inventory. The output of a processing department during a given period is measured in terms of *equivalent units* of production, which is the expression of the physical units of output in terms of doses or amount of work applied thereto.

The cost of production report generally consists of four sections:

1. *Physical flow* accounts for the physical flow of units in and out of a department.

2. *Equivalent production* is the sum of (a) units in process, restated in completed units and (b) total units actually produced. The computation of equivalent units of production depends on the flow of cost method-*weighted average* or *FIFO*.

3. *Costs to account for* accounts for the incurrence of costs that were (a) in process at the beginning of the period; (b) transferred in from previous departments; and (c) added by the department during the current period.

4. *Costs accounted for* accounts for the disposition of costs charged to the department that were (a) transferred out to the next department or finished goods inventory; (b) completed and on hand; and (c) in process at the end of the period. The total of the *Costs to account for* must equal the total of the *Costs accounted for.*

In computing the unit cost for a processing center, when a beginning inventory of work-in-process exists, two specific assumptions about the flow of costs are used—*weighted average* and *FIFO*. Under weighted average, the costs in the beginning inventory are averaged with the current period's costs to determine one average unit cost for all units passing through the cost center in a given month. Under FIFO, costs in the beginning inventory are not mingled with the current period's costs but transferred out as a separate batch of goods at a different unit cost from units started and completed during the period.

■ **Example**

The Portland Cement Manufacturing Company, Inc., manufactures cement. Its processing operations involve quarrying, grinding, blending, packing, and sacking. For cost accounting and control purposes, there are four processing centers: Raw Material No. 1, Raw Material No. 2, Clinker, and Cement. Separate cost of production reports are prepared in detail with respect to the foregoing cost centers. The following information pertains to the operation of Raw Material No. 2 Department for July 19A:

	Materials	Conversion
Units in process July 1		
800 bags	complete	60% complete
Costs	$12,000	$56,000
Units transferred out		
40,000 bags		
Current costs	$41,500	$521,500
Units in process, July 31		
5,000 bags	complete	30% complete

1. Using the weighted average method of costing, we can determine
   a. Equivalent production units and unit costs by elements
   b. Cost of work-in-process for July
   c. Cost of units completed and transferred
2. We can do the same thing, using the FIFO method of costing.

1 and 2 (a)

Computation of Output in Equivalent Units

	Physical Flow	Materials	Conversion
WIP, beginning	800(60%)		
Units transferred in	44,200		
Units to account for	45,000		
Units completed and transferred out	40,000	40,000	40,000
WIP, end	5,000(30%)	5,000	1,500
Units accounted for	45,000		
Equivalent units used for weighted average		45,000	41,500
Less: Old equivalent units for work done on beginning inventory in prior period		800	480
Equivalent units used for FIFO		44,200	41,020

1 (b) (c)

Cost of Production Report—Weighted Average Raw Material No. 2 Department for the Month Ended July 31, 19A

	WIP Beginning	Current Costs	Total Costs	Equivalent Units	Average Unit Cost
Materials	$12,000	$ 41,500	$ 53,500	45,000	$ 1.1889
Conversion costs	56,000	521,500	577,500	41,500	13.9156
	$68,000	563,000	631,000		$15.1045
Cost of goods completed 40,000 × $15.1045			$604,180		
WIP, end:					
Materials 5,000 × $1.1889	$ 5,944.50				
Conversion 1,500 × 13.9156	20,873.40	$ 26,817.90			
Total costs accounted		$631,000(rounded)			

2 (b) (c)

Cost of Production Report—FIFO Raw Material No. 2 Department for the Month Ended July 31, 19A

	Total Costs	Equivalent Units	Unit Costs
WIP, beginning	$ 68,000		
Current costs:			
Materials	41,500	44,200	$ 0.9389
Conversion costs	521,500	41,020	12.7133
Total costs to account for	$631,000		$13.6522
WIP, end:			
Materials			
5,000 × $0.9389	$ 4,694.50		
Conversion			
1,500 × $12.7133	19,069.95	23,764.45	
Cost of goods completed, 40,000 units:			
• WIP, beginning to be transferred out first	68,000		
• Additional costs to complete 800 × (1 − 0.6)			
× $12.7133	4,068.26		
• Cost of goods started and completed this month 39,200			
× $13.6522	535,166.24	$607,234.50	
Total costs accounted for		$631,000(rounded)	

Answers are summarized as follows:

1 and 2.

	Weighted Average		FIFO	
	Materials	Conversion	Materials	Conversion
a. Equivalent units	45,000	41,500	44,200	41,020
Unit costs	$1.1889	$13.9156	$0.9389	$12.7133
b. Cost of WIP	$26,817.90		$23,764.45	
c. Cost of units completed and transferred	$604,180		$607,234.50	

PRODUCT-FINANCING ARRANGEMENTS As per FASB 49, the arrangement involving the sale and repurchase of inventory is in substance a financing arrangement. It mandates that the product-financing arrangement be accounted for as a borrowing instead of a sale. In many cases, the product is stored on the company's (sponsor's) premises. Further, often the sponsor will guarantee the debt of the other entity.

Types of product-financing arrangements include:

• Sponsor sells a product to another business and agrees to reacquire the product or one basically identical to it. The established price to be paid by the sponsor typically includes financing and holding costs.

• Sponsor has another company buy the product for it and agrees to repurchase the product from the other entity.

• Sponsor controls the distribution of the product that has been bought by another company in accord with the aforementioned terms.

In all situations, the company (sponsor) either agrees to repurchase the product at given prices over specified time periods or guarantees resale prices to third parties.

When the sponsor sells the product to the other firm and in a related transaction agrees to repurchase it, the sponsor should record a liability when the proceeds are received to the degree the product applies to the financing arrangement. A sale should *not* be recorded and the product should be retained as inventory on the sponsor's books.

In the case where another firm buys the product for the sponsor, inventory is debited and liability credited at the time of purchase.

Costs of the product, except for processing costs, in excess of sponsor's original production cost or acquisition cost or the other company's purchase cost constitute finance and holding costs. The sponsor accounts for these costs according to its typical accounting policies. Interest costs will also be incurred in connection with the financing arrangement. These should be separately shown and may be deferred.

■ Example

On 1/1/19X1, a sponsor borrows $100,000 from another company and gives the inventory as collateral for the loan. The entry is

```
Cash        100,000
    Liability          100,000
```

Note that a sale is *not* recorded and the inventory remains on the books of the sponsor. In effect, inventory serves as collateral for a loan.

On 12/31/19X1, the sponsor pays back the other company. The collateralized inventory item is returned. The interest rate on the loan was 8%. Storage costs were $2,000. The entry is

```
Liability          100,000
Deferred Interest    8,000
Storage Expense      2,000
    Cash                    110,000
```

Typically, most of the product in the financing arrangement is eventually used or sold by the sponsor. However, in some cases, small amounts of the product may be sold by the financing entity to other parties.

The entity that gives financing to the sponsor is usually an existing creditor, nonbusiness entity, or trust. It is also possible that the financier may have been established for the *only* purpose of providing financing for the sponsor.

Footnote disclosure should be made of the particulars of the product-financing arrangement. *See also* Revenue Recognition Methods.

PRODUCTION MIX VARIANCE This is a cost variance that arises if the actual production mix deviates from the standard or budgeted mix. In a multiproduct, multiinput situation, the mix variances explain the portion of the *quantity (usage, or efficiency) variance* caused by using inputs (direct materials and direct labor) in ratios different from standard proportions, thus helping determine how efficiently mixing operations are performed. The *material mix variance* indicates the impact on material costs of the deviation from the budgeted mix. The *labor mix variance* measures the impact of changes in the labor mix on labor costs.

$$\begin{matrix} \text{Material} \\ \text{mix} \\ \text{variance} \end{matrix} = \left(\begin{matrix} \text{Actual units} \\ \text{used at} \\ \text{standard mix} \end{matrix} - \begin{matrix} \text{Actual units} \\ \text{used at} \\ \text{actual mix} \end{matrix} \right) \times \begin{matrix} \text{Standard} \\ \text{unit} \\ \text{price} \end{matrix}$$

$$\begin{matrix} \text{Labor} \\ \text{mix} \\ \text{variance} \end{matrix} = \left(\begin{matrix} \text{Actual hours} \\ \text{used at} \\ \text{standard mix} \end{matrix} - \begin{matrix} \text{Actual hours} \\ \text{used at} \\ \text{actual mix} \end{matrix} \right) \times \begin{matrix} \text{Standard} \\ \text{hourly} \\ \text{rate} \end{matrix}$$

Probable causes of unfavorable production mix variances are as follows: (1) capacity restraints force substitution; (1) poor production scheduling; (3) lack of certain types of labor; and (4) certain materials are in short supply.

■ Example

J Company produces a compound composed of Materials Alpha and Beta that is marketed in 20-pound bags. Material Alpha can be substituted for Material Beta. Standard cost and mix data have been determined as follows:

	Unit Price	Standard Unit	Standard Mix Proportions
Material Alpha	$3	5 lbs	25%
Material Beta	4	15	75
		20 lbs	100%

Processing each 20 pounds of material requires 10 hours of labor. The company employs two types of labor—skilled and unskilled—working on two processes, assembly and finishing. The following standard labor cost has been set for a 20-pound bag.

	Standard Hours	Standard Wage Rate	Total	Standard Mix Proportions
Unskilled	4 hrs	$2	$ 8	40%
Skilled	6	3	18	60
	10 hrs	$2.60	$26	100%

At standard cost, labor averages $2.60 per unit. During the month of December, 100 twenty-pound bags were completed with the following labor costs:

	Actual Hours	Actual Rate	Actual Wages
Unskilled	380 hrs	$2.50	$ 950
Skilled	600	3.25	1,950
	980 hrs	$2.96	$2,900

Material records show

Material Alpha actually used, 700 lbs @ $3.10
Material Beta actually used, 1,400 lbs @ 3.90

Using the previous formulas, the material mix variance and labor mix variance are computed as shown at bottom of page.

PRODUCTION YIELD VARIANCE Production yield variance is a difference between the actual yield and the standard yield. *Yield* is a measure of productivity. In other words, it is a measure of output from a given amount of input. For example, in the production of potato chips, we might expect a certain yield; such as 40% yield, or 40 pounds of chips for 100 pounds of potatoes. If the actual yield is less than the expected or standard yield for a given level of input, the yield variance is unfavorable. A yield variance is computed for labor as well as for materials. A *labor yield variance* is considered the result of the quantity and/or the quality of labor used. The yield variance explains the remaining portion of the *quantity variance* and is caused by a yield of finished product that does not correspond with the quantity that actual inputs should have produced. When there is no mix variance, the yield variance equals the quantity variance.

Material Mix Variance

	Actual Units Used at Standard Mix*	Actual Units at Actual Mix	Difference	Standard Unit Price	Variance (U or F)
Material Alpha	525 lbs	700 lbs	175U	$3	$525U
Material Beta	1,575	1,400	175F	4	700F
	2,100 lbs	2,100 lbs			$175F

*This is the standard mix proportions of 25% and 75% applied to the actual material units used of 2,100 pounds.

Labor Mix Variance

	Actual Hours Used at Standard Mix*	Actual Hours Used at Actual Mix	Difference	Standard Hourly Rate	Variance (U or F)
Unskilled	392 hrs	380 hrs	12F	$2	$24F
Skilled	588	600	12U	3	36U
	980 hrs	980 hrs			$12U

*This is the standard mix proportions of 40% and 60% applied to the actual total labor hours used of 980.

$$\text{Material yield variance} = \begin{pmatrix} \text{Actual units used at standard mix} & - \text{Actual output used at standard mix} \end{pmatrix} \times \text{Standard unit price}$$

$$\text{Labor yield variance} = \begin{pmatrix} \text{Actual hours used at standard mix} & - \text{Actual output hours used at standard mix} \end{pmatrix} \times \text{Standard hourly rate}$$

Probable causes of unfavorable production yield variances are (1) low-quality materials and/or labor; (2) faulty equipment; (3) improper production methods; and (4) an improper or costly mix of materials and/or labor.

■ Example

A company uses a standard cost system for its production of a chemical product. This chemical is produced by mixing three major raw materials, A, B, and C. The company has the following standards:

36 lbs of material A	@ 1.00	= $ 36.00
48 lbs of material B	@ 2.00	= 96.00
36 lbs of material C	@ 1.75	= $ 63.00
120 lbs of standard mix	@ 1.625	= $195.00

The company should produce 100 pounds of finished product at a standard cost of $1.625 per pound ($195/120 lbs). To convert 120 pounds of materials into 100 pounds of finished chemical requires 400 direct labor hours at $3.50 per hour, or $14 per pound. During the month of December, the company completed 4,250 pounds of output with the following labor: direct labor 15,250 hours @ $3.50. Material records show

Material A	1,160 lbs used
Material B	1,820
Material C	1,480

Material yield variance can be calculated as follows:

With a standard yield of 83⅓% (100/120), 4,250 pounds of completed output should have required 17,000 hours of direct labor (4,250 lbs × 400 direct labor hrs/100). Comparing the hours allowed for the actual input, 14,866.67 hours, with the hours allowed for actual output, 17,000 hours, we find a favorable labor yield variance of $7,466.66, as shown following:

Labor Yield Variance:

Actual hours at expected output	$52,033.34
Actual output (4,250 lbs × 400/100 = 17,000 hrs @ $3.50 or 4,250 lbs @ $14.00)	59,500
	$ 7,466.66*F*

PROFIT CENTER This is a responsibility center of an organization. It is the unit in an organization that is responsible for revenues earned and costs incurred. A manager of a profit center has control over both revenues and costs and attempts to maximize profit. Examples include a college book division of a publishing company, a houseware department in a retail store, and a product division. A profit center has the following characteristics: (1) its goal is to earn a profit; (2) its management is evaluated by means of contribution income statements, in terms of meeting sales and cost objectives; and (3) its management has the authority to make decisions regarding factors that determine the amount of profit, which may include selection of sales outlets, advertising policy, and selection of sources of supply. *See also* Responsibility Accounting; Segmental Reporting.

PROFIT VARIANCE Profit variance is a difference between actual profit and budgeted

	Actual Input Units at Standard Mix	Actual Output Units at Standard Mix*	Difference	Standard Unit Price	Variance (U or F)
Material A	1,338 lbs	1,275 lbs	63*U*	$1.00	$ 63*U*
Material B	1,784	1,700	84*F*	2.00	168*U*
Material C	1,338	1,275	63*U*	1.75	110.25*U*
	4,460	4,250			$341.25*U*

* This is the standard mix proportions of 30%, 40%, and 30% applied to the actual *output* units used of 4,250 lbs.

profit. Profit is affected by three basic items: sales price, sales volume, and costs. In a multiproduct firm, if all products are not equally profitable, profit is also affected by the mix of products sold. *See also* Contribution Margin; Profit Variance Analysis.

PROFIT VARIANCE ANALYSIS This, often called *gross profit analysis*, deals with how to analyze the profit variance which constitutes the departure between actual profit and the previous year's income or the budgeted figure. The primary goal of profit variance analysis is to improve performance and profitability in the future.

Profit, whether it is *gross profit* in *absorption costing* or *contribution margin* in *direct costing*, is affected by at least three basic items: sales price, sales volume, and costs. In addition, in a multiproduct firm, if not all products are equally profitable, profit is affected by the mix of products sold.

The difference between budgeted and actual profits are due to one or more of the following:
1. Changes in unit sales price and cost, called *sales price* and *cost price variances*, respectively. The difference between sales price variance and cost price variance is often called a *contribution-margin-per-unit variance* or a *gross-profit-per-unit variance*, depending upon the type of costing system, that is, absorption costing or direct costing. Contribution margin is considered a better measure of product profitability because it deducts from sales revenue only the variable costs that are controllable in terms of fixing responsibility. Gross profit does not reflect cost-volume-profit relationships. Nor does it consider directly traceable marketing costs.
2. Changes in the volume of products sold summarized as the *sales volume variance* and the *cost volume variance*. The difference between the two is called the *total volume variance*.

3. Changes in the volume of the more profitable or less profitable items, referred to as the *sales mix variance*.

Detailed analysis is critical to management when multiproducts exist. The volume variances may be used to measure a change in volume (while holding the mix constant) and the mix may be employed to evaluate the effect of a change in sales mix (while holding the quantity constant). This type of variance analysis is useful when the products are substituted for each other or when products that are not necessarily substitutes for each other are marketed through the same channel.

Types of Standards in Profit Variance Analysis

To determine the various causes for a favorable variance (an increase) or an unfavorable variance (a decrease) in profit we need some kind of yardstick to compare against the actual results. The yardstick may be based on the prices and costs of the previous year or any year selected as the base period. Some companies are summarizing profit variance analysis data in their annual report by showing departures from the previous year's reported income. However, one can establish a more effective control and budgetary method rather than the previous year's data. Standard or budgeted mix can be determined using such sophisticated techniques as *linear* and *goal programming*.

Single-Product Firms

Profit variance analysis is simplest in a single-product firm, for there is only one sales price, one set of costs (or cost price), and a unitary sales volume. An unfavorable profit variance can be broken down into four components: sales price variance, cost price variance, sales volume variance, and cost volume variance.

The *sales price variance* measures the impact on the firm's contribution margin (or gross profit) of changes in the unit selling price. It is computed as:

Sales price variance
= (Actual price − Budget price) × Actual sales

If the actual price is lower than the budgeted, for example, this variance is unfavorable; it tends to reduce profit. The *cost price variance*, on the other hand, is simply the summary of price variances for materials, labor, and overhead. (This is the sum of material price, labor rate, and factory overhead spending variances.) It is computed as:

Cost price variance
= (Actual cost − Budget cost) × Actual sales

If the actual unit cost is lower than budgeted, for example, this variance is favorable; it tends to increase profit. We simplify the computation of price variances by taking the sales price variance less the cost price variance and call it the *gross-profit-per-unit variance* or *contribution-margin-per-unit variance*.

The *sale volume variance* indicates the impact on the firm's profit of changes in the unit sales volume. This is the amount by which sales would have varied from the budget if nothing but sales volume had changed. It is computed as:

Sales volume variance
= (Actual sales − Budget sales) × Budget price

If actual sales volume is greater than budgeted, this is favorable; it tends to increase profit. The *cost volume variance* has the same interpretation. It is

(Actual sales − Budget sales) × Budget cost per unit

The difference between the sales volume variance and the cost volume variance is called the *total volume variance*.

▪ Example

The controller of the Royalla Publishing Company prepared the following comparative statement of operations for 19A and 19B.

	19A	19B
Sales in units	97,500	110,000
Selling price	$ 9.00	$ 8.80
Sales revenue	$877,500	$968,000
Cost of goods sold	$585,000	$704,000
Gross profit	$292,500	$264,000

The controller was very pleased with the performance of the company in 19A. Analyze the decline in gross profit between 19A and 19B by calculating:

(a) Sales price variance
(b) Cost price variance
(c) Sales volume variance
(d) Cost volume variance
(e) Total volume variance (sales volume variance − cost volume variance) or (sales mix variance + sales quantity variance)
(f) Sales mix variance
(g) Sales quantity variance

19A gross profit	$292,500
19B gross profit	264,000
Decrease in gross profit to be accounted for	$ 28,500

(a) *Sales price variance*:

19B actual sales revenue	$968,000
19B actual sales revenue at 19A price (110,000 @ $9)	990,000
	$ 22,000U

(b) *Cost price variance*:

19B actual	$704,000
19B actual at 19A cost per unit (110,000 @ $6*)	660,000
	$ 44,000U

*19A cost per unit = $585,000/97,500 = $6

(c) *Sales volume variance*:

19B actual volume at 19A price	$990,000 (110,000 × $9)
19A actual volume at 19A price	877,500
(19B actual − 19A actual) × 19A price	$112,500F

(d) *Cost volume variance:*

19B actual volume at 19A cost	$660,000 (110,000 × $6)
19A actual volume at 19A cost	585,000
(19B actual − 19A actual) × 19A cost	$ 75,000U

(e) *Total volume variance*

= Sales volume variance − Cost volume variance
= $112,500F − $75,000U = $37,500F

which is broken down into the sales mix variance and the sales quantity variance as follows:

(f) *Sales mix variance* = 0 since we have only one product in this problem.

(g) *Sales quantity variance*

19B Actual Volume	19A Budgeted Volume	Difference	19A Gross Profit per Unit*	Variance ($)
110,000	97,500	12,500F	$3	$37,500F

* 19A gross profit per unit = 19A selling price − 19A cost of goods sold = $9 − $6 = $3

The decline in gross profit of $28,500 can be explained as follows:

	Gains	Losses
Gain due to *favorable* sales volume variance	$112,500F	
Losses due to:		
Unfavorable sales price variance		$22,000U
Unfavorable cost price variance		44,000U
Unfavorable cost volume variance		75,000U
	$112,500F	$141,000U

The decrease in gross profit is thus accounted for:

$$141,000U − 112,500F = 28,500U$$

Multiproduct Firms

When a firm produces more than one product, there is a fourth component of the profit variance. This is the *sales mix variance*—the effect on profit of selling a different proportionate mix of products than that which has been budgeted. This variance arises when different products have different contribution margins. In a multiproduct firm, actual sales volume can differ from that budgeted in two ways. The total number of units sold could differ from the target aggregate sales. In addition, the mix of the products actually sold may not be proportionate to the target mix. Each of these two different types of changes in volume is reflected in a separate variance.

The total volume variance is divided into the two: the *sales mix variance* and the *sales quantity variance*. These two variances should be used to evaluate the marketing department of the firm. The sales mix variance shows how well the department has done in terms of selling the more profitable products, whereas the sales quantity variance measures how well the firm has done in terms of its overall sales volume. They are computed as:

Sales mix variance = (Actual sales at budget mix
        − Budget sales at budget mix)
            × Budget CM (or gross profit)/unit

Sales quantity variance = (Actual sales at budget mix
        − Actual sales at budget mix)
            × Budget CM (or gross profit)/unit

Total volume variance = (Actual sales at actual mix
        − Budget sales at budget mix)
            × Budget CM (or gross profit)/unit

■ Example

The Lake Tahoe ski store sells two ski models—model X and model Y. For the years 19X1 and 19X2, the store realized a gross profit of $246,640 and only $211,650, respectively. The owner of the store was astounded since the total sales volume in dollars and in units was higher for 19X2 than for 19X1, yet the gross profit achieved actually declined. Following are the store's unaudited operating results for 19X1 and 19X2. No fixed costs were included in the cost of goods sold per unit.

Year	Model X Selling Price	Cost of Goods Sold per Unit	Sales (in units)	Sales Revenue	Model Y Selling Price	Cost of Goods Sold per Unit	Sales (in Units)	Sales Revenue
1	$150	$110	2,800	$420,000	$172	$121	2,640	$454,080
2	160	125	2,650	424,000	176	135	2,900	510,400

Explain why the gross profit declined by $34,990. Include a detailed variance analysis of price changes and changes in volume both for sales and cost. Also subdivide the total volume variance into changes in price and changes in quantity.

Sales price and sales volume variances measure the impact on the firm's *CM* (or gross profit) of changes in the unit selling price and sales volume. In computing these variances, all costs are held constant in order to stress changes in price and volume. Cost price and cost volume variances are computed in the same manner, holding price and volume constant. All these variances for the Lake Tahoe ski store are computed following.

Sales Price Variance

Actual sales for 19X2:
Model X 2,650 × $160 = $424,000
Model Y 2,900 ×   176 =   510,400 $934,400
Actual 19X2 sales at 19X1 prices:
Model X 2,650 × $150 = $397,500
Model Y 2,900 ×   172 =   498,800   896,300
                                $ 38,100F

Sales Volume Variance

Actual 19X2 sales at 19X1 prices: $896,300
Actual 19X1 sales (at 19X1 prices):
Model X 2,800 × $150 = $420,000
Model Y 2,640 ×   172 =   454,080   874,080
                                $ 22,220F

Cost Price Variance

Actual cost of goods sold for 19X2:
Model X 2,650 × $125 = $331,250
Model Y 2,900 ×   135 =   391,500 $722,750
Actual 19X2 sales at 19X1 costs:
Model X 2,650 × $110 = $291,500
Model Y 2,900 ×   121 =   350,900   642,400
                                $ 80,350U

Cost Volume Variance

Actual 19X2 sales at 19X1 costs: $642,400
Actual 19X1 sales (at 19X1 costs):
Model X 2,800 × $110 = $308,000
Model Y 2,640 ×   121 =   319,440   627,440
                                $ 14,960U

Total volume variance = sales volume variance − cost volume variance = $22,220F − $14,960U = $7,260F

The total volume variance is computed as the sum of a sales mix variance and a sales quantity variance as follows:

Sales Mix Variance

	19X2 Actual Sales at 19X1 Mix*	19X2 Actual Sales at 19X2 Mix	Difference	19X1 Gross Profit per Unit	Variance ($)
Model X	2,857	2,650	207U	$40	$ 8,280U
Model Y	2,693	2,900	207F	51	10,557F
	5,550	5,550			$ 2,277F

* This is the 19X1 mix (used as standard or budget) proportions of 51.47% (or 2,800/5,440 = 51.47%) and 48.53% (or 2,640/5,440 = 48.53%) applied to the actual 19X2 sales figure of 5,550 units.

Sales Quantity Variance

	19X2 Actual Sales at 19X1 Mix*	19X1 Actual Sales at 19X1 Mix	Difference	19X1 Gross Profit per Unit	Variance ($)
Model X	2,857	2,800	57F	$40	$2,280F
Model Y	2,693	2,640	53F	51	2,703F
	5,550	5,440			$4,983F

* A favorable total volume variance is due to a favorable shift in the sales mix (that is, from Model X to Model Y) and also to a favorable increase in sales volume (by 110 units), which is shown as follows.

Sales mix variance	$2,277F
Sales quantity variance	4,983F
	$7,260F

However, there remains the decrease in gross profit. The decrease in gross profit of $34,990 can be explained as follows:

	Gains	Losses
Gain due to increased sales price	$38,100F	
Loss due to increased cost		80,350U
Gain due to increase in units sold	4,983F	
Gain due to shift in sales mix	2,277F	
	$45,360F	$80,350U

Hence, net decrease in gross profit = $80,350 − $45,360 = $34,990U.

Despite the increase in sales price and volume and the favorable shift in sales mix, the Lake Tahoe ski store ended up losing $34,990 compared to 19X1. The major reason for this comparative loss was the tremendous increase in cost of goods sold, as indicated by an unfavorable cost price variance of $80,350. The costs for both Model X and Model Y went up quite significantly over 19X1. The store has to take a close look at the cost picture. Even though only variable costs were included in cost of goods sold per unit, both variable and fixed costs should be analyzed in an effort to cut down on controllable costs. In doing that, it is essential that responsibility be clearly fixed to given individuals. In a retail business like the Lake Tahoe ski store, operating expenses such as advertising and payroll of store employees must also be closely scrutinized.

Sales Mix Analysis

Many product lines often include a lower margin price leader model and a high-margin deluxe model. For example, the automobile industry includes in its product line low-margin energy-efficient small cars and higher margin deluxe models. In an attempt to increase overall profitability, management would wish to emphasize the higher margin expensive items, but salespeople might find it easier to sell lower margin cheaper models. Thus, a salesperson might meet the unit sales quota with each item at its budgeted price but because of mix shifts could be far short of contributing his or her share of budgeted profit. Management should realize that (1) greater proportions of more profitable products mean higher profits and (2) higher proportions of lower margin sales reduce overall profit despite the increase in overall sales volume. That is to say that an unfavorable mix may easily offset a favorable increase in volume, and vice versa.

Performance Reports

Profit variance analysis aids in fixing responsibility by separating the causes of the change in profit into price, volume, and mix factors. With responsibility resting in different places, the segregation of the total profit variance is essential. The performance reports based on the analysis of profit variances must be prepared for each responsibility center, indicating the following:

1. Is it controllable?
2. Is it favorable or unfavorable?
3. If it is unfavorable, is it significant enough for further investigation?
4. Who is responsible for what portion of the total profit variance?
5. What are the causes for an unfavorable variance?
6. What is the remedial action to take?

The performance report must address these types of questions. The report is useful in two ways: (1) in focusing attention on situations in need of management action and (2) in increasing the precision of planning and control of sales and costs. The report should be produced as part of the overall standard costing and *responsibility accounting* system. *See also* Responsibility Accounting; Sales Mix Variance; Variance Analysis.

PROFITABILITY INDEX This, also called *excess present value index* or *cost-benefit ratio*, is the ratio of the total present value (PV) of future cash inflows to the initial investment (I). That is, PV/I. This index is primarily used as a means of ranking projects in *capital rationing* situations. In a single-project case, if the index is greater than 1, then you should accept the project. *See also* Capital Rationing.

PRO FORMA This refers to a financial statement or account that contains hypothetical (assumed) figures. The assumptions supporting the estimates are disclosed. In a sense, it is a what-if situation. The purpose is to show a proposed future financial condition.

PROGRAM EVALUATION AND REVIEW TECHNIQUE (PERT) PERT is a useful management tool for planning, scheduling, costing, coordinating, and controlling complex projects such as

• Formulation of a master budget
• Construction of buildings

• Installation of computers
• Scheduling the closing of books
• Assembly of a machine
• Research and development activities

Questions to be answered by PERT include

• When will the project be finished?
• What is the probability that the project will be completed by any given time?

The PERT technique involves the diagrammatic representation of the sequence of activities comprising a project by means of a *network*. The network (1) visualizes all of the individual tasks (activities) to complete a given job or program; (2) points out interrelationships; and (3) consists of activities (represented by arrows) and events (represented by circles), as shown following.

1. *Arrows*—represent tasks or activities that are distinct segments of the project requiring time and resources.

2. *Nodes* (*circles*)—symbolize events or milestone points in the project representing the completion of one or more activities and/or the initiation of one or more subsequent activities. An event is a point in time and does not consume any time in itself, as does an activity.

In a real-world situation, the estimates of completion times of activities will seldom be certain. To cope with the uncertainty in activity time estimates, the PERT proceeds

by estimating *three* possible duration times for each activity. As shown in Figure 1, the numbers appearing on the arrows represent these three time estimates which are needed to complete the various events. These time estimates are (1) the most optimistic time, labeled a; (2) the most likely time, m; and (3) the most pessimistic time, b.

For example, the optimistic time for completing activity B is 1 day, the most likely time is 2 days, but the pessimistic time is 3 days. The next step is to calculate an expected time, which is determined as follows:

$$t_e \text{ (expected time)} = (a + 4m + b)/6$$

For example, for activity B, the expected time is

$$(1 + 4(2) + 3)/6 = 12/6 = 2 \text{ days}$$

As a measure of variation (uncertainty) about the expected time, the standard deviation is calculated as follows:

$$\sigma = (b - a)/6$$

For example, the standard deviation of completion time for activity B is

$$(3 - 1)/6 = 2/6 = 0.33 \text{ days}$$

Expected activity times and their standard deviations are computed in this manner for all the activities of the network and arranged in the tabular format, as shown on top of page 360.

Figure 1 Network Diagram

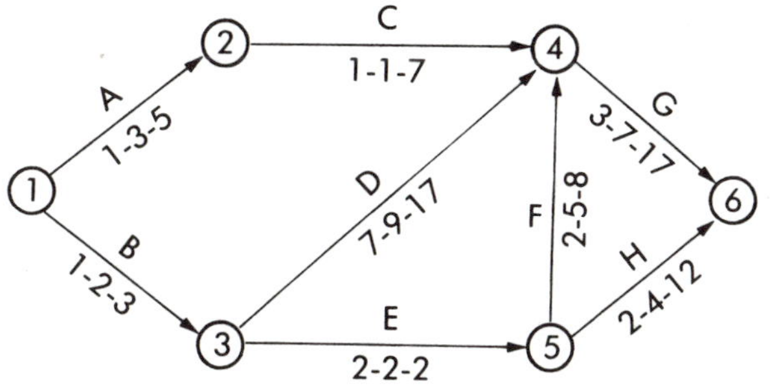

Activity	Predecessors	a	m	b	t_e	σ
A	None	1	3	5	3.0	0.67
B	None	1	2	3	2.0	0.33
C	A	1	1	7	2.0	1.00
D	B	7	9	17	10.0	1.67
E	B	2	2	2	2.0	0.00
F	E	2	5	8	5.0	0.67
G	C,D,F	3	7	17	8.0	2.33
H	E	2	4	12	5.0	1.67

To answer the first question, we need to determine the network's *critical path*. A path is a sequence of connected activities. In Figure 1, 1-2-4-6 would be an example of a path. The critical path for a project is the path that takes the longest amount of time. The sum of the estimated activity times for all activities on the critical path is the total time required to complete the project. These activities are "critical" because any delay in their completion will cause a delay in the project. The critical path is the minimum amount of time needed for the completion of the project. Thus, the activities along this path must be shortened in order to speed up the project. Activities not on the critical path are not critical, since they will be worked on simultaneously with critical path activities and their completion could be delayed up to a point without delaying the project as a whole.

An easy way to find the critical path involves the following two steps: (1) identify all possible paths of a project and calculate their completion times and (2) pick the one with the longest amount of completion time, which is the critical path.

(When the network is large and complex, we need a more systematic and efficient approach, which is reserved for an advanced management science text.)

In the example, we have:

Path	Completion Time
A-C-G	13 days (3 + 2 + 8)
B-D-G	20 days (2 + 10 + 8)
B-E-F-G	17 days (2 + 2 + 5 + 8)
B-E-H	9 days (2 + 2 + 5)

The critical path is B-D-G, which means it takes 20 days to complete the project.

The next important information we want to obtain is, What is the chance that the project will be completed within a contract time, say, 21 days? To answer the question, we introduce the standard deviation of total project time around the expected time, which is determined as follows:

Standard deviation (project)

$$= \sqrt{\frac{\text{Sum of the squares of the standard}}{\text{deviations of all critical path activities}}}$$

Using the standard deviation and table of areas under the normal distribution curve (see Appendix, Table 5), the probability of completing the project within any given time period can be determined.

Using the formula just given, the standard deviation of completion time (the path B-D-G) for the project is as follows:

$$\sqrt{\frac{(0.33)^2 + (1.67)^2 + (2.33)^2}{= \sqrt{0.1089 + 2.7889 + 5.4289}}}$$

$$= \sqrt{8.3267} = 2.885 \text{ days}$$

Assume the expected delivery time is, say, 21 days. The first step is to compute z, which is the number of standard deviations from the mean represented by our given time of 21 days. The formula for z is

$z = (\text{Delivery time} - \text{Expected time})/$
$\qquad\qquad\qquad\qquad \text{Standard deviation}$

Therefore, $z = (21 \text{ days} - 20 \text{ days})/2.885$ days $= 0.35$. The next step is to find the probability associated with the calculated value of z by referring to a table of areas under a normal curve (see Appendix, Table 5).

From Table 5 we see the probability is 0.63683, which means that there is close to a 64% chance that the project will be completed in less than 21 days.

Summary and Remarks

1. The expected completion time of the project is 20 days.
2. There is a better than 60% chance of fin-

ishing before 21 days. We can also obtain the chances of meeting any other deadline if we wish.

3. Activities B-D-G are on the critical path. They must be watched more closely than the others; for if they fall behind, the whole project falls behind.

4. If extra effort is needed to finish the project on time or before the deadline, we have to borrow resources (such as money and labor) from any activity *not* on the critical path.

5. It is possible to reduce the completion time of one or more activities, which will require an extra expenditure of cost. The benefit from reducing the total completion time of a project by accelerated efforts on certain activities must be balanced against the extra cost of doing so. A related problem is to determine which activities must be accelerated to reduce the total project completion time. Critical Path Method (CPM), also known as PERT/COST, is widely used to deal with this subject.

PERT is a technique for project management and control. It is *not* an optimizing decision model since the decision to undertake a project is initially assumed. It will not evaluate an investment project according to its attractiveness or the time specifications we observe.

PROGRAM-PLANNING-BUDGETING SYSTEM (PPBS)

PPBS is a planning-oriented approach to developing a program budget. A program budget is a budget in which expenditures are based primarily on programs of work and secondarily on character and object. It is a transitional type of budget, between the traditional character and object budget on the one hand and the performance budget on the other. The major contribution of PPBS lies in the planning process, that is, the process of making program policy decisions that lead to a specific budget and specific multi-year plans.

PROGRAM TRADING

This is a blanket term for strategies used by investors attempting to profit or *hedge* by trading stocks on New York exchanges against stock index futures in the Chicago future exchanges.

PROJECTED BENEFIT OBLIGATION

This is the actuarial discounted amount of future employee benefits to be paid using *future* salary levels for services rendered up to the current year. *See also* Pension Plans.

PROJECT SELECTION AND ZERO–ONE PROGRAMMING

A more general approach to solving *capital rationing* problems is the use of *zero–one* integer programming. Here the objective is to select the mix of projects that maximizes the net present value (NPV) subject to a budget constraint.

■ Example

A company with a fixed budget of $250,000 needs to select a mix of acceptable projects from the following:

Projects	I($)	PV($)	NPV($)
1	70,000	112,000	42,000
2	100,000	145,000	45,000
3	110,000	126,500	16,500
4	60,000	79,000	19,000
5	40,000	38,000	−2,000
6	80,000	95,000	15,000

Using the data just given, we can set up the problem as a zero–one integer programming problem such that

$$x_j = \begin{cases} 1 \text{ if project } j \text{ is selected} \\ 0 \text{ if project } j \text{ is not selected } (j = 1,2,3,4,5,6) \end{cases}$$

The problem then can be formulated as follows:

Maximize

$$NPV = \$42,000x_1 + \$45,000x_2 + \$16,500x_3 \\ + \$19,000x_4 - \$2,000x_5 + \$15,000x_6$$

subject to

$70,000x_1 + $100,000x_2 + $110,000x_3 + $60,000x_4$
$+ $40,000x_5 + $80,000x_6 \leq $250,000$
$$x_j = 0,1 \ (j = 1,2, \ . \ . \ . \ ,6)$$

Using the zero–one programming solution routine, the solution to the problem is

$$x_1 = 1, \ x_2 = 1, \ x_4 = 1$$

and the NPV is $106,000. Thus, projects 1, 2, and 4 should be accepted.

The strength of the use of zero–one programming is its ability to handle mutually exclusive and interdependent projects.

■ **Example**

Suppose that exactly one project can be selected from the set of projects 1, 3, and 5. Since either 1, 3, or 5 must be selected and only one can be selected, exactly one of the three variables x_1, x_3, or x_5 must be equal to 1 and the rest must be equal to 0. The constraint to be added is

$$x_1 + x_3 + x_5 = 1$$

Note that, for example, if $x_3 = 1$, then $x_1 = 0$ and $x_5 = 0$ in order for the constraint to hold.

■ **Example**

Suppose that projects 2 and 4 are mutually exclusive, which means neither, or either one of both (not both) should be selected. The constraint to be added:

$$x_2 + x_4 \leq 1$$

Note that the following three pairs satisfy this constraint:

$$x_2 = 0 \text{ and } x_4 = 0$$
$$x_2 = 1 \text{ and } x_4 = 0$$
$$x_2 = 0 \text{ and } x_4 = 1$$

But $x_2 = 1$ and $x_4 = 1$ violates this constraint, since $1 + 1 = 2 > 1$.

■ **Example**

Suppose if project 3 is selected then project 4 must be selected. In other words, a mutual dependence exists between projects 3 and 4. An example might be a project such as building a second floor, which requires the first floor to precede it. Then the constraint to be added is

$$x_3 \leq x_4$$

Note that if $x_3 = 1$, then x_4 must be equal to 1. However, x_4 can be equal to 1 and x_3 can be equal to either 1 or 0. That is, the selection of project 4 does not imply that project 3 must be selected. *See also* Capital Rationing; Integer Programming; Mutually Exclusive Investments; Zero–One Programming.

PROSPECTUS A prospectus is prepared by an entity that wishes to issue securities to investors. In the case of an issuance to the public, filing requirements of the Securities and Exchange Commission must be met. Included in the prospectus are financial statements, disclosures (e.g., lawsuit), business plans, overview of corporate operations, and information regarding officers.

A ''red herring'' is a preliminary prospectus that has not been finalized. Later, a statutory prospectus is prepared, which is the final version.

Prospectuses are also prepared by mutual funds and limited partnerships.

PROXY A proxy is the authorization given by a stockholder of a company to another to vote for him at an election (e.g., board of directors) or for a corporate resolution. The transfer is restricted in duration and usually is only for a specific occasion.

PURCHASE METHOD A business combination is accounted for under the purchase method when the acquiring company pays cash or incurs liabilities to buy the acquired company. *See also* Business Combinations.

Q

QUADRATIC PROGRAMMING (QP) QP is a special class of mathematical programming problems having a *quadratic* objective function and a *linear* constraint set. From the standpoint of solution methods, QP problems are relatively simple compared with other nonlinear programming forms. This is because the form of the QP problem is not too different from the standard linear programming (LP) problem. In fact, the strong similarity with the LP model has led to computational procedures that, with some modifications, utilize the simplex method to derive optimal solutions to QP problems. A classical example of a QP problem is the portfolio selection model as formulated by Harry Markowitz. The objective in the Markowitz model is to minimize some measure of risk associated with the portfolio (variance) while maximizing return on the total investment. The object is to determine the amount of funds to commit to each security from among a set of specified securities. In the area of cost accounting, the GP formulation was extended to the joint cost problem in order to determine optimal price and output policies. *See also* Mathematical Programming; Portfolio Theory and Capital Asset Pricing Model (CAPM).

QUALITATIVE ANALYSIS Accountants and financial managers must not forget the *qualitative* factors in decision making, in addition to the quantitative or financial factors highlighted by *incremental analysis* or otherwise. They are the factors relevant to a decision that are difficult to measure in terms of money. Qualitative factors may include (1) effect on employee morale, schedules, and other internal elements; (2) relationships with and commitments to suppliers; (3) effect on present and future customers; and (4) long-term future effect on profitability.

In some decision-making situations, qualitative aspects are more important than immediate financial benefit from a decision.

▪ Example

In selecting a laboratory site for a high-tech company, the proximity to leading academic institutions may be far more critical from a long-term standpoint than a short-term tax benefit offered by a particular state trying to obtain the laboratory.

QUALITY OF EARNINGS These are the accounting and financial characteristics that have an impact on the earning power of a firm, as shown in its net income figure. These characteristics are complex and interrelated, and are subject to wide varieties of interpretation by analysts, depending upon their own analytical objectives. Furthermore, measurements of some of the characteristics may be extremely difficult, elusive, and perhaps impossible. Nevertheless analysts cannot avoid sorting through the characteristics to determine which of them are favorable in terms of earnings quality and which are unfavorable, and to determine the degree to which they exist. They are then in a position to rank the relative quality of earnings of companies in an industry as well as to restate the companies' net incomes.

Favorable Characteristics in Earnings

• The degree to which the accounting policies employed reflect the economic reality of a company's transactions.

• The degree of realism used to develop estimates of current and future conditions; referring here to the degree of risk attached to estimates or assumptions that may ultimately prove overoptimistic or unwarranted.

• The degree to which sufficient provision has been made for the maintenance of assets and for the maintenance and enhancement of present and future earning power.

• The degree of earnings stability associated with a firm. This refers also to the degree to which income statement components are recurring in nature.

• The stability and growth trend of earnings as well as the predictability of factors that may affect their future levels.

Unfavorable Characteristics of Earnings

• The degree to which accounting changes that are inconsistent with economic reality have been made.

• The degree to which income manipulation exists.

• The degree to which unrealistic deferrals of costs exist.

• The degree to which a company has underaccrued or overaccrued its expenses.

• The degree to which a company has recognized revenue prematurely or belatedly.

• The degree to which unjustified reductions in discretionary costs have been made. Such reductions may deprive the business of expenditures needed for future growth.

• The degree to which highly subjective and uncertain accounting estimates are associated with the recognition of revenue and expense items. In general, the further revenue and expense recognition is removed from the point of cash receipt and payment, the less objective the transaction and the more subjective the interpretations involved.

• The degree to which assets are overstated and liabilities are understated.

• The degree of risk attached to the probability of future realization of different types of assets.

• The degree of operating leverage associated with the firm.

• The degree to which a firm is susceptible to the business cycle.

• The degree to which inflationary profits are included in net income.

The quality of the earnings figure of any given company for any particular time period is a matter of the degree to which favorable and unfavorable characteristics exist, and that the significance of the characteristics depends upon their relevance to and the point of view of the individual financial analyst.

QUANTITY DISCOUNT MODEL The *economic order quantity* (EOQ) model does not take into account quantity discounts, which is not realistic in many real-world cases. Usually, the more you order, the lower the unit price you pay. Quantity discounts are price reductions for large orders offered to buyers to induce them to buy in large quantities. If quantity discounts are offered, the buyer must weigh the potential benefits of reduced purchase price and fewer orders that will result from buying in large quantities against the increase in carrying costs caused by higher average inventories. Hence, the buyer's goal in this case is to select the order quantity that will minimize total costs, where total cost is the sum of carrying cost, ordering cost, *and* purchase cost:

Total cost = Carrying cost + Ordering cost + Purchase cost

$$= C \times (Q/2) + O(D/Q) + PD$$

where C = carrying cost per unit,
O = ordering cost per order,
D = annual demand,
P = unit price,
Q = order quantity.

A step-by-step approach to finding the economic order quanity *with* quantity discounts is summarized following.

1. Compute the *economic order quantity* (*EOQ*) when price discounts are ignored and the corresponding costs using the new cost formula just given. Note EOQ = $\sqrt{2OD/C}$.

2. Compute the costs for those quantities greater than the EOQ at which price reductions occur.

3. Select the value of Q that will result in the lowest total cost.

■ Example

Assume ABC store buys sets of steel at $40 per set from an outside vendor. ABC will sell 6,400 sets evenly throughout the year. ABC desires a 16% return on investment (cost of borrowed money) on its inventory investment. In addition, rent, taxes, and so on for each set in inventory is $1.60. The ordering cost is $100 per order.

Assume further that ABC was offered the following price discount schedule:

Order quantity(Q)	Unit price (P)
1 to 499	$40.00
500 to 999	39.90
1000 or more	39.80

First, the EOQ with no discounts is computed as follows:

$$\text{EOQ} = \sqrt{2(6,400)(100)/8.00}$$
$$= \sqrt{160,000} = 400 \text{ sets.}$$

Total cost = $8.00(400/2) + $100(6,400/400)
$\qquad\qquad$ + $40.00(6,400)

$\qquad\qquad$ = $1,600 + 1,600 + 256,000 = $259,200

We see that the value that minimized the sum of the carrying cost and the ordering cost but not the purchase cost was EOQ = 400 sets. As can be seen in Figure 1, the further we move from the point 400, the greater will be the sum of the carrying and ordering costs. Thus, 400 is obviously the only candidate for the minimum total cost value within the first price range. $Q = 500$ is the only candidate within the $39.90 price range, and $Q = 1,000$ is the only candidate within the $39.80 price bracket. These three quantities are evaluated in Table 1 and illustrated in Figure 1. We find that the EOQ *with* price discounts is 500 sets. Hence, ABC store is justified in going to the first price break, but the extra carrying cost of going to the second price break more than out-

Figure 1 Inventory Cost and Quantity

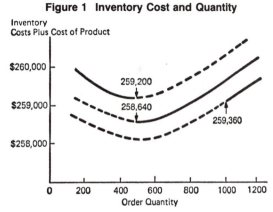

weighs the savings in ordering and in the cost of the product itself.

Table 1 Annual Costs With Varying Order Quantities

Order Quantity	400	500	1,000
Ordering cost			
$100 × (6,400/order quantity)	$ 1,600	$ 1,280	$ 640
Carrying cost			
$8 × (order quantity/2)	1,600	2,000	4,000
Purchase cost			
Unit price × 6,400	256,000	255,360	254,720
Total cost	$259,200	$258,640	$259,360

Advantages and Disadvantages of Quantity Discounts

Buying in large quantities has some favorable and some unfavorable features for a firm. The advantages are lower unit costs, lower ordering costs, fewer stockouts, and lower transportation costs. On the other hand, there are disadvantages, such as higher inventory carrying costs, greater capital requirement, and higher probability of obsolescence and deterioration.

QUANTITY THEORY OF MONEY This is the classical theory of the relationship between the money supply and the price level. The theory states that the level of prices in the economy is directly proportional to the quantity of money in circulation. That is, a given percentage change in the quantity of money will cause an equal percentage in the price level in the same direction. *See also* Equation of Exchange.

QUASI-REORGANIZATION A quasi-reorganization occurs when a company decides to eliminate a deficit in retained earnings through the restatement of assets to market value, liabilities, and stockholders' equity accounts. A company is provided with a fresh start when management believes that the business can become profitable. It allows for the business to continue in essence on the same basis as if legal reorganization had occurred, without the problem and cost typically associated with a legal reorganization. There must be approval from stockholders and creditors. The steps involved follow: (1) there is a write-down of assets to reflect their fair market value; (2) there is a restatement in the capital stock, resulting in additional paid-in-capital by lowering par value; and (3) there results a zero balance in retained earnings after the deficit is eliminated through the transfer of part of capital to the retained earnings account. Retained earnings will bear the quasi-reorganization date.

■ Example

A business having a $3,500,000 deficit undertakes a quasi-reorganization. There is an overstatement in assets of $800,000 compared to fair market value. The balances in capital stock and paid-in-capital are $5,000,000 and $1,500,000, respectively. The following entry is made to effect the quasi-reorganization:

Paid-in-Capital	1,500,000	
Capital Stock	2,800,000	
Assets		800,000
Retained Earnings		3,500,000

Note that the paid-in-capital account has been fully wiped out, so the remaining debit goes to capital stock.

R

RANDOM SAMPLE In random sampling there is an equal probability of each sampling unit being chosen. Further, every possible combination of sampling units has the same chance of being in the sample. The auditor has to be sure that the sample selected is representative of the population from which it is drawn.

A random sample typically involves the following steps:

• Relating identifying numbers (or letters) to sampling units in the population

• Deriving a random sample from the population with the aid of a random number table or a random number generator computer program

The sampling unit may be in physical or monetary terms. Examples of physical identifiers are check number, invoice number, page number, and warehouse row and bin number. Monetary units are in terms of cumulative dollar values in the population. In other words, whatever the order of physical units containing the dollars, their values are cumulative in dollar increments and the aggregate value at any point represents the last dollar included. The probability of choosing a physical unit increases in direct proportion to its dollar value. Thus, the sampling probabilities are proportional to size. *Note*: It is possible that one sampling unit may have more than one randomly selected dollar.

Random sampling may be used for nonstatistical and statistical applications. *See also* Sampling.

RANDOM WALK THEORY According to this theory, stock prices move in an unpredictable and random way due to stock market efficiency. A company's market price of stock goes randomly around real (intrinsic value). But there is a periodic change in the intrinsic value arising from new information. Present security prices are independent of previous ones. Hence, historical prices are not an accurate barometer of future prices.

According to random walk theory, financial information material enough to impact future value is available to knowledgeable investors. Thus, new data affecting stock price are immediately reflected in market value. At a particular point in time, market price is the optimum estimate of stock value, including all available information.

Random walk theorists do not reject the prediction of stock prices based on accurate forecasting of company earnings and dividends. But they do reject employing prior market price analysis in forecasting future market price. *See also* Efficient Market.

REAL ESTATE Generally, returns on real estate outperform those on stocks. Further, the standard deviation of real estate returns is typically less than the standard deviation of stock returns.

Types of real estate that the client may invest in include undeveloped land, residential rental property (e.g., single-family houses for rental, multi-unit apartments), and commercial property (e.g., office buildings, shopping centers, industrial property).

Besides location, the factors to be considered in making a particular real estate investment include method of financing the purchase of property, before-tax cash flow, after-tax cash flow, vacancy rate for rental property, gain or loss for tax purposes, and management problems.

Investing in Land

In real estate investing, land is in the forefront. While in 1989, real estate syndicates are down considerably, land investing is substantially up. Particular growth is in private pre-development land. The major reason for the interest in pre-development land was the Tax Reform Act of 1986 which eliminated many of the tax benefits of investing in commercial and residential property.

While some land investments are speculative, there are many land partnerships tied into specialized research and strong business planning. In analyzing the client's proposed land investment, the accounting practitioner should determine if the land arrangement is structured to eliminate serious risks, managerial ability, and marketing effectiveness.

Since land is not income-producing, there should be provision to retire the debt even if there is no salability of the property. Thus, there should be a lengthy period for the debt reduction (e.g., 8 years rather than 2 years).

If the debt schedule period is too short, foreclosures or requests for additional financing may ensue.

One type of land investment is undeveloped or underdeveloped lots already zoned for commercial development located by urban centers. Advantages of the urban strategy are that the urban centers will likely have future demand, rental income should be at competitive and consistent rates, and prime location exists. Disadvantages with the urban approach are the restricted choice of available undeveloped lots, metropolitan situated land is competitive, significant dependence upon the "downtown" development cycle, and metropolitan cities are more prone to crime and deterioration.

Determining the Cash Flow from Real Estate

A necessary task in analyzing an income-producing property is determining the before-tax cash flow. When the cash flow is known, we can figure the return on the investment, calculate the tax shelter, and evaluate the investment.

■ Example

Your client wanted to calculate the cash flow of a property offered to him for investment. We will go through this analysis, step by step, as an example of the process and format which the practitioner should follow. The client is considering a duplex apartment. The property is located in an attractive suburb. The cost of the building is $219,000 and a $175,000, 30-year mortgage at a 12% fixed rate is anticipated. The projected figures are based on the first full year of operation.

Step 1. Figuring Gross Income

The building has two three-bedroom apartments. To judge how much the apartments could rent for, your client compared his building to ones in the area which were similar in quality of location and construction.

He studied advertisements and questioned area real estate brokers. After weighing this information, he decided the three-bedroom could rent for $950. Thus, the total maximum yearly rental income was $22,800.

$$2 \times \$950 = \$1,900$$
$$\$1,900 \times 12 = \$22,800$$

Additional income of $800 from laundry fees would make the possible total gross income $23,600.

Step 2. Vacancy and Credit Losses

To estimate the reduction in gross income caused by vacancies and bad debts, your client looked at the result of the survey conducted by the local realtors and apartment associations. He estimated that the vacancy and bad debt rate would be 2% of possible gross income or $472 (2% of $23,600). See Table 1.

Step 3. Operating Expenses

For estimates of operating expenses, your client carefully examined the record of previous costs by category. He came up with the cost figures as shown in the chart, which are basically the previous costs plus adjustments for inflation.

Step 4. Net Operating Income

The projected operating expenses totaled $4,510 or 19.50% of gross operating income ($23,128). This left a net operating income (NOI) of $18,618 ($23,128 − $4,510). Now we proceed to calculating before-tax cash flow.

Step 5. Debt Service (Principal and interest payments)

Payments at 12% on a $175,000, 30-year fixed-rate mortgage would be $1800.08 per month or $21,601 annually (principal amount is $635).

Step 6. Before-Tax Cash Flow

The estimated before-tax cash flow was ($2,983) on an investment of $44,000 ($219,000 − $175,000). In order to compute after-tax cash flow, we have to add principal payments and deduct annual depreciation as follows:

Before-Tax Cash Flow	($2,983)
Add: Principal	635
Less: Depreciation	5,575
Taxable Income (loss)	$(7,923)
Client's Income Tax Rate	x .35
Value of Taxable Loss	$ 2,773

* Assumption: The depreciable base of the building is 70% of $219,000 = $153,300. Annual depreciation is therefore $5,575 ($153,300/27.5 years by straight line).

Table 1   Annual Property Operating Data
(12 months—projected)

Gross Scheduled Income		22,800
+ Other Income		800
Total Gross Income		23,600
− Vacancy/Credit Losses (2%)		472
Gross Operating Income (GOI)		23,128
Operating Expenses (with percent of GOI)		
Property insurance	1.93%	446
Real Estate Taxes	13.22%	3,058
Repairs and Maintenance	1.45%	335
Sewer and Water	2.90%	671
Total Operating Expenses (19.50%)		4,510
Net Operating Income (80.50%)		18,618
− Debt Service (Principal and Interest)		21,601
Before-Tax Cash Flow		(2,983)

Then after-tax cash flow is:

Before-Tax Cash Flow	$(2,983)
Add: Value of Taxable Loss	2,773
After-Tax Cash Flow	$(210)

Note: Due to the deductibility of interest payments and annual depreciation for income tax purposes, after-tax cash flow is reduced by a substantial amount. (In this example, after-tax was only −$210 as compared to before-tax of −$2,983. *Don't forget*: We did not even take into account the potential appreciation of the property. The return on the investment in this building should be calculated on the basis of both annual after-tax cash flows and the selling price of the property at the end of the holding period.

Determining the Value of Income-Producing Property

There are several rule-of-thumb methods to arrive at the estimated value of an income-producing property. They include:

• *Gross Income Multiplier*. Gross income multiplier is calculated as: Purchase price/gross rental income.

■ Example

In your client's example, the gross income multiplier is:

$$\$219,000/\$23,600 = 9.28.$$

A duplex in the similar neighborhood may be valued at "8 times annual gross." Thus, if its annual gross rental income amounts to $23,600, the value would be taken as $188,800 (8 x $23,600). *Warning*: This approach should be used with caution. Different properties have different operating expenses that must be taken into account in determining the value of a property.

• *Net Income Multiplier*. Net income multiplier is calculated as:

$$\text{Purchase price/net operating income (NOI)}$$

In your client's example, the net income multiplier is:

$$\$219,000/\$18,618 = 11.76$$

• *Capitalization rate*. Capitalization rate is almost the same as the net income multiplier, only used more often. It is the reciprocal of the net income multiplier. That is:

$$\text{Net operating income (NOI)/purchase price}$$

■ Example

The duplex's capitalization rate is $18,618/$219,000 = 8.5%. Whether it is over-priced or not depends on the rate of the similar type property derived from the market place. Suppose the market rate is 10%. That means the fair market value of the similar duplex is $18,618/10% = $186,180. Your client may be overpaying for this property.

How Much Can the Client Afford To Spend For Housing?

An accurate way to determine what kind of house the client can afford is to make two basic calculations: How much can the client pay each month for the long-term expenses of owning a home (e.g., mortgage payments, maintenance and operating expenses, insurance and property taxes)? And, how much cash does the client have to spend for the initial costs of the purchase (e.g., the down payment, points and closing cost)?

Many lenders use various rules of thumb to determine a borrower's housing affordability. They include:

• *35-Percent Rule of Thumb*. A borrower can afford no more than 35 percent of monthly take-home pay.

• *Multiple of Gross Earnings Rule*. The price should not exceed roughly 2 to 2½ times the family's gross annual income.

• *Percent of Monthly Gross Income Rule*. The monthly mortgage payment, property taxes and insurance should not exceed 25% to 28% of the family's monthly gross income, or about 35% for a Federal Housing Administration (FHA) or Veterans Administration (VA) mortgage.

See also Real Estate Investment Trust (REIT); Real Estate Syndicate.

REAL ESTATE INVESTMENT TRUSTS (REITs)

REITs are corporations that operate much like closed-end mutual funds, investing shareholders' money in diversified real estate or mortgage portfolios instead of stocks or bonds. Their shares trade on the major stock exchanges or over the counter.

By law, REITs must distribute 95% of their net earnings to shareholders, and in turn they are exempt from corporate taxes on income or gains. Since REIT earnings are not taxed before they are distributed, you get a larger percentage of the profits than with stocks. REIT yields are high, ranging between 5½ to 10½%.

Types of REITs

There are three types of REITs: (1) equity REITs invest primarily in income-producing properties; (2) mortgage REITs lend funds to developers or builders; and (3) hybrid REITs do both. Experts feel that equity REITs are the safest.

Basics About REITs

Where to buy	• Stockbrokers
Pluses	• Dividend income with competitive yields
	• Potential appreciation in price
	• A liquid investment in an illiquid area
	• Means of portfolio diversification and participation in a variety of real estate with minimal cash outlay
Minuses	• Possible glut in real estate or weakening demand
	• Market risk: possible decline in share price
Safety	• Low
Liquidity	• Very high: shares traded on major exchanges or over the counter and therefore sold at any time
Taxes	• Income subject to tax upon sale

How to Select a REIT

Before buying any REIT be sure to read the latest annual report, *The Value Line Investment Survey* or *Audit Investment's* Newsletter, *Realty Stock Review*. Check the following points.

• *Track record*—how long in business as well as solid dividend record.

• *Debt level*—make sure that the unsecured debt level is low.

• *Cash flow*—make sure that operating cash flow covers the dividend.

• *Adequate diversification*—beware of REITs investing in only one type of property.

• *Property location*—beware of geographically depressed areas.

• *Type of property*—nursing homes, some apartment buildings, shopping centers presently favored; "seasoned" properties preferred.

• *Aggressive management*—avoid REITs that do not upgrade properties.

• *Earnings*—monitor earnings regularly; be prepared to sell when the market of property location weakens.

See also Real Estate.

REAL ESTATE SALES FASB No. 66 deals with the accounting for sales of real estate. In the case of real estate sales (other than retail land sales), the accrual basis of accounting is generally used to recognize profit provided:

• Sale is complete (e.g., parties are bound and the risks of ownership have been transferred).

• Collectibility of the selling price is assured or can be estimated.

If these conditions are not met, revenue is deferred until they are satisfied.

Retail land sales should be recognized under accrual accounting provided all of the following criteria are satisfied:

• The refund period has expired.

• Cumulative payments of principal and interest equal or exceed 10% of the contract sales price.

• Collectibility of the receivables exists.

• There is nonsubordination of receivables.

• Development has been completed.

REAL ESTATE SYNDICATE A real estate syndicate (limited partnership) is an investment having potential for substantial gain. The *general partner* makes property investment and management decisions but has the entire liability. The general partner may be one or more individuals or a corporation. This partner sells participation units to *limited partners* whose obligations are typically limited to their investments. Ownership may be in unnamed properties (a blind pool) or in specific existing properties. *Caution*: Investors should know that often general partners make a lot of money by purchasing property themselves and selling them to other partners. In addition to cash investments, debt is often used as well in property acquisition.

A public limited partnership exists where the minimum investment is substantially less than the minimum investment necessary in a private offering. A public offering requires SEC registration.

The distribution to partners is decided upon by the general partner. A manager is typically retained to handle the affairs of the real estate holding.

Tax benefit is in the form of deductible depreciation and interest expense. Profits of partnership arrangements pass directly to the partners. Thus, no double taxation exists. *Note*: Losses on real estate investments that the taxpayer does not manage cannot exceed the amount for which he is at risk. "At risk" means the taxpayer cannot deduct a loss in excess of the adjusted cost basis. However, there is a phase-in period for the rules related to real estate in that the taxpayer can deduct 20% of the losses from passive rental properties in 1989, and 10% in 1990 provided the investment was made before enactment of the Tax Reform Act of 1986. Losses from investments made after enactment of the act are disallowed in the current year completely to the extent that they exceed passive income.

A limited partnership permits the investor to have diversification in real estate holdings compared to individual ownership.

Disadvantages of Limited Partnership

- Limited partners have little control.
- High fees charged by the general partner often range between 5% to 25%.
- The debt funds if not repaid will force foreclosure.
- There is a lack of marketability in limited partnership shares since they are not traded.

The investor should take into account the following when looking at real estate arrangements:

- Possible litigation against the partnership.
- Prior success or failure.
- Delays in payout to limited partners.
- Whether funds are invested in unspecified future projects or in identifiable ones.
- Whether limited partnership investment is publicly or privately received. A private offering is typically local and has a restricted number of investors.

See also Real Estate Investment Trusts (REITs); Limited Partnership; Basic Forms of Business Organization.

RECESSION This represents a lower phase of a business cycle, in which the economy's output (GNP), income, and employment is declining, coupled with a declining rate of business investment and consumer spending. Two to three successive quarterly declines in GNP is usually the sign of recession. Economists, however, have never made the distinction between recession and depression clear. It is the old rule of thumb that if your neighbor loses his or her job, it is a recession, and if you lose yours, it is a depression. *See also* Business Cycle; Depression.

RECONCILIATION This is a determination of the items necessary to bring the balances of two or more related accounts or statements into agreement.

A reconciliation statement shows the details of the differences between any two accounts. This type of statement may be used, for example, for the reconciliation of an account on the home office books containing transactions with a branch office. It would involve a showing of the balance of the branch office account and the corresponding home office account on the branch office books, as well as a listing of the details making up the differences.

A bank reconciliation can also be prepared. The purpose is to uncover any mistakes or irregularities in either the company's or the bank's records. The bank reconciliation should be prepared by one who does not have physical custody of the cash or who does not record cash transactions in the books of account.

A special four-column bank reconciliation (proof of cash) reconciles the book and bank balances at the start and end of the accounting period as well as cash receipts and cash payments for the period.

When preparing the bank reconciliation, the adjusted bank balance has to agree with the adjusted book balance. Journal entries are made to update the cash account so that it ties into the ending balance in the bank statement. Reconciling differences apply to (1) items shown on the company's books but not on the bank statement and (2) items presented on the bank statement but not on the depositor's books.

The bank balance is adjusted for items reflected on the company's books that are not on the bank statement. They include

Outstanding checks—the total of the outstanding checks is subtracted from the bank balance. The exception is an uncleared certified check, which is not deemed outstanding because both the company and bank know about it.

Deposits in transit—the deposits are added to the bank balance.

Errors in recording checks—mistakes, such as transposition errors, can be made in entering checks. For example, an item should be added to the bank balance when it was previously overstated on the books.

Bank errors in charging or crediting the company's account—if a company's account is charged by mistake for another firm's cleared check, the company's bank balance is understated. Thus, the company should add the amount of the check to its bank balance. On the other hand, if a deposit made by a firm is incorrectly credited to the account of another company, the latter should reduce its bank balance.

The book balance (cash account) is adjusted for items shown on the bank statement that are not reflected on the books. They include

Bank charges—fees for bank services reduce the book balance.

NSF checks—these are checks that have bounced due to inadequate funds in the customer's checking account. (NSF means Not Sufficient Funds.) The book balance is reduced for them.

Collections—notes and other items are collected by the bank for a fee. The proceeds received less the charge is credited to the firm's account. The net amount increases the book balance.

Interest earned—interest income credited by the bank on the checking account increases the book balance.

Errors on the books—various kinds of mistakes can be made on the books. Two examples of them and explanations of how they would be corrected follow (assume that the amount of the check is correct):

1. A check is written ($70) for more than the amount entered as a cash disbursement ($64). In this case, cash disbursements are understated by $6 and thus the book balance should be reduced by that amount.

2. A check is written ($110) for less than the amount shown as a cash disbursement ($118). Here, cash disbursements are over-

stated. Thus, the balance per books should be increased by \$8 to correct for the error.

■ Example

Smith Corporation provides the following information at December 31, 19X1:

- Balance per bank statement—December 31, 19X1, \$101,240
- Balance per books—November 30, 19X1, \$87,000
- Cash receipts for December, \$40,000
- Cash payments for December, \$38,000
- Outstanding checks—December 31, 19X1:
  - #108 for \$12,000
  - #112 certified check for \$7,000
  - #114 for \$5,000
- Received cash—December 31, 19X1, \$4,000; deposited on January 2, 19X2
- Return of \$300 check, made out to Lakeside Corporation, by the bank on December 26, 19X1, due to absence of countersignature
- Incorrect entry on bank statement for December 16, 19X1, deposit, \$2,010; actual deposit, \$2,100
- Erroneous charge of \$200 against Smith Corporation account for check issued by Stone Corporation
- December 20, 19X1: collection on a note receivable by bank for Smith Corporation, \$1,100, including \$100 in interest; collection charge, \$20
- Bank service charge for December 19X1 per debit memorandum, \$50
- Erroneous debit memorandum of December 21, 19X1 to charge the firm's Account for settlement of a bank loan in which check #82 was issued on December 20, 19X1, \$2,000
- Incorrect credit to Smith Corporation account for December 14, 19X1, Smart Corporation deposit, \$800

Balance per books—12/31/19X1		\$ 89,000*
Add: Collection on note receivable		
Principal	\$ 1,000	
Interest	100	1,100
		\$ 90,100
Deduct: Charge back of Lakeside check	\$ 300	
Service charge	50	
Collection charge	20	370
Adjusted book balance		\$ 89,730
Balance per bank—12/31/19X1		\$101,240
Add: Deposit in transit	\$ 4,000	
Error in deposit	90	
Check of Stone Corp. incorrectly charged to our account	200	
Debit memorandum of December 21	2,000	6,290
		\$107,530
Deduct: Outstanding checks		
#108	\$12,000	
#114	5,000	
	\$17,000	
Deposit of Smith Corp. credited to our account in error	800	17,800
Adjusted bank balance		\$ 89,730

* To determine the December book balance, the calculations are 87,000 + 40,000 − 38,000 = \$89,000.

Appropriate journal entries are

Cash	1,100	
Notes Receivable		1,000
Interest Income		100
Accounts Receivable	300	
Bank Charges	70	
Cash		370

REFINANCING OF SHORT-TERM DEBT TO LONG-TERM DEBT

A short-term obligation shall be reclassified as a long-term obligation in the following cases:

1. After the year-end of the financial statements but before the audit report is issued, the short-term debt is rolled over into a long-term obligation or an equity security is issued in substitution.

or

2. Prior to the audit report date, the company enters into a contract for refinancing of the current obligation on a long-term basis and *all* of the following are met:

• Agreement does not expire within one year.

• No violation of the agreement exists.

• The parties are financially capable of meeting the requirements of the agreement.

The proper classification of the refinanced item is under long-term debt and *not* stockholders' equity even if equity securities were issued in substitution of the debt. When short-term debt is excluded from current liabilities, a footnote should describe the financing agreement and the terms of any new obligation to be incurred.

If the amounts under the agreement for refinancing vary, the amount of short-term debt excluded from current liabilities will be the *minimum* amount expected to be refinanced based on conservatism. The exclusion from current liabilities cannot be greater than the net proceeds of debt or security issuances, or amounts available under the refinancing agreement.

Once cash is paid for the short-term debt even though the next day long-term debt of a similar amount is issued, the short-term debt shall be shown under current liabilities since cash was disbursed.

REGISTRATION STATEMENT

The registration statement is the disclosure document that must be filed with the SEC in order to issue securities to the public. The first part of the registration statement is a prospectus, and the second part contains supplemental data about the company of particular interest to the SEC. Management is legally liable for material misstatements or omissions in the registration statement. *See also* Prospectus.

REGRESSION ANALYSIS

This is a very popular statistical method used to project sales, cash flows, and earnings. It is also widely used to estimate the *cost-volume formula* (also called the *flexible budget formula*), which takes the following functional form:

$$y = a + bx$$

where y = the semivariable (mixed) costs to be broken up,

x = any given measure of activity such as production volume, machine hours, or direct labor hours,

a = the fixed cost component,

b = the variable rate per unit of x.

The regression method is a statistical procedure for estimating mathematically the average relationship between the dependent variable y and the independent variable x. *Simple regression* involves one independent variable, for example, direct labor hours (DLH) or machine hours alone, whereas *multiple regression* involves two or more activity variables. (We will assume simple *linear* regression throughout this discussion, which means that we will use the $y = a + bx$ relationship.)

In estimating the values of a and b, the regression method attempts to find a line of *best fit*. To find the line of best fit, a technique called the *method of least squares* is used.

Figure 1 Actual (y) Versus Estimated (y')

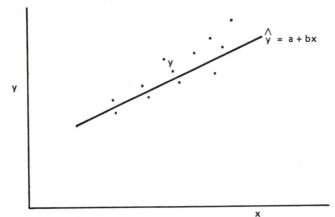

The Method of Least Squares

To explain the least-squares method, we define the error as the difference between the observed value and the estimated value of some semivariable cost and denote it with u. Symbolically:

$$u = y - y'$$

where y = observed value of a semivariable expense,

y' = estimated value based on $y' = a + bx$.

The least-squares criterion requires that the line of best fit be such that the sum of the squares of the errors (or the vertical distance in Figure 1 from the observed data points to the line) is a minimum, that is,

$$\text{Min } \Sigma u^2 = \Sigma(y - y')^2$$

Using differential calculus we obtain the following equations, called *normal equations*:

$$\Sigma y = n \cdot a + b \cdot \Sigma x$$
$$\Sigma xy = a \cdot \Sigma x + b \cdot \Sigma x^2$$

Solving the equations for b and a yields:

$$b = \frac{n \Sigma xy - (\Sigma x)(\Sigma y)}{n \Sigma x^2 - (\Sigma x)^2}$$

$$a = \bar{y} - b \bar{x} \text{ where } \bar{y} = \Sigma y/n \text{ and } \bar{x} = \Sigma x/n$$

The formula for a is a shortcut formula, which requires the computation of b first. This will save a considerable amount of time.

■ Example

To illustrate the computations of b and a, we will use the data following. All the sums required are computed and shown following.

DLH(X)	Factory Overhead (y)	xy	x^2
9 hours	$ 15	135	81
19	20	380	361
11	14	154	121
14	16	224	196
23	25	575	529
12	20	240	144
12	20	240	144
22	23	506	484
7	14	98	49
13	22	286	169
15	18	270	225
17	18	306	289
174 hours	$225	3,414	2,792

From the previous table:

$\Sigma x = 174 \quad \Sigma y = 225 \quad \Sigma xy = 3,414 \quad \Sigma x^2 = 2,792$

$\bar{x} = \Sigma x/n = 174/12 = 14.5$

$\bar{y} = \Sigma y/n = 225/12 = 18.75$

Substituting these values into the formula for b first:

$$b = \frac{n\Sigma xy - (\Sigma x)(\Sigma y)}{n\Sigma x^2 - (\Sigma x)^2}$$

$$= \frac{(12)(3,414) - (174)(225)}{(12)(2,792) - (174)^2} = \frac{1,818}{3,228} = 0.5632$$

$$a = \bar{y} - b\bar{x}$$
$$= (18.75) - (0.5632)(14.5) = 18.75 - 8.1664$$
$$= 10.5836$$

Our final regression equation is

$$y' = \$10.5836 + \$0.5632x$$

where y' = estimated factory overhead,
$\quad x$ = DLH.

RELATED PARTY TRANSACTIONS As per FASB 57, related party information should be disclosed in the financial statements. As per SAS 47, the auditor should know that the substance of a given transaction may be materially at variance with its legal form. If a client transacts business with another entity at more favorable terms than normal, a related party relationship may exist. The auditor should conduct substantive tests in such a way as to identify the existence and terms of related party transactions.

To identify transactions with related parties, the auditor should

• Review minutes of the board of directors

• Review transactions with major customers, suppliers, borrowers, and lenders

• Review large, unusual, and nonrecurring transactions

Once related party transactions have been identified, they should be examined so that the auditor can gain satisfaction as to the purpose, extent, and nature of the transactions. Further, the practitioner must satisfy himself or herself with the related party disclosures in the financial statements.

RELEVANT COSTING When analyzing the manufacturing and selling functions, account-

ants are constantly faced with the problem of choosing alternate courses of action. Typical questions to be answered include

1. What to make?
2. How to make it?
3. Where to sell the product or service?
4. What price should be charged?

In the short run, the accountant is typically confronted with the following nonroutine, nonrecurring types of decisions:

1. Accept or reject a special order.
2. Make or buy.
3. Add or drop a certain product line.
4. Utilize scarce resources.
5. Sell or process further.

In each of these situations, the ultimate decision rests upon cost data analysis. Cost data is important in many decisions, since they are the basis for profit calculations. However, not all costs are of equal importance in decision making, and accountants must identify the costs that are relevant to a decision. Such costs are called *relevant costs*. The relevant costs are the expected future costs, which differ between the decision alternatives. Therefore, the *sunk costs* are *not* relevant to the decision at hand because they are past and historical costs. The *incremental* or *differential* costs are *relevant* since they are the ones that differ between the alternatives. For example, in a decision on whether to sell an existing business for a new one, the cost to be paid for the new venture is relevant. However, the initial cost of the old business is not relevant to the decision because it is a sunk cost.

REORGANIZATION This is a major change in a company's financial structure as a result of an alteration in the rights and interests of stockholders. In effect, the failed business is reorganized so it can continue to operate as per Chapter 11 of the Bankruptcy Reform Act of 1978. A Chapter 11 reorganization may be initiated voluntarily by the debtor or involuntarily by creditors. *See also* Business Failure.

RESEARCH AND DEVELOPMENT COSTS

Research is the testing done in search for a new product, service, process, or technique. Research can also be aimed at deriving a material improvement to an existing product or process. Development is the translation of the research into a design for the new product or process. Development may also result in material improvement in an existing product or process. As per FASB 2, research and development costs are expensed as incurred. However, R&D costs incurred under contract for others that are reimbursable are charged to a receivable account rather than expensed. Further, materials, equipment, and intangibles purchased from others that have alternative future benefit in R&D activities are capitalized. The depreciation or amortization on such assets is classified as R&D expense. If no alternative future use exists, the costs should be expensed.

R&D costs include the salaries of personnel involved as R&D activities. R&D costs also include a rational allocation of indirect (general and administrative) costs. If a group of assets are acquired, allocation should be made to those that relate to R&D efforts. When a business combination is accounted for as a purchase, R&D costs are assigned their fair market value.

Expenditures paid to others to conduct R&D activities are expensed.

Examples of R&D activities include
• Formulation and design of product alternatives and testing thereof
• Laboratory research
• Engineering functions until the point the product satisfies operational requirements for manufacture
• Design of tools, molds, and dies involving new technology
• Preproduction prototypes and models

• Pilot plant costs

Examples of activities that are not for R&D include:
• Quality control
• Seasonal design changes
• Legal costs of obtaining a patent
• Market research
• Identifying breakdowns during commercial production
• Engineering follow-up in the initial stages of commercial production
• Rearrangement and start-up activities, including design and construction engineering
• Recurring and continuous efforts to improve the product
• Commercial use of the product

FASB 2 does not apply to regulated industries and to the extractive industries (e.g., mining).

According to FASB 86, costs incurred for computer software to be sold, leased, or otherwise marketed are expensed as R&D costs until technological feasibility exists, as indicated by the development of a detailed program or working model. After technological feasibility exists, software production costs should be deferred and recorded at the lower of unamortized cost or net realizable value. Examples of such costs include debugging the software, improvements to subroutines, and adaptions for other uses. Amortization begins when the product is available for customer release. The amortization expense should be based on the higher of (1) the percent of current revenue to total revenue from the product and (2) the straight-line amortization amount.

As per FASB 68, if a business enters into an arrangement with other parties to fund the R&D efforts, the nature of the obligation must be determined. In the case where the entity has an obligation to repay the funds irrespective of the R&D results, a liability has to be recognized with the related R&D expense. The journal entries are

Cash
  Liability
Research and Development Expense
  Cash

A liability does not exist when the transfer of financial risk involved to the other party is substantive and genuine. If the financial risk applicable with R&D is transferred because repayment depends only on the R&D possessing future economic benefit, the company accounts for its obligation as a contract to conduct R&D for others. In this case R&D costs are capitalized and revenue is recognized as earned and becomes billable under the contract. Footnote disclosure is made of the terms of the R&D agreement, the amount of compensation earned, and the costs incurred under the contract.

When repayment of loans or advances to the company depends only on R&D results, such amounts are deemed R&D costs incurred by the company and charged to expense.

If warrants or other financial instruments are issued in an R&D arrangement, the company records part of the proceeds to be provided by the other parties as paid-in-capital based on their fair market value on the arrangement date.

RESIDUAL INCOME (RI)

RI is the operating income that an *investment center* is able to earn above some minimum return on its assets. It is a popular alternative performance measure to *return on investment (ROI)*.

RI is computed as:

RI = Net operating income
       − (Minimum rate of return on investment
                         × Operating assets)

Residual income, unlike ROI, is an absolute amount of income rather than a rate of return. When RI is used to evaluate divisional performance, the objective is to maximize the total amount of residual income, not to maximize the overall ROI percentage figure.

■ Example

Assume that operating assets are $100,000, net operating income is $18,000, and the minimum return on assets is 13%. Residual income is $18,000 − (13% × $100,000) = $18,000 − $13,000 = $5,000.

RI is sometimes preferred over ROI as a performance measure because it encourages managers to accept investment opportunities that have rates of return greater than the charge for invested capital. Managers being evaluated using ROI may be reluctant to accept new investments that lower their current ROI even though the investments would be desirable for the entire company. Advantages of using residual income in evaluating divisional performance include (1) it is an economic income taking into account the opportunity cost of tying up assets in the division; (2) the minimum rate of return can vary depending on the riskiness of the division; (3) different assets can be required to earn different returns depending on their risk; (4) the same asset may be required to earn the same return regardless of the division it is in; and (5) maximizing dollars rather than a percentage leads to goal congruence. *See also* Divisional Performance Evaluation.

RESPONSIBILITY ACCOUNTING

This is the system for collecting and reporting revenue and cost information by areas of responsibility. It operates on the premise that managers should be held responsible for their performance, the performance of their subordinates, and for all activities within their responsibility center. Responsibility accounting, also called *profitability accounting* and *activity accounting*, has the following advantages:

1. It facilitates delegation of decision making.

2. It helps management promote the concept of management by objective, in which managers agree on a set of goals. The manager's

performance is then evaluated based on his or her attainment of these goals.

3. It provides a guide to the evaluation of performance and helps to establish standards of performance that are then used for comparison purposes.

4. It permits effective use of the concept of *management by exception*, which means that the manager's attention is concentrated on the important deviations from standards and budgets.

Types of Responsibility Centers

A well-designed responsibility accounting system establishes responsibility centers within the organization. *A responsibility center* is defined as a unit in the organization that has control over costs, revenues, and/or investment funds. Responsibility centers can be one of the following types:

Cost center—the unit within the organization that is responsible only for costs. Examples include the production and maintenance departments of a manufacturing company, and the admissions department of a university. *Variance analysis* based on *standard costs* and *flexible budgets* would be a typical performance measure of a cost center.

Profit center—the unit that is held responsible for the revenues earned and costs incurred in that center. Examples might include a sales office of a publishing company, an appliance department in a retail store, and an auto repair center in a department store. *The contribution approach to cost allocation* is widely used to measure the performance of a profit center.

Investment center—the unit within the organization that is held responsible for the costs, revenues, and related investments made in that center. The corporate headquarters or division in a large decentralized organization would be an example of an investment center. *Return on investment* and *residual income* are two key performance measures of an investment center.

Figure 1 (p. 381) illustrates the manner in which responsibility accounting can be used within an organization and highlights profit and cost centers.

Cost Center Performance and Standard Costs

One of the most important phases of responsibility accounting is establishing standard costs and evaluating performance by comparing actual costs with the standard costs. The difference between the actual costs and the standard costs, called the *variance*, is calculated for individual *cost centers*. Variance analysis is a key tool for measuring performance of a cost center.

The standard cost is based on physical and dollar measures; it is determined by multiplying the standard quantity of an input by its standard price. Two general types of variances can be calculated for most cost items: (1) *a price variance* and (2) *a quantity variance*. The price variance is calculated as follows:

$$\begin{aligned}
\text{Price} &= \text{Actual} \times \left(\text{Actual} - \text{Standard} \right) \\
\text{variance} &\quad \text{quantity} \quad \left(\text{price} \quad \text{price} \right) \\
&= AQ \times (AP - SP) \\
&= \underset{(1)}{(AQ \times AP)} - \underset{(2)}{(AQ \times SP)}
\end{aligned}$$

The quantity variance is calculated as follows:

$$\begin{aligned}
\text{Quantity} &= \left(\text{Actual} - \text{Standard} \right) \times \text{Standard} \\
\text{variance} &\quad \left(\text{quantity} \quad \text{quantity} \right) \quad \text{price} \\
&= (AQ - SQ) \times SP \\
&= \underset{(2)}{(AQ \times SP)} - \underset{(3)}{(SQ \times SP)}
\end{aligned}$$

Figure 2 (page 382) shows a general model (3-column model) for variance analysis that incorporates the items (1), (2), and (3) from the previous equations.

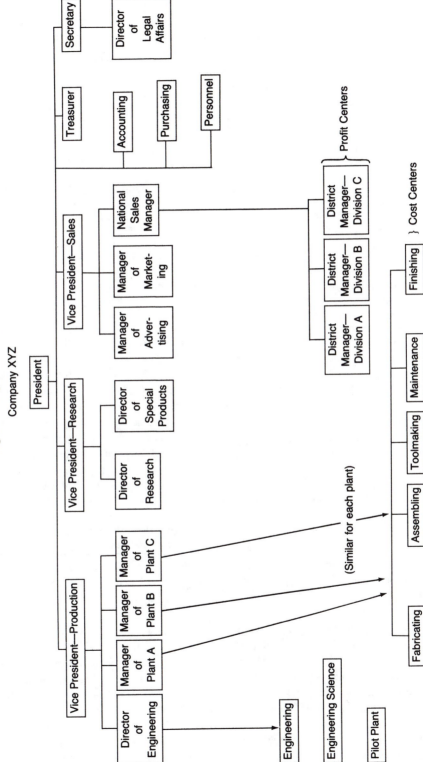

Figure 1 Organization Chart
Company XYZ

Figure 2 A General Model for Variance Analysis for Variable Manufacturing Costs

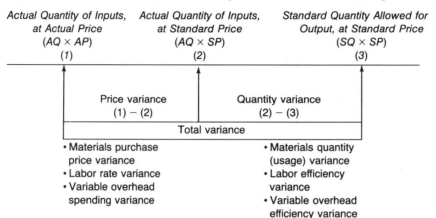

Advantages and Disadvantages of Standard Costing

Standard costing has many advantages, including

1. Aiding in cost control and performance evaluation.
2. "Red flagging" current and future problems through the "management by exception" principle.
3. Improving performance by recommending paths for corrective action in cost reduction.
4. Fixing responsibility.
5. Being a vehicle of communication between top management and supervisors.
6. Establishing selling prices and transfer prices.
7. Determining bid prices on contracts.
8. Setting business goals.
9. Aiding in the planning and decision-making processes.
10. Simplifying bookkeeping procedures and saving clerical costs. Standard costing is not without some drawbacks, however, such as the possible biases involved in deriving standards and the disfunctional effects of setting improper norms and standards.

We will now illustrate by example variance analysis for each of the variable manufacturing cost items.

Materials Variances

A materials price variance is isolated at the time of purchase of the material. Therefore, it is normally computed based on the actual quantity purchased. The purchasing department is responsible for any materials price variance that might occur. The materials quantity (usage) variance is computed based on the actual quantity used. Note that the production department is responsible for any materials quantity variance that might occur. The possible causes for *unfavorable* materials variances are given following.

Possible Causes for Unfavorable Materials Variances

1. *Materials price variance*
   a. Inaccurate standard prices
   b. Failure to take a discount on quantity purchases
   c. Failure to shop for bargains
   d. Inflationary cost increases
   e. Scarcity in raw material supplies resulting in higher prices
   f. Purchasing department inefficiencies
2. *Materials quantity (usage) variance*
   a. Poorly trained workers
   b. Improperly adjusted machines
   c. Use of improper production method

d. Outright waste on the production line
e. Use of a lower grade material purchased in order to economize on price

■ Example 1

ABC Corporation uses a standard cost system. The standard variable costs for Product J are as follows:

Materials: 2 lbs at $3 per lb
Labor: 1 hr at $5 per hr
Variable overhead: 1 hr at $3 per hr

During March, 25,000 pounds of material were purchased for $74,750 and 20,750 pounds of material were used in producing 10,000 units of finished product. Direct labor costs incurred were $49,896 (10,080 direct labor hours) and variable overhead costs incurred were $34,776. Using the general model (3-column model), the materials variances are presented below.

It is important to note that the amount of materials purchased (25,000 pounds) differs from the amount of materials used in production (20,750 pounds). The materials purchase price variance was computed using 25,000 pounds purchased, whereas the material quantity (usage) variance was computed using the 20,750 pounds used in production. A total variance cannot be computed because

of the difference. Alternatively, we can compute the materials variances as follows:

Materials purchase price variance
$$= AQ \times (AP - SP) = (AQ \times AP) - (AQ \times SP)$$
$$= 25{,}000 \text{ lbs } (\$2.99 - \$3)$$
$$= \$74{,}750 - \$75{,}000 = \$250F$$

Materials quantity (usage) variance
$$= (AQ - SQ) \times SP$$
$$= (20{,}750 \text{ lbs} - 20{,}000 \text{ lbs}) \times \$3$$
$$= \$62{,}250 - \$60{,}000 = \$2{,}250U$$

Labor Variances

Labor variances are both isolated when labor is used for production. They are computed in a manner similar to the materials variances, except that in the 3-column model the terms "hours" and "rate" are used in place of the terms "quantity" and "price." The production department is responsible for both the prices paid for labor services and the quantity of labor services used. Therefore, the production department must explain why any labor variances occur (see following).

Possible Causes for Unfavorable Labor Variances

1. *Labor price (rate) variance*
   a. Increase in wages
   b. Poor scheduling of production resulting in overtime work

Materials Variances

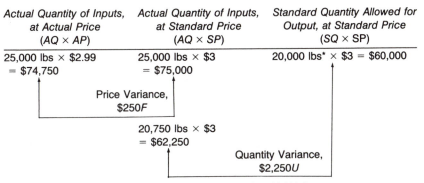

Actual Quantity of Inputs, at Actual Price (AQ × AP)	Actual Quantity of Inputs, at Standard Price (AQ × SP)	Standard Quantity Allowed for Output, at Standard Price (SQ × SP)
25,000 lbs × $2.99 = $74,750	25,000 lbs × $3 = $75,000	20,000 lbs* × $3 = $60,000

Price Variance, $250F

20,750 lbs × $3 = $62,250

Quantity Variance, $2,250U

* 10,000 units actually produced × 2 lbs allowed per unit = 20,000 lbs

c. Use of workers commanding higher hourly rates than contemplated in the standards

2. *Labor efficiency variance*
   a. Poor supervision
   b. Use of unskilled workers paid lower rates or the wrong mixture of labor for a given job
   c. Use of poor quality machinery
   d. Improperly trained workers
   e. Poor quality of materials requiring more labor time in processing
   f. Machine breakdowns
   g. Employee unrest
   h. Production delays due to power failure

■ Example 2

Using the same data given in Example 1, the labor variances can be calculated as shown below.

Variable Overhead Variances

The variable overhead variances are computed in a way very similar to the labor variances. The production department is usually responsible for any variable overhead variance that might occur. Some of the possible causes for any overhead variance are given following. Variances for fixed overhead are of questionable usefulness for control purposes since these variances are usually beyond the control of the production department.

Possible Causes for Unfavorable Variable Overhead Variances

1. *Variable overhead spending variance*
   a. Increase in supplier prices
   b. Increase in labor rates
   c. Inaccurate standards
   d. Waste
   e. Theft of supplies
2. *Variable overhead efficiency variance*
   a. Poorly trained workers
   b. Use of poor quality materials
   c. Use of faulty equipment
   d. Poor supervision
   e. Employee unrest
   f. Work interruptions
   g. Poor production scheduling
   h. A lack of automation and computerization in processing

Labor Variances

Actual Hours of Input, at the Actual Rate $(AH \times AR)$	Actual Hours of Input, at the Standard Rate $(AH \times SR)$	Standard Hours Allowed for Output, at the Standard Rate $(SH \times SR)$
10,080 hrs × $4.95 = $49,896	10,080 hrs × $5 = $50,400	10,000 hrs* × $5 = $50,000

Rate Variance, $504F	Efficiency Variance, $400U

Total Variance, $104F

* 10,000 units actually produced × 1 hr allowed per unit = 10,000 hrs. Note that the symbols (AQ, SQ, AP, and SP) have been changed to (AH, SH, AR, and SR) to reflect the terms "hour" and "rate." Alternatively, we can calculate the labor variances as follows:

Labor rate variance $= AH \times (AR - SR) = (AH \times AR) - (AH \times SR)$
$= 10,080$ hrs $(\$4.95 - \$5) = \$49,896 - \$50,400 = \$504F$

Labor efficiency variance $= (AH - SH) \times SR$
$= (10,080$ hrs $- 10,000$ hrs$) \times \$5 = \$50,400 - \$50,000$
$= \$400U$

■ Example 3

Using the same data given in Example 1, the variable overhead variances can be computed as shown below.

Mix and Yield Variances

The material quantity variance is divided into a material mix variance and a material yield variance. The material mix variance measures the impact of the deviation from the standard mix on material costs, while the material yield variance reflects the impact on material costs of the deviation from the standard input material allowed for actual production. The material mix variance is computed by holding the total input units constant at their actual amount. On the other hand, the material yield variance is computed by holding the mix constant at the standard amount.

The computations for labor mix and yield variances are the same as those for materials. If there is no mix, the yield variance is the same as the quantity (or usage) variance.

Probable Causes of Unfavorable Mix Variances

1. When capacity restraints force substitution
2. Poor production scheduling
3. Lack of certain types of labor
4. Certain materials are in short supply

Probable Causes of Unfavorable Yield Variances

1. The use of low-quality materials and/or labor
2. The existence of faulty equipment
3. The use of improper production methods
4. An improper or costly mix of materials and/or labor

See also Production Mix Variance; Production Yield Variance.

RETAIL INVENTORY METHOD   The retail inventory method is used by retail stores to determine the valuation of ending inventory. A cost to retail ratio is determined which is then applied to the final inventory stated at selling price. See also Inventory Valuation.

Variable Overhead Variances

Actual Hours of Input, at the Actual Rate ($AH \times AR$)	Actual Hours of Input, at the Standard Rate ($AH \times SR$)	Standard Hours Allowed for Output, at the Standard Rate ($SH \times SR$)
10,080 hrs × $3.45 = $34,776	10,080 hrs × $3 = $30,240	10,000 hrs* × $3 = $30,000

Spending Variance, $4,536U

Efficiency Variance, $240U

Total Variance, $4,776

* 10,000 units actually produced × 1 hr allowed per unit = 10,000 hrs. Alternatively, we can compute the variable overhead variances as follows:

Variable overhead spending

$$variance = AH \times (AR - SR)$$
$$= (AH \times AR) - (AH \times SR) = 10,080 \text{ hrs}$$
$$(\$3.45 - \$3) = \$34,776 - \$30,240 = \$4,536U$$

$$\text{Variable overhead efficiency variance} = (AH - SH) \times SR$$
$$= (10,080 \text{ hrs} - 10,000 \text{ hrs}) \times \$3$$
$$= \$30,240 - \$30,000 = \$240U$$

RETIREMENT AND PENSION PLANNING

Many people do not prepare for retirement even though it is a major event in their lives. Retirement planning involves an explicit consideration of present versus future needs and an examination of how present resources may be allocated to serve future needs. A financial advisor such as a financial planner, a CPA, or a life insurance agent may be called upon to advise clients on the type of retirement plan necessary to meet their particular needs.

The first step in retirement planning is to develop retirement goals. Once they have been set, specific savings plans aimed at achieving them should be developed. It is essential to economic security in old age to provide some income to accomplish retirement goals. Means of saving for retirement are social security, employer retirement and pension plans, annuities, and individual retirement and savings plans. An easy way to plan for retirement is to state retirement income objectives as a percentage of present earnings. For example, if one desires a retirement income of 70% of his or her final take-home pay, the amount necessary to fund this need can be determined.

Types of Pension and Retirement Plans

Two major sources of retirement income are company-sponsored pension plans and individual retirement plans. They are summarized following:

Company-sponsored pension plans
- Qualified company retirement plans
- Profit-sharing plans
- 401(k) salary reduction plans
- Tax-sheltered annuities (TSA)
- Employee stock ownership plans (ESOP)
- Simplified employee pension plan (SEP)

Individual retirement plans
- Individual retirement accounts (IRAs)
- Keoghs
- Annuities

Company-Sponsored Pension Plans

Qualified company retirement plans—the IRS permits a corporate employer to make contributions to a retirement plan that is qualified. *Qualified* means that it meets a number of specific criteria in order to deduct from taxable income contributions to the plan. The investment income of the plan is allowed to accumulate untaxed.

Profit-sharing plans—a type of defined contribution plan. Unlike other qualified plans, employees may not have to wait until retirement to receive distributions. Since the company must contribute only when it earns a profit, the amount of benefit at retirement is highly uncertain.

401(k) salary reduction plans—in addition to, or in place of, a qualified pension plan or profit-sharing plan, one may set up a 401(k) salary reduction plan, which defers a portion of the salary for retirement. This is like building a nest egg for the future by taking a *cut* in pay. Tax savings more than offset a paper cut (on paper) since employees end up with more take-home pay and more retirement income.

■ Example

A client saves 10% of his $40,000-a-year salary in a 401(k) plan. He is married with two children, is the only wage earner in the family, and does not itemize deductions. How will the client fare with a 401(k) plan and without one?

Take-Home Pay

	With 401(k) Plan	Without 401(k) Plan
Base pay	$40,000	$40,000
Salary reduction	4,000	None
Taxable income	$36,000	$40,000
Federal and FICA taxes	8,159	9,279
Savings after taxes	None	4,000
Take-home pay	$27,841	$26,721
Extra take-home pay under 401(k) $1,120		

Retirement income will grow faster inside a tax-sheltered plan, such as 401(k), than outside one. This is because the interest earned will go untaxed and keep compounding.

Tax-sheltered annuities (TSA)—if one is an employee of a nonprofit institution, he or she is eligible for a TSA. A TSA is similar to the 401(k), but one may withdraw the funds at any age for any reason without tax penalty. He or she must pay ordinary taxes on all withdrawals.

Employee stock ownership plans (ESOP)—a stock bonus plan. The contributions made by the employer are tax deductible.

Simplified employee pension (SEP)—a plan whereby an employer makes annual contributions on the employee's behalf to an individual retirement account set up by the employee.

Individual Retirement Plans

Individual Retirement Accounts (IRAs)—if one does not have a company retirement plan or would like to supplement a company plan through additional private savings, the benefits of tax deferral can also be attained through individual-oriented investments, such IRAs, Keoghs, and annuities.

The IRA is a retirement savings plan that individuals set up themselves. The IRA is a qualified individual retirement plan whereby contributions not only grow tax free but are also either tax deductible or not included in their income. Under the Tax Reform Act of 1986, however, a person who is covered by an employer's retirement plan or who files a joint return with a spouse who is covered by such a plan may be entitled to only a partial deduction or no deduction at all, depending on the adjusted gross income (AGI). The deduction begins to decrease when the taxpayer's income rises above a certain level and is eliminated altogether when it reaches a higher level. The deduction

is reduced or eliminated entirely depending on filing status and income, as follows:

If Filing Status Is	Deduction Is Reduced if AGI Is Within Range of	Deduction Is Eliminated if AGI Is
Single or Head of Household	$25,000—$35,000	$35,000 or more
Married—joint return, or Qualifying widow(er)	$40,000—$50,000	$50,000 or more
Married—separated return	$ 0—$10,000	$10,000 or more

A person *not* covered by an employee retirement plan can still take a full IRA deduction of up to $2,000 or 100% of compensation, whichever is less.

Keoghs—a person who is self-employed may set up a Keogh plan. Keogh contributions are tax sheltered and their earnings are tax deferred. The overall federal limit on annual contributions is 25% of annual compensation or $30,000, whichever is less.

Annuities—a savings account with an insurance company or other investment company. A person makes either a lump-sum deposit or periodic payments to the company and at retirement is "annuitized"—receives regular payments for a specified time period (usually a certain number of years or for the rest of life). All of the payments build up tax free and are taxed only when withdrawn at retirement, a time when an individual is usually in a lower tax bracket. Annuities pay off at retirement; life insurance pays off at death.

Annuities come in two basic varieties: fixed and variable.

Fixed rate annuities—the insurance company guarantees principal plus a minimum rate of interest. If one has little tolerance for risk, the fixed annuity is an ideal investment. In buying a fixed annuity, be aware of two interest rates. One is the minimum guaranteed rate, which applies for the duration of the contract. The other is the "current" rate of interest, which reflects market conditions.

Variable annuities—the company does not provide the same guarantee as fixed annuities. The company invests in common stocks, corporate bonds, or money market instruments, and the investment value fluctuates with the performance of these investments. Note that with a variable annuity, a policyholder bears the risk of the investment options. The good thing is that most companies allow switching to another fund within the variable variety. Note that annuities can be for everybody. For young people, the vehicles are an excellent forced savings plan. For older people, they are tax-favored investments that can guarantee an income for life.

Pitfalls of Annuities

• Penalties for early withdrawals of money imposed by the IRS and insurance company.

• Surrender charges if a policyholder decides to cash in the contract early.

• The so-called nonqualified annuities, which are annuities with the tax-deferral feature but which are paid for with after-tax dollars. Qualified annuities, on the other hand, are used to fund such vehicles as Individual Retirement Accounts (IRAs) and pension plans. In a qualified annuity, the contributions not only grow tax free but are also either tax deductible or not included in one's income.

Unlike pension plans and IRAs, there are no limitations on the amunt to be contributed to an annuity.

RETURN This is a key consideration in the investment decision. It is the reward for investing. The investor must compare the expected return for a given investment with the risk involved. The return on an investment consists of the following sources of income: (1) periodic cash payments, called *current income*, and (2) appreciation (or depreciation) in market value, called *capital gains* (or *losses*).

Current income, which is received on a periodic basis, may take the form of interest, dividend, rent, and the like. Capital gains or losses represent changes in market value.

A capital gain is the amount by which the proceeds from the sale of an investment exceeds its original purchase price. If the investment is sold for less than its purchase price, then the difference is a capital loss.

The way we measure the return on a given investment depends primarily on how we define the relevant period over which we hold our investment, called the holding period. We use the term *holding period return* (HPR), which is the total return earned from holding an investment for that period of time. It is computed as follows:

$$\text{HPR} = \frac{\text{Current income} + \text{Capital gain (or loss)}}{\text{Purchase price}}$$

In the case of stock, we use the following symbols:

$$r = \frac{D_1 + (P_1 - P_0)}{P_0}$$

where r = expected return for a single period,

D_1 = dividend at the end of the period,

P_1 = price per share at the end of the period,

P_0 = price per share at the beginning of the period.

In words,

$$r = \frac{\text{Dividends} + \text{Capital gain}}{\text{Beginning price}}$$

$$= \text{Dividend yield} + \text{Capital gain yield}$$

■ Example

Consider the investment in stock A and B over a one-year period of ownership:

	Stock	
	A	B
Purchase price (begininng of year)	$100	$100
Cash dividend received (during the year)	13	18
Sales price (end of year)	107	97

The current income from the investment in stocks A and B over the one-year period are $13 and $18, respectively. For stock A, a capital gain of $7 ($107 sales price − $100 purchase price) is realized over the period. In the case of stock B, a $3 capital loss ($97 sales price − $100 purchase price) results.

Combining the capital gain return (or loss) with the current income, the total return on each investment is summarized following.

| | Stock | |
Return	A	B
Current income	$13	$18
Capital gain (loss)	7	(3)
Total return	$20	$15

Thus, the holding period return on investments A and B are

$$\text{HPR (stock A)} = \frac{\$13 + (\$107 - \$100)}{\$100} = \frac{\$13 + \$7}{\$100}$$

$$= \frac{\$20}{\$100} = 20\%$$

$$\text{HPR (stock B)} = \frac{\$18 + (\$97 - \$100)}{\$100} = \frac{\$18 - \$3}{\$100}$$

$$= \frac{\$15}{\$100} = 15\%$$

See also Annual Percentage Rate (APR); Arithmetic Average Return Versus Geometric Average Return; Bond Yield Mean—Effective Rate of Return on a Bond; Yield Spread.

RETURN ON PENSION PLAN ASSETS The return (interest and dividends) on the fair market value of pension plan assets acts to decrease the pension expense provision for the year. *See also* Pension Plans.

REVENUE EXPENDITURE A revenue expenditure is an expenditure that only benefits less than a year and is therefore immediately expensed. An example is a repair to a fixed asset (e.g., tuneup). *See also* Capital Expenditure.

REVENUE RECOGNITION METHODS Revenue may be recognized under different methods depending on the particular circumstances. Revenue is associated with a gross increase in assets or a decrease in liabilities. The methods that may be used include realization, completion of production, during production, and cash basis.

Realization—revenue is recognized when goods are sold or services are performed. It results in an increase in net assets. This method is used almost all of the time. At realization, the earnings process is complete. Further, realization is consistent with the accrual basis, meaning that revenue is recognized when earned rather than when received. Realization should be used when the selling price is determinable, future costs can be estimated, and an exchange has taken place that can be objectively measured. There must exist a reasonable basis to determine anticipated bad debts. There are exceptional situations in which another method of revenue recognition should be used. These are now discussed.

At the completion of production—revenue is recognized prior to sale or exchange. There must exist a stable selling price, absence of material marketing costs to complete the final transfer, and interchangeability in units. This approach is used with agricultural products, byproducts, and precious metals when the aforementioned criteria are met. It is also used in accounting for construction contracts under the completed contract method.

During production—revenue recognition is made in the case of long-term production situations where an assured price for the completed item exists by contractual agreement and a reliable measure of the degree of completion at various stages of the production process is possible. An example is the percentage of completion method used in accounting for long-term construction contracts.

Construction contracts—under the completed contract method, revenue should not be recognized until completion of a contract. The method should be used only when the use of the percentage of completion method is inappropriate.

Under the percentage of completion method, revenue is recognized as production activity is occurring. The gradual recognition of revenue levels out earnings over the years and is more realistic since revenue is recognized as performance takes place. This method is preferred over the completed contract method and should be used when reliable estimates of the extent of completion of each period is possible. If not, the completed contract method should be used. Percentage of completion results in a matching of revenue against related expenses in the benefit period.

Using the cost-to-cost method, revenue recognized for the period equals:

$$\frac{\text{Actual costs to date}}{\text{Total estimated costs}} \times \text{Contract price}$$

$$= \text{Cumulative revenue}$$

Revenue recognized in prior years is deducted from the cumulative revenue to determine the revenue in the current period. An example follows:
- Cumulative Revenue (1–4 years)
- *Revenue Recognized* (1–3 years)
- Revenue (Year 4–current year)
- Revenue less expenses equals profit

■ Example

In year 4 of a contract, the actual costs to date were $50,000. Total estimated costs are $200,000. The contract price is $1,000,000. Revenue recognized in the prior years (years 1–3) were $185,000.

$$\frac{\$50,000}{\$200,000} \times \$1,000,000$$

$$= \$250,000 \text{ Cumulative revenue}$$

Cumulative revenue	$250,000
Prior year revenue	185,000
Current year revenue	$ 65,000

Regardless of whether the percentage of completion method or the completed contract method is used, conservatism dictates that an obvious loss on a contract should immediately be recognized even before contract completion.

Journal entries under the construction methods using assumed figures are presented below.

In the last year when the construction project is completed, the following additional entry is made to record the profit in the final year:

	Percentage of Completion	Completed Contract
Progress Billings on Construction-in-Progress	Total billings	Total billings
Construction-in-Progress	Cost + Profit	Cost
Profit	Incremental profit for last year	Profit for all the years

Construction-in-progress less Progress billings is shown net. Usually, a debit figure results, which is shown as a current asset.

	Percentage of Completion		Completed Contract	
Construction-in-Progress	100,000		100,000	
Cash		100,000		100,000
Construction costs				
Progress Billings Receivable	80,000		80,000	
Progress Billings on Construction-in-Progress		80,000		80,000
Periodic bililngs				
Construction-in-Progress	25,000		No entry	
Profit		25,000		
Yearly profit recognition based on percentage of completion during the year				

Construction-in-progress is an inventory account for a construction company. If a credit balance occurs, the net amount is shown as a current liability.

Cash basis—in the case of a company selling inventory, the accrual basis is used. However, when certain circumstances exist, the cash basis of revenue recognition is used. Namely, revenue is recognized upon collection of the account. The cash basis instead of the accrual basis must be used when one or more of the following exist:

• Selling price is not objectively determinable at the time of sale.

• Inability to estimate expenses at the time of sale.

• Risk exists as to collections from customers.

• Uncertain collection period.

Revenue recognition under the installment method equals the cash collected times the gross profit percentage. Any gross profit not collected is deferred on the balance sheet until collection occurs. When collections are received, realized gross profit is recognized by debiting the deferred gross profit account. The balance sheet presentation is

> Accounts receivable (Cost + Profit)
> Less: Deferred gross profit
> Net accounts receivable (Cost)

It is important to note that a service business that does not deal in inventory (e.g., accountant, doctor, lawyer) has the option of either using the accrual basis or cash basis. *See also* Franchise Fee Revenue; Product-Financing Arrangements; Revenue Recognition When A Right of Return Exists.

REVENUE RECOGNITION WHEN A RIGHT OF RETURN EXISTS

In the situation when a buyer has a right of returning the merchandise bought, the seller can recognize revenue only at the time of sale, in accordance with FASB 48, provided that *all* of the following conditions are satisfied:

• Selling price is known.

• Buyer has to pay for the goods even if the buyer is unable to resell them. An example is a sale of a good from a manufacturer to a wholesaler. No provision must exist that the wholesaler has to be able to sell the item to the retailer.

• If the buyer loses the item or it is damaged in some way, the buyer still has to pay for it.

• Purchase by the buyer of the item has economic feasibility.

• Seller does not have to render future performance in order that the buyer will be able to resell the goods.

• Returns may be reasonably estimated.

In case any one of the previous criteria are not met, revenue must be deferred along with deferral of related expenses until the criteria have been satisfied or the right-of-return provision has expired. An alternative to deferring the revenue would be to record a memo entry as to the sale.

The ability of a company to predict future returns involves consideration of the following:

• Predictability is detracted from when there is technological obsolescence risk of the product, uncertain product demand changes, or other material external factors.

• Predictability is lessened when there is a long time period involved for returns.

• Predictability is enhanced when there exists a large volume of similar transactions.

• Seller has previous experience in estimating returns for similar products.

• Nature of customer relationship and types of product involved.

FASB 48 does not apply to dealer leases or real estate transactions, nor to service industries. *See also* Revenue Recognition Methods.

REVIEW A review is the next step above a compilation. There is some assurance expressed on the financial statements. A review is mostly composed of inquiry and analytical procedures applied to financial information so that the accountant has a reasonable basis to express limited assurance that no material adjustments have to be made to the financial statements in order for them to be in conformity with GAAP (or another comprehensive basis of accounting).

Review procedures do *not* involve a study and appraisal of internal control or the gathering of competent evidential matter. Thus, an opinion cannot be expressed. Although the accountant may look to areas that materially affect the financial statements, the review engagement may not be relied upon to disclose all significant matters that may be revealed if an audit engagement was involved.

In a review engagement, the practitioner should

• Obtain a letter of engagement.

• Obtain familiarity with the accounting policies employed in the industry.

• Obtain an understanding of the organization and operations of the client, including operating locations.

• Become familiar with the nature of the client's balance sheet and income statement accounts.

• Look at the client's production, distribution, and compensation methods.

• Understand the product line or services performed by the client.

• Note related-party transactions.

• Conduct inquiry and analytical procedures, including

Client independence.

Basis of accounting followed.

Procedures to record, classify, and summarize transactions.

Adequacy of disclosures.

Comparing current year financial information to prior year financial data.

Comparing actual figures to budgeted figures.

Identifying abnormal changes.

Comparing financial information with nonfinancial data (e.g., sales to employees).

Looking at the minutes of stockholders' and board of directors' meetings.

• Read the financial statements and related footnotes.

• Obtain a report from another accountant who is involved with reviewing a material component of the entity.

• Inquire about changes in business activities, accounting methods, and practices.

• Resolve incomplete, inaccurate, or questionable matters.

• Obtain a client representation letter, if desired.

• Document review procedures in the workpapers.

• Prepare the review report.

The following should be contained in the review report:

• Identification of the financial statements.

• Statement that the review was performed in accord with standards established by the AICPA.

• Statement that all information included in the financial statements is the representation of management (owners).

• Definition of a review in that it consists mostly of inquiries of company personnel and analytical procedures to financial data.

• Statement that a review is significantly less in scope than an audit. There is no expression of an opinion on the financial statements taken as a whole.

• If warranted, the issuance of limited assurance. The accountant may state that he or she is not aware of any needed material modifications to the financial statements to make them into conformity with GAAP (or another comprehensive basis of accounting).

• Disclosure of any material modifications that are needed to the financial statements.

• Completion date of the review.

• Accountant's signature.

Each page of the reviewed financial statements should be labeled "See Accountant's Review Report." The practitioner may also want to expand the label to include "and the Notes to the Financial Statements." Further, each page of the financial statements may be labeled "unaudited."

When the accountant is prevented from conducting necessary review procedures, a review report may *not* be issued. Instead, a compilation report may be called for. *Caution*: Professional judgment has to be exercised considering the reasons for the preclusion of the audit report.

In case independence is impaired, a review report may not be issued.

The accountant may issue a review report on only *part* of the financial statements (e.g., balance sheet).

An accountant who was originally retained to perform an audit may be asked to step down to a lower level of service (audit to a review or compilation). The accountant must consider the following before agreeing to such a move:

• Client reasons for the change, including scope limitations

• Degree of additional audit procedures to finalize the audit engagement

• Client cost of performing the additional auditing procedures

Special Note: If the accountant is not permitted by the client to inquire with the client's legal counsel regarding litigation claims or the client refuses to provide a representation letter, a scope limitation exists which prevents the issuance of an opinion. This type of scope limitation is such that it would prevent an accountant from issuing a compilation or review report. However, if proper justification exists for the step-down, the account-

ant's report should *not* make reference to the change in engagement or to the application of any audit procedures performed. The compilation or review report may be rendered. *See also* Compilation.

RISK   Risk refers to the variability of cash flow (or earnings) around the expected value (return). Risk can be measured in either absolute or relative terms. Statistics such as *standard deviation* and *coefficient of deviation* are used to measure risk.

First, the expected value, A, is

$$\bar{A} = \sum_{i=1}^{n} A_i P_i$$

where A_i = the value of the ith possible outcome,

P_i = the probability that the ith outcome will occur,

n = the number of possible outcomes.

Then, the absolute risk is measured by the standard deviation:

$$\sigma = \sum_{i=1}^{n} (A_i - \bar{A})^2 P_i$$

The relative risk is measured by the coefficient of variation, which is $\sigma/\bar{A}$

■ **Example**

The ABC Corporation is considering investing in one of two mutually exclusive projects. Depending on the state of the economy, the projects would provide the following cash inflows in each of the next 5 years:

State	Probability	Proposal A	Proposal B
Recession	0.3	$1,000	$ 500
Normal	0.4	2,000	2,000
Boom	0.3	3,000	5,000

To compute the expected value (A), the standard deviation (σ), and the coefficient of variation, it is convenient to set up the following tables:

For proposal A:

$A_i(\$)$	P_i	A_iP_i ($)	$(A_i - \bar{A})$ ($)	$(A_i - \bar{A})^2$ ($)
1,000	0.3	300	−1,000	1,000,000
2,000	0.4	800	0	0
3,000	0.3	900	1,000	1,000,000
		$\bar{A} = 2,000$		$\sigma^2 = 2,000,000$

Since $\sigma^2 = 2,000,000$, $\sigma = 1,414$. Thus:

$$\frac{\sigma}{\bar{A}} = \frac{\$1,414}{\$2,000} = 0.71$$

For proposal B:

A_i ($)	P_i	A_ip_i ($)	$(A_i - \bar{A})$ ($)	$(A_i - \bar{A}^2)$ ($)
500	0.3	150	−1,950	3,802,500
2,000	0.4	800	−450	202,500
5,000	0.3	1,500	2,550	6,502,500
		$\bar{A} = 2,450$		$\sigma^2 = 10,507,500$

Since $\sigma^2 = 10,507,500$, $\sigma = \$3,242$. Thus:

$$\frac{\sigma}{\bar{A}} = \frac{\$3,242}{\$2,450} = 1.32$$

Therefore, proposal A is relatively less risky than proposal B, as indicated by the lower coefficient of variation.

Sources of Risk

There are the following different sources of risk involved in investment and financial decisions. Investors and decision makers must take into account the type of risk underlying an asset.

1. *Business risk*—caused by fluctuations of earnings before interest and taxes (operating income). Business risk depends on variability in demand, sales price, input prices, and amount of operating leverage.

2. *Liquidity risk*—represents the possibility that an asset may not be sold on short notice for its market value. If an investment must be sold at a high discount, then it is said to have a substantial amount of liquidity risk.

3. *Default risk*—the risk that a borrower will be unable to make interest payments or principal repayments on debt. For example, there is a great amount of default risk inherent in the bonds of a company experiencing financial difficulty.

4. *Market risk*—Prices of all stocks are correlated to some degree with broad swings in the stock market. Market risk refers to changes in a stock's price that result from changes in the stock market as a whole, regardless of the fundamental change in a firm's earning power.

5. *Interest rate risk*—refers to the fluctuations in the value of an asset as the interest rates and conditions of the money and capital markets change. Interest rate risk relates to fixed income securities such as bonds. For example, if interest rates rise (fall), bond prices fall (rise).

6. *Purchasing power risk*—relates to the possibility that an investor will receive a lesser amount of purchasing power than was originally invested. Bonds are most affected by this risk since the issuer will be paying back in cheaper dollars during an inflationary period.

7. *Systematic and unsystematic risk*—Many investors hold more than one financial asset. The portion of a security's risk, called unsystematic risk, can be controlled through diversification. This type of risk is unique to a given security. Business, liquidity, and default risks fall in this category. Nondiversifiable risk, more commonly referred to as systematic risk, results from forces outside the firm's control and are therefore not unique to the given security. Purchasing power, interest rate, and market risks fall into this category. This type of risk is measured by the *beta* coefficient.

Risk Analysis

Risk analysis is the process of measuring and analyzing the risks associated with financial and investment decisions. It is important especially in making capital investment decisions because of the large amount of capital involved and the long-term nature of the investment being considered. The higher the risk associated with a proposed project, the greater the return that must be earned to compensate for that risk. There are several methods for the analysis of risk, including *risk-adjusted discount rate*, *certainty equivalent*, *Monte Carlo simulation*, sensitivity analysis, and *decision trees*. *See also* Beta Coefficient; Capital Asset Pricing Model (CAPM); Return; Risk Analysis in Capital Budgeting; Risk-Return Trade-off.

RISK ANALYSIS IN CAPITAL BUDGETING Risk

analysis is important in making capital investment decisions because of the large amount of capital involved and the long-term nature of the investments being considered. The higher the risk associated with a proposed project, the greater the rate of return that must be earned on the project to compensate for that risk.

Since different investment projects involve different risks, it is important to incorporate risk into the analysis of capital budgeting. There are several methods for incorporating risk, including
1. Probability distributions
2. Risk-adjusted discount rate
3. Certainty equivalent
4. Simulation
5. Sensitivity analysis
6. Decision trees (or probability trees)

Probability Distributions

Expected values of a probability distribution may be computed. Before any capital budgeting method is applied, compute the expected cash inflows or, in some cases, the expected life of the asset.

■ Example 1

A firm is considering a $30,000 investment in equipment that will generate cash savings from operating costs. The following estimates regarding cash savings and useful life, along with their respective probabilities of occurrence, have been made:

Annual Cash Savings		Useful Life	
$ 6,000	0.2	4 years	0.2
8,000	0.5	5 years	0.6
10,000	0.3	6 years	0.2

Then, the expected annual saving is

$$\begin{aligned} \$ 6,000 \ (0.2) &= \$1,200 \\ 8,000 \ (0.5) &= \ 4,000 \\ 10,000 \ (0.3) &= \ \underline{3,000} \\ & \ \ \ \ \ \$8,200 \end{aligned}$$

The expected useful life is

$$\begin{aligned} 4 \ (0.2) &= 0.8 \\ 5 \ (0.6) &= 3.0 \\ 6 \ (0.2) &= \underline{1.2} \\ & \ 5 \ \text{years} \end{aligned}$$

The expected NPV is computed as follows (assuming a 10% cost of capital):

$$\begin{aligned} \text{NPV} = PV - I &= \$8,200 \ (PVIFA_{10\%,5}) - \$30,000 \\ &= \$8,200 \ (3.791) - \$30,000 \\ &= \$31,086 - \$30,000 = \$1,086 \end{aligned}$$

The expected IRR is computed as follows: by definition, at IRR,

$$I = PV$$
$$\$30,000 = \$8,200 \ (PVIFA_{i,5})$$
$$PVIFA_{i,5} = \frac{\$30,000}{\$8,200} = 3.659$$

which is about halfway between 10% and 12% in Table 4 in the Appendix, so that we can estimate the rate to be 11%. Therefore, the equipment should be purchased, since (1) NPV = $1,086, which is positive, and/or (2) IRR = 11%, which is greater than the cost of capital of 10%.

Risk-Adjusted Discount Rate

This method of risk analysis adjusts the cost of capital (or discount rate) upward as projects become riskier. Therefore, by increasing the discount rate from 10% to 15%, the expected cash flow from the investment must be relatively larger or the increased discount rate will generate a negative NPV and the proposed acquisition/investment would be turned down.

The use of the risk-adjusted discount rate is based on the assumption that investors demand higher returns for riskier projects. The expected cash flows are discounted at the risk-adjusted discount rate and then the usual capital budgeting criteria such as NPV and IRR are applied.

■ Example 2

A firm is considering an investment project with an expected life of 3 years. It requires an initial investment of $35,000. The firm estimates the following data in each of the next 3 years:

After-Tax Cash Inflow	Probability
−$5,000	0.2
$10,000	0.3
30,000	0.3
50,000	0.2

Assuming that a risk-adjusted required rate of return (after taxes) of 20% is appropriate for the investment projects of this level of risk, compute the risk-adjusted NPV.

First:

$\bar{A} = -\$5,000(0.2) + \$10,000(0.3) + \$30,000(0.3)$
$\qquad + \$50,000(0.2) = \$21,000$

The expected NPV = $21,000 $(PVIFA_{20\%,3})$
− $35,000 = 21,000 (2.106) − $35,000
= $44,226 −$35,000 = $9,226.

Certainty Equivalent

The certainty equivalent approach to risk analysis is drawn directly from the concept of utility theory. This method forces the decision maker to specify at what point the firm is indifferent to the choice between a certain sum of money and the expected value of a risky sum.

Once certainty equivalent coefficients are obtained, they are multiplied by the original cash flow to obtain the *equivalent certain* cash flow. Then, the accept-or-reject decision is made, using the normal capital budgeting criteria. The risk-free rate of return is used as the discount rate under the NPV method and as the cutoff rate under the IRR method.

■ Example 3

XYZ, Inc., with a 14% cost of capital after taxes, is considering a project with an expected life of 4 years. The project requires an initial certain cash outlay of $50,000. The expected cash inflows and certainty equivalent coefficients are as follows:

Year	After-Tax Cash Flow ($)	Certainty Equivalent Coefficient
1	10,000	0.95
2	15,000	0.80
3	20,000	0.70
4	25,000	0.60

The risk-free rate of return is 5%; compute the NPV and IRR. The equivalent certain cash inflows are obtained as follows:

Year	After-Tax Cash Inflow ($)	Certainty Equivalent Coefficient	Equivalent Certain Cash Inflow ($)	PV at 5%	PV ($)
1	10,000	0.95	9,500	0.9520	9,044
2	15,000	0.80	12,000	0.9074	10,884
3	20,000	0.70	14,000	0.8630	12,096
4	25,000	0.60	15,000	0.8223	12,345
					44,369

$$\text{NPV} = \$44,369 - \$50,000 = -\$5,639$$

By trial and error, we obtain 4% as the IRR. Therefore, the project should be rejected, since (1) NPV = −$5,639, which is negative and/or (2) IRR = 4% is less than the risk-free rate of 5%.

Simulation

This risk analysis method is frequently called Monte Carlo simulation. It requires that a probability distribution be constructed for each of the important variables affecting the project's cash flows. Since a computer is used to generate many results using random numbers, project simulation is expensive.

Sensitivity Analysis

Forecasts of many calculated NPVs under various alternative functions are compared to see how sensitive NPV is to changing conditions. It may be found that a certain variable or group of variables, once their assumptions are changed or relaxed, drastically alters the NPV. This results in a much riskier asset than was originally forecast.

Decision Trees

Some firms use decision trees (probability trees) to evaluate the risk of capital budgeting proposals. A decision tree is a graphical method of showing the sequence of possible outcomes. A capital budgeting tree would show the cash flows and NPV of the project under different possible circumstances. The decision tree method has the following advantages: (1) it visually lays out all the possible outcomes of the proposed project and makes management aware of the adverse possibilities and (2) the conditional nature of successive years' cash flows can be expressly depicted. The primary disadvantage is that most problems are too complex to permit year-by-year depiction. For example, for a 3-year project with three possible outcomes following each year, there are 27 paths. For a 10-year project (again with three possible outcomes following each year) there will be about 60,000 paths.

■ Example 4

A firm has an opportunity to invest in a machine that will last 2 years, initially cost $125,000, and has the following estimated possible after-tax cash inflow pattern: In year 1, there is a 40% chance that the after-tax cash inflow will be $45,000, a 25% chance that it will be $65,000, and a 35% chance that it will be $90,000. In year 2, the after-tax cash inflow possibilities depend on the cash inflow that occurs in year 1; that is, the year 2 after-tax cash inflows are conditional probabilities. Assume that the firm's after-tax cost of capital is 12%. The estimated conditional after-tax cash inflows (ATCI) and probabilities are given following.

If ATCI1 = $45,000		If ATCI1 = $65,000		If ATCI1 = $90,000	
ATCI2($)	Probability	ATCI2($)	Probability	ATCI2($)	Probability
30,000	0.3	80,000	0.2	90,000	0.1
60,000	0.4	90,000	0.6	100,000	0.8
90,000	0.3	100,000	0.2	110,000	0.2

Then the decision tree—which shows the possible after-tax cash inflow in each year, including the conditional nature of the year 2 cash inflow and its probabilities—can be depicted as follows:

Time 0	Time 1	Time 2	NPV at 12%	Joint Probability	Expected NPV
		$ 30,000	−$60,905[a]	0.120[b]	−$7,309
	$45,000	60,000	−36,995	0.160	−5,919
		90,000	−13,085	0.120	−1,570
		80,000	−3,195	0.050	−160
−$125,000	65,000	90,000	4,775	0.150	716
		100,000	12,745	0.050	637
		90,000	27,100	0.035	949
	90,000	100,000	35,070	0.280	9,820
		110,000	43,040	0.035	1,506
				1.000	−$1,330

$$^a \text{NPV} = PV - I = \frac{\$45,000}{(1 + 0.12)} + \frac{\$30,000}{(1 + 0.12)^2} - \$125,000$$

$$= \$45,000 \, (PVIF_{12\%,1}) + \$30,000 \, (PVIF_{12\%,2}) - \$125,000$$

$$= \$45,000 \, (0.893) + \$30,000 \, (0.797) - \$125,000$$

$$= \$40,185 + \$23,910 - \$125,000 = -\$60,905$$

^{b} Joint probability = (0.4)(0.3) = 0.120

The last column shows the calculation of expected NPV, which is the weighted average of the individual path NPVs where the weights are the path probabilities. In this example, the expected NPV of the project is −$1,330, and the project should be rejected.

Correlation of Cash Flows Over Time

When cash inflows are independent from period to period, it is fairly easy to measure the overall risk of an investment proposal. In some cases, however, especially with the introduction of a new product, the cash flows experienced in early years affect the size of the cash flows in later years. This is called the time dependence of cash flows, and it has the effect of increasing the risk of the project over time.

■ Example 5

Janday Corporation's after-tax cash inflows (ATCI) are time-dependent, so that year 1 results (ATCI1) affect the flows in year 2 (ATCI2), as follows:

If ATCI1 is $8,000 with a 40% probability, the distribution for ATCI2 is

0.3	$ 5,000
0.5	10,000
0.2	15,000

If ATCI1 is $15,000 with a 50% probability, the distribution for ATCI2 is

0.3	$10,000
0.6	20,000
0.1	30,000

If ATCI1 is $20,000 with a 10% chance, the distribution for ATCI2 is

0.1	$15,000
0.8	40,000
0.1	15,000

The project requires an initial investment of $20,000 and the risk-free rate of capital is 10%.

The company uses the expected NPV from decision tree analysis to determine whether the project should be accepted. The analysis is below.

Since the NPV is positive ($5,306), Janday Corporation should accept the project.

Normal Distribution and NPV Analysis

With the assumption of independence of cash flows over time, the expected NPV would be

$$NPV = PV - I = \sum_{t=1}^{n} \frac{\bar{A}_t}{(1+r)^t} - I$$

The standard deviation of NPVs is

Time 0	Time 1	Time 2	NPV at 10%	Joint Probability	Expected NPV
		$ 5,000	−$8,598[a]	0.12[b]	−$1,031
	$ 8,000	10,000	−4,463	0.20	−893
		15,000	−331	0.08	−26
		10,000	1,901	0.15	285
−20,000	15,000	20,000	10,165	0.30	3,050
		30,000	18,429	0.05	921
		15,000	10,576	0.01	106
	20,000	40,000	31,238	0.08	2,499
		50,000	39,502	0.01	395
				1.00	$5,306

[a] NPV = PV − I = $8,000 PVIF_{10,1} + $5,000 PVIF_{10,2} −$20,000
= $8,000 (0.9091) + $5,000 (0.8264) − $20,000 = $8,598
[b] Joint probability of the first path = (0.4) (0.3) = 0.12

$$\sigma = \sqrt{\sum_{t=1}^{n} \frac{\sigma_t^2}{(1 + r)^{2t}}}$$

The expected value ($\bar{A}$) and the standard deviation (σ) give a considerable amount of information by which to assess the risk of an investment project. If the probability distribution is normal, some probability statement regarding the project's NPV can be made. For example, the probability of a project's providing NPV of less or greater than zero can be computed by standardizing the normal variate x as follows:

$$z = \frac{x - NPV}{\sigma}$$

where x = the outcome to be found,

NPV = the expected NPV,

z = the standardized normal variate whose probability value can be found in Table 5 in the Appendix.

■ Example 6

Assume an investment with the following data:

	Period 1	Period 2	Period 3
Expected cash inflow ($\bar{A}$)	$5,000	$4,000	$3,000
Standard deviation (σ)	1,140	1,140	1,140

Assume that the firm's cost of capital is 8% and the initial investment is $9,000. Then the expected NPV is

$$NPV = PV - I$$

$$= \frac{\$5,000}{(1 + 0.08)} + \frac{\$4,000}{(1 + 0.08)^2} + \frac{\$3,000}{(1 + 0.08)^3}$$
$$- \$9,000$$

$$= \$5,000(PVIF_{8,1}) + \$4,000(PVIF_{8,2})$$
$$+ \$3,000(PVIF_{8,3}) - \$9,000$$

$$= \$5,000(0.926) + \$4,000(0.857)$$
$$+ \$3,000(0.794) - \$9,000$$

$$= \$4,620 + \$3,428 + \$2,421 - \$9,000$$
$$= \$1,430$$

The standard deviation about the expected NPV is

$$\sigma = \sqrt{\sum_{t=1}^{n} \frac{\sigma_t^2}{(1 + r)^{2t}}}$$

$$= \sqrt{\frac{\$1,430^2}{(1 + 0.08)^2} + \frac{\$1,430^2}{(1 + 0.08)^4} + \frac{\$1,430^2}{(1 + 0.08)^6}}$$

$$= \sqrt{\$2,788,411} = \$1,670$$

The probability that the PV is less than zero is then:

$$z = \frac{x - NPV}{\sigma}$$

$$= \frac{0 - \$1,430}{\$1,670} = -0.863$$

The area of normal distribution that is z standard deviations to the left or right of the mean may be found in Table 5 in the Appendix. A value of z equal to -0.863 falls in the area between 0.1949 and 0.1922 in Table 5. Therefore, there is approximately a 19% chance that the project's NPV will be zero or less. Putting it another way, there is a 19% chance that the IRR of the project will be less than the risk-free rate.

CAPM in Capital Budgeting

Portfolio considerations play an important role in the overall capital budgeting process. Through diversification, a firm can stabilize earnings, reduce risk, and thereby increase the market price of the firm's stock. The *beta* coefficient can be used for this purpose.

The capital asset pricing model (CAPM) can be used to determine the appropriate cost of capital. The NPV method uses the cost of capital as the rate to discount future cash flows. The IRR method uses the cost of capital as the cutoff rate. The required rate of return, or cost of capital according to the CAPM, or security market line (SML), is equal to the risk-free rate of return (r_f) plus a risk premium equal to the firm's beta coefficient (b) times the market risk premium ($r_m - r_f$):

$$r_j = r_f + b(r_m - r_f)$$

■ Example 7

A project has the following projected cash flows:

Year 0	Year 1	Year 2	Year 3
$(400)	$300	$200	$100

The estimated beta for the project is 1.5. The market return is 12%, and the risk-free rate is 6%. Then the firm's cost of capital, or required rate of return is

$$r_j = r_f + b(r_m - r_f) = 6\% + 1.5(12\% - 6\%) = 15\%$$

The project's NPV can be computed using 15% as the discount rate:

Year	Cash Flow ($)	PV at 15%	PV ($)
0	(400)	1.000	(400)
1	300	0.870	261
2	200	0.756	151
3	100	0.658	66
			78[a]

[a] NPV

The project should be accepted since its NPV is positive, that is, $78. Also, the project's IRR can be computed by trial and error. It is almost 30%, which exceeds the cost of capital of 15%. Therefore, by that standard also the project should be accepted. *See also* Beta Coefficient; Capital Asset Pricing Model (CAPM); Risk.

RISK PREMIUM　This is the amount by which the required return on an asset or security exceeds the *risk-free rate*, r_f. In terms of the *capital asset pricing model* (CAPM), it can be expressed as $b (r_m - r_f)$, where b is the security's *beta* coefficient, a measure of *systematic risk*, and r_m is the required return on the market portfolio. The risk premium is the additional return required to compensate investors for assuming a given level of risk. The higher this premium, the more risky the security, and vice versa. *See also* Beta Coefficient; Capital Asset Pricing Model (CAPM).

RISK-RETURN TRADE-OFF　Integral to the theory of finance and investment is the concept of a risk-return trade-off. All financial decisions involve some sort of risk-return trade-off. The greater the risk associated with any financial decision, the greater the return expected from it. For example, in the case of working capital management, the less inventory a firm keeps, the higher the expected return (since less of the firm's current assets is tied up), but also the greater the risk of running out of stock and thus losing potential revenue.

Risk, along with the return, is a major consideration in investment decisions. The investor must compare the expected return from a given investment with the risk associated with it. Generally speaking, the higher the risk undertaken, the more ample the return, and conversely, the lower the risk, the more modest the return. (See Figure 1, page 401.) In the case of investment stock, the investor would demand higher return from a speculative stock to compensate for the higher level of risk.

Proper assessment and balance of the various risk-return trade-offs is part of creating a sound financial and investment plan.

ROUND LOT　A round-lot transaction involves units of 100 shares each. *See also* Odd-Lot; Stock Orders.

RULE OF 78　The Rule of 78, sometimes called the *Sum of the Digits*, is a method that banks use to develop a loan amortization schedule. It results in a borrower paying more interest in the beginning of a loan when he or she has the use of more of the money and less and less interest as the debt is reduced. Therefore, it is important to know how much interest can be saved by prepaying after a certain month and how much of the loan is still owed.

Figure 1 Return Versus Risk

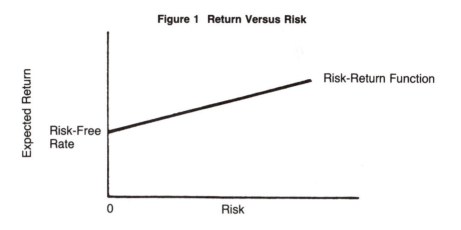

■ Example

Assume you borrow $3,180 ($3,000 principal and $180 interest) for 12 months, so your equal monthly payment is $265 ($3,180/12). You want to know how much interest you save by prepaying after six payments. You might guess $90 ($180 × 6/12), reasoning that interest is charged uniformly each month. Good guess but wrong. Here is how the Rule of 78 works.

1. First, add up all the digits for the number of payments scheduled to be made, in this case the sum of the digits 1 through 12.

$$(1 + 2 + 3 \ldots + 12 = 78)$$

Generally, you can find the sum of the digits (SD) using the following formula:

$$SD = n(n + 1)/2 = 12(12 + 1)/2$$
$$= (12)(13)/2 = 156/2 = 78$$

where n = the number of months.
(The sum of the digits for a 4-year (48 months) loan is 1,176 [(48)(48 + 1)/2 = (48)(49)/2 = 1,176)]. See Table 1, page 402 (Loan Amortization Schedule).

2. In the first month, before making any payments, you have the use of the entire amount borrowed. You thus pay 12/78ths (or 15.39%) of the total interest in the first payment. In the second month, you pay 11/78ths (14.10%); in the third, 10/78ths (12.82%); and so on down to the last payment, 1/78ths (1.28%). Thus, the first month's total payment of $265 contains $27.69 (15.39% × $180) in interest and $237.31 ($265 − $27.69) in principal. The twelfth and last payment of $265 contains $2.30 (1.28% × $180) in interest and $262.70 in principal.

3. In order to find out how much interest is saved by prepaying after the sixth payment, you merely add up the digits for the remaining six payments. Thus, using the previous formula, 6(6 + 1)/2 = 21. This means that 21/78ths of the interest, or $48.46 (21/78 × $180), will be saved.

4. To calculate the amount of principal still owed, subtract the total amount of interest already paid, $131.54 ($180 − $48.46), from the total amount of payments made, $1,590 (6 × $265), giving $1,458.46. Then subtract this from the original $3,000 principal, giving $1,541.54 still owed.

5. Does it pay to pay off after the sixth payment? It depends on how much return you can get from investing elsewhere. In this example, you needed $1,541.54 to pay off the loan to save $48.46 in interest. For loans of longer maturities, the same rules apply, though the actual sum of the digits will be different. Thus, for a 48-month loan, you would pay in the first month 48/1176ths of the total interest, in the second month, 47/1176ths, and so on.

Table 1   Loan Amortization Schedule
(Based on a loan of $3,180 [$3,000 principal and $180 interest])

Payment Number	Fraction (Percent) Earned by Lender	Monthly Payment	Interest	Principal
1	12/78 (15.39%)	$ 265	$ 27.69[a]	$ 237.31[b]
2	11/78 (14.10%)	265	25.39	239.61
3	10/78 (12.82%)	265	23.08	241.92
4	9/78 (11.54%)	265	20.77	244.23
5	8/78 (10.26%)	265	18.46	246.54
6	7/78 (8.97%)	265	16.15	248.85
7	6/78 (7.69%)	265	13.85	251.15
8	5/78 (6.41%)	265	11.54	253.46
9	4/78 (5.13%)	265	9.23	255.77
10	3/78 (3.85%)	265	6.92	258.08
11	2/78 (2.56%)	265	4.62	260.38
12	1/78 (1.28%)	265	2.30	262.70
78	78/78 (100%)	$3,180	$180.00	$3,000.00

[a] $27.69 = $180.00 × 12/78 (15.39%)
[b] $237.31 = $265 − $27.69

RULE OF 72 AND RULE OF 69   To determine how many years it takes to *double* investment money, the *rule of 72* is used. Under it, dividing the number 72 by the fixed rate of return equals the number of years it takes for annual earnings from the investment to double. That is,

$$72/r \text{ (in percent)}$$

▪ Example

Assume you bought a piece of property yielding an annual return of 25%. Then the investment will double in less than 3 years.

$$72/25 = 2.88 \text{ years}$$

The *rule of 69*, which is very similar to the rule of 72, states that an amount of money invested at r percent per period will double in

$$69/r \text{ (in percent)} + 0.35 \text{ periods}$$

▪ Example

Using the same data from the previous example,

$$69/25 + 0.35 = 2.76 + 0.35 = 3.11 \text{ years}$$

S

SAFE HARBOR RULE This rule by the SEC protects a registrant and independent CPA from lawsuits for a subsequently proved inaccurate projection as long as it was made in ''good faith'' and the assessment was reasonably based. The plaintiff has the burden of proof to establish that the forecasts and projections did *not* have a reasonable basis or were *not* disclosed in good faith.

SAFETY STOCK This is extra units of inventory a firm must carry as protection against possible stockouts. The safety stock must be carried when the firm is not certain about either the demand of the product or lead time or both. *See also* Inventory Planning and Control; Optimal Reorder Point.

SALES-LEASEBACK ARRANGEMENT The lessor sells property and then leases it back for use. One reason for this transaction may be that the lessor was in need of funds. *See also* Leases.

SALES MIX VARIANCE This is the effect on profit of selling a different proportionate mix of products than had been budgeted. This variance arises when different products have different contribution margins. The sales mix variance shows how well the department has done in terms of selling the more profitable products, while the *sales volume variance* measures how well the firm has done in terms of its sales volume.

Sales mix variance = (Actual sales at budgeted mix
  − Actual sales at actual mix)
    × Budgeted contribution margin per unit

■ Example

Assume that the XYZ Company has the following expected contribution margin (CM) for 19A:

Product A	30 units at $2.00 per unit of CM	$ 60.00
Product B	70 units at $1.00 per unit of CM	70.00
		$130.00

Assume actual CMs for the year are

Product A	45 units at $1.75	$ 78.75
Product B	50 units at $1.25	62.50
		$141.25

Then the sales mix variance is computed as follows:

	Actual Sales at Budgeted Mix*	Actual Sales at Actual Mix	Difference	Budgeted CM	Variance ($)
Product A	28.5 units	45	16.5 units	$2.00	$33.00F
Product B	66.5	50	16.5	1.00	16.50U
	95.0	95			$16.50F

* This is the budgeted sales mix proportions of 30% and 70% applied to 95 units actually sold.

See also Profit Variance Analysis; Sales Volume Variance.

SALES PRICE VARIANCE   This is the difference between actual selling price per unit and the budgeted selling price per unit multiplied by the actual number of units sold.

Sales price variance
= (Actual price − Budgeted price) × Actual sales

If the actual price is greater than the budgeted price, a variance is favorable; otherwise, it is unfavorable. *See also* Profit Variance Analysis.

SALES-TYPE LEASE   The lessor is a manufacturer or dealer in the rental property. The lessor records profit on the assumed sale of the item in the year of lease and interest revenue over the life of the lease. *See also* Leases.

SALES VOLUME VARIANCE   Sales volume (quantity) variance is the difference between the actual number of units sold and the budgeted number multiplied by the budgeted selling price per unit.

Sales price variance
= (Actual sales − Budgeted sales) × Budgeted price

If the actual sales is greater than the budgeted sales, a variance is favorable; otherwise, it is unfavorable. Responsibility for the sales volume variance usually rests with the marketing department. *See also* Profit Variance Analysis.

SAMPLING   In their examinations of financial statements, auditors often encounter balances resulting from many small repetitive transactions. Clearly, it is not cost effective to in-spect every transaction or document for a particular characteristic. Auditors typically select a *sample* of transactions and examine those items for desired characteristics. Then, on the basis of the findings in the sample, they make inferences about the true (but unknown) occurrence of the characteristics in the audit *population*. There are two basic methods of selecting samples from populations: nonstatistical (judgment or nonrandom) sampling and statistical (random or probability) sampling.

Nonstatistical Sampling

In nonstatistical sampling, personal knowledge and opinion are used to identify those items from the population that are to be included in the sample. Nonstatistical sampling therefore relies on the auditor's seasoned experience in drawing an appropriate sample. This technique is used primarily when the audit population consists of either a small number of high-dollar-value items or items with an immaterial aggregate amount. The auditor uses professional judgment to decide how many and which items should be included in the sample. For example, this method typically would be used in selecting 20 additions to property and equipment, worth $200,000, for vouching when total additions consist of 40 items aggregating $250,000.

Statistical Sampling

In statistical sampling, all the items in the population have a chance of being chosen in the sample. It relies on the laws of probability in selecting the sample data. In auditing, this method of sampling is used primarily when making judgments about an audit population consisting of a large number of homogeneous items. For example, an auditor may use this technique to estimate the percentage of deviation from an established internal control procedure relating to sales when 85,000 sales transactions have been processed during the year.

Statistical Selection

Random selection of the sample is an indispensable part of any statistical sampling plan. The underlying basic concepts of a simple random sample are (1) every item in the population has an equal chance of being chosen for inclusion in the sample and (2) the auditor selecting the sample will not influence or bias the selection in any way. The most common ways to select random samples are

1. *Simple (unrestricted) random sampling*—selects samples by methods that allow each possible sample to have an equal probability of being picked and each item in the entire population to have an equal chance of being included in the sample. The methods of selection are typically either by reference to a table of random numbers or to a computer program that generates random numbers.

2. *Systematic sampling*—elements are selected from the population at a uniform interval that is measured in time, order, or space. This method differs from simple random sampling in that each item has an equal chance of being selected but each sample does not have an equal chance of being selected. Compared to random sampling, systematic sampling is a more efficient, faster sampling methodology since it consists of basically counting out the sampling units using a uniform interval. In simple random sampling, a one-to-one relationship must be set up between the sampling units and a table of random numbers (which may be generated through computer programs). In addition, a systematic sample is considered less random than the simple random sample because the former may introduce a bias into the sampling

process if there is a cyclical pattern in the population being tested that may coincide with the interval being used to select the sample.

3. *Stratified sampling*—the population is divided into relatively homogeneous groups, called *strata*, according to a common characteristic (such as the stratification of total credit sales into open account sales and credit card sales). For this purpose, one of two approaches can be used. Either we select at random from each stratum a specified number of items corresponding to the proportion of that stratum in the population as a whole or we draw an equal number of items from each stratum and give weight to the results according to the stratum's proportion of total population. With either approach, stratified sampling guarantees that every item in the population has a chance of being selected.

4. *Cluster (block) sampling*—the population is divided into groups, called *clusters*. A random sample is then selected from the clusters. A cluster consists of contiguous transactions. For example, a cluster selected from a population of all vouchers processed for the year 19X1 might be all vouchers processed on March 3, June 20, and September 10, 19X1. This sample includes only three sampling units out of 250 business days since the sampling unit in this example is a period of time rather than the individual transaction. This method is not widely used in auditing.

See also Audit.

SCATTERGRAPH METHOD The scattergraph method is a graphical procedure used to separate a mixed (semivariable) cost into the fixed and the variable cost portion. In this method, a semivariable expense is plotted on the vertical axis (or y-axis) and activity measure is plotted on the horizontal axis (or x-axis). Then a *regression* line is fitted by visual inspection of the plotted x-y data, as shown in the figure on page 406. The scattergraph method is relatively easy to use and simple to understand. However, it should be used with extreme caution, because it does not provide an objective test for assuring that the regression line drawn is the most accurate fit for the underlying observations. *See also* Cost Behavior Analysis; Cost Behavior Patterns.

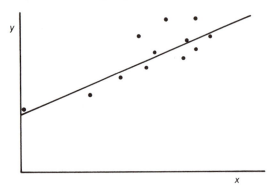

SECURITY VALUATION The process of determining security valuation involves finding the present value of an asset's expected future cash flows using the investor's required rate of return. Thus, the basic security valuation model can be defined mathematically as follows:

$$V = \sum_{t=1}^{n} \frac{C_t}{(1 + r)^t}$$

where V = intrinsic value or present value of an asset,

C_t = expected future cash flows in period $t = 1, \ldots, n$,

r = investor's required rate of return.

See also Bond Valuation; Common Stock Valuation.

SEGMENTAL REPORTING Financial reporting for business segments is useful in evaluating segmental performance, earning potential, and risk. Segmental reporting may be by industry, foreign geographic area, export sales, major customers, and governmental contracts. The financial statement presentation for segments may appear in the body, footnotes, or separate schedule to the financial statements. Segmental information is not required for nonpublic companies or in interim reports. An industry segment sells merchandise or renders services to outside customers. Segmental information assists financial statement users in analyzing financial statements by allowing improved assessment of an enterprise's past performance and future prospects.

Segmental data occurs when a company prepares a full set of financial statements (balance sheet, income statement, statement of cash flows, and related footnotes). Segmental data is shown for each year presented. Information reported is a disaggregation of consolidated financial information.

Accounting principles employed in preparing financial statements should be used for segmental information, except that numerous intercompany transactions eliminated in consolidation are included in segmental reporting on a gross basis.

Reporting Requirements

A segment must be reported if one or more of the following criteria are met:

• Revenue is 10% or more of total revenue.

• Operating income or loss is 10% or more of the combined operating profit.

• Identifiable assets are 10% or more of the total identifiable assets.

Factors to be considered when determining industry segments are

• Nature of the product. Related products or services have similar purposes or end uses (e.g., similarity in profit margins, risk, and growth).

• Nature of the production process. Homogeneity may be indicated when there is interchangeable production or sales facilities, equipment, service groups, or labor force.

• Nature of the market. Similarity exists in geographic markets serviced or types of customers serviced.

Reportable segments are determined by

• Identifying specific products and services

• Grouping those products and services by industry line into segments

• Selecting material segments to the company as a whole

A grouping of products and services by industry lines should take place. A number of approaches are possible. However, not one method is appropriate in determining industry segments in every case. In many cases, management judgment is necessary to determine the industry segment. A starting point in deriving an industry segment is by *profit center*. A profit center is a component that sells mostly to outsiders for a profit.

When the profit center goes across industry lines, it should be broken down into smaller groups. A company in many industries not accumulating financial information on a segregated basis must disaggregate its operations by industry line.

Although worldwide industry segmentation is recommended, it may not be practical to gather. If foreign operations cannot be disaggregated, the firm should disaggregate domestic activities. Foreign operations should be disaggregated where possible and the remaining foreign operations treated as a single segment.

As per FASB 14, a segment that was significant in the past, even though not meeting the 10% test in the current year, should still be reported upon if it is expected that the segment will be significant in the future.

Segments should constitute a substantial portion, meaning 75% or more of the company's total revenue to outside customers. The 75% test is applied separately each year. However, in order to derive 75%, as a matter of practicality, not more than 10 segments should be shown. If more than 10 are identified, it is possible to combine similar segments.

Note that even though intersegmental transfers are eliminated in the preparation of consolidated financial statements, they are includable for segmental disclosure in determining the 10% and 75% rules.

In applying the 10% criteria, the accountant should note the following:

• *Revenue*—a separation should exist between revenue to unaffiliated customers and revenue to other business segments. Transfer prices are used for intersegmental transfers. Accounting bases followed should be disclosed.

• *Operating profit or loss*—operating earnings of a segment excludes general corporate revenue and expenses that are not allocable, interest expense (unless the segment is a financial type, such as one involved in banking), domestic and foreign income taxes, income from unconsolidated subsidiaries or investees, income from discontinued operations, extraordinary items, cumulative effect of a change in accounting principles, and minority interest. Note that directly traceable and allocable costs should be charged to segments when applicable thereto.

• *Identifiable assets*—assets of a segment include those directly in it and general corporate assets that can rationally be allocated to it. Allocation methods should be consistently applied. Identifiable assets include those consisting of a part of the company's investment in the segment (e.g., goodwill). Identifiable assets do not include advances or loans to other segments except for income therefrom that is used to compute the results of operations (e.g., a segment of a financial nature).

■ Example

A company provides the following data regarding its business segments and overall operations:

	Segment A	Segment B	Company*
Revenue	$2,000	$1,000	$12,000
Direct costs	500	300	5,000
Company-wide costs (allocable)			800
General company costs (not allocable)			1,700

* Excludes segment amounts

Company-wide costs are allocable based on the ratios of direct costs. The tax rate is 34%.

The profits to be reported by segment and for the company as a whole are as follows:

	Segment A	Segment B	Company
Revenues	$2,000	$1,000	$15,000
Less:			
Direct costs	(500)	300	5,800
Indirect costs (allocated)			
$800 × $500/$5,800	(69)		
$800 × $300/$5,800		(41)	
			(800)
Segment margin	$1,431	$ 659	
General company costs			(1,700)
Income before tax			$ 6,700
Income tax (34%)			2,278
Net income			$ 4,422

Disclosures

Disclosures are not required for 90% enterprises (e.g., a company that derives 90% or more of its revenue, operating profit, and total assets from one segment). In effect, that segment is the business. The dominant industry segment should be identified.

Disclosures to be made by segments include

• Aggregate depreciation, depletion, and amortization expense.

• Capital expenditures.

• Company's equity in vertically integrated unconsolidated subsidiaries and equity method investees. Note the geographic location of equity method investees.

• Effect of an accounting principle change on the operating profit of the reportable segment. Also include its effect on the company.

• Material segmental accounting policies not already disclosed in the regular financial statements.

• Transfer price used.

• Allocation method for costs.

• Unusual items affecting segmental profit.

• Type of products.

Consolidation Aspects

If a segment includes a *purchase method* consolidated subsidiary, the required segmental information is based upon the consoli-

dated value of the subsidiary (e.g., fair market value and goodwill recognized) and *not* on the values recorded in the subsidiary's own financial statements. However, transactions between the segment and other segments, which are eliminated in consolidation, are included in reportable segmental information.

Segmental data is *not* required for *unconsolidated subsidiaries* or other *unconsolidated investees*. Note that each subsidiary or investee is subject to the rules of FASB 14 that segment information be reported.

Some types of typical consolidation eliminations are *not* eliminated when reporting for segments. For instance, revenue of a segment includes intersegmental sales and sales to unrelated customers.

A full set of financial statements for a foreign investee that is *not* a subsidiary does not have to disclose segmental information when presented in the same financial report of a primary reporting entity except if the foreign investee's separately issued statements already disclose the required segmental data.

Other Requirements

Segmental disclosure is also required when

• 10% or more of revenue or assets is associated with a foreign area. Presentation must be made of revenue, operating profit or loss, and assets for foreign operations in the aggregate or by geographic locality. A foreign geographic area is a foreign country or group of homogeneous countries. Factors considered in deriving this grouping decision are proximity, economic affinity, and similar business environments.

• 10% or more of sales is to one customer. A group of customers under common control is construed as one customer.

• 10% or more of revenue is obtained from domestic government contracts or a foreign government.

In the previous cases, the source of the

segmental revenue should be disclosed along with the percentage so derived.

In some instances, restatement of prior period information is required for comparative reasons. The nature and effect of restatement should be disclosed. Restatement is needed when financial statements of the company as a whole have been restated. Also, restatement occurs when there is a pooling of interests. Restatement is also needed when a change has occurred in grouping products or services for segment determination or change in grouping of foreign activities into geographic segments.

As per FASB 24, segmental data are not required in financial statements that are presented in another company's financial report if those statements are

• Combined in a complete set of statements and both sets are presented in the same report

• Presented for a foreign investee (not a subsidiary of the primary enterprise) unless the financial statements disclose segment information (e.g., those foreign investees for which such information is already required by the SEC)

• Presented in the report of a nonpublic company

If an investee uses the cost or equity method and is not exempted by one of the previous provisions, its full set of financial statements presented in another enterprise's report must present segmental information if such data are significant to statements of the primary enterprise. Significance is determined by applying the percentage tests of FASB 14 (i.e., 10% tests) in relation to financial statements of the primary enterprise without adjustment for the investee's revenue, operating results, or identifiable assets.

SELL-OR-PROCESS-FURTHER DECISION When
two or more products are produced simultaneously from the same input by a joint process, these products are called *joint products*.

The term *joint costs* is used to describe all the manufacturing costs incurred prior to the point where the joint products are identified as individual products, referred to as the *split-off point*. At the split-off point, some of the joint products are in final form and salable to the consumer, whereas others require additional processing. In many cases, the company might have the option: It can sell the products at the split-off point or process them further for increased revenue. In connection with this type of decision, joint costs are considered irrelevant, since the joint costs have already been incurred at the time of the decision and therefore are *sunk* costs. The decision will rely exclusively on additional revenue compared to the additional costs incurred due to further processing.

■ Example

Assume a company produces three products, A, B, and C, from a joint process. Joint production costs for the year were $120,000. Product A may be sold at the split-off point or processed further. The additional processing requires no special facilities and all additional processing costs are variable. Sales values and cost needed to evaluate the company's production policy regarding product A follow:

Units Produced	Sales Value at Split-off	Additional Cost and Sales Value After Further Processing	
		Sales	Cost
3,000	$60,000	$90,000	$25,000

Should product A be sold at the split-off point or processed further? To answer this question all we need to do is compare incremental revenue with the incremental costs as follows:

Incremental sales revenue	$30,000 ($90,000 − $60,000)
Incremental costs, additional processing	25,000
Incremental gain	$ 5,000

Therefore, product A should be processed further. Keep in mind that the joint production cost of $120,000 is not included in the analysis since it is a sunk cost and therefore irrelevant to the decision.

SENSITIVITY ANALYSIS Sensitivity analysis, or post-optimality analysis, is a technique for determining how the optimal solution to a *linear programming* problem changes if the problem data such as objective function coefficients or right-hand side values change. To an alert accountant and financial analyst, the optimal solution not only provides answers—given assumptions about resources, capacities, and prices in the problem formulation—but should raise questions about what would happen *if* conditions should change. Some of these changes might be imposed by the environment, such as changes in resource costs and financial and product market conditions. Some, however, represent questions raised by the decision maker because they are changes that he or she can initiate, such as enlarging capacities or adding new activities. Sensitivity analysis is essentially a *what-if (simulation)* technique that is most effective in attacking the uncertainty or risk about the future. *See also* Linear Programming (LP); Simulation.

SERIAL BOND A serial bond is a bond issue that matures in installments. The time intervals for the maturity dates are usually equally spaced. Each installment may have a different interest rate associated with it. The portion due within the year is classified as a current liability, with the balance being presented as a noncurrent liability.

Serial bonds are widely used by school districts and other taxing authorities that borrow money to finance public projects, for example, a new public school, public water/ sewage treatment facilities, and the like. The money is borrowed based upon agreement that a specific tax will be levied to pay off the obligation. As the taxes are collected, the cash is used to pay off the indebtedness.

■ Example

Serial bonds carrying 7% interest payable (3½% semiannually) are sold to yield 5% per annum with the following maturity dates: $10,000 at the end of 12 months; $20,000 at the end of 18 months; and $30,000 at the end of 24 months. The calculations are

	Price	Premium
Serial No. 1 (due in 12 months = 2 interest periods)		
Principal: $10,000 × 0.95181	$ 9,518	
Interest: $10,000 × 1.92742	675	
	10,193	$ 193
Serial No. 2 (due in 18 months = 3 interest periods)		
Principal: $20,000 × 0.92861	18,572	
Interest: $20,000 × 2.85602	1,999	
	20,571	571
Serial No. 3 (due in 24 months = 4 interest periods)		
Principal: $30,000 × 0.90595	27,179	
Interest: $30,000 × 3.76197	3,950	
	31,129	1,129
Total All Serials	$61,893	
Total Premium* on All Serials		$1,893

* This issue is sold at a premium since its interest rate (7%) is greater than the yield rate (5%).

The corresponding entry to record the sale of the bonds would be

Cash	61,893	
Serial Bonds Payable		60,000
Premium on Bonds Payable		1,893

SETTLEMENT IN PENSION PLAN   A settlement occurs when there is a complete or partial discharge of the employer's obligation under the plan. *See also* Pension Plans.

SHADOW PRICE   Shadow price in *linear programming* (LP) is imputed value, not an actual value; that is, maximum price that management is willing to pay for an extra unit of a given scarce resource. For example, an accountant and financial manager who have solved an LP problem might wish to know whether it pays to add capacity in hours in a particular department. The manager would be interested in the monetary value to the firm of adding, say, an hour per week of assembly time. This monetary value is usually the additional profit that could be earned. This amount is the shadow price. A shadow price is, in a way, an *opportunity cost*—the profit that would be lost by not adding an additional hour of capacity. To justify a decision in favor of a short-term capacity decision, the manager must be sure that the shadow price exceeds the actual price of that expansion.

■ Example

Suppose that the shadow price of an hour of the assembly capacity is $6.50, whereas the actual market price is $8. That means it does not pay to obtain an additional hour of the assembly capacity. *See also* Linear Programming (LP).

SHARPE SINGLE-INDEX MODEL   The number of data inputs for even a moderate-sized portfolio using the Markowitz portfolio selection model (*quadratic programming* model) can be quite staggering. William Sharpe developed a model that drastically reduced the data requirements necessary to perform portfolio analysis. The Sharpe model is called the single-index or market index model. Sharpe suggests that all securities are linearly related to a market index. This relationship can be expressed through the equation:

$$r_j = a + b_{r_m} + u_j$$

where a = alpha and b = beta, the index of systematic risk, which represents the individual securities' relationship with the market. The random error u_j represents the unsystematic or nonmarket-related return of an individual asset. Securities are assumed to be related to one another through their relationship with the market. Rather than computing the covariances of all combinations of securities in a portfolio, the Sharpe model assumes that all securities are related to one another through their relationship with a market index such as the Standard & Poor's 500 Index. *See also* Beta Coefficient; Portfolio Theory and Capital Asset Pricing Model (CAPM).

SHORT SELLING   Selling short a stock is an approach used by an investor to gain when the price of a stock drops. The investor attempts to sell high and buy low. To undertake a short sale the broker borrows the security from someone else and then sells it for the investor to another. Proceeds from the sale are kept in the brokerage account. Later on, the investor buys the shares back. The investor can ''sell short against the box'' when he or she sells short shares actually owned (not borrowed shares). The investor loses money if the repurchase price is higher than the original selling price.

To undertake a short sale, the short seller must have a margin account. The Federal Reserve mandates that a short seller must have in a margin account cash or securities worth at least 50% of the market value of the stock he or she wants to sell short. Stock can only be sold short on an "up tick." However, over-the-counter stocks may be sold short at any time. Short sellers typically pay no interest charge but will pay brokerage commissions on the selling price and repurchase price.

Situations Where Short Selling May Be Advisable

• Expectation of a price decline in the stock.

• Desire to postpone showing a gain and paying taxes on it from one year to the next. For instance, 100 shares of XYZ Company bought at $20 now have a market price of $32. If the investor sells now, a tax must be paid on the gain. If it is desired to postpone the gain to next year, the investor can short XYZ Company stock against the box. The broker will retain the certificate in a vault and sell it short. Since the investor owns the stock and has sold it short, he or she has a hedge against increases or decreases in stock price. If the stock goes to $45 per share by the time it is sold in the next year, an additional gain of $13 per share is made but there is a $13 loss on the stock sold short.

• Desire to protect oneself when for some reason the investor cannot currently sell the stock. For example, an investor may purchase stock through a payroll purchase plan at the end of the quarter but may not obtain the certificate until a number of weeks later. It may be advisable for the investor to sell the shares short to lock in the gain.

■ Example

An investor sells short 100 shares of ABC Company stock having a market price of $60. Thus, the selling price is $6,000. The broker holds onto the proceeds of the short sale in "street name." If the investor buys the stock back at $50, a $10 per share profit is earned, or a total of $1,000.

SIMPLE RATE OF RETURN   Simple (accounting, or unadjusted) rate of return is a measure of profitability obtained by dividing the expected future annual net income by the required investment. Sometimes the *average* investment rather than the original initial investment is used as the required investment, which is called *average rate of return*.

■ Example

Consider the following investment:

Initial investment	$8,000
Estimated life	20 years
Expected annual net income	$700

Then, the simple rate of return is $700/$8,000 = 8.75%. Using the average investment, which is usually assumed to be one half of the original investment, the average rate of return will be doubled, as follows:

$$\$700/1/2(\$8,000) = \$700/\$4,000 = 17.5\%$$

SIMPLE REGRESSION   This involves one independent (explanatory) variable in regression analysis. For example, total factory overhead is explained by only one activity variable (such as either direct labor hours or machine hours). Also, an asset's return is a function of the return on a market portfolio (such as Standard & Poor's 500). It takes the following form:

$$y = a + bx$$

where y = dependent variable,
   x = independent variable,
   a = constant,
   b = slope.

See also Multiple Regression; Regression Analysis.

SIMPLEX METHOD OF LP   The simplex method is a computational method of solving a *linear programming (LP)* problem. It is an algorithm, which is a reiterative computational procedure, such that successively larger (smaller) values of the objective function in a maximization (minimization) problem are obtained at each step. The procedure is guaranteed to yield the optimal solution in a finite number of steps. The simplex method is capable of solving large-scale problems, whereas the *graphical method* can typically solve a two-variable problem. In practical applications of LP, computer software packages that employ the simplex method are available for obtaining optimal solutions. *See also* Linear Programming (LP); Graphical Method of LP.

SIMULATION   This is an attempt to represent a real-life system via a model to determine how a change in one or more variables will affect the rest of the system. Simulation will not provide an optimal solution to a problem except by trial and error. It will provide comparisons of alternative systems or how a particular system works under specified conditions. It is a technique used for *what-if* scenarios. The advantages of simulation are (1) when a model has been constructed, it may be used over and over to analyze different types of situations; (2) it allows modeling of systems whose solutions are too complex to describe by one or several mathematical relationships; (3) it requires a lower level of mathematical skill than do optimization models; and (4) it is usually cheaper than building the actual system and testing it in operation. Financial models that are used to generate budgets and help answer a variety of what-if questions are examples of simulation. *See also* Budgeting Models; Corporate Planning Models; Financial Models; Monte Carlo Simulation; Optimization Models; Sensitivity Analysis; Simulation Models.

SIMULATION MODELS   These are basically *what-if* models that attempt to simulate the effects of alternative policies and assumptions about the firm's external environment. They are basically a tool for management's laboratory. They are detailed representations of the real world. Most *financial and budgeting models* are simulation models that are

designed primarily for generating projected financial statements, budgets, and special reports, and for performing a variety of what-if analyses in an effort to find the best course of action for the company. Thanks to computer software such as spreadsheets and financial modeling languages, more and more companies are building and using modeling for their planning and decision-making efforts. Another type of simulation is *Monte Carlo simulation*, which is used when a system has a random, or chance, component. *See also* Budgeting Models; Corporate Planning Models; Financial Models.

SINGLE-PREMIUM WHOLE LIFE (SPWL) IN-SURANCE   SPWL insurance is a policy with a low-risk investment flavor. For a minimum amount of $5,000, paid once, a policyholder gets a paid-up insurance policy. The money is invested at a guaranteed rate of interest, for one year or longer. SPWL has the following features:

1. Cash value earns interest immediately at competitive rates.
2. May borrow interest earned annually after first year.
3. May take out a loan for up to 90% of principal at lower rates.
4. Receive permanent life insurance coverage.
5. Withdrawals and loans before age 59½ are subject to a nondeductible 10 percent tax penalty. They used to be 100 percent tax-free.
6. Tax-deferred accumulation of cash values.
7. Tax-free death benefits to named beneficiaries.

Minuses of SPWL include:
1. There are usually surrender charges if the money is taken out.
2. Interest rate is generally guaranteed for only one year and could drop.

When shopping for SPWL, it is advisable to get answers to the following questions:

1. What is the net interest rate at which the cash value will grow? The net interest rate is the yield after subtracting costs of the insurance and administrative expenses.
2. What is the surrender charge?
3. Are there any loan-processing fees? What is the loan interest rate?
4. Is there a bailout plan, which enables one to cash in the policy without penalty if interest rates drop below the initial rate?

SINKING FUND A sinking fund represents cash or assets placed into a fund periodically and the return earned thereon (e.g., interest income, dividend income) which is accumulated for a specific purpose, such as to pay off debt at maturity, retire stock, or for capital expansion. Some bond issues require that the company establish a sinking fund to redeem the bonds at maturity. The cash and securities comprising the sinking fund are usually shown as a single amount under long-term investments.

SOCIAL ACCOUNTING, DISCLOSURE, AND AUDIT Social accounting is a branch of accounting that aids a business in determining whether society benefits from the goals and programs of the business. It therefore provides information on the social and environmental impacts of doing business. It discloses the social costs and benefits of business activities. It also involves an audit in connection with the performance of its public interest, nonprofit, social activities. These audits usually are performed primarily for internal benefit and typically are not released to the public. The social audit may be performed routinely by internal or external consulting groups, as part of regular internal audits. These evaluations consider social and environmental impacts of corporate activities.

SOLVENCY MEASURES Solvency is the ability of a company to meet its long-term debt payments (principal and interest). Long-term creditors (e.g., suppliers, loan officers) are interested in whether the company will have adequate funds to satisfy obligations when they mature. Consideration is given to the long-term financial and operating structure of the business. An analysis is made of the magnitude of noncurrent liabilities and the realization risk in noncurrent assets. Corporate solvency also depends on earning power since a company will not be able to satisfy its obligations unless it is profitable.

When it is practical for the financial analyst to do so, he or she should use market value of assets instead of book value in ratio computations since it is more representative than true worth.

Measures of long-term debt paying ability include:

• *Long-term debt to stockholders' equity*— high leverage indicates risk because it may be difficult for the company to meet interest and principal payments as well as obtain further reasonable financing. The problem is particularly acute when a company has cash problems. Excessive debt means less financial flexibility because the entity will have more of a problem in obtaining funds during a tight money market.

• *Cash flow to long-term debt*—evaluates the adequacy of available funds to satisfy noncurrent obligations.

• *Net income before taxes and interest to interest (interest coverage ratio)*—indicates the number of times interest expense is covered. It is a safety margin indicator because it shows the degree of decline in income that a company can tolerate.

• *Cash flow generated from operations plus interest to interest*—indicates available cash to meet interest charges. Cash not profit pays interest.

• *Net income before taxes and fixed charges to fixed charges*—helps in appraising a firm's ability to meet fixed costs. A low ratio points to risk because when corporate activity falls, the company is unable to meet its fixed charges.

• *Cash flow from operations plus fixed charges to fixed charges*—a high ratio indicates the ability of the company to meet its fixed charges. Further, a company with stability in operations is better able to meet fixed costs.

• *Noncurrent assets to noncurrent liabilities*—Long-term debt is ultimately paid from long-term assets. Thus, a high ratio affords more protection for long-term creditors.

• *Retained earnings to total assets*—the trend in this ratio reflects the firm's profitability over the years.

■ Example

The following partial balance sheet and income statement data are provided for Company D:

Long-term assets	$700,000
Long-term liabilities	500,000
Stockholders' equity	300,000
Net income before tax	80,000
Cash flow provided from operations	100,000
Interest expense	20,000
Average norms taken from competitors:	
Long-term assets to long-term liabilities	2.0
Long-term debt to stockholders' equity	0.8
Cash flow to long-term liabilities	0.3
Net income before tax plus interest to interest	7.0

Company D's ratios are

Long-term assets to long-term liabilities	1.4
Long-term debt to stockholders' equity	1.67
Cash flow to long-term liabilities	0.2
Net income before tax plus interest to interest	5.0

After comparing the company's ratios with the industry norms, it is evident that the firm's solvency is worse than its competitors' due to the greater degree of long-term liabilities in the capital structure and lower interest coverage.

SPECIAL-PURPOSE FINANCIAL STATEMENT
A special-purpose financial statement is one useful just to *limited* users. In certain instances, a company may prepare such statements to accompany certified general-purpose financial statements. Usually, specialized statements are prepared when firms file specified data useful in governmental and trade statistics.

SPECIAL REPORTS The independent CPA may be asked to conduct necessary procedures in order to issue a special report. As per SAS 14, the major categories of special reports are

• Reports on financial statements not prepared in accordance with GAAP but rather with another comprehensive basis

• Reports on specific items, elements, or accounts of a financial statement

• Reports on compliance with a contract related to audited financial statements

• Reports on data includable in prescribed forms or schedules

SPECIAL TERMINATION BENEFITS TO EMPLOYEES An expense should be accrued when an employer offers special termination benefits to an employee, he accepts the offer, and the amount is subject to reasonable estimation. The amount equals the current payment plus the discounted value of future payments.

When it can be objectively measured, the effect of changes on the employer's previously accrued expenses applicable to other employee benefits directly associated with employee termination should be included in measuring termination expense.

■ Example

On 1/1/19X1, as an incentive for early retirement, the employee receives a lump sum payment today of $50,000 plus payments of $10,000 for each of the next 10 years. The discount rate is 10%. The journal entry is

Expense	111,450	
Estimated Liability		111,450
Present value $10,000 × 6.145* =	61,450	
Current payment	50,000	
Total	$111,450	

    * Present value factor for $n = 10$, $i = 10\%$ is 6.145.

See also Pension Plans.

SPEECH RECOGNITION SOFTWARE Speech recognition products allow the accountant and financial executive to verbally command the microcomputer to perform such tasks as spreadsheet, data base management, and word processing. Software and hardware (boards) exist so one can input data by talking to the computer, move the cursor, and fill in information on a spreadsheet. For example, Super Soft's Scratch Pad with Voice Drive™ is a voice-driven spreadsheet that gives the PC the ability to recognize speech and translate it into commands that the system's spreadsheet comprehends. Computer-voice Corporation's board permits the user to insert voice messages into a Symphony worksheet or document. IBM's Personal Computer Voice Communications Option™, which is an adapter card, supports voice recognition, voice storage, voice synthesis, and telephone management. It allows the IBM PC to read aloud answers to data base questions. Dragon Systems™ has a program allowing IBM PC-AT users to recognize thousands of words spoken by the same individual.

SPOILAGE This refers to *unacceptable* production units that are disposed of at salvage value. Financial management should know the nature and cause of the spoilage so corrective action can be taken, if possible. The spoilage may apply to completed or partially completed goods. Net spoilage cost equals:

Total manufacturing cost to the rejection point
    + Disposal costs (or − Net disposal value)

The two types of spoilage are *normal* and *abnormal*.

Normal spoilage occurs even when manufacturing is running efficiently. It is expected in the production process and is not controllable by management in the short term. Costs of normal spoilage are deemed an element of the cost of making *good* units and are therefore inventoriable product costs. The costs should be accumulated separately and allocated to work-in-process or finished goods, depending on the point in the production process at which the spoilage occurred. *Recommendation*: When normal spoilage occurs at a specific point in the manufacturing process, the cost should be allocated over all units that have passed this point. For example, if spoilage took place upon completion of the goods, no cost of normal spoilage would be allocated to ending work-in-process.

Abnormal spoilage is spoilage that is not anticipated to take place under efficient manufacturing conditions. It is *not* an inherent element in the production process. Abnormal spoilage is typically considered controllable by the factory foreman and results from an unfavorable condition. Examples are abnormal spoilage due to breakdown in equipment and inferior materials. Costs of abnormal spoilage should be charged off as a loss for the current period. It is recommended that the loss account be shown as a separate item when a detailed income statement is prepared to highlight the problem.

■ **Example**

A job order calls for 1,200 shirts. Product costs are materials $1.75, labor $5, and overhead $3. One hundred shirts are spoiled and have to be sold as seconds for $5 each. Assume spoilage occurred as a result of a specific job order. The entries are

Work-in-Process	11,700	
Materials Inventory		2,100
Salaries Payable		6,000
Applied Overhead		3,600
Spoiled Goods Inventory	500	
Work-in-Process		500
Finished Goods	11,200	
Work-in-Process		11,200

As a result, the recorded cost of manufacturing the shirts is $11,200 and the unit cost per shirt is $10.18 ($11,200/1,100 good shirts).

SPREAD   A spread is buying a call option (long position) and the writing of a call option (short position) in the same stock. A sophisticated investor may write numerous spreads to profit from differences in option premiums. There is significant return potential with high risk. The kinds of spreads include:

• *Vertical*—the purchase and writing of two contracts at different exercise prices with the same expiration date.

• *Horizontal*—the purchase and writing of two options with the same exercise price but for different periods.

• *Diagonal*—combination of horizontal and vertical spread.

A spread requires the investor to both purchase and sell a call. The gain or loss from a spread position depends on the change between two option prices as the price of the stock rises or falls. The price spread is the difference between two option prices.

A speculator using a vertical bull spread expects a rise in stock price, but the strategy lowers risk. A ceiling on gain or loss exists.

A speculator employing a vertical spread anticipates a declining stock price. The investor sells short the call with the lower strike price and puts a cap on upside risk by purchasing a call with a higher strike price.

A spread may be bought to maximize return or to lower risk. They are *not* traded on listed exchanges but instead have to be acquired through brokerage firms that are members of the Put and Call Brokers and Dealers Association.

Computer analysis helps with this type of investment.

SPREADSHEETS   These permit values (numeric data or formulas) and text (words, labels) to be entered at any location on an electronic columnar pad. They are entered in cells identified by row and column locations. They resemble a grid. Mathematical relationships can be expressed between different areas on the sheet. *Remember*: When one number is altered, every other number related to it is similarly changed. For example, you can study how earnings change as sales change, which is helpful for forecasting and modeling purposes. What-if answers come forth easily. The accuracy of a spreadsheet depends on the reliability of the formulas governing the relationship between various figures. In formulating a spreadsheet, you should follow a standardized sequential operation that is logical and consistent.

In moving data into a consolidation worksheet, beware that data will not go into a "protected cell."

Tip: Spreadsheets allow for applications in audit, tax, financial planning, and management service.

Evaluation of Spreadsheets

In evaluating spreadsheets, you must take into account the availability of the following features:

• Maximum number of columns and rows.

• Ease of use and flexibility, such as the ability to maneuver within the spreadsheet.

• Availability of template programs.

• Formulas involved and functions to be performed.

• Existence of minimum, maximum, and random functions.

• Mathematical functions, including cross-footing, extensions, absolute value, average value, logarithms, square root, trigonometric, and statistics. The spreadsheet program should allow for your own mathematical formulations.

• Recalculation order, such as row versus column.

• Existence of data base commands within the spreadsheet. This eliminates the need to find a program that can import data from another data base program.

• Alpha and numeric functions, which permit the entry of labels and mathematical calculations.

• Logic functions, so the accountant can utilize conditional values.

• Transposition ability to interchange the presence of cells, columns, or rows.

• Ability of what-if calculations. Formulas are the means by which mathematical and what-if calculations are performed. What-if analysis shows the effect of changes on another specific variable or on the whole picture (financial statements, budget, and financial analysis).

• Sorting and searching capabilities, such as the ability to arrange and access data in alphabetical and numerical sequence.

• Iteration, referring to changing a variable what-if situation. In changing a variable dependent upon another variable, which in turn is dependent on a third variable, it becomes apparent that an exact recalculation is often impossible. Iteration eliminates this problem by overcoming the circular reference structure.

• Inserting, editing, deleting, copying, retaining, and outputting functions. Included are column and row functions such as copying, moving, adding, or deleting multiple columns or rows.

• Spreadsheet consolidation (linking) where columns from one spreadsheet can be moved to another.

• Locking (protecting) and unlocking (unprotecting) cells. This capability refers to the protection of cells so contents in rows and columns will not be accidentally destroyed by the operator entering data over them.

• The number of different worksheets that can be displayed in the different windows.

• Ability to link parts of files created by one module with those created by another (i.e., a change in the value in the spreadsheet will automatically update the information in a letter produced by a word processing program).

Spreadsheet Applications

The applications of spreadsheets to the accounting practitioner are unlimited.

• Any imaginable type of what-if analysis involving alternative situations (e.g., what the client's tax liability will be, assuming different tax options are taken; what is the effect on the accounts if taxes are increased by 4%?).

• Preparing working papers (e.g., trial balances).

• Preparing financial statements.

• Planning budgets and forecasts.

• Preparing and analyzing payroll.

• Analyzing revenue by volume, price, and product-service mix.

• Analyzing expenses.

• Specifying costs in terms of volume, price, and category.

• Converting from cash to accrual basis and vice versa.

• Aging accounts receivable.

• Managing inventory.

  • Inventory extensions and footings.

  • Determining inventory management figures, including estimated sales and carrying costs per unit.

  • Production forecasts.

  • Economic order quantity.

• Liability valuation (such as aging accounts payable) and liability classification (such as breaking down notes payable into current and noncurrent portions).

• Expense calculations and reports such as for depreciation.

• Breakdown of expenses by category (e.g., selling expenses into promotion and entertainment, commissions, and travel).

• Analyzing cash flow (e.g., debt levels, interest rates) and balancing the checkbook.

• Performing integrated business plans in which income statements, balance sheets, statements of cash flow, and other related schedules can be integrated into one model.

• Analyzing financial statements.
  • Ratio computations.
  • Earnings per share.
  • Rate of return (i.e., assets, equity).
  • Cost-revenue relationship (i.e., advertising to sales).
  • Input-output relationship, such as effect of volume on costs.
  • Horizontal and vertical analysis.
• Financial aspects of the business.
  • Capital expenditure analysis.
  • Capital budgeting analysis.
  • Future value analysis.
  • Break-even analysis.
  • Managing assets.
  • Lease versus buy.
  • Productivity measures.
  • Loan amortization tables.
  • Acquisitions analysis of other companies.
  • Investment selection.
  • Preparing portfolio investment transactions and balances.
  • Optimal financing mix (i.e., debt-equity).
• Cost and managerial accounting.
  • Divisional and departmental performance evaluation (i.e., cost center).
  • Product line measures.

• Overhead calculations.
• Variance determination (standard to actual, budget to actual) in dollars and percentage terms.
• Job costing.
• Tax preparation and planning.
• CPA firm practice management.
  • Time sheets by employee for control and billing purposes.
  • Client statistics for evaluation and reporting purposes.
  • Arriving at answers in seconds when meeting with the client without having to redo calculations manually.

• Generate data files compatible with certain statistical packages for conducting regression analysis and other statistical procedures. (Here, a single data file may be used for multiple applications.)

• Marketing aspects, such as product line appraisal by market share, revenue and costs by geographic area, and sales by customer.

Linking spreadsheets together enables you to carry labels, numbers, and formulas from one spreadsheet to another automatically. For example, a spreadsheet may use the input from several hundred numbers that result in ten final numbers. These ten numbers may then be transferred to another spreadsheet without having to input the hundred numbers again. Also, you can place formulas and labels of columns and rows from one spreadsheet to another.

Turner Hall Publishing's Note™ lets you embed comments within the 1–2–3 spreadsheet with ease. Comments can either be highlighted or concealed. The software allows you to attach notes to specific cells to document the details of the worksheet. You can note the assumptions for a formula or the source of an input value. Pad is a 1–2–3 file that has to be used to link Note It and 1–2–3. The notepad should be placed in an empty area of the spreadsheet. If it is put in a place that will be manipulated, it will be erased with new data.

Avoiding Errors

Spreadsheet errors and disasters can be avoided if certain controls are practiced and work is documented. The Spreadsheet Auditor™ utility package by Consumers Software can be used to verify formulas in a spreadsheet by printing them in the same gridlike format as a spreadsheet. It tells the accountant which formulas have problems. It shows in a two-dimensional grid the formulas that conform to the spreadsheet format. The software also assists in documenting the spreadsheet by preparing a permanent record. The Spreadsheet Auditor provides the derivation of each cell. Spreadsheet Auditor has cross- and circular referencing, capability for macro extension, and side printing of the spreadsheet. It lets the user avoid spreadsheet disasters. The program becomes more essential with the greater sophistication of a spreadsheet. There is a sideprint feature that permits the accountant or financial manager to print wide spreadsheets or audit reports sideways.

Cambridge Software's Spreadsheet Analyst™ for Lotus 1–2–3 has an automatic scan to assist in finding errors, cross-referencing, a circular reference locator, and probing. Thus, it lets you ascertain the logic behind the worksheet and trace formulas and values flowing into certain cells. It allows for documenting the worksheet and identifying specific problems. *See also* Template.

STANDARD DEVIATION This is a statistic that measures the tendency of data to be spread out. Accountants and financial managers can make important inferences from past data with this measure. The standard deviation, denoted with and read as *sigma*, is defined as follows:

$$\sigma = \sqrt{\frac{(x - \bar{x})^2}{n - 1}}$$

where $\bar{x}$ is the mean.

■ Example

One and one-half years of quarterly returns are listed below for Amko Motors stock.

Time Period	x	$(x - \bar{x})$	$(x - \bar{x})^2$
1	10%	0	0
2	15	5	25
3	20	10	100
4	5	−5	25
5	−10	−20	400
6	20	10	100
	60		650

From the previous table, note that

$$\bar{x} = 60/6 = 10\%$$
$$\sigma = \sqrt{(x - \bar{x})/n - 1} = \sqrt{650/(6 - 1)}$$
$$= 130 = 11.40\%$$

The Amko Motors stock has returned on the average 10% over the last six quarters, and the variability about its average return was 11.40%. The high standard deviation (11.40%) relative to the average return of 10% indicates that the stock is very risky.

Standard deviation is also a measure of the dispersion of a probability distribution. It is the square root of the mean of the squared deviations from the *expected value* $E(x)$.

$$\sigma = \sqrt{\Sigma (x_i - E(x))^2 \, p_i}$$

It is commonly used as an absolute measure of risk. The higher the standard deviation, the higher the risk. *See also* Decision Making Under Uncertainty.

STATEMENT OF AFFAIRS This shows a company's assets at anticipated liquidation values. Liabilities are shown at the estimated amounts that would be received by creditors upon corporate liquidation. Forced liquidation values will typically be less than historical cost. Emphasis is placed on the legal status or resources and claims against them.

The financial statement is appropriate in cases of actual or pending bankruptcy. Creditors and owners use the statement to estimate amounts realizable upon asset disposition and the priority of claims. Another possible use is by a creditor who desires to look at pessimistic figures for the firm in the event severe financial difficulties arise. In this case, a worst case scenario is presented.

A typical Statement of Affairs presents the following information:

Assets
Assets pledged with fully secured creditors
Assets pledged with partially secured creditors
Free assets
Liabilities
Liabilities having priorities
Fully secured liabilities
Partially secured liabilities
Unsecured creditors

A trustee often prepares a realization and liquidation report showing financial activities for the accounting period. The following information is usually given:

Assets realized
Assets not realized
Assets acquired
Liabilities liquidated
Liabilities not liquidated
Liabilities incurred
Expenses
Revenues

■ Example

Company XYZ is bankrupt. The historical cost of assets and liabilities is $800,000 and $300,000, respectively. If not for forced-liquidation, the market value of the net assets would be slightly higher than historical cost. However, the liquidation value of the assets and liabilities is $700,000 and $300,000, respectively. The Statement of Affairs follows.

Company XYZ
Statement of Affairs
December 31, 19X1

Assets	$700,000	Liabilities	$300,000
		Stockholders' equity	400,000
		Total liabilities	
Total assets	$700,000	and equity	$700,000

As a result of liquidation, the company suffers a loss of $100,000 representing the difference between net assets on a historical cost basis ($500,000) and liquidation value basis ($400,000).

STATEMENT OF CASH FLOWS As per FASB 95, a Statement of Cash Flows is required in the annual report. In addition, separate reporting is mandated for certain information applicable to noncash investments and financing transactions. The objective of the statement is to furnish useful data regarding a company's cash receipts and cash payments for a period. There should exist a reconciliation between net income and net cash flow from operations. Further, the net effects of operating transactions that impact earnings and operating cash flow in different periods should be disclosed.

The Statement of Cash Flows explains the change in *cash and cash equivalents* for the period. A cash equivalent is a short-term very liquid investment satisfying the following criteria:

• Easily convertible into cash.
• Very near the maturity date so there is hardly any chance of change in market value due to interest rate changes. Typically, this criterion is solely applicable to investments having original maturities of 3 months or less.

Some examples of cash equivalents are commercial paper, money market fund, and Treasury bills. Disclosure should be made of the company's policy for determining which items represent cash equivalents. A change in such policy is accounted for as a change in accounting principle, which requires the restatement of previous year's financial statements for comparative purposes.

The Statement of Cash Flows classifies cash receipts and cash payments as arising from investing, financing, or operating activities.

Investing activities include making and collecting loans, buying and selling fixed assets, and purchasing debt and equity securities in other entities. Cash inflows from investing are comprised of

- Collections or sales of loans made by a company and of another firm's debt instruments that were purchased by the company
- Receipts from sales of equity securities of other companies
- Amount received from disposing of fixed assets

Cash outflows for investing activities include

- Disbursements for loans made by the company and payments to buy debt securities of other entities
- Disbursements to buy equity securities of other companies
- Payments to buy fixed assets

Included in financing activities are receiving equity funds and furnishing owners with a return on their investment. Also included is debt financing and repayment or settlement of debt. Another element is obtaining and paying for other resources derived from creditors on noncurrent credit.

Cash inflows from financing activities are comprised of

- Funds received from the sale of stock
- Funds obtained from the incurrence of debt

Cash outflows for financing activities include

- Dividend payments
- Repurchase of stock
- Paying off debt
- Other principal payments to long-term creditors

Operating activities relate to manufacturing and selling goods or the rendering of services. They do not apply to investing or financing functions. Cash flow derived from operating activities typically apply to the cash effects of transactions entering into profit computation.

Cash inflows from operating activities include

- Cash sales or collections on receivables arising from the initial sale of merchandise or rendering of service.
- Cash receipts from returns on loans, debt securities, or equity securities of other entities. Included are interest and dividends received.
- Receipt of a litigation settlement.
- Reimbursement under an insurance policy.

Cash outflows for operating activities include

- Cash paid for raw material or merchandise for resale
- Principal payments on accounts payable arising from the initial purchase of goods
- Cash payments to suppliers
- Employee payroll expenditures
- Payments to governmental agencies (e.g., taxes, penalties, fees)
- Payments to lenders and other creditors for interest
- Lawsuit payment
- Charitable contributions
- Cash refund to customers for defective merchandise

If a cash receipt or cash payment applies to more than one classification (investing, financing, operating), classification is made as to the activity that is the main source of that cash flow. For instance, the purchase and sale of equipment to be used by the company is typically construed as an investing activity.

In the case of foreign currency cash flows, use the exchange rate at the time of the cash flow in reporting the currency equivalent of foreign currency cash flows. The impact of changes in the exchange rate on cash balances held in foreign currencies shall be shown as a separate element of the reconciliation of the change in cash and cash equivalents for the period.

The Statement of Cash Flows presents the net source or application of cash by operating, investing, and financing activities. The net effect of these flows on cash and cash equivalents for the period shall be reported so that the beginning and ending balances of cash and cash equivalents may be reconciled.

The *direct method* is preferred in that companies should report cash flows from operating activities by major classes of gross cash receipts and gross cash payments and the resulting net amount. A company using the direct method should separately present the following types of operating cash receipts and cash payments:

• Cash received from customers, licensees, and lessees
• Receipts from dividend and interest
• Other operating cash receipts
• Cash paid to employees and suppliers for goods or services
• Cash paid to advertising agencies and insurance companies
• Payment of interest
• Tax payments
• Other operating cash payments

Additional breakdowns of operating cash receipts and disbursements may be made to enhance financial reporting. For example, a manufacturing company may divide cash paid to suppliers into payments applicable to inventory acquisition and payments for selling expenses.

Although the direct method is preferred, a company has the option of using the indirect (reconciliation) method. Under the indirect method, the company reports net cash flow from operating activities indirectly by adjusting profit to reconcile it to net cash from operating activities. This is shown in the operating section within the body of the statement or in a separate schedule. If presented in a separate schedule, the net cash flow from operating activities is presented as a single line item. The adjustment to reported earnings involves

• Effects of deferrals of past operating cash receipts and cash payments (e.g., changes in inventory and deferred revenue), and accumulations of anticipated future operating cash receipts and cash payments (e.g., changes in receivables and payables)
• Effects of items whose cash impact relates to investing or financing cash flows (e.g., depreciation expense, amortization expense, gain and loss on the sale of fixed assets, and gain or loss on the retirement of debt)

From the above discussion, we can see that there is basically one difference in statement presentation between the direct and indirect methods. It solely relates to the operating section. Under the direct method, the operating section presents gross cash receipts and gross cash payments from operating activities with a reconciliation of net income to cash flow from operations in a separate schedule. Under the indirect method, gross cash receipts and gross cash payments from operating activities are *not* shown. Instead, there is only presented the reconciliation of net income to cash flow from operations in the operating section *or* in a separate schedule with the final figure of cash flow from operations presented as a single line item in the operating section.

Within the Statement of Cash Flows, there should be separate presentation of cash inflows and cash outflows from investing and financing activities. For example, the purchase of fixed assets is an application of cash, whereas the sale of a fixed asset is a source of cash. Both are shown separately to aid readers in analyzing the financial statements.

Debt incurrence would be a source of cash, whereas debt payment would be an application of cash. Thus, $800,000 cash received from debt incurrence would be shown as a source, whereas the payment of debt of $250,000 would be presented as an application. The net effect is $550,000.

Separate disclosure shall be made of investing and financing activities impacting upon assets or liabilities that do *not* affect cash flow. This disclosure may be footnoted or shown in a schedule. Further, a transaction having cash and noncash elements should be discussed but only the cash aspect should be shown in the Statement of Cash Flows. Examples of noncash activities of an investing and financing nature are bond conversion, purchase of a fixed asset by the incurrence of a mortgage payable, capital lease, and nonmonetary exchange of assets.

Cash flow per share shall *not* be shown in the financial statements since it will detract from the importance of the earnings per share statistic.

An analysis of the Statement of Cash Flows assists creditors and investors in

• Evaluating the entity's ability to obtain positive future net cash flows

• Appraising the company's ability to satisfy debt

• Analyzing the firm's dividend-paying ability

• Establishing an opinion regarding the company's capability to derive outside financing

• Formulating when a difference exists between net income and cash flow

• Evaluating the impact on the firm's financial position of cash and noncash investing and financing transactions

▪ Example

Summarized following is financial information for the current year for Company M, which provides the basis for the statements of cash flows:

Company M
Consolidated Statement of Financial Position

	1/1/X1	12/31/X1	Change
Assets:			
Cash and cash equivalents	$ 600	$ 1,665	$1,065
Accounts receivable (net of allowance for losses of $600 and $450)	1,770	1,940	170
Notes receivable	400	150	(250)
Inventory	1,230	1,375	145
Prepaid expenses	110	135	25
Investments	250	275	25
Property, plant, and equipment, at cost	6,460	8,460	2,000
Accumulated depreciation	(2,100)	(2,300)	(200)
Property, plant, and equipment, net	4,360	6,160	1,800
Intangible assets	40	175	135
Total assets	$8,760	$11,875	$3,115
Liabilities:			
Accounts payable and accrued expenses	$1,085	$ 1,090	$ 5
Interest payable	30	45	15
Income taxes payable	50	85	35
Short-term debt	450	750	300
Lease obligation	—	725	725
Long-term debt	2,150	2,425	275
Deferred taxes	375	525	150
Other liabilities	225	275	50
Total liabilities	4,365	5,920	1,555
Stockholders' equity:			
Capital stock	2,000	3,000	1,000
Retained earnings	2,395	2,955	560
Total stockholders' equity	4,395	5,955	1,560
Total liabilities and stockholders' equity	$8,760	$11,875	$3,115

Source: Statement of Financial Accounting Standards No. 95, *Statement of Cash Flows*, 1987, Appendix C, Example 1, pp. 44–51. Reprinted with permission of the Financial Accounting Standards Board.

Company M
Consolidated Statement of Income
for the Year Ended December 31, 19X1

Sales	$13,965
Cost of sales	(10,290)
Depreciation and amortization	(445)
Selling, general, and administrative expenses	(1,890)
Interest expense	(235)
Equity in earnings of affiliate	45
Gain on sale of facility	80
Interest income	55
Insurance proceeds	15
Loss from patent infringement lawsuit	(30)
Income before income taxes	1,270
Provision for income taxes	(510)
Net income	$ 760

The following transactions were entered into by Company M during 19X1 and are reflected in the previous financial statements:

a. Company M wrote off $350 of accounts receivable when a customer filed for bankruptcy. A provision for losses on accounts receivable of $200 was included in Company M's selling, general, and administrative expenses.

b. Company M collected the third and final annual installment payment of $100 on a note receivable for the sale of inventory and collected the third of four annual installment payments of $150 each on a note receivable for the sale of a plant. Interest on these notes through December 31 totaling $55 was also collected.

c. Company M received a dividend of $20 from an affiliate accounted for under the equity method of accounting.

d. Company M sold a facility with a book value of $520 and an original cost of $750 for $600 cash.

e. Company M constructed a new facility for its own use and placed it in service. Accumulated expenditures during the year of $1,000 included capitalized interest of $10.

f. Company M entered into a capital lease for new equipment with a fair value of $850. Principal payments under the lease obligation totaled $125.

g. Company M purchased all of the capital stock of Company S for $950. The acquisition was recorded under the purchase method of accounting. The fair values of Company S's assets and liabilities at the date of acquisition are presented below:

Cash	$ 25
Accounts receivable	155
Inventory	350
Property, plant, and equipment	900
Patents	80
Goodwill	70
Accounts payable and accrued expenses	(255)
Long-term note payable	(375)
Net assets acquired	$950

h. Company M borrowed and repaid various amounts under a line-of-credit agreement in which borrowings are payable 30 days after demand. The net increase during the year in the amount borrowed against the line-of-credit totaled $300.

i. Company M issued $400 of long-term debt securities.

j. Company M's provision for income taxes included a deferred provision of $150.

k. Company M's depreciation totaled $430, and amortization of intangible assets totaled $15.

l. Company M's selling, general, and administrative expenses included an accrual for incentive compensation of $50 that has been deferred by executives until their retirement. The related obligation was included in other liabilities.

m. Company M collected insurance proceeds of $15 from a business interruption claim that resulted when a storm precluded shipment of inventory for one week.

n. Company M paid $30 to settle a lawsuit for patent infringement.

o. Company M issued $1,000 of additional common stock of which $500 was issued for cash and $500 was issued upon conversion of long-term debt.

p. Company M paid dividends of $200.

Based on the financial data from the preceding example, the following computations illustrate a method of indirectly determining cash received from customers and cash paid to suppliers and employees for use in a statement of cash flows under the direct method:

Cash received from customers during the year:

Customer sales		$13,965
Collection of installment payment for sale of inventory		100
Gross accounts receivable at beginning of year	$2,370	
Accounts receivable acquired in purchase of Company S	155	
Accounts receivable written off	(350)	
Gross accounts receivable at end of year	(2,390)	
Excess of new accounts receivable over collections from customers		(215)
Cash received from customers during the year		$13,850

Cash paid to suppliers and employees during the year:

Cost of sales		$10,290
General and administrative expenses	$1,890	
Expenses not requiring cash outlay (provision for uncollectable accounts receivable)	(200)	
Net expenses requiring cash payments		1,690
Inventory at beginning of year	(1,230)	
Inventory acquired in purchase of Company S	(350)	
Inventory at end of year	1,375	
Net decrease in inventory from Company M's operations		(205)
Adjustments for changes in related accruals:		
Account balances at beginning of year		
Accounts payable and accrued expenses	$1,085	
Other liabilities	225	
Prepaid expenses	(110)	
Total	1,200	
Accounts payable and accrued expenses acquired in purchase of Company S	255	
Account balances at end of year		
Accounts payable and accrued expenses	1,090	
Other liabilities	275	
Prepaid expenses	(135)	
Total	(1,230)	
Additional cash payments not included in expense		225
Cash paid to suppliers and employees during the year		$12,000

Presented on page 427 is a statement of cash flows for the year ended December 31, 19X1, for Company M. This statement of cash flows illustrates the direct method of presenting cash flows from operating activities.

Company M
Consolidated Statement of Cash Flows
for the Year Ended December 31, 19X1
Increase (Decrease) in Cash and Cash Equivalents

Cash flows from operating activities:		
Cash received from customers	$13,850	
Cash paid to suppliers and employees	(12,000)	
Dividend received from affiliate	20	
Interest received	55	
Interest paid (net of amount capitalized)	(220)	
Income taxes paid	(325)	
Insurance proceeds received	15	
Cash paid to settle lawsuit for patent infringement	(30)	
Net cash provided by operating activities		$1,365
Cash flows from investing activities:		
Proceeds from sale of facility	600	
Payment received on note for sale of plant	150	
Capital expenditures	(1,000)	
Payment for purchase of Company S, net of cash acquired	(925)	
Net cash used in investing activities		(1,175)
Cash flows from financing activities:		
Net borrowings under line-of-credit agreement	300	
Principal payments under capital lease obligation	(125)	
Proceeds from issuance of long-term debt	400	
Proceeds from issuance of common stock	500	
Dividends paid	(200)	
Net cash provided by financing activities		875
Net increase in cash and cash equivalents		1,065
Cash and cash equivalents at beginning of year		600
Cash and cash equivalents at end of year		$1,665

Reconciliation of net income to net cash provided by operating activities:

Net income		$ 760
Adjustments to reconcile net income to net cash provided by operating activities:		
Depreciation and amortization	$ 445	
Provision for losses on accounts receivable	200	
Gain on sale of facility	(80)	
Undistributed earnings of affiliate	(25)	
Payment received on installment note receivable for sale of inventory	100	
Change in assets and liabilities net of effects from purchase of Company S:		
Increase in accounts receivable	(215)	
Decrease in inventory	205	
Increase in prepaid expenses	(25)	
Decrease in accounts payable and accrued expenses	(250)	
Increase in interest and income taxes payable	50	
Increase in deferred taxes	150	
Increase in other liabilities	50	
Total adjustments		605
Net cash provided by operating activities		$1,365

Supplemental Schedule of Noncash Investing and Financing Activities

The company purchased all of the capital stock of Company S for $950. In conjunction with the acquisition, liabilities were assumed as follows:

Fair value of assets acquired	$1,580
Cash paid for the capital stock	(950)
Liabilities assumed	$ 630

A capital lease obligation of $850 was incurred when the company entered into a lease for new equipment.

Additional common stock was issued upon the conversion of $500 of long-term debt.

Disclosure of Accounting Policy

For purposes of the statement of cash flows, the company considers all highly liquid debt instruments purchased with a maturity of three months or less to be cash equivalents.

Presented below is Company M's statement of cash flows for the year ended December 31, 19X1, prepared using the indirect method.

Company M
Consolidated Statement of Cash Flows
for the Year Ended December 31, 19X1
Increase (Decrease) in Cash and Cash Equivalents

Cash flows from operating activities:		
Net income		$ 760
Adjustments to reconcile net income to net cash provided by operating activities:		
Depreciation and amortization	$ 445	
Provision for losses on accounts receivable	200	
Gain on sale of facility	(80)	
Undistributed earnings of affiliate	(25)	
Payment received on installment note receivable for sale of inventory	100	
Change in assets and liabilities net of effects from purchase of Company S:		
Increase in accounts receivable	(215)	
Decrease in inventory	205	
Increase in prepaid expenses	(25)	
Decrease in accounts payable and accrued expenses	(250)	
Increase in interest and income taxes payable	50	
Increase in deferred taxes	150	
Increase in other liabilities	50	
Total adjustments		605
Net cash provided by operating activities		1,365

Cash flows from investing activities:		
Proceeds from sale of facility	600	
Payment received on note for sale of plant	150	
Capital expenditures	(1,000)	
Payment for purchase of Company S, net of cash acquired	(925)	
Net cash used in investing activities		(1,175)
Cash flows from financing activities:		
Net borrowings under line-of-credit agreement	300	
Principal payments under capital lease obligation	(125)	
Proceeds from issuance of long-term debt	400	
Proceeds from issuance of common stock	500	
Dividends paid	(200)	
Net cash provided by financing activities		875
Net increase in cash and cash equivalents		1,065
Cash and cash equivalents at beginning of year		600
Cash and cash equivalents at end of year		$1,665

Supplemental Disclosures of Cash Flow Information

Cash paid during the year for:	
Interest (net of amount capitalized)	$220
Income taxes	325

Supplemental Schedule of Noncash Investing and Financing Activities

The company purchased all of the capital stock of Company S for $950. In conjunction with the acquisition, liabilities were assumed as follows:

Fair value of assets acquired	$1,580
Cash paid for the capital stock	(950)
Liabilities assumed	$ 630

A capital lease obligation of $850 was incurred when the company entered into a lease for new equipment.

Additional common stock was issued upon the conversion of $500 of long-term debt.

Disclosure of Accounting Policy

For purposes of the statement of cash flows, the company considers all highly liquid debt instruments purchased with a maturity of 3 months or less to be cash equivalents.

STATISTICAL SOFTWARE Software packages for models have statistical functions, including standard deviation, multiple regression, correlation, univariate and multivariate analysis, frequency distributions, cross tabulations, log-linear modeling, cluster analysis, variance analysis, factor analysis, time series analysis, matrix, and data graphing of statistical information.

A model base management system generates mathematical models and can change and store components. There is also an interrelationship between the models and the data base. A hierarchical set of alternatives can be selected by a decision maker to reach an objective.

■ Example

SPSS Incorporated's SPSS/PC™ statistical package greatly assists the financial manager in performing extensive statistical analysis. The executive can use up to 200 variables per record, inclusive of factors obtained directly from the data file and those obtained from the analysis.

STATUTORY AUDIT A statutory audit is one performed to comply with particular requirements set forth by a regulatory agency.

STOCK-INDEX FUTURES A stock-index futures contract is an agreement to purchase or sell a broad stock market index, including the New York Stock Exchange Composite Stock Index, S&P 500 Stock Index, and the Value Line Composite Stock Index. For an investor with limited funds, an S&P 100 futures contract may be entered into because of the lower margin deposit required. With a stock index futures contract, the investor is able to "play" the general change in the overall stock market. Rather than a particular stock, the "market as a whole" is bought and sold. If one expects a bull market but cannot predict an increase in price of a specific company, the purchase (long position) of a stock-index future is advantageous. On the other hand, if an investor wants to protect the portfolio from a drop in value due to a bear market, he or she can sell a stock-index future. *See also* Futures Contract.

STOCK OPTION PLAN A contractual privilege provided to a company's officers and other employees giving them the right to buy a given number of shares of the company's stock, at a stated price, within a specified time period. Usually, such rights are given to corporate employees as compensation for services or as incentives.

Noncompensatory plans are *not* primarily designed to provide employees compensation for services rendered. No compensation expense is recognized. A noncompensatory plan has *all* of the following characteristics:

1. All employees are offered stock on some basis (e.g., equally, percent of salary).
2. Most full-time employees may participate.
3. A reasonable period of time exists to exercise the options.
4. The price discount for employees on the stock is not better than that afforded to corporate stockholders if there was an additional issuance to the stockholders.

The purpose of a noncompensatory plan is to obtain funds and to induce greater widespread ownership in the company among employees.

Accounting for a noncompensatory stock plan is one of simple sale. The option price is the same as the issue price.

A compensatory plan exists if any one of the four criteria are *not* met. Consideration received by the firm for the stock equals the cash, assets, or employee services obtained.

In a compensatory stock option plan for executives, compensation expense should be recognized in the year in which the services are performed. The deferred compensation is determined at the measurement date as the difference between the market price of the stock at that date and the option price. When there exists more than one option plan, compensation cost should be computed separately for each. If treasury stock is used in the stock option plan, its market value and not cost is to be used in measuring the compensation.

The measurement date is the date upon which the number of shares to be issued and the option price are known. The measurement date cannot be changed by provisions that reduce the number of shares under option in the case of employee termination. A new measurement date occurs when an option renewal takes place. The measurement date is not altered when stock is transferred to a trustee or agent. In the case of convertible stock being awarded to employees, the measurement date is the one upon which the conversion rate is known. Compensation is measured by the higher of the market price of the convertible stock or the market price of the securities to which the convertible stock is to be converted.

There may be a postponement in the measurement date to the end of the reporting year if all of the following conditions exist:

• A formal plan exists for the award.

• The factors determining the total dollar award is designated.

• The award relates to services performed by employees in the current year.

■ Example

On 1/1/19X1, 1,000 shares are granted under a stock option plan. At the measurement date, the market price of the stock is $10 and the option price is $6. The amount of the deferred compensation is

Market price	$10
Option price	6
Deferred compensation	$ 4
Deferred compensation equals:	
1,000 shares × $4 = $4,000	

Assume the employees must perform services for 4 years before they can exercise the option.

On 1/1/19X1, the journal entry to record total deferred compensation cost is

Deferred Compensation Cost	4,000	
Paid-in-Capital—Stock Options		4,000

Deferred compensation is a contra account against stock options to derive the net amount under the capital stock section of the balance sheet.

On 12/31/19X1, the entry to record the expense is

Compensation Expense	1,000	
Deferred Compensation		1,000
$4,000/4 years = $1,000		

The capital stock section on 12/31/19X1 would show stock options as follows:

Stock options	$4,000
Less: Deferred compensation	1,000
Balance	$3,000

Compensation expense of $1,000 would be reflected for each of the next 3 years as well.

At the time the options are exercised when the market price of the stock at the exercise date exceeds the option price, an entry must be made for stock issuance.

Assuming a par value of $5 and a market price of $22, the journal entry for the exercise is

Cash ($6 × 1,000)	6,000	
Paid-in-Capital—Stock Options	4,000	
Common Stock ($5 × 1,000)		5,000
Paid-in-Capital		5,000

If the market price of the stock was below the option price, the options would lapse, requiring the following entry:

Paid-in-Capital—Stock Options	4,000	
Paid-in Capital		4,000

Note: In the case where an employee leaves after finishing the required service years, no effect is given to recorded compensation and the nonexercised options are transferred to paid-in-capital. In the situation where the employee leaves before the exercise period, previously recognized compensation is adjusted currently.

If the grant date is prior to the measurement date, we have to estimate the deferred compensation costs until the measurement date so that compensation expense is recognized when services are performed. The difference between the actual figures and estimates are treated as a change in estimate during the year in which the actual cost is determined.

When the measurement date comes after the grant date, compensation expense for each period from the date of award to the measurement date should be based on the market price of the stock at the close of the accounting period.

In a variable plan granted for previous services, compensation should be expensed in the period the award is granted.

When the employee performs services for several years prior to the stock being issued, an accrual should be made during these periods for compensation expense applicable to the stock issuance related thereto.

When employees receive cash in settlement of a previous option, the cash paid is used to measure the compensation. If the ultimate compensation differs from the amount initially recorded, an adjustment should be made to the original compensation. It is accounted for as a change in estimate.

The accrual of compensation expense may necessitate estimates that have to be revised later. An example is when an employee resigns from the company and hence does not exercise his stock option. Compensation expense should be reduced when employee termination occurs. The adjustment is accounted for as a change in estimate.

Footnote disclosure for a stock option plan includes the status of the plan, number of shares under option, option price, number of shares exercisable, and the number of shares issued under the option during the year.

Compensation expense is deductible for tax purposes when paid, but deducted for book purposes when accrued. This results in interperiod income tax allocation involving a deferred income tax credit. If for some reason reversal of the temporary difference will not occur, a permanent difference exists that does not affect profit. The difference should adjust paid-in-capital in the period the accrual takes place.

STOCK ORDERS

Various stock orders may be placed by the investor through the broker, including:

• *Market order*—the purchase or sale of stock is at the current market price.

• *Limit order*—a purchase of stock is at no more than a given price or a sale is at no less than a stated price. The broker retains the order until a stipulated date or until terminated by the investor.

■ Example

A limit order is placed to buy at $30 or less a stock now selling at $32. If the stock goes up to $40, the broker will not purchase it; if it declines to $30, the broker buys it immediately.

• *Stop-loss order*—an order to buy or sell a stock when it increases to or declines below a stipulated price. Assume 100 shares of ABC Company are owned having a current price per share of $25. A stop-loss order is given to sell the stock if it declines to $20. By selling the stock at a predetermined price, the investor is insulated from further declines in stock price.

• *Time order*—an order is placed for the broker to sell at a given price during a specified time period or until the order is canceled. Assume the investor desires to sell 100 shares of XYZ Company at $60 per share. The investor believes the stock price will go up to $60 in one month. It is currently $55. The investor places a time order with the broker to sell the shares at $60, specifying a limit of one month.

STOCK RIGHT

In a stock rights offering, existing common stock owners have a *preemptive right* allowing them to maintain their percentage interest in the company. They can buy new shares before they are issued to the public.

■ Example

An investor owns 5% of ABC Company. The company decides to issue 6,000 additional shares. The investor has the right to purchase 300 shares of the new issue.

The right permits the investor to buy new common stock at an exercise (subscription) price for a short time, typically no more than several weeks. The exercise price is less than the current market price of the stock.

■ Example

A company has 4,000,000 shares outstanding and desires to issue another 100,000 shares. Each current stockholder will receive one right per share owned. Hence, a stockholder needs 40 rights to purchase one new share.

Advantages to investors of the stock rights option are to lower the exercise price and to avoid paying a brokerage commission.

If a stockholder does not desire to purchase additional shares, he can sell the rights in the secondary market. Obviously, if a right is not used prior to the expiration date, its value is lost.

A right's value is dependent upon whether a stock is traded *rights-on* or *rights-off* (ex-rights). In a *rights-on* situation, the stock is traded with rights attached so the investor who buys a share receives the attached stock right. In a *rights-off* situation, the stock and rights are separable and are traded in different markets. Regardless of the form of the rights, the value of a right equals:

$$\frac{\text{Market price of current stock} - \text{Exercise price of new stock}}{\text{Number of rights to purchase one share}}$$

■ Example

The current market price of stock is $40. The new share has an exercise price of $32. An investor desires four rights to buy one new share. The right equals

$$\frac{\$40 - \$32}{4} = \frac{\$8}{4} = \$2$$

If the stock continues around a $40 price, the value of the right is $2.

STOCK TYPES

• *Blue chip stocks* are securities of high-quality companies with a long earnings and dividend record. They are considered long-term investments. There is dependable return with little risk. Investors who want to avoid risk are attracted to them. An example is General Electric.

• *Growth stocks* are those having a long-term record of above-average earnings and appreciation in price. However, they may fluctuate in price. There is low or no dividends because profits are retained for future expansion. Growth stocks typically grow faster than the economy and the industry they are in. Younger people find growth stocks attractive for retirement planning. An example is a high-tech company, such as one in robotics.

• *Income stocks* have higher average and dividend payout ratios. They are attractive to investors desiring high current income with minimal risk. There is less emphasis on appreciation in market price. Older people relying on fixed income find them particularly suitable. Income stocks may also be advisable when uncertainty exists in the economy. Income stocks are typically of companies in stable industries, such as utilities.

• *Cyclical stocks* are securities having market price and profits change with the business cycle. Examples are airlines and steel companies.

• *Defensive stocks* are least impacted by economic downturns. They are consistent and safe securities. However, a lower return is earned. They are recommended for an older individual who wishes to avoid downside risk in the economy. Recession-resistant companies include pharmaceuticals and utilities.

• *Speculative stocks* do not have a long-term track record of high profits and dividends. Uncertainty exists as to future market price of the stock. Although significant risk exists for loss, there is the potential for high return. An example is a penny stock of a new company.

STOCK WARRANT   A stock warrant is the option to buy a specified number of shares at a given price for a stated time period. The subscription price *exceeds* the current market price. A warrant may or may not be on a one-to-one basis with the common stock held. Warrants are much longer in life than stock options. They typically have an exercise period of several years. Some do not have a maturity date.

Usually, warrants are issued as sweeteners for a debt or equity issue. The company may be able to float a bond at a lower interest rate. Most warrants are detachable from the bond and have their own market price. Thus, warrants may be exercised while the bond continues to exist. Warrants are traded on organized exchanges, including the American Stock Exchange (where most are traded) and the New York Stock Exchange.

Warrants are not often issued and are not available for all securities. There are no dividends or voting rights associated with them. The warrant holder indirectly participates in the appreciation in market price of the related common stock. The price of a warrant is typically listed along with that of the common stock.

If the market price of the common stock increases, the warrant holder may either sell it in the secondary market (since the warrant will also go up in value) or exercise the warrant to obtain the stock. Trading in warrants is speculative due to the potential fluctuation in return, since the value of the warrant depends on the related common stock.

■ Example

A warrant of ABC company stock enables the holder to buy one share for $30. If the stock rises above $30, the warrant increases in value. If the stock falls below $30, the warrant's value is lost.

Typically, the exercise price of a warrant is constant over the warrant's life. However, the price of some warrants may increase as the expiration date approaches. Exercise price is adjusted for stock dividends and stock splits.

The return on a warrant for a holding period not exceeding one year is

$$\frac{\text{Selling price} - \text{Purchase price}}{\text{Purchase price}}$$

■ Example

A warrant costing $15 is sold for $18. The return is

$$\frac{\$18 - \$15}{\$15} = \frac{\$3}{\$15} = 20\%$$

If the holding period exceeds one year, the return equals

$$\frac{\dfrac{\text{Selling price} - \text{Purchase price}}{\text{Years}}}{\text{Average investment}}$$

■ Example

Assume a warrant costing $10 is sold for $15 after 4 years. The return is

$$\frac{\dfrac{\$15 - \$10}{5}}{\dfrac{\$15 + \$10}{2}} = \frac{\$1.00}{\$12.50} = 8\%$$

The value of the warrant is greatest when the market price of the related stock equals or exceeds the warrant's exercise price. The value of a warrant equals:

(Market price of common stock − Exercise price of warrant) × Number of common stock shares bought for one warrant

■ Example

A warrant has an exercise price of $40. Two warrants equal one share. The market price of the stock is $50. The value of the warrant is

$$(\$50 - \$40) \times 0.5 = \$5$$

Generally, the market value of a warrant exceeds its intrinsic value, or *premium*, because of the speculative nature of warrants. As the value of a warrant increases, the premium usually goes down. Premium equals:

Value of premium = Market price of warrant
                              − Intrinsic value

■ Example

The warrant in the prior example has a market price of $7. Thus, the premium is $2 ($7 − $5).

■ Example

A company issues 400 bonds worth $400,000. One bond has 6 warrants attached. Each warrant allows the investor to buy one share of stock at $14. The warrant will have no value at the issue date if the stock has a price below $14. If the stock rises to $22, the warrant will be worth $8. Thus, 6 warrants are worth $48 (6 × $8).

■ Example

A company's common stock has a market price of $50 per share. One warrant can be used to buy one share at $42 in the next 2 years. The intrinsic (minimum) value per warrant is $8 [($50 − $42) × 1]. Since the warrant has 2 years remaining and can be used for speculative purposes, it may be traded at an amount in excess of $8. If the warrant is selling at $11, it has a premium of $3.

Even if the stock is selling below $42 per share, there may be a market value to the warrant because speculators may want to buy it if they anticipate future appreciation in market price of the stock. For example, if the common stock was at $40, there is a negative intrinsic value of $2, but the warrant may have a dollar value of $1 arising from positive expectations of an increase in market price of the stock.

Leveraging may be done to maximize return.

■ Example

An investor has $10,000 of available funds. If common stock is bought at $50 per share, then 200 shares could be purchased. If market price goes to $55, there is a gain of $1,000. However, if the $10,000 was invested in warrants having a price of $5 per share, then 2,000 warrants could have been bought (assuming 1 warrant = 1 share). If the price of the warrant increases by $5, the gain is $10,000. The return on the warrant is 100%, while the return on the common stock is only 10%. *Warning*: If the market price of the stock dropped by $5, the investor would lose $1,000. But if he or she invested in the warrants, the entire $10,000 would be lost, assuming that no warrant premium exists.

If an investor is to achieve maximum price potential from a warrant, the market price of the common stock must equal or exceed the warrant's exercise price. Further, lower priced issues provide greater leverage opportunity. *Recommendation*: A warrant with a low unit price causes higher price volatility and less downside risk, and thus is preferred to a warrant with a high unit price.

The investor may use warrants to protect a speculative transaction. For instance, an investor sells a stock short and the price increases. The speculator cannot keep the short position continually open; it may be too costly to wait until a drop in market price. The investor may protect the short sale by buying a warrant, fixing the purchase price and limiting the potential loss on the trade.

■ Example

An investor sells short 100 shares at $12 each. He then buys warrants for 100 shares at $10 each. The cost of the option is $3 per share, or a total of $300. In essence, the investor is buying the stock at $13 per share. If the stock increases above $12, the loss is limited to $1 per share.

Advantages of Warrants

• The price of the warrant is tied into the related common stock.

• The low unit cost permits the investor to obtain leverage from a smaller investment thus enhancing return. The low unit cost also involves less downside risk.

Disadvantages of Warrants

• No dividends are received.
• The entire investment in the warrant may be lost if market price of the stock declines.

Accounting by the Issuer of Stock Warrants

For the issuing company, warrants are common stock equivalents and as such dilute earnings per share.

If bonds are issued along with *detachable* stock warrants, the portion of the proceeds applicable to the warrants is credited to paid-in-capital. The basis for allocation is the relative values of the securities at the time of issuance. In the event that the warrants are *not detachable*, the bonds are accounted for solely as convertible debt. There is *no* allocation of the proceeds to the conversion feature.

■ Example

A $20,000 convertible bond is issued at $21,000 with $1,000 applicable to stock warrants. If the warrants are not detachable, the entry is

Cash	21,000	
Bonds Payable		20,000
Premium on Bonds Payable		1,000

If the warrants are detachable, the entry is

Cash	21,000	
Bonds Payable		20,000
Paid-in-Capital—Stock Warrants		1,000

In the event that the proceeds of the bond issue were only $20,000 instead of $21,000 and $1,000 could be attributable to the warrants, the entry is

Cash	20,000	
Discount	1,000	
Bonds Payable		20,000
Paid-in-Capital—Stock Warrants		1,000

See also Options: Calls and Puts; Stock Right.

STOP-LOSS ORDER   *See* Stock Orders.

STRADDLE
This is an integration of a call and put on the identical stock with the same strike price and exercise date. A speculator trading on both sides of the market uses it. The speculator is looking for a material change in stock price in either direction to obtain a gain in excess of the cost of both options. A loss equal to the cost of the options will occur if a significant price movement does not take place. Thus, there is high risk with this investment strategy. The straddle holder may increase profit potential but also has risk by closing one option prior to closing the other.

■ Example

A call and put are bought on a March option for $6 each when the stock price is $50. The total investment is $1,200 ($600 × 2). At expiration, the stock rises to $75. There is a profit on the call of $19 ($25 − $6) and a loss on the put of $6. The net gain is $13, or $1,300 in total.

STRATIFIED SAMPLING
When using stratified sampling, the auditor segregates the population into homogeneous subgroups (strata). The auditor then samples each strata. The sample results should be separately appraised and combined to provide an estimate of the population characteristics. Homogeneity is enhanced when very high or low value items are segregated into individual strata. Homogeneity in population improves the efficiency of the sample. Thus, usually fewer items have to be examined to appraise several strata separately than to evaluate the whole population. Stratification benefits the sampling proc-

ess and enhances auditor ability to relate sample selection to the materiality and turnover of items. The type of audit procedures applied to each stratum may vary based on individual circumstances and the nature of the environment. An application of stratified sampling is when total accounts receivable (population) is broken down into groups based on dollar balances for confirmation purposes. An illustration follows:

Stratum	Method of Selection Used	Type of Confirmation
All accounts of $50,000 or more	100% confirmed	Positive
All other accounts under $50,000	Random number table selection	Positive

Stratification can also be applied to type of transaction and by transaction frequency. Stratification is recommended in the case where a variable under scrutiny changes substantially within different parts of the population. This approach is usually used in classical variables sampling and often in attributes sampling. *See also* Sampling.

SUBSEQUENT EVENT   A subsequent event is an important occurrence between the date of the financial statements and the audit report date. It requires footnote disclosure because of its significance to financial readers of the statements. It may have an influence upon their decisions. Usually, the subsequent event has a material effect upon financial position or operating performance. Examples are when the company is accused of an illegal act by the government, extraordinary loss, lawsuit, and a permanent decline in the market price of stock investments.

SUBSTANTIVE TEST   A substantive test substantiates the validity of account balances. There exist the following three types of substantive tests: (1) transaction tests; (2) tests of balances; and (3) analytical review. The

purpose of testing transactions and balances is to obtain evidence of the correctness of recording transactions and deriving account balances. Attention is given to identifying irregularities. To ascertain the validity of financial statement numbers, statistical sampling may be employed. Transaction tests occur periodically throughout the year or at year-end. A transaction test is when, for instance, the auditor traces a cash payment from the cash disbursements journal to the cash account in the general ledger for agreement. A test of balances is when the auditor compares the book balance of cash to the bank balance. This test is performed about year-end. Another substantive test is computing dividend revenue on stocks owned and substantiating the amount recorded. In an analytical review, the CPA looks to the reasonableness of financial statement items by examining relationships. Discrepancies are noted. For example, if promotion and entertainment expense to sales went from 2% last year to 30% this year, a "red flag" exists. Analytical review procedures may be applied to overall corporate financial data, information for business segments, and to individual items. When reasonable relationships exist, there is corroborating evidence to the account balance. *See also* Analytical Procedures; Transaction Test.

SUPPLY-SIDE ECONOMICS VERSUS DEMAND-SIDE ECONOMICS   Supply-side economics aims at achieving efficiency through economic policies and measures designed to stimulate production. On the other hand, *demand-side economics* focuses on regulating aggregate demand. *Keynesian economics*, since it tends to focus on fiscal and monetary policies to control aggregate demand, has been characterized as demand-side economics. Supply-side economics relies heavily on the direct use of *incentives*. For example, reductions in marginal tax rates—the taxes paid on the last dollar of taxable income—

provide direct incentives to work, save, and invest, thereby stimulating aggregate supply rather than aggregate demand. Tight monetary control to curb inflation is another principal prescription of supply-side economics. *See also* Keynesian Economics.

SYSTEMATIC SAMPLING This consists of sequencing all items of the population. Sampling units are put in order (e.g., numerical). Audit software that has routines for systematic sampling is available. The auditor then divides the population into *n* intervals of equal size based on the number of sampling units that must be chosen for the sample (*n*). He or she then chooses a sampling unit from each of the derived intervals. The selection interval can be determined by dividing the population size (*N*) by the required sample size (*n*).

■ Example

The auditor is examining 1,000 sales invoices from a population of 20,000 invoices. One random starting point is employed. Each 20th invoice is chosen. In order that 1,000 invoices are selected, the auditor moves up or down from the random starting point. If a random starting point of invoice number 100 is selected, invoice number 80 (100 − 20) and 60 (100 − 40) are included in the sample, as well as every twentieth invoice number after 100 (i.e., 120, 140, 160, and so on). If the auditor selected 10 random starting points, 100 invoices (1,000/10) would be selected for audit. Thus, the auditor would select every two hundredth invoice number (20,000/100) before and after each random beginning point.

■ Example

The population is 10,000 units and the sample size is 1,000 units. The auditor selects a random starting point between 1 and the sampling interval of 10 (10,000/1,000). This forces the auditor to choose the first sampling unit from the first interval. After including the random start unit as part of the sample, the accountant then sequentially selects every tenth item of the population. Typically, this approach results in a true random sample. Note that if a cyclical pattern in the population exists that coincides with the selection interval, a bias may result; that is, if every tenth sampling unit or multiple of 10 happens to be a departmental manager, then based on the random start, the sample derived may yield either all departmental managers or none. However, the possibility of introducing a bias into the sample as a result of a cyclical pattern in the population would be minimized by picking multiple starting points in the selection process. But if multiple starting points are chosen, then the sampling interval that was previously selected must be multiplied by the number of random starts so that the required sample size is unchanged.

When there is no numerical sequence to a population, the auditor will find it easier to use a systematic random sample rather than a pure random sample. If documents, records, or transactions are unnumbered, there is no need with systematic sampling to number them physically. If random number table selection was involved, the drawback would be to require numbering. With systematic sampling, the auditor uses the sampling interval as the basis to select the document to examine.

Systematic sampling may be employed for both statistical and nonstatistical sampling. *See also* Sampling.

SYSTEMS SOFTWARE This usually is for a particular micro to facilitate use. It is a buffer (communication) between the accountant or application programs (e.g., spreadsheet) and the hardware (including operating peripherals). It includes operating systems and programming languages (e.g., BASIC). Systems software reconciles the differences between different models of micros and permits the accountant to work with whatever model is involved.

The operating system is a collection of general-purpose programs. The operating system is executed when the computer is turned on. It acts as an interface among the operator, the computer, and the applications software. *Key point*: The operating system supports the input, output, processing, storage, and control activities of the micro. It contains the instructions to the hardware for allowing access to the computer memory.

Functions of the operating system include loading and executing programs, keeping track of information within memory and/or external storage sources, transferring information between hardware elements of the micro system, and directing computer operations.

Important: The operating system includes utilities (common functions) such as changing files, backup of file data, and printing information. It has a minimum main storage, thus reducing the storage that can be used for applications.

IBM batch programs enable the carrying out of a series of DOS commands at one time. *Save Valuable Time*: A batch file conducts the DOS commands sequentially as if they were manually typed. A batch file is identified with the .BAT file name extension. For example, AUTO-EXEC.BAT™ provides start-up commands to configure the system as needed. There can also be more than one batch program run, referred to as a chain of two or more programs. IBM batch programs allow for program looping, conditional tests, and program branching. Two or more batch programs can be chained, passing information between them.

Computers of different manufacturers may be able to use the same application programs if they run on the same operating system (e.g., MS-DOS). They are referred to as clones or compatibles.

What You Need to Know: Multitasking operating systems permit several application programs to share the processor and other operating facilities. The advantage is that you can go from task to task quickly or do more than one task at the same time. Multitasking, multiuser operating systems include Microsoft's Xenix™ and AT&T's Unix™.

Window operating systems represent an alternative operating environment to MS-DOS (called DOS shells). These operating systems in effect surround DOS with a shell, turning the display into a menu-oriented "desktop" for selecting and running PC applications. Each window operating system is slightly different from the others but has the basic ultimate objective of loading alternative DOS and taking control of the machine. Examples are Microsoft Windows,™ IBM's Topview,™ Digital Research GEM Desktop™, and Quarterback Office System's DesqView™. They enable the user to present the display into a menu-oriented desktop with features such as concurrency, multiple windowing, cutting and pasting, and file switching for dedicated applications. They are in a sense an alternative operating environment substitute for integrated software. The windowing operating systems provide the convenience of integrated software without being limited to one package and requiring the replacement of the installed applications base.

The windows allow for *mundane* multitasking (not real multitasking) where you can switch quickly from one program to another program so they seem to be running simultaneously. For example, you can move from a data base to a spreadsheet very fast. The ability to change the nature of the window presents significant power.

T

TAX PLANNING Tax planning is done by a tax practitioner to minimize the income tax liability of a client. To do so, it is essential to analyze the tax consequences of alternative client decisions. Is the client missing any tax-saving opportunities? A long-term tax-planning strategy should be developed that takes into account the client's age, income, liquidity needs, family status, estate-planning preferences, and so on. There are many comprehensive tax publications to refer to, such as those published by Prentice Hall Information Services.

Reasons to Postpone Taxes

• Client will be in a lower tax bracket in a future year.

• Client lacks the funds to meet the present tax requirement.

• Client can earn a return on the funds that he or she would have had to pay the federal and local taxing authorities.

• Client, by deferring payment of taxes, will be paying in cheaper dollars because of the inflationary effect.

• Client may possibly avoid the tax payment.

Recommendation: Have the client properly time the receipt of income and the payment of expenses to minimize the tax payment, particularly if the client's income is on the borderline between two tax brackets. A good tax strategy is to receive income in a year in which it will be taxed at a lower rate and to pay tax-deductible expenses in a year in which it will receive the most benefit.

■ Example

Your client is in a high tax bracket this year but expects to be in a lower one next year. The client should increase tax-deductible expenses in the high tax year (e.g., making a thirteenth mortgage payment). The client should delay receiving income in the high tax year (e.g., have the employer pay a bonus next year for the services rendered in the prior year).

It may be advantageous for your client to defer the receipt of salaries, bonuses, commissions, and professional fees to the following year so that the tax may be postponed until the filing of next year's tax return. (This assumes that tax rates will be the same or decline the following year.) Also, money has a time value since it could be invested with the expectation of a return.

Your client may take advantage of a de-

440

ferred-compensation agreement, representing a contract for payments of current services to be made in the future. As a result, there are tax savings in the current year.

Tax-Exempt Income

Sources of tax-exempt income should be searched out. There is a tax-free buildup for certain types of life insurance and deferred annuity policies. Taxes may be postponed on the interest earned until the policy matures.

Funds received from a life insurance contract paid to beneficiaries when the insured dies is generally not taxable. Also, disability benefits and health insurance benefits are excludable when attributable to premiums paid by the holders. Casualty insurance proceeds not exceeding the basis of assets are also tax exempt.

The client should try to obtain tax-exempt income whenever possible. The client receives the full benefit of that income because taxes are not paid on it. Thus, tax-free income is worth much more than taxable income. You can determine the equivalent taxable income as follows:

$$\text{Equivalent taxable income} = \frac{\text{Tax-free income}}{1 - \text{Marginal tax rate}}$$

Interest earned on municipal bonds used for traditional governmental purposes and qualified private activity bonds is not subject to federal tax and is exempt from tax of the state in which the bond was issued.

Interest on U.S. government bonds are fully taxed by the federal government but exempt from state and local taxes.

You must disclose on the client's tax return the amount of tax-exempt income received.

Delaying Paying Tax on Interest

The client can defer reporting interest as income if he or she keeps U.S. savings bonds after their maturity date or has a tax-free exchange of the U.S. bonds for another non-transferable U.S. obligation.

The client can postpone taxes by buying a U.S. Series EE savings bond. The bonds are issued on a discount basis with interest represented by yearly increases in the redemption value. Tax on the interest may be postponed until the maturity date of the bond or when redeemed. Further, taxes may still be postponed by converting the Series EE bond to a Series HH bond at maturity.

Defer interest income by purchasing financial instruments (e.g., certificates of deposit, Treasury bills, U.S. savings bonds) maturing in a later year. Taxes are not due on the interest until the investment matures and the interest income is made available.

Be careful: Interest on zero-coupon bonds is taxable even before the interest is received.

Stock Transactions

A technique for postponing the tax on the gain from a disposition of stock while simultaneously protecting that gain is to sell short. If the client owns appreciated stock, he or she may sell short near the end of the year and then deliver the stock to the dealer and realize the gain after the new year.

Tax Strategies If the Client Has Children

The client can engage in several income-shifting strategies to shift income to his or her children. The client can give the child money to buy U.S. savings bonds or to purchase an annuity from an insurance company. Parents can give appreciating assets (e.g., growth stocks) to their young children. Caution must be exercised since there may be a gift tax consequence if the value of the gift is in excess of $10,000 ($20,000 where the taxpayer and spouse make a joint election). There may be no tax until the asset is sold or the annuity payments start. If the sale takes place after the child is 14, the capital gain is taxed at the child's *lower* tax rate.

Net unearned income is taxed at the parent's rate if the child is under age 14. However, in general, the first $1,000 of net unearned income is taxed at the child's lower rate. *Recommendation*: The client should structure the child's investments so the child recognizes only $1,000 of net unearned income in a particular year, with the excess deferred until the child is 14.

It pays to shift income to children over 14, such as through a savings account in the child's name, say for a college education.

Interest Deduction

Mortgage interest is deductible only on the client's first and second homes (e.g., vacation home). He or she cannot deduct interest on that portion of a mortgage loan that exceeds the cost of the property including improvements. However, the client can deduct the interest on loan proceeds in excess of the cost (plus improvements) of the property but limited to its fair market value if the funds are used to pay educational or medical expenses. Excess mortgage proceeds not used for medical or education expenses will be treated in a manner similar to personal interest. Points paid to obtain a *new* mortgage are tax deductible. *Beware*: Points incurred on the refinancing of a mortgage are only deductible over the life of the loan unless the proceeds of the refinanced mortgage are used for home improvements.

■ Example

The client paid $100,000 for a home and made capital improvements of $10,000. He or she can borrow up to $110,000 and the interest will be entirely deductible. The client may use the available funds to meet payments on credit card balances and auto loans.

Interest on personal loans (e.g., auto loans, credit cards, and interest on tax deficiencies) is being phased out. Allowable interest deductions for personal loans are

| 1989 | 20% of interest incurred |
| 1990 | 10% of interest incurred |

Tax Strategy: Have the client take out a mortgage loan and use the proceeds to buy personal items (e.g., an auto) so that he or she may get a tax deduction for the interest.

If the client uses credit cards for expenses just prior to year-end, he or she can still claim a current year deduction even though the bill is not paid until next year.

Interest on debt incurred for investment purposes may be partially or totally deductible. However, interest is disallowed on debt used to acquire securities that generate tax-free income.

Self-Employed Client

A home office deduction is limited to the net income arising from the trade or business. The home office deduction in excess of net income may be carried forward to future years.

In general, the client can immediately expense up to $10,000 of equipment acquired in a particular year. The amount that may be expensed must be reduced, dollar for dollar, to the extent that the cost of the equipment exceeds $200,000.

Pension Plan Considerations

There are various types of pension plans. One may set up an Individual Retirement Account (IRA) and/or Keogh plan. There are also employer-sponsored pension and profit-sharing plans. The client is not usually taxed on pension monies until he or she begins to make withdrawals from the plans. If the client withdraws money from a pension plan, he or she can avoid taxes by rolling it over into another qualified pension plan within 60 days. The client is not taxed until he or she later takes those funds out.

Individual Retirement Account

If an individual is working and not covered by (i.e., not an active participant in) another retirement plan, he or she may deduct an annual IRA contribution of up to $2,000 ($4,000 if both husband and wife are working). The deduction is treated as an adjustment to gross income in arriving at adjusted gross income. If the client is working and is an active participant in another retirement plan, he or she may deduct IRA contributions (up to $2,000) if the adjusted gross income is below $25,000 a year ($40,000 for a married couple filing a joint return). However, if the client is an active participant in another retirement plan, he or she may not make deductible IRA contributions if the adjusted gross income is in excess of $35,000 a year ($50,000 for a joint return). The deduction will be disallowed proportionately as adjusted gross income increases within the phase-out range (i.e., $25,000–$35,000 for single taxpayers and $40,000–$50,000 for married taxpayers filing a joint return). *Warning*: If one spouse is an active participant in another retirement plan, then both spouses will be subject to the phase-out rules.

Even if the IRA contribution is not deductible, the client does not have to pay tax now on the return earned from the IRA investment. The interest earned on the account is tax-deferred until withdrawn. Hopefully, at retirement, the taxable income will be lower and will result in less tax. Even if the lower retirement tax rate is not expected, the tax-deferred aspect is desirable so as to spread taxable income over several years or to lower taxable income in any one particular year.

Keogh Plan

Keogh pension plans are for self-employed individuals who may contribute up to 20% of the net self-employed income (before considering the deduction), up to a maximum of $30,000 per year. The monies earn interest without being currently taxed. A client may have a Keogh even though he or she has an IRA. A client may also have a Keogh plan for his or her self-employed income even though the client belongs to an employer's retirement plan. A client cannot withdraw Keogh funds without penalty until age 59½, and withdrawals must commence by age 70½. Under certain circumstances, one can, with stringent limitations, borrow against the funds in the Keogh.

A distribution from a retirement plan that equals 50% or more of the balance in the plan may be rolled over into an IRA or Keogh without being taxed as current income.

401(k) Plans

The employer may offer a contributory employee pension plan, allowing the employee to voluntarily put in some of his or her current income together with the employer's contribution. The employee's money is deducted from current income.

The 401(k) Plans are salary-reduction plans, permitting the employee to deposit into a retirement account, through the company, part of his or her income. The plan enables the employee to defer taxes on part of his or her salary. The limitation on compensation that can be deferred was $7,000 in 1987. This amount was indexed for inflation using the Consumer Price Index starting in 1988. Money may be withdrawn with minimal or no penalty in the event of financial hardship. Loans are allowed from 401(k) plans but not from IRAs. FICA tax is not deducted on contributions to salary reduction plans.

Real Estate Transactions

The client can avoid *current* tax on a sale of a home if the adjusted sales price of the former residence is used to purchase a new home. Further, if a homeowner is 55 or older, there is available a one-time exclusion on the first $125,000 of the profit on the sale of the home.

Gifts

Gifts are not included in the taxable income of the recipient. They may be taxed to the donor. Nonliquid holiday gifts or bonuses received from the employer are also tax free. The client can make a gift to another person which is exempt up to $10,000 per year ($20,000 if the gift is from a taxpayer and his or her spouse). *See also* Tax Software.

TAX SHELTER   A tax shelter is a tax-favored investment engaged in usually by a partnership or joint venture. Typically, the investment requires a sizable sum of money and high risk.

The tax shelter investment typically results in losses, generally noncash in nature (e.g., depreciation) or arising from accelerated payments that go to the benefit of the individual taxpayer and may be used to offset other income. The result is the lowering of taxable income. Although the Tax Reform Act of 1986 has eliminated mostly all tax shelters, there are some that still exist. An example is a working interest in oil and gas properties. Tax shelters in real estate have been virtually eliminated. It should be noted that deductible real estate losses are capped at $25,000 but are reduced for taxpayers with adjusted gross incomes between $100,000 and $150,000. Losses are not deductible within the $25,000 cap unless the client actively participates in managing the property and owns at least 10% of the property for the entire year. The $25,000 cap is to be reduced by 50% of the amount by which the taxpayer's adjusted gross income is in excess of $100,000. Active participation mandates that the client be involved in the operations on a regular, continuous, and substantial basis. Losses over $25,000 may only be applied against gains

from other passive investments. *Recommendation*: If the client has tax-sheltered losses, he or she should invest in a profitable general partnership or an "S" corporation.

Losses on real estate investments (e.g., Real Estate Investment Trusts) that the client does not manage cannot exceed the amount for which he or she is at risk. "At risk" means that the client cannot deduct a loss that exceeds the adjusted cost basis (cost and improvements) of the property. However, there is a phase in period for the rules related to real estate in that the client can deduct 20% of the losses from passive rental properties in 1989 and 10% in 1990, provided the investment was made before the enactment of the Tax Reform Act of 1986 (10/22/86). Losses from investments made subsequent to enactment are disallowed in the current year completely to the extent that they exceed passive income.

Since the maximum tax rate is 28%, there is much less of an incentive to invest in real estate tax shelters. Income from the sale of tax shelter assets is subject to the ordinary income tax rates.

TAX SOFTWARE   In choosing tax software, it is imperative that your microcomputer system and the nature of your practice be considered. Tax packages have to be compatible with the user's hardware and its components. Also, tax software should be acquired that integrates with the present accounting software used in keeping your client's books. Time and cost savings will ensue. Consideration should always be given to the vendor's ability to update the tax packages for recent changes in the tax laws. It is also preferred that the software being tested be analyzed by independent consultants before distribution, such as by a national CPA firm. The practitioner should also thoroughly test the software prior to use to assure that it will do what it is supposed to, given the nature of the tax issue and your practice. For example, it must be able to generate accurate forms and schedules as well as minimizing the taxpayer's liability. It should not only prepare the appropriate returns but also provide itemized listings to support the numbers such as 1099s.

Input of data may either be through preprinted forms, interview schedules, or client-prepared information. Obviously, tax software must have good documentation. The manuals should be clear, understandable, and user-friendly. Client data of a recurring nature should be retained in the form of diskette so that it will not have to be input each period. Also, output forms have to meet Internal Revenue Service and local tax agency requirements, and at the same time meet client and practitioner requirements (i.e., compatibility with the practitioner's standard policies).

Amps Tax ™ by Amps Software has many input items along with HELP commands. It generates reports detailing carry backs and carry forwards. It contains, for example, the order that carry overs should be applied and contains the complex logic for minimum tax calculations.

Volts Tax Software Pack™ by Hanover Software is a tax preparation package enabling the user to immediately input data when interviewing the client. If desired, information sheets can also be filled out by clients and then entered.

Micro-Tax™ by Microcomputer Tax Systems has different modules to satisfy different needs (i.e., individual returns, corporate returns, partnership returns).

Tax-planning and compliance software, in general, furnishes the minimum tax that will result under alternative tax options (what-if analysis). There should also be a software feature to override the least tax in the event of extenuating circumstances (i.e., the client is in a new business expecting significantly more profit in future years). The tax-planning result should be clear and under-

standable to the client. Typically, it should indicate for each tax strategy recommendation the tax liability that would result along with all major supporting calculations by category.

To meet tax-planning needs, the software must be flexible to derive a fairly accurate predictable conclusion. It should have sufficient integrative ability in terms of prospectively determining the different tax liabilities depending on alternative scenarios, potential tax consequences, ability to change one variable and see its effect on others, and ability to use alternative tax rate schedules depending on changing circumstances. However, excessive variables should be avoided since too much complexity may occur.

Ernst and Whinney's Tax-Plan™ handles planning for carry backs and carry forwards. Tax Plan can handle the calculations of tax liability, refunds, carry backs, and so on.

A-plus Tax™ of Arthur Andersen can accommodate many what-if situations. It can consolidate multiple work and trial balances. It provides many forms and supporting schedules. The Professional Tax Plan Program enables one to project and plan tax alternatives and investments.

The Tax Planning Template™ by Permar and Associates can be used with Lotus 1–2–3 or Symphony.

Of course, the tax practitioner may also develop his or her own tax-planning program with the aid of an electronic spreadsheet (e.g., Lotus 1–2–3).

Tax research assistance may be obtained by accessing on-line data bases like the AICPA's Lexis System™. To use, a keyword or group of words is entered (e.g., accelerated cost recovery system) and relevant literature references are generated. *See also* Tax Planning.

TECHNICAL ANALYSIS   In the opinion of technical analysts, market direction and magnitude can be predicted. The stock market is analyzed via numerous indicators, such as studying economic variables. Companies' stock prices usually move with the market since they react to a host of demand and supply forces. Technical analysts attempt to forecast short-term price changes and then recommend when to buy and sell. A consistent pattern in prices or a relationship between stock price and other market data is searched out. Technical analysts also prepare charts and graphs of market data over time, including prices and volume.

A sample company's stock chart follows:

Figure 1 Sample Company Stock Chart

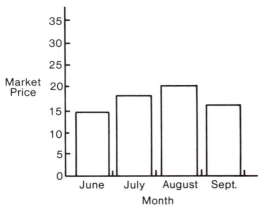

Some terms used in technical analysis follow:

• *Momentum*—the degree of change in stock price or a market index over a specified time period.

• *Accumulation*—an increase in stock price with significant volume that is going from "weak hands" to "strong hands."

• *Distribution*—a decrease in stock price on significant volume that is going from "strong hands" to "weak hands."

• *Resistance phase*—the time interval in which stock prices move with difficulty.

• *Consolidation phase*—the time period when prices move within a narrow band.

• *Bellwether stock*—a stock that typifies market condition (e.g., IBM).

The two major tools used are key indicators and charting.

Key Indicators

There are several indicators reflective of market and stock performance, including trading volume, market breadth, Barron's Confidence Index, mutual fund cash position, short selling, odd-lot theory, and the Index of Bearish Sentiment.

Trading volume—indicative of the health of the market. Price follows volume. For instance, a higher price may be anticipated with increased volume.

Market volume depends on supply/demand and reflects strength or weakness in the market. There is a strong market when volume increases as prices rise. A weak market is indicated when volume increases as prices drop.

When supply exceeds demand, prices decline and vice versa. An examination of demand/supply concentrates on the short run rather than the long run.

Volume is closely tied into the change in stock price. A bullish market occurs if a new high occurs on heavy trading volume. But a new high on light volume is construed as a temporary occurrence. A new low with light volume is deemed significantly better than one with high volume since fewer investors are involved. A high volume with a new low price is a particularly bearish sign.

In the case where prices reach a new high on increased volume, there may exist a potential reversal when current volume is less than the previous rally's volume. A rally with declining volume is questionable and may foreshadow a price reversal. There is a bullish sign when prices rise after a long decline and then reach a level equal to or greater than the prior trough. A bullish sign exists when volume on the secondary trough is less than the first one. It is a bearish sign when price declines on heavy volume; it is indicative of a reversal in trend.

A *selling climax* occurs when there is a price decline for a long time period at an increasing rate coupled with increased volume. Subsequent to the selling climax, it is anticipated that prices will increase, and the low at the climax point is not expected to be violated for a long time. At the culmination of a bear market, a selling climax often takes place.

If prices have been increasing for several months, a low price increase together with high volume is a bearish indicator.

An *upside/downside index* reveals the difference between stock volume advancing and declining. It is typically based on a 10-day or 30-day moving average. Changes in market direction may be reviewed by examining the index. The sustenance of a bull market depends on strong buying.

The *final stage* in a major increase in stock price is referred to as the *exhaustion move*. It takes place when price and volume decline quickly. A trend reversal is indicated.

Muller and Company has a "net volume" service for major listed securities. *Accumulation* occurs when net volume increases. *Distribution* occurs when net volume decreases. When net volume is constant or rises when prices are dropping, there is accumulation under weakness and an expected reversal exists. However, constant or declining net volume with a price increase points to distribution under strength and an expected reversal.

Market breadth—refers to the dispersion of a general price increase or decrease. It may aid as an advance indicator of a major decline or increase in stock prices. It may be useful in evaluating the prime turning points in the market based on stock market cycles. In a bull market, there is a long time period in which particular securities reach their peak slowly, with the number of individual peaks increasing as market averages move to a turning point. In a bear market, the prices of numerous securities decline materially in a short time period. In determining market weakness, the investment analyst examines whether many stocks are declining in price while the averages increase. In predicting the culmination of a bear market, consideration is given to the extent of selling pressure.

With a market breadth indicator, there is a measurement of the activity of a broader group of securities than that contained in a restricted market average (e.g., Dow Jones Industrial Average). The Dow Jones Industrial Average may not be representative of the entire market since emphasis is given to large companies in the weighting process. Market breadth may relate to advances and declines in all securities on an exchange.

A sign that the bull market may be ending is when the Dow Jones Industrial Average is increasing but the number of declining issues continually outnumber the advancing ones. This indicates that conservative investors are purchasing blue chips but do not have confidence in the overall market. An upturn in the market is pointed to when the Dow Jones Industrial Average is declining but advances recurringly exceed declines.

An assumption of breadth analysis is that numerous stocks decline in price for a short period in a bear market. An examination of the change in market breadth may aid in forecasting a sell-off in stock. In the final phase of a bear market, the net advance-decline line decreases by several thousand, Dow Jones Industrials decline several percentage points, and trading volume materially rises.

Market breadth can also be used to evaluate specific stocks. Net advances or declines may be appraised.

■ Example

ABC Company trades 200,000 shares for the day, with 120,000 rising in price, 70,000 decreasing in price, and 10,000 having no change. The net volume difference is therefore 50,000 traded on upticks. An examination should be made of any divergence between the price trend and the net volume of the company. If there is a divergence, the security analyst may anticipate a reversal in the price trend. Accumulation is evident when there exists declining price and increasing net volume.

Barron's Confidence Index—if the security analyst looks at what bond traders are doing now, he can predict what stock traders will be doing later. A lead time of several months is typically assumed. *Barron's* publishes the index each week. It equals:

$$\frac{\text{Yield on Barron's 10 top-grade corporate bonds}}{\text{Yield on Dow Jones 40 bond average}}$$

■ Example

The Dow Jones yield is 14%, while the Barron's yield is 13%. The Confidence Index equals:

$$\frac{13\%}{14\%} = 92.9\%$$

There is a lower yield in the numerator since it is comprised of higher quality bonds. Less risk generates a lower return. Because top-grade bonds have lower yields than lower grade ones, the index will be less than 100%. Typically, the trading range goes between 80% to 95%. If bond investors are bullish, there is a small difference between the yields on high-grade and low-grade bonds.

In bearish times, bond investors desire to hold top-quality issues. Investors who continually place funds in average or lower quality bonds will demand a higher yield for greater risk. In this case, the index will drop due to a larger denominator. When much confidence exists, investors will be inclined toward lower grade bonds, causing the yield on high-grade bonds to decline while the yield on low-grade bonds will increase.

Mutual fund cash position—by looking at the pattern of mutual funds, the security analyst may formulate the purchasing potential of large institutional investors. The In-

vestment Company Institute publishes the following useful ratio:

$$\frac{\text{Mutual fund cash and cash equivalents}}{\text{Total assets}}$$

A change in the statistic reveals the thinking of institutional portfolio management. The ratio is typically between 5% to 25%. If the cash position is 15% or more of assets, there is a material amount of purchasing power, which may point to a stock market increase. The higher the cash position, the more bullish the sign. When cash is invested, stock prices will rise. A low cash position is a bearish indicator.

Short selling—takes place when investors are of the opinion that stock prices will decline. Technical analysts are interested in the number of shares sold short. They also appraise for the month the ratio of:

$$\frac{\text{Reported short interest position}}{\text{Daily average value}}$$

Short interest refers to the number of stocks sold short at a particular time. A bullish sign is a high ratio, while a bearish sign is a low ratio. Typically, the ratio for all stocks on the New York Stock Exchange is between 1.0 and 1.75. A sign of a market low is when the short-interest ratio is 2.0 or more.

The following of short sales by the security analyst is referred to as a *contrary opinion rule*. Some analysts are of the opinion that an increase in the number of short sellers is a bullish indication. It is believed that short sellers become emotional and overreact. Further, the short seller will subsequently buy the short-sold stock. An increase in short sales and volume will result in additional market supply. Then when there is a drop in the market, short sellers will reacquire their shares, generating increased market demand.

There are some security analysts, however, that are of the opinion that increased short selling points to a downward and technically weak market that is caused by pessimism. The short seller is anticipating a drop in stock prices.

The Wall Street Journal, for example, publishes the amount of short interest on the New York Stock Exchange and the American Stock Exchange. Through an examination of short interest, the security analyst can predict future market demand and ascertain if the current market is pessimistic or optimistic. A significant short interest in a stock may raise the question of its being overvalued.

Limitations of Short-Interest Information

• Short interest may follow a similar pattern to market price changes.

• Data may not be available for some time after the short sales take place (e.g., 2 weeks).

Odd-lot theory—holds that knowledgeable investors should sell when small traders are buying and buy when they are selling. Statistics on odd-lot volume activity can be found in *The Wall Street Journal* and *Barron's*. *Note*: In the SEC Statistical Bulletin, volume is expressed in dollars.

The odd-lot index is the ratio of odd-lot buys to odd-lot sells. The ratio typically falls between 0.40 and 1.60. Some technical analysts evaluate the ratio of total odd-lot volume to round-lot volume, and the ratio of odd-lot short sales to total odd-lot sales. These statistics may verify conclusions formed through the evaluation of the ratio of odd-lot selling volume to odd-lot buying volume.

As per the theory, the small trader is correct most of the time but does not recognize key market turns. For instance, odd-lot traders properly begin selling some of their stocks in an up market; but as the market continues to improve, the small traders attempt to make a killing by initiating a significant buy position. This will occur just prior to a market drop (e.g., stock market crash on October

19, 1987). Similarly, odd-lotters will initiate selling significantly just before the end of a bear market. The technical analyst concludes that a market turn is eminent in case odd-lot volume rises in an increasing stock market.

Index of Bearish Sentiment—prepared by Investors Intelligence and based on the opposite of investment advisory service recommendations. The index is based on contrary opinion, in that you should do the opposite of that recommended in the reports of investment advisory firms. According to Investors Intelligence, when 42% or more of advisory services are bearish, the market will rise. When 17% or less of the services are bearish, the market will drop.

The index equals:

$$\frac{\text{Number of services that are bearish}}{\text{Total number of services providing an opinion}}$$

A movement approaching 10% indicates the Dow Jones Industrial Average is shortly going to go from bullish to bearish. When the index nears 60%, the Dow Jones Industrial Average is shortly going to move from bearish to bullish. It is expected that the advisory services are trend followers instead of anticipators. Hence, the services' least bearish reports mean the market will decline, and the most bearish reports mean the market will rise.

Option trading activity in calls and puts—by examining the trading activity in options, the investment analyst can forecast market trends. The put-call ratio equals:

$$\frac{\text{Put Volume}}{\text{Call Volume}}$$

The ratio rises when there is greater put activity due to investor pessimism around market bottom. The ratio decreases because of greater call activity arising from optimism around the market peak.

The option buy (initial option transaction reflecting a long position) call percentage equals:

$$\frac{\text{Open buy call transactions}}{\text{Total call volume}}$$

A high ratio indicates investor optimism, while a low ratio infers caution.

Charting

Three basic kinds of charts are line, bar, and point-and-figure. With a line or bar chart, the vertical line indicates price while the horizontal one reflects time. On a line chart, closing prices are connected using a straight line. With a bar chart, vertical lines are at each time period. The high and low prices are indicated at the top and bottom of each bar. There is a horizontal line across the bar indicating the ending price.

Point-and-figure charts reveal emerging price patterns in the overall market and for particular stocks. Typically, the closing price is only charted. X connotes a price increase while 0 signifies a decrease. The time horizon covered may be one year or less for active securities and more than one year for those that are inactive.

Point-and-figure charts reveal a vertical price scale. Plots on the chart are made when there is a price change by a predetermined amount. There is a depiction of substantial changes and their reversal. Significance of movement depends on the investment analyst's perspective. Closing prices or interday prices may be used in evaluation depending on time constraints. Typically, predetermined figures are 1 or 2 points for medium-priced stocks, 3 or 5 points for high-priced stocks, and ½ point for low-priced stocks. Usually, charts have specific volume information.

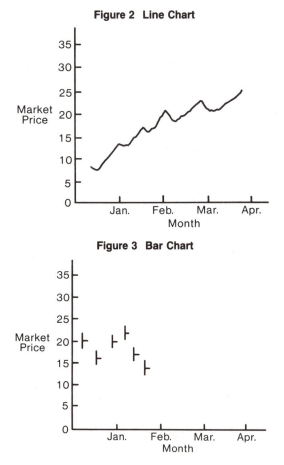

Figure 2 Line Chart

Figure 3 Bar Chart

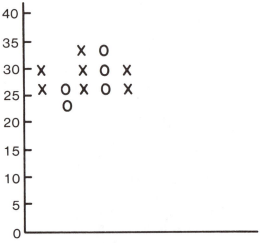

Figure 4 Point-and-Figure Chart

The technical analyst plots prices depicting a trend in a single column, moving to the next column only if a trend in reversal occurs. The price is typically rounded to the nearest dollar and the beginning rounded price is plotted first. No entry is made if the rounded price remains the same. A different rounded price is plotted. If new prices are in the same direction, they are shown in the same column. A reversal starts a new column.

Information is provided about resistance levels (points). Market direction is indicated by a breakout from the resistance level. The longer the sideways movement prior to a break, the more the stock can rise in price.

The charts help to identify if the market is in a major upturn or downturn and if a reversal in trend is likely. The price that may be accomplished by a particular stock or market average is also revealed. The degree of price swing possible may also be evident.

Moving average—can be looked at to appraise intermediate and long-term stock movements. By comparing the change in current prices to the long-term moving average of prices, a reversal in a major uptrend in price of a specific stock or general market may be revealed. A moving average reveals the direction and degree of change of highly volatile numbers.

It is computed by averaging a portion of the series and then adding the next number to the numbers already averaged, omitting the first number and deriving a new average.

Typically, a 200-day moving average of daily closing prices is used. The average price is usually graphed on stock charts to uncover direction. A "buy" signal exists when the 200-day average line is constant or increases after a decline and when the daily stock price moves up above the average line.

A "buy" recommendation is indicated when stock price increases above the 200-day line, then proceeds down toward it but not through it, and then goes up again. A "sell" recommendation occurs when the average line is constant or moves down after a rise and when the daily stock price goes down through the average line. A sell is also indicated when stock price is below the average line, then rises toward it, but rather than going through it the price drops down again.

Relative strength analysis—a stock price may be predicted by appraising *relative strength* equal to

$$\frac{\text{Monthly average stock price}}{\text{Monthly average market index (or industry group index)}}$$

Another approach is to determine the ratio of specific industry group price indexes to the total market index.

If a stock or industry group shows better performance than the overall market, the stock is viewed favorably because strong stocks and groups typically become stronger. There may be a differentiation made between relative strength in an upward versus declining market. If a stock does better than the market average in an advance, it may shortly turn around. However, if the stock does better than the rest of the market in a decline, that stock will typically remain strong.

Support and resistance levels—the lower end of a trading range is the support level, whereas the upper end is the resistance level. Support exists when a stock goes to the lower level of trading since new investors may now want to acquire it. In that case, new demand takes place in the market. Resistance occurs when a security approaches the high side of the normal trading range. Investors who bought on a prior high may deem this as an opportunity to sell the stock at a gain. If market price exceeds the resistance point or is below the support point (in a breakout, investors assume the stock is trading in a

Table 1   Moving Average

Day	Index	Three-Day Moving Total	Three-Day Moving Average
1	115		
2	122		
3	108	345 (Days 1–3)	115 (345/3)
4	111	341 (Days 2–4)	113.7 (341/3)

new range and that higher or lower trading values may occur.

Figure 5 Support and Resistance

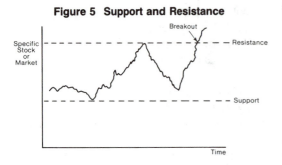

Dow Theory—looks at the movement in the Dow Jones Industrial Average and the Dow Jones Transportation Average. According to the theory, the trend in the overall market is essential because it indicates the end of both bull and bear markets. It is an after-measure with no prediction ability. It does not forecast the timing of a reversal but only confirms that a reversal has taken place.

There are three movements going on simultaneously:

• *Primary trend* is bullish or bearish and typically lasts 28 to 33 months.

• *Secondary trend* runs counter to the primary movement and typically lasts 3 weeks to 3 months.

• Daily fluctuation comprises the first two movements of the market.

Secondary movements and daily variability are important since they show a long-term primary market trend.

A major primary increase in market averages coexists with intermediate secondary downward reactions, eliminating a significant amount of the prior rise. At the end of each reaction, a price recovery takes place falling short of the previous high. If subsequent to an unsuccessful recovery, a downward reaction goes below the low point of the last previous reaction, the market is in a primary downturn.

Figure 6 Dow Theory Chart

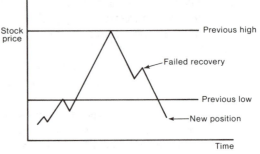

The rationale for the Dow Theory is that the market is increasing when the cyclical movements of the market averages increase over time and the successive market lows get higher; the market is down when the successive highs and successive lows in the stock market are lower than the prior highs and lows. Some technical analysts believe the movement of the Dow Jones Transportation Average must confirm the action of the Dow Jones Industrial Average to indicate that there is a bull or bear market occurring. Other technical analysts are of the opinion that employing the Dow Jones Industrial Average in this way has lost substantial reliability because these two averages do not typically move in a similar pattern.

TELECOMMUNICATIONS   This applies to communications between computers in different locations—usually some distance apart. To communicate properly, the computers must use the same standard transmission procedure (protocols). A good communications program will have several protocol options, permitting communication with different types of equipment. Although it usually occurs over telephone lines, radio waves and satellite are possible.

A protocol translates signals so it is comprehendible by the computer. Popular examples are ASCII, XModem, and Kermit. ANSI is a protocol allowing for the transfer of graphics. Telink is a protocol enabling batch file transfer. A computer with a communications board (RS–232C Serial Port), telecommunications software, and a modem are necessary for asynchronous communication (a terminal may also be used, preferably a smart terminal). The software is required to communicate between computers within the company, in time-sharing situations, and to access on-line data bases.

Communications packages typically reserve part of the computer memory as a buffer. Financial data can be downloaded from a mainframe, mini, or micro. Information is put in the capture buffer awaiting later disposition (e.g., saving to disk or printing the information out with a printer). Alternatively, one can load financial data from a disk into the buffer for telecommunication transmission (uploading) to another computer in ASCII if asynchronous communication is used (as opposed to synchronous communication). The information-handling functions are the core of the telecommunications program. The software aids the manipulation of information coming over the modem. Some communications packages have the ability for error checking of information received. Examples of popular communications software are Microstuf's Crosstalk™ and Hayes Smartcom II™. Lattice's Side-Talk™ transfers files or receives mail while the computer is being used for other things.

Desirable Features in Telecommunications Programs

- Menus including help
- Selected baud rates
- Telephone directory storage
- Automatic log-on procedures
- Automatic redial
- Selection of file transfer protocols
- Capture function enabling the writing to disk of the contents on the screen

Communications software allows accountants in multiple offices in different geographic areas to communicate with each other, such as by electronic mail, or to transfer files and documents between offices. For example, a report draft might be sent to another practice office to obtain a concurring review and/or further instructions may be sent to participating offices. Information may be transferred from a distant data base to do spreadsheet analysis. Bulletin boards can enable the CPA to share current accounting and auditing information with clients. An example is Deloitte, Haskins and Sells' PC Forum™.

A serial interface hooks up the computer to other remote computers with the use of a modem. Baud refers to the serial information transfer speed. The rate equals the number of bits-per-second (BPS) transmitted. The 300-, 1,200-, and 2,400-BAUD modems are usually used. *Recommendation*: Use a faster modem when typing is at a minimum and uploading or downloading is at a maximum. A good modem is Hayes Smartcom 2400™. Drawbacks to faster modems are poorer transmission on-line quality and increased cost. Typically, higher speed modems are compatible with lower speed modems. *Warning*: Do not purchase one without this downward capability.

Tip: If the typical usage is to access an on-line service where the major purpose is reading information and typing replies or messages, a 300-BPS modem is adequate.

Security modems exist, such as IT&T's Security Modem™. They allow only authorized users to access confidential information. The IT&T modem has three graduated levels of security and stores security codes for users. On receiving the correct password, the modem sends instructions to hang up and makes the call-back on a second line to prevent any risk of interception. With the Cermetek Microelectronics' Security Modem™, there are built-in audit trail capabilities to monitor who is accessing private files.

Most telecommunications to Information Services is asynchronous. However, it is possible to use an application for synchronous communication between a PC and mainframe. This will allow micros to communicate with corporate mainframes that are synchronous. Hayes Synchronous Interface™ makes synchronous communications software independent of hardware. Note that synchronous is faster and more error free than asynchronous. Synchronous communication permits greater use of micros as a communication to mainframes.

TEMPLATE Many spreadsheet programs have templates, or overlay programs, to go with the specific spreadsheet program used, to enhance productivity. Templates, or overlays, are guides in preparing the spreadsheet and are predetermined files, including formulas and row and column labels for specific applications. In essence, they are worksheet models to solve particular kinds of problems. Templates (models) permit the referencing of cells and formulations of interrelated formulas and functions. They are reused for similar situations. Templates are ideal for worksheets whose structure and formulas are flexible to encompass numerous types of tasks.

After the accountant or financial manager loads in the spreadsheet, the template file comes next. All that remains is to put in the numbers. The variables and formulas are placed in the template. The template in effect has the model in it. Data is input and the outcome obtained. Templates may be ''canned'' or specially prepared by the practitioner. When templates are canned, template designs are included in the documentation. Templates may be modified to achieve the client's particular requirements.

Remember: Templates can come as separate programs or be part of a sophisticated spreadsheet package. A good supplier of canned templates is 4–5–6 World of California. When internally prepared, the template must be well documented so it is comprehend-

ible by later users, who may have to make desired changes to it. *Note*: Multiple templates can be linked together to formulate more complex applications. They are good for standardized operations. One spreadsheet template may be used to begin or add to another template. For instance, predefined templates are a routine set of calculations that may be copied into other worksheets to derive a broader template.

Take full advantage: Templates may be used for all kinds of accounting and financial applications. For example, templates exist for inventory counts, computing inventory values, depreciation schedules, analyzing revenue and expenses, and financial analysis. CPA+™ is a comprehensive set of accounting templates to perform functions of general ledger, financial statements, accounts payable, accounts receivable, and payroll. As mentioned earlier, 4–5–6 offers a host of templates and add-on utilities. The practitioner may also download templates from numerous sources, such as the Lotus Forum on Compu-Serve.

In consolidating spreadsheet templates, the practitioner may add rows and columns where each cell must match. *See also* Spreadsheet.

10-K This is the annual filing that public companies have to make with the Securities and Exchange Commission. Included are financial statements and supplementary data. Detailed schedules in support of financial statement figures are given. Some types of disclosures provided are revenue, operating earnings, segmental sales and profit, and general business data. The 10-K is more inclusive than the annual report. *See also* 10-Q.

10-Q This is the quarterly filing of public companies with the Securities and Exchange Commission. Interim financial statements with related footnotes are provided. The statements may or may not be audited. Data may be for one quarter and/or cumulative from the beginning of the year. Comparisons are provided to prior similar periods. *See also* 10-K.

TERM STRUCTURE OF INTEREST RATES

The term structure of interest rates, also known as a *yield curve*, shows the relationship between length of time to maturity and yields of debt instruments. Other factors such as default risk and tax treatment are held constant. An understanding of this relationship is important to corporate treasurers who must decide whether to borrow by issuing long- or short-term debt. It is also important to investors who must decide whether to buy long- or short-term bonds. Fixed income security analysts should investigate the yield curve carefully in order to make judgments about the direction of interest rates. A yield curve is simply a graphical presentation of the term structure of interest rates. A yield curve may take any number of shapes, that is, a flat (vertical) yield curve (Figure 1-A), a positive (ascending) yield curve (Figure 1-B), an inverted (descending) yield curve (Figure 1-C), and a humped (ascending and then descending) yield curve (Figure 1-D). As to the shape of the yield curve that changes over time, there are three major explanations, or theories, of yield curve patterns. They are the (1) expectation theory; (2) liquidity preference theory; and (3) market segmentation, or "preferred habitat," theory.

Expectation Theory

The expectation theory postulates that the shape of the yield curve reflects investors' expectations of future short-term rates. Given the estimated set of future short-term interest rates, the long-term rate is then established as the geometric average of future interest rates.

■ Example

At the beginning of the first quarter of the year, suppose a 91-day T-bill yields a 6% annualized yield and the expected yield for a 91-day T-bill at the beginning of the second quarter is 6.4%. Under the expectation theory, a 182-day T-bill is equivalent to having successive 91-day T-bills and thus should offer investors the same annualized yield. Therefore, a 182-day T-bill issued at the beginning of the first quarter of the year should yield 6.2%, which is an arithmetic mean (average) of successive 91-day T-bills.

$$1/2 \ (6.00 + 6.40) = 1/2 \ (12.40) = 6.20\%$$

Mathematically, a current long-term yield is a geometric average of current and successive short-term yields, or

$$(1 + {_tR_n})^n = (1 + {_tR_1})(1 + {_{t+1}r_1}) \ . \ . \ . \ (1 + {_{t+n-1}r_1})$$

where the subscripts to the left of the variable, $t, t + 1, \ . \ . \ . \ ,$ signify the period, and the subscripts to the right, $1, 2, \ . \ . \ . \ , n$ signify the maturity of the debt instrument. R is the

Figure 1 Alternative Term-Structure Patterns

A Flat	B Ascending	C Descending	D Humped
Yield	Yield	Yield	Yield
Years to Maturity	Years to Maturity	Years to Maturity	Years to Maturity

current yield, and r is a future (expected) yield.

A positive (ascending) yield curve (Figure 1-B) implies that investors expect short-term rates to rise, whereas a descending (inverted) yield curve (Figure 1-C) implies that they expect short-term rates to fall.

■ Example

Suppose a current 2-year yield is 9%, or $_tR_2$ = 0.09, and a current 1-year yield is 7%, or $_1R_t$ = 0.07.

Then the expected 1-year future yield $_{t+1}r_1$ is 0.11037, or 11.04%:

$$(1 + {_tR_2})^2 = (1 + {_tR_1})(1 + {_{t+1}r_1})$$
$$(1.09)^2 = (1.07)(1 + {_{t+1}r_1})$$
$$1.1881 = (1.07)(1 + {_{t+1}r_1})$$
$$(1 + {_{t+1}r_1}) = 1.1881/1.07$$
$$_{t+1}r_1 = 1.11037 - 1 = 0.11037 = 11.04\%$$

Liquidity Preference Theory

The liquidity preference theory contends that risk-averse investors prefer short-term bonds to long-term bonds because long-term bonds have a greater chance of price variation, that is, carry greater interest rate risk. Accordingly, the theory states that rates on long-term bonds will generally be above the level called for by the expectation theory. Current long-term bonds should include a liquidity premium as additional compensation for assuming *interest rate risk*. This theory is nothing but a modification of the expectation theory.

Mathematically, a current 2-year rate is a geometric average of a current and a future 1-year rate *plus* a liquidity risk premium L:

$$(1 + {_tR_2})^2 = (1 + {_tR_1})(1 + {_{t+1}r_1}) + L$$

Because of a liquidity premium, a yield curve would be upward sloping rather than vertical when future short-term rates are expected to be the same as the current short-term rate.

Market Segmentation (Preferred Habitat) Theory

The market segmentation theory does not recognize expectations and emphasizes the rigidity in loan allocation patterns by lenders. Some lenders (such as banks) are required by law to lend primarily on a short-term basis. Other lenders (such as life insurance companies and pension funds) prefer to operate in the long-term market. Similarly, some borrowers need short-term money (e.g., to build up inventories), while others need long-term money (e.g., to purchase homes). Thus, under this theory, interest rates are determined by supply and demand for loanable funds in each maturity market spectrum.

THEORY OF CAPITAL STRUCTURE   The theory of capital structure is closely related to the firm's *cost of capital*. Capital structure is the mix of the long-term sources of funds used by the firm. The primary objective of capital structure decisions is to maximize the market value of the firm through an appropriate mix of long-term sources of funds. This mix, called the optimal capital structure, will minimize the firm's overall cost of capital. However, there are arguments about whether an optimal capital structure actually exists. The arguments center on whether a firm can, in reality, affect its valuation and its cost of capital by varying the mixture of the funds used. There are four different approaches to the theory of capital structure:
1. Net operating income (NOI) approach
2. Net income (NI) approach
3. Traditional approach
4. Modigliani-Miller (MM) approach
All four use the following simplifying assumptions:
1. No income taxes are included.
2. The company's dividend payout is 100%.
3. No transaction costs are incurred.

4. The company has constant earnings before interest and taxes (EBIT).
5. There is a constant operating risk.

Given these assumptions, the company is concerned with the following three rates:

1.
$$k_i = \frac{I}{B}$$

where k_i = yield on the firm's debt (assuming a perpetuity),
I = annual interest charges,
B = market value of debt outstanding.

2.
$$k_e = \frac{EAC}{S}$$

where k_e = the firm's required rate of return on equity or cost of common equity (assuming no earnings growth and a 100% dividend payout ratio),
EAC = earnings available to common stockholders,
X = market value of stock outstanding.

3.
$$k_o = \frac{EBIT}{V}$$

where k_o = the firm's overall cost of capital (or capitalization rate),
EBIT = earnings before interest and taxes (or operating earnings),
$V = B + S$ and is the market value of the firm.

In each of the four approaches to determining capital structure, the concern is with what happens to k_i, k_e, and k_o when the degree of leverage, as denoted by the debt/equity (B/S) ratio, increases.

The Net Operating Income (NOI) Approach

The net operating income approach suggests that the firm's overall cost of capital, k_o, and the value of the firm's market value of

debt and stock outstanding, V, are both independent of the degree to which the company uses leverage. The key assumption with this approach is that k_o, is constant regardless of the degree of leverage.

■ Example 1

Assume that a firm has $6,000 in debt at 5% interest; that the expected level of EBIT is $2,000; and that the firm's cost of capital, k_o, is constant at 10%. The market value (V) of the firm is computed as follows:

$$V = \frac{EBIT}{k_o} = \frac{\$2,000}{0.10} = \$20,000$$

The cost of external equity (k_e) is computed as follows:

$$EAC = EBIT - I = \$2,000 - (\$6,000 \times 5\%)$$
$$= \$2,000 - \$300 = \$1,700$$
$$S = V - B = \$20,000 - \$6,000 = \$14,000$$
$$k_e = \frac{EAC}{S} = \frac{\$1,700}{\$14,000} = 12.14\%$$

The debt/equity ratio is

$$\frac{B}{S} = \frac{\$6,000}{\$14,000} = 42.86\%$$

Assume now that the firm increases its debt from $6,000 to $10,000 and uses the proceeds to retire $10,000 worth of stock and also that the interest rate on debt remains at 5%.

The value of the firm now is

$$V = \frac{EBIT}{k_o} = \frac{\$2,000}{0.10} = \$20,000$$

The cost of external equity is

$$EAC = EBIT - I = \$2,000 - (\$10,000 \times 5\%)$$
$$= \$2,000 - \$500 = \$1,500$$
$$S = V - B = \$20,000 - \$10,000 = \$10,000$$
$$k_o = \frac{EAC}{S} = \frac{\$1,500}{\$10,000} = 15\%$$

The debt/equity ratio is now

$$\frac{B}{S} = \frac{\$10,000}{\$10,000} = 100\%$$

Figure 1 Cost of Capital: Net Operating Income Approach

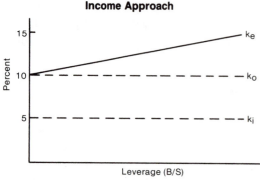

Since the NOI approach assumes that k_o remains constant regardless of changes in leverage, the cost of capital cannot be altered through leverage. Hence, this approach suggests that there is no one optimal capital structure, as evidenced in Figure 1.

The Net Income (NI) Approach

Unlike the net operating income approach, the net income approach suggests that both the overall cost of capital, k_o and the market value of the firm, V, are affected by the firm's use of leverage. The critical assumption with this approach is that k_i and k_e remain unchanged as the debt/equity ratio increases.

■ Example 2

Assume the same data given in Example 1 except that k_e equals 10%. The value of the firm, V, is computed as follows:

$$EAC = EBIT - I = \$2,000 \\ - (\$6,000 \times 5\%) = \$1,700$$

$$V = S + B = \frac{EAC}{k_e} + B$$

$$= \frac{\$1,700}{0.10} + \$6,000$$

$$= \$17,000 + 6,000 = \$23,000$$

The firm's overall cost of capital is

$$k_o = \frac{EBIT}{V} = \frac{\$2,000}{\$23,000} = 8.7\%$$

The debt/equity ratio in this case is

$$\frac{B}{S} = \frac{\$6,000}{\$17,000} = 35.29\%$$

Now assume as before that the firm increases its debt from $6,000 to $10,000, uses the proceeds to retire that amount of stock, and that the interest rate on debt remains at 5%. Then the value of the firm is

$$EAC = EBIT - I = \$2,000 \\ - (\$10,000 \times 5\%) = \$1,500$$

$$V = S + B = \frac{EAC}{k_e} + B$$

$$= \frac{\$1,500}{0.10} + \$10,000$$

$$= \$15,000 + \$10,000 = \$25,000$$

The overall cost of capital is

$$k_o = \frac{EBIT}{V} = \frac{\$2,000}{\$25,000} = 8\%$$

The debt/equity ratio is now

$$\frac{B}{S} = \frac{\$10,000}{\$15,000} = 66.67\%$$

The NI approach shows that the firm is able to increase its value, V, and lower its cost of capital, k_o, as it increases the degree of leverage. Under this approach, the optimal capital structure is found farthest to the right in Figure 2.

Traditional Approach

The traditional approach to valuation and leverage assumes that there is an optimal capital structure and that the firm can increase its

Figure 2 Cost of Capital: Net Income Approach

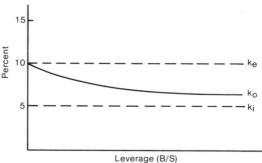

value through leverage. This is a moderate view of the relationship between leverage and valuation that encompasses all the ground between the NOI approach and the NI approach.

■ Example 3

Assume the same data given in Example 1. Assume, however, that k_e is 12%, rather than the 12.14% or 10% with the NOI or NI approaches illustrated previously. The value of the firm is

$$EAC = EBIT - I = \$2,000$$
$$- (\$6,000 \times 5\%) = \$1,700$$

$$V = S + B = \frac{EAC}{k_e} + B$$

$$= \frac{\$1,700}{0.12} + \$6,000$$

$$= \$14,167 + \$6,000 = \$20,167$$

The overall cost of capital is

$$k_o = \frac{EBIT}{V} = \frac{\$2,000}{\$20,167} = 9.9\%$$

The debt/equity ratio is

$$\frac{B}{S} = \frac{\$6,000}{\$14,167} = 42.35\%$$

Assume, as before, that the firm increases its debt from \$6,000 to \$10,000. Assume further that k_i rises to 6% and k_e at that degree of leverage is 14%. The value of the firm, then, is

$$EAC = EBIT - I$$
$$= \$2,000 - (\$10,000 \times 6\%)$$
$$= \$2,000 - \$600 = \$1,400$$

$$V = S + B = \frac{EAC}{k_e} + B$$

$$= \frac{\$1,400}{0.14} + \$10,000 = \$10,000 + \$10,000$$

$$= \$20,000$$

The overall cost of capital is

$$k_o = \frac{EBIT}{V} = \frac{\$2,000}{\$20,000} = 10.0\%$$

the debt/equity ratio is

$$\frac{B}{S} = \frac{\$10,000}{\$10,000} = 100\%$$

Thus the value of the firm is lower and its cost of capital slightly higher than when the debt is \$6,000. This result is due to the increase in k_e and, to a lesser extent, the increase in k_i. These two observations indicate that the optimal capital structure occurs before the debt/equity ratio equals 100%, as shown in Figure 3.

Miller-Modigliani (MM) Position

Miller-Modigliani (MM) advocates that the relationship between leverage and valuation is explained by the NOI approach. More specifically, MM's propositions are summarized following.
1. The market value of the firm and its cost of capital are independent of its capital structure.
2. k_e increases so as to exactly offset the use of cheaper debt money.
3. The cutoff rate for capital budgeting decisions is completely independent of the way in which an investment is financed.

Factors Affecting Capital Structure

Many financial managers believe, in practice, that the following factors influence financial structure:
1. Growth rate of future sales

Figure 3 Capital Structure vs. Cost of Capital

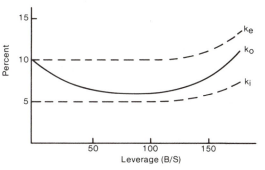

2. Stability of future sales

3. Competitive structures in the industry

4. Asset makeup of the individual firm

5. Attitude of owners and management toward risk

6. Control position of owners and management

7. Lenders' attitude toward the industry and a particular firm

See also Cost of Capital; Leverage.

THINKING PROGRAMS Accountants and financial executives often have to prepare written reports, such as management letters and specialized analyses of operations. Writing skills may be aided with respect to organization, clarity, and communication by using thinking software. "Idea" (outline) programs enable the user to sequence his or her thoughts in proper order. Outline processors allow accountants and financial managers to formulate a logical outline from random ideas entered into the computer. The computer has the information labeled, organized, and structured. A certain set of information can be a major category, while other pieces are identified as subordinates. In effect, we have a "brainstorm" processor for the practitioner to improve the quality of report writing with minimum time and effort.

Living Videotext's "Think Tank"™ breaks a piece of information into component parts by testing them as a headline within the outline. Each headline becomes a separate component. Text material is entered below each headline. The software enables the accountant or financial person to continually check with the main outline to assure the writer is still on the right track. Ashton-Tate's Framework™ idea processor allows for the grouping of several different frames in subsections of an outline.

THREE-WAY ANALYSIS This involves the computation of three variances for factory overhead: *spending*, *efficiency*, and *volume*. The budget variance in the *two-way analysis* is

separated into spending and efficiency variances. When an analysis of historical costs permits the estimation of variable and fixed overhead but the accounting records do not allow the separation of actual overhead costs into their variable and fixed elements, this three-way analysis of overhead variance is used. The three-way analysis provides the following reconciliation between and actual and applied overhead:

Actual	Flexible Budget	Flexible Budget	Applied Costs
Actual factory overhead costs	$(AH \times SR)$ for variable + Budgeted fixed overhead costs	$(SH \times SR)$ for variable + Budgeted fixed overhead costs	$(SH \times SR)$ for variable + Fixed overhead rate × Activity allowed

Three-way	Spending Variance	Efficiency Variance	Volume Variance
Two-way		Budget Variance	Volume Variance

where AH = actual hours used,
  SH = standard hours allowed,
  SR = standard overhead rate.

See also Responsibility Accounting; Two-Way Analysis; Variance Analysis.

TIME AND BILLING SOFTWARE (T&B) T&B software keeps track of hours incurred—by activity—of different staff for a particular client. Sources of time information are hourly rates, time sheets, practice management reports, and financial reports. At the end of a period, there is a bill prepared based on hours worked and billing rate. In case a flat fee is involved, hourly data aid the accountant or financial consultant in appraising staff productivity. The software also provides for employee expenses chargeable to the client. The hourly rate may be adjusted depending on the client serviced (e.g., higher fees for clients where legal exposure is greater). T&B

programs can give projected fees to current and prospective clients for an engagement.

Software can provide analyses of actual, budget, and variance figures for chargeable and nonchargeable time by type of function performed, and in the aggregate.

Features of Time and Billing Software

• Input controls of the system to appraise reasonableness of data.

• Flexibility in billing and management report format.

• Accommodation of different coding schemes.

• Generation of statements when required for specific clients (e.g., a bill for a particular tax, audit, or management advisory service).

• Ability to update one file while working on another file.

• Recurring billing (e.g., a client is billed monthly for a flat fee).

• Program flexibility such as in allowing itemized transaction billing, automatic billing codes, and free-form billing.

• Past-due reports and statements, including aging.

• Monthly summaries.

• Client past history reports (e.g., billings to client, when payments are made, last time fee was increased).

• Sort capability.

• Productivity report capability such as analyzing the profitability of staff operating at a given pay rate.

• Allowance for multiple-rate billing when the same staff person is charged out at different hourly rates, based on different jobs done or type of client serviced.

• Hours of nonbillable activity by type.

• Percentage of change in time to perform a task compared to the previous year.

• Advance billings.

• Comparison of expected billing rate with actual billing rate.

• Months having the most unbillable time.

• Trend in uncollectible client accounts.

• Evaluation of the reasonableness of the relationship between billable and nonbillable time.

• Extent of time lost in trying to get new business that was not forthcoming.

• Evaluation of overtime. Is it excessive?

• Partial billings and billing adjustments.

• Categorization of clients (e.g., new client, long-term client).

• Classification of fee arrangement (e.g., minimum fee, hourly fee, per-diem rate, flat fee).

• Aged unbilled work-in-process by client.

• Evaluation of client complaint to fee charged.

• Utilization of time percentages. Some packages incorporate a clock/timer that permits you to maintain a running tally of hours spent on a particular work area.

• Output of exception reports, such as jobs that are overdue.

An example of a time and billing package is Systematic Data Marketing Corporation's Time Management and Billing System.™ It prepares invoices and statements, maintains and controls accounts receivable and cash receipts, and generates the following reports and graphs:

• *Client or activity analysis report*—computes the billings of the firm by client or activity.

• *Employee analysis and history report*—measures staff productivity and profitability. It provides employee hours charged, billing, reimbursable expenses, and so on.

• *Billing history graphs*—generates a bar graph comparing billed versus billable amounts for clients.

• *Miscellaneous schedules and reports*—includes aged work-in-process schedules, activity summary, billing worksheet by client, automatic retainer billing, and aged accounts receivable schedules.

UniLink's Professional Time and Billing™ has an unlimited number of clients/ engagements, on-line data verification, work-in-process aging, finance/late charge capability, progress billing, and user-defined selection fields within the client and engagement files for selective management reporting. It also contains employee, partner, firm service code, and client realization in productivity reports.

TIME VALUE OF MONEY AND ITS APPLICATIONS

The time value of money is a critical consideration in financial and investment decisions. For example, compound interest calculations are needed to determine future sums of money resulting from an investment. Discounting, or the calculation of present value, which is inversely related to compounding, is used to evaluate future cash flow associated with capital budgeting projects. There are plenty of applications of time value of money in accounting and finance. We will discuss the concepts, calculations, and applications of future values and present values.

Future Values—Compounding

A dollar in hand today is worth more than a dollar to be received tomorrow because of the interest it could earn from putting it in a savings account or placing it in an investment account. Compounding interest means that interest earns interest. For the discussion of the concepts of compounding and time value, let us define:

F_n = Future value
= The amount of money at the end of year n

P = Principal
i = Annual interest rate
n = Number of years

Then:

F_1 = Amount of money at end of year 1
= Principal and interest = $P + iP = P(1 + i)$

F_2 = Amount of money at end of year 2 = $F_1(1 + i)$
= $P(1 + i)(1 + i) = P(1 + i)^2$

The future value of an investment compounded annually at rate i for n years is $F_n = P(1 + i)^n = P.\ FVIF_{i,n}$ where $FVIF_{i,n}$ is

the future value interest found in Table 1 in the Appendix.

■ Example 1

Paul Nani places \$1,000 in a savings account earning 8% interest compounded annually. How much money will he have in the account at the end of 4 years?

$$F_n = P(1 + i)^n$$
$$F_4 = \$1,000\ (1 + 0.08)^4$$

From Table 1 in the Appendix, the $FVIF$ for 4 years at 8% is 1.361. Therefore:

$$F_4 = \$1,000\ (1.36) = \$1,361$$

■ Example 2

Steve Hahn invested a large sum of money in the stock of Sigma Corporation. The company paid a \$3 dividend per share. The dividend is expected to increase by 20% per year for the next 3 years. He wishes to project the dividends for years 1 through 3.

$$F_n = P(1 + i)^n$$
$$F_1 = \$3(1 + 0.2)^1 = \$3\ (1.200) = \$3.60$$
$$F_2 = \$3(1 + 0.2)^2 = \$3\ (1.440) = \$4.32$$
$$F_3 = \$3(1 + 0.2)^3 = \$3\ (1.728) = \$5.18$$

Intrayear Compounding

Interest is often compounded more frequently than once a year. Banks, for example, compound interest quarterly, daily, and even continuously. If interest is compounded m times a year, then the general formula for solving for the future value becomes

$$F_n = P\left(1 + \frac{i}{m}\right)^{n \cdot m} = P \cdot FVIF_{i/m,n \cdot m}$$

The formula reflects more frequent compounding $(n \cdot m)$ at a smaller interest rate per period (i/m). For example, in the case of semiannual compounding $(m = 2)$, the previous formula becomes

$$F_n = P\left(1 + \frac{i}{2}\right)^{n \cdot 2} = P \cdot FVIF_{i/2,n \cdot 2}$$

As m approaches infinity, the term $(1 + i/m)^{n \cdot m}$ approaches $e^{i \cdot n}$ where e is approximately 2.71828, and F_n becomes

$$F_n = P \cdot e^{i \cdot n}$$

The future value increases as m increases. Thus, continuous compounding results in the maximum possible future value at the end of n periods for a given rate of interest.

■ Example 3

Assume that $P = \$100$, $i = 12\%$, and $n = 3$ years. Then:

Annual compounding ($m = 1$):
$$F_3 = \$100(1 + 0.12)^3 = \$100(1.404)^3 = \$140.49$$

Semiannual compounding ($m = 2$):
$$F_3 = \$100\left(1 + \frac{0.12}{2}\right)^{3.2} = \$100(1 + 0.06)^6$$
$$= \$100(1.419) = \$141.90$$

Quarterly compounding ($m = 4$):
$$F_3 = \$100\left(1 + \frac{0.12}{4}\right)^{3.4} = \$100(1 + 0.3)^{12}$$
$$= \$100(1.426) = \$142.60$$

Monthly compounding ($m = 12$):
$$F_3 = \$100\left(1 + \frac{0.12}{12}\right)^{3.12}$$
$$= \$100(1 + 0.01)^{36} = \$100(1.431)$$
$$= \$143.10$$

Continuous compounding ($e^{i \cdot n}$):
$$F_3 = \$100 \cdot e^{(0.12 \cdot 3)}$$
$$= \$100(2.71828)^{0.36}$$
$$= \$100(1.433) = \$143.30$$

Future Value of an Annuity

An annuity is defined as a series of payments (or receipts) of a fixed amount for a specified number of periods. Each payment is assumed to occur at the end of the period. The future value of an annuity is a compound annuity that involves depositing or investing an equal sum of money at the end of each year for a certain number of years and allowing it to grow.

Let: S_n = the future value on an n-year annuity
$\quad\quad A$ = the amount of an annuity

Then we can write:

$$S_n = A(1 + i)^{n-1} + A(1 + i)^{n-2} + \ldots + A(1 + i)^0$$
$$= A[(i + i)^{n-1} + (1 + i)^{n-2} + \ldots + (1 + i)^0]$$
$$= A \cdot \sum_{t=0}^{n-1} (1 + i)^t$$
$$= A \frac{[(1 + i)^n - 1]}{i} = A \cdot FVIFA_{i,n}$$

where $FVIFA_{i,n}$ represents the future value interest factor for an n-year annuity compounded at i percent and can be found in Table 2 in the Appendix.

■ Example 4

Lisa Clarke wishes to determine the sum of money she will have in her savings account at the end of 6 years by depositing $1,000 at the end of each year for the next 6 years. The annual interest rate is 8%. The $FVIFA_{8\%,6 \text{ years}}$ is given in Table 2 in the Appendix as 7.336. Therefore:

$$S6 = \$1,000 \ (FVIFA_{8,6}) = \$1,000 \ (7.336) = \$7,336$$

Present Value—Discounting

Present value is the present worth of future sums of money. The process of calculating present values, or discounting, is actually the opposite of finding the compounded future value. In connection with present value calculations, the interest rate i is called the discount rate. Recall that

$$F_n = P(1 + i)^n$$

Therefore:

$$P = \frac{F_n}{(1 + i)^n} = F_n\left[\frac{1}{(1 + i)^n}\right] = F_n \cdot PVIF_{i,n}$$

where $PVIF_{i,n}$ represents the present value interest factor for $1 and is given in Table 3 in the Appendix.

■ Example 5

John Jaffe has been given an opportunity to receive $20,000 6 years from now. If he can earn 10% on his investments, what is the most he should pay for this opportunity?

To answer this question, one must compute the present value of $20,000 to be received 6 years from now at a 10% rate of discount. F_6 is $20,000, i is 10%, which equals 0.1, and n is 6 years. $PVIF_{10,6}$ from Table 3 is 0.565.

$$P = \$2,000 \left[\frac{1}{(1 + 0.1)^6} \right]$$
$$= \$20,000(PVIF_{10,6})$$
$$= \$20,000(0.565) = \$11,300$$

This means that John Jaffe, who can earn 10% on his investment, could be indifferent to the choice between receiving $11,300 now or $20,000 6 years from now since the amounts are time equivalent. In other words, he could invest $11,300 today at 10% and have $20,000 in 6 years.

Present Value of Mixed Streams of Cash Flows

The present value of a series of mixed payments (or receipts) is the sum of the present value of each individual payment. We know that the present value of each individual payment is the payment times the appropriate *PVIF*.

■ Example 6

Bonnie Brown has been offered an opportunity to receive the following mixed stream of revenue over the next 3 years:

Year	Revenue
1	$1,000
2	2,000
3	500

If she must earn a minimum of 6% on her investment, what is the most she should pay today? The present value of this series of mixed streams of revenue follows:

Year	Revenue ($)	×	PVIF	=	Present Value
1	1,000		0.943		$ 943
2	2,000		0.890		1,780
3	500		0.840		420
					$3,143

Present Value of an Annuity

Interest received from bonds, pension funds, and insurance obligations all involve annuities. To compare these financial instruments, we need to know the present value of each. The present value of an annuity (p_n) can be found by using the following equation:

$$P_n = A \cdot \frac{1}{(1 + i)^1} + A \cdot \frac{1}{(1 + i)^2} + \ldots + A \cdot \frac{1}{(1 + i)^n}$$
$$= A \left[\frac{1}{(1 + i)^1} + \frac{1}{(1 + i)^2} + \ldots + \frac{1}{(1 + i)^n} \right]$$
$$= A \cdot \sum_{t=1}^{n} \frac{1}{(1 + i)^t}$$
$$= A \cdot \frac{\left[1 - \frac{1}{(1 + i)^n} \right]}{i} = A \cdot PVIFA_{i,n}$$

where $PVIFA_{i,n}$ represents the appropriate value for the present value interest factor for a $1 annuity discounted at i percent for n years, which is found in Table 4 in the Appendix.

■ Example 7

Assume that the revenues in Example 6 form an annuity of $1,000 for 3 years. Then the present value is

$$P_n = A \cdot PVIFA_{i,n}$$
$$P_3 = \$1,000 \ (PVIFA_{6,3}) = \$1,000 \ (2.673) = \$2,673$$

Perpetuities

Some annuities go on forever. Such annuities are called perpetuities. An example of a perpetuity is preferred stock, which yields a constant dollar dividend indefinitely. The present value of a perpetuity is found as follows:

$$\text{Present value of a perpetuity} = \frac{\text{Receipt}}{\text{Discount rate}} = \frac{A}{i}$$

■ Example 8

Assume that a perpetual bond has an $80-per-year interest payment and that the discount rate is 10%. The present value of this perpetuity is

$$P = \frac{A}{i} = \frac{\$80}{0.10} = \$800$$

Applications of Future Values and Present Values

Future and present values have numerous applications in accounting, finance, and investments, which will be discussed throughout the Encyclopedia. Five of these applications follow.

Deposits to Accumulate a Future Sum (or Sinking Fund)

An individual might wish to find the annual deposit (or payment) that is necessary to accumulate a future sum. To find this future amount (or sinking fund) we can use the formula for finding the future value of an annuity.

$$S_n = A \cdot FVIFA_{i,n}$$

Solving for A, we obtain:

$$\text{Sinking fund amount} = A = \frac{S_n}{FVIFA_{i,n}}$$

■ Example 9

Karen Black wishes to determine the equal annual end-of-year deposits required to accumulate $5,000 at the end of 5 years, when her son enters college. The interest rate is 10%. The annual deposit is

$$S_5 = \$5,000$$
$$FVIFA_{10,5} = 6.105 \quad \text{(from Table 2)}$$
$$A = \frac{5,000}{6.105} = \$819$$

In other words, if she deposits $819 at the end of each year for 5 years at 10% interest, she will have accumulated $5,000 at the end of the fifth year.

Amortized Loans

If a loan is to be repaid in equal periodic amounts, it is said to be an amortized loan. Examples include auto loans, mortgage loans, and most commercial loans. The periodic payment can easily be computed as follows:

$$P_n = A \cdot PVIFA_{i,n}$$

Solving for A, we obtain:

$$\text{Amount of loan} = A = \frac{P_n}{PVIFA_{i,n}}$$

■ Example 10

Kim Naomi has a 40-month auto loan of $5,000 at a 12% annual interest rate. He wants to find out the monthly loan payment amount.

$$i = 12\%/12 \text{ months} = 1\%$$
$$P_{40} = \$5,000$$
$$PVIFA_{1,40} = 32.835 \quad \text{(from Table 4)}$$

Therefore:

$$A = \frac{\$5,000}{32.835} = \$152.28$$

So, to repay the principal and interest on a $5,000, 12%, 40-month loan, Kim Naomi has to pay $152.28 a month for the next 40 months.

■ Example 11

Assume that a firm borrows $2,000 to be repaid in three equal installments at the end of each of the next 3 years. The bank wants 12% interest. The amount of each payment is

$$P_3 = \$2,000$$
$$PVIFA_{12,3} = 2.402$$

Therefore:

$$A = \frac{\$2,000}{2.402} = \$832.64$$

Each loan payment consists partly of interest and partly of principal. The breakdown is often displayed in a loan amortization schedule. The interest component is larger in the first period and subsequently declines, whereas the principal portion is smallest in the first period and increases thereafter, as shown in the following example.

▪ Example 12

Using the same data as in Example 11, we set up the following amortization schedule:

Year	Payment	Interest	Repayment of Principal	Remaining Balance
1	$832.64	$240.00[a]	$592.64	$1,407.36
2	832.64	168.88	663.76	743.60
3	832.83[b]	89.23	743.60[c]	

[a] Interest is computed by multiplying the loan balance at the beginning of the year by the interest rate. Therefore, interest in year 1 is $2,000(0.12) = $240; in year 2 interest is $1,407.36(0.12) = $168.88; and in year 3 interest is $743.60(0.12) = $89.23. All figures are rounded.
[b] Last payment is adjusted upward
[c] Not exact because of accumulated rounding errors

Rates of Growth

In finance, it is necessary to calculate the compound annual interest rate, or rate of growth, associated with a stream of earnings.

▪ Example 13

Assume that the Geico Company has earnings per share of $2.50 in 19X1, and 10 years later the earnings per share has increased to $3.70. The compound annual rate of growth of the earnings per share can be computed as follows:

$$F_n = P \cdot FVIF_{i,n}$$

Solving this for FVIF, we obtain

$$FVIF_{i,n} = \frac{F_n}{P}$$

$$FVIF_{i,10} = \frac{\$3.70}{\$2.50} = \$1.48$$

From Table 3 an *FVIF* of 1.48 at 10 years is at $i = 4\%$. The compound annual rate of growth is therefore 4%.

Bond Values

Bonds call for the payment of a specific amount of interest for a stated number of years and the repayment of the face value

at the bond's maturity. Thus a bond represents an annuity plus a lump sum. Its value is found as the present value of this payment stream. The interest is usually paid semiannually.

$$V = \sum_{t=1}^{n} \frac{I}{(1 + r)^t} + \frac{M}{(1 + r)^n}$$

$$= I(PVIFA_{r,n}) + M(PVIF_{r,n})$$

where I = interest payment per period,
M = par value, or maturity value, usually $1,000,
r = investor's required rate of return,
n = number of periods.

▪ Example 14

Assume there is a 10-year bond with a 10% coupon, paying interest semiannually and having a face value of $1,000. Since interest is paid semiannually, the number of periods involved is 20 and the semiannual cash inflow is $100/2 = $50.

Assume that investors have a required rate of return of 12% for this type of bond. Then the present value (V) of this bond is

$$V = \$50(PVIFA_{6,20}) + \$1,000\ (PVIF_{6,20})$$
$$= \$50(11.470) = \$1,000(0.312)$$
$$= \$573.50 + \$312.00 = \$885.50$$

Note that the required rate of return (12%) is higher than the coupon rate of interest (10%), and so the bond value (or the price investors are willing to pay for this particular bond) is less than its $1,000 face value.

TOTAL PROJECT APPROACH   Total project approach (or comparative statement approach) is an approach that looks at all the items of revenue and cost data under two alternatives and compares the net income or contribution margin results. Other approaches are the *incremental analysis* and the *opportunity cost approach*.

▪ Example

Assume the SBC Company is planning to expand its productive capacity. The plans consist of purchasing a new machine for $50,000 and disposing of the old machine without receiving anything. The new machine has a 5-year life. The old machine has a 5-year remaining life and a book value of $12,500. The new machine will reduce variable operating costs from $35,000 per year to $20,000 per year. Annual sales and other operating costs are shown below.

	Present Machine	New Machine
Sales	$80,000	$80,000
Variable costs	35,000	20,000
Fixed costs:		
Depreciation		
(straight-line)	2,500*	10,000
Insurance, taxes,		
etc.	4,000	4,000

* Note that the depreciation expense of $2,500 of the old machine is irrelevant because it is a *sunk* cost.

The total project approach results in the following:

	Present Machine	New Machine	Increment (or difference)
Sales	$80,000	$80,000	—
Less: Variable costs	35,000	20,000	$(15,000)
Contribution margin	$45,000	$60,000	$ 15,000
Less: Fixed costs			
Depreciation	—	10,000	10,000
Other	4,000	4,000	—
Net income	$41,000	$46,000	$ 5,000

The schedule for the total project approach shows an increase in profit of $5,000 with the purchase of the new machine. *See also* Incremental Analysis; Opportunity Cost Approach.

TRADING ON EQUITY This, also known as *financial leverage*, means the use of borrowed funds in the capital structure of a firm. Trading *profitably* on the equity, also known as *positive (favorable) financial leverage*, means that the borrowed funds generate a higher rate of return than the interest rate paid for the use of the funds. The excess accrues to the benefit of the owners because it magnifies, or increases, their earnings. *See also* Financial Leverage; Leverage.

TRANSACTION TEST A transaction test is an audit procedure involving the examination of specific transactions and related documentation. It is an element of the testing process to determine the degree to which the CPA may rely on internal controls to uncover errors. Evidence is obtained to assist in rendering an audit opinion with respect to the fairness of financial statement presentation. Test of transactions include the substantiation of dollar amounts such as through recalculations, and tracing transactions from initiation to culmination in the financial statements. But it should be noted that transaction tests are of significantly less scope than analytical review. The procedure involved is to select a specified number of specific transactions for testing in order to ascertain whether proper controls exist. The ensuing error rate is computed. If there is an acceptable error rate, reliance can be placed on the client's recording and posting of transactions. Transaction tests provide the auditor with guidance in deriving the scope of the audit needed. Test of transactions is significantly used in substantive testing as well as in the area of internal control. *See also* Compliance Test; Substantive Test.

TRANSFER PRICING Goods and services are often exchanged between various divisions of a decentralized organization. A major goal of transfer pricing is to enable divisions that exchange goods or services to act as independent businesses. The question then is, What monetary values should be assigned to these exchanges or transfers? Market price? Some kind of cost? Some version of either? Unfortunately, there is no single transfer price that will please everybody—that is, top management, the selling division, and the buying division. Various transfer pricing schemes are available, such as *market price*, *cost-based price*, or *negotiated price*.

The choice of a transfer pricing policy (i.e., which type of transfer price to use) is normally decided by top management. The decision will typically include consideration of the following:

• *Goal congruence*—Will the transfer price promote the goals of the company as a whole? Will it harmonize the divisional goals with organizational goals?

• *Performance evaluation*—Will the selling division receive enough credit for its transfer of goods and services to the buying division? Will the transfer price hurt the performance of the selling division?

• *Autonomy*—Will the transfer price preserve autonomy, the freedom of the selling and buying division managers to operate their divisions as decentralized entities?

• Other factors such as minimization of tariffs and income taxes and observance of legal restrictions.

Transfer prices can be based on
• Market price
• Cost-based price—variable or full cost
• Negotiated price
• General formula, which is usually the sum of variable costs per unit and opportunity costs for the company as a whole (lost revenue per unit on outside sales)

Market Price

Market price is the best transfer price, in the sense that it will maximize the profits of the company as a whole if it meets the following two conditions: (1) there exists a competitive market price and (2) divisions are independent of each other. If either one of these conditions is violated, market price will not lead to an optimal economic decision for the company.

Cost-Based Price—Variable or Full Cost

Cost-based transfer price, another alternative transfer pricing scheme, is easy to understand and convenient to use. But there are some disadvantages, including

• Inefficiencies of selling divisions are passed on to the buying divisions with little

incentive to control costs. The use of standard costs is recommended in such cases.

• The cost-based method treats the divisions as cost centers rather than profit or investment centers. Therefore, measures such as ROI and RI cannot be used for evaluation purposes.

The variable cost-based transfer price has an advantage over the full cost method because in the short run it may tend to ensure the best utilization of the overall company's resources. The reason is that, in the short run, fixed costs do not change. Any use of facilities, without incurrence of additional fixed costs, will increase the company's overall profits.

Negotiated Price

A negotiated price is generally used when there is no clear outside market. A negotiated price is a price agreed upon between the buying and selling divisions that reflects unusual or mitigating circumstances. This method is widely used when no intermediate market price exists for the product transferred and the selling division is assured of a normal profit.

■ Example 1

Company X just purchased a small company that specializes in the manufacture of part No. 323. Company X is a decentralized organization and will treat the newly acquired company as an autonomous division called Division B with full profit responsibility. Division B's fixed costs total $30,000 per month, and variable costs per unit are $18. Division B's operating capacity is 5,000 units. The selling price per unit is $30. Division A of Company X is currently purchasing 2,500 units of Part No. 323 per month from an outside supplier at $29 per unit, which represents the normal $30 price less a quantity discount. Top management of the company must decide what transfer price should be used.

Top management may consider the following alternative prices:

(a) $30 market price
(b) $29—the price that Division A is currently paying to the outside supplier
(c) $23.50 negotiated price, which is $18 variable cost plus ½ of the benefits of an internal transfer [($29 − $18) × ½]
(d) $24 full cost, which is $18 variable cost plus $6 ($30,000/5,000 units) fixed cost per unit
(e) $18 variable cost

We will discuss each of these prices:

(a) $30 would not be an appropriate transfer price. Division B cannot charge a price more than the price Division A is paying now ($29).
(b) $29 would be an appropriate transfer price if top management wants to treat the divisions as autonomous investment centers. This price would cause all of the benefits of internal transfers to accrue to the selling division, with the buying division's position remaining unchanged.
(c) $23.50 would be an appropriate transfer price if top management wants to treat the divisions as investment centers but wants to share the benefits of an internal transfer equally between them, as follows:

Variable costs of Division B	$18.00
½ of the difference between the variable costs of Division B and the price Division A is paying ($29 − $18) × ½	5.50
Transfer price	$23.50

Note that $23.50 is just one example of a negotiated transfer price. The exact price depends on how the benefits are divided.

(d) $24 [$24 = $18 + ($30,000/5,000 units)] would be an appropriate transfer price if top management treats divisions like cost centers with no profit responsibility.

All benefits from both divisions will accrue to the buying division. This will maximize the profits of the company as a whole but affect adversely the performance of the selling division. Another disadvantage of this cost-based approach is that inefficiencies (if any) of the selling division are being passed on to the buying division.

(e) $18 would be an appropriate transfer price for guiding top management in deciding whether transfers between the two divisions should take place. Since $18 is less than the outside purchase price of the buying division and the selling division has excess capacity, the transfer should take place because it will maximize the profits of the company as a whole. However, if $18 is used as a transfer price, then all of the benefits of the internal transfer accrue to the buying division and it will hurt the performance of the selling division.

General Formula

It is not easy to find a cure-all answer to the transfer pricing problem, since the three problems of goal congruence, performance evaluation, and autonomy must all be considered simultaneously. It is generally agreed, however, that some form of competitive market price is the best approach to the transfer pricing problem. The following formula would be helpful in this effort:

$$\text{Transfer price} = \text{Variable costs per unit} + \text{Opportunity costs per unit for the company as a whole}$$

Opportunity costs are defined here as net revenue foregone by the company as a whole if the goods and services are transferred internally. The reasoning behind this formula is that the selling division should be allowed to recover its variable costs plus opportunity cost (i.e., revenue that it could have made

Figure 1

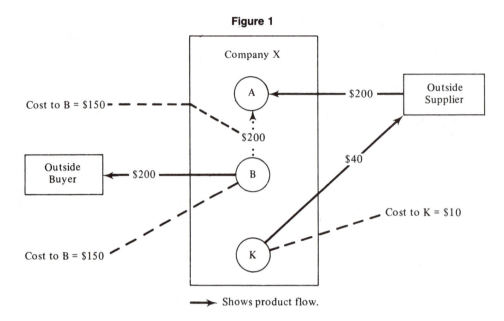

Shows product flow.

by selling to an outsider) of the transfer. The selling department should not have to suffer lost income by selling within the company.

■ Example 2

Company X has more than 50 divisions, including A, B, and K. Division A, the buying division, wants to buy a component for its final product and has an option to buy from Division B or from an outside supplier at the market price of $200. If Division A buys from the outside supplier, it will in turn buy selected raw materials from Division K for $40. This will increase its contribution to overall company profits by $30 ($40 revenue minus $10 variable costs). Division B, on the other hand, can sell its component to Division A or to an outside buyer at the same price. Division B, working at full capacity, incurs variable costs of $150. Will the use of $200 as a transfer price lead to optimal decisions for the company as a whole? Figure 1 depicts the situation.

The optimal decision from the viewpoint of Company X as a whole can be looked at in terms of its net cash outflow, as follows:

	Division A's Action	
	Buy From B	Buy From Outsider
Outflow to the company as a whole	$(150)	$(200)
Cash inflows	—	to B: $50($200 − $150)
		to K: $30($ 40 − $ 10)
Net cash outflow to the company as a whole	$(150)	$(120)

To maximize the profits of Company X, Division A should buy from an outside supplier. The transfer price that would force Division A to buy outside should be the sum of variable costs and opportunity costs, that is,

$$\$150 + \$50 + \$30 = \$230 \text{ per unit}$$

In other words, if Division B charges $230 to Division A, Division A will definitely buy from the outside source for $200.

TRANSFER OF RECEIVABLES AND RECOURSE

According to FASB 77, a sale is recorded for the transfer of receivables with recourse if *all* of the following criteria are satisfied:

1. The transferor gives up control of the future economic benefits applicable to the receivables (e.g., repurchase right).
2. The liability of the transferor under the recourse provisions is estimable.
3. The transferee cannot require the transferor to repurchase the receivables unless there is a recourse provision in the contract.

When the transfer is treated as a sale, gain or loss is recognized for the difference between the selling price and the net receivables. The selling price includes normal servicing fees of the transferor and appropriate probable adjustments (e.g., debtor's failure to pay on time, effects of prepayment, and defects in the transferred receivable). Net receivables equal gross receivables plus finance and service charges minus unearned finance and service charges.

In case the selling price varies during the term of the receivables due to a variable interest rate provision, the selling price is estimated with the use of an appropriate "going market interest rate" at the transfer date. Later changes in the rate cause a change in estimated selling price, not in interest income or interest expense.

If one of the aforementioned criteria is not satisfied, a liability is recognized for the proceeds received.

Footnote disclosures include

• Amount received by transferor

• Balance of the receivables at the balance sheet date

TREASURY STOCK Treasury stock is issued shares that have been bought back by the company. The two methods to account for treasury stock are

1. *Cost method*—Treasury stock is recorded at the cost to purchase it. If treasury stock is later sold above cost, the entry is

Cash
    Treasury Stock
    Paid-in-Capital

If treasury stock was sold instead at below cost, the entry is

Cash
Paid-in-Capital—Treasury Stock (up to amount available)
Retained Earnings (if paid-in-capital is unavailable)
    Treasury Stock

If treasury stock is donated, only a memo entry is needed. When the treasury shares are later sold, the entry based on the market price at that time is

Cash
    Paid-in-Capital—Donation

An appropriation of retained earnings equal to the cost of treasury stock on hand is required.

Treasury stock is shown as a reduction from total stockholders' equity.

2. *Par value method*—Treasury stock is recorded at its par value when bought. If treasury stock is purchased at more than par value, the entry is

Treasury Stock—Par Value
Paid-in-Capital—original premium per share
Retained Earnings—if necessary
    Cash

If treasury stock is purchased at less than par value, the entry is

Treasury Stock—Par Value
    Cash
    Paid-in-Capital

Upon sale of the treasury stock above par value, the entry is

Cash
    Treasury Stock
    Paid-in-Capital

Upon sale of the treasury stock at less than par value, the entry is

Cash
Paid-in-Capital (amount available)
Retained Earnings (if paid-in-capital is insufficient)
 Treasury Stock

An appropriation of retained earnings equal to the cost of the treasury stock on hand is required. Treasury stock is shown as a contra account to the common stock it applies to under the capital stock section of stockholders' equity.

TREASURY STOCK METHOD This method is used to compute the common stock equivalency of options and warrants in the earnings per share statistic. *See also* Earnings per Share.

TREND ANALYSIS A common method for forecasting sales or earnings is the use of trend analysis, which is a special case of regression analysis. This method involves a regression whereby a trend line is fitted to a time series of data. The trend line equation can be shown as

$$y = a + bx$$

The formulas for the coefficients a and b are essentially the same as the ones for simple regression. However, for regression purposes, a time period can be given a number so that $\Sigma x = 0$. When there is an odd number of periods, the period in the middle is assigned a zero value. If there is an even number, then -1 and $+1$ are assigned the two periods in the middle, so that again $\Sigma x = 0$.

With $\Sigma x = 0$, the formula for b and a reduces to the following:

$$b = \frac{n\Sigma xy}{n\Sigma x^2}$$

$$a = \Sigma y/n$$

■ Example

Case 1 (odd number)
 19X1 19X2 19X3 19X4 19X5
 $x = $ -2 -1 0 $+1$ $+2$

Case 2 (even number)
 19X1 19X2 19X3 19X4 19X5 19X6
 $x = $ -3 -2 -1 $+1$ $+2$ $+3$

In each case, $\Sigma t = 0$.

■ Example

Consider TDK Company whose historical earnings per share (EPS) follow:

Year	EPS
19X1	$1.00
19X2	1.20
19X3	1.30
19X4	1.60
19X5	1.70

Since the company has f years' data, which is an odd number, the year in the middle is assigned a zero value.

Year	x	EPS(y)	xy	x^2
19X1	-2	$1.00	-2.00	4
19X2	-1	1.20	-1.20	1
19X3	0	1.30	0	0
19X4	$+1$	1.60	1.60	1
19X5	$+2$	1.70	3.40	4
	0	$6.80	1.80	10

$$b = \frac{(5)(1.80)}{(5)(10)} = \frac{9}{50} = \$0.18$$

$$a = \frac{\$6.80}{5} = \$1.36$$

Therefore, the estimated trend equation is

$$\hat{y} = \$1.36 + \$0.18x$$

where $\hat{y}$ = estimated EPS,
 x = year index value.

To project 19X6 sales, we assign $+3$ to the x value for the year 19X6. Thus:

$$\hat{y} = \$1.36 + \$0.18(+3)$$
$$= \$1.36 + \$0.54$$
$$= \$1.90$$

See also Regression Analysis.

TREND (HORIZONTAL) ANALYSIS This looks at the trend in accounts over the years and aids in identifying areas of wide divergence mandating further attention. Horizontal analysis may also be presented by showing trends relative to a base year.

■ Example

X Company's revenue in 19X1 was $200,000 and in 19X2 was $250,000. The percentage increase equals

$$\frac{\text{Change}}{\text{Prior year}} = \frac{\$50,000}{\$200,000} = 25\%$$

See also Vertical Analysis.

TROUBLED DEBT RESTRUCTURING   In a troubled debt restructuring, the debtor has financial problems and is relieved of part or the full amount of the obligation by the creditor. The concession is from debtor-creditor agreement, imposed by law, or relates to foreclosure and repossession. Troubled debt restructurings may include

• Debtor gives creditor receivables from third parties or other assets in satisfaction of the obligation.

• Debtor transfers stock to creditor to satisfy the debt.

• Modification of the terms of obligation, including reducing the interest rate, extending the maturity date, or downwardly adjusting the face amount of the debt.

The debtor recognizes an extraordinary gain (net of tax) on the restructuring but the creditor recognizes a loss. The loss may be ordinary or extraordinary depending on whether the creditor's arrangement is unusual and infrequent. Generally, the loss is deemed ordinary.

Debtor

The gain to the debtor equals the difference between the fair value of the assets exchanged and the book value of the obligation including accrued interest. Additionally, there may be a gain on disposal of assets exchanged in the transaction equal to the difference between the fair market value and the book value of the transferred assets. The latter gain or loss is *not* a gain or loss on restructuring but instead an ordinary gain or loss relating to asset disposal.

■ Example

A debtor transfers assets having a fair market value of $70 and a book value of $50 to settle a payable having a carrying value of $85. The gain on restructuring is $15 ($85 − $70). The ordinary gain is $20 ($70 − $50).

A debtor may provide the creditor with an equity interest. The debtor records the equity securities issued based on fair market value and not the recorded value of the debt extinguished. The excess of the recorded payable satisfied over the fair value of the issued securities represents an extraordinary item.

A modification in terms of an initial debt contract is accounted for prospectively. A new interest rate may be determined based on the new terms. This interest rate is then used to allocate future payments to lower principal and interest. When the new terms of the agreement result in the sum of all the future payments to be *less* than the carrying value of the payable, the payable is reduced and a restructuring gain recorded for the difference. Future payments are deemed a reduction of principal only. Interest expense is not recorded.

A troubled debt restructuring may result in a *combination* of concessions to the debtor. This may take place when assets or an equity interest are given in *partial* satisfaction of the obligation and the balance is subject to a modification of terms. Two steps are involved: (1) the payable is reduced by the fair value of the assets or equity transferred and (2) the balance of the debt is accounted for as a ''modification of terms'' type restructuring.

Direct costs, such as legal fees, incurred by the debtor in an equity transfer reduce the fair value of the equity interest. All other costs reduce the gain on restructuring. If there is no gain involved, they are expensed.

■ Example

The debtor owes the creditor $200,000 and has expressed that due to financial problems there may be difficulty in making future payments. Footnote disclosure of the problem should be made by both debtor and creditor.

■ Example

The debtor owes the creditor $80,000. The creditor relieves the debtor of $10,000. The balance of the debt will be paid at a subsequent time.

The journal entry for the debtor is

Accounts Payable	10,000	
Extraordinary Gain		10,000

The journal entry for the creditor is

Ordinary Loss	10,000	
Accounts Receivable		10,000

■ Example

The debtor owes the creditor $90,000. The creditor agrees to accept $70,000 in full satisfaction of the obligation.

The journal entry for the debtor is

Accounts Payable	20,000	
Extraordinary Gain		20,000

The journal entry for the creditor is

Ordinary Loss	20,000	
Accounts Receivable		20,000

The debtor should disclose the following in the footnotes:

• Particulars of the restructuring agreement
• The aggregate and per share amounts of the gain on restructuring
• Amounts that are contingently payable, including the contingency terms

Creditor

The creditor's loss is the difference between the fair value of assets received and the book value of the investment. When terms are modified, the creditor recognizes interest income to the degree that total future payments are greater than the carrying value of the investment. Interest income is recognized using the effective interest method. Assets received are reflected at fair market value. When the book value of the receivable is in excess of the aggregate payments, an ordinary loss is recognized for the difference. All cash received in the future is accounted for as a recovery of the investment. Direct costs of the creditor are expensed.

The creditor does not recognize contingent interest until the contingency is removed and interest has been earned. Further, future changes in the interest rate are accounted for as a change in estimate.

The creditor discloses the following in the footnotes:

• Loan commitments of additional funds to financially troubled companies
• Loans and/or receivables by major type
• Debt agreements in which the interest rate has been downwardly adjusted, including an explanation of the circumstances
• Description of the restructuring terms

TRUST A trust is a fiduciary relationship in which a trustee holds property for the benefit of a beneficiary. The grantor creates the trust. There is a distinction between the corpus (property) and income generated from it. The trust agreement stipulates the manner of distribution of principal and income. A trust is typically created by the owner of property who transfers property to the trustee. The administration of a trust typically is done without any court interference. The administration is usually in the form of managing funds to provide money to an income beneficiary and then to a remainderman.

A trust is a special form of ownership that provides sound management of assets and insulates them from tax and creditors. Trusts transfer property ownership to a third party, the trust, while permitting the real owner to keep control by appointing himself, another person, or a financial institution to act as trustee. The trustee assures that the beneficiaries receive proper benefit.

Advantages of Having a Trust

• Avoiding the costs applicable to outright ownership of property

• Improves administrative convenience

• Shelters owner from lawsuits and creditors

• Enables faster inheritance

• May reduce the tax burden

• Tailored to meet obligations

• Management may be done by a trusted third party

• Property is transferred to minors without the need for a guardian

• Protects inheritor's principal against unwise spending

Flexibility: One can empower the trustee with as much or as little power to make decisions as desired.

An irrevocable trust transfers trust assets outside the grantor's ownership and is immune from lawsuits and creditors' claims against the grantor. Irrevocable trusts established prior to death are not included in the deceased probatable estate, reducing access to the decedent's property from creditors' claims. However, this does not guard against estate taxation.

Irrevocable and revocable living trusts are not includable in the probate of the decedent's estate and thus result in faster inheritance. Because trusts are not included in the probatable estate, probate costs are lower since they depend on the estate's size.

To enable the trust's income to be taxed at the lower marginal tax rate of the beneficiary instead of the higher marginal tax rate of the grantor, the following conditions have to exist:

• The grantor relinquishes his or her reversionary interest in both the principal and income of the trust for at least more than 10 years or the beneficiary's lifetime.

• The grantor relinquishes control over the income payable to persons other than himself or herself during the trust period.

• The grantor gives up certain administrative powers (e.g., grantor cannot reacquire the trust capital).

• The grantor cannot revoke the trust.

• The trust's income cannot be distributed or accumulated for future disposition to the grantor or his or her spouse, nor can it be used to meet the grantor's support obligations (e.g., payment of college tuition for children).

Warning: Revocable trusts provide no tax advantages to the grantor and thus should be considered for nontax reasons.

Recommendation: Use an irrevocable trust when the grantor's main concern is to transfer part of his or her assets prior to death so as to lower estate taxes. The appreciation in value of the trust is not subject to gift or estate taxes.

T-STATISTICS   T-statistics (or *t*-value) is a measure of the statistical significance of an independent variable, x, in explaining the dependent variable y. It is determined by dividing the estimated regression coefficient, b, by its standard error, s_b. It is then compared with the table *t*-value. (See Table 6 in the Appendix). Thus, the *t*-statistic measures how many standard errors the coefficient is away from zero. Generally, any *t*-value greater than $+2$ or less than -2 is acceptable. The higher the *t*-value, the greater the confidence we have in the coefficient as a predictor. Low *t*-values are indications of low reliability of the predictive power of that coefficient. *See also* Cost Behavior Analysis; Regression Analysis.

TURNOVER   This refers to the number of times an asset (e.g., inventory, accounts receivable) is replaced during an accounting period, typically one year. Usually, turnover is the ratio of sales to a balance sheet item, such as sales to fixed assets. A high turnover rate is favorable because it indicates the efficient utilization of assets.

■ **Example**

Beginning and ending inventory are $30,000 and $40,000, respectively. Cost of sales is $300,000. Inventory turnover equals

$$\text{Inventory turnover} = \frac{\text{Cost of sales}}{\text{Average inventory}}$$
$$= \frac{\$300,000}{\$35,000} = 8.6 \text{ times}$$

See also Balance Sheet Analysis.

TWO-WAY ANALYSIS Two-way analysis of variance is the computation of two variances—*price* and *quantity* variances for di-

rect materials and direct labor, and *budget* and *volume* variances for factory overhead. The budget variance is the difference between actual overhead costs and the budget overhead based on standard hours allowed. The volume variance (denominator variance) is the difference between denominator volume and actual volume multiplied by a predetermined fixed overhead rate. The two-way analysis for factory overhead stops here; it does not break up the budget variance into *spending* and *efficiency* variances. See the general model that provides the two-way and three-way analyses for factory overhead that follows.

See also Three-Way Analysis; Variance Analysis.

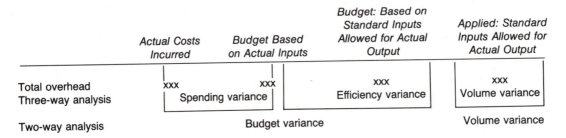

	Actual Costs Incurred	Budget Based on Actual Inputs	Budget: Based on Standard Inputs Allowed for Actual Output	Applied: Standard Inputs Allowed for Actual Output
Total overhead Three-way analysis	xxx	xxx	xxx	xxx
		Spending variance	Efficiency variance	Volume variance
Two-way analysis		Budget variance		Volume variance

U

UTILIZATION OF SCARCE RESOURCES In general, the emphasis on products with higher contribution margin maximizes a firm's total net income, even though total sales may decrease. This is not true, however, where there are constraining factors and scarce resources. The constraining factor is the factor that restricts or limits the production or sale of a given product. The constraining factor may be machine hours, labor hours, or cubic feet of warehouse space. *Special Note*: In the presence of these constraining factors, maximizing total profits depends on getting the highest contribution margin *per unit* of the factor (rather than the highest contribution margin per unit of product output).

■ Example

Assume that a company produces two products, A and B, with the following contribution margins (CM) per unit.

	A	B
Sales	$8	$24
Variable costs	6	20
CM/unit	$2	$ 4
Annual fixed costs		$42,000

As is indicated by CM per unit, B is more profitable than A since it contributes more to the company's total profits than A ($4 vs. $2). But let us assume that the firm has a limited capacity of 10,000 labor hours. Further, assume that A requires 2 labor hours to produce and B requires 5 labor hours. One way to express this limited capacity is to determine the contribution margin per labor hour.

	A	B
CM/unit	$2.00	$4.00
Labor hours required per unit	2	5
CM per labor hour	$1.00	$ .80

Since A returns the higher CM per labor hour, it should be produced and B should be dropped.

VALIDITY TEST A validity test is an audit technique to determine whether a recorded financial statement item has been properly stated. When performing validity tests, the auditor attempts to satisfy himself of the accuracy, appropriateness, relevance, and authorization of recorded transactions by the entity. The approach utilized in testing activity is dependent upon the nature and dollar magnitude of the transactions involved. When transactions are tested, the auditor may employ a number of techniques to choose a reliable sample and undertake various tests on the transactions.

VARIANCE ANALYSIS A standard cost is a predetermined cost of manufacturing, servicing, or marketing an item during a given future period. It is based on current and projected future conditions. The norm is also dependent upon quantitative and qualitative measurements. Standards are set at the beginning of the period. Examples are sales quotas, standard costs (e.g., material price, wage rate), and standard volume.

Variance analysis compares standard to actual performance. Variances may be as detailed as necessary, considering the cost-benefit relationship. Evaluation of variances may be done yearly, quarterly, monthly, daily, or hourly, depending on the importance of identifying a problem quickly. Since the managerial accountant does not know actual figures (e.g., hours spent) until the end of the period, variances can only be arrived at then. A material variance requires highlighting who is responsible and taking corrective action. Insignificant variances need not be looked into further unless they recur repeatedly and/or reflect potential difficulty.

One measure of materiality is to divide the variance by the standard cost. A variance of less than 5% may be deemed immaterial. In some cases, materiality is looked at in terms of dollar amount or volume level. For example, the cost accountant may set a policy looking into any variance that exceeds $10,000 or 20,000 units, whichever is less. Guidelines for materiality also depend upon the nature of the particular element as it affects corporate performance and decision making. For example, where the item is critical to the future functioning of the business (i.e., critical part, promotion, repairs), limits for materiality should be such that reporting is encouraged. Further, statistical techniques can be used to ascertain the significance of cost and revenue variances.

Often the reason for the variance is out-of-date standards or a poor budgetary process. Thus, it may not be due to actual performance.

Standards and variance analyses resulting therefrom are essential in financial analysis and decision making.

Advantages of Standards and Variances

- Assist in decision making.
- Formulate selling price.
- Set and evaluate corporate objectives.
- Cost control.
- Highlight problem areas through the "management by exception" principle.
- Pinpoint responsibility for undesirable performance so that corrective action may be taken. Variances in product activity (cost, quantity, quality) are typically the foreman's responsibility. Variances in sales are often the responsibility of the marketing manager. Variances in profit usually relate to overall operations. It should be noted that if variances indicate strengths, they should be further taken advantage of.
- Facilitate communication within the organization.
- Assist in planning by forecasting needs (e.g., cash requirements).
- Establish bid prices on contracts.

Setting Standards

Standards are based on the particular situation being appraised. Some examples follow.

Situation	Standard
Cost reduction	Tight
Pricing policy	Realistic
High-quality goods	Perfection

Types of Standards

- *Basic*—not changed from period to period. They form the basis to which later period performance is compared. What is unrealistic about it is that no consideration is given to a change in the environment.

- *Maximum efficiency*—perfect standards assuming ideal, optimal conditions. Realistically, certain inefficiencies will occur.
- *Currently attainable*—based on efficient activity. They are possible but difficult to achieve. Considered are normal occurrences, such as anticipated machinery failure.
- *Expected*—figures that come very close to actual figures.

Sales Variances

Sales variances are computed to gauge the performance of the marketing function.

■ Example

Western Corporation's budgeted sales for 19X1 were

Product A: 10,000 units at $6 per unit	$ 60,000
Product B: 30,000 units at $8 per unit	240,000
Expected sales revenue	$300,000

Actual sales for the year were

Product A: 8,000 units at $6.20 per unit	$ 49,600
Product B: 33,000 units at $7.70 per unit	254,100
Actual sales revenue	$303,700

There is a favorable sales variance of $3,700, consisting of the sales price variance and the sales volume variance.

The sales price variance equals

Actual selling price vs. Budgeted selling price
× Actual units sold

Product A ($6.20 vs. $6 × 8,000)	$1,600 Favorable
Product B ($7.70 vs. $8 × 33,000)	9,900 Unfavorable
Sales price variance	$8,300 Unfavorable

The sales volume variance equals

Actual quantity vs. Budgeted quantity
× Budgeted selling price

Product A (8,000 vs. 10,000 × $6)	$12,000 Unfavorable
Product B (33,000 vs. 30,000 × $8)	24,000 Favorable
Sales volume variance	$12,000 Favorable

Cost Variances

When a product is made or a service is performed, the managerial accountant has to compute these three measures:

1. Actual cost equals actual price times actual quantity, where actual quantity equals actual quantity per unit of work times actual units of work produced.

2. Standard cost equals standard price times standard quantity, where standard quantity equals standard quantity per unit of work times actual units of work produced.

3. Control variance equals actual cost less standard cost.

Control variance has the following elements:

• Price (rate, cost) variance (Standard price vs. Actual price × Actual quantity)

• Quantity (usage, efficiency) variance (Standard quantity vs. Actual quantity × Standard price)

These are computed for both material and labor.

A variance is unfavorable when actual cost is higher than standard cost.

Material Variances

The cost accountant can use the material price variance to evaluate the activity of the purchasing department and to see the impact of raw material cost changes on profitability. The material quantity variance is the responsibility of the production supervisor.

■ Example

The standard cost of one unit of output (product or service) was $15: three pieces at $5 per piece. During the period, 8,000 units were made. Actual cost was $14 per unit; two pieces at $7 per piece.

Material Control Variance	
Standard quantity × Standard price (24,000 × $5)	$120,000
Actual quantity × Actual price (16,000 × $7)	112,000
	$ 8,000F

Material Price Variance	
Standard price vs. Actual price × Actual quantity ($5 vs. $7 × 16,000)	$ 32,000U

Material Quantity Variance	
Standard quantity vs. Actual quantity × Standard price (24,000 vs. 16,000 × $5)	$ 40,000F

The manager may not be able to control material price variances when higher prices are due to inflation or shortage situations.

The reason as well as the responsible party for an unfavorable material variance follow:

Reason	Responsible Party
Overstated price paid	Purchasing
Failure to detect defective goods	Receiving
Inefficient labor or poor supervision	Foreman
Poor mix in material	Production manager
Rush delivery of materials	Traffic
Unfavorable quantity variance	Foreman
Unexpected change in production volume	Sales manager

To correct for an unfavorable material price variance, the manager can increase selling price, substitute cheaper materials, change a production method or specification, or engage in a cost-reduction program.

Labor Variances

The standard labor rate should be based on the contracted hourly wage rate. Where salary rates are set by union contract, the labor rate variance will usually be minimal. Labor efficiency standards are typically estimated by engineers on the basis of an analysis of the production operation.

Labor variances are determined in a manner similar to that in which material variances are determined.

■ Example

The standard cost of labor is 4 hours times $9 per hour, or $36 per unit. During the period, 7,000 units were produced. The actual cost is 6 hours times $8 per hour, or $48 per unit.

Labor Control Variance	
Standard quantity × Standard price (28,000 × $9)	$252,000
Actual quantity × Actual price (42,000 × $8)	336,000
	$ 84,000U

Labor Price Variance	
Standard price vs. Actual price × Actual quantity ($9 vs. $8 × 42,000)	$ 42,000F

Labor Quantity Variance	
Standard quantity vs. Actual quantity × Standard price (28,000 vs. 42,000 × $9)	$126,000U

Possible reasons for a labor price variance and the one responsible follow.

Reason	Responsible Party
Use of overpaid or excessive number of workers	Production manager or union contract
Poor job descriptions	Personnel
Overtime	Production planning

In the case of a shortage of skilled workers, it may be impossible to avoid an unfavorable labor price variance.

The cause and responsible entity for an unfavorable labor efficiency variance follow.

Cause	Responsible Entity
Inadequate supervision	Foreman
Improper functioning of equipment	Maintenance
Insufficient material supply or poor quality	Purchasing

Overhead Variances

The overhead variance comprises the controllable and volume variances. Relevant computations follow.

• Overhead control variance equals actual overhead versus standard overhead (standard hours times standard overhead rate).

• Controllable variance equals actual overhead versus budget adjusted to standard hours. *Note*: Budget adjusted to standard hours equals fixed overhead plus variable overhead (standard hours times standard variable overhead rate).

• Volume variance equals standard overhead versus budget adjusted to standard hours.

■ Example

The following data are provided:

Budgeted overhead (includes fixed overhead of $7,500 and variable overhead of $10,000)		$17,500
Budgeted hours		10,000
Actual overhead		$ 8,000
Actual units produced		800
Standard hours per unit of production		5
Preliminary calculations:		
Budgeted fixed overhead ($7,500/10,000 hrs)		$ 0.75
Budgeted variable overhead ($10,000/10,000 hrs)		1.00
Total budgeted overhead ($17,500/10,000 hrs)		$ 1.75
Standard hours (800 units × 5 hrs per unit)		4,000

Overhead Control Variance		
Actual overhead		$ 8,000
Standard overhead		
Standard hours	4,000 hrs	
Standard overhead rate	× $1.75	7,000
		$ 1,000U

Controllable Variance		
Actual overhead		$ 8,000
Budget adjusted to standard hours		
Fixed overhead	$7,500	
Variable overhead (Standard hours × Standard variable overhead rate 4,000 × $1)	4,000	11,500
		$ 3,500F

Volume Variance	
Standard overhead	$ 7,000
Budget adjusted to standard hours	11,500
	$ 4,500U

The controllable variance is the responsibility of the foreman, since he influences actual overhead incurred. The volume variance is the responsibility of management executives and production managers, since they are involved with plant utilization.

Variable overhead variance information is helpful in arriving at the output level and output mix decisions. It also assists in appraising decisions regarding variable inputs. Fixed overhead variance data provide information regarding decision-making astuteness when buying some combination of fixed plant size and variable production inputs.

Possible Reasons for a Recurring Unfavorable Overhead Volume Variance

- Buying the wrong size plant
- Improper scheduling
- Insufficient orders
- Shortages in material
- Machinery failure
- Long operating time
- Inadequately trained workers

When idle capacity exists, this may indicate long-term operating planning problems.

Variances to Evaluate Marketing Effort

Prior to setting a marketing standard in a given trade territory, the manager should examine prior, current, and forecasted conditions for the company itself and the given geographical area. Standards will vary depending upon geographical location. In formulating standard costs for the transportation function, minimum cost traffic routes should be selected on the basis of the given distribution pattern.

Standards for advertising costs in particular territories will vary depending upon the types of advertising media needed, which are in turn based on the type of customers the advertising is intended to reach as well as the nature of the competition.

Some direct-selling costs can be standardized, such as product presentations for which a standard time per sales call can be established. Direct-selling expenses should be related to distance traveled, frequency of calls made, and so on. If sales commissions are based on sales generated, standards can be based on a percentage of net sales.

Time and motion studies are usually a better way of establishing standards than prior performance, since the past may include inefficiencies.

Cost variances for the selling function may pertain to the territory, product, or personnel.

Salesperson Variances

The manager should appraise salesforce effectiveness within a territory, including time spent and expenses incurred.

■ Example

Sales data for a company follow.

Standard cost	$240,000
Standard salesperson days	2,000
Standard rate per salesperson day	$ 120
Actual cost	$238,000
Actual salesperson days	1,700
Actual rate per salesperson day	$ 140

Total Cost Variance

Actual cost	$238,000
Standard cost	240,000
	$ 2,000F

The control variance is broken down into salesperson days and salesperson costs.

Variance in Salesperson Days

Actual days vs. Standard days × Standard rate per day (1,700 vs. 2,000 × $120)	$ 36,000F

The variance is favorable because the territory was handled in fewer days than expected.

Variance in Salesperson Costs

Actual rate vs. Standard rate × Actual days ($140 vs. $120 × 1,700)	$ 34,000U

An unfavorable variance results because the actual rate per day is greater than the expected rate per day.

■ Example

A salesperson called on 55 customers and sold each an average of $2,800 worth of merchandise. The standard number of calls is 50, and the standard sale is $2,400. Variance analysis looking at calls and sales follows.

Total Variance	
Actual calls × Actual sale 55 × $2,800	$154,000
Standard calls × Standard sale 50 × $2,400	120,000
	$ 34,000

The elements of the $34,000 variance are

Variance in Calls	
Actual calls vs. Standard calls × Standard sale (55 vs. 50 × $2,400)	$ 12,000

Variance in Sales	
Actual sale vs. Standard sale × Standard calls ($2,800 vs. $2,400 × 50)	$ 20,000

Joint Variance	
(Actual calls vs. Standard calls) × (Actual sale vs. Standard sale) (55 vs. 50) × ($2,800 vs. $2,400)	$ 2,000

Warehousing Costs Variances

Variances in warehousing costs can be calculated by looking at the cost per unit to store the merchandise and the number of orders anticipated.

■ Example

The following information applies to a product:

Standard cost	$12,100
Standard orders	5,500
Standard unit cost	$ 2.20
Actual cost	$14,030
Actual orders	6,100
Actual unit cost	$ 2.30

Total Warehousing Cost Variance	
Actual cost	$14,030
Standard cost	12,100
	$ 1,930U

The total variance is segregated into the variance in orders and variance in cost.

Variance in Orders	
Actual orders vs. Standard orders × Standard unit cost 6,100 vs. 5,500 × $2.20	$1,320U

Variance in Cost	
Actual cost per unit vs. Standard cost per unit × Actual orders $2.30 vs. $2.20 × 6,100	$ 610U

Conclusion

Variance analysis is essential to the organization for the appraisal of all aspects of the business, including manufacturing, marketing, and service. Unfavorable variances must be examined to ascertain whether they are controllable by management or uncontrollable because they relate solely to external factors. When controllable, immediate corrective action must be undertaken to handle the problem. If a variance is favorable, an examination of the reasons for it should be made so that corporate policy may include the positive aspects found. Further, the responsible entity for a favorable variance should be recognized and rewarded.

VERTICAL ANALYSIS   In vertical analysis, a significant item on a financial statement is used as a base value and all other items on the financial statement are compared to it. In performing vertical analysis for the balance sheet, total assets is assigned 100%. Each asset is expressed as a percentage of total assets. Total liabilities and stockholders' equity are also assigned 100%. Each liability and stockholders' equity account is then expressed as a percentage of total liabilities and stockholders' equity. In the income statement, net sales is given the value of 100% and all other accounts are appraised in comparison to net sales. The resulting figures are then given in a common size statement.

Vertical analysis points to possible problem areas to be evaluated by the financial analyst.

■ Example

X Company
Common Size Income Statement
for the Year Ended 12/31/19X5

Sales	$40,000	100%
Less: Cost of sales	10,000	25%
Gross profit	$30,000	75%
Less: Expenses	4,000	10%
Net income	$26,000	65%

Vertical analysis is helpful in disclosing the internal structure of the business. It shows the relationship between each income statement account and revenue. It indicates the mix of assets that produces the income and the mix of the sources of capital, whether by current or long-term liabilities or by equity funding. Besides making internal evaluation possible, the results of vertical analysis are also employed to appraise the company's relative position in the industry. *See also* Trend (Horizontal) Analysis.

W

WEIGHTED AVERAGE This is an average of observations having different degrees of importance or frequency. The formula for a weighted average is

$$\text{Weighted average} = \Sigma wz$$

where $x =$ the data values and $w =$ relative weight assigned to each observation, expressed as a percentage or relative frequency. *See also* Mean.

WEIGHTED-AVERAGE COSTING VERSUS FIRST-IN, FIRST-OUT

In process costing, two typical assumptions are made regarding the flow of costs of the beginning work-in-process inventory. They are weighted-average costing and first in, first out (FIFO) costing.

Weighted-average costing is a procedure for computing the unit cost of a process by which the beginning work-in-process inventory costs are added to the costs of the current period, and a weighted average is obtained by dividing the combined costs by equivalent units. Thus, there is only one average cost for goods completed. *Equivalent units* under weighted-average costing may be computed as follows:

Units completed + (Ending work-in-process
$\qquad \times$ Degree of completion [%])

On the other hand, under *FIFO*, beginning work-in-process inventory costs are separated from added costs applied in the current period. Thus, there are two unit costs for the period: (1) beginning work-in-process units completed and (2) units started and completed in the same period. Under FIFO, the beginning work-in-process is assumed to be completed and transferred first. Equivalent units under FIFO costing may be computed as follows:

Units completed + (Ending work-in-process
$\qquad \times$ Degree of completion [%])
− (Beginning work-in-process
$\qquad \times$ Degree of completion [%])

■ Example

To illustrate, the following data relate to the activities of Department A during the month of January:

	Units
Beginning work-in-process	
(100% complete as to materials;	
⅔ complete as to conversion)	1,500
Started this period	5,000
Completed and transferred	5,500
Ending work-in-process	
(100% complete as to materials;	
⁶⁄₁₀ complete as to conversion)	1,000

Equivalent production in Department A for the month is computed using *weighted-average costing*, as follows:

	Materials	Conversion Costs
Units completed and transferred	5,500	5,500
Ending work-in-process		
Materials (100%)	1,000	
Conversion costs (60%)		600
Equivalent production	6,500	6,100

Equivalent production in Department A for the month is computed using *FIFO costing*, as follows:

	Materials	Conversion Costs
Units completed and transferred	5,500	5,500
Ending work-in-process		
Materials (100%)	1,000	
Conversion costs (60%)		600
Equivalent production	6,500	6,100
Minus: Beginning work-in-process		
Materials (100%)	1,500	
Conversion costs ($\frac{2}{3}$)		1,000
	5,000	5,100

See also Process Costing.

WORKING CAPITAL MANAGEMENT Net working capital equals current assets less current liabilities. Management of working capital entails considering two related problems: (1) managing the firm's investment in current assets and (2) managing the firm's use of short-term or current liabilities. Involved are decisions on how assets should be financed (e.g., short-term debt, long-term debt, or equity). Managing working capital involves a trade-off between return and risk. If funds go from fixed assets to current assets, there is a reduction in liquidity risk, greater ability to obtain short-term financing, and enhanced flexibility because the entity can more readily adjust current assets to changes in sales volume. But less of a return is earned because the yield on fixed assets is more than that of current assets. Financing with noncurrent debt has less liquidity risk than financing with current debt. However, long-term debt often has a higher cost than short-term debt because of the greater uncertainty, which detracts from overall return.

Rule of Thumb: The longer the time period involved to buy or produce goods, the more working capital is required. Working capital also applies to the volume of purchases and the cost per unit. For example, if you can receive a raw material in 2 weeks, you need less of an inventory level than if 2 months lead time is involved. *Tip*: Purchase material early if significantly lower prices are available and if the material's cost savings exceed inventory carrying costs. *See also* Accounts Receivable Management; Cash Management; Inventory Planning and Control.

WORKING PAPERS As per Statement on Auditing Standards No. 41, working papers are required on an audit engagement. They assist in performing and reviewing audit work. The form and content of the working papers may vary depending on the nature of the particular engagement. Further, the auditor may supplement working papers by other means. Working papers should show that the field-work standards have been met. In this regard, there should be documentation that a study and analysis of the internal control structure has been undertaken. Further, the work performed and by whom should be spelled out along with audit findings. *See also* Audit.

YIELD   The cost of a corporate bond is expressed in terms of yield. Two types of yield calculations are

1. *Simple Yield*

$$\frac{\text{Nominal interest}}{\text{Present value of bond}}$$

It is not as accurate as yield to maturity.

2. *Yield to Maturity* (effective interest rate)

$$\frac{\text{Nominal interest} + \dfrac{\text{Discount}}{\text{Years}} - \dfrac{\text{Premium}}{\text{Years}}}{\dfrac{\text{Present value} + \text{Maturity value}}{2}}$$

■ Example

A $100,000, 10%, 5-year bond is issued at 96. The simple yield is

$$\frac{\text{Nominal interest}}{\text{Present value of bond}} = \frac{\$10,000}{\$96,000} = 10.42\%$$

The yield to maturity is

$$\frac{\text{Nominal interest} + \dfrac{\text{Discount}}{\text{Years}}}{\dfrac{\text{Present value} + \text{Maturity value}}{2}} = \frac{\$10,000 + \dfrac{\$4,000}{5}}{\dfrac{\$96,000 + \$100,000}{2}}$$

$$\frac{\$10,800}{\$98,000} = 11.02\%$$

When a bond is issued at a discount, the yield (effective interest rate) is greater than the nominal (face, coupon) interest rate.

When a bond is issued at a premium, the yield is less than the nominal interest rate. *See also* Bond Accounting; Bond Yield.

YIELD SPREAD   This is the difference between the yields received on two different types of bonds with different ratings. In times of economic uncertainty, the yield spread increases because investors demand higher premiums on risky issues to compensate for the increased chance of default. *See also* Bond Ratings.

Z

ZERO-BASE BUDGETING (ZBB)
ZBB is budgeting from scratch as if the budget was being started for the first time. The steps involved in ZBB are

• Ascertain objectives and activities required

• Evaluate alternative ways of accomplishing each activity

• Appraise alternative budget figures for different activity levels

• Formulate performance measures

• Rank activities in the order of their importance

ZBB usually begins with the decision units that are at the lowest levels in the firm for which a budget is formulated. *Decision packages* are prepared for each unit. The packages describe alternative means of accomplishing a task, including the manager's recommended way. The cost and time associated with the recommended and alternative means of carrying out the task are specified. Top management may decide not to fund the project, fund it as recommended by the manager, or proceed with the project according to one of the alternative approaches (e.g., less costly).

An illustrative decision package follows:

**Decision Package
Task A**

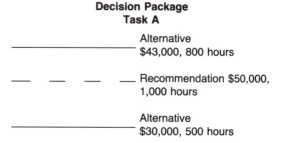

Alternative
$43,000, 800 hours

Recommendation $50,000, 1,000 hours

Alternative
$30,000, 500 hours

The problem with ZBB is cost versus benefit. The significant cost involved to prepare a ZBB may outweigh the benefits to be derived. *See also* Budgeting for Profit Planning.

ZERO-COUPON BOND
This is a bond sold at a deep discount. The interest, instead of being paid out directly, is added to the principal semiannually, and both the principal and the accumulated interest are paid at maturity. Although a fixed rate is implicit in the discount and the specific maturity, they are not fixed income securities in the traditional sense because they provide for no periodic income. Although the interest on the bond is paid at maturity, accrued interest, though not received, is taxable yearly as ordinary income. Zero-coupon bonds have two basic advan-

tages over regular coupon-bearing bonds: (1) a relatively small investment is required to buy these bonds and (2) a specific yield is assured throughout the term of the investment.

ZERO–ONE PROGRAMMING This is a special case of *integer programming* where integer variables are restricted to values of either zero or one. In a *capital rationing* problem, the decision variables are restricted to either zero or one, implying total investment (inclusion in a portfolio) or no investment (exclusion from the portfolio). *See also* Capital Rationing; Integer Programming; Project Selection and Zero–One Programming.

Z SCORES: FORECASTING BUSINESS FAILURES The recent past has witnessed an increasing trend in bankruptcies. Will your client go bankrupt? Is the company you are working for on the verge of bankruptcy? Who will go bankrupt—your major customer, your important supplier, your borrower? If you can predict with reasonable accuracy that the company you are interested in is developing financial distress, you could better protect yourself and recommend means for corrective action.

In 1968, using a blend of the traditional financial ratios and a statistical method known as multiple discriminant analysis (MDA), Edward Altman developed a bankruptcy prediction model that produces a Z score as follows:

$$Z = 1.2*X_1 + 1.4*X_2 + 3.3*X_3 + 0.6*X_4 + 0.999*X_5$$

where:

X_1 = Working capital/Total assets,
X_2 = Retained earnings/Total assets,
X_3 = Earnings before interest and taxes (EBIT)/Total assets,
X_4 = Market value of equity/Book value of debt,
X_5 = Sales/Total assets.

Altman also established the following guidelines for classifying firms:

Z score	Probability of Failure
1.8 or less	Very high
1.81–2.99	Not sure
3.0 or higher	Unlikely

The Z score is known to be about 90% accurate in forecasting business failure one year in the future and about 80% accurate in forecasting it two years in the future. For a more detailed discussion of Z Score, see Edward I. Altman, "Financial Ratios, Discriminant Analysis, and the Prediction of Corporate Bankruptcy," *Journal of Finance*, September 1968.

Now we will illustrate the computation by setting up a Z score spreadsheet using a computer program like Lotus 1-2-3. Table 1 (page 490) shows the 7-year financial history and the Z scores of Navistar International (formerly, International Harvestor).

After creating the data worksheet and calculating the Z scores, it is a good idea to develop a graph for these values, as shown in Figure 1 (page 491).

The graph shows that Navistar International performed at the edge of the ignorance zone ("unsure area") for the years 1975 through 1979. Since 1980, though, the company started signaling a sign of failure. However, by selling stock and assets, the firm managed to survive. Since 1982, the company showed an improvement in its Z scores, but it still has a long way to go.

More Applications of the Z Score

Accountants and financial managers apply Z score in numerous ways. For example,
1. *Financial management analysis*—The score can indicate whether capital expansion and dividends should be curtailed to keep needed funds within the business.

Table 1 Navistar International Z Score Data and Score

| | Balance Sheet | | | | | | | Income Statement | | Stock Data | Calculations | | | | | | Miscellaneous Graph Values | | | |
| | Current Year Assets | Total Assets | Current Liabilities | Total Liabilities | Retained Earnings | Net Worth | Working Capital | Sales | EBIT | Market Value | WC/TA | RE/TA | EBIT/TA | MKT/TL | SALES/TA | Z Score | TOP GRAY | BOTTOM GRAY | Year |
Year	CA	TA	CL	TL	RE	NW	WC	SALES	EBIT	MKT						A	B	C	X
1979	3266	5247	1873	3048	1505	2199	1393	8426	719	1122	0.2655	0.2868	0.1370	0.3681	1.6059	3.00	2.99	1.81	1979
1980	3427	5843	2433	3947	1024	1896	994	6000	−402	1147	0.1701	0.1753	−0.0688	0.2906	1.0269	1.42	2.99	1.81	1980
1981	2672	5346	1808	3864	600	1482	864	7018	−16	376	0.1616	0.1122	−0.0030	0.0973	1.3128	1.71	2.99	1.81	1981
1982	1656	3699	1135	3665	−1078	34	521	4322	−1274	151	0.1408	−0.2914	−0.3444	0.0412	1.1684	−0.18	2.99	1.81	1982
1983	1388	3362	1367	3119	−1487	243	22	3600	−231	835	0.0065	−0.4423	−0.0687	0.2677	1.0708	0.39	2.99	1.81	1983
1984	1412	3249	1257	2947	−1537	302	155	4861	120	575	0.0477	−0.4731	0.0369	0.1951	1.4962	1.13	2.99	1.81	1984
1985	1101	2406	988	2364	−1894	42	113	3508	−242	570	0.0470	−0.7872	−0.1006	0.2411	1.4580	0.22	2.99	1.81	1985

Figure 1 Altman's Z Score Graph

Navistar International

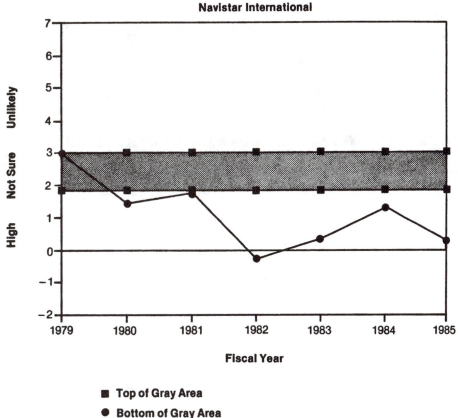

Fiscal Year

■ **Top of Gray Area**
● **Bottom of Gray Area**

2. *Merger analysis*—The Z score can help identify potential problems with a merger candidate.

3. *Loan credit analysis*—Bankers and lenders can use it to determine if they should extend a loan. Other creditors such as vendors have used it to determine whether to extend credit.

4. *Investment analysis*—The Z score model can help an investor in selecting stocks of potentially troubled companies.

5. *Auditing analysis*—External CPA auditors are able to use this technique to assess whether the client will continue as a going concern. If not, disclosure is required in the audit report.

6. *Legal analysis*—Those who manage other people's investments tend to get sued if the investment goes sour. The Z score can help either side of the argument.

Appendix

Table 1   Future Value of $1

$$F_n(1 + i)^n = FVIF_{i,n}$$

Periods	4%	6%	8%	10%	12%	14%	20%
1	1.040	1.060	1.080	1.100	1.120	1.140	1.200
2	1.082	1.124	1.166	1.210	1.254	1.300	1.440
3	1.125	1.191	1.260	1.331	1.405	1.482	1.728
4	1.170	1.263	1.361	1.464	1.574	1.689	2.074
5	1.217	1.338	1.469	1.611	1.762	1.925	2.488
6	1.265	1.419	1.587	1.772	1.974	2.195	2.986
7	1.316	1.504	1.714	1.949	2.211	2.502	3.583
8	1.369	1.594	1.851	2.144	2.476	2.853	4.300
9	1.423	1.690	1.999	2.359	2.773	3.252	5.160
10	1.480	1.791	2.159	2.594	3.106	3.707	6.192
11	1.540	1.898	2.332	2.853	3.479	4.226	7.430
12	1.601	2.012	2.518	3.139	3.896	4.818	8.916
13	1.665	2.133	2.720	3.452	4.364	5.492	10.699
14	1.732	2.261	2.937	3.798	4.887	6.261	12.839
15	1.801	2.397	3.172	4.177	5.474	7.138	15.407
20	2.191	3.207	4.661	6.728	9.646	13.743	38.338
30	3.243	5.744	10.063	17.450	29.960	50.950	237.380
40	4.801	10.286	21.725	45.260	93.051	188.880	1469.800

Table 2 Future Value of an Annuity of $1

$$S_n = \frac{(1 + i)^n - 1}{i} = FVIFA_{i,n}$$

Periods	4%	6%	8%	10%	12%	14%	20%
1	1.000	1.000	1.000	1.000	1.000	1.000	1.000
2	2.040	2.060	2.080	2.100	2.120	2.140	2.220
3	3.122	3.184	3.246	3.310	3.374	3.440	3.640
4	4.247	4.375	4.506	4.641	4.779	4.921	5.368
5	5.416	5.637	5.867	6.105	6.353	6.610	7.442
6	6.633	6.975	7.336	7.716	8.115	8.536	9.930
7	7.898	8.394	8.923	9.487	10.089	10.730	12.916
8	9.214	9.898	10.637	11.436	12.300	13.233	16.499
9	10.583	11.491	12.488	13.580	14.776	16.085	20.799
10	12.006	13.181	14.487	15.938	17.549	19.337	25.959
11	13.486	14.972	16.646	18.531	20.655	23.045	32.150
12	15.026	16.870	18.977	21.395	24.133	27.271	39.580
13	16.627	18.882	21.495	24.523	28.029	32.089	48.497
14	18.292	21.015	24.215	27.976	32.393	37.581	59.196
15	20.024	23.276	27.152	31.773	37.280	43.842	72.035
20	29.778	36.778	45.762	57.276	75.052	91.025	186.690
30	56.085	79.058	113.283	164.496	241.330	356.790	1181.900
40	95.026	154.762	259.057	442.597	767.090	1342.000	7343.900

Table 3 Present Value of $1

$$P = \frac{1}{(1 + i)^n} = PVIF_{i,n}$$

Periods	4%	5%	6%	8%	10%	12%	14%	16%	18%	20%	22%	24%	26%	28%	30%	40%
1	0.962	0.952	0.943	0.926	0.909	0.893	0.877	0.862	0.847	0.833	0.820	0.806	0.794	0.781	0.769	0.714
2	0.925	0.907	0.890	0.857	0.826	0.797	0.769	0.743	0.718	0.694	0.672	0.650	0.630	0.610	0.592	0.510
3	0.889	0.864	0.840	0.794	0.751	0.712	0.675	0.641	0.609	0.579	0.551	0.524	0.500	0.477	0.455	0.364
4	0.855	0.823	0.792	0.735	0.683	0.636	0.592	0.552	0.516	0.482	0.451	0.423	0.397	0.373	0.350	0.260
5	0.822	0.784	0.747	0.681	0.621	0.567	0.519	0.476	0.437	0.402	0.370	0.341	0.315	0.291	0.269	0.186
6	0.790	0.746	0.705	0.630	0.564	0.507	0.456	0.410	0.370	0.335	0.303	0.275	0.250	0.227	0.207	0.133
7	0.760	0.711	0.665	0.583	0.513	0.452	0.400	0.354	0.314	0.279	0.249	0.222	0.198	0.178	0.159	0.095
8	0.731	0.677	0.627	0.540	0.467	0.404	0.351	0.305	0.266	0.233	0.204	0.179	0.157	0.139	0.123	0.068
9	0.703	0.645	0.592	0.500	0.424	0.361	0.308	0.263	0.225	0.194	0.167	0.144	0.125	0.108	0.094	0.048
10	0.676	0.614	0.558	0.463	0.386	0.322	0.270	0.227	0.191	0.162	0.137	0.116	0.099	0.085	0.073	0.035
11	0.650	0.585	0.527	0.429	0.350	0.287	0.237	0.195	0.162	0.135	0.112	0.094	0.079	0.066	0.056	0.025
12	0.625	0.557	0.497	0.397	0.319	0.257	0.208	0.168	0.137	0.112	0.092	0.076	0.062	0.052	0.043	0.018
13	0.601	0.530	0.469	0.368	0.290	0.229	0.182	0.145	0.116	0.093	0.075	0.061	0.050	0.040	0.033	0.013
14	0.577	0.505	0.442	0.340	0.263	0.205	0.160	0.125	0.099	0.078	0.062	0.049	0.039	0.032	0.025	0.009
15	0.555	0.481	0.417	0.315	0.239	0.183	0.140	0.108	0.084	0.065	0.051	0.040	0.031	0.025	0.020	0.006
16	0.534	0.458	0.394	0.292	0.218	0.163	0.123	0.093	0.071	0.054	0.042	0.032	0.025	0.019	0.015	0.005
17	0.513	0.436	0.371	0.270	0.198	0.146	0.108	0.080	0.060	0.045	0.034	0.026	0.020	0.015	0.012	0.003
18	0.494	0.416	0.350	0.250	0.180	0.130	0.095	0.069	0.051	0.038	0.028	0.021	0.016	0.012	0.009	0.002
19	0.475	0.396	0.331	0.232	0.164	0.116	0.083	0.060	0.043	0.031	0.023	0.017	0.012	0.009	0.007	0.002
20	0.456	0.377	0.312	0.215	0.149	0.104	0.073	0.051	0.037	0.026	0.019	0.014	0.010	0.007	0.005	0.001
21	0.439	0.359	0.294	0.199	0.135	0.093	0.064	0.044	0.031	0.022	0.015	0.011	0.008	0.006	0.004	0.001
22	0.422	0.342	0.278	0.184	0.123	0.083	0.056	0.038	0.026	0.018	0.013	0.009	0.006	0.004	0.003	0.001
23	0.406	0.326	0.262	0.170	0.112	0.074	0.049	0.033	0.022	0.015	0.010	0.007	0.005	0.003	0.002	
24	0.390	0.310	0.247	0.158	0.102	0.066	0.043	0.028	0.019	0.013	0.008	0.006	0.004	0.003	0.002	
25	0.375	0.295	0.233	0.146	0.092	0.059	0.038	0.024	0.016	0.010	0.007	0.005	0.003	0.002	0.001	
26	0.361	0.281	0.220	0.135	0.084	0.053	0.033	0.021	0.014	0.009	0.006	0.004	0.002	0.002	0.001	
27	0.347	0.268	0.207	0.125	0.076	0.047	0.029	0.018	0.011	0.007	0.005	0.003	0.002	0.001	0.001	
28	0.333	0.255	0.196	0.116	0.069	0.042	0.026	0.016	0.010	0.006	0.004	0.002	0.002	0.001	0.001	
29	0.321	0.243	0.185	0.107	0.063	0.037	0.022	0.014	0.008	0.005	0.003	0.002	0.001	0.001	0.001	
30	0.308	0.231	0.174	0.099	0.057	0.033	0.020	0.012	0.007	0.004	0.003	0.002	0.001	0.001	0.001	
40	0.208	0.142	0.097	0.046	0.022	0.011	0.005	0.003	0.001	0.001						

Table 4 Present Value of an Annuity of $1

$$P_n = \left[\frac{1 - \dfrac{1}{(1+i)^n}}{i}\right] = PVIFA_{i,n}$$

Periods	4%	5%	6%	8%	10%	12%	14%	16%	18%	20%	22%	24%	26%	28%	30%	40%
1	0.962	0.952	0.943	0.926	0.909	0.893	0.877	0.862	0.847	0.833	0.820	0.806	0.794	0.781	0.769	0.714
2	1.886	1.859	1.833	1.783	1.736	1.690	1.647	1.605	1.566	1.528	1.492	1.457	1.424	1.392	1.361	1.224
3	2.775	2.723	2.673	2.577	2.487	2.402	2.322	2.246	2.174	2.106	2.042	1.981	1.868	1.816	1.816	1.589
4	3.630	3.546	3.465	3.312	3.170	3.037	2.914	2.798	2.690	2.589	2.494	2.404	2.320	2.241	2.166	1.879
5	4.452	4.330	4.212	3.993	3.791	3.605	3.433	3.274	3.127	2.991	2.864	2.745	2.635	2.532	2.436	2.035
6	5.242	5.076	4.917	4.623	4.355	4.111	3.889	3.685	3.498	3.326	3.167	3.020	2.885	2.759	2.643	2.168
7	6.002	5.786	5.582	5.206	4.868	4.564	4.288	4.039	3.812	3.605	3.416	3.242	3.083	2.937	2.802	2.263
8	6.733	6.463	6.210	5.747	5.335	4.968	4.639	4.344	4.078	3.837	3.619	3.421	3.241	3.076	2.925	2.331
9	7.435	7.108	6.802	6.247	5.759	5.328	4.946	4.607	4.303	4.031	3.786	3.566	3.366	3.184	3.019	2.379
10	8.111	7.722	7.360	6.710	6.145	5.650	5.216	4.833	4.494	4.192	3.923	3.682	3.465	3.269	3.092	2.414
11	8.760	8.306	7.887	7.139	6.495	5.988	5.453	5.029	4.656	4.327	4.035	3.776	3.544	3.335	3.147	2.438
12	9.385	8.863	8.384	7.536	6.814	6.194	5.660	5.197	4.793	4.439	4.127	3.851	3.606	3.387	3.190	2.456
13	9.986	9.394	8.853	7.904	7.103	6.424	5.842	5.342	4.910	4.533	4.203	3.912	3.656	3.427	3.223	2.468
14	10.563	9.899	9.295	8.244	7.367	6.628	6.002	5.468	5.008	4.611	4.265	3.962	3.695	3.459	3.249	2.477
15	11.118	10.380	9.712	8.559	7.606	6.811	6.142	5.575	5.092	4.675	4.315	4.001	3.726	3.483	3.268	2.484
16	11.652	10.838	10.106	8.851	7.824	6.974	6.265	5.669	5.162	4.730	4.357	4.033	3.751	3.503	3.283	2.489
17	12.166	11.274	10.477	9.122	8.022	7.120	6.373	5.749	5.222	4.775	4.391	4.059	3.771	3.518	3.295	2.492
18	12.659	11.690	10.828	9.372	8.201	7.250	6.467	5.818	5.273	4.812	4.419	4.080	3.786	3.529	3.304	2.494
19	13.134	12.085	11.158	9.604	8.365	7.366	6.550	5.877	5.316	4.844	4.442	4.097	3.799	3.539	3.311	2.496
20	13.590	12.462	11.470	9.818	8.514	7.469	6.623	5.929	5.353	4.870	4.460	4.110	3.808	3.546	3.316	2.497
21	14.029	12.821	11.764	10.017	8.649	7.562	6.687	5.973	5.384	4.891	4.476	4.121	3.816	3.551	3.320	2.498
22	14.451	13.163	12.042	10.201	8.772	7.645	6.743	6.011	5.410	4.909	4.488	4.130	3.822	3.556	3.323	2.498
23	14.857	13.489	12.303	10.371	8.883	7.718	6.792	6.044	5.432	4.925	4.499	4.137	3.827	3.559	3.325	2.499
24	15.247	13.799	12.550	10.529	8.985	7.784	6.835	6.073	5.451	4.937	4.507	4.143	3.831	3.562	3.327	2.499
25	15.622	14.094	12.783	10.675	9.077	7.843	6.873	6.097	5.467	4.948	4.514	4.147	3.834	3.564	3.329	2.499
26	15.983	14.375	13.003	10.810	9.161	7.896	6.906	6.118	5.480	4.956	4.520	4.151	3.837	3.566	3.330	2.500
27	16.330	14.643	13.211	10.935	9.237	7.943	6.935	6.136	5.492	4.964	4.525	4.154	3.839	3.567	3.331	2.500
28	16.663	14.898	13.406	11.051	9.307	7.984	6.961	6.152	5.502	4.970	4.528	4.157	3.840	3.568	3.331	2.500
29	16.984	15.141	13.591	11.158	9.370	8.022	6.983	6.166	5.510	4.975	4.531	4.159	3.841	3.569	3.332	2.500
30	17.292	15.373	13.765	11.258	9.427	8.055	7.003	6.177	5.517	4.979	4.534	4.160	3.842	3.569	3.332	2.500
40	19.793	17.159	15.046	11.925	9.779	8.244	7.105	6.234	5.548	4.997	4.544	4.166	3.846	3.571	3.333	2.500

Table 5   Normal Distribution Table

Areas Under the Normal Curve

.9648

Mean 1.81

Z	0	1	2	3	4	5	6	7	8	9
0.0	0.5000	0.5040	0.5080	0.5120	0.5160	0.5199	0.5239	0.5279	0.5319	0.5359
0.1	0.5398	0.5438	0.5478	0.5517	0.5557	0.5596	0.5636	0.5675	0.5714	0.5753
0.2	0.5793	0.5832	0.5871	0.5910	0.5948	0.5987	0.6026	0.6064	0.6103	0.6141
0.3	0.6179	0.6217	0.6255	0.6293	0.6331	0.6368	0.6406	0.6443	0.6480	0.6517
0.4	0.6554	0.6591	0.6628	0.6664	0.6700	0.6736	0.6772	0.6808	0.6844	0.6879
0.5	0.6915	0.6950	0.6985	0.7019	0.7054	0.7088	0.7123	0.7157	0.7190	0.7224
0.6	0.7257	0.7291	0.7324	0.7357	0.7389	0.7422	0.7454	0.7486	0.7517	0.7549
0.7	0.7580	0.7611	0.7642	0.7673	0.7703	0.7734	0.7764	0.7794	0.7823	0.7852
0.8	0.7881	0.7910	0.7939	0.7967	0.7995	0.8023	0.8051	0.8078	0.8106	0.8133
0.9	0.8159	0.8186	0.8212	0.8238	0.8264	0.8289	0.8315	0.8340	0.8365	0.8389
1.0	0.8413	0.8438	0.8461	0.8485	0.8508	0.8531	0.8554	0.8577	0.8599	0.8621
1.1	0.8643	0.8665	0.8686	0.8708	0.8729	0.8749	0.8770	0.8790	0.8810	0.8830
1.2	0.8849	0.8869	0.8888	0.8907	0.8925	0.8944	0.8962	0.8980	0.8997	0.9015
1.3	0.9032	0.9049	0.9066	0.9082	0.9099	0.9115	0.9131	0.9147	0.9162	0.9177
1.4	0.9192	0.9207	0.9222	0.9236	0.9251	0.9265	0.9278	0.9292	0.9306	0.9319
1.5	0.9332	0.9345	0.9357	0.9370	0.9382	0.9394	0.9406	0.9418	0.9430	0.9441
1.6	0.9452	0.9463	0.9474	0.9484	0.9495	0.9505	0.9515	0.9525	0.9535	0.9545
1.7	0.9554	0.9564	0.9573	0.9582	0.9591	0.9599	0.9608	0.9616	0.9625	0.9633
1.8	0.9641	(0.9648)	0.9656	0.9664	0.9671	0.9678	0.9686	0.9693	0.9700	0.9706
1.9	0.9713	0.9719	0.9726	0.9732	0.9738	0.9744	0.9750	0.9756	0.9762	0.9767
2.0	0.9772	0.9778	0.9783	0.9788	0.9793	0.9798	0.9803	0.9808	0.9812	0.9817
2.1	0.9821	0.9826	0.9830	0.9834	0.9838	0.9842	0.9846	0.9850	0.9854	0.9857
2.2	0.9861	0.9864	0.9868	0.9871	0.9874	0.9878	0.9881	0.9884	0.9887	0.9890
2.3	0.9893	0.9896	0.9898	0.9901	0.9904	0.9906	0.9909	0.9911	0.9913	0.9916
2.4	0.9918	0.9920	0.9922	0.9925	0.9927	0.9929	0.9931	0.9932	0.9934	0.9936
2.5	0.9938	0.9940	0.9941	0.9943	0.9945	0.9946	0.9948	0.9949	0.9951	0.9952
2.6	0.9953	0.9955	0.9956	0.9957	0.9959	0.9960	0.9961	0.9962	0.9963	0.9964
2.7	0.9965	0.9966	0.9967	0.9968	0.9969	0.9970	0.9971	0.9972	0.9973	0.9974
2.8	0.9974	0.9975	0.9976	0.9977	0.9977	0.9978	0.9979	0.9979	0.9980	0.9981
2.9	0.9981	0.9982	0.9982	0.9983	0.9984	0.9984	0.9985	0.9985	0.9986	0.9986
3.0	0.9987	0.9990	0.9993	0.9995	0.9997	0.9998	0.9998	0.9999	0.9999	1.0000

Table 6   T-Table (Values of t)

d.f.	$t_{.100}$	$t_{.050}$	$t_{.025}$	$t_{.010}$	$t_{.005}$	d.f.
1	3.078	6.314	12.706	31.821	63.657	1
2	1.886	2.920	4.303	6.965	9.925	2
3	1.638	2.353	3.182	4.541	5.841	3
4	1.533	2.132	2.776	3.747	4.604	4
5	1.476	2.015	2.571	3.365	4.032	5
6	1.440	1.943	2.447	3.143	3.707	6
7	1.415	1.895	2.365	2.998	3.499	7
8	1.397	1.860	2.306	2.896	3.355	8
9	1.383	1.833	2.262	2.821	3.250	9
10	1.372	1.812	2.228	2.764	3.169	10
11	1.363	1.796	2.201	2.718	3.106	11
12	1.356	1.782	2.179	2.681	3.055	12
13	1.350	1.771	2.160	2.650	3.012	13
14	1.345	1.761	2.145	2.624	2.977	14
15	1.341	1.753	2.131	2.602	2.947	15
16	1.337	1.746	2.120	2.583	2.921	16
17	1.333	1.740	2.110	2.567	2.898	17
18	1.330	1.734	2.101	2.552	2.878	18
19	1.328	1.729	2.093	2.539	2.861	19
20	1.325	1.725	2.086	2.528	2.845	20
21	1.323	1.721	2.080	2.518	2.831	21
22	1.321	1.717	2.074	2.508	2.819	22
23	1.319	1.714	2.069	2.500	2.807	23
24	1.318	1.711	2.064	2.492	2.797	24
25	1.316	1.708	2.060	2.485	2.787	25
26	1.315	1.706	2.056	2.479	2.779	26
27	1.314	1.703	2.052	2.473	2.771	27
28	1.313	1.701	2.048	2.467	2.763	28
29	1.311	1.699	2.045	2.462	2.756	29
inf.	1.282	1.645	1.960	2.326	2.576	inf.

The t-value describes the sampling distribution of a deviation from a population value divided by the standard error.

Degrees of freedom (d.f.) are in the first column. The probabilities indicated as subvalues of t in the heading refer to the sum of a one-tailed area under the curve that lies outside the point t.

For example, in the distribution of the means of samples of size $n = 10$, d.f. $= n - 2 = 8$; then 0.025 of the area under the curve falls in one tail outside the interval $t \pm 2.306$.

INDEX OF ENTRIES